Hitler's *Luftwaffe* Infantry

DEDICATION
For my mother and father
2019 – RIP

Hitler's *Luftwaffe* Infantry

The German Air Force Field Divisions, 1942–1945

Dr Antonio J. Muñoz

AN IMPRINT OF PEN & SWORD BOOKS LTD
YORKSHIRE – PHILADELPHIA

First published in Great Britain in 2025 by
FRONTLINE BOOKS
an imprint of Pen & Sword Books Ltd
Yorkshire – Philadelphia

Copyright © Dr Antonio J. Muñoz, 2025

ISBN 978-1-03613-033-6

The right of Dr Antonio J. Muñoz to be identified as the author of this work has been asserted by him in accordance with the Copyright, Designs and Patents Act 1988.

A CIP catalogue record for this book is available from the British Library.

All rights reserved. No part of this book may be reproduced, transmitted, downloaded, decompiled or reverse engineered in any form or by any means, electronic or mechanical including photocopying, recording or by any information storage and retrieval system, without permission from the Publisher in writing. NO AI TRAINING: Without in any way limiting the Author's and Publisher's exclusive rights under copyright, any use of this publication to 'train' generative artificial intelligence (AI) technologies to generate text is expressly prohibited. The Author and Publisher reserve all rights to license uses of this work for generative AI training and development of machine learning language models.

Typeset by Concept, Huddersfield, West Yorkshire, HD4 5JL
Printed on paper from a sustainable source by
CPI Group (UK) Ltd, Croydon CR0 4YY

The Publisher's authorised representative in the EU for product safety is Authorised Rep Compliance Ltd, Ground Floor, 71 Lower Baggot Street, Dublin D02 P593, Ireland – www.arccompliance.com

For a complete list of Pen & Sword titles please contact
PEN & SWORD BOOKS LTD
47 Church Street, Barnsley, South Yorkshire, S70 2AS, England
E-mail: enquiries@pen-and-sword.co.uk
Website: www.pen-and-sword.co.uk
or
PEN & SWORD BOOKS
1950 Lawrence Rd, Havertown, PA 19083, USA
E-mail: uspen-and-sword@casematepublishers.com
Website: www.penandswordbooks.com

Contents

List of plates	vi
List of tables	vii
Introduction	1
1. *Luftwaffen-Felddivision*	9
2. *Luftwaffen-Felddivision*	17
3. *Luftwaffen-Felddivision*	27
4. *Luftwaffen-Felddivision*	34
5. *Luftwaffen-Felddivision*	41
6. *Luftwaffen-Felddivision*	55
7. *Luftwaffen-Felddivision*	68
8. *Luftwaffen-Felddivision*	77
9. *Luftwaffen-Felddivision*	82
10. *Luftwaffen-Felddivision*	93
11. *Luftwaffen-Felddivision*	102
12. *Luftwaffen-Felddivision*	118
13. *Luftwaffen-Felddivision*	138
14. *Luftwaffen-Felddivision*	148
15. *Luftwaffen-Felddivision*	159
16. *Luftwaffen-Felddivision*	184
17. *Luftwaffen-Felddivision*	201
18. *Luftwaffen-Felddivision*	210
19. *Luftwaffen-Sturm-Division*	220
20. *Luftwaffen-Sturm-Division*	235
Division Meindl / 21. Luftwaffen-Felddivision	248
22. *Luftwaffen-Felddivision*	282

Appendices
  I. Active *Luftwaffe* divisions, 1 November 1943 285
  II. Insignia of the *Luftwaffe* field divisions 286
Notes 289
Bibliography 313
Name Index 319
Unit Index 324

List of plates

German troops inspecting a French 155mm heavy artillery piece.

This father and son duo served in the same air force field unit.

Marching to the front, 1944.

German *Luftwaffe* infantry interrogating a suspected partisan, Central Russia, 1942.

A bunker on the Leningrad front, winter of 1942/1943.

Training in the field, 1943.

The commander of *15. Luftwaffen Felddivision*, General Alfred Mahncke.

Marching to the front, 1943.

The men of a Luftwaffe infantry squad before a patrol, some time in 1943.

NCO Friedrich Sass.

Generalmajor Eugen Meindl, the commander of *Luftwaffe Felddivision Meindl / 21. Luftwaffe Felddivision.*

Luftwaffe infantry in the autumn of 1942.

A typical *Luftwaffe* trooper on the Eastern Front.

Men from a *Luftwaffe* field division move forward during the 1944 summer battles in France.

Company muster in southern France, spring 1944.

Two comrades from *Flieger-Regiment 13*, summer 1942.

List of tables

1. Employment of *2. Luftwaffen-Felddivision*, 1942–1944 25
2. Combat readiness of divisions under Army Group North 127
3. Strength of *Felddivision 12 (L)*, March 1945 133
4. Axis Order of Battle, Army Group Don, December 1942 170
5. Available weaponry, 12 February 1943 185
6. Location of *16. Luftwaffen-Felddivision* units on 1 June 1943 187
7. Ground and air losses, 6 June–29 September 1944 198
8. Declared fortresses by the German High Command 203
9. Weapons in the 19th *Luftwaffe* Division, 1 April 1944 227
10. Corps and Army Posting for *20. Luftwaffen-Sturm-Division* 246
11. *Luftwaffe* field division men transferred into the paratroopers, 14 December 1943 268
12. Employment of *Division Meindl / 21. Luftwaffen-Felddivision / Felddivision 21 (L)* 279

Introduction

Hermann Göring: The Force Behind the Creation of the *Luftwaffe* Field Divisions

The history of the German air force field divisions which fought during the Second World War is tied to the history of a former First World War German fighter pilot named Hermann Wilhelm Göring, who had served alongside Baron Manfred Albrecht von Richthofen in *Jagdgeschwader 1* (1st Fighter Wing). More commonly referred to by the pilots as the *Fliegenden Zirkus* ('Flying Circus'), *Jagdgeschwader 1* was the scourge of the Entente fighter pilots, scoring an impressive number of combat kills during the war. The unit's commander, Baron von Richthofen, would be responsible for downing no fewer than eighty enemy planes before he himself was finally shot down and killed on 21 April 1918. When Richthofen died, Göring assumed command of *Jagdgeschwader 1* and led the unit until the end of the war in November 1918. In May, about a month after Richthofen's death, Hermann Göring was awarded the *Pour le Mérite* (nicknamed the 'Blue Max') for gallantry in action. This was the highest military award that one could receive in Imperial Germany. Göring did not go through the war unscathed. On one occasion he was shot down and barely survived the crash.

After the war, like most German veterans, Göring found it difficult to readjust to civilian life. This was particularly true given that the Germany Göring and others of his generation had grown up in no longer existed. In its place the Allies had created a democratic government known as the Weimar Republic. In addition, huge swathes of land had been lost by Imperial Germany, as well as all her overseas colonies. To add insult to injury, Germany had been forced to pay huge war reparations, causing untold misery and pain for everyday Germans. Göring chafed at such a harsh peace settlement. Like many of his generation, his politics eventually led him to a more radical party. Göring joined the nascent Nazi Party in late 1922. He had met and befriended Adolf Hitler a year earlier, at a Party meeting. In 1923 Friedrich Ebert, the president of the Weimar Republic, informed the French and English governments that Germany was temporarily suspending payments of war reparations because the nation lacked the funds. The British government grimaced but in the end accepted the German explanation as a *fait accompli*. The French, however, who had suffered most from German aggression, and whose northern lands had been ravaged by the war, were not so understanding. In retaliation, France occupied the Ruhr region of Germany, with its vast deposits of coal, and announced that they would receive their war reparations by seizing German coal.

A German wartime propaganda etching, depicting a Luftwaffe infantryman faithfully standing watch.

The Weimar government was incensed that France had occupied sovereign German territory and was now requisitioning German coal. In response to this, Ebert told the German miners to remain home. The logic of this was that if the miners did not dig up the coal, the French could not seize it. The miners, however, demanded that they be paid to stay home, as they needed to feed their families and pay their rent. Ebert agreed to this. The way that the Weimar Republic did this was to simply print more paper money. However, very quickly inflation began to rise, to the point where people's bank savings were rendered worthless. A man might have saved all his life to accumulate 10,000 *Reichsmarks* in a savings account, but now that money could not even buy him a loaf of bread. The hyperinflation in Germany in 1923 also created more Nazi Party members than ever before, as many Germans, bitter at having lost their savings, and not being able to afford food or rent, became radicalized. Only in 1924, with the Dawes Plan, was the runaway inflation controlled and the value of the *Reichsmark* rose once again. But by then the damage had been done.

Based on this instability, a small nationalist party in Germany tried to take advantage by staging a coup. When Hitler attempted his *Putsch* in Munich on 8–9 November 1923, it ended in failure. Sixteen Nazis were eventually killed during the coup attempt, and many were also wounded, including Göring. His wound was in the groin, and even after several operations, the pain was insufferable. The physician who was treating him prescribed morphine as the only palliative care that could alleviate the unbearable pain Göring experienced on a daily basis. Before long, he became addicted to the drug, and would spend the rest of his life as a morphine addict. The stock market crash of 1929, and the subsequent depression, only served to worsen the situation for everyday Germans. John Maynard Keynes, the famous English economist, had taken a look at the Versailles treaty and remarked that because of its harshness, it would bring about another world war. Unfortunately, he was proven right. Even the former French commander, Marshal Ferdinand Foch, had realized the harshness of the treaty imposed on Germany and commented: 'This is not a treaty; this is a twenty-year armistice.' His prediction was off by only a few months. Given all of this, and the political chaos in Germany in the 1920s and 1930s, it is hardly surprising that Hermann Göring and millions of other Germans openly resented the Treaty of Versailles and the Weimar Republic.

As stated previously, in 1922, during a rally protesting the Treaty of Versailles, Hermann Göring met Adolf Hitler, an up-and-coming right-wing nationalist orator who would eventually lead the *Nationalsozialistische Deutsche Arbeiterpartei* (NSDAP, 'National Socialist German Workers Party'). The party had grown from a small, fringe party known as the *Deutsche Arbeiterpartei* (DAP) that had existed from 1919 to 1920, when the title was changed to the NSDAP. In 1921 Hitler became its leader. The NSDAP, whose members were known as 'Nazis', were rabidly anti-Semitic and ultra-nationalistic. The Nazi Party was also an exclusionary party, meaning that only people of Aryan descent were allowed to join. The party's platform seemed to appeal to Göring's conservative mind. Like millions of other Germans, he became a member of the Nazi Party and a follower of Adolf Hitler.

In January 1933 President Paul von Hindenburg appointed Hitler as Chancellor of Germany. Hitler wasted no time in appointing his friend of ten years, Göring, to a high post in the government. On 11 April 1933 Göring was appointed Minister President of Prussia, a position that he held until 23 April 1945. He was also given a mostly ceremonial title, *Reichsstatthalter der Preussen* ('National Governor of Prussia'), a position which he held for roughly the same period of time as Minister President of Prussia. Two years later, on 1 March 1935, he was appointed *Oberbefehlshaber der deutschen Luftwaffe* ('Commander-in-Chief of the German Air Force'). In 1936 Hitler appointed Göring to lead the so-called Four-Year Plan, a series of economic measures that the general public was told would make Germany economically self-sufficient. The real motive of the Four-Year Plan, however, was to prepare Nazi Germany for another war. After the fall of France in 1940, Hitler bestowed another honorary title on Hermann Göring: *Reichsmarschall des Grossdeutschen Reiches* ('National Marshal of the Greater German Nation').

The Creation of the Air Force Field Divisions

By 1941 Hermann Göring was at the peak of his power, influence and popularity. Since 1935 he had sought to strengthen and enlarge the German Air Force. He was particularly proud of the fact that part of the basic training for all *Luftwaffe* personnel, instituted by him, was political indoctrination. While all members of the German *Wehrmacht* (armed forces) had to swear a personal oath of loyalty to Adolf Hitler, the *Heer* (army) had never instituted political indoctrination on a grand scale. This meant that for the most part air force personnel tended to be more politically reliable.

Göring suffered two embarrassments in 1940. First, he had promised Hitler that 'his' *Luftwaffe* could prevent the British Expeditionary Force from being evacuated at Dunkirk. In the end, 338,000 troops – mostly British, but some French – reached safety in England. They escaped without any heavy weapons, but these men could be rearmed and would fight again. Although the Germans won a tactical victory at Dunkirk, they incurred a strategic defeat. However, because this was the first time that Göring had failed Hitler, and because of their eighteen-year friendship, the *Führer* did not demote the *Reichsmarschall*. Nevertheless, Hitler made it clear that Göring had let him down and Göring swore to himself not to allow such a failure to occur again. But then his *Luftwaffe* lost the air battle over Britain, which lasted from 10 July to 31 October 1940. In fairness to Göring, it was Hitler who altered the *Luftwaffe*'s strategy from targeting radar installations, RAF airfields and aircraft manufacturing plants[1] to concentrating instead on bombing civilian targets as a way of crushing the will of the British. The bombing of British population centres had the opposite effect, as the people of the United Kingdom became more resolute and determined to defeat the Nazis. It also gave the RAF enough breathing room to recover from its heavy losses. That in turn helped the British to defeat the *Luftwaffe* during the Battle of Britain.

All of these political and personal setbacks would feature prominently in the mind of Hermann Göring, when in the spring of 1942 the German Army made a reasonable request that appeared to further diminish the *Reichsmarschall*'s power. Fresh from its heavy losses during the Soviet winter counteroffensive, and facing huge personnel shortages, the *Oberkommando der Wehrmacht* (Armed Forces High Command) and the *Ostheer* (Eastern Army) petitioned for those 200,000 excess *Luftwaffe* personnel to be transferred directly into the army, and retrained as infantry. The German Army also requested that 20,000 members of the *Kriegsmarine* (Navy) be likewise transferred to the *Heer* (Army). The *Heer* had been smart to point out that the expected growth of the *Luftwaffe* had not occurred, giving Göring no excuse why he shouldn't turn these men over to the army. Indeed, by the spring of 1942 the *Luftwaffe* did not possess enough aircraft to create the squadrons for which these ground crews and airmen were being kept. Fearing that his personal power within Hitler's circle would be further diminished, and incensed at the army's request, Göring vowed to Hitler that he would never transfer a single 'national socialist airman' into the *Heer*. Instead, he convinced the *Führer* to allow him to create a series of air force infantry divisions, which he titled *Luftwaffen-Felddivisionen* ('Air Force Field Divisions'), from the 200,000 men that the *Ostheer* wished to use as replacements for its depleted divisions. Göring argued that *Luftwaffe* officers could handle ground troops, given their 'fervent National Socialist ideology'. He also boasted that all the men in the Luftwaffe possessed this 'National Socialist spirit'. Somehow this Nazi fervour was supposed to make these air force personnel into effective combat troops. Unfortunately for the *Heer*, and for the overall German war effort, Hitler agreed with Göring's proposal. The German Army High Command was left dumbfounded. Apparently, a rival army, made up of air force personnel, would now be created. It was bad enough that the SS had begun to create its own private army (the *Waffen SS*). Now the *Luftwaffe* was going into this line of 'business' as well.

It was thus that a valuable pool of replacements for the much-battered German divisions on the Eastern Front was squandered on infantry divisions that, at best, would be mediocre. Instead of retraining these excess air force personnel as infantrymen and using them to strengthen the veteran German divisions, these airmen were to be employed in poorly established *Luftwaffe* field divisions. So badly did these air force field divisions perform that on 1 November 1943 the German Army had to assume control of them. Those air force divisions that were not already destroyed were reorganized and reinforced with a sprinkling of army veterans, which, it was hoped, might bring these mostly ineffective divisions up to parity with the rest of the *Heer*. They also attempted to reorganize them more effectively. Initially, the field divisions had consisted of two weak infantry regiments (instead of three), and only one artillery battalion, instead of an artillery regiment containing three battalions. The divisional support units were likewise smaller, and these too had to be expanded.

Hermann Göring, who was initially enthusiastic about forming 'his' infantry divisions, soon lost interest in them as reports began to pile up about the weakness and ineffectiveness of these units. Losing face yet again in the eyes of the *Führer*, he soon turned his attention to another pet project: the establishment of an air force armoured force. Göring's neglect only increased as the air force infantry divisions met with further calamity and disaster at the front. To Göring's mind, their poor showing only served to embarrass him in front of the *Führer*.

In an attempt to regain the *Führer's* favour, Göring concentrated on supporting and touting the German parachute divisions and the elite Hermann Göring Panzer and Panzer Grenadier Divisions that he would eventually create. Better armed and organized, and equipped with tanks and other armoured fighting vehicles, these divisions proved to be the equal of their *Heer* counterparts. For the rest of the war, Göring made sure to supply these units with quality men and materiel, while totally disregarding the needs of the air force field divisions. In fact, when the German Army assumed control of these divisions in November 1943, he demanded the removal of all *Flak* battalions from these divisions, so the 'loathed army' would not get their hands on them. Ironically, this partisan-motivated and petty decision further weakened the field divisions because now they had to fight without their *Flak* battalions, which often served as their best defence against armoured forces.

Toward a Reckoning

The creation of the *Luftwaffe* field divisions was the result of a political and personal decision trumping military necessity. The logical decision should have been to transfer the excess air force personnel into the *Heer*. By choosing political expediency and compromise (Göring still held some influence with Hitler), some 200,000 men were squandered in formations that proved to be not worth raising. Ironically, Hermann Göring had tried to dissuade Hitler from invading the USSR, but he was unable to convince the *Führer* that the *Luftwaffe*, and indeed, the entire *Wehrmacht*, was not up to the task of defeating the 'Russian Bear'.

In the spring of 1942, however, Göring was able to convince the *Führer* that raising infantry formations manned and staffed by air force personnel, supposedly all imbued with Nazi fanaticism, was a brilliant concept. It was madness, but it fitted neatly into Hitler's strategy of keeping the various factions under his command in competition, all vying for power and influence. Further, the concept of overlapping areas of command and control appealed to the Nazi leader, as his underlings would have to go to him for a decision, because he was the final arbiter in these matters of overlapping commands. That, of course, is what Hitler wanted, so that his underlings would always be at some level of rivalry with one another, and thus too busy to plot any coups against the *Führer*. It was a stratagem geared to keep him from losing power, but it was a wasteful one.

Another factor that sealed the fate of these air force field divisions, even before they were created, was Göring's decision to ignore tried and tested German Army divisional organizational structure. Other factors also ensured that these divisions would not succeed. The increasing pressures of the war, especially the stresses and demands of the Eastern Front, eventually caused Ernst Udet, who was in charge of *Luftwaffe* procurement, to commit suicide over the ever-increasing demands made by Erhard Milch, the Inspector General of the *Luftwaffe*. These demands dealt with airplane production, as well as the production of *Flak* guns and other equipment, and also controlled the delivery and distribution of these weapons. However efficient factories and workers may have been, German industry in the early to mid-1940s could not accomplish the high production figures that Milch was now demanding.[2] In addition, Göring's lack of attention to detail and strategic planning had created a *Luftwaffe* that was established as a tactical weapon, but not as a strategic air force. The *Luftwaffe* could support the *Heer* but was wholly incapable of launching a prolonged air operation, either as a protracted bombing campaign, or for some other strategic goal. The *Luftwaffe* employed light and medium bombers but the Third Reich never produced heavier, four-engined bombers on the scale necessary for such operations. Instead, the few four-engined planes that were available were used for either reconnaissance or special missions.

Göring's failures as head of the *Luftwaffe* eventually began to see the light of day. As his ineptitude began to show, his influence with the *Führer* began to wane. This made Göring all the more defensive and paranoid. His drug addiction didn't help him either. So when in the spring of 1942 the German Army made the sound request of asking for 200,000 excess Luftwaffe personnel, Göring absolutely refused. He simply believed that giving in to the army's wishes was a sign that his power was diminishing and his influence with Hitler was similarly decreasing. Göring's incompetence, coupled with his fear of losing whatever power and influence he had, was the catalyst that set into motion the establishment of the *Luftwaffe* field divisions. In terms of human lives lost as a result of this selfish decision, it was an unforgivable military blunder to try to create infantry divisions from within the German air force. The professional ground fighting force was the *Heer*. To send air force officers and enlisted men into a ground battle, especially the meat-grinder that was the Russian Front, with little or no training, was totally senseless and irresponsible. This is a perfect paradigm of how personal and political considerations can often damage military goals. The human tragedy of Göring and Hitler's choice is that many German airmen died, whose lives might have been spared had they gone through proper army training.

1. Luftwaffen-Felddivision

This division was the first official unit raised (not including Division-Meindl). It was formed in *Luftgau I* (Air Force District No. 1), in Konigsberg, East Prussia. The majority of the division was trained at *Heerestruppenübungsplatz Gross-Born* (Army Troop Training Ground Gross-Born). The infantry recruits came from *Flieger-Regiment 10*, a cadre regiment under the command of *Oberst* Robert Pistorius,[1] which had been established on 1 April 1939 in Neukuhren, from *Flieger-Ausbildungs-Regiment 10*. In November 1941 *Flieger-Regiment 10* was moved to the Maubeuge region of Belgium and northern France. The new division's infantry complement lacked a regimental headquarters, but did have four independently led *Luftwaffe Jäger* battalions. The formation eventually received an anti-tank battalion, comprising a company of towed 75mm Pak 40 anti-tank guns, a 37mm *Flak* company mounted on halftracks, and an assault gun battery of *Sturmgeschütz III* assault guns. The *Sturmgeschütz III* assault gun was basically a turretless armoured vehicle carrying the 75mm L24 anti-tank gun.[2] This assault gun battery, in effect, acted as the third company in the anti-tank battalion. It was organized from 19 October to 7 November 1942 at *Truppenübungsplatz Ohrdruf* (Troop Training Ground Ohrdruf) in Thuringia. A few of the component parts of the division were organized in the area behind the front lines of *58. Infanterie-Division, XXXVIII. Armeekorps*, near the Volkov river in June 1942.[3]

Instead of a regular artillery regiment of three to four artillery battalions, *1. Luftwaffen-Felddivision* only had one artillery battalion with three artillery batteries. Smaller, company-sized formations in the division included a *radfahr* (cycling) company (*Radfahr Kompanie der Luftwaffen-Felddivision 1*), which performed reconnaissance missions for the division, an engineer company, a *signals* (communications) company and a *pionier* (engineer) company. Overall, the division was far smaller than a regular German infantry division. As far as support services were concerned, the company-sized units were wholly inadequate. However, the division did contain an entire *Flak* battalion that quite often served in an anti-tank role.

On 1 November 1943 the army assumed control of the air force field divisions. However, Göring, who wished to keep as much control of his forces as possible, withdrew the *Flak* battalions from these divisions and returned them to *Luftwaffe* service. For example, the *Flak* battalion in *1. Luftwaffen-Felddivision* was detached from the division and redesignated as *I. Flak-Abteilung/Flak-Regiment 40*. The withdrawal of the *Flak* battalions from the *Luftwaffe* field divisions diminished the fighting value of these units even further.

As stated earlier, the original cadre of men for this division came from *Flieger Regiment 10*, which was a training and replacement regiment for the Air Force. *Oberst* Robert Pistorius led this regiment from its formation on 1 April 1939 until 23 November of that same year. In July 1942 the regiment was disbanded because its men had been used to form the cadre of *1. Luftwaffen-Felddivision*.

The first divisional commander was *Generalleutnant* (Lieutenant General) Gustav Wilke, who led the division from 30 September 1942 until 15 June 1943, when *Oberst* Anton Longin assumed temporary command. On 23 July 1943 Wilke resumed command and led the division until 1 November 1943, when *Generalmajor* (Major General) Rudolf Petrauschke took over command. As stated previously, on 1 November 1943 the *Heer* assumed all responsibility for the surviving air force field divisions. They were now to be referred to as *Felddivision 1 (L)*, where the 'L' represented the word *Luftwaffe* (air force), thus denoting their original branch of service. *1. Luftwaffen-Felddivision* made its appearance on the Eastern Front in November 1942. The division was part of a major reinforcement of Army Group North, in anticipation of a coming Soviet winter offensive in and around the area of *16.* and *18. Armee*. In addition, *69. Infanterie-Division* had been brought in from southern Norway and sent to the western edge of the Pogostje cauldron, in the Volkhov region. In the meantime, *9.* and *10. Luftwaffen-Felddivisionen* were sent to garrison the Oranienbaum pocket. This pocket (which the Russians referred to as a bridgehead) lay to the west of the city of Leningrad, skirting the Gulf of Finland. It was 65km long and 25km deep. For some reason, the Germans never attempted to destroy the pocket. This was a serious mistake, for when the Russians launched their offensive, they attacked from it, aiding the Red Army drive to break the siege of Leningrad. When the division arrived in the region of Army Group North, it was ordered to relieve the much battered and weary *250. Infanterie-Division (spanische) 'Blau Division'*[4] in and around the city of Novgorod on the northern edge of Lake Ilmen. It was hoped that the presence of the lake, plus the Volkhov river in front of Novgorod, would act as a natural defensive barrier that the air force men, unaccustomed to the rigours of the Russian front, could use to defend themselves against any Soviet attack. Initially, in November 1942, the division was under the command of *X. Armeekorps/16. Armee* but in December it was transferred to the *XXXVIII. Armeekorps/18. Armee*.

The amount of training that the division had received in Germany had been so scant and lacking that it had to be continued at the front. This was one of the reasons why the Novgorod sector was chosen for this small and untried unit. The *Oberkommando des Heeres* (OKH, Army High Command) felt that the naturally defensible terrain might help make up for the lack of training and combat experience. This plan worked while the Novgorod sector was not the main focus of Soviet attention and intentions, but this all changed to the Germans' disadvantage once a serious attack in this region was planned by STAVKA (the Main Command of the Armed Forces of the USSR) and launched in January 1944. Thus, *1. Luftwaffen-Felddivision* had had about a year in which to get accustomed

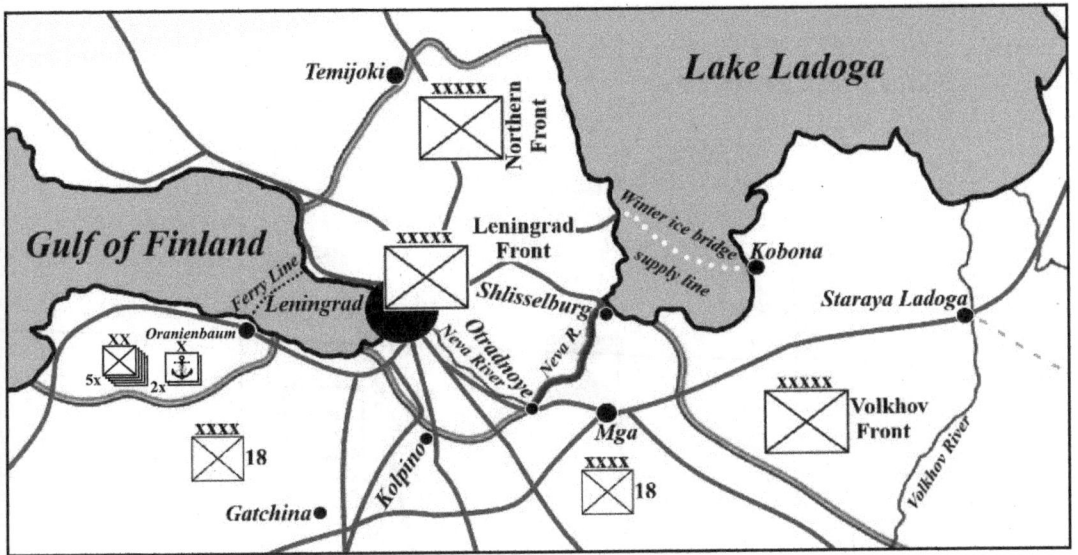

The Leningrad Front in the fall of 1941.

to the almost daily ritual of battery and counter-battery fire between the opposing sides' artillery units, and the occasional infantry probes across the lines. It didn't take the Russians long to realize that they were dealing with a second-rate (at best) infantry formation. In fact, this may well have been the reason why this part of the front was chosen as one of the focal points of their northern regional winter offensive in January 1944. If they concentrated on breaking through this relatively weak division, they could penetrate the German lines much more easily than anywhere else.

1. Luftwaffen-Felddivision was a division in name only. It remained in defensive positions in and around Novgorod and under *XXXVIII. Armeekorps / 18. Armee* for most of its time at the front, beginning in December 1942, although it was briefly transferred to the control of *16. Armee* between August and September 1943. It spent most of the winter of 1942/1943 and all of 1943 fighting off relatively small Soviet penetrations and defending against guerrilla raids in the rear. These attacks were mostly probing sorties, designed to discover the division's weaknesses and defensive positions.

In July 1943, while *1. Luftwaffen-Felddivision* was under the *XXXVIII. Armeekorps*, it formed part of the corps' right flank, alongside *217. Infanterie-Division* and the *(lettische) SS-Freiwilligen-Brigade* (Latvian SS Volunteer Brigade). On 28 October 1943 the division had an effective 'bayonet strength' of only 2,779 men, while the total bayonet strength of the entire corps was a mere 6,429 men.[5] In the early morning hours of 15 January 1944 the relative quiet of the Novgorod region on the Volkhov Front was shattered by the massive artillery barrage that heralded the start of the new Soviet winter offensive.[6] The first assault was directed to the north of the positions of *Felddivision 1 (L)* in the region of *28. Jäger-Division*.

Wave after wave of Red Army infantry battalions stormed the German defensive positions along the Volkhov river, but *Jäger-Regiment 49* and *Jäger-Regiment 83*, whose men hailed from Silesia, held their ground long enough for

12 Hitler's *Luftwaffe* Infantry

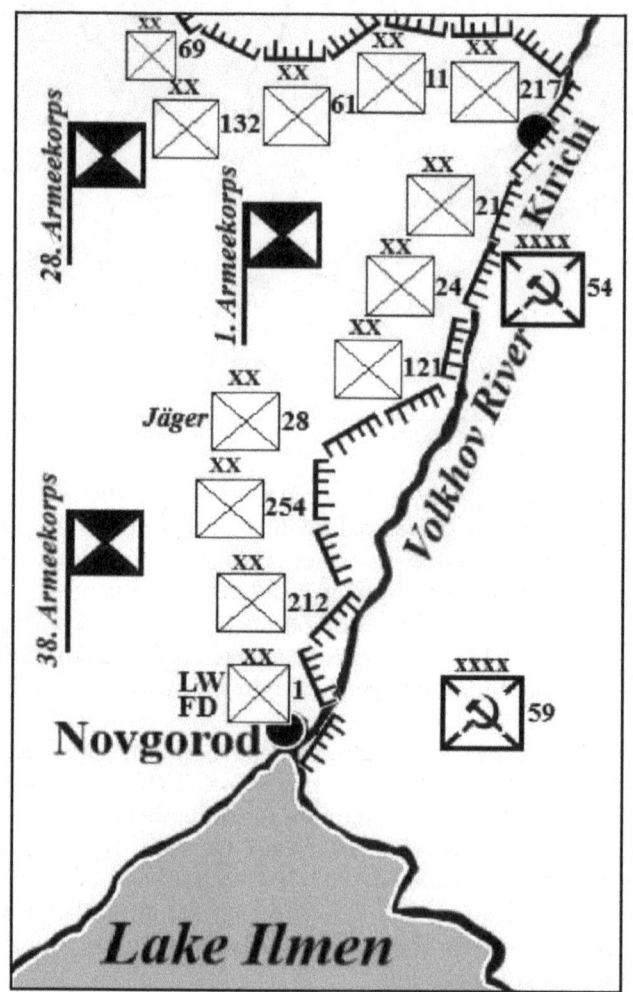

1. Luftwaffen-Felddivision in the Novgorod-Lake Ilmen region, January 1943.

the assault to stall in their sector. The initial attack from the bridgehead positions near Teremets and across the Volkhov river collapsed under the intense fire of *28. Jäger-Division*. The prolonged artillery barrage by the batteries of *Artillerie-Regiment 28* finally cracked the ice-covered Volkhov and thick chunks of ice began to break and float away, destroying the natural frozen path that had allowed for the Soviet attack to proceed in the first place.

Now the Soviets turned their attention to Novgorod itself and its defenders, the men of *1. Luftwaffen-Felddivision*. As discussed above, in November 1943 the division had been inducted into the German Army from the air force and redesignated as *Felddivision 1 (L)*. This was in keeping with the standing order to induct all air force field divisions into the German Army, as well as to reorganize

1. Luftwaffen-Felddivision

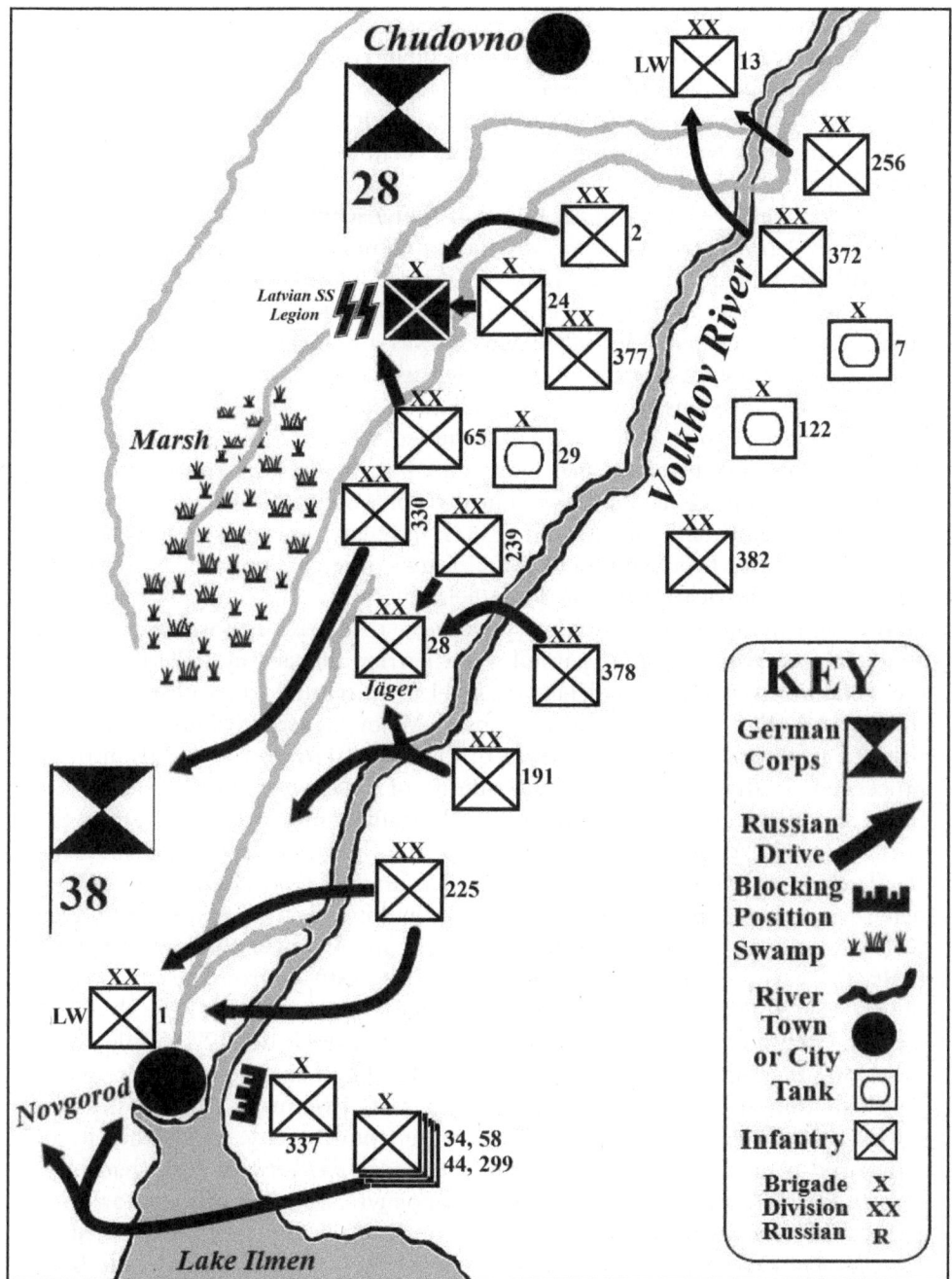

The Soviet Leningrad-Novgorod offensive, January 1944. The detail shows the Soviet attacks in the Novgorod-Chudovno region. The Russians were able to outflank *1. Luftwaffen-Felddivision* by crossing over a frozen section of Lake Ilmen.

and supply them with a sprinkling of army personnel. It was hoped that by adding key soldiers from the *Heer*, especially junior infantry officers, these air force field divisions could be salvaged and be of some use. The German army concerns over these units was justified by *Felddivision 1 (L)*, which in the first two weeks of the Soviet Leningrad-Novgorod offensive, took casualties of over 1,300 men killed or wounded.[7]

In November 1943 *Generalmajor* Rudolf Petrauschke had taken command of *Felddivision 1 (L)*. Petrauschke was the former commander of *Fliegerregiment 82*, and had led that unit with the rank of *Oberst* (Colonel). The Russians had a year to study these *Luftwaffe* field divisions and derive an estimation of their abilities and deficiencies. I don't believe it was a coincidence that the Soviets began to direct the focal points of their offensives at the front lines held by these air force field divisions whenever possible. *Felddivision 1 (L)* in particular was woefully unprepared to hold back a determined Soviet assault. The guns of the division's anti-tank battalion had long since been withdrawn in order to help form another air force field division. The division's only anti-tank protection was a mere fifteen anti-tank guns. It didn't even have any *Flak* guns to fall back on, since they too had been withdrawn (on Göring's orders). The scene was thus set for the eventual defeat of this air force field division.

Although the division lacked heavy weapons to defend against an armoured attack, it was favoured by the natural water barrier afforded by Lake Ilmen and the Volkhov river. But in mid-January 1944 these natural water obstacles were frozen hard. The Soviets managed to insert Major General Sviklin's 58th Rifle Brigade across Lake Ilmen, just south of the city of Novgorod, and from there proceeded to attack the rear area positions of *Felddivision 1 (L)*. The Soviet thrust cut the western and southern roads leading into the city, leaving the northern road as the only exit. Inside the city, the *Grenadier-Regiment 503* and the *II. Abteilung/Artillerie-Regiment 290*, as well as units of *Felddivision 1 (L)*, took up defensive positions in the outskirts of the city and in the city itself.[8] General Ivan Korovnikov, who was in overall charge of the attack, saw a window of opportunity thrown open when his leading forces drove westward from the city as far as the *Rollbahn* (runway) and decided to commit the 372nd and 225th Rifle Divisions as well. Eventually Korovnikov also sent into the breach the 299th Rifle Regiment, and the 34th and 44th Brigades. Now the German defenders were being attacked from three sides: west, south and east. Eventually, the 225th Rifle Division would cut the northern escape route from the city. Inside the city of Novgorod panic began to set in. The riflemen of *Felddivision 1 (L)* had been thrown off guard by this sudden flanking manoeuvre, but their officers now tried to establish some sort of a defence. In the ruins of the city they were joined by *Kampfgruppe Furguth*, the only available corps reserve, which had already been brought up.[9] In the city, *II. Abteilung/Artillerie-Regiment 290* provided covering fire. After two days of intense fighting, the German units were ordered to withdraw.

The last intact ammunition dump in the city was blown up during the night of 19 January 1944 so the Russians could not capture it, and afterwards a breakout order was sent out. Not many German soldiers were able to escape the Soviet encirclement. Of *Kampfgruppe Furguth*, for example, only one officer and around 100 men reached the German lines. The remnants of *Felddivision 1 (L)* were combined with the survivors of *28. Jäger-Division* and *Kavallerie-Regiment Nord*. This battle group, nicknamed *Kampfgruppe Speth*, numbered only about 2,200 men. In effect, *Felddivision 1 (L)* had ceased to exist. By 2 February 1944 the battlegroup represented about a quarter of the total 'bayonet' strength of *XXXIV. Armeekorps*. This corps now had about 9,100 combat troops, not including support personnel. At the beginning of February 1944 the entire front line from the Volkhov river by Lake Ilmen to Kirishi was held by the *XXXVIII. Armeekorps*, with *21.* and *96. Infanterie-Division* and *Felddivision 13 (L)*. The 9,000 or so survivors of the much-reduced *XXXVIII. Armeekorps* were now attached to *XXVIII. Armeekorps*.[10] The infantrymen from *Felddivision 1 (L)* continued to serve under *Kampfgruppe Speth* until April 1944, when the division was officially dissolved. In reality, *Felddivision 1 (L)* had ceased to function as a division around the time of the breakout from the city of Novgorod between 19 and 21 January 1944. The remnants of the *Luftwaffe* infantry from *Felddivision 1 (L)* were eventually reassigned to the Silesian *28. Jäger-Division*, which was also virtually wiped out and was in the process of reforming.

Command Structure of *1. Luftwaffen-Felddivision*

Commanders:
    Generalleutnant Gustav Wilke, 30/09/42–17/01/43
    Generalmajor Werner Zech, 18/01/43–14/06/43
    Oberst Anton Longin, 15/06/43–23/07/43
    Generalleutnant Gustav Wilke, 23/07/43–01/11/43
    Generalmajor Rudolf Petrauschke, 01/11/43–02/44
Ia:
    Major Herbert Schmidt, 01/10/42–01/11/43
Ib:
    Major Karl Seehars, 02/05/43–12/07/43
    Hauptmann Walter Segebarth, 13/07/43–01/44
IIa:
    Hauptmann Mans, 10/12/43–?
    CO *I. Jäger-Bataillon / 1. Luftwaffen-Felddivision*:
    Major Bodo Ahlhorn, 10/42–29/03/43
    CO *II. Jäger-Bataillon / 1. Luftwaffen-Felddivision*

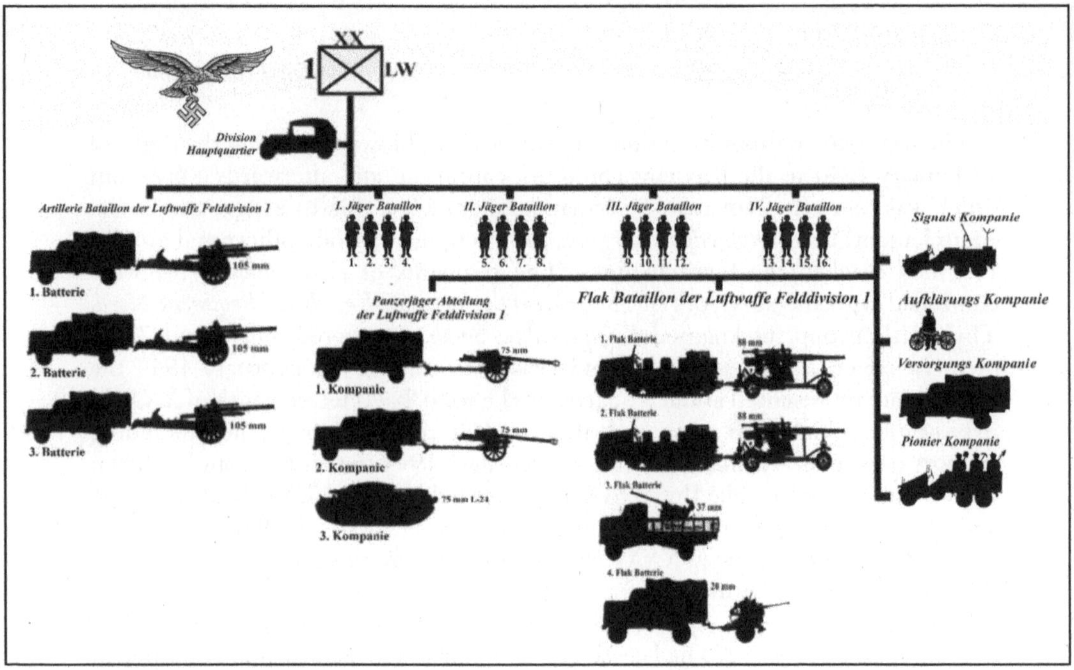

Structure of *1. Luftwaffen-Felddivision*, December 1942.

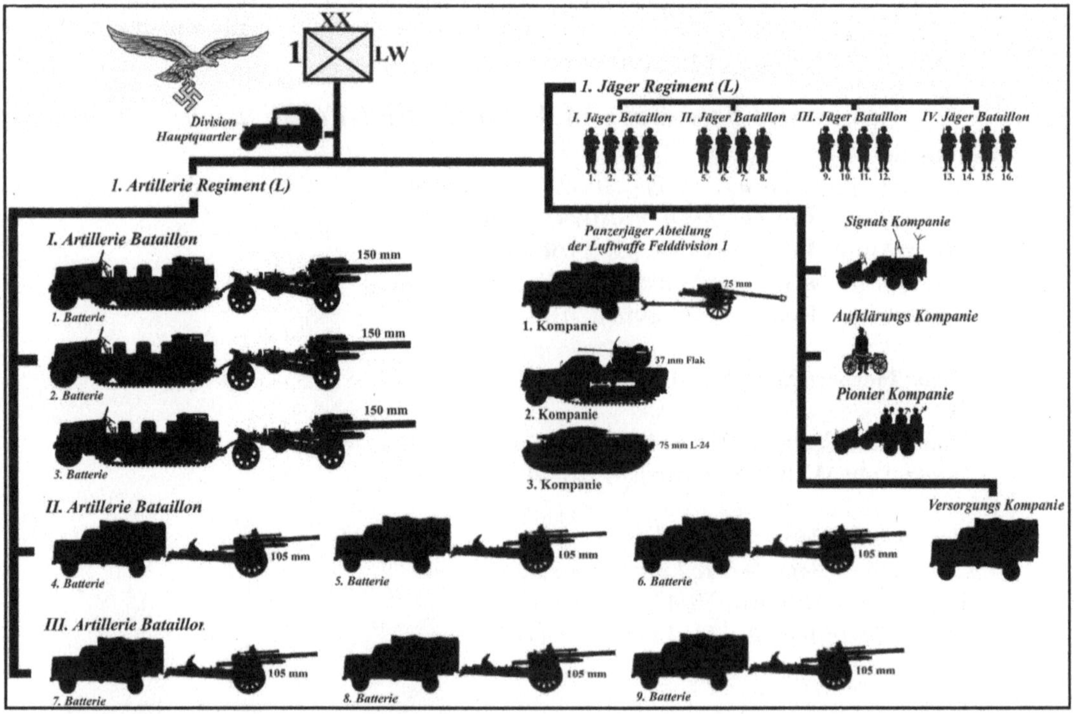

Structure of *Felddivision 1 (L)*, December 1943.

2. Luftwaffen-Felddivision

This division had a similar origin to *1. Luftwaffen-Felddivision*, having been formed in September 1942 at Troop Training Ground Gross-Born under *Luftgau III* (Air Force District No. 3). Just like *1. Luftwaffen-Felddivision*, the unit's infantry complement contained no regimental headquarters, but did have four independently led *Jäger* battalions. In November 1942 the worsening situation on the Russian front forced the quick transfer of the partly trained division to the area of Army Group Centre, where it was employed in defensive positions around the city of Smolensk.

There was no regimental artillery. Instead, the division could count on one artillery battalion of three batteries, equipped with Czechoslovakian 75mm Skoda Model 15 mountain guns. The unit also contained a three-company anti-tank battalion, which consisted of a towed *PAK* (anti-tank) company, a *Flak* (anti-aircraft) company and an assault gun battery of *Sturmgeschütz III* assault guns. There was also a *Flak* battalion attached to the division. Engineer and signals companies rounded out the basic organization. One source also states that the division contained a bicycle company that operated as the divisional reconnaissance unit, but this might have been added later. This 'compact' divisional organization was a recipe for failure in the field, given that the size of these so-called 'divisions' was in reality a medium brigade at best. The harsh and brutal conditions on the Eastern Front, coupled with the poorly constructed *Luftwaffe* field divisions, with their inadequately trained men and officers, would eventually prove the undoing of this and most of the other divisions that Hermann Göring insisted would prove themselves in battle because of their 'National Socialist fervour'.[1] When the army took over these divisions in November 1943, they tried to reorganize them and fill them with army veterans. By the time those changes were instituted, more than half of the divisions had already been destroyed.

Command of *2. Luftwaffen-Felddivision* was entrusted to *Oberst* Hellmuth Pätzold and records indicate that the division was initially stationed in the region of Smolensk under *VI. Armeekorps, 9. Armee*. Soon, however, the untried and half-trained unit was shifted to a position some 18km south-southwest of the important town of Byeloye (Bjeloje in German), where it came under the control of *XXX. Armeekorps*. In early October an attempt was made to solidify the front lines of *2. Luftwaffen-Felddivision*. To this end *Kampfgruppe Schafer*, a force made up of men from *246. Infanterie-Division* and *I. Bataillon/3. Regiment Brandenburg*, was organized and sent into the defence lines to 'stiffen' the positions of this air force infantry division.[2] This remedy would only prove temporary, however, and the weight of the enemy attack would eventually force the collapse of *2. Luftwaffen-Felddivision*.

It was in and around the town of Batutino that on the night of 25 November 1942, in the middle of a driving snowstorm, the Red Army flung no fewer than ten rifle and five tank divisions at the front lines of *2. Luftwaffen-Felddivision* and its neighbour to the north, *246. Infanterie-Division*. The situation for the Germans was made all the worse by the large frontage that each division was expected to hold. If a German division were lucky, it was given about 20–25km of front lines to guard. Even for a regular-sized German infantry division, these frontages were hard to hold. The air force field divisions, most of which were the size of a brigade, were wholly incapable of holding such a long front line. Adding to the problem

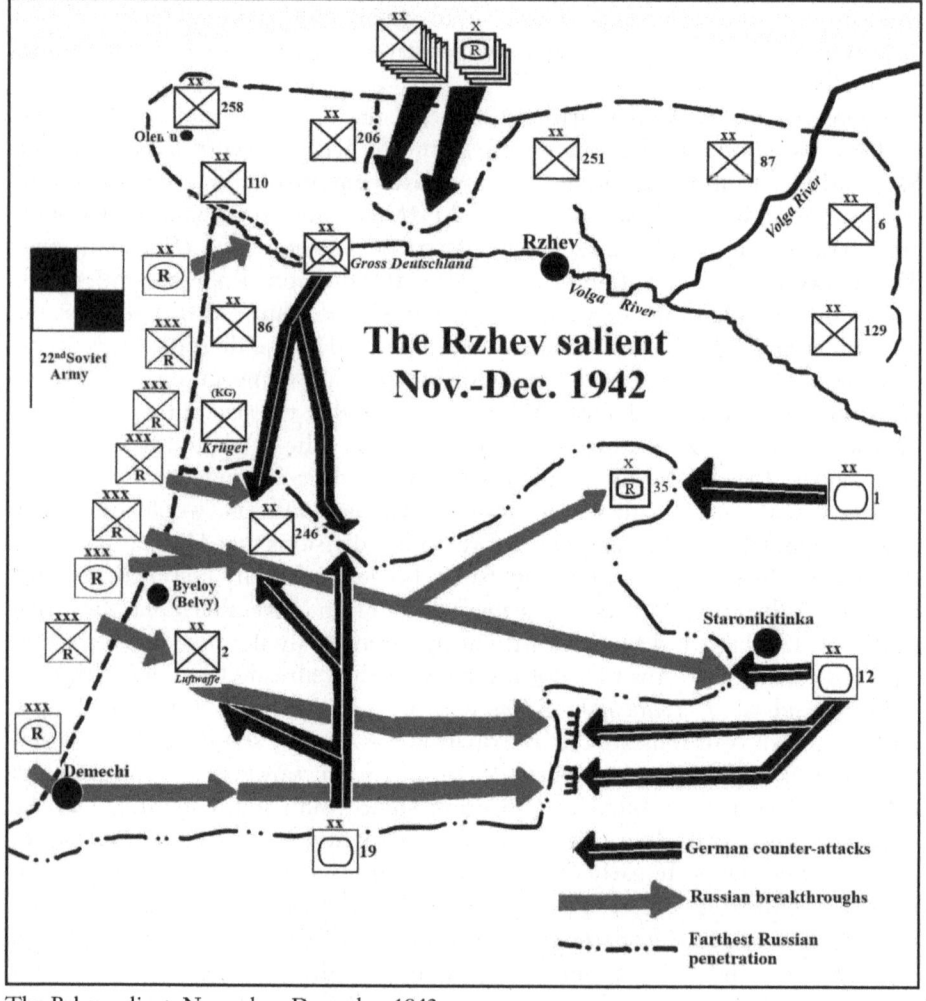

The Rzhev salient, November–December 1942.

of this massive attack was the partisan menace, which caused countless losses behind the lines among the inexperienced soldiers of *2. Luftwaffen-Felddivision*. The front lines of the *Luftwaffe* men broke on the first day of the attack, with some troops giving way to panic.[3] The front lines of *246. Infanterie-Division* held until 14 December 1942, despite the fact that its left flank began to be enveloped as early as 27 November 1942.

Enemy armoured attacks were launched against *2. Luftwaffen-Felddivision* and the neighbouring unit on its right flank, *246. Infanterie-Division*, as early as 25 and 29 November respectively. Russian T-34 tanks penetrated the southernmost positions of *2. Luftwaffen-Felddivision* at Demechi on 25 November 1942. It wasn't until 9 December that Soviet mechanized forces broke through the *Luftwaffe* infantry screen further north. The Germans realized the danger and immediately threw in two reserve divisions, *20. Panzer-Division* and the *SS-Kavallerie-Division Florian Geyer*. In addition, the decision was quickly made to employ a third unit, *156. Infanterie-Division*, which was now moved forward to help stiffen what used to be the defence lines of *2. Luftwaffen-Felddivision*.

Three days later Soviet armoured units were rushing through the village of Turovo, just south of Byeloye. The situation worsened when the Red Army's 35th Tank Brigade almost reached the village of Bulygma, several kilometres southeast of Byeloye. Only through the prompt arrival of two additional divisions, *19. Panzer-Division* and *Infanterie-Division 'Groß Deutschland' (motorisiert)*, did the Germans avert a complete military disaster.

The Red Army attack against *2. Luftwaffen-Felddivision* south of Byeloye in November–December 1942 was serious, but by 1 January 1943 the lines south of Byeloye had been stabilized, thanks in part to the quick actions of Army Group Centre. However, *2. Luftwaffen-Felddivision* was shattered.

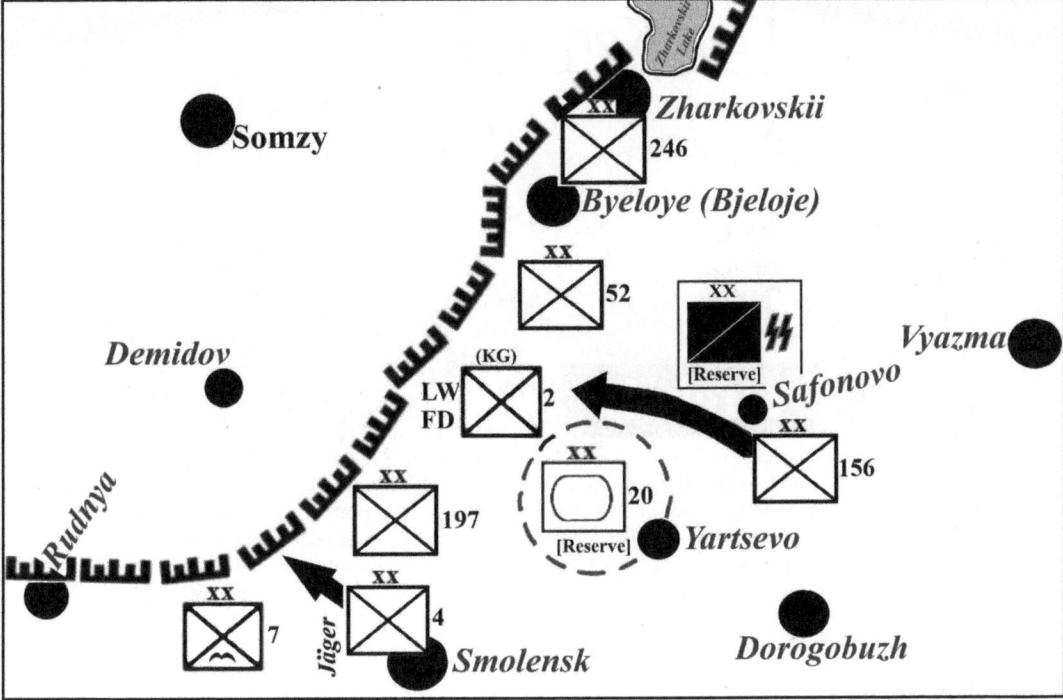

The positions of *II. Luftwaffen-Feldkorps*, comprising *Felddivision 2 (L), 3 (L), 4 (L),* and *6 (L)*. On 1 October 1943 the corps and its divisions numbered around 21,000 men. This corps, therefore, was the strength of a reinforced German infantry division from the 1939 period. As the war dragged on, the Germans reduced the number of men needed for an infantry division to be considered at 'full strength'. By 1944 an infantry division of around 10,000–12,000 men was considered full strength.

The rapid collapse of *2. Luftwaffen-Felddivision*, coupled with the calamitous military situation that its defeat presented to Army Group Centre, was a public relations nightmare for *Reichsmarschall* Hermann Göring, whose enemies in Hitler's inner circle made sure to mention this defeat more than once to the *Führer*. The collapse of resistance by *2. Luftwaffen-Felddivision*, so quickly and so fully, was a psychological blow to Göring's ego. The fact that his 'National Socialist' airmen had endured such a complete and utter defeat only proved once and for all that the *Heer* had been right all along in their estimation of what would happen if these air force field divisions were established. It was now obvious to all that the transfer of 200,000 airmen from the *Luftwaffe* into the German Army would have made a more positive impact on the course of the war.[4] The rapid collapse of *2. Luftwaffen-Felddivision* also affirmed the observations made by Soviet intelligence on the weaknesses of these air force ground units. Author Colonel Albert Seaton expressed it succinctly when he wrote:

> In early October Yeremenko's Kalinin Front attacked 3rd Panzer Army in the sector held by a Luftwaffe field corps, the offensive being so heavy that a half trained and inexperienced Luftwaffe division broke almost immediately, some of it running away in panic. Within a matter of hours Yeremenko's men were pouring through the ten-mile gap into the rear. Göring, whose honor was involved by the failure of the Luftwaffe ground troops, had immediately allocated reinforcement Flak batteries and 600 aircraft to the sector and, with their assistance, the situation was temporarily brought under control.[5]

That the unit remained in existence at all to serve into 1943 was a tribute not to its men and officers, but to German Army organizational command and control effectiveness. On 25 May 1943 the remnants of *2. Luftwaffen-Felddivision* were temporarily attached to *XLIII. Armeekorps*. Although the majority of these *Luftwaffe* soldiers were physically fit young men, they nevertheless lacked vital infantry training and equipment. General Weidling had been particularly derogatory about these *Luftwaffe* field divisions, and when the decision was made on 17 June 1943 to group four air force field divisions into a corps-sized unit, he prophesied calamitous consequences. On 14 September 1943 OKH ordered that Army Group Centre's boundary be shifted south of Nevel.[6] Then *XLIII. Armeekorps*, containing the *83.*, *205.*, and *263. Infanterie-Division*, were transferred to Army Group North. Although Hermann Göring had supplied *II. Luftwaffen Feldkorps* with an ample number of *Flak* units, it was still considered inadequate by the army. *Generalleutnant* Otto Heidkämper, who at the time was chief of the general staff for *3. Panzerarmee*, related how *II. Luftwaffen Feldkorps* was well equipped, but its units, especially *2. Luftwaffen-Felddivision*, were weak.[7] By now it was becoming painfully clear that *II. Luftwaffen-Feldkorps* and its air force divisions were poorly trained and organized. Now this weak German corps was placed at a critical point, covering the junction between Army Group North and Army Group Centre.[8] In vain, Heidkämper warned that placing such a weak force at so critical a juncture was asking for trouble, but his warnings were ignored. It was a tactical mistake on the part of the German command that would have strategic consequences.

The Red Army attack concentrated on an area between Rossedenye and Volchi Gory. Then, supported by T-34 tanks and *Ilyushin Il-2* ground-attack fighter-bombers (nicknamed '*Sturmovik*'), the Red Army advanced northwest and southeast of Bolshaya, threatening the deep flank of 2. *Luftwaffen-Felddivision*.[9] German Army fears were once again realized on 6 October 1943 when 2. *Luftwaffen-Felddivision*, under the strain of another determined Red Army tank attack, broke once again. According to *Generalleutnant* Heidkämper, 2. *Luftwaffen-Felddivision* was completely crushed and was 'without combat value'.[10] The tear in the German lines left a 16km gap, which the Russians took full advantage of. The Red Army poured through the gap, utterly nullifying the so-called 'Panther' positions, upon which Hitler, and indeed the entire *Ostheer*, were pinning their hopes of halting the Red Army. The OKW War Diary described the situation:

> At 10:00 a.m. on 6 October the offensive opened with an attack by 3rd & 4th Shock Armies both of the Kalinin Front side by side, supported by tanks and bombers. The half trained and inexperienced 2. *Luftwaffen-Felddivision* of Schlemm's *II. Luftwaffen-Feldkorps* broke almost immediately, some of the troops giving way to panic, and within a matter of hours Soviet forces were pouring through a 10-mile [16km] gap. Nevel was taken and the next day the lateral railway line connecting both army corps was broken.[11]

By exploiting the weak boundary between Army Groups North and Centre, and by attacking the feeble and inexperienced 2. *Luftwaffen-Felddivision*, the Soviets caught the Germans by surprise and were able to exploit their breakthrough. *Grenadier-Regiment 547 (83. Infanterie-Division)*, and units of 2. *Luftwaffen-Felddivision* fought stubbornly to hold the city of Nevel. While *III. Bataillon/Grenadier-Regiment 547* fought to keep hold of Bardino, *II. Bataillon/Grenadier-Regiment 547*, together with the survivors of 2. *Luftwaffen-Felddivision*, now fought their way out of the city of Nevel.[12] On 26 November 1943 a wide gap still separated the remnants of 2. *Luftwaffen-Felddivision* and *197. Infanterie-Division*. It was now that *SS-Kavallerie-Division 'Florian Geyer'* was thrown into the breach in order to stem the Russian advance. The German counterattack to retake Nevel eventually drew in the entire *II. Luftwaffen-Feldkorps* and its air force field divisions, thus weakening its original positions in and around Vitebsk. Due to heavy losses, 2. and 3. *Luftwaffen-Felddivisionen* were disbanded in late November, and their remnant parts began the process of being absorbed into 6. *Luftwaffen-Felddivision*.

On 13 December 1943 the Russians launched another attack, this time in the region of *IX. Armeekorps*. This Soviet offensive crashed headlong against the lines held by *87., 129.* and *252. Infanterie-Divisionen*, as well as *20. Panzer-Division* and *Felddivision 6 (L)*, with the remnants of *Felddivision 2 (L)*. During the fighting in

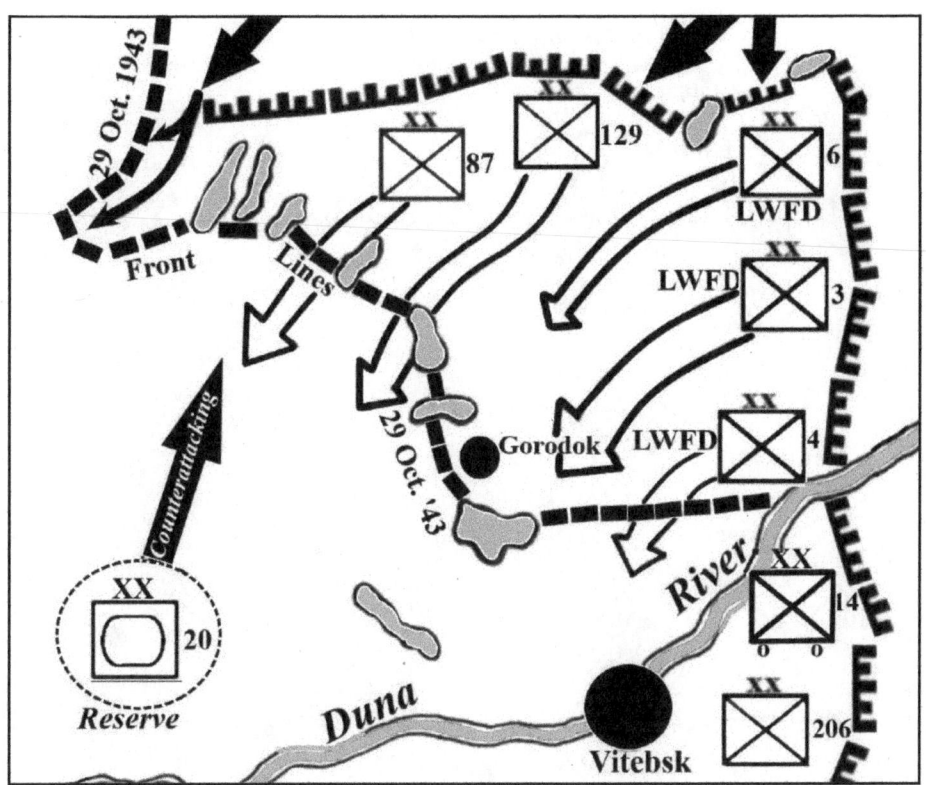

Positions of *2. Luftwaffen-Felddivision* as of 2 October 1943. The Red Army launched a massive attack which tore through the ranks of *2. Luftwaffen-Felddivision* like tissue paper. The breakthrough occurred just southeast of Nevel and eventually reached Gorodok, just northeast of Vitebsk, by 29 October 1943.

December 1943 *4. Luftwaffen-Felddivision* took heavy losses just northeast of Vitebsk. Even before the Soviet offensive, the German High Command was fed up with the ineptitude of *Felddivision 2 (L)*. According to German Army reports, while the unit had lost only 722 men between 6 and 12 October 1943, material losses had included large numbers of weapons: 2,648 rifles, 1,175 pistols, 552 machine guns, 26 anti-tank guns, 31 mortars, 38 20mm *Flak* guns and 4 88mm *Flak* guns.[13] It was not possible to explain the high losses in weapons compared to the number of men lost other than to think that many soldiers simply dropped their weapons and ran away or surrendered. Either way, it spoke volumes about the poor fighting quality of this unit.

The conclusion was unavoidable, and reflected what the army had said in the spring of 1942 about the establishment of these *Luftwaffe* divisions. Once again, Göring was shamed and embarrassed. The German Army now demanded that *Felddivision 2 (L)* be disbanded, and took great pleasure in pointing out the discrepancy in weapons lost compared to men killed or wounded. The decision to

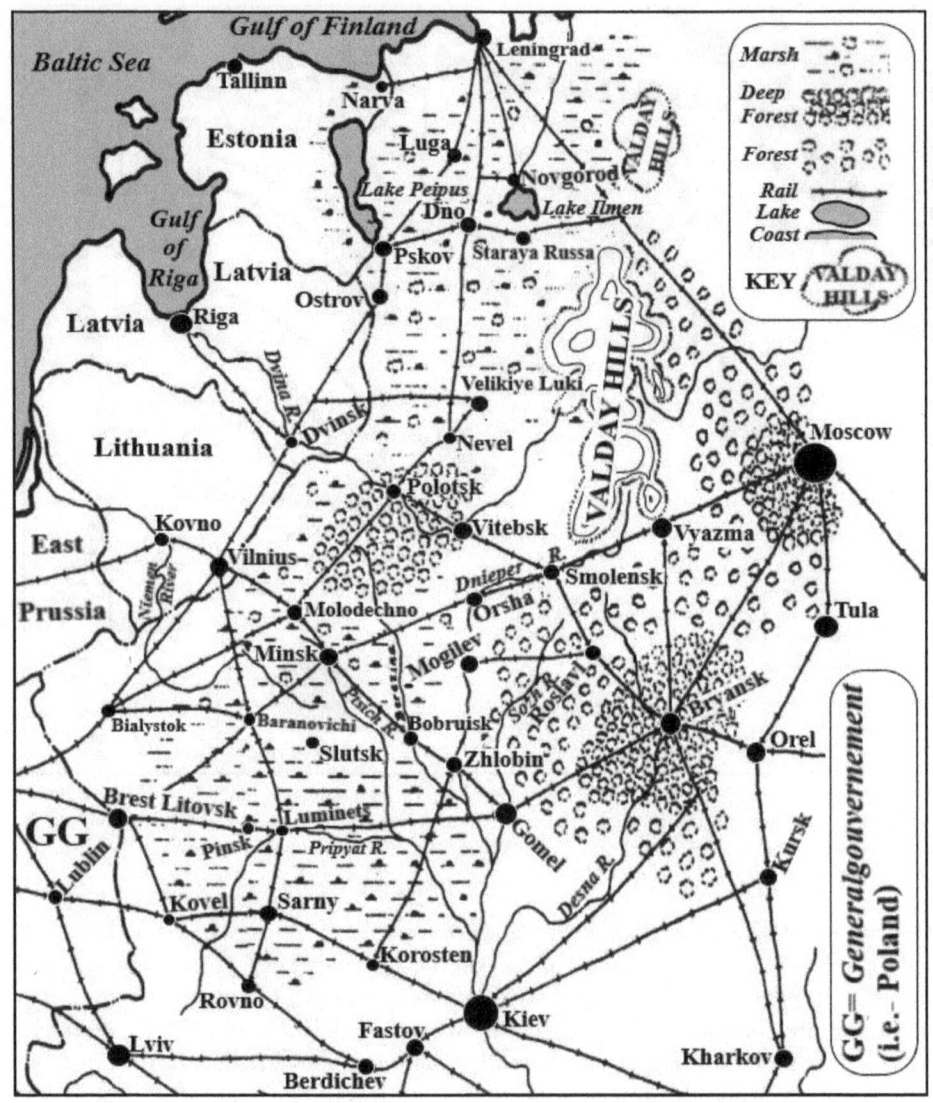

Main rail lines in the Baltic States, Belarus, northwestern Ukraine and central Russia.

disband the 'luckless' division was made official on 17 January 1944, with its remnants being absorbed by *Felddivision 6 (L)*.[14] Some army divisional and corps commanders were far more critical of the unit's poor performance, calling the *Luftwaffe* soldiers 'gutless'. Hermann Göring was said to have been furious that this *Luftwaffe* division had humiliated him in such a manner. Furtively, the army generals were gloating that their predictions had been proven true.

The *Flak* battalion of *Felddivision 2 (L)*, designated *IV. Abteilung* in the divisional artillery regiment, was detached and used to create *I. Flak-Bataillon* of

Table 1. Employment of *2. Luftwaffen-Felddivision*, 1942–1944.

Date		Corps	Army	Army Group	Location
1942	Nov.	VI. Armeekorps	9. Armee	Mitte	Smolensk
	Dec.	XXX. Armeekorps	9. Armee	Mitte	Smolensk
1943	Jan.	XLI. Panzerkorps	9. Armee	Mitte	Smolensk
	Feb.–April	II. Luftwaffen-Feldkorps	3. Panzerarmee	Mitte	Nevel
	May	XLIII. Armeekorps F[15]	3. Panzerarmee	Mitte	Velish
	June–8 Nov.	II. Luftwaffen-Feldkorps[16]	3. Panzerarmee	Mitte	Nevel
	9 Nov.–31 Dec.	IX. Armeekorps	3. Panzerarmee	Mitte	Vitebsk
1944	Jan.–June	LIII. Armeekorps	3. Panzerarmee	Mitte	Vitebsk

Flak-Regiment 50 (motorisiert). Two separate sources state that the remnant parts of *Felddivision 2 (L)* that were still intact were absorbed into *Felddivision 3 (L)* and *Felddivision 4 (L)*.[17] This, however, contradicts another report that claims the division was absorbed by *Felddivision 6 (L)*. The answer to this apparent contradiction could be that all three *Felddivisionen* received some part of the now defunct division. For example, *II. Jäger-Bataillon* of *Felddivision 2 (L)* was redesignated as *II. Bataillon* of *Jäger-Regiment 53 (L)* of *Felddivision 6 (L)*,[18] while *III. Artillerie-Abteilung* of *Felddivision 2 (L)* was also absorbed into *Felddivision 6 (L)*, becoming *IV. Artillerie-Abteilung* of *Artillerie-Regiment 6 (L)*. These units were themselves destroyed in July 1944 during the Soviet summer offensive launched against Army Group Centre.[19] Yet another source states that *Felddivision 4 (L)* and *Felddivision 6 (L)* absorbed the vestiges of *Felddivision 2 (L)*.[20] The Post Office Company of the disbanded division was transferred over to *3. Kavallerie-Brigade*.[21]

Command Structure of *2. Luftwaffen-Felddivision*

Commanders:
 Divisional CO:
  Oberst Hellmuth Pätzold,[22] 09/42–12/42
  Oberst Carl Becker, 01/0143–17/01/43
  Oberst Hellmuth Pätzold, 18/01/43–09/1943
  General der Flieger Alfred Schlemm, 09/43–12/43
 Ia:
  Major Gottfried Fischer, 10/42–30/10/43
  Hauptmann Herbert Schmidt,[23] 01/11/43–11/11/43
 Ib:
  Major Wilhelm Schwarz, 02/09/43–01/44
 IVb:
  Oberstarzt Dr Carl Nordwig,[24] 01/04/43–11/43
 V:
  Hauptmann Herbert Scholz, 10/42–10/43
 WuG:[25]
  Leutnant Hans Basedow, 10/42–10/43

CO *I. Jäger-Bataillon / 2. Luftwaffen-Felddivision*:
  Major Horst Fliesbach, 10/42–10/43
  Major Paul Hedenus, 10/43–01/11/43
CO *II. Jäger-Bataillon / 2. Luftwaffen-Felddivision*:
  Oberstleutnant Hasso Hemmer, 01/10/42–31/10/42
  Major Ernst Wagner, 01/11/42–10/43
CO *III. Jäger-Bataillon / 2. Luftwaffen-Felddivision*:
  Oberst Wilhelm Waldschmidt,[26] 19/02/43–09/06/43
  Hauptmann Hans-Juergen Rosenthal, 10/06/43–11/43
CO *IV. Jäger-Bataillon / 2. Luftwaffen-Felddivision*:
  Hauptmann Bogert, 10/42–11/42
  Oberst Bruno Scheloske, 03/43–12/43
  Oberstleutnant Carl (Karl) Schmitz,[27] 06/43–24/07/43
  Hauptmann Alfons Sarnitz,[28] 01/1943–31/05/43
  Hauptmann Hans-Juergen Rosenthal, ?–10/05/43
CO *Luftwaffen-Artillerie-Regiment 2*:
  Oberleutnant Kurt Zausch, 07/43–01/11/43
Also in the division:
  Oberleutnant Karl Seibold
  Hauptmann Bruno Scheloske,[29] 12/42–31/01/43

Major Otto Stolle was appointed to the divisional staff of *2. Luftwaffen-Felddivision* on 5 December 1942. He was then promoted to *Oberstleutnant* on 1 April 1943. *Oberstleutnant* Kurt Zausch was transferred to *2. Luftwaffen-Felddivision* and appointed commander of the divisional artillery regiment. On 1 September 1943 he was promoted to *Oberst*. The organizational structure of *2. Luftwaffen-Felddivision* in November 1942 resembled the initial table of organization of *1. Luftwaffen-Felddivision*.

3. Luftwaffen-Felddivision

This division began forming at Troop Training Ground Gross-Born in Pomerania on 19 September 1942.[1] The four *Jäger* battalions that formed the core of the division came from *Luftgau III* (Berlin). The unit's infantry complement contained no regimental headquarters, but did have four independently led *Jäger* battalions. The rest of the division was composed of an artillery battalion with three artillery batteries, an anti-tank company, a *Flak* company, an engineer company, a signals company, and supply and support troops. Later on in 1943, the anti-tank company of the division was expanded to a battalion composed of three companies. The artillery battalion contained three batteries. One source states that the division also had a bicycle company that acted as the reconnaissance and fusilier unit within the division. Again, the structure of this formation was more the size of a reinforced brigade rather than a full division. In November 1942, after only two months of training, the division was attached to *VI. Armeekorps, 9. Armee*.[2] It remained in the Nevel area until January 1943, when it was transferred to *XLI. Panzerkorps, 9. Armee* and stationed in and around the city of Vitebsk.

In November 1942 the division was transferred to the central sector of the Russian Front and began an additional two-month training period, performing anti-partisan duties in the rear of Army Group Centre. Divisional units took on the protection of towns, railways, munitions, bridges and food-dumps as they acclimated to the Russian Front. In February 1943 the division was attached to

Positions of *3. Luftwaffen-Felddivision* from January to February 1943.

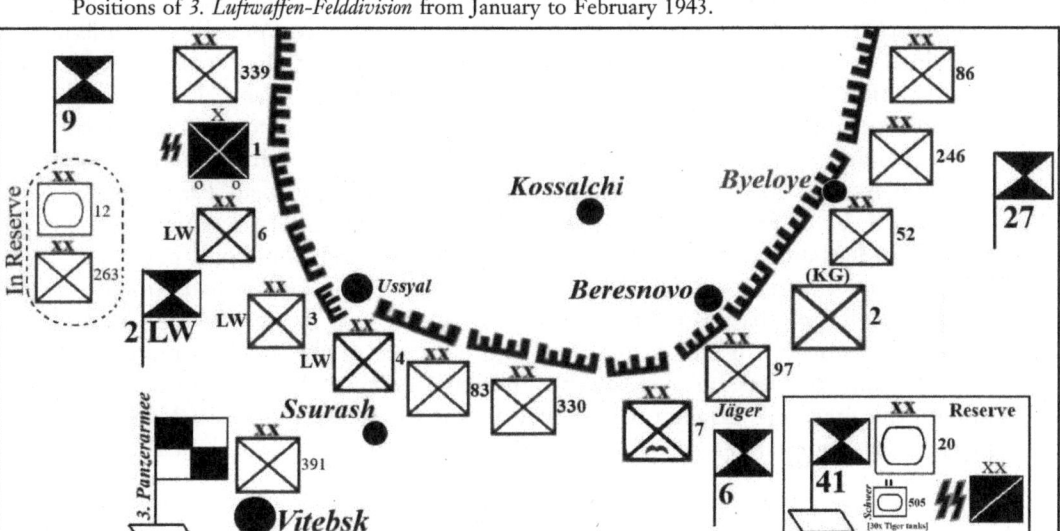

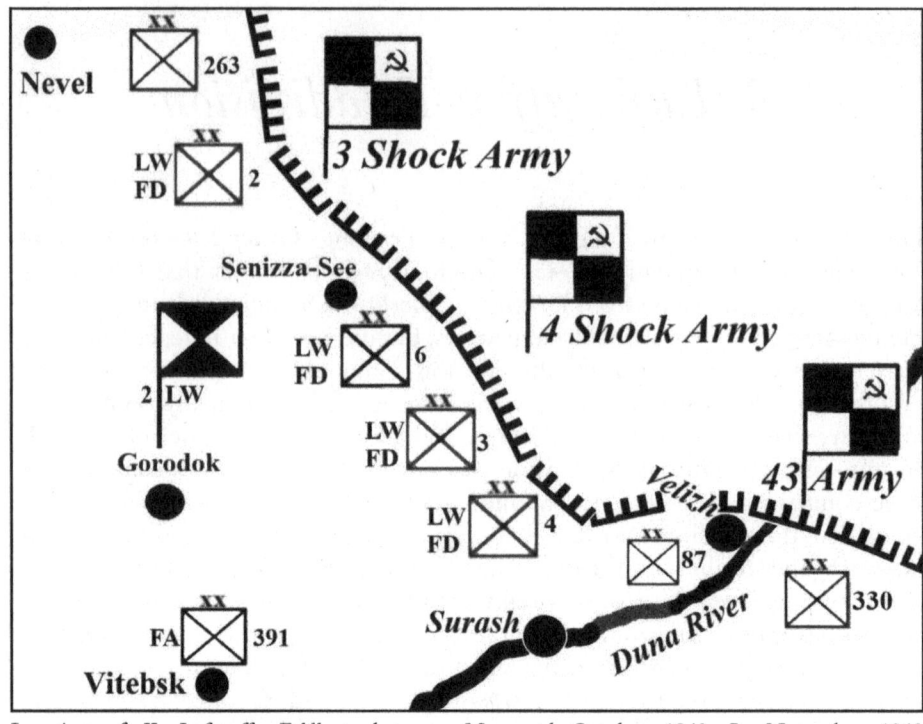

Location of *II. Luftwaffen-Feldkorps* between May and October 1943. In November 1943 *330. Infanterie-Division* was disbanded.

the newly formed *II. Luftwaffen-Feldkorps*, part of *3. Panzerarmee*. In the summer of 1943 the division found time to reorganize. The artillery battalion was expanded and a regimental headquarters staff was formed. The existing artillery battalion now became *III. Artillerie-Abteilung* of the new *Luftwaffen-Artillerie-Regiment 3*. It retained its old organization of two artillery batteries and one *Sturmgeschütz* battery. *I.* and *II. Artillerie-Abteilung* were completely new and contained two artillery batteries apiece. The 4th Artillery Battalion was simply a redesignation of the divisional *Flak* battalion (*Flak-Bataillon 3 der 3. Luftwaffen-Felddivision*). The 5th Battalion was the division's anti-tank company, which now expanded to three companies. Shortly thereafter, this '5th Battalion' was detached from *Luftwaffen-Artillerie-Regiment 3*, becoming instead *Panzerjäger-Abteilung 3 der 3. Luftwaffen-Felddivision*. Although the artillery regiment contained four battalions, this was deceptive, since each of them could only count on two batteries apiece, except for the 3rd Artillery Battalion (which had an additional assault gun battery). Still, when the time came, *Luftwaffen-Artillerie-Regiment 3* proved a useful formation. The batteries of the artillery regiment often became the last bulwark of the division's defence. Several times in its history the division's last line of defence was the artillery regiment. Wilhelm Gareis, the commander of *Luftwaffen-Artillerie-Regiment 3*, was killed while leading his unit on 18 December 1943. For his actions, he was awarded the much-coveted Knight's Cross. The award was issued on 5 February 1944.³

The division also performed anti-partisan operations, alongside seasoned units, against Russian guerrilla bands, remaining engaged between the Nevel region and Vitebsk from November 1942 to October 1943. The order for the division to serve initially in the rear of Army Group Centre was calculated to do two things. First, it was to accustom the former *Luftwaffe* airmen and their units, most of whom were not considered combat ready by the German Army, to the intense and arduous fighting that so characterized the Russian Front. Second, the *Luftwaffe* field divisions were often used behind the lines as part of the new German anti-guerrilla policy that was instituted in the summer of 1942. The forces available for anti-partisan warfare were to be immediately augmented by second and third echelon units. Now not only were the police and SS units charged with this war behind the lines, but army training, school units and *Luftwaffe* ground troops as well were earmarked for these operations, which were considered less strenuous than front-line service.⁴ This new policy had been created because of the growing Soviet partisan menace. Additionally, the region between Vitebsk and Nevel, where the 2., 3., 4. and 6. *Luftwaffen-Felddivisionen* operated, was heavily infested with Russian partisans.

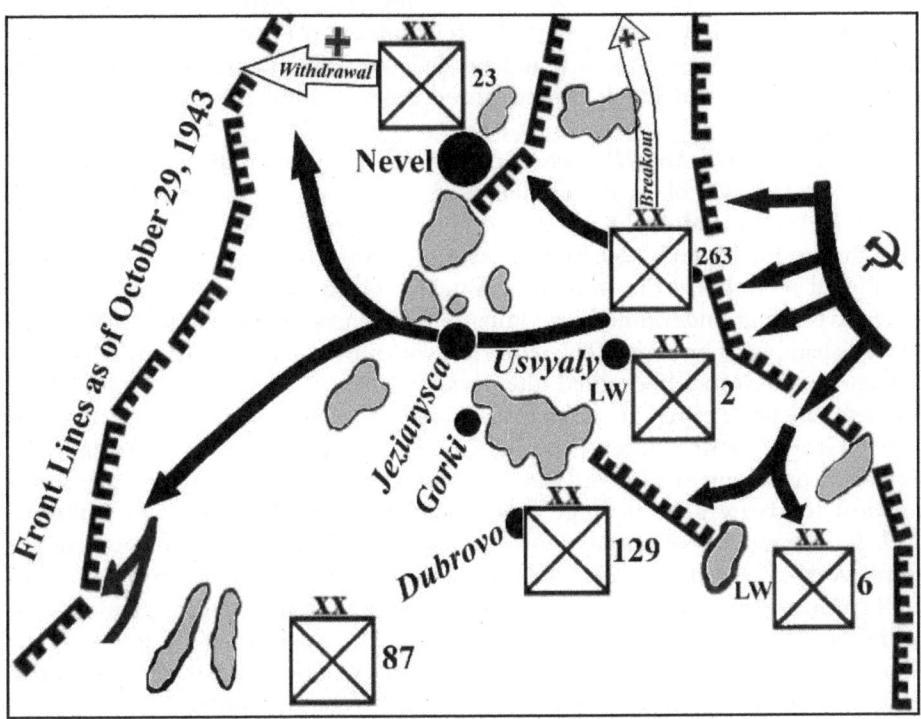

The Red Army drive north of Vitebsk in late October 1943 took a heavy toll on many of the Heer and Luftwaffe divisions located there, but *3. Luftwaffen-Felddivision* was especially hard-hit.

In late February 1943 all these units took part in an anti-guerrilla drive to eliminate a strong Russian partisan force in the Surazh rayon.[5] This region lay between the front-line positions of *3. Panzerarmee* and the city of Vitebsk, with its vital supply base for the Germans. In October 1943 the Red Army began a great offensive that attacked the left wing of *2. Luftwaffen-Felddivision* in and around the city of Nevel, in the region separating Army Group North from Army Group Centre. Another Soviet offensive, intended to support the October 1943 attack around Nevel, was launched in December 1943 around Gorodok. In this new attack *Felddivision 3 (L)* sustained heavy losses.[6] Initially, the front lines of the *3., 4.* and *6. Luftwaffen-Felddivisionen* were located between Lake Sadratch and southwards to Lake Losvida in October 1943.[7] The attack began on 6 October 1943 and was concentrated almost exclusively against the front lines of *2. Luftwaffen-Felddivision*, whose positions were located on the left flank of *6. Luftwaffen-Felddivision* between Lake Semniza and Lake Jeseritche. This was an area about 10km north of Bol. Budniza. By 12 October the Russians had broken through the lines of *2. Luftwaffen-Felddivision* and its neighbour to the left, *263. Infanterie-Division*.[8] The battle for the breakthrough reached its climax on 24 December 1943 when the Soviet 5th Tank Corps drove a wedge between the *129. Infanterie-Division* and the *Felddivision 3 (L)*, driving into Gorodok. This move forced *129. Infanterie-Division, 14. Infanterie-Division (motorisiert)* and *Felddivision 3 (L)* and *Felddivision 4 (L)* to withdraw to Losvida a day later.[9] The Soviet attack now veered south and headed towards Vitebsk. It bypassed that major city and, when finally halted, stood 30km behind the front lines of the *Felddivision 3 (L)*.

As already stated, the *Heer* assumed control of these divisions in November 1943.[10] During October, it was deployed defensively in the aftermath of the Soviet Nevel–Gorodok and Vitebsk offensives, formations strategically significant for the Red Army's objective of severing Army Group Centre. The division attempted to stabilize the front near Vitebsk, but heavy attrition and deficient infantry training undermined its combat effectiveness. These factors culminated in its disbandment by early 1944, with survivors redistributed to other divisions.[11]

Capturing Gorodok enabled the Russians to cut the important Polotsk–Vitebsk rail line, which acted as a vital link between Army Group North and Army Group Centre. After the 5th Russian Tank Corps broke through the defensive positions of *129. Infanterie-Division* and *Felddivision 3 (L)*, they drove forward to create a deep bulge in the German line. The order to withdraw *129. Infanterie-Division, Felddivision 3 (L)* and *Felddivision 6 (L)* was given in the third week of December 1943. The divisions were to disengage on the night of 17/18 December, while *Felddivision 3 (L)* and *Felddivision 6 (L)* were to proceed to a line between Lake Vymno and Vyshedki.[12] The Soviets closely followed the German withdrawal. Several attempts by Soviet troops to break through north of these positions were stopped by *IX. Armeekorps*. During the night of 19/20 December *Felddivision 6 (L)* was withdrawn and relocated to the region northwest of Lake Losvida.

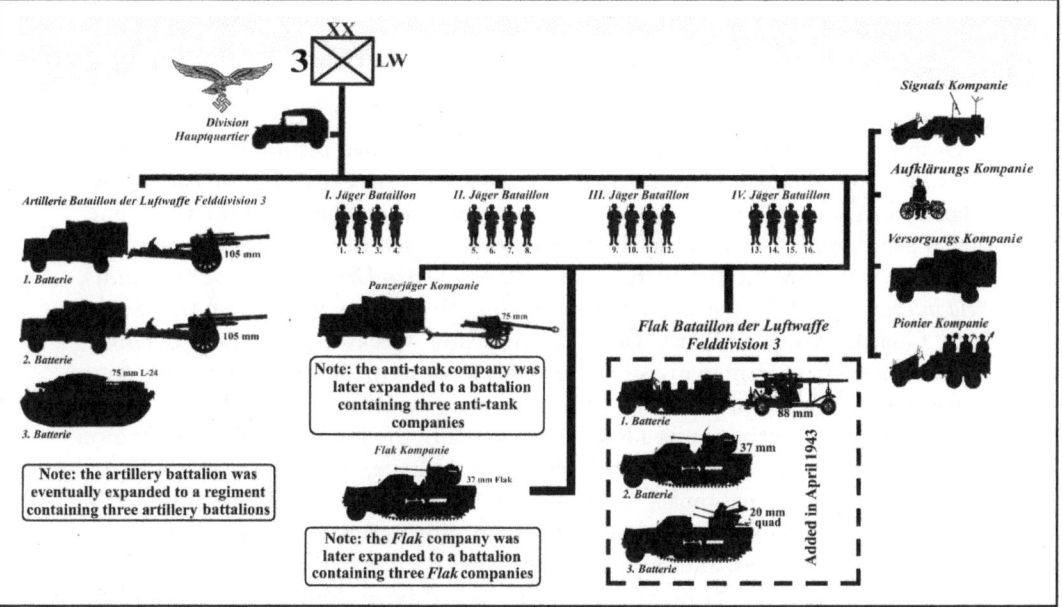

3. Luftwaffen-Felddivision in November 1942.

3. Luftwaffen-Felddivision in June 1943. In November 1943 the *Flak* battalion was withdrawn and returned to *Luftwaffe* service when the army assumed control of the air force field divisions. This further weakened the combat abilities of the division.

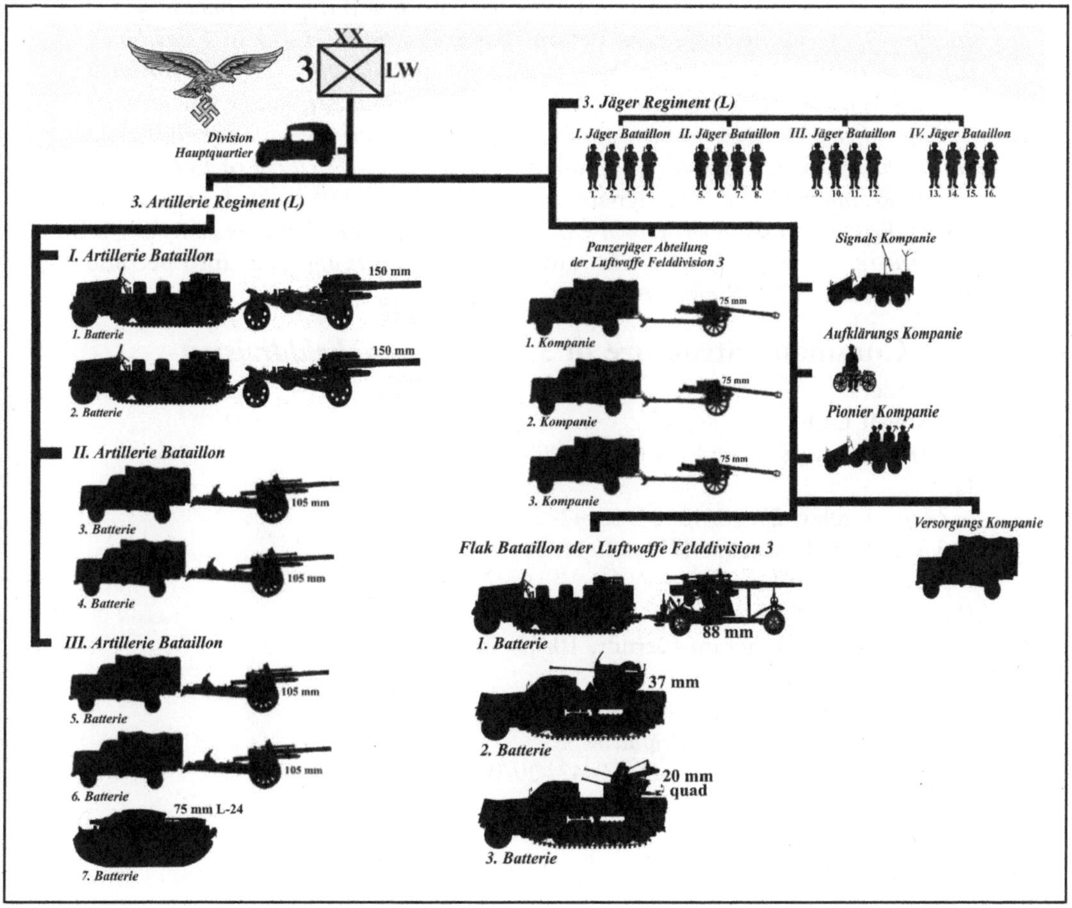

Despite a terrible snowstorm, the Red Army offensive resumed on 9 January 1944. No fewer than fifty-six infantry divisions, three cavalry divisions, five infantry brigades and twenty-two tank brigades now crashed into the front lines of *3. Panzerarmee*. On that day a gap was forced open between *Felddivision 3 (L)* and what was now the battlegroup of *129. Infanterie-Division*. These two units, *Felddivision 3 (L)* in particular, were facing the entire weight of the Soviet 11th Guards Army and 5th Tank Corps. After weeks of non-stop defensive battles, these two German divisions were too weak to prevent the Red Army from moving through their positions and advancing south. Adding further to the problem for the Germans was a Red Army attack in the Gorodok–Sirotino region by 4th Shock Army. Against this determined advance, *3. Panzerarmee* only had seventy-five operational tanks. Although the Soviets had taken a heavy toll of the Germans, they themselves had suffered even more grievous losses. The Soviet offensive finally stalled, and on 17 January 1944 the 1st Baltic Front called off all offensive operations.[13] However, the damage had been done and on 22 January 1944 OKH ordered the dissolution of *Felddivision 3 (L)* (although one source makes the claim that the order was issued on 17 January 1944).[14] Numerous sources all agree that the division's remnants were absorbed into *4.* and *6. Luftwaffen-Felddivisionen*.[15] On 12 February 1944 the actual dissolution of the division occurred. The divisional staff, coupled with *I.* and *II. Jäger-Bataillonen* of *Luftwaffen-Jäger-Regiment 5*, now became *Jäger-Regiment 51 (L)* of *Felddivision 4 (L)*. In addition, *III.* and *IV. Jäger-Bataillonen* of *Luftwaffen-Jäger-Regiment 6* were used to form *Jäger-Regiment 52 (L)* of *Felddivision 6 (L)*. *I. Artillerie-Abteilung* of *3. Luftwaffen-Felddivision* was redesignated as *I. Artillerie-Abteilung* of *Artillerie-Regiment 6 (L)*, *Felddivision 6 (L)*. Similarly, *II. Artillerie-Abteilung* of *Luftwaffen-Artillerie-Regiment 3* was redesignated as *III. Artillerie-Abteilung* of *Luftwaffen-Artillerie-Regiment 4 (L)*, *Felddivision 4 (L)*. Finally, *IV. (Flak) Artillerie-Abteilung* of *Luftwaffen-Artillerie-Regiment 3* was returned to the *Luftwaffe* branch to become *I. Flak-Abteilung, Flak-Regiment 43*.[16]

Command Structure of *3. Luftwaffen-Felddivision*

Commanders:
Divisional CO:
Generalmajor Robert Pistorius, 26/09/42–24/01/44[17]
Ia:
Major Egeler, 27/10/42–31/10/42
Major Paul Passlick, 01/11/42–11/43
Major i.G. Orthmann[18]
IIa:
Oberstleutnant Joachim Gerndt, 10/42–01/44
V:
Leutnant Bodemann, 10/42–11/43
CO *Luftwaffen-Artillerie-Regiment 3*:
Oberstleutnant Karl Glaesel, 10/42–29/01/43

Oberst Wilhelm Gareis,[19] 29/01/43–18/12/43
CO *I. Bataillon / 3. Luftwaffen-Felddivision*:
Hauptmann Johann Briegel, 10/42–08/43
Major Hermann Dieketter, 09/43–01/11/43
CO *II. Bataillon / 3. Luftwaffen-Felddivision*:
Hauptmann Ostermeyer, 10/42–01/43
Major Lottens, 02/43–03/43
Major Alfred Norsen, 29/03/43–?
CO *II. Bataillon / 3. Luftwaffen-Felddivision*:
Major Wilhelm Schwarz,[20] 01/11/42–30/11/42
CO *III. Bataillon / 3. Luftwaffen-Felddivision*:
Major Andreas Bauer, 10/42–10/43
CO *IV. Bataillon / 3. Luftwaffen-Felddivision*:
Hauptmann Engelbert Melitz, 10/42–01/05/43
Hauptmann der Reserve Hans-Joachim Schawdtke, 06/43–?
CO *Luftwaffen-Artillerie-Regiment 3*:
Oberstleutnant Karl Gläsel, 10/42–29/01/43
Oberst Wilhelm Gareis, 29/01/43–04/02/43
Major Heinz Erbe, 04/02/43–01/11/43

Make up of the 1943 artillery regiment:
 I. Artillerie-Abteilung: 2 batteries (new)
 II. Artillerie-Abteilung: 2 batteries (new)
 III. Artillerie-Abteilung: 2 artillery and 1 *Sturmgeschütz* battery
 IV. Artillerie-Abteilung: divisional *Flak* battalion
 V. Artillerie-Abteilung: divisional *panzerjäger* battalion

4. Luftwaffen-Felddivision

This air force field division began forming in *Luftgau III* (Berlin) at Troop Training Ground Gross-Born. The men came from *Flieger-Ausbildungsregiment 14*, which was based in Klagenfurt, Austria. *Major* Axel Freiherr von Jena led this training/cadre regiment, the roots of which were derived from *Flieger-Ersatz-Abteilung 14*, which was formed on 1 April 1939 and was renamed and expanded into a regiment in early 1942. By September 1942 its training battalions were on their way to becoming part of *4. Luftwaffen-Felddivision*. This division initially contained no regimental headquarters, but did have four *Jäger* battalions. However, this changed in the third week of January 1944, when three regiments were organized for the division.[1] Officially, these regiments were created in the autumn of 1943, but the order did not take effect until 17 January 1944. Most likely then, the regimental headquarters were not established until February 1944 or March (at the latest). Notice also that the creation of these regimental headquarters occurred after the *Heer* absorbed the *Luftwaffe* divisions in November 1943.

In keeping with the initial table of organization implemented for the *Luftwaffe* field divisions, the rest of the division was organized as follows. It contained an artillery battalion with three batteries, an anti-tank battalion (three companies), a *Flak* battalion (three companies), an engineer company, a bicycle company (acting as the unit's reconnaissance unit), a signals company, and supply and support troops. The artillery battalion contained two batteries of 105mm *Nebelwerfer* Type 40 rocket launchers. Each of these two batteries contained six tubes apiece. The third battery in the battalion was made up of five *Sturmgeschütz III* assault guns. These self-propelled guns were fabricated on the outdated *Panzer III* chassis and carried the short-barrelled 75mm L-24 anti-tank gun.[2] *XIII. Fliegerkorps* had directed that the training for the 2., 3. and *4. Luftwaffen-Felddivisionen* was to be completed by 10 October 1942, since the situation on the Russian Front necessitated more reinforcements.[3] The initial commander of this division was *Oberst* Rainer Stahel, but his tenure was brief; at the end of November 1942 he left the division in central Russia and went on to command an emergency ad hoc battle group formed from *Luftwaffe* ground personnel in southern Russia.[4] He led this unit from November 1942 until the end of January 1943, at which point he was posted to *Luftflotte-Kommando 4*.

4. Luftwaffen-Felddivision arrived in the central sector of the Russian Front in late October 1942 and was posted to *2. Luftwaffen-Feldkorps*, west of Velish and north of Surash.[5] This unit, along with the rest of the *Luftwaffe* field divisions, was under Göring's Basic Order No. 12[6] which requested the *Heer* to place these units in 'quiet' sectors of the front, as well as to assist them with training and support.[7] The order might have better read that these divisions should have been employed *behind* the lines, since no part of the Russian Front could, in all fairness, be considered 'quiet'. In accordance with Basic Order No. 12, *II. Luftwaffen-Feldkorps* was made subordinate to *LIX. Armeekorps*.[8] *4. Luftwaffen-Felddivision* remained in the region of Velish until the late summer of 1943, when it was shifted to positions north of the Duna river and further west of Velish. The division now settled to a series of artillery duels and small-scale feints and penetrations, during which the Soviets attempted to gauge the strengths and weaknesses of the airmen and their division. A small report, dated 4 March 1943, described a typical engagement:

> We received hostile enemy fire of all calibres in the right and middle corps positions, and behind the lines north of Novosokoniki. An Ober Jäger and an Obergefreiter of the 3rd Jäger Battalion of the 4th Air Force Field Division were reported missing after a reconnaissance mission. After penetration of an enemy reconnaissance into the main line of defence, a Gefreiter of the

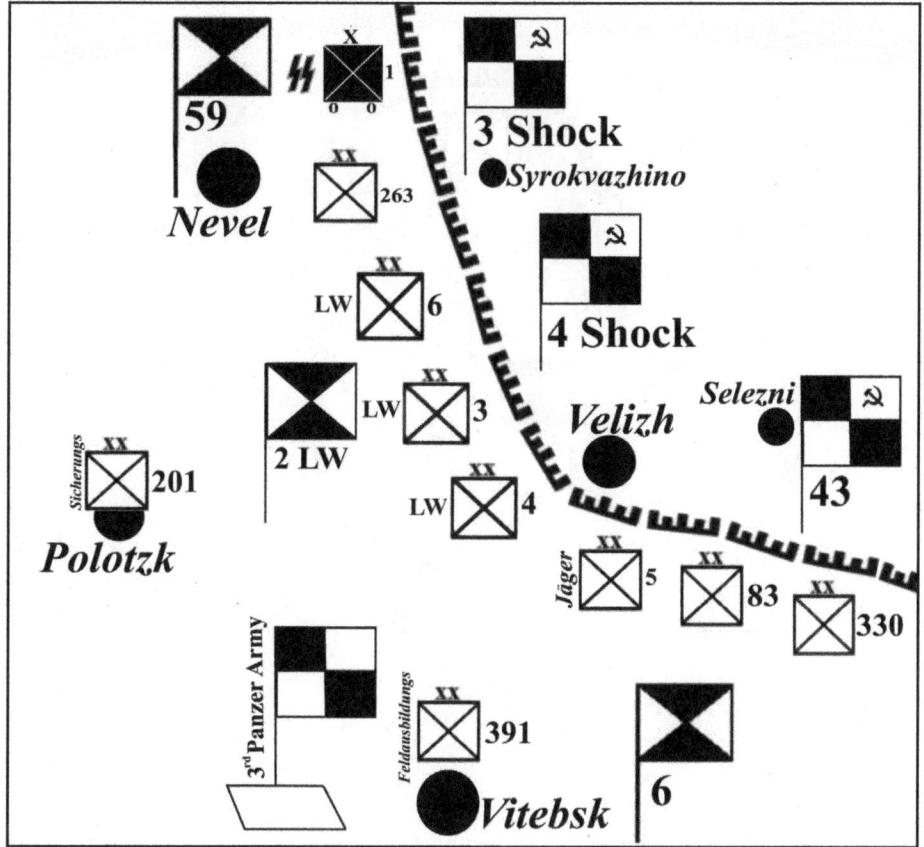

Defensive position and location of *4. Luftwaffen-Felddivision* from February to June 1943.

36 Hitler's *Luftwaffe* Infantry

4th Company, Grenadier-Regiment 90 (20 Motorized Infantry Division) was reported missing.[9]

During the summer of 1943 the division acquired two regimental headquarters for its *Jäger* battalions and also organized an artillery regimental headquarters, although this did not become active until the autumn. It was achieved by redesignating the existing artillery battalion as *III. Artillerie-Abteilung*, the *Flak-Abteilung* became *IV. Artillerie-Abteilung*, while the anti-tank battalion became *V. Artillerie-Abteilung*. *I.* and *II. Artillerie-Abteilungen* in the regiment were raised from scratch and only contained two artillery batteries apiece. In total, the artillery regiment could count on twelve batteries.[10] This organization was temporary, however, as *IV. Artillerie-Abteilung* (the division's *Flak* battalion) was detached in October 1943 and transferred out of the division to be redesignated *II. Flak-Abteilung* of *Flak-Regiment 8*.[11] In addition, in January 1944 *II. Artillerie-Abteilung* of

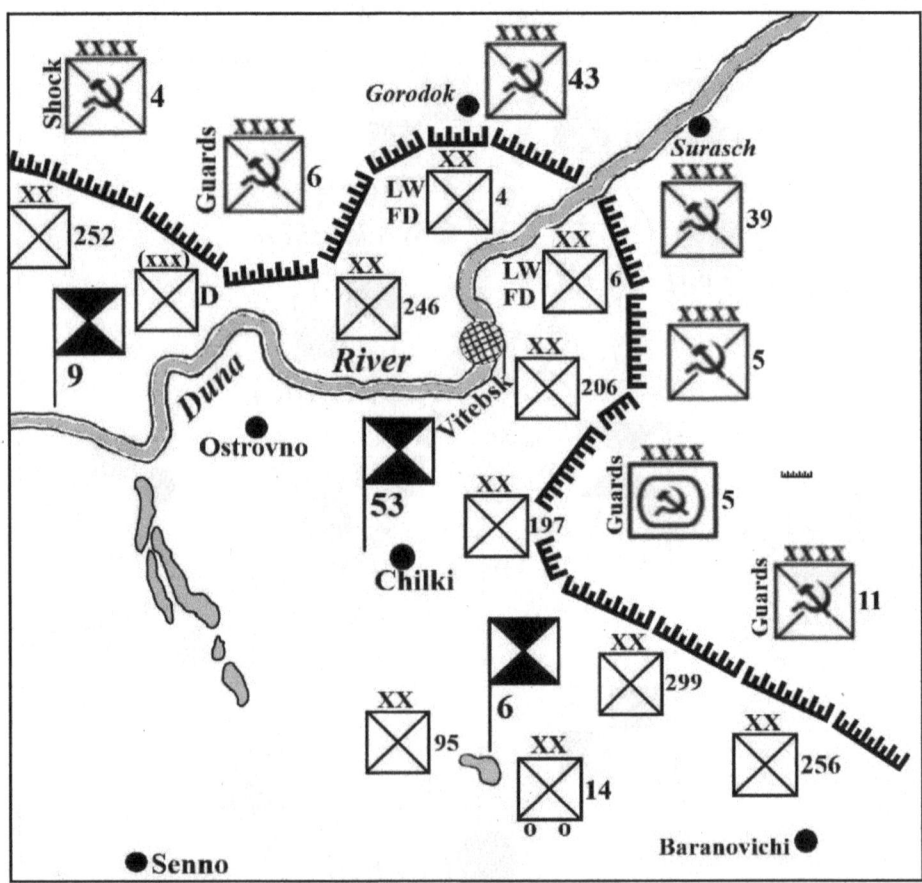

Positions of *Felddivision 4 (L)* north of Vitebsk shortly before the Red Army launched its 1944 summer offensive on 22 June, mocking the German invasion date of the Soviet Union three years earlier.

Artillerie-Regiment 3 (L) was redesignated *III. Artillerie-Abteilung, Artillerie-Regiment 4 (L)*. In that month the division still remained attached to *LIII. Armeekorps*.[12]

In the winter of 1943/1944, as *Felddivision 3 (L)* disintegrated, *Felddivision 4 (L)* was able to form a third *Jäger-Regiment* from the remnants of that unit:[13] its *I.* and *II. Jäger-Bataillone* became *I.* and *II. Jäger-Bataillone* of *Jäger-Regiment 49 (L)*, while *III.* and *IV. Jäger-Bataillone* were grouped together to form *Jäger-Regiment 50 (L)*. The headquarters for these regiments were formed from the staffs of *Grenadier-Regiment 486*[14] and *Grenadier-Regiment 286* respectively. Meanwhile, *I.* and *II. Jäger-Bataillone* of the disbanded *Felddivision 3 (L)* were now used to form *Jäger-Regiment 51 (L)*. During the initial days and weeks of the Soviet attack against the German positions in and around Nevel, the division was transferred into the *Heer* as *Felddivision 4 (L)* under the command of General Gollwitzer's *LIII. Armeekorps*. This occurred around the middle of December 1943 northeast of Vitebsk.[15] During the spring of 1944 *Felddivision 4 (L)* continued to regroup and reorganize itself while building up large earthen fortifications and other defensive works in its positions north and northwest of Vitebsk. Its neighbour to the east of its positions was *Felddivision 6 (L)*, with *Korpsabteilung D* defending positions to the west.[16]

When the Soviet 1944 summer offensive began on 22 June, *LIII. Armeekorps* managed to hold its positions throughout the first day of the assault. Soviet planners had originally intended for their leading units to advance headlong into Vitebsk as part of their offensive schedule, but by 31 May 1944 the plan had been altered: now the Russians would attack that important Belorussian city by enveloping it from both flanks.[17] By the evening of 24 June *LIII. Armeekorps* was cut off in Vitebsk and the surrounding countryside. Now began a fierce and desperate battle for the city. The defenders had nowhere to retreat to. As the Red Army advanced, the Germans were squeezed into an ever-smaller pocket. Inside the pocket were *Felddivision 4 (L)* and *Felddivision 6 (L)*, as well as *206.* and *246. Infanterie-Divisions*, plus elements of *197. Infanterie-Division*.[18] During the fighting for the city *Felddivision 4 (L)* was hit hard. The Soviets had thrown masses of infantry against the trench lines of the air force soldiers. To support their infantry, the Red Army had committed numerous tank brigades from their 39th and 43rd Soviet Armies.[19] This prevented the air force field division's employment by *3. Panzerarmee* to plug the gap between *LIII. Armeekorps* and *VI. Armeekorps* on the right flank.[20] The commander of *LIII. Armeekorps*, *General der Infanterie* Friedrich Gollwitzer, requested permission for an immediate breakout of his divisions from the Vitebsk encirclement.[21] Time was of the essence, every hour that passed without a breakout attempt meant that the encircled German forces were driven together in an ever-smaller circle. When permission to break out was finally given on 26 June, it was too late.[22] German reconnaissance aircraft located the leading elements of *LIII. Armeekorps* about 10km southwest of Vitebsk.[23] In *LIII. Armeekorps'* sector the initial attempt to break out of Vitebsk began to stall, as stated by the following situation report dated 8.25am on 26 June

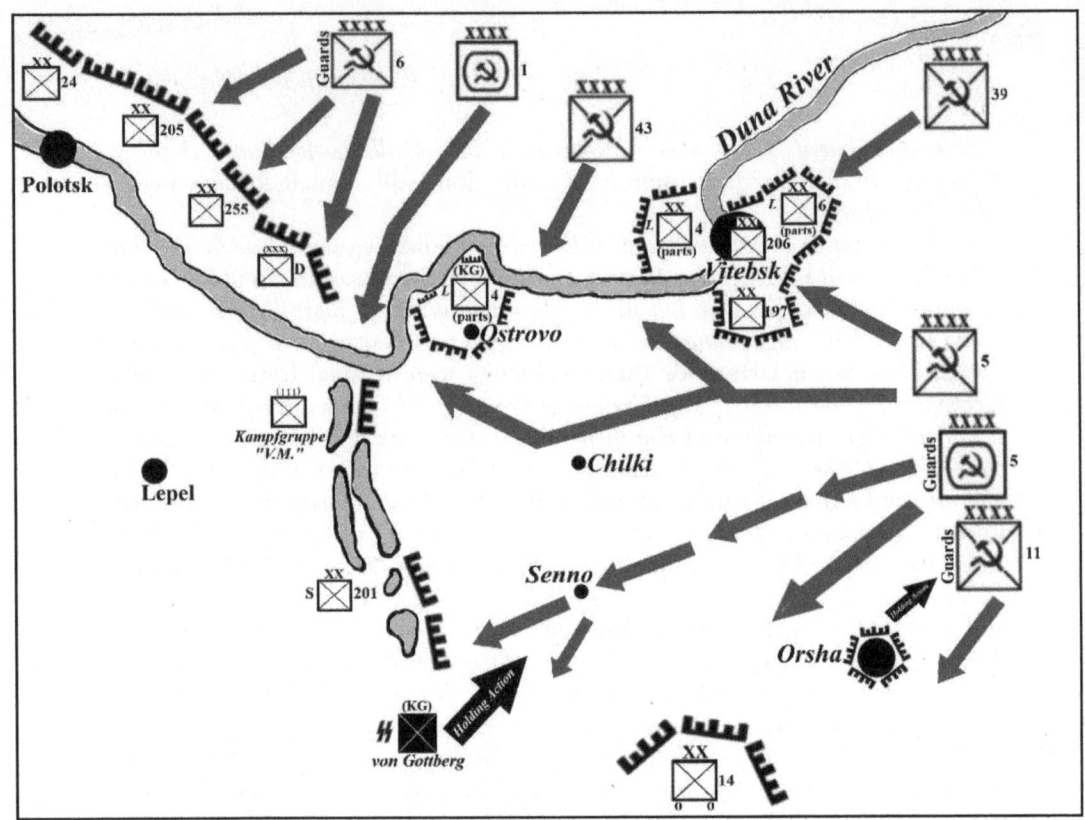

The end of *Felddivision 4 (L)* came during the breakout from the Vitebsk pocket in late June 1944, in the midst of the Soviet 1944 summer offensive.

1944: 'As early as 08.25 hours Corps reported that *4. Felddivision (L)* was surrounded in Ostrovo and requested a supply drop of ammunition and rations onto the town. This meant the corps was bottled up in two separate parts.'[24]

The narrow strip of land east of Beshenkovichi and southwest of Vitebsk was designated as the objective of the breakout.[25] The Germans did not get much further. After four days of fierce fighting, and now entirely surrounded, General Gollwitzer radioed one last communication to the High Command of Army Group Centre. His final message was sent at 1.12pm on 25 June 1944 and read as follows: 'Situation fundamentally fluid. Complete encirclement. *Field Division 4 (L)* no longer exists. *246. Infanterie-Division* and *Field Division 6 (L)* heavily engaged on several fronts. Several penetrations, bitter street fighting, with no quarter given.'[26]

On 27 June 1944, just two days after this message was sent, *Generalleutnant* Robert Pistorius, the last commander of *Felddivision 4 (L)*, fell in combat during the breakout from the Vitebsk pocket.[27] By the night of 27/28 June *General der Infanterie* Friedrich Gollwitzer, the commander of *LIII. Armeekorps*, assessed that only *246. Infanterie-Division* was still resisting, while both *Luftwaffe* divisions and elements of the *197. Infanterie-Division* had been completely wiped out. Of the 28,000 men trapped in the Vitebsk pocket, eventually 22,000–23,000 were captured and about 5,000 were killed.[28] Strangely, a German order of battle for

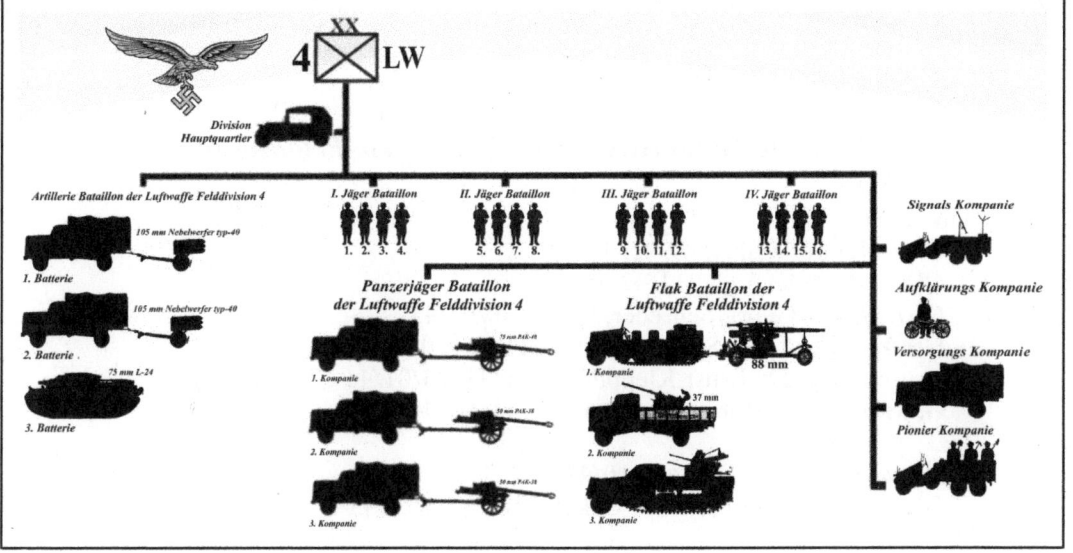

4. Luftwaffen-Felddivision in December 1942.

15 July 1944 still listed *LIII. Armeekorps* as active and *Felddivision 4 (L)* as still combat worthy. Just four days later, on 19 July, this wishful thinking on the part of the Army High Command was tempered by a note that simply said '*Ort Umbekannt*' ('location unknown').[29] The reality was that the division had been completely smashed by 27 June 1944. Officially, *Felddivision 4 (L)* was ordered to be disbanded, effective on 3 August 1944, on orders from *Organizations Abteilung der OKH* (*Org.Abt. / OKH*). The German Army High Command also ordered that whatever remnants from the division remained intact should be transferred over to *Korpsabteilung H* (Army Corps Detachment 'H').

4. Luftwaffen-Felddivision in October 1943.

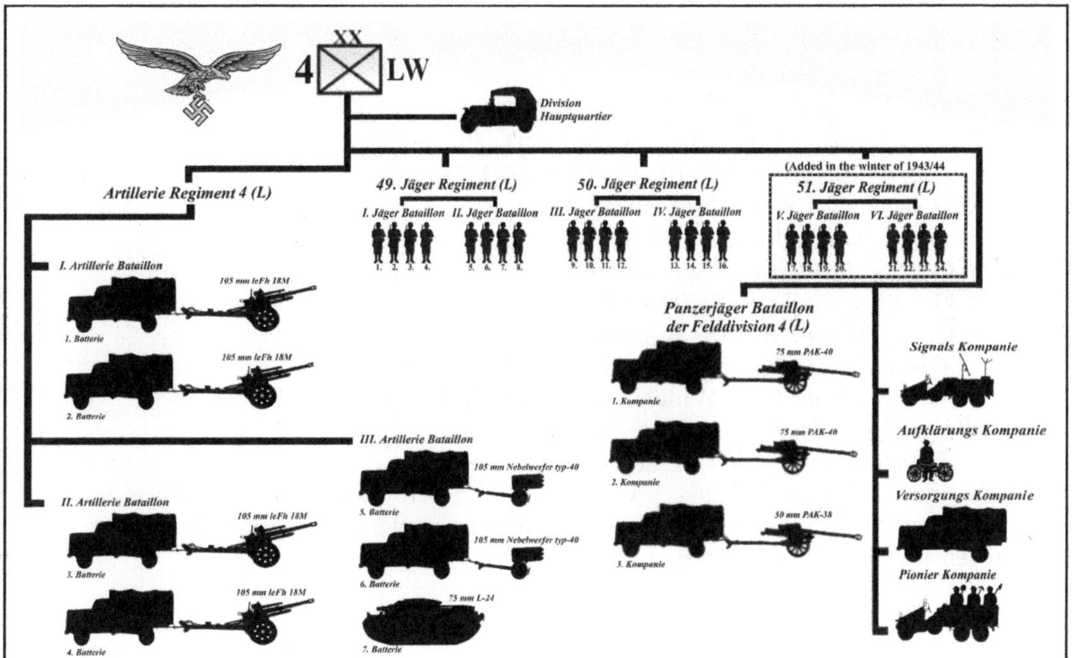

Command Structure of 4. Luftwaffen-Felddivision
Commanders:
Divisional CO:
Oberst Rainer Stahel, 09/42–11/42
Oberst Wilhelm Völk, 11/42–04/43
Oberst Hans-Georg Schreder, 04/43–30/07/43
Generalmajor Hans Sauerbrey,[30] 05/11/43–20/11/43
Generalmajor Dr Ernst Klepp,[31] 20/11/43–24/01/44
Generalleutnant Robert Pistorius, 01/44–06/44
Ia:
Oberleutnant Karl Schuetz, 10/42–11/43
Oberstleutnant Freiherr von Uckermann,[32] 10/12/43–?
Ib:
Hauptmann Hans-Christian Strackerjahn,[33] 01/10/42–14/04/43
Major Wilhelm Schwarz, 06/05/43–01/09/43
IIa:
Hauptmann Karl Schütz, 11/42–?
Oberleutnant Dr Heinemann
IVb:
Oberstarzt Dr Werner Darge, 01/04/43–?
V:
Leutnant Walter Hoffmann, 10/42–10/43
CO *I. Jäger-Bataillon / 4. Luftwaffen-Felddivision*:
Major der Reserve Hans Wahnschaffe, 01/12/42–01/43
Hauptmann Walter Nitzschke, 01/43–01/11/43
CO *II. Jäger-Bataillon / 4. Luftwaffen-Felddivision*:
Hauptmann Alfred Kment, 29/03/43–26/08/43
CO *III. Jäger-Bataillon / 4. Luftwaffen-Felddivision*:
Hauptmann Albert Sartori, 02/43–01/11/43
CO *IV. Jäger-Bataillon / 4. Luftwaffen-Felddivision*:
Oberstleutnant Ernst Wenzel, 29/03/43–29/09/43
Oberstleutnant Emil Deffner, 24/09/43–12/43
CO *Luftwaffen-Jäger-Regiment 49*:[34]
Oberstleutnant Ernst Wenzel[35]
CO *Luftwaffen-Jäger-Regiment 50*[36]
CO *Luftwaffen-Jäger-Regiment 51*[37]
CO *Luftwaffen-Artillerie-Regiment 4*:
Oberstleutnant Georg Hollunder, 09/42–13/02/43
Oberstleutnant Fritz Winkler, 13/02/43–01/11/43
Panzerjäger-Abteilung 4 (L) / Felddivision 4 (L):
Hauptmann Siegfried Vehlow, 25/06/43–?

Hauptmann Georg Tempel was transferred to *4. Luftwaffen-Felddivision* on 1 August 1943. He served in the division in an unknown capacity until June 1944, when the division was destroyed.

5. Luftwaffen-Felddivision

The creation of *5. Luftwaffen-Felddivision* began with its initial training at Troop Training Ground Mlawa (Mielau), in southeast Prussia, in September 1942.[1] Another source, however, states that it was formed at Troop Training Ground Gross-Born.[2] It is possible that the component parts of this division were created in both troop training grounds, which would explain the seeming contradiction. *Flieger Regiment 16* was one of the training and replacement units of the German Air Force that were used to help form this division. Like the other initial *Luftwaffe* field divisions, the unit contained four *Jäger* battalions with no regimental headquarters. Like the *3., 4., 6., 9.* and *10. Luftwaffen-Felddivisionen, 5. Luftwaffen-Felddivision* initially contained only one artillery battalion, composed of two batteries of 105mm Type 40 *Nebelwerfers* (rocket launchers). The third battery in the battalion was intended to have been made up of five *Sturmgeschütz III* assault guns, but in this division assault guns were only issued to *3. Kompanie* of the anti-tank battalion (*Panzerjäger-Abteilung der 5. Luftwaffen-Felddivision*). Therefore, the artillery battalion could only count on two batteries with a total of twelve barrels.[3] The division's *panzerjäger* (anti-tank) battalion contained three companies.

1. and *2. Panzerjäger Kompanie* contained mainly captured and outdated towed anti-tank guns from France, although there were a few German-made 50mm

The German 150mm Type 40 *Nebelwerfer* rocket launcher. Given its configuration, it was capable of firing six 150mm rockets instantly, one after the other.

anti-tank guns that were equally ineffective against most Russian tanks. The French anti-tank guns in these companies, the 47mm SA Model 1937, was to prove obsolete for the Eastern Front.[4] The only half-worthy anti-tank unit in the division was *3. Panzerjäger Kompanie*, which contained an assault gun battery armed with the 75mm L48 anti-tank gun. The divisional *Flak* Battalion contained three *Flak* companies and was armed with the single barrel 20mm *Flak 38*, the 37mm *Flak 37* and the 88mm *Flak 36* guns. The division also possessed a *radfahr* (bicycle) company that was referred to as *Radfahr-Kompanie* (cycling company) and acted as a reconnaissance unit. There was also an engineer company, a signals company and a *versorgungs* (supply) column.

Overall, this type of organization was typical of the Table of Organization and Equipment (TO&E) of the *Luftwaffe* field divisions. However, as previously stated, this style of formation proved to be ineffective, especially on the Eastern Front, with its harsh and brutal conditions. In fact, these formations, although divisional in name, probably had the combat effectiveness of a small infantry brigade (at best). *5. Luftwaffen-Felddivision* had hardly completed its cursory initial training when it was transferred by rail to the southern sector of the Eastern Front on 1 November 1942.[5] It had gone through a very short training period, after which the unit was rapidly transported through Poland, central and southern Russia and into the Crimea. It settled in and around Simferopol but its stay in the Crimea was brief.

By Christmas Day the division had orders to cross the Kerch Strait in order to assist *Heeresgruppe A*, as the situation had worsened on account of the Red Army's winter counter-offensive, which had begun on 19 November 1942.[6] On 1 January 1943 it was sent to the Caucasus, where the men were placed into defensive positions in and around the city of Krasnodar.[7] The *Luftwaffe* troops remained in this type of positional war under the control (at various times) of *V.*, *XLIV.* and *LII. Armeekorps*, *17. Armee*. The division was given this relatively easy assignment behind the front lines so the men could acclimatize to the Russian Front. It was also there to 'stiffen' the Romanian Cavalry Corps, which was fighting south of Krasnodar on the front line and had already shown signs of cracking.[8]

By mid-January 1943 *5. Luftwaffen-Felddivision*, along with *97. Jäger-Division*, *101. Jäger-Division* and *198 Infanterie-Division*, formed the bulwark of the Krasnodar defence. These divisions were all under the command of *XLIV. Armeekorps*, which had been moved into this area in order to bolster the defence of the Romanian formations. On 16 January 1943 the hammer came down when three Red Army divisions (later joined by a fourth) launched a serious attack on the Romanian 9th Cavalry Division. The Romanians were holding a front line some 42km (28 miles) long. The Soviets soon expanded their assault by attacking *125. Infanterie-Division*, which was holding the front line on the left flank of the 9th Cavalry Division. The line could not hold, and the Soviets broke through in the sector of the 3rd Cavalry Regiment *'Rosiori'*. The breach, west of Lambina Hill, near Maraket, was about 2–3km deep by around 3.5–4km wide.

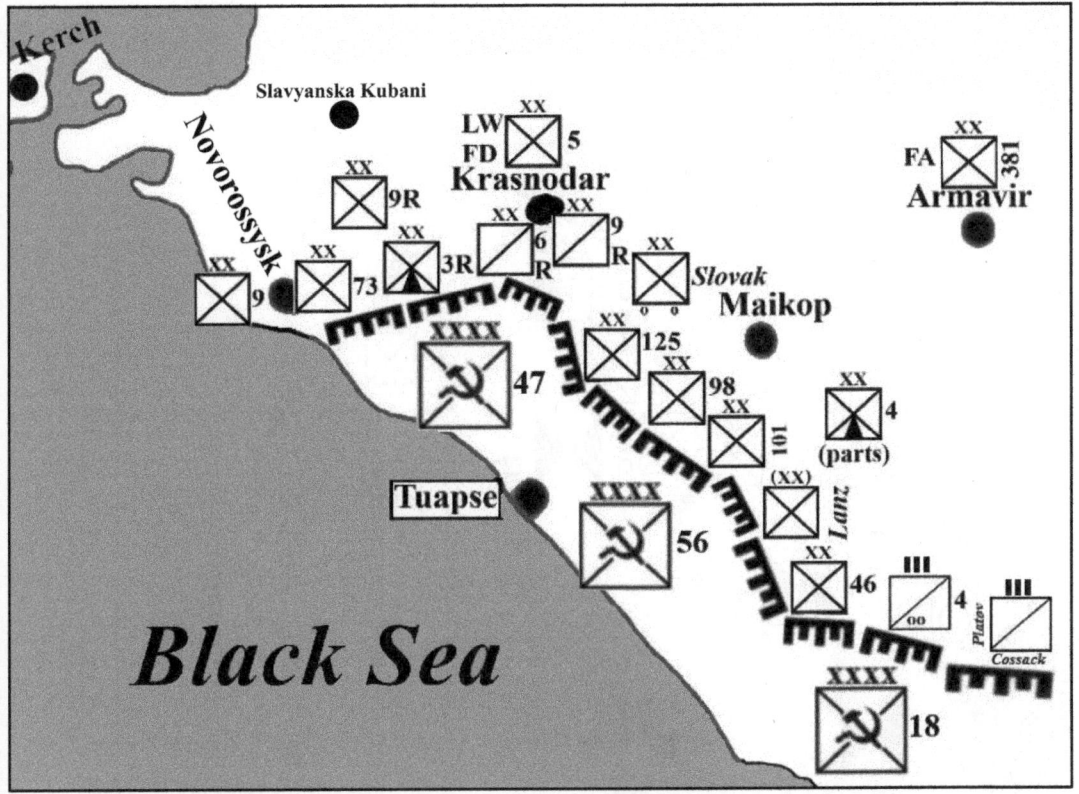

In December 1942 *5. Luftwaffen-Felddivision* arrived on the Eastern Front and from January 1943 was stationed in Krasnodar. Still in the process of forming, it was tasked with keeping the German supply and communications lines free of partisan interruptions. The front line here remained static from November 1942 to January 1943.

Now the Red Army increased their attacks against the Romanian Cavalry Corps, launching another heavy attack against the 6th Cavalry Division on 18 January, but the arrival of German support helped the Romanians to repel these attacks. The transfer of *XLIV. Armeekorps* into this area was the direct result of the Soviet plan (code-named 'Operation Mountain') to take Krasnodar and prevent the withdrawal of *1. Panzerarmee* from the Caucasus.[9] To this end, the Soviet 56th Army had launched its offensive on 11 January 1943. The Romanian Cavalry Corps, located nearby, was too weak to hold the Russian drive on its own. Many of the German divisions under the command of *XLIV. Armeekorps* were greatly reduced in the fighting. For example, *101. Jäger-Division* was so weakened by losses that it was subsequently referred to as *Kampfgruppe Busche*.[10] Similarly, *5. Luftwaffen-Felddivision* was referred to as *Kampfgruppe Kohl*,[11] although not because the unit had been reduced in heavy fighting, since it had only recently been committed. In fact, the division had been split up. An OKW situation map dated 1 February 1943 listed clearly that *5. Luftwaffen-Felddivision* had been divided into three parts: one with the Romanian Cavalry Corps, another with *XLIV. Armeekorps* and the third with *XLIX. Gebirgs Armeekorps*.[12] The withdrawal of *1. Panzerarmee* through Rostov and the retreat of *17. Armee* to the Kuban bridgehead continued into February 1943. That part of *5. Luftwaffen-Felddivision*

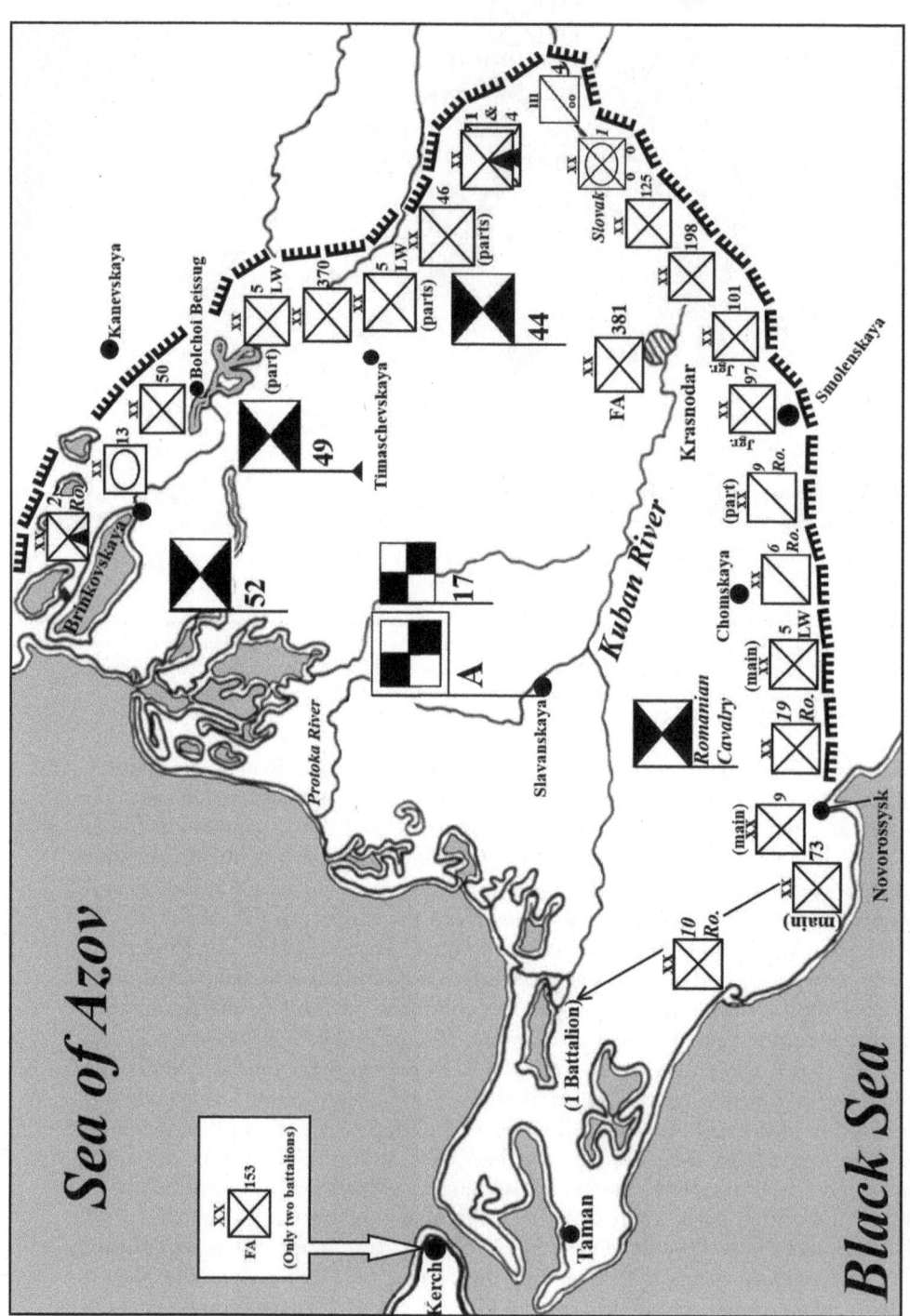

The German military situation, 21 February 1943.

which was forced to retreat northwards with *1. Panzerarmee* withdrew from the Terek river to the Don with other divisions:

> Marching at night, they pulled out of the Promised Land of Caucasian oil – the regiments of the Terek divisions who had fought their way to the very gates of Grozny and had got within an arm's reach of Baku. They were the Berlin *3. Panzer-Division* and parts of *5. SS-Panzer-Grenadier-Division 'Wiking'*, along with the Brandenburg, Lower Saxon, Silesian, Anhalt and Austrian Regiments of *13. Panzer-Division, 111., 370.* and *50. Infanterie-Division*, and *5. Luftwaffen-Felddivision*.[13]

All the while, Soviet divisions pressed their attacks against the retreating German forces. Russian guerrilla units also did their best to blow up bridges, harass the withdrawing Axis forces and kill as many enemy soldiers as they could get their hands on. The German reaction to these communist guerrilla methods was brutish, and served to further alienate a population that had initially been overwhelmingly friendly to the Axis cause. The German commanders began a systematic campaign of retaliation shootings against the local populace for every partisan attack that took place.[14] Of course, this was exactly what the Russian guerrillas were hoping for.

In February 1943 *5. Luftwaffen-Felddivision* remained in the Kuban area, still under *17. Armee*. By 12 February 1943, along with *97.* and *101. Jäger-Division*, it was committed to defending Novorossisk under *V. Armeekorps*.[15] This was in reaction to a Soviet naval landing on 4 February 1943 in and around that Caucasian Black Sea port.[16] The month of March saw *5. Luftwaffen-Felddivision* and the rest of *17. Armee* making a slow, fighting withdrawal into the Taman peninsula. On 3 April 1943 the Soviets again launched a major attack against *97. Jäger-Division*, which at the time was defending the approaches to Krymskaya. On 4 April the Germans launched a counterattack aimed at relieving the pressure on *97. Jäger-Division*. In this counterattack, elements of *13. Panzer-Division*, the 19th Romanian Infantry Division and *5. Luftwaffen-Felddivision* were used to plug the 1.5km-wide breach in the German line,[17] with the assault gun battery of *5. Luftwaffen-Felddivision* proving particularly useful.[18] By 17 April 1943 the general situation in the region of Krymskaya had been stabilized. *Generalleutnant* Ernst Rupp, the commander of *97. Jäger-Division*, thanked the units of *V. Armeekorps* in a brief divisional communiqué dated 17 April 1943:[19]

> In an indescribably difficult struggle the division, with the help of elements of a Panzer-Division (13.), a Luftwaffe field division (5.) and a Romanian infantry division (19), in cooperation with corps artillery and the Luftwaffe, which supported with strong artillery fire and numerous aircraft, frustrated the breakthrough attempt of five Russian divisions and two tank formations. The leaders and troops have made superhuman efforts. The success was paid for with much sacrifice. However, it was decisive for the overall situation in the bridgehead.[20]

On 3 May 1943 the Russians launched yet another major attack, this time south of Krymskaya. Once again, the assault gun battery of *5. Luftwaffen-Felddivision*, along with elements of *Sturmgeschütz-Brigade 249*, was committed to support *9. Infanterie-Division* and the 19th Romanian Infantry Division. As General Rupp's statement above detailed, German losses were heavy. *5. Luftwaffen-Felddivision* had performed well in spite of its numerous materiel, technical and tactical deficiencies, but it suffered such heavy losses that by the beginning of May 1943 it was little more than a combat group.

The remnants of *5. Luftwaffen-Felddivision* were finally withdrawn from the Taman peninsula at the end of May 1943 and by 2 June 1943 three battalions were already on the Crimean side of the Kerch Strait.[21] The division's battle group was immediately put to work in the Crimea, performing security duty. It wasn't until the beginning of July 1943, however, that the remaining two battalions in the Kuban bridgehead were transported into the Crimea. In the meantime, the summer months were spent trying to reorganize the division. One part of this was the expansion of the divisional artillery battalion into a complete five-battalion artillery regiment. The existing two artillery batteries of the artillery battalion became *III. Artillerie-Abteilung* in the new artillery regiment, while the divisional *Flak* battalion became *IV. Artillerie-Abteilung* and the anti-tank battalion became *V. Artillerie-Abteilung*. In addition, two completely new artillery battalions were planned, which would become *I.* and *II. Artillerie-Abteilung*. However, due to lack of guns, these two artillery battalions were never

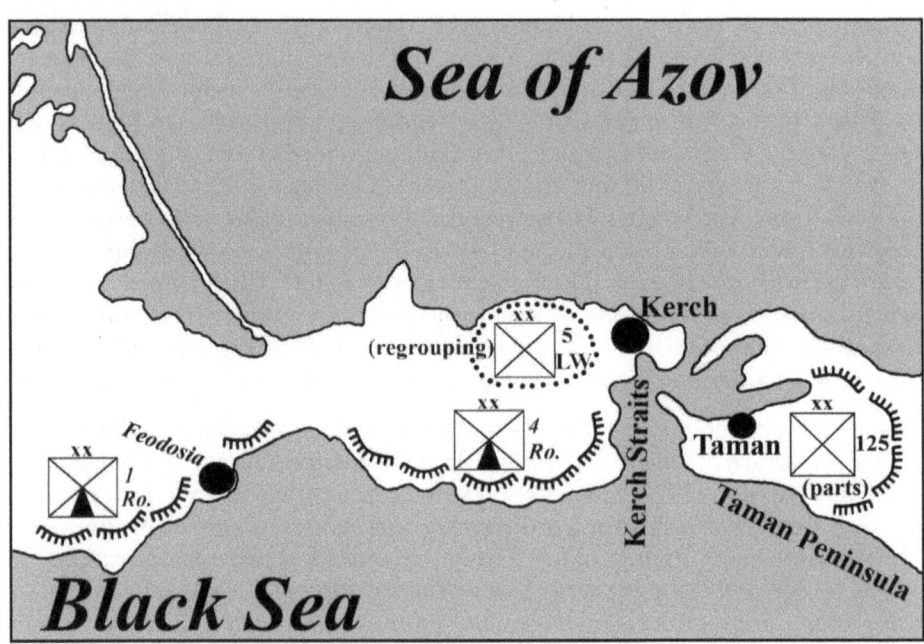

Location of *5. Luftwaffen-Felddivision*, June 1943.

formed.[22] The two planned infantry regiments for the division, *Luftwaffen-Jäger-Regiment 9* and *Luftwaffen-Jäger-Regiment 10*, began organizing in the spring of 1943 in eastern Crimea. Each was to contain three *Luftwaffe Jäger* battalions, numbered *I., II.* and *III.*

By 3 August 1943, *5. Luftwaffen-Felddivision* was still located on the Crimean side of the Kerch Strait, performing coastal guard duty and reorganizing. Events on the ground, however, overtook the plans for the continued rebuilding of the division. By September the military situation of *6. Armee* had become extremely precarious. Whatever forces were available were sent to reinforce this German army, including the still incompletely reformed *5. Luftwaffen-Felddivision*, which was transferred from the Crimea. By the middle of September 1943 it was situated north of Melitopol, alongside part of *15. Luftwaffen-Felddivision*. Another part of *15. Luftwaffen-Felddivision* was located in Melitopol itself, and in the northern suburbs. In anticipation of transferring the *1.–6.* and *9.–21. Luftwaffen-Felddivisionen*, Hermann Göring sent a telex to OKH, informing them of his plans to reclaim the *Flak* battalions that had been originally allocated to the *Luftwaffe* field divisions. The German Armed Forces High Command war diary for 20 September 1943 also noted that as a result of Göring's decision, a substantial number of personnel would be diverted back into the *Luftwaffe*.[23] They included 10,000 men of the field divisions, who were now to be transferred into the parachute forces, and 6,000 specialty personnel, who would be transferred from the field divisions into units of the *Luftwaffe*.[24] Additionally, the remains of *15. Luftwaffen-Felddivision* were now absorbed into *5. Luftwaffen-Felddivision*, beginning with the headquarters.[25] This occurred around Melitopol.

On 26 September 1943 a massive Soviet offensive began in the German front lines in and around Melitopol.[26] By 9 October Russian forces had captured half of the city. During the intense fighting that ran into the third week of October, the Russians finally broke through the lines of *6. Armee.*

By 2 November Soviet mechanized forces had reached Perekop, effectively cutting off Axis forces still in the Crimea.[27] *6. Armee* had been virtually destroyed during the month of October 1943. In November the formation was sent to the Nikolayev area for coastal guard. However, as a result of heavy losses, the division had to disband the following units:

Headquarters of *Jäger-Regiment 10 (L)*
I. Jäger-Bataillon
II. Jäger-Bataillon[28]
V. Artillerie-Abteilung (L)[29]
Pioneer-Kompanie 5 (L)
Signals-Kompanie 5 (L)
III. Bataillon / Jäger-Regiment 9 (L)[30]
Flak Abteilung 5 (L)[31]

15. Luftwaffen-Felddivision was largely defeated during the defence of Melitopol and suffered heavy losses. The fighting in the city was particularly fierce and

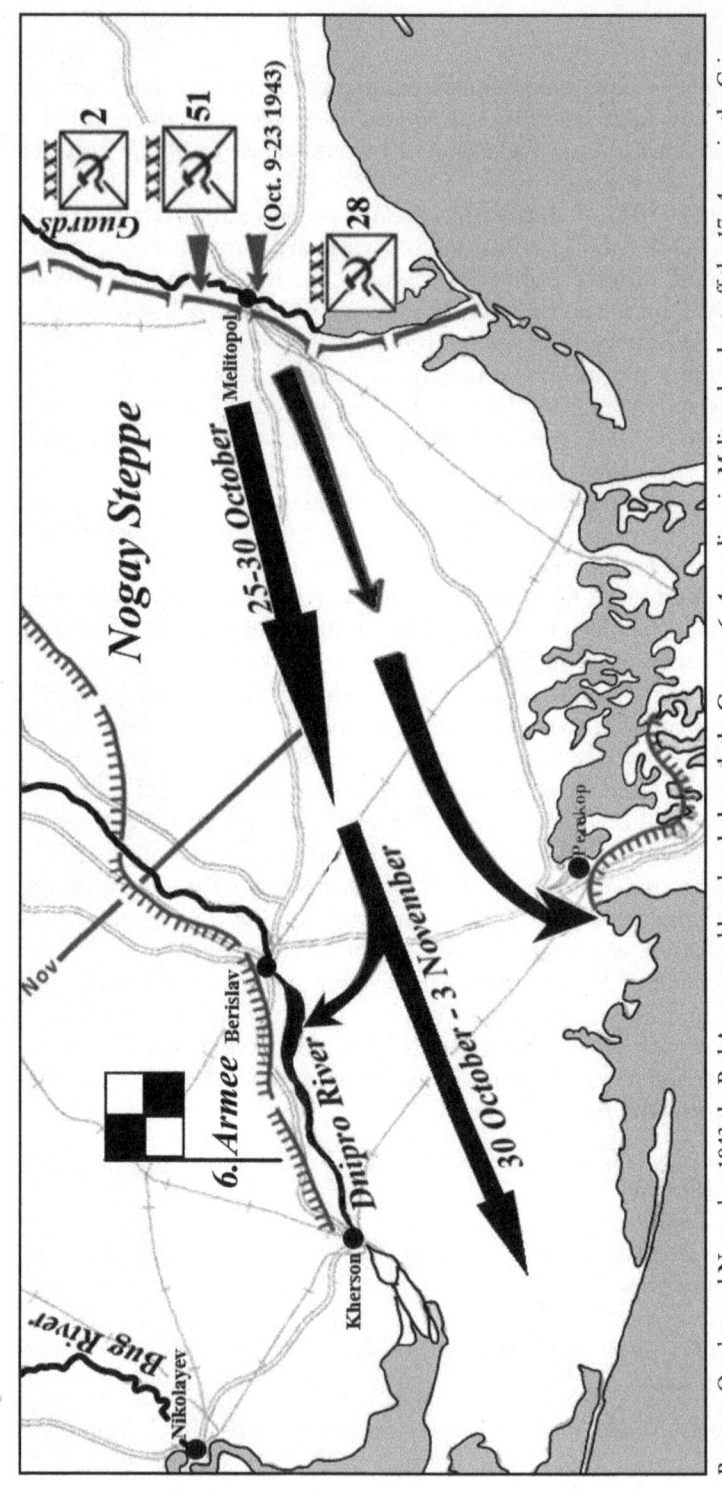

Between October and November 1943 the Red Army was able to break through the German 6. *Armee* lines in Melitopol and cut off the 17. *Armee* in the Crimea.

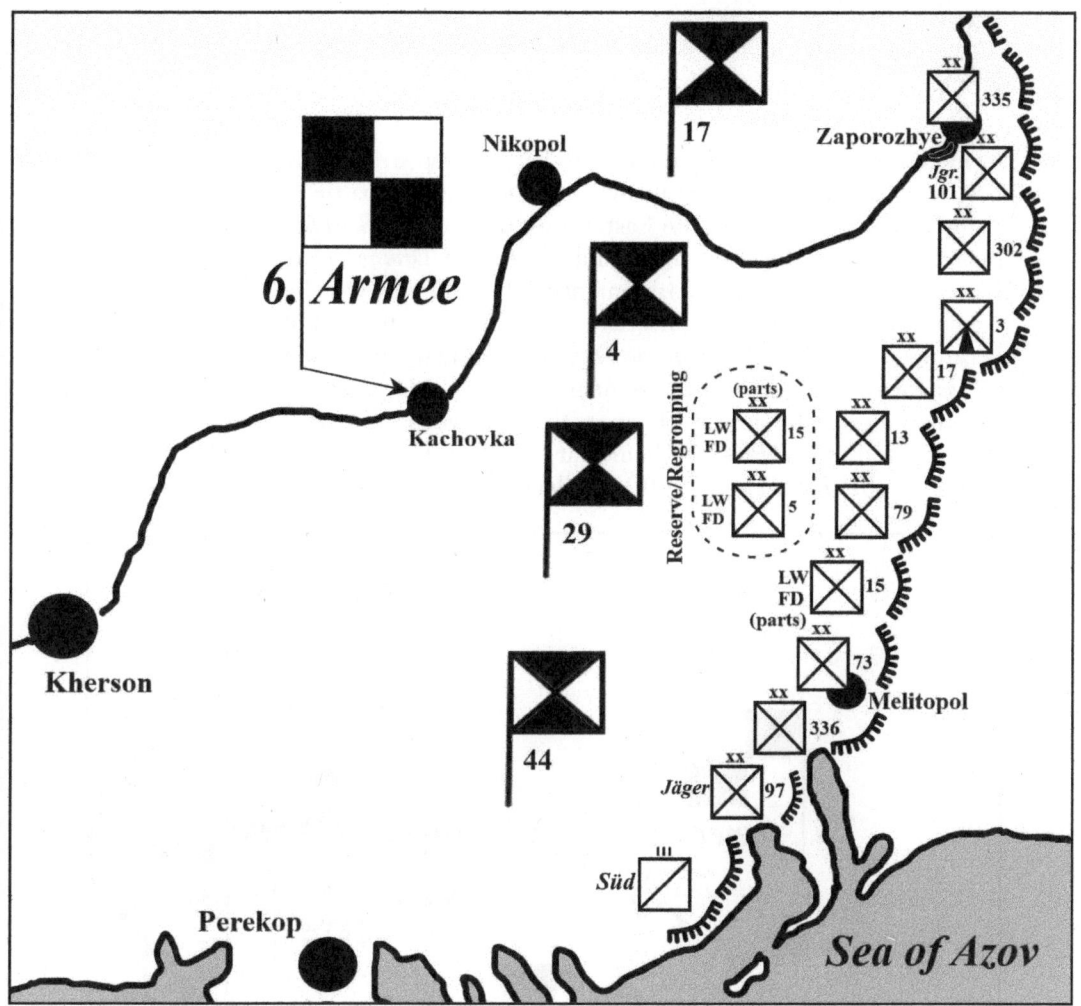

Positions of *5.* and *15. Luftwaffen-Felddivisionen* under the German *6. Armee*, mid-September 1943.

brutal. From all accounts, it appears that the Soviet 51st Army took very few prisoners during the first and second week of October 1943 (at the start of the offensive). On 21 October 1943 the remnants of *15. Luftwaffen-Felddivision*, unfit for further front-line action, were sent to defence lines just south of the city of Nikolayev, by the coast, to protect the shores of the mouth of the Dnieper river. The threat of a Soviet naval landing was small but the possibility could not be ruled out. Using what was left of the division to guard the coast seemed a logical choice for the German high command to make. The survivors were now under the command of *Befehlshaber West-Taurien* (German Military Commander West-Taurien), a rear area German military command that had by necessity been forced to take control of front-line units and positions.

In February 1944 *LXXII. Armeekorps* was created from the staff of the then disbanded *Befehlshaber West-Taurien*. This corps immediately became part of what was an attempt to reconstitute *6. Armee*. On 1 November 1943 the division was officially renamed *Felddivision 5 (L)*.[32] This was a mere technicality, since the formation had by then been reduced to battlegroup strength. Still, it operated as best it could, much like the many other skeletal and battle-weakened German Army divisions fighting in the East. Other units under *Befehlshaber West-Taurien* included the 1st Slovak Division and *17. Panzer-Division* (November 1943). In December the Romanian 24th Infantry Division relieved *17. Panzer-Division*, which was now placed as *6. Armee* reserve.[33] What remained of *Felddivision 5 (L)* became attached to *79. Infanterie-Division* in January 1944. In early March 1944 *79. Infanterie-Division* and the remnant parts of *Felddivision 5 (L)* were fighting together along the lower Dnieper river between *370. Infanterie-Division* at Kherson and *304. Infanterie-Division* at Berisslav. By the middle of March 1944, however, the *Felddivision 5 (L)* battlegroup had been moved southwest of

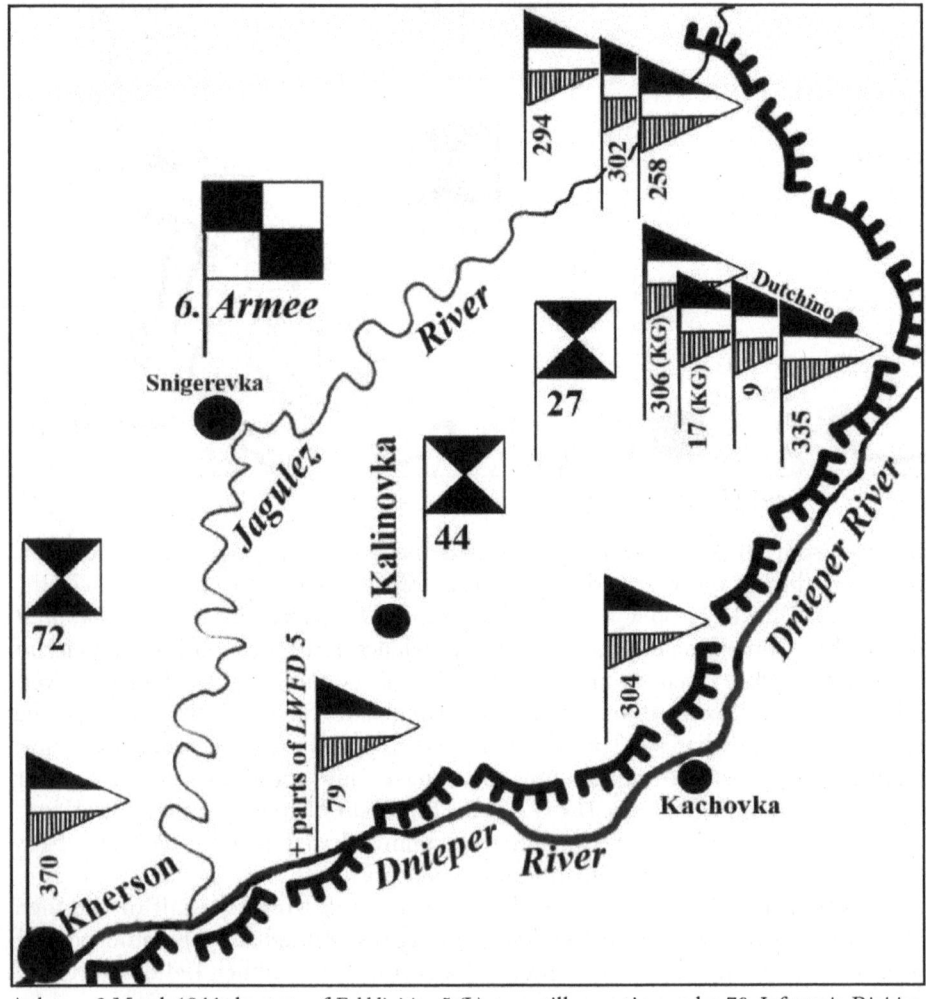

As late as 3 March 1944 elements of *Felddivision 5 (L)* were still operating under *79. Infanterie-Division*.

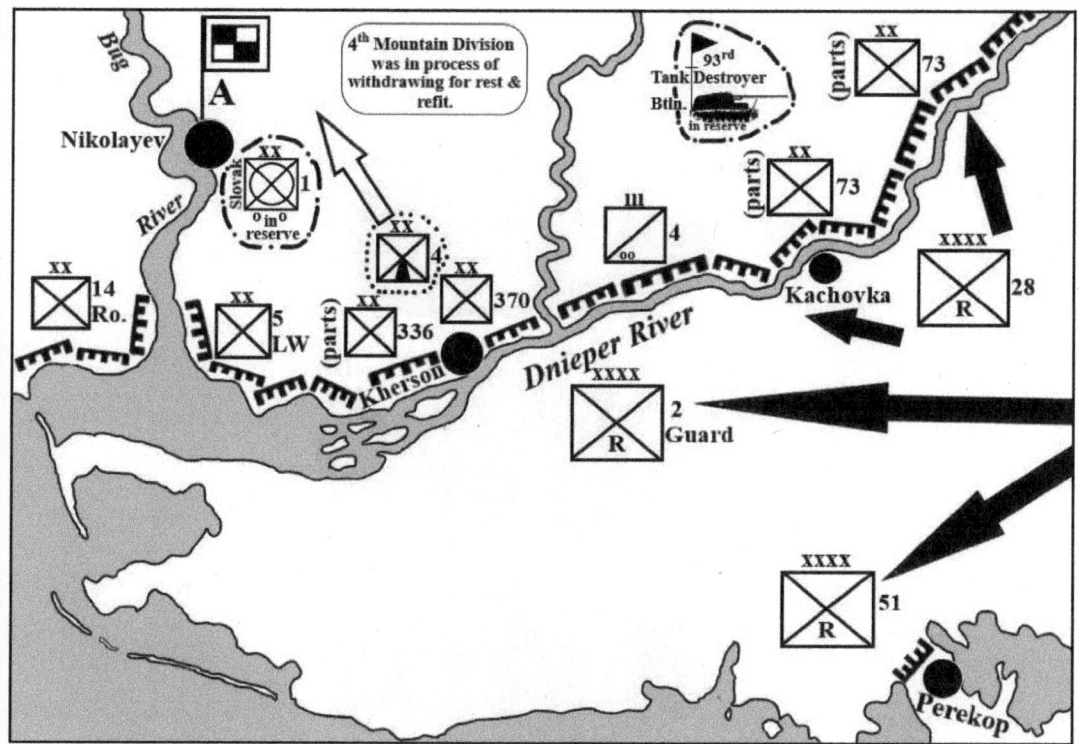

Location of the remnants of *Felddivision 5 (L)* and other units of *6. Armee*, 20 January 1944.

Nikolayev, and positioned behind the vast expanse of the Bug river estuary – that part of the river which empties into the Black Sea. Further south, on the right flank, the Romanian 15th Infantry Division covered the southern flank of the *Luftwaffe kampfgruppe*. Units of the Romanian 4th Army Corps were positioned on the left flank of the battlegroup, also behind the Bug river.[34] A Soviet drive beginning on 20 March once again battered the tired German and Romanian divisions along the defence lines of *6. Armee*. By 28 March 1944 Soviet armoured columns had broken through the defence lines of *XXIX. Armeekorps* and were driving to Beresovka, threatening to envelop the entire right wing of *6. Armee* and the whole of *8. Armee*. If they succeeded, these two German armies would be trapped with their backs against the shores of the Black Sea.

The *Felddivision 5 (L)* battlegroup, along with the rest of *8. Armee*, now withdrew from their defensive positions on the western bank of the Bug river. By 16 April they were located southwest of Odessa, by the Dniester river estuary. Again, the battlegroup had been assigned a relatively quiet and easily defensible area, this time under the control of the Romanian 3rd Army Corps. At the beginning of May 1944 the remnants of the division were finally disbanded and shared between the *76., 304., 320.* and *335. Infanterie-Divisionen*.[35] In particular, *76.* and *304. Infanterie-Divisionen* received the bulk of the air force soldiers.[36] The only strong combat infantry unit in the division, *Jäger-Regiment 9 (L)*, was absorbed into *76. Infanterie-Division*.

Felddivision 5 (L) was formally dissolved on 9 October 1944. It had fought as a battlegroup from November 1943 till May 1944 (seven months). It is almost

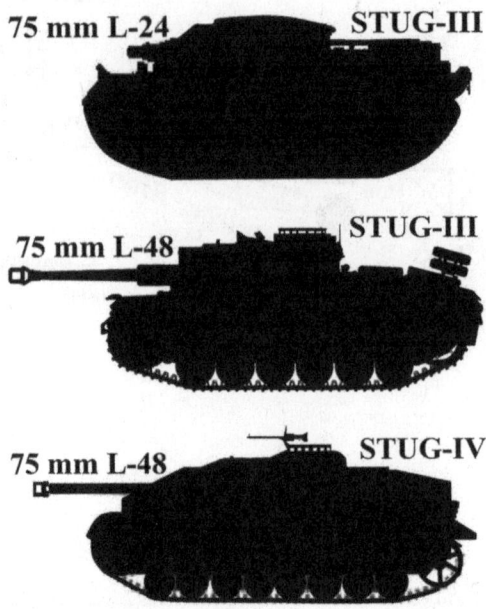

The three most common armoured vehicles employed in the *Luftwaffen-Felddivisionen*, specifically the *Ausführung D*, the *Ausführung G* and the *Ausführung H* variants of the *Sturmgeschütz III/IV*.

certain that after *Field Division 15 (L)* was shattered at Melitopol its surviving forces were absorbed into *Felddivision 5 (L)*. It is equally probable that this allowed *Felddivision 5 (L)* to carry on for as long as it did. However, the mere fact that the division survived on its own from November 1942 until August 1943 – a span of ten months – is a tribute to its officers and airmen. Although it sustained heavy losses, the unit continued to endure and persevere. And that *5. Luftwaffen-Felddivision / Felddivision 5 (L)* managed to serve fairly well, in spite of its brief, meagre training, poor organization and total lack of proper equipment, places it a mark above *2., 3.* and *4. Luftwaffen-Felddivisionen*. The assault gun battery of the divisional anti-tank battalion in particular distinguished itself in the Caucasus and in the Kuban bridgehead. It was eventually transferred into *Felddivision 22 (L)* before finally being handed over to *Felddivision 21 (L)*. Given its relatively long and good combat history, in spite of being decimated at Melitopol, we can consider this division as one of the best of the twenty-two *Luftwaffe* field infantry divisions.[37]

Command Structure of *5. Luftwaffen-Felddivision*

Commanders:
  Divisional CO:
    Generalmajor Hans-Joachim von Arnim, 10/42–11/42
    Oberst Hans-Bruno Schulz-Heyn, 25/11/42–10/12/43
    Generalmajor Botho Graf von Hülsen, 10/03/44–1/06/44

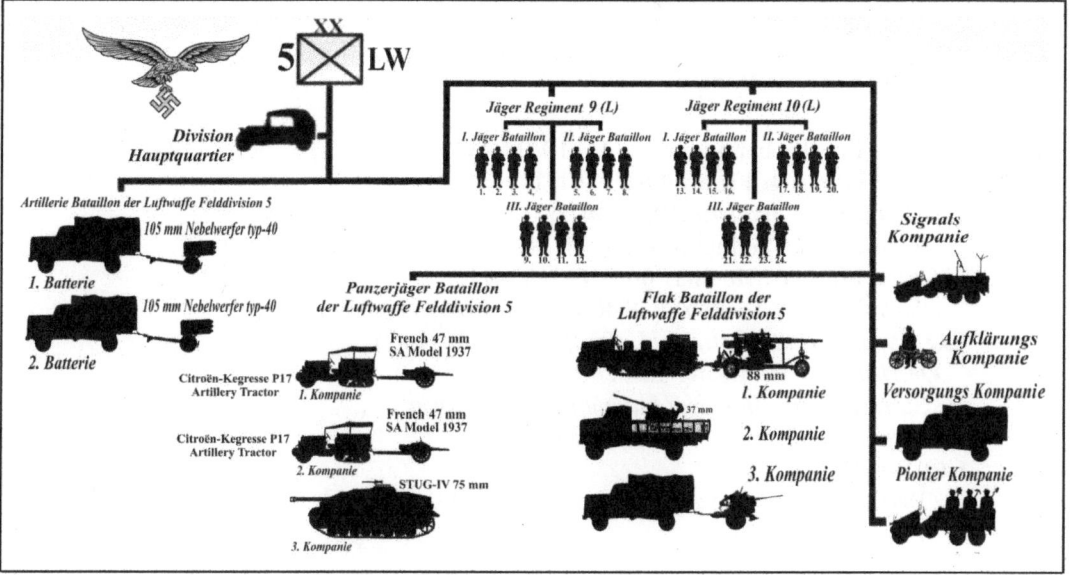

5. *Luftwaffen-Felddivision*, December 1942.

Ib:
    Major Karl-Heinz Puschner, 07/09/43–01/11/43
IVb:
    Oberstarzt Dr Werner Darge, 01/04/43–?
CO *Luftwaffen-Jäger-Regiment 9*:
    Oberst Hans Borckenhagen, 12/42–09/43
    Oberstleutnant Hermann Helbig, 03/09/43–01/11/43
CO *I. Bataillon / Luftwaffen-Jäger-Regiment 9*:
    Major Erich Roesner, 11/42–31/12/42
    Oberst Tillo Schaefer, 01/01/43–25/01/43[38]
CO *Luftwaffen-Jäger-Regiment 10*:
    Oberst Anton Schub, 12/42–07/43

5. *Luftwaffen-Felddivision*, August 1943.

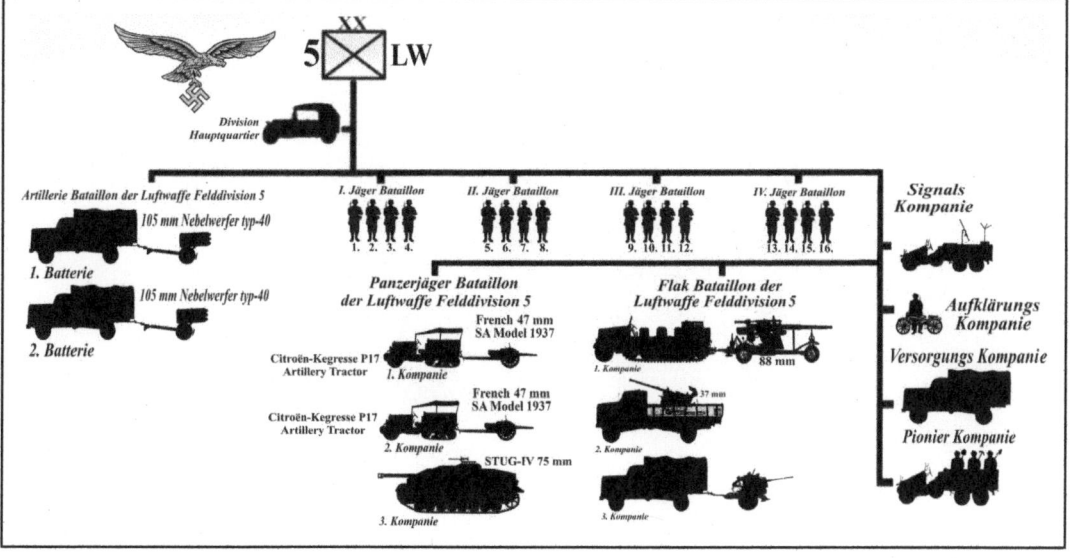

Oberst Friedrich Lampe, 07/43–10/08/43
Major Heinrich Frohn, 08/43–01/11/43
CO *Luftwaffen-Artillerie-Regiment 5*:
Oberstleutnant Wilhelm Mann, 01/43–06/03/43
Oberst Herbert Mueller, 06/03/43–11/43
Major Max Graf von Schall-Riaucour, 11/43–12/43
CO *Sturmgeschütz-Batterie/Luftwaffen-Felddivision 5*:
Oberleutnant Wolfgang Bach
Ia. *Sturmgeschütz-Batterie/Luftwaffen-Felddivision 5*:
Hauptwachmeister Hermann Christ[39]
CO *Sanitäts Abteilung*:
Oberfeldarzt Dr Alexander Schulz, 22/06/43–08/43

6. Luftwaffen-Felddivision

This division was formed in the autumn of 1942 at Training Camp Gross-Born from *Luftwaffen-Flieger-Regiment 21*. This training regiment had initially been stationed at Magdeburg but was later transferred to Reims. The commander of *Luftwaffen-Flieger-Regiment 21* was *Oberstleutnant* Günther Hartung. He was relieved of his command on 19 September 1942 when the regiment was disbanded and its battalions redesignated as *Jäger-Bataillonen* and assigned to the forming 6. *Luftwaffen-Felddivision*. This air force division contained the typical complement of four *Jäger* battalions, plus smaller supporting units. There was no initial regimental headquarters. The artillery battalion comprised two towed artillery batteries and an assault gun battery. The division was kitted out with Czechoslovak Army equipment.

In December 1942 the division was sent by rail to Nevel. It then moved forward and by 23 January 1943 was situated in the front lines near the towns of Ossikino and Tschernosen, just south of Velikiye Luki and southeast of Lake Ssenniza.[1] This region had been the scene of heavy fighting ever since November 1942 when Velikiye Luki had been surrounded by strong enemy forces. Inside the city were 7,500 German troops under *Oberstleutnant* von Saß.[2] Many of the troops inside the surrounded town were from *83. Infanterie-Division*, which had been established on 1 December 1939 as part of the Sixth Wave, using men from Lower Saxony.

The German defenders had to cover an area of some 13 square miles. By the end of December 1942 only two strong points inside the city were still in German hands: the railway station and the Citadel itself. OKW knew this area of the Russian Front needed reinforcements, and earmarked 6. *Luftwaffen-Felddivision* as one of several formations sent to this region of the front, alongside other German Army and *Luftwaffe* field divisions that had been rushed from their bases in the *Reich*. These army forces were the so-called *Walküre* (Valkyrie) divisions that from 15 December 1941 had been quickly organized and put together, using training and replacement troops as well as troops who were convalescing after being wounded. In total, four *Walküre* divisions were created: *328., 329., 330.* and *331 Infanterie-Divisionen*.

On 16 January 1943 Velikiye Luki fell to Soviet forces. On the same day the Red Army launched eight formations against the two German divisions. The Red Army forces included:

708th Rifle Division
47th Mechanized Rifle Brigade
56th Engineer Brigade

85th Corps Artillery Regiment
793rd Divisional Artillery Regiment
923rd Divisional Artillery Regiment
78th Tank Brigade
   263rd Tank Battalion with T-60 tanks
   264th Tank Battalion with T-34 tanks
   a motorized rifle battalion
   technical support company
77th BM-13 Katyusha (Rocket Launcher) Brigade.

Facing this superior Red Army force in the area of Lashni Belodedovo were the Pomeranian regiments of *32. Infanterie-Division* and *6. Luftwaffen-Felddivision*.[3]

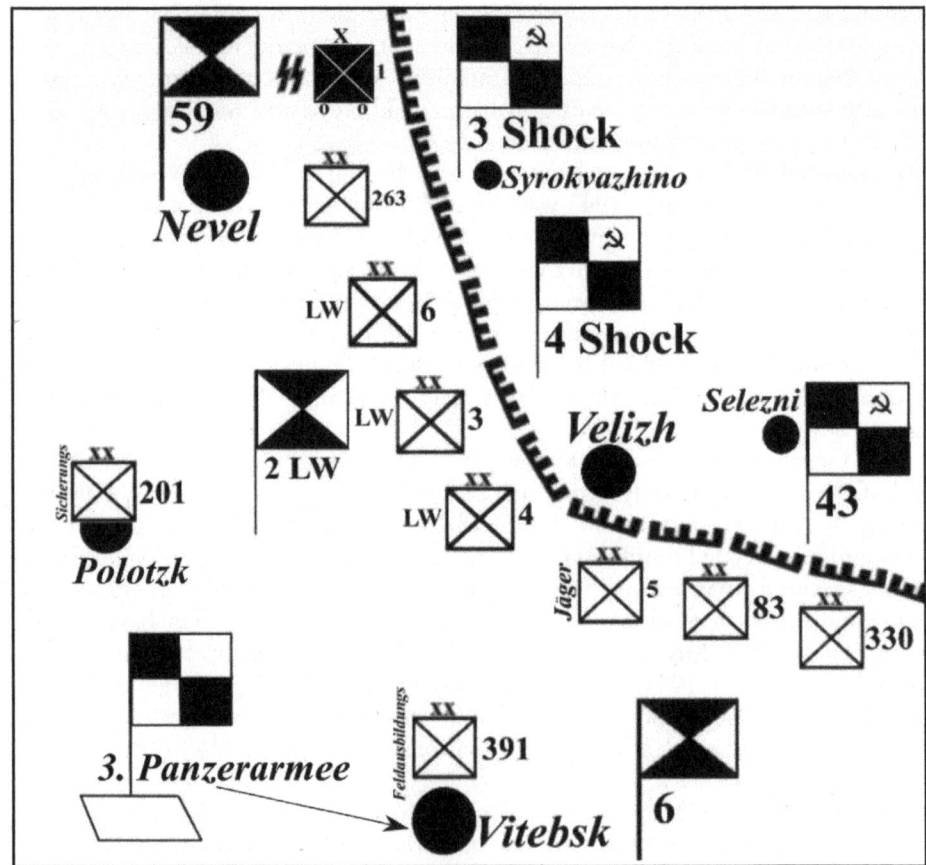

General area of operations for *6. Luftwaffen-Felddivision* during 1943. The decision to use *General der Fallschirmjäger* Alfred Schlemm's *2. Luftwaffen Feldkorps* with its weak air force divisions as the lynchpin of the defences between Army Groups North and Centre in the Polotsk-Nevel region was a mistake on the part of the German command. The Soviets took advantage of this mistake, and struck German forces stationed there, with overwhelming force.

It would need the addition of ten other German divisions to finally halt this Soviet assault. Additionally, the Thuringian and Saxon regiments of *87. Infanterie-Division*, whose front lines wavered but never broke during these attacks, firmly held the left flank of *6. Luftwaffen-Felddivision*. This helped to eventually check the Red Army advance. The *2., 3., 4.* and *6. Luftwaffen-Felddivisionen* were assigned to *II. Luftwaffen-Feldkorps*. The arriving *Luftwaffe* field divisions were placed into the area south of Veliki Luki and southeast of Nevel from January 1943. Here, these units took on defensive positions southeast of Lake Ssenniza. The defence lines of *6. Luftwaffen-Felddivision* remained mostly unchanged in the same area around Ossokino until March 1943. By 27 July 1943 the division had been shifted south to Kapustino, about 20km east of Nevel.[4]

In May 1943 two *Jäger* battalions from the division were employed in an anti-partisan drive which began on 17 May 1943. The operation was titled *Maigewitter* (May Thunderstorm). The German combat groups were arranged as follows:

Kampfgruppe Oberstleutnant Abel
Staff, *Panzergrenadier-Regiment 28*
Reinforced *Panzer-Aufklärungs-Abteilung 8*
II. Jäger-Bataillon / 6. Luftwaffen-Felddivision
Zwei Züge (2 platoons) *der Panzer-Pionier-Bataillon 59*

Kampfgruppe Oberstleutnant Neise
Panzergrenadier-Regiment 8
Four 'alarm' companies from *8 Panzer-Division*
Ostkompanie 59
Zwei Züge (2 platoons) *der Panzer-Pionier-Bataillon 59*

Kampfgruppe Major von Renteln
Kosaken-Infanterie-Bataillon 623
Kosaken-Infanterie-Bataillon 625
Kosaken-Infanterie-Kompanie 638
Ein Züg (1 platoon) *der Panzer-Pionier-Bataillon 59*

Kampfgruppe Oberst von Scotti
Staff, *Panzer-Artillerie-Regiment 80*
I. Jäger-Bataillon / 6. Luftwaffen-Felddivision
Kosaken-Infanterie-Bataillon 631
Ost-Bataillon Hensen
Zwei Züge (2 platoons) *der Panzer-Pionier-Bataillon 59*[5]

The anti-partisan operation was concentrated against the guerrillas operating in and around the Gorodok–Vischedki–Mesha highway and the Duna Forest region.[6] By 18 May one combat group had broken through the partisan defences of the Alexiev Partisan Brigade (containing five battalions). Total losses on the Axis side were 21 dead (including 5 non-Germans), 76 wounded (including 18 non-Germans) and 2 missing (including a non-German). Partisan losses were

398 dead, 78 taken prisoner and 14 who had deserted, plus 1,679 people who were apprehended and accused of being a *partisanhelfer* (partisan helper). The division received reinforcements in the summer of 1943 because of the installation of the two regimental staffs for the infantry battalions, *Jäger-Regiment 11 (L)* and *Jäger-Regiment 12 (L)*; *Luftwaffen-Artillerie-Regiment 6* was also organized that same summer. The original artillery battalion in the division was redesignated *III. Artillerie-Bataillon* in the newly formed artillery regiment, while the division's *Flak* abteilung was redesignated *IV. Artillerie-Abteilung/Luftwaffen-Artillerie-Regiment 6*. On 6 October 1943, *6. Luftwaffen-Felddivision* was hit by a Russian offensive geared to create a wedge between Army Groups North and Centre. The offensive was part of a broader Soviet strategy to destabilize the German front by severing the connection between major army groups, thereby weakening their operational cohesion and creating opportunities for deeper penetrations. This occurred while the division was reforming.

The division's Flak battalion was withdrawn and became *I. Abteilung/Flak-Regiment 34 (motorisiert)*.[7] The division's anti-tank battalion was also grouped into the new regiment as *V. Artillerie-Abteilung/Luftwaffen-Artillerie-Regiment 6*. This decision was later reversed so that the anti-tank battalion remained an independent formation within the division.[8] The artillery regiment also created *I.* and *II. Artillerie-Abteilungen* as well as the regimental staff for the regiment.[9] According to orders dated 1 November 1943 the regiment was redesignated *Artillerie-Regiment 6 (L)*.[10] The divisional leadership was changed with the inclusion of army officers throughout the ranks. The division was now renamed as *Felddivision 6 (L)*. When the Soviets launched their second Smolensk operation in October 1943, the Red Army drive eventually crushed both *Felddivision 2 (L)* and *Felddivision 3 (L)*, leaving only remnant parts which were absorbed by *Felddivision 4 (L)* and *Felddivision 6 (L)* on 17 January 1944.[11] This allowed *Felddivision 6 (L)* to form a third *Jäger-Regiment* at the beginning of 1944. The unit now contained the following infantry regiments, formed from the following *Heer* and *Luftwaffe* formations:

- 1. *Jäger-Regiment 52 (L)*: formed from the staff of *Grenadier-Regiment 471* and *Luftwaffen-Jäger-Bataillon 3/3* and *4/3*;[12]
- 2. *Jäger-Regiment 53 (L)*: a new regimental staff, plus *Luftwaffen-Jäger-Bataillone 1/6* and *2/2*;[13] and
- 3. *Jäger-Regiment 54 (L)*: formed from the staff of *Grenadier-Regiment 459*, with *III.* and *IV. Luftwaffen-Jäger-Bataillone*.

Other units in the division were also affected during this reorganization:

- *Fusilier-Bataillon 6 (L)*: this unit, formed in March 1944 from elements of *Felddivision 2 (L)*, *Felddivision 3 (L)* and *Felddivision 6 (L)*, was organized in the vicinity of Vitebsk; it would act as the division's reconnaissance formation.

- *Sturmgeschütz-Abteilung 6 (L)*: this assault gun battalion was formed using *III. Sturmgeschütz Batterie* of the original artillery battalion as a cadre. The unit was eventually detached from the division and redesignated *Sturmgeschütz Abteilung 1006*, becoming a corps troop of *3. Panzerarmee.*[14]
- *Feldersatz-Bataillon 6 (L)*: formed from the training and replacement companies of *Felddivision 2 (L)*, *Felddivision 3 (L)* and *Felddivision 6 (L)*.
- *Nachrichten Abteilung 6 (L)*: created from the division's original signals company. It reached battalion strength in January 1944.
- *Panzer-Jäger-Abteilung 6 (L)*: basically the same unit that was formed when the division was established in the autumn of 1942. It continued to have three companies.
- *Pionier-Bataillon 6 (L)*: formed using the engineer companies from *Felddivision 2 (L)*, *Felddivision 3 (L)* and *Felddivision 6 (L)*. The staff for the battalion was formed from *216. Pionier-Bataillon*, which was a *Heer* formation.[15]
- *Artillerie-Regiment 6 (L)*: staff headquarters came from *Luftwaffen-Artillerie-Regiment 2*, along with *I.* and *III. Artillerie-Abteilung / Luftwaffen-Artillerie-Regiment 6* and *I. Bataillon / Luftwaffen-Artillerie-Regiment 3*, plus *III. Bataillon / Luftwaffen-Artillerie-Regiment 2*.

The division's artillery regiment now contained four artillery battalions. *I.–III. Artillerie-Abteilungen / Artillerie-Regiment 6 (L)* each contained three batteries of four 105mm le-FH howitzers. *IV. Artillerie-Abteilung* was weaker, comprising two batteries of French-made 155mm *Grande Puissance Filloux* (GPF) *modèle 1917* howitzers and one battery of 150mm sFH-18 German howitzers. The three batteries of *IV. Artillerie-Abteilung* each had four guns apiece. Altogether, the division could count on 48 guns (36 light and 12 heavy),[16] and it would need every one of them, as it experienced some of the fiercest fighting between October 1943 and its final death throes in June/July 1944. In November 1943 the engineer company was enlarged to battalion size. Later, in January 1944 the signals (communications) company was likewise expanded into a battalion. As the division transferred into the army in November 1943 another Soviet offensive began which eventually forged a breach between Army Groups North and Centre in the region of Nevel. During the autumn of 1943 *II. Luftwaffen-Feldkorps* was holding a front line that was 80km long.[17]

This was a military misjudgement that was just asking for trouble. Nevertheless, most German Army divisions covered from 30 to 50km apiece, so 80km for four divisions may have seemed reasonable. The problem was that the four *Luftwaffe* divisions under this corps, *Felddivision 2 (L)*, *3 (L)*, *4 (L)* and *6 (L)*, had not yet completed their expansion and reorganization, and other than *Felddivision 6 (L)* they were still the size of a brigade each. In early October 1943 *Felddivision 6 (L)* was located in and around Tschurilovo, directly east of Lake Ssenniza. When the Soviet attack began, *Felddivision 6 (L)* was pushed back on its left flank south of Lake Ssenniza under heavy pressure. Between 7 and 25 October

1943 it made a fighting withdrawal between Lake Ssennitza and Lake Sadratsch, in the region of Rudnya. The retreat then continued until the end of the month, when German forces reached the so-called 'Panther Position'. This defence line was nowhere near completed, and would not hold back the Soviets for any appreciable amount of time. It was no surprise then, when this 'Panther Position' was breached northeast of Gorodok on 26 October 1943.[18] On 26 November 1943 the Red Army took Sselitsche and widened the breach between Army Groups North and South. The gap was now 20km wide and getting bigger. Both Army Groups sent combat groups to try to plug the gap but they only managed to slow down the enemy drive, without halting it. On 9 December a light frost came down and covered the cold countryside.

The Soviets struck again four days later, on 13 December. Their attack this time was aimed at units of *3. Panzerarmee*.[19] On 17 December 1943 the Germans withdrew towards Gorodok, via Gnilitschi and Tscherny. The next day they reached Frolov. By 19 December 1943 *Felddivision 6 (L)* had withdrawn to an area between Dubrova and Smolovka. On 25 December it reached Grabniza and Gorodok, just 18km northwest of Vitebsk. It was on Christmas Eve that the fiercest combat between the Soviets and units of *3. Panzerarmee* reached its zenith when no fewer than 37 rifle divisions, a cavalry division and 15 tank brigades crashed headlong into the front lines of *3. Panzerarmee*. A breakthrough by the

The Red Army offensive against the lynchpin connecting the southern tip of *Heeresgruppe Nord* with the northern tip of *Heeresgruppe Mitte* proved successful. Particularly hard-hit were *129. Infanterie-Division* and *Felddivision 6 (L)*. The gap that appeared in the German lines could only be partially sealed by the employment of SS and Police units that normally would have been employed against the partisans. This Red Army attack was assisted by approximately 10,000 guerrilla fighters located in the Senno region.

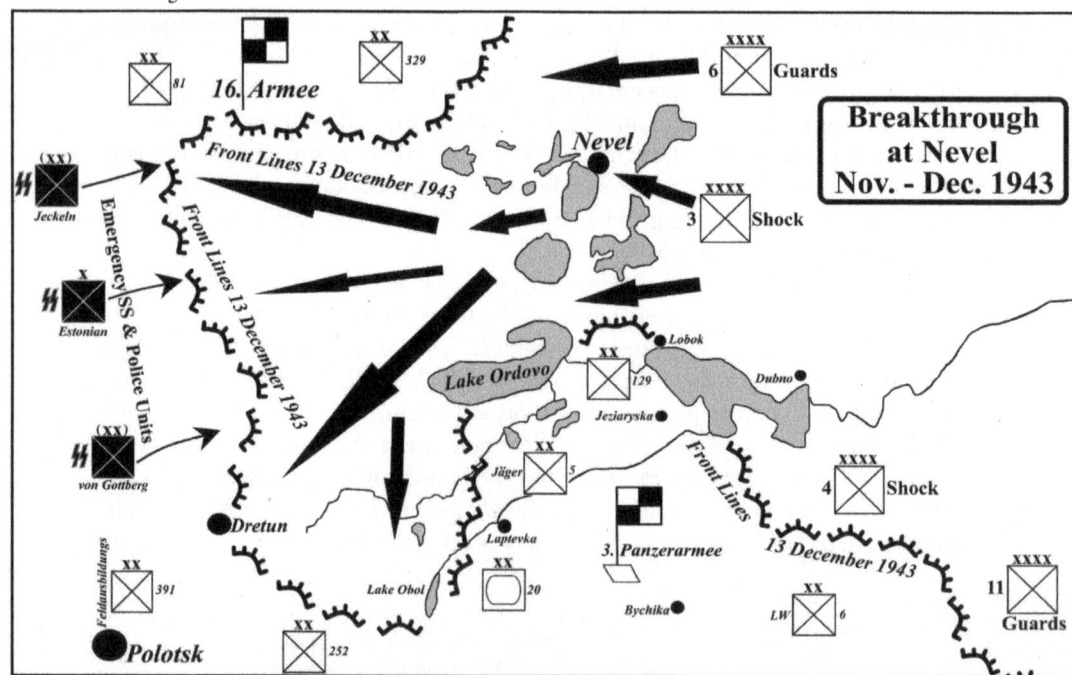

Author's line drawing of the armoured 'Nashorn' (rhinoceros) tank-destroyer, which carried the accurate and deadly 88mm PAK-43 anti-tank gun. *Schwere Panzerjäger-Abteilung 519* (519th Heavy Tank Destroyer Battalion) was equipped with these vehicles.

5th Soviet Tank Corps between *Felddivision 3 (L)* and *129. Infanterie-Division* saw Soviet tanks driving headlong into Gorodok. After the city fell, *129. Infanterie-Division* and *14. Infanterie-Division (motorisiert)*, plus *Felddivision 3 (L)* and *Felddivision 4 (L)*, withdrew to blocking positions in and around Losvida. *Felddivision 6 (L)* now lay directly in front of the Soviet drive. Heavy fighting was reported between 24 and 27 December. The Red Army advance continued into January 1944. On 9 January 1944, in a blinding snowstorm, the Red Army attacked with a total of 56 rifle divisions, 3 cavalry divisions, 5 rifle brigades and 22 tank brigades.

Facing this formidable horde were eighteen tired, depleted and worn-out German divisions of *3. Panzerarmee*. Though exhausted, the German formations held their ground, causing the equally tired Soviet units to cease operations for three days. On 13 January 1944 this small respite was shattered when over 200 Red Army bombers dropped their heavy bombloads on the front lines of *Felddivision 6 (L)*.[20] When *Felddivision 6 (L)* began to be pushed back, the arrival of *Panzerjäger-Abteilung 519* temporarily stabilized the situation. The *Luftwaffe* and *Heer* troops fought for their lives south of Lake Naroch, and only managed to halt the Soviet attack with the greatest difficulty. On 20 January 1944 the commander of *Felddivision 6 (L)*, *Generalleutnant* Rudolf Peschel, was awarded the much-coveted Knight's Cross for his leadership of the division during these tough withdrawal battles. The German *Landsers* in *Felddivision 6 (L)* were also rewarded when one of their own, *Obergefreiter* Heinz Reichmann, who was serving in *8. Kompanie / Jäger-Regiment 54 (L)*, was also awarded the Knight's Cross. Reichmann received his country's highest award alongside his divisional commander, *Generalleutnant* Peschel.[21] Losses on the German side were heavy, but the Russian formations had taken severe casualties.

At this time *LIII. Armeekorps* was composed of *12. Infanterie-Division*, a battlegroup of *87. Infanterie-Division*, a battlegroup of *6. Felddivision (L)*, *4. Felddivision (L)* and *3. Felddivision (L)*.[22] In February 1944 the *20. Panzer-Division (IX Armeekorps)* was transferred to the control of *LIII. Armeekorps*. In the first three weeks of

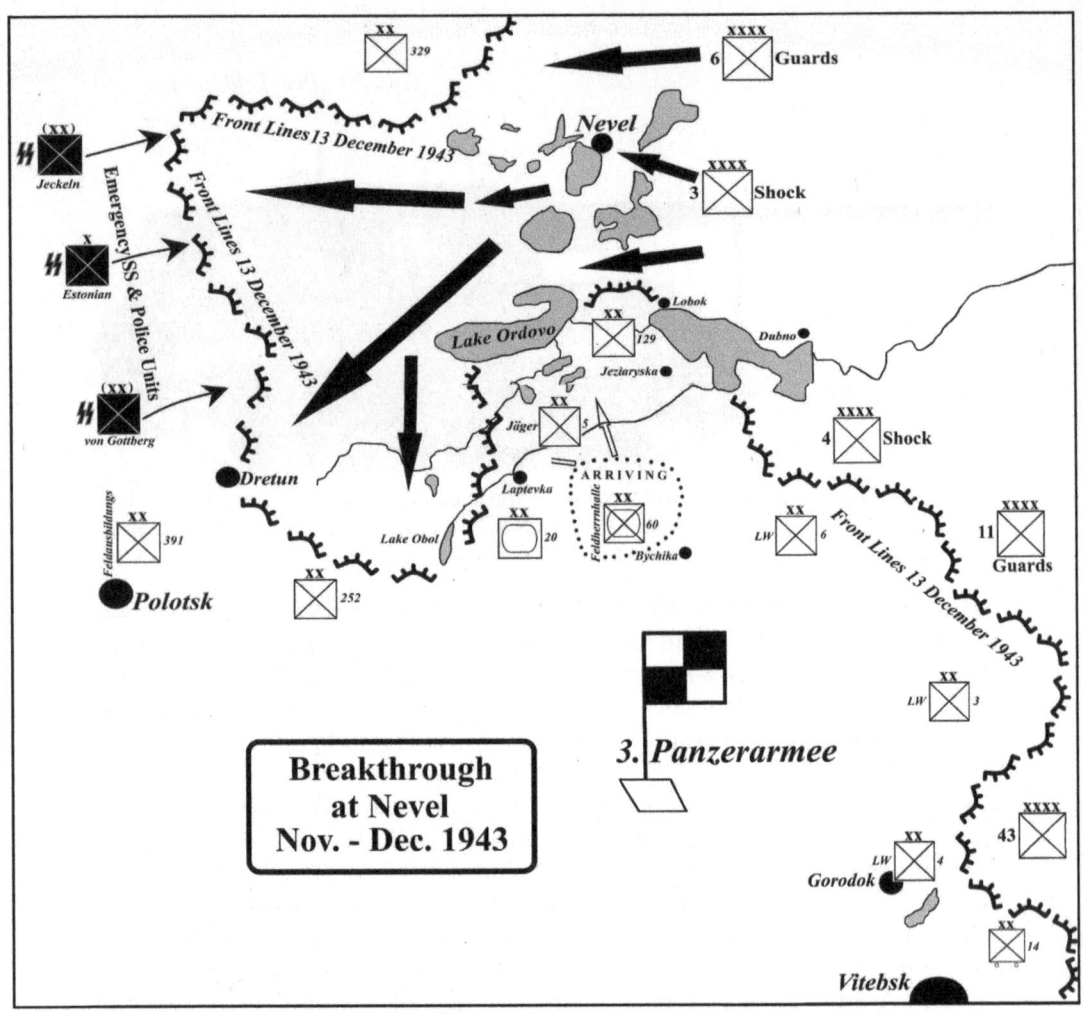

Complete disaster was averted south of Lake Ordovo by the timely employment of *20. Panzerdivision*, as well as the newly arriving *60. Panzergrenadier Division Feldherrnhalle*.

February 1944 the Red Army concentrated on tightening its noose around Vitebsk. By 17 February the 4th Shock Army and 33rd Army had managed to penetrate northeast and south of Vitebsk. The 4th Shock Army had reached the Duna river bend, just west of Vitebsk. In March 1944 Soviet attention was redirected at German forces in Kovel. The region around Vitebsk was relegated to trench warfare and artillery duels, with the occasional enemy probe. This respite gave the formations of *LIII. Armeekorps* some much-needed rest and allowed its divisions, including *Felddivision 6 (L)*, to regroup and replenish their depleted line companies. The division now built defensive wooden and earthen works along its front lines.

This was in keeping with orders issued by *LIII. Armeekorps* to all of its divisions. The men of *Pionier-Bataillon 6 (L)* particularly distinguished themselves during these early spring months by creating a huge number of bunkers and trenches. The engineers were so effective in this mission that the battalion garnered praise

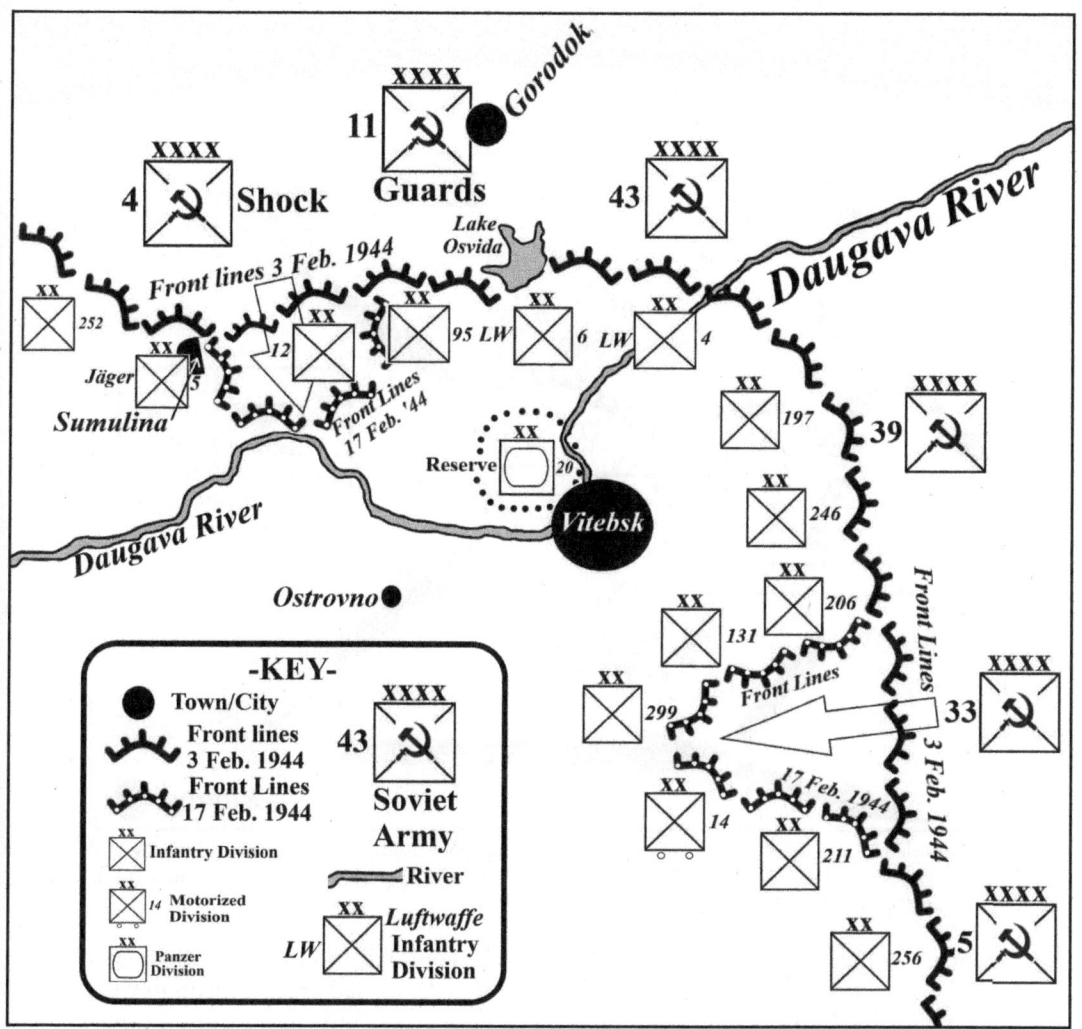

German positions in and around Vitebsk, 3–17 February 1944.

in the German Army High Command War Diary, which personally mentioned the unit and one of its company commanders: *Oberleutnant* Walter Zurmühlen, commanding officer of *1. Kompanie*. Zurmühlen would go on to receive the Knight's Cross.[23]

Although the Germans had taken advantage of the relatively quiet spring months of 1944 to build substantial fortifications, no amount of defensive works was going to stop the Red Army's 1,670,000 men from breaking through the lines of Army Group Centre. These Soviet troops were supported by 5,818 tanks and assault guns, 32,718 artillery pieces and rocket launchers, and close to 8,000 combat aircraft. The Soviet summer offensive, which began on 22 June 1944, would bring about the destruction of *Felddivision 6 (L)*, which up until then, had managed to survive through an influx of replacements from other shattered units and the tenacity and determination of its officers and men. In fact, the Soviet summer offensive of 1944 would almost completely wipe out Army Group

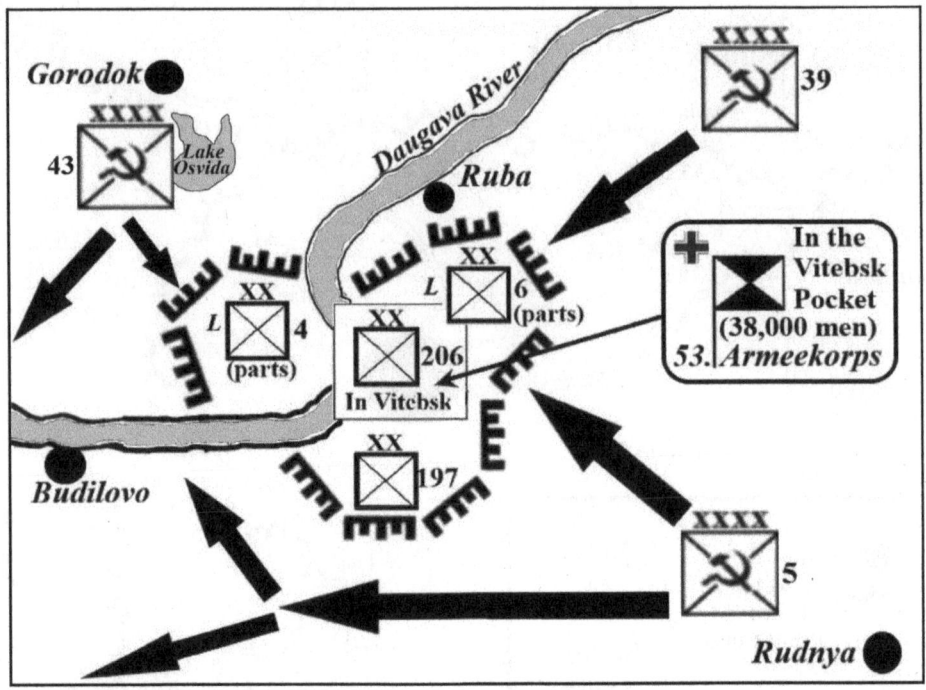

The destruction of several air force field divisions in June 1944. *Felddivision 6 (L)* was surrounded on three sides just northeast of the outskirts of Vitebsk, and was slowly pushed into the city, where it was annihilated, alongside other divisions of *LIII. Armeekorps*.

Centre. When the Soviets finally attacked, General Friedrich Gollwitzer's *LIII. Armeekorps* was initially unaffected. The Red Army had broken through west of Vitebsk, and was headed towards the Daugava river. This move caused Gollwitzer to ask permission to withdraw his corps from the outer Vitebsk defence lines to a much closer line of defence, which would make it harder for the enemy to trap his corps.[24] After much hesitancy, Hitler gave his permission that same day at around 6.30pm. It was a rare moment indeed, when the *Führer* consented to a withdrawal, even a tactical one. This move was also geared towards reducing the front lines of *LIII. Armeekorps* and establishing a reserve. However, the collapse of *VI. Armeekorps* on 24 June on the right flank of Gollwitzer's corps forced him to send what remained of *Felddivision 4 (L)* to try to reestablish contact with *VI. Armeekorps*. Events were now moving more quickly than the German corps commander could react to, given the fact that any major move had to be approved from above, sometimes as high up the chain of command as Hitler himself. By 25 June *LIII. Armeekorps* was surrounded in and around Vitebsk with the following units: elements of *197. Infanterie-Division*; *206. Infanterie-Division*; *246. Infanterie-Division*; *Felddivision 4 (L)* and *Felddivision 6 (L)*.

On the same day that *LIII. Armeekorps* was surrounded, *3. Panzerarmee* granted permission for *General der Infanterie* Gollwitzer to break out from the pocket with his men. Army headquarters could only recommend a breakout in a southwesterly direction towards Chodzy. The only stipulation to the order to break out was that the *Führer* was demanding that *206. Infanterie-Division* hold Vitebsk as a *Festung* (fortress). This was a veritable death sentence for the men of the division. Hitler was convinced that the Red Army flooding westwards could be halted in the same manner that his order of 'no retreat' had eventually halted the Soviet winter offensive of 1941/1942. But what Hitler failed to comprehend was that the end of the Soviet offensive in the spring of 1942 had been due to other factors. Nevertheless, until the end of the war Hitler persisted in establishing fortified localities that were grandiosely named *Festungen*. The withdrawal attempts of *LIII. Armeekorps* proved futile. By 25/26 June *Felddivision 4 (L)* no longer existed. Corps reports from those last days in June state that both *Felddivision 6 (L)* and *246. Infanterie-Division* were heavily engaged from multiple sides and could not withdraw.[25] This meant that any organized defence line on a corps level was no longer possible. No German relief forces were available to help with the breakout from outside the pocket, as every unit under *3. Panzerarmee* was committed. For a time, elements of *95.* and *197. Infanterie-Division*, including *201. Sicherungs-Division*, attempted to keep a narrow corridor open for *LIII. Armeekorps* and for the defence of the western Dvina (Daugava in Latvian, Duna in German) river sector north of Beshenkovichi. Unfortunately, this only lasted for a very brief time. The corps apparently pushed southwest from Vitebsk to within 5–6km of its objective breakout point before it was overwhelmed by Soviet forces and effectively annihilated.[26]

Thus ended the history of *6. Luftwaffen-Felddivision / Felddivision 6 (L)*. The entire lifespan of the unit had been 21 months – just shy of two years. The division had benefited greatly by the addition of reinforcements from two other *Luftwaffe* field divisions that had been destroyed and disbanded. Its performance during the bitter fighting between October 1943 and April 1944 was considered good, since they were able to make a fighting withdrawal without collapsing

6 Luftwaffen-Felddivision in November 1942.

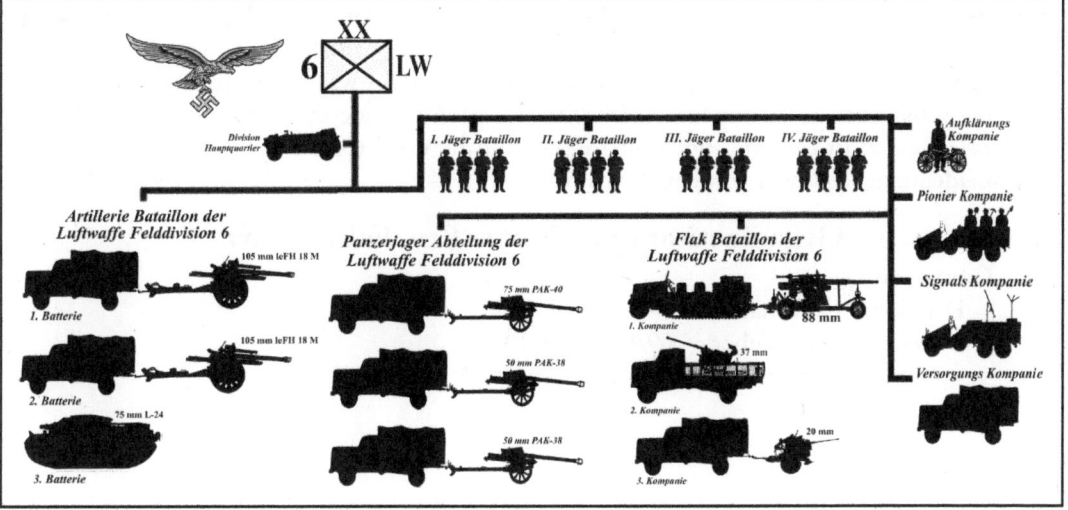

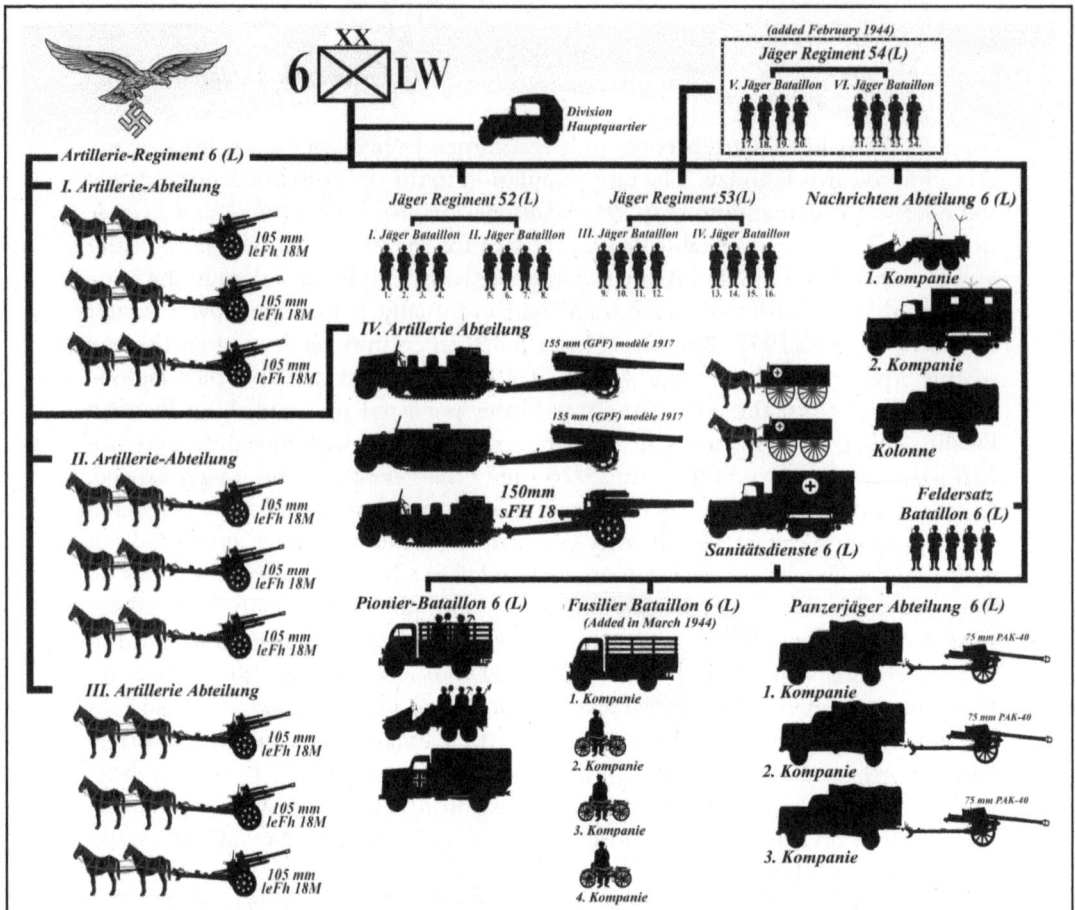

6. *Luftwaffen-Felddivision* in October 1943. A month later the title was changed to *Felddivision 6 (L)*.

altogether. The fact that the unit did not break apart completely should not entirely be attributed to receiving replacements and reinforcements; some credit must be given to the unit's former *Luftwaffe* airmen as well. We must remember, however, that during this time period the *Heer* had taken over the division and infused it with a good number of *Heer* officers and men. This means that credit for the survivability of the unit must be characteristic of the improvements that the army made to these air force field divisions. The performance of the division prior to the army assuming control in November 1943 was lacklustre and mediocre, but even so it was far better than the performance of 2. or 3. *Luftwaffen-Felddivision*. In the end, not much else could be expected from the unit and its inadequate start as a combat formation.

Organization of 6. *Luftwaffen-Felddivision*

Commanders:
  Divisional Commanders:
    Oberst Ernst Weber,[27] 09/42–16/11/42
    Generalleutnant Rüdiger von Heyking, 25/11/42–04/11/43

Generalleutnant Rudolf Peschel,[28] 31/10/43–29/06/44
Ia:
Hauptmann Ernst Friedrichsen, 10/42–09/12/43
Oberstleutnant Georg Zabel, 10/12/43–30/06/44
IIa:
Hauptmann Emmerich, 10/12/43–?
WuG:
Oberleutnant Rene Suetterlin, 10/42–01/11/43
V:
Major Otto Rothmayer, 10/42–01/11/43
CO *I. Jäger-Bataillon / 6. Luftwaffen-Felddivision*:
Oberstleutnant Wilhelm Arns, 10/42–02/43
Hauptmann Willi Maass, 02/43–06/43
Hauptmann Huhmann, 06/43–01/11/43
CO *II. Jäger-Bataillon / 6. Luftwaffen-Felddivision*:
Oberstleutnant Karl Fischer, 10/42–03/43
Major Paul Bureck, 29/03/43–05/43
Oberst Wilhelm Waldschmidt,[29] 15/06/43–31/07/43
CO *III. Jäger-Bataillon / 6. Luftwaffen-Felddivision*:
Major Walter Ross, 10/42–11/43
Major Hugo Novak, 02/43–01/11/43
CO *IV. Jäger-Bataillon / 6. Luftwaffen-Felddivision*:
Major Walter Schmidt-Künitz, 10/42–01/11/43
CO *Luftwaffen-Jäger-Regiment 52*[30]
CO *Luftwaffen-Jäger-Regiment 53*[31]
CO *Luftwaffen-Jäger-Regiment 54*[32]
CO *I. Artillerie-Abteilung / Luftwaffen-Felddivision 6*:
Oberst Walter Graepel, 10/42–10/43
CO: *Luftwaffen-Artillerie-Regiment 6*
Oberst Walter Graepel, 11/43–?

7. Luftwaffen-Felddivision

Initially, 7. *Luftwaffen-Felddivision* was formed at Troop Training Ground Gross-Born, but training was soon shifted to Troop Training Ground Mlawa in November 1942. This formation was one of the earliest division-sized *Luftwaffe* field units to see action,[1] aside from the regiments that served under *Luftwaffen-Felddivision-Meindl* in northern Russia during the winter of 1941/1942.[2] The men used to form this division came from *Luftgau III* and *Luftgau IV*. Unlike its predecessors, the initial 'rifle' complement of 7. *Luftwaffen-Felddivision* only included three *Jäger* battalions instead of the usual four.[3] It wasn't until December 1942 that *IV. Jäger-Bataillon* was added to the division. This was accomplished at the front in southern Russia by the addition of several *Luftwaffe* troops gathered from various ground crews and supply, signals and service units operating behind the front lines. The divisional artillery battalion contained two towed 105mm le-FH 18 howitzer batteries (with four guns each), while *III. Batterie* was equipped with five *Sturmgeschütz III* assault guns.[4] This artillery battalion was slightly more powerful than had originally been planned, as the artillery battalions of *1., 2., 7.* and *8. Luftwaffen-Felddivision* were to have received Czech-made 75mm Skoda Model 15 (K-15) mountain guns for their *1.* and *2. Artillerie-Batterie*.[5]

It was therefore unusual that 7. *Luftwaffen-Felddivision* had been able to acquire heavier artillery pieces for its *1.* and *2. Artillerie-Batterie*. As with many *Luftwaffe* field division assigned to the Eastern Front, the artillery pieces were all towed by *Opel Blitz* trucks or *Raupenschlepper Ost* tracked prime movers, when available. The divisional *Flak* battalion contained the allocated table of organization

Author's line drawing of the Czech-made Skoda Model 15 mountain gun.

Author's rendering of a *Raupenschlepper Ost* tracked prime mover.

strength of two 20mm *Flak* batteries and a 88mm *Flak* battery. The total number included the normal complement of 24 20mm and 4 88mm *Flak* guns. The anti-tank battalion of the division was excellently armed for a *Luftwaffe* field division. Although *1.* and *2. Panzerjäger-Kompanie* had three outdated 50mm PAK 38 anti-tank guns, they were also equipped with the more than adequate 75mm PAK 40 anti-tank gun, which was capable of defeating most Soviet tanks. *1. Kompanie* had three of these weapons, while *2. Kompanie* was slightly better off, having four. *3. Panzerjäger Kompanie* did not possess the 75mm PAK 40 guns, but did have nine of the virtually obsolescent 50mm PAK 38 anti-tank guns. It was hoped that what striking power couldn't accomplish would somehow be made up in numbers. Overall, the division's anti-tank battalion was slightly better off than most of the other *Luftwaffe* divisional anti-tank units.

The remainder of 7. *Luftwaffen-Felddivision* was composed of a supply company, an engineer company, a communications company and a *radfahr* (bicycle) company acting as the divisional reconnaissance unit.[6]

As in all *Luftwaffe* field divisions, the divisional support elements were too small and wholly inadequate to properly support a division-sized formation. Training of this and other *Luftwaffe* divisions proved to be short-lived and rudimentary, as the worsening military situation on the Russian Front required the immediate employment there of these and other units. Two regiments had been planned for the division, *Jäger-Regiment 13 (L)* and *Jäger-Regiment 14 (L)*, but the rapid deployment of the division into combat prevented their development.[7] On 19 November 1942 the Soviets launched their winter offensive against the weakly held flanks of the Axis armies strung out along the Don and Volga rivers. Employing huge numbers of tank, cavalry and infantry formations, Russian forces

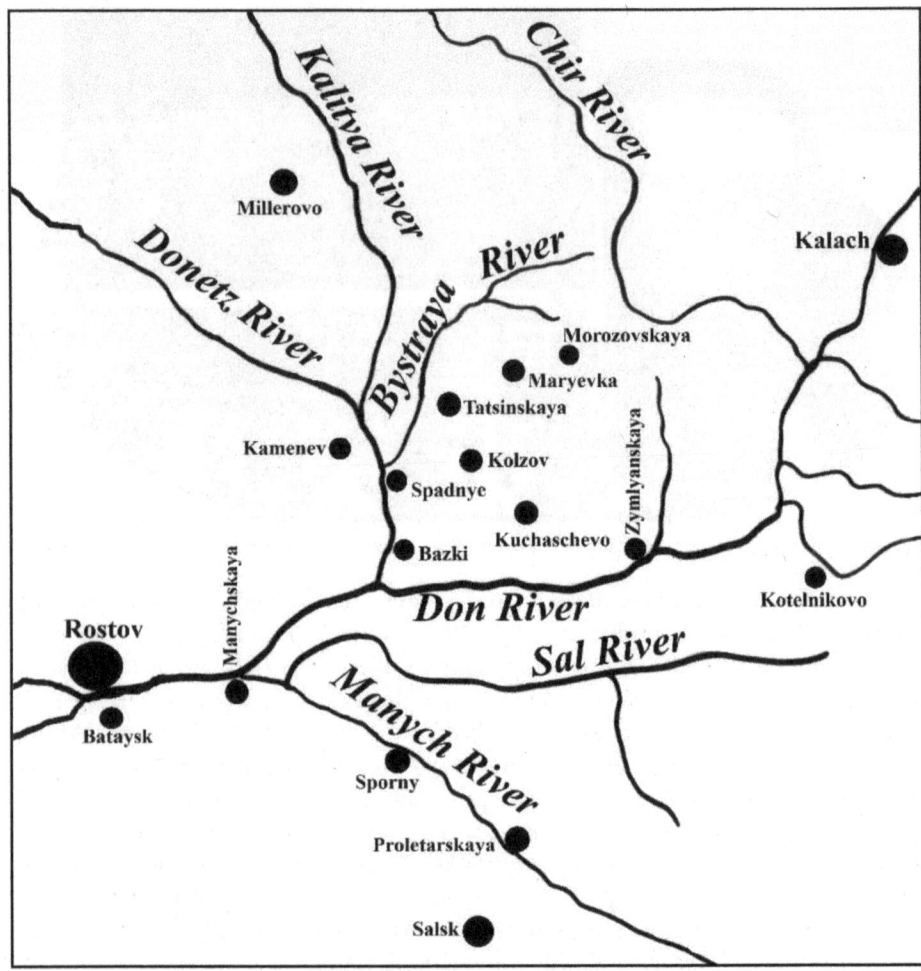

The region of the Don river bend, where most of the heavy fighting would take place during the relief effort to break out German forces from the Stalingrad pocket.

quickly broke out of their bridgehead at Kremenskaya and tore a 32km gap in the front lines of the 3rd Romanian Army.

Similarly, the 4th Romanian Army, covering the right flank of *6. Armee* and *4. Panzerarmee*, was likewise pierced and routed. The points of the Russian pincers met at Kalatsch on 23 November, effectively cutting off the twenty or so divisions of *6. Armee* and parts of *4. Panzerarmee* in and around Stalingrad.[8] Eventually, Adolf Hitler authorized a relief operation, codenamed *Unternehmen Wintergewitter* (Operation Winter Storm). Field Marshal Fritz-Erich von Manstein would lead this drive at the head of the newly created Army Group Don, which had been established on 21 November 1942.[9] Army Group Don, which on 12 February 1943 was redesignated Army Group South, had been created in

November 1942 from the headquarters staff of *11. Armee*, and embarked on preparations for the Stalingrad relief effort beginning on 1 December 1942. The main brunt of the attack would be made by the recently refreshed Panzer-Divisions of *LVII. Panzerkorps* (*6.* and *23. Panzer-Divisionen*).

A secondary effort would be made by *XLVIII. Panzerkorps*, which was located on the Chir river front with *22. Panzer-Division* and the 1st Romanian Armoured Division. These two divisions were removed from the corps and in their place OKW assigned the arriving *11. Panzer-Division*, *336. Infanterie-Division* and *7. Luftwaffen-Felddivision*.[10] On 22 December Army Group Don was composed primarily of *Armee-Abteilung Hoth*, which included the 6th and 7th Romanian Army Corps. In addition, *8. Luftwaffen-Felddivision* was allocated as the group reserve, and was listed as still arriving. Acting as a reserve, and directly under the command of *Armee-Abteilung Hoth*, was *16. Infanterie-Division (motorisiert)*. The 6th Romanian Corps contained the remnants of the 1st, 2nd and 18th Romanian Infantry Divisions, while the 7th Romanian Corps was composed of the 4th Romanian Infantry and parts of the 8th Romanian Cavalry Division.

Operations of Army Detachment Hollidt from December 1942 to January 1943. *7.* and *8. Luftwaffen-Felddivisionen* were a part of this attempt to relieve the German *6. Armee* at Stalingrad.

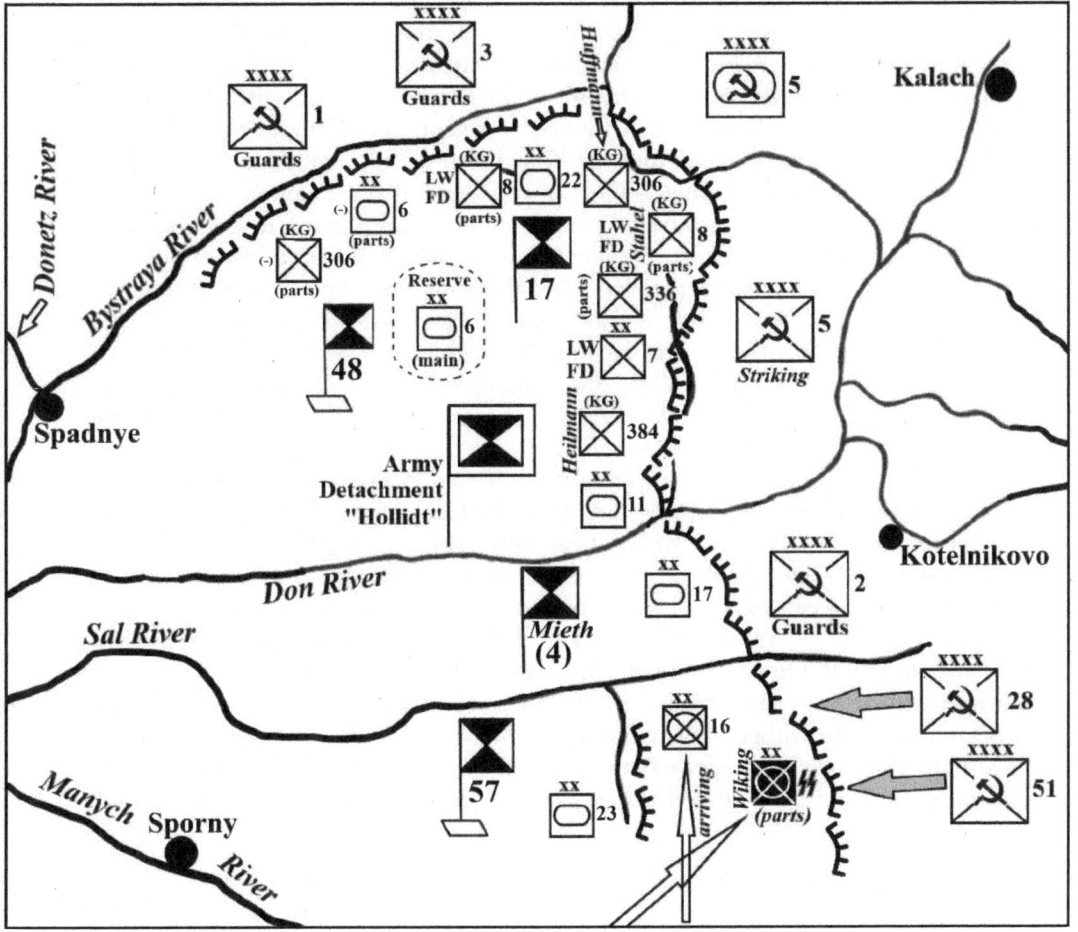

In addition, the 5th Romanian Cavalry Division, together with another part of the 8th Romanian Cavalry Division, was assigned as the reserve for *Armee-Abteilung Hoth* (alongside *16. Infanterie-Division*).

As stated, *Armeegruppe Don* included *LVII. Panzerkorps*, initially with *6.* and *23. Panzer-Divisionen*, but later with the addition of *17. Panzer-Division* and *15. Luftwaffen-Felddivision*. Another tank corps, *XLVIII. Panzerkorps*, contained *336. Infanterie-Division, 7. Luftwaffen-Felddivision* and *11. Panzer-Division*. Remnants of *384. Infanterie-Division*, nicknamed *Gruppe Heilmann* and *Gruppe Adam*, were fighting independently but attached to the Army Group.[11] The 3rd and 4th Romanian Armies (or what was left of them) were also made a part of *Armeegruppe Don*, as was the *6. Armee* trapped in Stalingrad. At first, *7. Luftwaffen-Felddivision* was assigned to *Korps Mieth* (*General der Infanterie* Friedrich Mieth) of *Armee-Abteilung Hollidt*.[12] On paper, the division was listed under *I. Luftwaffen-Feldkorps*, but this was merely a formality. The division was one of the units now earmarked for *Unternehmen Wintergewitter*. Its sister division, *8. Luftwaffen-Felddivision*, had already been selected to perform blocking actions and had been ordered to advance from its assembly point at Morozovsk. Preparations for this drive were begun on 1 December 1942.

The plan was to employ *LVII. Panzerkorps*, with its *6.* and *23. Panzer-Divisionen*, then arriving from the Caucasus, as the primary unit of the main assault. *LVII. Panzerkorps* would advance northeast from the vicinity of Kotelnikovo towards Stalingrad. Meanwhile, *XLVIII. Panzerkorps*, with *22. Panzer-Division* and the 1st Romanian Armoured Division, would make the secondary effort.[13] They were to strike towards Kalach out of the small bridgehead along the convergence of the Don and Chir rivers. General von Paulus's *6. Armee* was to concentrate its entire armoured complement of eighty tanks in the southwest part of the pocket in order to coordinate a breakout from within, the hope being that *6. Armee* and *Armee-Abteilung Hollidt* could link up, thus breaking the encirclement.[14] The arriving *7. Luftwaffen-Felddivision, 336. Infanterie-Division* and *11. Panzer-Division* were to assume the positions of *XLVIII. Panzerkorps* on the upper Chir river line,[15] while the Romanian 6th and 7th Army Corps were supposed to cover the flanks of *LVII. Panzerkorps*. The attack was to commence at daybreak on 8 December.

Events developed against the Germans, however. For one thing, the divisions of *LVII. Panzerkorps*, which were coming from the Caucasus, were late in arriving. In addition, the Soviets began to put heavy pressure on the Stalingrad pocket, so much so that Paulus had to commit his armour in order to halt the Soviet attempts to crush his trapped army. That meant that his eighty remaining tanks could not be used to help break out of the pocket. To make matters conclusively dire for *6. Armee*, Adolf Hitler eventually forbade *6. Armee* from withdrawing. Meanwhile, on the Chir river front, the Red Army launched a new series of attacks beginning 3 December. This caused von Manstein to commit the divisions of *XLVIII. Panzerkorps* in order to support what was left of the 3rd Romanian Army. That meant that *22. Panzer-Division* and the 1st Romanian Armoured Division could not support the Stalingrad relief attempt. Because of this, *XLVIII. Panzerkorps* was assigned the arriving 7. *Luftwaffen-Felddivision, 336. Infanterie-Division* and *11. Panzer-Division*. The changing military situation forced OKH to instruct *Heeresgruppe Don* to employ the arriving 7. and *8. Luftwaffen-Felddivisionen* in defensive operations. On 6 December *336. Infanterie-Division* assumed defensive positions on the Chir river, between Nizhna Chirskaya and Surovikino. A day later *11. Panzer-Division* arrived there as well, with 7. *Luftwaffen-Felddivision* following close behind. *Generalmajor* F.W. von Mellenthin, the recently appointed commander of *XLVIII. Panzerkorps*, recalled in his memoirs his estimate of the arriving divisions, including his evaluation of 7. *Luftwaffen-Felddivision*:

> These troops differed greatly in quality. 11th Panzer and the 336. Infantry were excellent divisions but the Luftwaffe field division was less satisfactory. These divisions were a creation of Göring who aspired to command ground troops as well as the Luftwaffe. His divisions were given excellent human material and the best of equipment, but their training was quite inadequate. They were commanded by air force men who knew nothing about land fighting. The Ia of this particular Luftwaffe division was a charming fellow, whom I had known as Air Liaison Officer of the 3. Corps in 1939. He had then carried out his duties very well, but he had no idea of the responsibilities of the Ia of an ordinary infantry division.[16]

Mellenthin's estimate of 7. *Luftwaffen-Felddivision* would prove to be mostly precise, although his comment about these divisions being given the 'best equipment' wasn't exactly true for most of them. However, he was correct in the rest of his observation, for when events took a more serious turn in the lower Chir river region, the division proved wholly inadequate:

> Here, on the Lower Chir, from its junction with the Don to a point some 45 miles [70km] upstream, the only troops on the ground, apart from a few anti-aircraft groups, were alarm units which had been set up from B-echelon elements and Sixth Army men returning from leave. These were later augmented by the two Luftwaffe divisions, which, after originally being earmarked for Army Detachment Hollidt, had been found only conditionally employable owing to their complete lack of battle experience and shortage of trained officers and NCOs.[17]

Now *11. Panzer-Division* withdrew from its positions covering the Soviet bridgehead at Kalinovski and moved to Nizhna Chirskaya, to try to force a passage over the half-frozen Don river in an effort to link up with Hoth's relieving force.

The sector facing the Kalinovski bridgehead was now taken over by 7. *Luftwaffen-Felddivision* and a few alarm units.[18] Here the division would remain until January 1943, suffering heavy casualties in the process.[19] Soon the division was forced to operate as a component part of *336. Infanterie-Division*, in order to avoid complete annihilation. This situation continued well into 1943 as

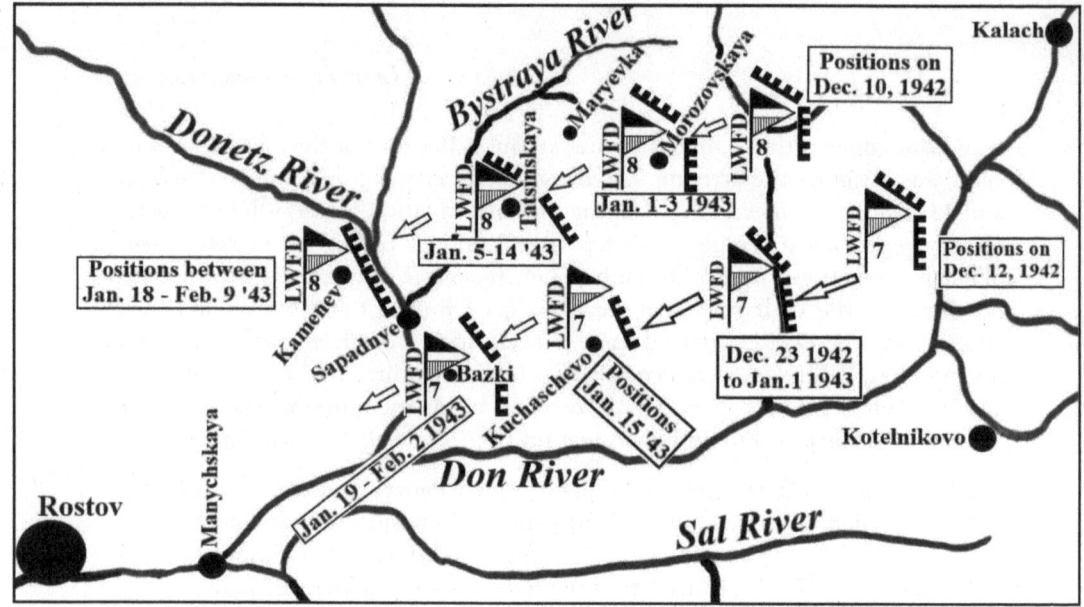

Route of retreat for *7.* and *8. Luftwaffen-Felddivision*, December 1942–February 1943.

the German forces withdrew from the Don and Chir rivers.[20] By 12 December 1942 the division had withdrawn past Aleshkin, some 20km northwest of Popov. By 23 December it was located west of the Zymla river, by Vorobyeve and Sisovo. The division remained in these positions until 1 January 1943, at which time it began to withdraw further west, following the German withdrawal. On 15 January 1943 *7. Luftwaffen-Felddivision* passed the town of Kuschachevo. On 19 January it crossed the lower Don river by Bazki and reached Borodin on 9 February. Three days later the division was 53km further west, at Schachty. During January *7. Luftwaffen-Felddivision* and *336. Infanterie-Division* were attached to *XLVIII. Panzerkorps* but by 21 February *7. Luftwaffen-Felddivision* was attached to *Korps Mieth*.[21] This corps was led by *General der Infanterie* Friedrich Mieth, and had been established in January 1943.[22] The corps headquarters controlled the following formations:

- *336. Infanterie-Division* + *7. Luftwaffen-Felddivision*
- *Gruppe Major Burgstaller* (*Kampfgruppe der 22. Panzer-Division*), located in Starobelsk in January 1943[23]
- *Gruppe Heitmann* (unknown composition)
- *Gruppe Stab der 384. Infanterie-Division*
- *Gruppe (Reiner) Stahel* (*Luftwaffen-Infanterie Kampfgruppe*)

In March and April 1943 the division's remnants were shifted to *XXIX. Armeekorps* and attached to *15. Luftwaffen-Felddivision* on the Mius river.[24] Plans were now implemented to disband *7. Luftwaffen-Felddivision* and use its surviving parts to rebuild *15. Luftwaffen-Felddivision*. Notably, the anti-tank battalion of *7. Luftwaffen-Felddivision* was redesignated as the new anti-tank battalion of *15. Luftwaffen-Felddivision*.[25] The divisional artillery battalion was also handed over to *15. Luftwaffen-Felddivision*, as well as other remaining parts. Strangely, even though it never employed any regimental headquarters for its *Jäger* battalions, two *Jäger* regiments were listed as having been assigned to the division.[26] These were *Jäger-Regiment 13 (L)* and *Jäger-Regiment 14 (L)*. 7. *Luftwaffen-Felddivision* was short-lived: in fact, the unit lasted no more than six months from its formation until its disbandment. Even the Romanians resented and scorned these German *Luftwaffe* formations, largely because they saw them as better armed, yet still being defeated. One author put it thus:

> The Luftwaffe field divisions, despite a very high educational standard of recruit and a good complement of motor vehicles, were notoriously inexperienced and poorly led, and were eventually all disbanded. Basing his decision on little more than racial arrogance, Hitler sent 7. and *8. Luftwaffen Fielddivisionen* to provide stiffening for 3rd Romanian Army at Stalingrad, and 5th Luftwaffe Field Division to the Caucasus to stiffen the Cavalry Corps. All of them broke down within days of commitment and proved as big a burden on the German Army as did its allies.[27]

Shortly before 7. *Luftwaffen-Felddivision* was disbanded, one of its officers was awarded the prized Knight's Cross. This was *Oberleutnant* Emil Eitel, born on 6 June 1915 in Riedelberg, Bavaria. He was promoted to *Oberleutnant* on 1 June 1942 and became commander of *IV. Jäger-Bataillon* on 13 September 1942. On 3 February 1943 he was assigned to command *III. Jäger-Bataillon/ Luftwaffen-Jäger-Regiment 30 (15. Luftwaffen-Felddivision)*. He was awarded the German Cross in Gold on 17 April 1943.[28] On 1 August 1943 he was promoted to *Hauptmann*. His leadership of *III. Jäger-Bataillon* during the fighting for Semaki resulted in the award of the much-prized Knight's Cross. He was relieved of his command on 15 November 1943 after he fell ill with jaundice and an infection. After recuperating, he returned as commander of *III. Jäger-Bataillon/*

7. *Luftwaffen-Felddivision* in November 1942.

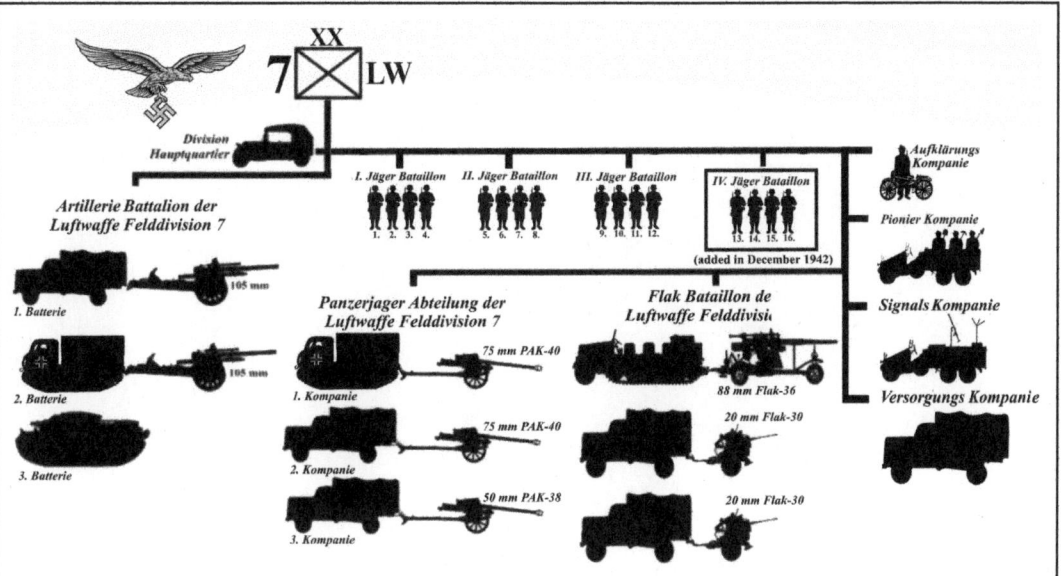

Luftwaffen-Jäger-Regiment 30 on 20 January 1944, and would remain in that post until 14 September 1944, when he was killed fighting in the Latvian town of Ergli.

Organization of 7. *Luftwaffen-Felddivision*

Commanders:
  Divisional CO:
   Generalmajor Wolf Freiherr von Biedermann,[29] 09/42–03/43
   Generalleutnant Willibald Spang,[30] 09/01/43–14/02/43[31]
  Ia:
   Major August Fischer-See,[32] 12/42–01/43
  CO *I. Jäger-Bataillon / 7. Luftwaffen-Felddivision*:
   Hauptmann Hans Mueller-Gebuehr, 10/42–30/11//42
   Major Guido von Suchodol-Maculan,[33] 01/12/42–03/43
  CO *II. Jäger-Bataillon / 7. Luftwaffen-Felddivision*:
   Hauptmann Ernst Ottenberg, 12/42–03/43
  CO *IV. Jäger-Bataillon / 7. Luftwaffen-Felddivision*:
   Oberleutnant Emil Eitel, 13/09/42–02/02/43
  CO *Artillerie-Abteilung 5*:
   Oberstleutnant Reinhold Bluhm, 02/43–?

8. Luftwaffen-Felddivision

The core of this division was formed from *Flieger-Regiment 42*[1] and the unit began training at Troop Training Ground Mlawa in East Prussia. *Flieger-Regiment 42* was an expansion of *Flieger-Ersatz-Abteilung 42*. This unit had been created on 1 April 1939 as an air force replacement battalion and in 1941 was stationed at Salzwedel in *Luftgau XI* (Hannover). It was expanded and renamed *Flieger-Regiment 42* that same year, and moved outside Germany. On 29 October 1942 the regiment was disbanded and its two battalions became the core of *8. Luftwaffen-Felddivision*.[2] The division was assigned the normal complement of three anti-tank companies and three *Flak* batteries. The artillery battalion comprised two batteries of 75mm Czech-made (Skoda Model K-15) mountain guns and a battery of *Sturmgeschütz III* assault guns. The rest of the division comprised a signals company, an engineer company and a supply column. The first commander of the division was *Luftwaffe Oberst* Hans Heidemeyer, who led the unit from its inception in October 1942 until 1 January 1943. The division had only received rudimentary training before it was shipped off to southern Russia early in November 1942. Two regiments, numbered *Jäger-Regiment 15* and *Jäger-Regiment 16*, were supposed to have been formed but because the formation was committed so rapidly and destroyed just as quickly, this never occurred.[3] The structure of *8. Luftwaffen-Felddivision* was the same as its sister division, *7. Luftwaffen-Felddivision*. The division was initially attached to *XVII. Armeekorps*, the corps headquarters of which was used to form *Armee-Abteilung Hollidt* of *Heeresgruppe Don*.[4] *Heeresgruppe Don* existed from 21 November 1942 to 12 February 1943 and consisted of the following armies:

- 12/42: *Heeresgruppe Hoth* (*4. Panzerarmee* (parts) and 4th Romanian Army (remnants)), *6. Armee* (trapped in the Stalingrad pocket), *Kampfgruppe Hollidt*, 3rd Romanian Army (remnants)
- 01/43: *Heeresgruppe* (*4. Panzerarmee* (parts) and 4th Romanian Army (remnants)), *6. Armee* (trapped in the Stalingrad pocket), *Armee-Abteilung Hollidt*, 3rd Romanian Army (remnants)
- 02/43: *1. Panzerarmee, 4. Panzerarmee, Armee-Abteilung Hollidt*, 3rd Romanian Army (remnants), 4th Romanian Army (remnants), *6. Armee* (surrendered 02/02/43).

In September 1942 *294. Infanterie-Division* had been attached to the Italian 8th Army. Two months later, in November, this German infantry division was assigned to *XVII. Armeekorps*,[5] as one of a series of German units that were sent to form a relief force to break through the Soviet forces and relieve the encircled

6. *Armee* at Stalingrad. The massive Soviet winter counteroffensive, begun on 19 November 1942, had torn numerous gaps in both flanks of *6. Armee*. The lines of the 3rd and 4th Romanian Armies had been broken, and soon the Italian 8th Army suffered the same fate. When *8. Luftwaffen-Felddivision* arrived in southern Russia, there was apparently a *Luftwaffe* unit that had been formed in southern Russia and was earmarked for absorption into the division. This unit had preceded the arrival of the division and was led by *Luftwaffe Oberst* Rainer Stahel. The *Luftwaffe* ground units operating under Stahel's command were apparently rear area *Luftwaffe* supply and support troops, ground crews and airmen from the airfield security units and even *Flak* troops. Stahel's command had been hastily formed, grouped together and deployed, pending the arrival of the division proper.

Stahel's command had been organized behind the lines of Army Group South soon after the German forces in Stalingrad became surrounded. It had initially been earmarked for the forming *15. Luftwaffen-Felddivision*, but that order was cancelled and the unit was now to be absorbed by the arriving *8. Luftwaffen-Felddivision*. Nevertheless, *Kampfgruppe Stahel* would operate independently of *8. Luftwaffen-Felddivision* for most of December 1942 and into early January

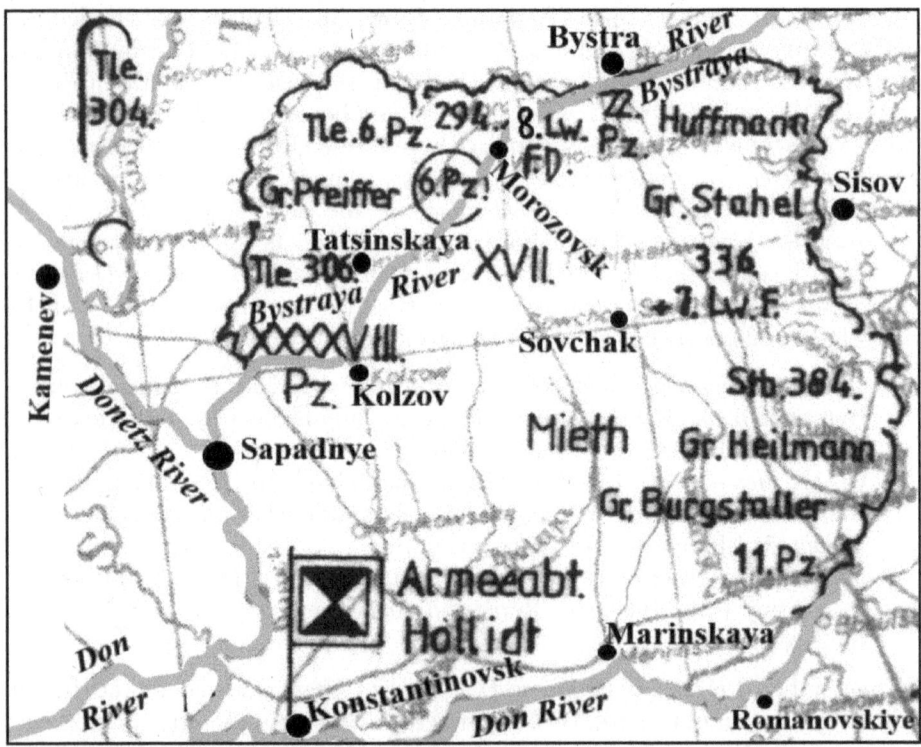

Positions of *Army Detachment Hollidt* on 1 January 1943. Notice that *Luftwaffe Kampfgruppe Stahel* was operating independently of *8. Luftwaffen-Felddivision*, which was located northwest of *Gruppe Stahel*.

1943. According to one source, on paper at least *Kampfgruppe Stahel* was listed as part of *8. Luftwaffen-Felddivision* as of 18 December 1942, even though at the time it was serving as part of the 3rd Romanian Army.[6] Initially, the arriving *8. Luftwaffen-Felddivision* was assigned as a reserve division of *Heeresgruppe Don*. Events on the ground, however, necessitated the deployment of *8. Luftwaffen-Felddivision* and every other available rear area formation as early November 1942. The division arrived by rail and detrained in the town of Morozovsk. It next moved as a unit through the town of Nizhne Chirskaya. Author Kevin Ruffner described what transpired next:

> With the anti-tank battalion in advance, 8. Luftwaffen-Felddivision marched across the snow-swept steppes toward Stalingrad. Unfamiliar with the terrain, the division had little intelligence regarding the extent of the Russian breakthrough. Expecting to find retreating German troops, 8. Luftwaffen-Felddivision ran headlong into the Soviet pincers and was scattered in a matter of hours. The division established a collection point at Nizhne Chirskaya near the confluence of the Don and Chir rivers, where the survivors of the bloody battle gathered. When only 12 men returned from the advance elements of the division, the commander of the division's anti-tank battalion committed suicide.[7]

The unit had been posted to the Zymlya river sector between the Chir and Don river bend. It was there that the line companies of the division suffered severe losses due to the relentless attacks by elements of the Soviet 5th Striking Army.

As the line companies of the division made a fighting withdrawal, they took heavy losses. At this point the division was split into several battle groups.[8] In the last week of November the Russian 24th and 25th Tank Corps had begun operations between Tatsinskaya and Maryevka, between the Donets and Don rivers.[9] The remnants of *8. Luftwaffen-Felddivision* had withdrawn in late December and set up defensive positions in and around the city of Tatsinskaya. On its left flank the Romanian 7th Cavalry Division was laying a thin screen of defences to the north, but this was quickly brushed aside by elements of the Soviet 1st Guards Army.[10] Only by the arrival of other German reinforcements was disaster averted in this sector, and the remnants of *8. Luftwaffen-Felddivision*, on the left flank, were able to hold their ground. These new reinforcements included *19. Panzer-Division* and parts of *3. Gebirgs-Division*, brought in from *Heeresgruppe Mitte*. Two additional divisions, *304. Infanterie-Division* and *7. Panzer-Division*, had arrived from garrison duty in France.[11] This did not prevent the Russian 24th Tank Corps from attacking the town of Tatsinskaya and wreaking havoc on the partly trained and now splintered *8. Luftwaffen-Felddivision*. In December the four *Luftwaffe Jäger* battalions were quickly reduced to two through heavy losses.[12] The divisional anti-tank battalion was likewise completely lost during these fierce winter months.[13] Another recently created air force field division, *15. Luftwaffen-Felddivision*, also helped to defend Tatsinskaya, but they could not prevent the city from eventually falling into Soviet hands.[14]

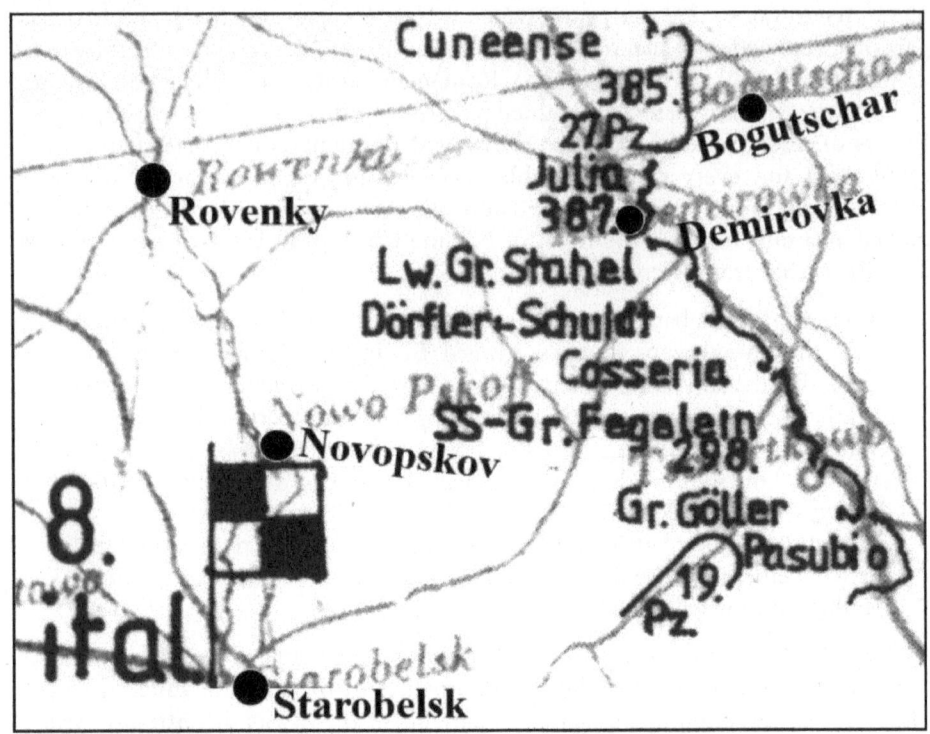

Luftwaffe Group Stahel with the 8th Italian Army, January 1943. Stahel's unit was an infantry formation raised from the first organized elements of *4. Luftwaffen-Felddivision*.

German *kriegsgliederung karte* showing Army Group Don. This headquarters was established on 21 November 1942, employing the staff of *11. Armee*. On 12 February 1943 the Army Group was renamed Army Group South.

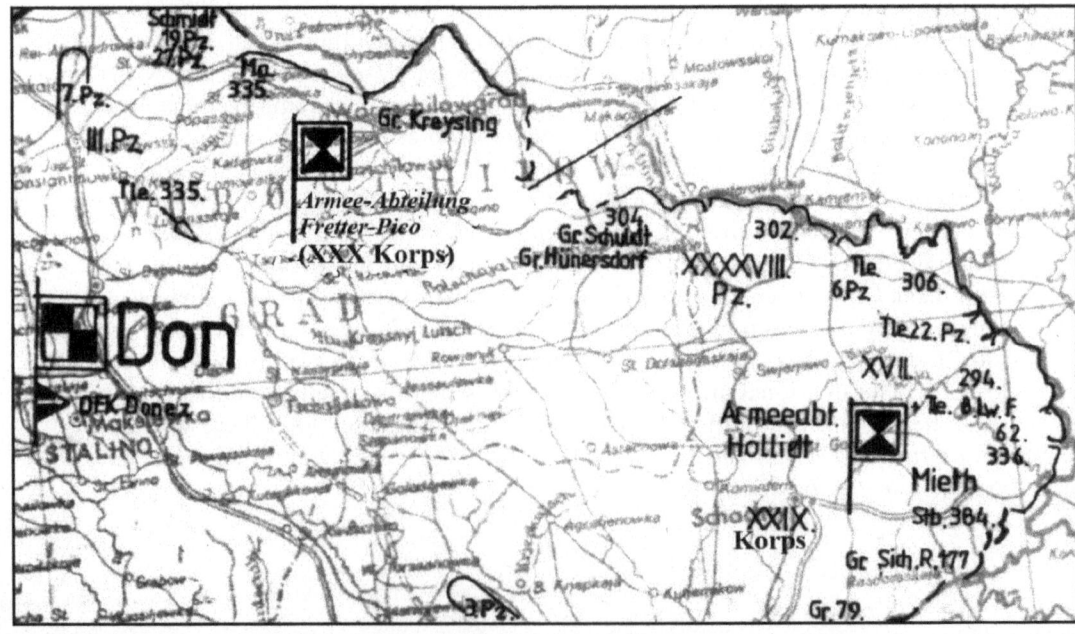

The remnants of *8. Luftwaffen-Felddivision* followed the withdrawal of other German forces from the Caucasus in January and February 1943. This occurred while elements of the division were still operating under *XVII. Armeekorps*, *Armee-Abteilung Hollidt*. In March 1943 the remaining elements of the division were shifted to *III. Panzerkorps, 1. Panzerarmee*, and placed in the region of the Mius river. During April and May the remaining battle-worthy divisional units were absorbed into *15. Luftwaffen-Felddivision*. Having existed for only three or four months, *8. Luftwaffen-Felddivision* has the dubious distinction of being considered one of the worst units raised under the auspices of the German *Luftwaffe*. As for *Oberst* Rainer Stahel, his career would eventually gain him promotion to general. His experiences during the fighting on the Don river bend gained him the reputation of being a tough, brutal commander. In the summer of 1944 he defended Vilnius in Lithuania from Red Army forces for a while, gaining the nickname 'the Defender of Vilnius'. This led Adolf Hitler to promote Stahel as *Kampf Kommandant* (battle commander) of Warsaw in July 1944. Stahel's headquarters in Warsaw was surrounded by Polish Home Army units during the initial stages of the Warsaw Uprising and he remained trapped there with his staff until German forces finally relieved them.[15]

Organization of *8. Luftwaffen-Felddivision*

Commanders:
  Divisional Commander:
    Oberst Hans Heidemeyer, 10/42–01/01/43 (partly)
    Oberst Rainer Stahel, 12/43–01/01/43 (partly)
    Generalleutnant Willibald Spang, 02/01/43–14/02/43
  CO *Artillerie-Abteilung / 8. Luftwaffen-Felddivision*:
    Oberst Herbert Mueller, 10/42–08/02/43
    Oberstleutnant Fritz Winkler, 09/02/43–13/02/43
  CO *I. Jäger-Bataillon / 8. Luftwaffen-Felddivision*:
    Oberstleutnant Hans Reuter
  CO *II. Jäger-Bataillon / 8. Luftwaffen-Felddivision*:
    Hauptmann Hans-Helmuth Steuer,[16] 15/02/43–20/05/43
  CO *III. Jäger-Bataillon / 8. Luftwaffen-Felddivision*:
    Hauptmann Bruno Holtz, 10/42–12/42
  CO *IV. Jäger-Bataillon / 8. Luftwaffen-Felddivision*:
    Oberstleutnant Hans Stein, 10/42–12/42
  CO *Flak-Abteilung der 8. Luftwaffen-Felddivision*:
    Hauptmann Christian von Steiglitz, 12/42–03/01/43[17]
    Major Kurt Ulmer, in the divisional staff,[18] 16/11/42–15/02/43, then again: 01/05/43–28/05/43

Eduard Winkelbauer (born 7 March 1898) was promoted to *Oberstleutnant* on 1 December 1942. On 6 March 1943 he was transferred to *8. Luftwaffen-Felddivision*.

9. Luftwaffen-Felddivision

The ninth consecutively numbered *Luftwaffe* field division was organized at Troop Training Ground Arys in East Prussia and at Troop Training Ground Mielau (Mlawa) in Poland. *Flieger-Regiment 62* was used as the basis for *9. Luftwaffen-Felddivision*.[1] According to official records, this division was the first to be formed employing two regimental headquarters to control its infantry battalions.[2] In addition, the unit had six *Jäger* battalions instead of the usual four. This meant that both regiments had a complement of three infantry battalions apiece. The artillery regiment was supposed to contain three artillery battalions, but strangely there was no third battalion, only the *I.* and *II. Artillerie-Abteilungen*.[3] The rest of this division comprised a fusilier battalion, an anti-tank battalion, an engineer battalion, a *Flak* battalion and a signals company. The *Flak* battalion was considered the *IV. Artillerie-Abteilung* in the artillery regiment. The fusilier battalion was to act as the divisional reconnaissance formation. The division was sent by rail to northern Russia in December 1942. It was placed on the eastern tip of the Oranienbaum pocket, an area west of Leningrad along the coast of the Gulf of Finland.

The Oranienbaum pocket – an area some 65km long and 25km deep that was controlled by Russian forces – had existed since 7 September 1941, when German forces had cut off the Red Army units there, preventing them from withdrawing east towards Leningrad. The Germans had never bothered to reduce the Russian pocket, despite several opportunities to do so. The Oranienbaum pocket eventually became a thorn in the rear of the German lines near Leningrad and would eventually cause the rapid demise of both *9.* and *10. Luftwaffen-Felddivision* in 1944. In effect, leaving the pocket intact was a tactical mistake that eventually turned into a strategic defeat for Army Group North.

As stated earlier, there had been several opportunities to destroy the pocket (which the Soviets referred to as a bridgehead). The last had occurred in the late summer of 1942, when *11. Armee* had been sent to the Leningrad Front after its successful capture of Sevastopol in the Crimea. The plan was to employ *11. Armee* to help capture Leningrad itself, but from the very beginning this scheme was doomed to failure. For one thing, OKW did not bring the entire *11. Armee* to the Leningrad Front. It only sent two corps (*XXX.* and *LIV. Armeekorps*), with only four divisions (*28. Jäger*, and *50.*, *72.* and *132. Infanterie-Division*). This meagre number of reinforcements would prove insufficient to storm Leningrad in a frontal assault. The German high command would have done better to use these divisions to destroy the Oranienbaum pocket, a move that would have freed more German divisions for the storming of Leningrad.

In addition, as soon as these four divisions reached Army Group North, they were committed to countering by Soviet attacks along the Leningrad and Volkov front. The newly established *III. Luftwaffen-Feldkorps* arrived in the region of the Oranienbaum pocket in February 1943 and took over control of *9.* and *10. Luftwaffen-Felddivisionen*, which were tasked with helping to guard the pocket. Eventually, *III. (germanische) SS-Panzerkorps* would also arrive, in late November 1943. Between 8 and 12 December 1943 this SS panzer corps relieved *L. Armeekorps*, which up until then had been tasked with guarding the pocket.

III. (germanische) SS-Panzerkorps sounded like a powerful armoured unit, but in reality it only contained *11. SS-Panzergrenadier Division Nordland* and *SS-Panzergrenadier Brigade Nederland* (basically one-and-a-half armoured infantry divisions). Initially, *9. Luftwaffen-Felddivision* was assigned to *L. Armeekorps*, *18. Armee*.[4] In addition, *69. Infanterie-Division* had already been brought in from southern Norway and was placed in positions on the western edge of the Pogoste pocket, under *XXVI. Armeekorps*, while *1. Luftwaffen-Felddivision* had gone to relieve the weary and battered *250. Infanterie-Division (spanische)*, known also as the *Blau Division*, or Blue Division at Novgorod, under *XXXVIII. Armeekorps*. These reinforcements were needed, but half of them (*1.*, *9.* and *10. Luftwaffen-Felddivisionen*) had arrived at the front without any actual combat infantry experience.[5] While *9. Luftwaffen-Felddivision* began moving to the Leningrad Front as early as late November 1942, some parts of the unit were still arriving as late as January and February 1943.[6]

The lack of training and the arrival of the division in parts were weaknesses that were forgiven during the initial months stationed in the Leningrad sector. This was because Russian military moves were, for the moment, concentrated in the sector of *16. Armee*, and parts of *18. Armee* further east. This left the Oranienbaum sector fairly quiet. Enemy activity in this region was for the present limited to artillery duels and occasional enemy reconnaissance probes. The front lines held by both *9.* and *10. Luftwaffen-Felddivisionen* were quite long. Both divisions covered a sector 48km long on the eastern half of the Oranienbaum pocket. *10. Luftwaffen-Felddivision* was responsible for 27km from the region near Zasstrove to Korovino, while *9. Luftwaffen-Felddivision* held the remaining 21km up to Peterhof and the sea coast. Initially, their positions were located between Krasnoye Selo and Volossovo.[7] In December 1942 the divisional headquarters was located at Ropscha, while the regimental headquarters of *Jäger-Regiment 17 (L)* and *Jäger-Regiment 18 (L)* were situated at Sanino and Korovino respectively.

From December 1942 until March 1943 *II. Jäger-Bataillon* of *Jäger-Regiment 17* was detached from *9. Luftwaffen-Felddivision* and was employed south of Lake Ladoga as a reinforcement for *227. Infanterie-Division* of *XXVI. Armeekorps*. Moving out from Volossovo in the middle of a snowstorm, *II. Jäger-Bataillon* travelled northeast. It fought under *227. Infanterie-Division* through the winter months. When the thaw arrived, it fought in the fly-infested swamps of the Volkhov Front until it was withdrawn in March 1943.[8]

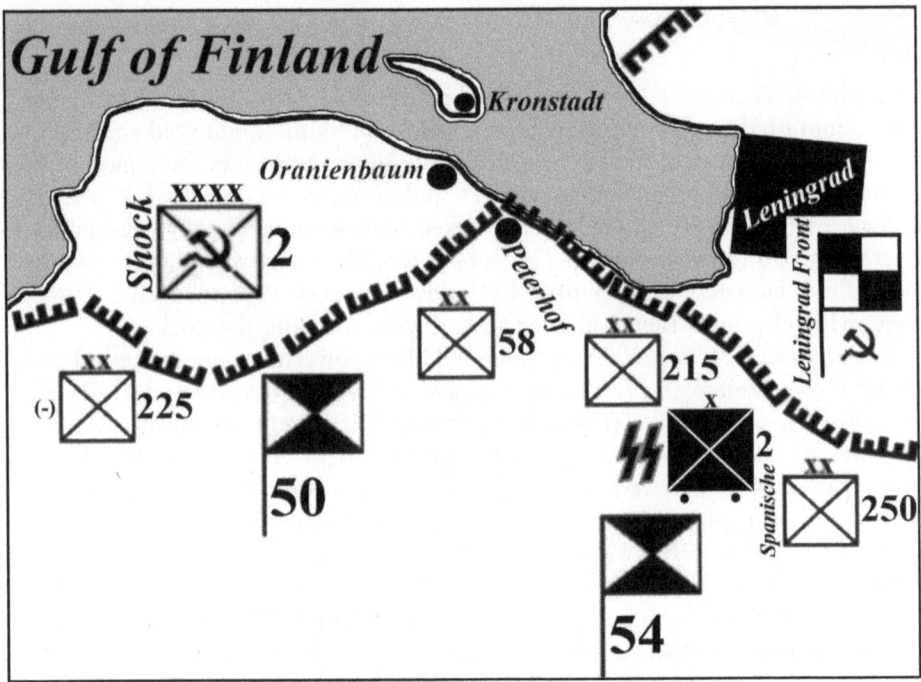

The Oranienbaum pocket in November 1942, just before the arrival of *9. Luftwaffen-Felddivision*. From February to December 1942, *376. Grenadier-Regiment* (of *225. Infanterie-Division*) was fighting in the Demyansk Pocket and was therefore detached from its parent division.

The military situation in the region of the Oranienbaum pocket in December 1942. While *9. Luftwaffen-Felddivision* had already established itself in the Peterhof area, its sister division, *10. Luftwaffen-Felddivision*, was only just arriving.

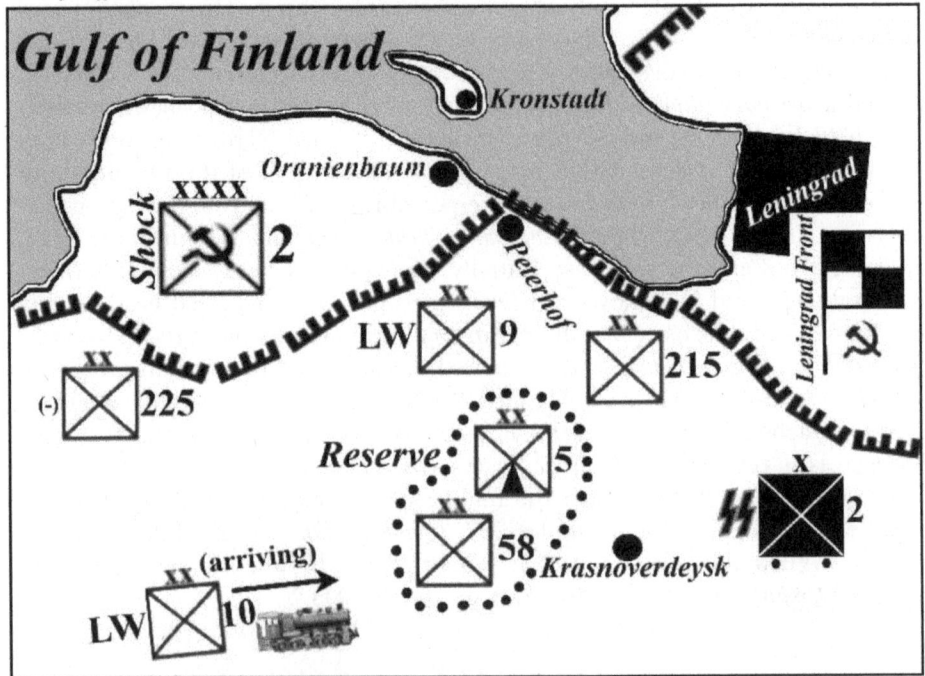

A month earlier, in February 1943, *9. Luftwaffen-Felddivision* received a small artillery reinforcement when *1. Batterie* of *Heeres-Küsten-Artillerie-Abteilung 708* was attached to its artillery regiment. Officially, this coastal artillery battalion was supposed to contain three batteries of 150mm sFH-18 field guns. However, it contained four captured French 145mm *modele 1916 Saint-Chamond* heavy artillery guns. Due to the ever-growing partisan menace behind the front lines, several *Jagdkommandos* (hunter groups) were formed to both secure the rear areas behind the front lines, and seek out and destroy the Russian guerrillas, if possible. *9.* and *10. Jäger-Kompanie* of the adjacent *10. Luftwaffen-Felddivision*, which happened to be equipped with bicycles, were merged with *2. Kompanie* of *Ost-Bataillon 661* and *3. Kompanie* of *Ost-Bataillon 665*.

In this way, a four-company strong hunter group was organized. A *Waffen und Gerät* (Weapons and Equipment) roster of available weapons for *9. Luftwaffen-Felddivision*, dated 23 May 1943, clearly showed that as far as small weapons were concerned, the unit was well armed: 18,625 rifles, 2,677 pistols, 110 mortars and 37 machine guns.[9] These numbers were impressive given that the division only possessed about 10,000 men in total. However, it was another matter as far as heavy weapons were concerned (that is, artillery and anti-tank guns). For example, in January 1944, when the Soviet 2nd Shock Army broke out of the Oranienbaum pocket and overwhelmed both *Luftwaffe* formations, *9. Luftwaffen-Felddivision* only had fifteen anti-tank guns with which to try to halt the Soviet assault.[10] This lack of proper heavy anti-tank weapons, not to mention insufficient munitions, was particularly acute. A report during the summer months of 1943 clearly showed the growing problem:

> The situation at the front was odd. The number of personnel at the front was no longer suitable. The soldiers could not properly occupy a long running trench line. Therefore, strong points were formed that lay 100 metres apart, and in between ran NCOs, hoping to catch Russians who were trying to penetrate. These NCOs were to call in an artillery barrage, although the artillery only had enough projectiles for a five-minute barrage.[11]

The divisional battle lines of both *9.* and *10. Luftwaffen-Felddivisionen* during the summer of 1943 stretched out from Peterhof and the coast to Zasstrove, a distance of about 70km. This was clearly too long a frontage for either unit to hold properly. The problem should have been apparent to the corps and army commanders, but either its solution was prevented by ignorance on their part, or more likely, they had neither local nor strategic reserves to reinforce the overstretched air force defence lines. On 1 November 1943 all *Luftwaffe* field divisions still in existence were taken over by the German Army, whereupon *9. Luftwaffen-Felddivision* was redesignated *Felddivision 9 (L)*. The structure of the division, instead of being reinforced, was actually reduced, in keeping with Göring's desire to retain the *Flak* battalions within the air force. The main change for *Felddivision 9 (L)*, therefore, was the loss of the divisional *Flak* battalion, which eventually became *I. Flak-Abteilung* of *Flak-Regiment 2 (motorisiert)*. This meant that the division now had to face any possible Russian attack with thirty-six fewer guns. Clearly, this decision to remove the *Flak* battalions weakened the *Luftwaffe* field divisions and endangered the German military situation wherever these air force field divisions happened to be stationed.

An attempt was made to shorten the front lines of *Felddivision 9 (L)* when the commander of *III. Luftwaffen-Feldkorps*, whose HQ was located in the town of Shakh, ordered that the new main line of resistance for the division would now run from Peterhof to Petrovskaya.[12] In addition, the new divisional headquarters was now to be located in the town of Ropscha.[13] But this was only a half-measure since it did not address the actual problem, which was that, comparatively speaking, the Soviet infantry and mechanized forces arrayed against the front lines of *Felddivision 9 (L)* were overwhelmingly superior in size and firepower to the *Luftwaffe* division. This was simply a recipe for disaster. Small reinforcements made their way to the German forces surrounding the Oranienbaum pocket. However, these forces were small and did not benefit the German defence in a significant way. These minor reinforcements therefore did not aid *Felddivision 9 (L)* directly, but it did free up some elements of *11. SS-anzergrenadier Division Nordland* to help support the *Luftwaffe* divisions in the eastern and southeastern half of the pocket.

For example, *SS Pionier-Bataillon 11* was temporarily detached from its parent division, *11. SS-Panzergrenadier-Division Nordland*, and assigned to a sector of the front at the boundary between *Felddivision 9 (L)* and *Felddivision 10 (L)*. It was felt that this boundary was particularly vulnerable to enemy penetration. But in the end, all these small half-measures proved too little, too late. Substantial Soviet forces had been gathering in the Oranienbaum pocket since November 1943 and the Leningrad Front had been steadily building up what the Russians referred to as the Oranienbaum bridgehead. Little by little, the Soviets had ferried the units of the 2nd Shock Army into the area that had up until then been only weakly defended by four Russian infantry divisions and two naval infantry brigades. By 14 January 1944 – the date of the attack – the Soviets had ferried numerous divisions into the pocket, including 600 artillery pieces and a substantial number of tanks and assault guns.[14]

The German lines were already stretched. For example, the *SS Nederland Brigade*, which had around 6,000 men in total, was covering a front line of some 15km. The *SS Nordland Division*, with 14,500 men, held a front line that was 24km long. The *Luftwaffe* divisions contained about 10,000 men each. While *10. Luftwaffen-Felddivision* had to defend a front line that was 17km long, *9. Luftwaffen-Felddivision* was slightly better off, having only some 15km to control. The problem for the Germans came to a head on the night of 13/14 January 1944 when the 2nd Shock Army began its breakout from the Oranienbaum pocket with an initial artillery barrage of over 100,000 shells that pounded the positions of *III. (germanische) SS-Panzerkorps* and *III. Luftwaffen-Feldkorps*.[15] In addition, the Soviets mobilized 42 rifle divisions and 9 tank corps from their

Leningrad Front and threw them against the lines of *18. Armee*. The bombardment of the positions of *III. (germanische) SS-Panzerkorps* was a deception, however. The commander of the 2nd Shock Army, Lieutenant General I.I. Fedyuninsky, had planned his attack very well. Employing three naval infantry brigades to cover 43km of the Oranienbaum front, Fedyuninsky massed no fewer than eight rifle divisions and a tank division on a front only 10.5km wide. The Soviets created false radio messages and troop movements to convince the Germans that forces were massing in the sector of *III. (germanische) SS-Panzerkorps*, when in reality Fedyuninsky only had two naval infantry brigades in that sector.[16] This allowed him to concentrate massive firepower against the *Luftwaffe* field divisions, whose poor combat efficiency, no doubt, had not remained concealed from the Soviet command.[17]

On the German side confusion reigned. While *III. (germanische) SS-Panzerkorps* braced for an attack that never came, the lines of the *Luftwaffe* soldiers, already greatly weakened, simply melted away under the concentrated Russian assault. The recipe for disaster that had been simmering for months now

The Red Army offensive of January 1944, known as Neva-2. The drive ended the siege of the Soviet pocket around Oranienbaum, and created a land-link to Leningrad. It also created a land-link south of Lake Ladoga. In the process, *Felddivision 9 (L)* and *Felddivision 10 (L)* were wrecked. Aware of the weakness of the Luftwaffe field divisions, the Soviets concentrated their main line of attack on the front lines of the Luftwaffe units.

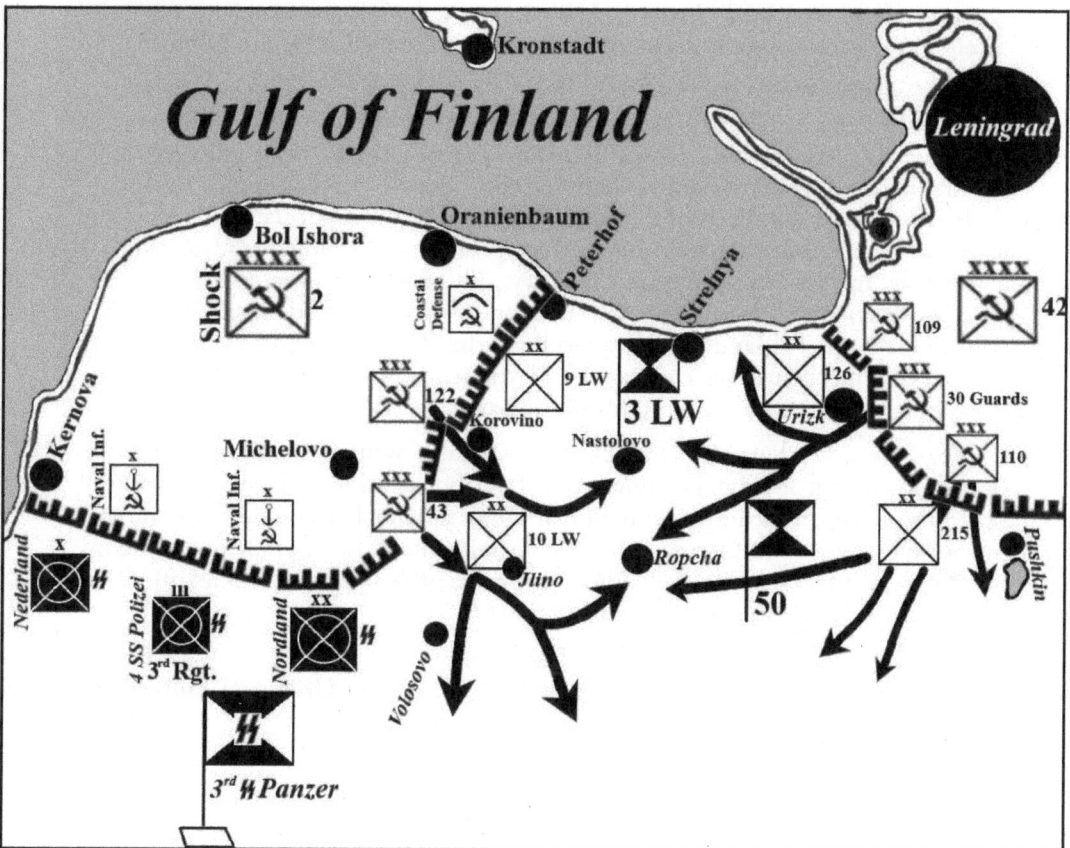

suddenly came to the boil. A heavy price was paid for the German disregard of this problem. One report described in this way:

> The full weight of the attack fell on *Felddivision 9 (L)* to the east of the pocket. Remnants of the *Felddivision 9 (L)* escaped the Soviets but fell back in a wild retreat and were not combat worthy. The net result was that a major, unrepairable breakthrough was made in the northern wing of *18. Armee* within a few hours of the beginning of the attack.[18]

The Soviets had concentrated the bulk of their 43rd and 122nd Corps between Korovino and Zasstrove, leaving only the 50th Coastal Brigade to man the front lines facing *Felddivision 9 (L)* from Peterhof to Korovino. This allowed the 11th and 43rd Rifle Divisions and the 152nd Tank Division to hit the left flank of the *Luftwaffe* division. When the Soviets brought up the 131st, 168th and 196th Rifle Divisions to quickly follow up the initial attack units, they formed an overwhelming force that simply steamrollered through the *Luftwaffe* positions. The Soviets concentrated these six divisions in a 6km-wide assault on *Felddivision 9 (L)* between Korovino and Jlino, guaranteeing a successful breakthrough.[19] The other 4.5km of front lines out of the total 10.5km designated as the breakout point were assigned to divisions ordered to attack *Felddivision 10 (L)*. The *SS-Pionier-Bataillon 11*, which had been stationed between the two air force units, was quickly surrounded and had to fight its way out of a veritable sea of Red Army tanks and infantry. They took heavy losses before part of the battalion was able to extricate itself and rejoin its parent division. One source described their predicament:

> The Nordland units that had been deployed in the vicinity of the Luftwaffe field divisions suffered most on the first day of the offensive. This was particularly true for *SS-Pionier-Bataillon 11*, which had been engaged in building up defensive positions between the *Luftwaffe 9. Feld Division (L)* and *10. Felddivision (L)*. Parts of the battalion absorbed the full force of the initial Soviet attack, but they held on to their positions in vicious hand-to-hand fighting against tank-supported infantry. The cost, however, was terrible: *2. Kompanie, SS-Pionier-Bataillon 11* alone lost a hundred men killed or wounded on 14 January. Despite this, the *Waffen-SS* troops held on doggedly by themselves even as the inexperienced neighbouring Luftwaffe troops fell back rapidly – often in near panic.[20]

In *18. Armee* headquarters, intelligence estimates written months before and based on combat intelligence now proved all too prescient. Extensive warnings had been issued regarding enemy preparations to launch a double envelopment operation against the German forces arrayed around Leningrad, undoubtedly during the winter of 1943/1944. The focal points of this probable Soviet offensive were identified as three key areas of the front:

(1) the Novgorod region south of Leningrad;[21]
(2) the western part of the Leningrad region between Urizk and Pulkovo; and

(3) the Oranienbaum pocket, where *Felddivision 9 (L)* and *Felddivision 10 (L)* covered the rearward positions of *126. and 215. Infanterie-Divisionen* on the westernmost part of the Leningrad Front.

However, the *Heer* failed to replace with more reliable formations these *Luftwaffe* field divisions, likely due to a lack of available forces.[22] It seems that the Soviets had planned their offensive specifically targeting these Air Force field divisions. On 17 January 1944 OKH approved measures geared towards the withdrawal of Army Group North to more tenable positions. One of these measures called for the withdrawal of *Felddivision 9 (L)* and *126. Infanterie-Division* from the Urizk-Strelnya-Peterhof region, where the remnants of both divisions had been pushed by the dual Russian drive from Oranienbaum and Leningrad.[23] The attempt to break out of the encirclement began on 18 January, but Soviet forces simply sliced into the withdrawing columns of both divisions. An Army High Command report for 19 January presented a clear summary of the situation. It stated that communications with *Felddivision 9 (L)* had been lost:

> 19 January 1944: *3. SS-Panzerkorps* attack with tank support on Popscha, employing six tanks. With attacks on highway to the south of Kipen, four enemy tanks were destroyed. Kipen was lost. Over the activity of Feld Division 9 (L), no news is available.[24]

In reality, *Felddivision 9 (L)* had been destroyed between 14 and 18 January 1944. It simply ceased to exist. The unit was recorded as officially wiped out on the night of 19 January, north of Krasnoye Selo and Ropscha, while it was attempting to reach the lines of General Wegener's *L. Armeekorps*.[25] The remnants had come under the command of *Oberst* Fischer, the commander of *126. Infanterie-Division*, after *Oberst* Michael, the CO of *Felddivision 9 (L)*, had fallen in combat, while leading his men.[26] A naval artillery unit, *Marine-Artillerie-Abteilung 530*, under *Korvettenkapitän* Schenke, had tagged along as well. *Grenadier-Regiment 424* of *126. Infanterie-Division* had led the assault group for the breakout. By now, all that remained of the regiment was a greatly weakened infantry battalion of 150 men (a company in strength) and a few remaining anti-tank guns. This, however, contradicts one source that stated: 'The majority of *126. Infanterie-Division*, as well as *Feld Division 9 (L)* and *Marine-Artillerie-Abteilung 530* made it through.'[27]

Losses for *Felddivision 9 (L)* between 14 January and 1 March 1944 included 315 killed, 1,196 wounded and 1,548 missing – most of whom were probably captured.[28] Since the division began the battle with a strength of some 7,000–8,000 men, we can surmise that perhaps around 4,000–4,500 men survived to be distributed to other German units. One source stated that *Felddivision 9 (L)* and *Felddivision 10 (L)* had around 10,000 men each.[29] If this is true, then about 6,000–6,500 men survived to be employed in other units once the division was disbanded. Most likely, the majority of these 'survivors' were rear area support troops, since the 'bayonet' strength of the division on 14 January was at around 2,000 men. Those rear support elements of *Felddivision 9 (L)* that had managed to avoid the Russian pincers were redistributed to other formations a few months later, in March and April 1944.

Author George Nafziger states that the unit's survivors were distributed to the *61., 225.* and *227. Infanterie-Divisionen*.[30] He seems to be quoting verbatim from author Werner Haupt, who also lists these divisions as beneficiaries of the demise of *Felddivision 9 (L)*. Haupt goes even further, saying that the anti-tank battalion of the division was redesignated as the anti-tank battalion of *225. Infanterie-Division*.[31] This seems unlikely since reports state that only a few anti-tank guns from *Felddivision 9 (L)* made it through to German lines. In any case, there were only fifteen anti-tank guns in the division before the start of the Russian offensive. Therefore, if indeed the division's anti-tank battalion became the new anti-tank battalion for *225. Infanterie-Division*, it must have been very greatly reduced. However, the claim of a direct transfer of anti-tank units is also echoed in an extremely authoritative and scholarly study, so cannot be discounted outright.[32] The same source also states that the division's artillery regiment was not disbanded until May 1944, and that the *Jäger* regiments were likewise disbanded only in July 1944. These last two statements seem quite unbelievable. It is extremely unlikely that any units of *Felddivision 9 (L)* survived into the summer months of 1944. It is more likely that these formations were not struck from the German field post rolls until June and July 1944.

This happened quite often when German units were destroyed, especially during the particularly disastrous 1944–1945 period. This may explain how these statements could have been made. Captured German records clearly state that the majority of the infantry and combat support units that were still in existence in March and April 1944 were assigned to *126. Infanterie-Division*, which was built back up with these and other bits and pieces. In addition, the newly organized *20. Waffen-Grenadier-Division der SS (estnische Nr. 1)*, made up of Estonians with a German cadre staff, was given the administrative section that had belonged to *Felddivision 9 (L)*. Similarly, the HQs of *III. (germanische) SS-Panzerkorps, 11. SS-Panzergrenadier-Division Nordland* and *4. SS-Panzergrenadier-Brigade Nederland* each received several truck columns from both *Felddivision 9 (L)* and *Felddivision 10 (L)*.[33] One final, scholarly German source admits that part of *Felddivision 9 (L)* was absorbed into *225. Infanterie-Division*, but the clear beneficiary was *126. Infanterie-Division*.[34]

Whichever may be the case, *Felddivision 9 (L)* ceased to function as a division in the third week of January 1944. It had proved to be a characteristic *Luftwaffe* field division, with various deficiencies and inadequacies. All of these failings were not lost on the enemy, who used these weaknesses to their advantage by coordinating, whenever possible, offensives at focal points in the German defence lines where these *Luftwaffe* divisions were posted. Heavy German losses on the Russian Front, exacerbated by lack of proper reinforcements and replacements, and the exigencies of war which these shortcomings created, sometimes compelled the *Ostheer* to station the *Luftwaffe* divisions in positions and situations that accelerated their demise and destruction. This was clearly the case with *Felddivision 9 (L)*.

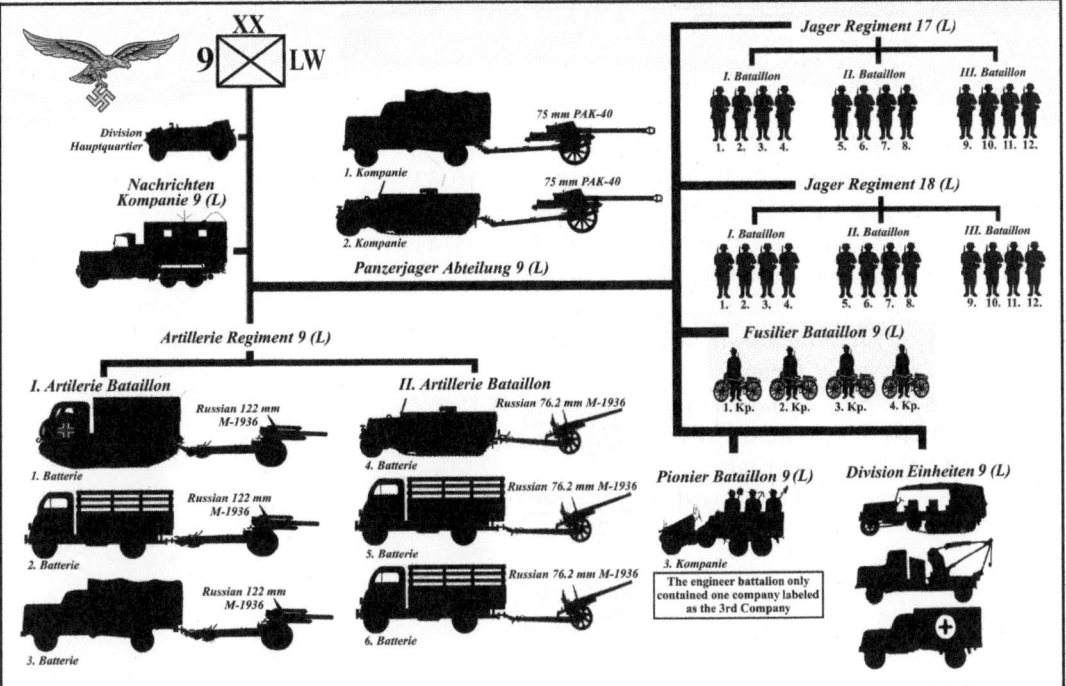

9. Luftwaffe Felddivision, December 1942.

This division's history therefore epitomizes the military performance of a stereotypical *Luftwaffe* field unit.[35]

Organization of *9. Luftwaffen-Felddivision*

Commanders:
  Divisional Commanders:
    Generalmajor Hans Erdmann, 08/10/42–11/08/43
    Oberst Heinrich Geerkens,[36] 12/08/43–25/08/43
    Generalmajor Anton-Carl Longin, 26/08/43–05/11/43
    Generalleutnant Paul Winter, 05/11/43–25/11/43
    Generalmajor Ernst Michael, 25/11/43–22/01/44 (killed in action 22/01/44)
    Generalleutnant Hans-Kurt Höcker, 02/44–28/09/1944
IIa:
  Hauptmann der Reserve von Dehn-Rotfelser, 10/42–?
Ia:
  Major Egeler, 04/10/42–09/12/42
  Oberst Heinrich Geerkens, 10/12/42–12/08/43[37] and 26/08/43–31/10/43
  Oberstleutnant i.G. Ernst-Friedrich Biehler, 01/11/43–14/01/44
  Oberst Lassmann, 15/01/44–22/01/44
Ib:
  Hauptmann Dr Adolf Ulmer, 15/06/43–?
CO *Artillerie-Regiment 9 (L)*:
  Oberst Rudolf Schiffer, 01/07/43–31/10/43
  Oberst Engelbert Massing, 01/11/43–22/01/44

CO *Luftwaffen-Jäger-Regiment 17*:
  Oberst Dr Jur. Emil Stephan, 02/04/42–10/42[38]
  Oberst Carl Rütgers, 10/42–17/08/43
  Oberst Geerkens, Heinrich, 18/08/43–1/11/43
CO *I. Jäger-Bataillon / Jäger-Regiment 17 (L)*:
  Major Erich Ostertag, 10/42–11/42
CO *II. Jäger-Bataillon / Jäger-Regiment 17 (L)*:
  Hauptmann Pirner
CO *IV. Jäger-Bataillon / Jäger-Regiment 18 (L)*:
  Major Hans Stein,[39] 01/10/42–12/42
CO *Sanitäts-Kompanie*:
  Oberfeldarzt Dr Eduard Schuh, 15/07/43–02/44

10. Luftwaffen-Felddivision

Fliegerregiment 72, originally led by *Oberst* Herbert Pfeiffer and stationed in the town of Detmold, Westphalia, was the cadre unit used to create *10. Luftwaffen-Felddivision* between October and December 1939.[1] The division was organized around two *Jäger* regiments: *Luftwaffen-Jäger-Regiment 19* and *Luftwaffen-Jäger-Regiment 20*, with three battalions each.[2] The divisional artillery regiment was well armed, having four artillery battalions instead of the usual two or three. This was achieved by completely outfitting the unit with *Luftwaffe* equipment. *IV. Artillerie-Bataillon* was the heavy unit, being equipped with the deadly 88mm *Flak*-36 anti-aircraft gun.[3] This was deadly against enemy aircraft and tanks alike, but was unsuitable as an indirect fire artillery weapon. *IV. Artillerie-Abteilung* was eventually designated as the divisional *Flak* battalion, but in keeping with the standard *Luftwaffe* field division organization, it remained under the control of the divisional artillery regiment.

The rest of the artillery regiment was organized as follows: *I. Artillerie-Abteilung* contained two light artillery batteries made up of twelve 105mm *Nebelwerfer-40* rocket launchers[4] and two batteries armed with captured Russian artillery pieces; *II. Artillerie-Abteilung* contained two batteries armed with the Czech-made 75mm K15 mountain gun and two batteries of captured Russian guns; and *III. Artillerie-Abteilung* had two batteries of 20mm *Flak* guns and one battery of 37mm *Flak* guns. These lower-calibre *Flak* guns were great for direct fire infantry support against low-flying enemy aircraft and even against light tanks and other lightly armoured enemy vehicles, but were not actual artillery, so could not offer the indirect fire support that artillery is supposed to provide. The rest of the division comprised an anti-tank battalion, plus engineer, signals and supply companies. There was also a divisional *Luftwaffen-Radfahr-Aufklärungs-Kompanie* (bicycle reconnaissance company), which served as the unit's eyes and ears.[5]

The airmen who filtered into *10. Luftwaffen-Felddivision* were typical. They had a high degree of education by 1940 standards, with most having completed high school or higher. With few exceptions, the men were physically fit. A typical example was Corporal von Zerneck, who began his career in the German *Luftwaffe* as a member of *6./Jagdgeschwader 53* in 1939. This unit had been established in 1937, so it was one of the oldest German fighter wings of the Second World War. It employed various versions of the *Messerschmitt Bf-109* fighter throughout the war. Later, Airman von Zerneck was posted to *Luftwaffekontrollkomission III* in 1941, but by December 1942 had been sent to the forming *Luftwaffen-Jäger-Regiment 20*. The Russians eventually captured von Zerneck in January 1944, and he returned home to Germany two years later, in 1946. He was one of the lucky ones.⁶

Command of *10. Luftwaffen-Felddivision* was initially entrusted to 46-year-old *Generalmajor* Walter Wadehn, who led the division until it was taken over by the army on 1 November 1943, at which time he was reassigned to the paratrooper forces. In 1944 he led *8. Fallschirmjäger-Division* on the Western Front. On 5 January 1945 he was killed in action while still leading that division.⁷ When the *Heer* assumed command of *10. Luftwaffen-Felddivision*, *Generalleutnant* Hermann von Wedel was posted as the new commanding officer. Wedel had what appears to be a regular army career. In 1942 he had been leading *Grenadier-Regiment 4* of the East Prussian *32. Infanterie-Division*. He was promoted to *Generalmajor* on 1 September 1943 and quickly elevated to the rank of *Generalleutnant* when he accepted command of *10. Luftwaffen-Felddivision*.⁸

The division was sent to the Oranienbaum sector of the Leningrad Front in December 1942 and was initially placed under the direct control of *18. Armee*.⁹ Eventually, it was assigned to *L. Armeekorps* while *III. Luftwaffen-Feldkorps* was being established. It was intended that this new air force corps should assume control of both *9. Luftwaffen-Felddivision* and *10. Luftwaffen-Felddivision*. The positions that *10. Luftwaffen-Felddivision* took up in late December 1942 were on the eastern side of the Oranienbaum pocket. In January 1943 the military situation all along the Russian Front became critical as in numerous places the Russians were pressing home attacks aimed at tearing holes in the German lines. Indeed, so critical was this situation that many units had arrived at the front with little or no training or preparation as quoted here: '10. Luftwaffen-Felddivision (Major General von Wedel) was transferred directly from the homeland to the Oranienbaum front without any infantry experience.'¹⁰

Plans had been written up during the spring and summer of 1942 that called for the elimination of the Oranienbaum pocket by German forces in the autumn of 1942 as part of a wider plan to alter the military situation in the region of Army Group North. There were four operational goals:

- *Unternehmen Nordlicht* (Operation Northern Lights): the conquest of Leningrad;
- *Unternehmen Schlingpflanze* (Operation Creeper): the expansion of the Demyansk pocket;
- *Unternehmen Moorbrand* (Operation Peat Fire): the elimination of the Pogostje pocket; and
- *Unternehmen Bettelstab* (Operation Beggar Stick): the destruction of the Oranienbaum bridgehead.¹¹

Had the Germans been able to raise sufficient units, air support, ammunition and other supplies to launch these attacks, their military situation in the region of Army Group North would have been greatly improved. However, they lacked the resources for conducting these attacks while they were heavily engaged in southern Russia and, perhaps more significantly, the plans failed to raise any real enthusiasm on the part of the Army Group commander and his staff.[12] As a result, as 1943 approached, the bulge behind the front lines of Army Group North west of Leningrad remained intact. This was a mistake, as the pocket would eventually threaten the entire army group. In southern Russia, German armies were reeling: *6. Armee* was surrounded at Stalingrad and *Heeresgruppe Süd* was fighting to extricate itself from the Caucasus. All the while, Soviet forces were aiming to cut the Germans off by taking the key city of Rostov. In the central and northern parts of the Eastern Front the situation was much the same. The Russians were continuing to apply pressure all along the front, in order to prevent the Germans from being able to rest and regroup.

German military reversals in southern Russia prompted the withdrawal of the divisions of *11. Armee* that had been sent north to help launch the planned attacks there. This force had only recently arrived in the Leningrad sector after capturing Sevastopol in the Crimea. It was the withdrawal of this force which gave General Govorov, commanding the Leningrad Front, and General Meretskov, commanding the Volkhov Front, the chance they were waiting for to launch simultaneous attacks against the German *LIV.* and *XXVI. Armeekorps*.[13] The siege of Leningrad had been going on for too long, despite numerous attempts by the Soviet army to raise it. In late January and early February 1943, knowing that the German front lines had been weakened, Govorov and Meretskov made another attempt, this time in the area between Schlusselberg by Lake Ladoga and Kolpino, some 28km to the southwest. The aim was to link up in a double envelopment using a pincer movement from east (the Leningrad Front) and west (the Volkhov Front).[14] The Soviets arrayed their 42nd, 55th and 67th Armies inside the Leningrad pocket and prepared to launch them against the German units between Schlusselberg and Kolpino. Simultaneously, the 2nd Striking, 8th and 54th Armies would attack from outside the encircled city in an effort to destroy the German army corps in between. When the offensive began, the Germans, already struggling to find reinforcements for their southern armies, were at a loss to find forces to help repel this latest Russian attack. No division-sized units were available so the German command resorted to borrowing battalions and companies from other parts of the front and sending them into the fighting as small reinforcements for the already greatly weakened German units. In this way one battalion from each of the two *Jäger* regiments of *10. Luftwaffen-Felddivision* were detached and sent to the threatened sector. In early January 1943 one of these battalions was part of a battle group sent to reinforce the Spanish volunteers of *250. Infanterie-Division*, holding the region in and around Krasny Bor, just south of Kolpino, and the outermost focal point on the Leningrad side of the double-pronged enemy pincer movement. The *Kampfgruppe* was organized as follows:

- 1 battalion from *Luftwaffen-Jäger-Regiment 19*[15]
- 1 battalion from *Luftwaffen-Jäger-Regiment 20*
- 22 anti-tank guns from *Panzerjäger-Abteilung 563*[16]
- 4 Tiger tanks from *schwere-Panzer-Abteilung 502*.[17]

Other formations sent to help repel the Soviet offensive included *Grenadier-Regiment 374* of *207. Sicherungs-Division*, the Latvian and Flemish SS legions and two regiments of *24. Infanterie-Division*.[18] The arrival of this small but strong combat group was to temporarily prevent the Germans from losing Krasny Bor, a vital city bordering the front lines of *212. Infanterie-Division* and *250. Infanterie-Division* on its right flank.[19] The assault group made up of *Luftwaffe* infantry and Tiger tanks went into action on 11 January 1943. The battle raged fiercely. In the city, the Spaniards fought off wave after wave of Russian attacks with daggers, entrenching tools and hand-grenades.[20] The battle raged on until 27 February 1943. Unfortunately for the Germans, the city was eventually lost, but not before it cost the Soviets over 11,000 men killed out of an original force of 33,000 grouped into four divisions: the 43rd, 45th, 63rd and 72nd Rifle Division.[21] After the situation had calmed down in the Lake Ladoga region, the battalions borrowed from *10. Luftwaffen-Felddivision* were eventually returned to the parent formation.

The front line assumed by the division in mid-January 1943 had not basically changed by the spring. It ran from the coast on the western part of the Oranienbaum pocket, through an area south of Kernovo, Gorbovizy, Voronina and Lopuschinka.[22] In November 1943 *10. Luftwaffen-Felddivision* was transferred into the army. According to Göring's plan, the unit's *Flak* battalion was detached and sent back for service in the *Luftwaffe*, becoming *II. Flak-Abteilung* of *Flak-Regiment 32 (motorisiert)*. However, the remainder of what was now *Felddivision 10 (L)* continued relatively unchanged in terms of organization. Records for the division as of 16 January 1944 show that its main components were: *Jäger-Regiment 19 (L)*, *Jäger-Regiment 20 (L)*, *Artillerie-Regiment 10 (L)*, *Fusilier Bataillon 10 (L)*[23] and *Panzerjäger-Bataillon 10 (L)*.[24]

The arrival of units belonging to *III. (germanische) SS-Panzerkorps*, beginning in late November or early December 1943, enabled the eventual shifting of the defence lines from the western part of the Oranienbaum pocket to the eastern side. This was accomplished as elements of the SS panzer corps took over the positions formerly held by *Felddivision 9 (L)* and *Felddivision 10 (L)*.[25] In fact, this transfer of positions had begun in early December 1943, as the following account relates:

On 4 December 1943, in the pitch darkness of night, the *III. (germanische) SS-Panzerkorps* arrived by railway transport to the Volossovo railway station. At midday on 5 December the Corps was unloaded and was transferred to the forest camp near Klopitzy. *SS-Pionier-Bataillon 11* and the engineer companies of *SS-Regiment Norge* and *SS-Regiment Danmark* had been sent from SS Troop Training Ground Beneschau and had only now just reached the designated area before the other parts of the division at the Oranienbaum pocket. On 6 December they unloaded the engineer troops in Volossovo and partially reached the area of Klopitzy by forced march. The engineer companies of the SS regiments were subordinated to *SS-Pionier-Bataillon 11* for tactical control and supply. Arms and all weapons, including vehicles used by these two engineer companies in each regiment, were dragged along and attached to the *SS-Pionier-Bataillon 11*. Two days later that large SS Engineer component assumed the defensive positions and mine fields which had been established earlier by *10. Felddivision (L)*.[26]

All these new measures, which began to take effect in early January 1944 and reinforced the German forces holding the Soviet units in the Oranienbaum pocket, were to prove ineffectual, however. Just as the Germans had been sending units to help reinforce *III. Luftwaffen-Feldkorps*, the Russians had been secretly ferrying across divisions into the pocket. Some slight changes in the pocket had occurred. For example, in January 1943 the Russians had been facing only *III. Luftwaffen-Feldkorps* and its two divisions, *9.* and *10. Luftwaffen-Felddivisionen*. At that point, the coastal town of Peterhof was in Soviet hands.[27] By January 1944, however, the town was under German control and *III. (germanische) SS-Panzerkorps* had arrived to lend their help in containing the pocket. The commanders of both *Luftwaffe* divisions along the Oranienbaum pocket knew when the expected Russian attack would take place. General Reinhard Gehlen, the head of the *Abwehr* (German Armed Forces Intelligence Service) on the Eastern Front, had conveyed to all pertinent German commanders in the field that the expected attack would take place at the beginning of January 1944. This is confirmed by an autobiographical study written by a former member of the communications company for *Felddivision 10 (L)*, and published in 2013. *Gefreiter* Ferdinand Müller said it was common knowledge among those who were in charge.[28]

The Soviet offensive, begun on the night of 13/14 January 1944, altered for ever the military situation on the Leningrad Front. The initial Russian artillery bombardment lasted a full 65 minutes and was quickly followed by an attack on the right flank of *Felddivision 10 (L)* by no fewer than six Russian divisions.[29] One eyewitness report says that units of *III. (germanische) SS-Panzerkorps* began to be bombarded by all kinds of artillery, including naval guns from ships anchored by the coast in the Gulf of Finland, at around 7.00am on 14 January 1944.[30] Another source breaks down the Soviet attack as follows: the 48th, 90th, 98th and 43rd Rifle Divisions plus the 152nd Tank Division attacked *Felddivision 10 (L)*'s positions, while the 11th and 131st Rifle Divisions attacked *Felddivision 9 (L)* on a very narrow part of the front, alongside the attacking formations that broke through the lines of *Felddivision 10 (L)*.[31] On the border between *Felddivision 9 (L)* and *Felddivision 10 (L)* lay the town of Petrovskaya. One report of the artillery barrage and its after-effects described it this way:

> At 06:00 hours they found themselves under intense artillery bombardment from guns of all calibres. Bunkers had been pounded flat into the earth by heavy naval guns firing from ships in the Gulf of Finland. Trees had been torn to jagged splinters of no more than 6 or 7 feet in height. Shortly later, all those who remained in place had to face the first Russians, who came

forward into the wooded area, dressed in white winter clothing. Little by little the weapons of the nearby Luftwaffe field soldiers fell silent. The Luftwaffe field soldiers were, for the most part, totally out of the action. Those who had not been killed, wounded or captured had fled in panic as far as they could.[32]

Another description of the initial assault was much simpler and to the point: 'The first German unit to be caught in the Soviet onslaught was the 10. Luftwaffe Field Division. It instantly fell apart, leaving a gap through which the Reds poured with tanks and infantry.'[33] Having almost no training, most of the unit collapsed.

However, as discouraging as these descriptions were, there were some parts of *Felddivision 10 (L)* that were resisting. The focal points of this resistance centred on the towns of Lopochinka, Sherebyatki, Llino and Saostrovje.[34] Zaastrove fell quickly, but Kapyloschka and Dyatlezy held on for a while. These points of resistance were like small and ineffective breakwaters in a sea of enemy units as the Red Army tanks and troops swarmed forwards. At the beginning of the Red Army offensive, *Felddivision 10 (L)* had a listed strength of only eleven anti-tank guns.[35] By 15 January the situation was already critical. The only unit that the Germans could afford to shift towards the Oranienbaum pocket was *61. Infanterie-Division*, but it would take at least a few days for the unit to arrive. Until then, *III. (germanische) SS-Panzerkorps* could only spare *I. Bataillon* of *SS-Panzergrenadier-Regiment 23 Norge*. This battalion was added to stiffen what remained of *Felddivision 10 (L)*.[36] In fact, one source states that this battalion, together with the survivors of *SS-Pionier-Bataillon 11*, and supported by *SS-Artillerie-Regiment 11*, was supposed to counterattack the enemy penetration.[37] It is most likely that these small units simply helped to hold the breakthrough for a time. By 17 January the German retreat had begun:

> The sector commander, Hauptsturmführer Rudolf Saalbach decided to withdraw on 17 January to a better line of defence to the southwest. At the time his command consisted of the Reconnaissance Battalion Nordland, *1. Kompanie/SS-Pionier-Bataillon 11* and a mixed combat detachment scraped together from *10. Luftwaffen-Felddivision*.[38]

By 17 January *Felddivision 10 (L)* fell apart. It could no longer be considered a cohesive division. Although the bulk of the division quickly disintegrated, there were instances where officers and men of the division grimly held their positions for days, completely encircled, before being overrun or able to withdraw. One such case was that of the commander of *Jäger-Regiment 19 (L)*, *Oberst* Paul Matussek, who was awarded the Deutsches Kreuz in Gold (German Cross in Gold) for his heroic command of the regiment during the fierce battles in January 1944. One source says that *Oberst* Matussek received this award on 25 November 1943, months before the Soviet offensive was launched,[39] but this is incorrect. The actual date of the award was 7 February 1944.[40] The date indicates that the actions for which he was recognized most likely occurred during the Soviet breakout from the pocket and subsequent dissolution of the division. Reports about the unit's destruction were succinct:

> The Division was crushed on 17 January. Its remnants withdrew along the Baltic until reaching Narva before being dissolved. This is also confirmed by another account, which also gives January 17th as the date the unit was smashed: 'By 17 January, the 10. Luftwaffe Field Division was smashed. It suffered further losses in the initial retreats through the Baltic area of the Soviet Union to the Narva and was disbanded shortly thereafter.'[41]

By 23 January the front lines had been dramatically altered. The Russians had succeeded in breaking out of the Oranienbaum pocket, linking up with the Leningrad Front and finally releasing the German grip on the city of Leningrad. In the wake of the Russian drive, the German forces of Army Group North were reeling back, heading towards the borders of Estonia and Latvia. Many units from the Oranienbaum and Leningrad sectors were no longer intact, and ad hoc battle groups were common. One such group, *Kampfgruppe Helling*, was composed of men from *SS-Pionier-Bataillon 1* and survivors of *Felddivision 10 (L)*.[42] By 26 January 1944 *III. (germanische) SS-Panzerkorps* had withdrawn to positions in and around Narva, along the Estonian–Russian border. Soon *11. SS-Panzergrenadier-Division Nordland* and the survivors of *Felddivision 10 (L)* dug in around Kingisepp and prepared to attempt to stop the 2nd Shock Army from gaining further ground.[43] In February 1944 *Felddivision 10 (L)* was officially disbanded. The bulk of the division's survivors seem to have been absorbed by *170. Infanterie-Division*.[44] However, author Kevin Ruffner also states that a good portion of *Felddivision 9. (L), 10. (L)* and *21. (L)*, who endured up until their unit's destruction, transferred into another *Luftwaffe* formation: 'A number of members of the 9., 10., and 21. Felddivision (L) joined 2. Flak-Division in the spring of 1944 after the retreat to the Narva river line.'[45]

Thus ended the history of *Felddivision 10 (L)*. The unit had existed for only about thirteen months, most of which had been spent in a relatively quiet sector of the front. Once the Russian forces made a serious assault, though, it did not take long for the division to crumble. Given the relatively similar histories of *9.* and *10. Luftwaffen-Felddivisionen*, we can say that both divisions performed about the same. We must take into account, however, that *Felddivision 10 (L)* had the support of a solid left flank held by *11. SS-Panzergrenadier-Division Nordland*. Additionally, *SS-Pionier-Bataillon 1*, plus *I. Bataillon, SS-Panzergrenadier-Regiment 23 Norge* and *I. Bataillon, SS-Panzergrenadier-Regiment 48 General Seyffardt* were sent to stiffen *Felddivision 10 (L)* in order to help contain the Soviet attack. This move delayed the enemy advance, although not because of any renewed *Luftwaffe* fervour; rather it was the tenacity of the *Waffen-SS* units that stalled the enemy. Finally, *Felddivision 10 (L)* did not find itself surrounded like *Felddivision 9 (L)*, and had a rear to withdraw to. Even so, in spite of these added benefits to its tactical advantage, *Felddivision 10 (L)* performed slightly below the mediocre standards of its sister unit, *Felddivision 9 (L)*.

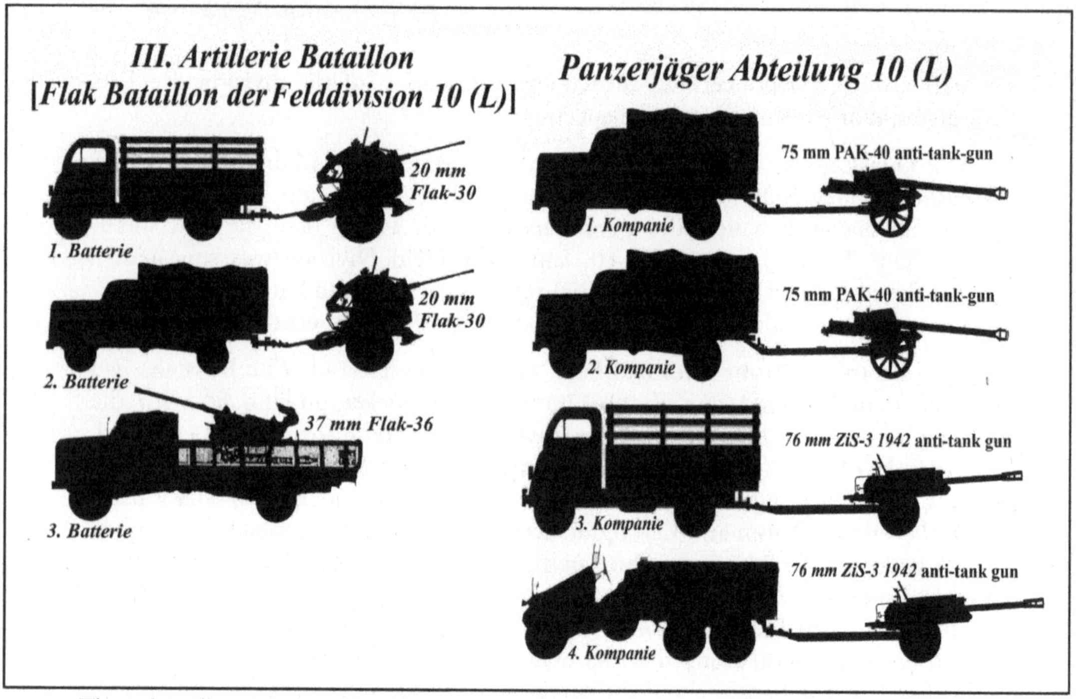

III. Artillerie Bataillon
[Flak Bataillon der Felddivision 10 (L)]

1. Batterie — 20 mm Flak-30

2. Batterie — 20 mm Flak-30

3. Batterie — 37 mm Flak-36

Panzerjäger Abteilung 10 (L)

1. Kompanie — 75 mm PAK-40 anti-tank-gun

2. Kompanie — 75 mm PAK-40 anti-tank-gun

3. Kompanie — 76 mm ZiS-3 1942 anti-tank gun

4. Kompanie — 76 mm ZiS-3 1942 anti-tank gun

The 3rd Artillery Battalion (actually a *Flak* battalion) and the anti-tank battalion of *10. Luftwaffe Felddivision / Felddivision 10 (L)*, December 1942. A 4th Artillery Battalion (really a heavy *Flak* battalion containing 88mm *Flak* guns) also existed. It was withdrawn from the division in November 1943.

10. Luftwaffe Felddivision / Felddivision 10 (L), December 1942.

10 LW

- Nachrichten Kompanie 10 (L)
- Pionier Kompanie 10 (L)
- Division Hauptquartier
- Fusilier Kompanie der Felddivison 10 (L)

Jager Regiment 19 (L)
- I. Bataillon — 1. 2. 3. 4.
- II. Bataillon — 5. 6. 7. 8.
- III. Bataillon — 9. 10. 11. 12.

Jager Regiment 20 (L)
- I. Bataillon — 1. 2. 3. 4.
- II. Bataillon — 5. 6. 7. 8.
- III. Bataillon — 9. 10. 11. 12.

Artillerie Regiment 10 (L)

IV. Artillerie Bataillon [Flak Bataillon 10 (L)] = This *Flak* battalion was withdrawn in November 1943.

- 1. Batterie — 88 mm Flak-36
- 2. Batterie — 88 mm Flak-36
- 3. Batterie — 88 mm Flak-36

I. Artillerie Bataillon
- 1. Batterie — 150 mm Nebelwerfer
- 2. Batterie — 150 mm Nebelwerfer
- 3. Batterie — Russian 122 mm M-1936
- 4. Batterie — Russian 122 mm M-1936

II. Artillerie Bataillon
- 5. Batterie — Skoda 75 mm M-15
- 6. Batterie — Skoda 75 mm M-15
- 7. Batterie — Russian 76.2 mm M-1936
- 8. Batterie — Russian 76.2 mm M-1936

Division Einheiten 10 (L)

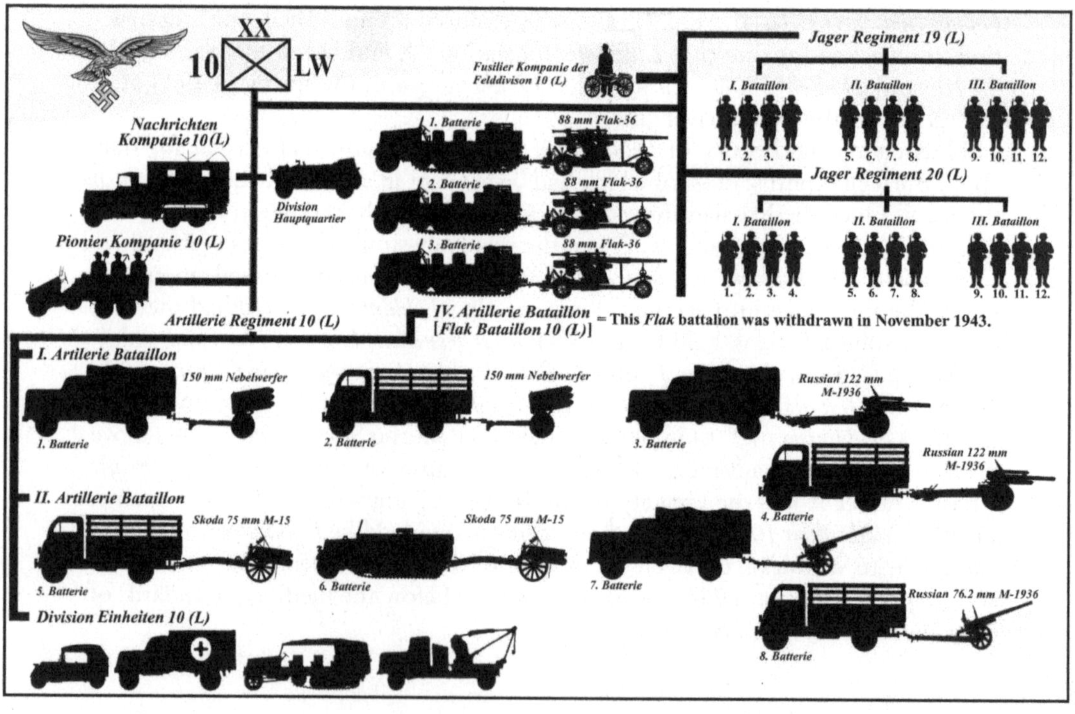

Organization of *10. Luftwaffen-Felddivision*

Commanders:
Divisional Commanders:
Generalmajor Walther Wadehn, 28/11/42–04/11/43
Generalmajor Hermann von Wedel, 05/11/43–05/02/44[46]
Ia:
Hauptmann Kurt Orthmann, 25/11/42–24/05/43
Oberst Guenther Clodius, 25/05/43–09/12/43
Oberstleutnant i.G. Henning Eppendorff, 10/12/43–02/44
Ib:
Major Hermann Kretschmer, 10/42–21/12/42
Major Josef Waibel,[47] 22/12/42–02/43
Major Hermann Kretschmer, 02/43–11/43
IIa:
Oberleutnant Fritz Zenker, 02/43–11/43
Oberstleutnant Ludwig Engel, 11/43–02/44
IIb:
Leutnant der Reserve Dr Georg Matt, 10/42–11/43
O1:
Oberleutnant Alfred Petermann, 10/42–11/43
O2:
Oberleutnant Karl-Hermann Stockhaus, 10/42–11/43
O3:
Oberleutnant Ernst Spiller, 10/42–11/43
WuG:
Hauptmann Richard Drobeck, 10/42–11/43
IVa:
Standartenjunker [Leutnant] Friedrich-Wilhelm Schwier, 10/42–11/43
Standartenjunker [Leutnant] Johannes Pulina, 11/43–02/44
IVb:
Oberstabarzt Dr Carl Weber, 01/04/42–01/08/43
CO *Luftwaffen-Artillerie-Regiment 10*:
Oberst Ludwig Meyer, 02/43–11/43
CO *Jäger-Regiment 19 (L)*:
Oberst Paul Matussek, 29/03/43–02/44
CO *I. Bataillon/Jäger-Regiment 19 (L)*:
Major Alfred Rein, 10/42–12/42
CO *II. Bataillon/Jäger-Regiment 19 (L)*:
Major Dr Walter Weiss,[48] 02/43–31/07/43
CO *III. Bataillon/Jäger-Regiment 19 (L)*:
Hauptmann Karl Burbach, 10/42–12/42
CO *Jäger-Regiment 20 (L)*:
Oberst Karl Mehnert,[49] 29/03/43–01/11/4

11. Luftwaffen-Felddivision

This division was formed at Troop Training Camp Munsterlager, in *Luftgau IV* (Dresden region), in October 1942. The cadre used to create this new unit was *Flieger-Regiment 31*, which had been stationed at Hilversum since 1941.[1] The main components of the division were as follows:

Luftwaffen-Jäger-Regiment 21
  I. Jäger-Bataillon
  II. Jäger-Bataillon
  III. Jäger-Bataillon
  13. Infanteriegeschütz-Kompanie
  14. Panzerjäger-Kompanie
Luftwaffen-Jäger-Regiment 22
  I. Jäger-Bataillon
  II. Jäger-Bataillon
  III. Jäger-Bataillon
  13. Infanteriegeschütz-Kompanie
  14. Panzerjäger-Kompanie
Luftwaffen-Flak-Bataillon 11
  1. Flak Batterie (6 × 20mm *Flak* guns)
  2. Flak Batterie (6 × 20mm *Flak* guns)
  3. Flak Batterie (3 × quadruple 20mm *Flak* guns)
  4. Flak Batterie (4 × 88mm *Flak* guns)
Luftwaffe-Pionier-Bataillon 11
  1. Pionier-Kompanie
  2. Pionier-Kompanie
  3. Pionier-Kompanie
Luftwaffen-Artillerie-Regiment 11
  I. Artillerie-Abteilung
    1. Artillerie-Batterie (4 × German 75mm howitzers)
    2. Artillerie-Batterie (4 × German 75mm howitzers)
  II. Artillerie-Abteilung
    1. Artillerie-Batterie (4 × German 75mm howitzers)
    2. Artillerie-Batterie (4 × German 75mm howitzers)
Luftwaffen-Radfahr-Kompanie 11
Luftwaffen-Nachrichten-Kompanie 11
Luftwaffen-Versorgungs-Einheit 11

This organization would later be altered. The greatest modification would be made to the divisional artillery regiment, which would undergo a dramatic strengthening – so much so, that by 30 August 1943 the regiment would be composed of three artillery battalions instead of two. Additionally, *I. Artillerie-Abteilung* would now have three batteries instead of its initial complement of two. Similarly, *II. Artillerie-Abteilung* was reinforced by the addition of a third artillery battery. Finally, the new *III. Artillerie-Abteilung* contained two artillery batteries. The regimental order of battle now looked like this:

Luftwaffen-Artillerie-Regiment 11 / Artillerie-Regiment 11 (L)
 I. Artillerie-Abteilung
  1. *Artillerie-Batterie* (4 × German 75mm howitzers)
  2. *Artillerie-Batterie* (4 × German 75mm howitzers)
  3. *Artillerie-Batterie* (4 × German 75mm howitzers)
 II. Artillerie-Abteilung
  4. *Artillerie-Batterie* (4 × French 75mm *canon de 75 modèle 1897* howitzers)
  5. *Artillerie-Batterie* (4 × French 75mm *canon de 75 modèle 1897* howitzers)
  6. *Artillerie-Batterie* (4 × French 75mm *canon de 75 modèle 1897* howitzers)
 III. Artillerie-Abteilung
  7. *Artillerie-Batterie* (4 × French 75mm *canon de 75 modèle 1897* howitzer).
  8. *Artillerie-Batterie* (4 × French 75mm *canon de 75 modèle 1897* howitzer).[2]

These French-made artillery pieces were modified for Second World War battlefield conditions. For example, the large wooden wheels used in the First World War were replaced with the standard all-metal wheels employed by current German anti-tank guns. The gun shield was the one typically used for the German PAK-40 75mm anti-tank gun. A long, tubular muzzle flash was added at the end of the barrel to reduce both noise and muzzle flash. The initial commander of *11. Luftwaffen-Felddivision* was *Generalleutnant* Karl Drum, the former Chief of the Inspector of Air Reconnaissance Forces and Operations in Berlin.[3] Assigning this specialized officer to lead what was basically an infantry unit was a waste of talent, but was typical of how the *Luftwaffe* sometimes squandered its skilled manpower on these field divisions. Although the division did not initially contain an anti-tank battalion, that deficiency was soon partly remedied. By the spring of 1943 the organization for the divisional anti-tank battalion had been established on paper as follows:

Luftwaffen-Panzerjäger-Abteilung 11
 1. *Panzerjäger-Kompanie (motorisiert)* (9 × 50mm Pak-38 and
  5 × 75mm Pak-40)
 2. *Panzerjäger-Kompanie (motorisiert)* (9 × 50mm Pak-38 and
  5 × 75mm Pak-40)
 3. *Sturmgeschütz III batterie* (4 × *STUG-III* 75mm L-48 assault guns)

However, according to one source, only the battalion headquarters and *1. Panzerjäger-Kompanie* were ever created.[4]

The divisional support elements had also grown, and by August 1943 the division had the following support units:

1. Schwer-(Raupenschlepper)-Motorisiert Versorgungs Kompanie
2. Leicht (motorisiert) Versorgungs Kompanie
3. Leicht (motorisiert) Versorgungs Kompanie
Schlachten-Kompanie
Feldbäkerei
Verwaltungskompanie
Krankenkompanie (motorisiert)
Krankenwagen-Kompanie
9/III Luftwaffen-Feldlazarett-Kompanie (motorisiert)
Veterinär Kompanie (motorisiert)
Motorwartungs Zug
Luftwaffe Feldgendarmerie Trupp
Feldpostamt (motorisiert)

11. Luftwaffen-Felddivision left Germany in January 1943 for Greece because of the increase in guerrilla activity there from the autumn of 1942.[5] It reached Athens in that same month and was immediately made a reserve formation of *12. Armee*. In fact, an advance element of the division, *I. Jäger-Bataillon, Luftwaffen-Jäger-Regiment 21.*, had arrived in Athens on 29 December 1942.[6] Of this advance group, twenty-two men were sent to the island of Crete in preparation for the division being posted to that Greek island. On 3 February 1943 the entire division was moved to the island, as well as to surrounding islands that were deemed vital, and became part of the German garrison on Crete.[7] The division remained on Crete in March and April and adapted quickly to the routine of occupation duty.[8] Although it could be lonely work, employment in this type of military duty was far preferable to front-line combat in Russia. One published report states that the division was stationed in Attika in March 1943.[9] Another report states that the unit did not reach the mainland and the city of Athens until the end of April 1943.[10] The confusion derives from the fact that the division moved in several tranches.

The leading element of *11. Luftwaffen-Felddivision, Luftwaffen-Jäger-Regiment 21*, actually arrived in Attika by the end of March 1943, after an increase in guerrilla activity had forced the German command to recall the division to Athens. The unit was reinforced and immediately placed on railway security duty between Athens and the area just north of Lamia.[11] It wasn't long before *11. Luftwaffen-Felddivision* had its first major engagement with the Greek guerrillas. That initial clash occurred on 4 May 1943, in the region of Larissa, Katerini and Elasson. On 17 May 1943 *I. Jäger-Bataillon, Luftwaffen-Jäger-Regiment 21*, was sent by air transport to occupy the island of Milos, halfway between Athens and Crete. Meanwhile, *II.* and *III. Jäger-Bataillon* of *Luftwaffen-Jäger-Regiment 21* were sent to protect the Corinth Canal. That was as close as the division's units came to entering the Peloponnese.[12] One company was detached and ordered to the island

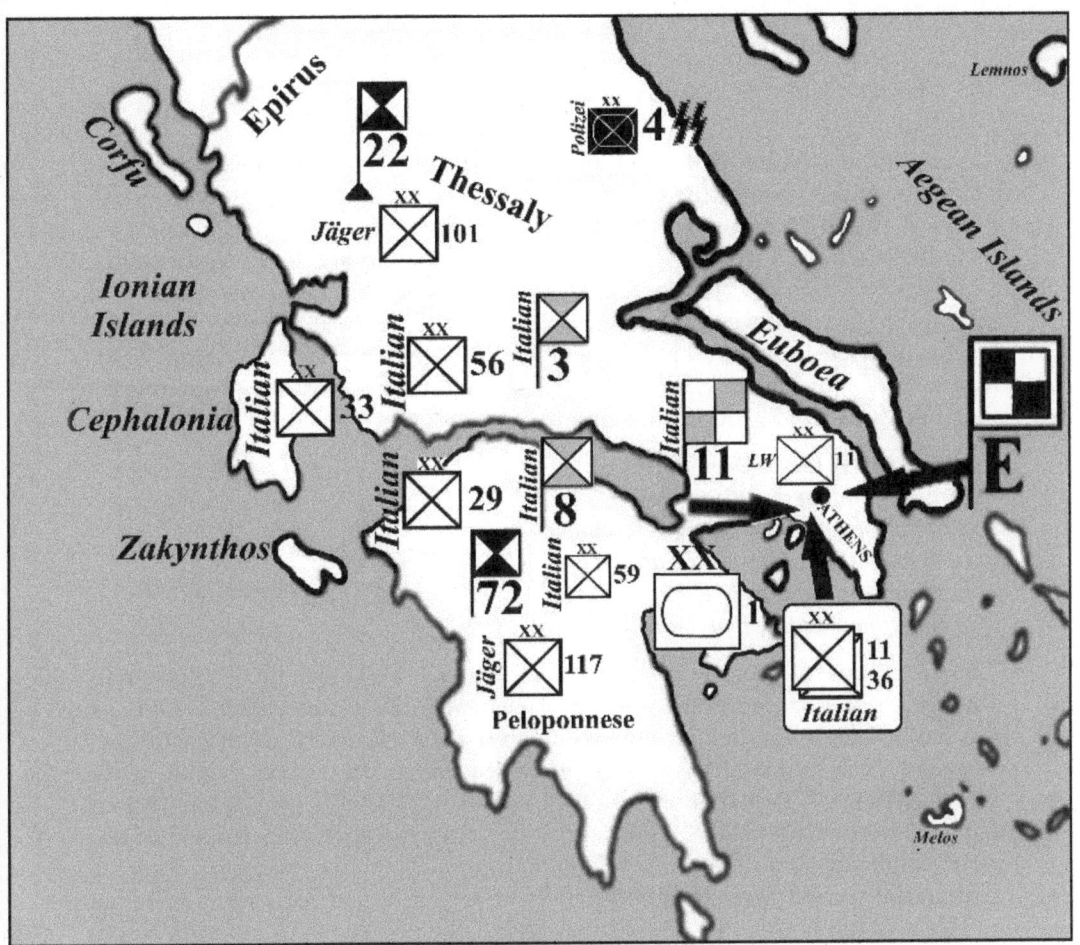

11. Luftwaffen-Felddivision in Athens, Greece, mid-1943.

of Salamis. All of these moves were geared as part of German security precautions based on fears of an impending Allied move against Axis forces in Greece. However, that fear proved to be unfounded when British and American forces landed in Sicily in July 1943. When Italy surrendered on 8 September 1943 *11. Luftwaffen-Felddivision* was one of many German units in the Balkans that moved to disarm as many Italian formations as possible.

The great fear was that the Italian arms would either be handed over to the Greek and Yugoslav guerrillas, or would be seized by them in exchange for free passage for Italian divisions going home. It was also feared that the Italians might join the partisans. In fact, some Italian units joined the guerrillas. One element of *11. Luftwaffen-Felddivision* actually advanced as far as the Albanian-Greek border and disarmed parts of the Italian 11th Army in that region, as well as Italian forces in Attika and the Corinth Canal region.[13] On 17 October part of the division was used in conjunction with a regiment of the *Brandenburg* commandos against Greek guerrillas in the region of Thebes and Eleusis. Another consequence of the Italian surrender in September 1943 was that the British had been able to occupy several Greek islands in the Aegean Sea. Concerned that these moves would bring

Turkey closer to the Allied camp, or that these islands could be used as staging points for an invasion of the Greek mainland, the German leadership of *Heeresgruppe E* proposed to retake the islands. The forces gathered for this purpose included various German formations from the *Brandenburg* commandos, *22. Infanterie-Division (Luftlande)*, as well as *11. Luftwaffen-Felddivision*. The principal islands that were to be recaptured included Stampalia, Levita, Leros and Calino. Ferried in by air, *11. Kompanie* of *III. Jäger-Bataillon, Luftwaffen-Jäger-Regiment 21*, quickly took Stampalia.[14] The assault on Leros was planned using four battalion-sized groups, including:

Brandenburg Küstenjäger Kompanie
Pionier Landungskompanie 780
1 battalion of *fallschirmjäger* troopers
II. Bataillon, Infanterie Regiment 16
II. Bataillon, Infanterie Regiment 65
II. Bataillon, Luftwaffen-Jäger-Regiment 22

The battalions of *Infanterie Regiment 16* and *65* belonged to *22. Infanterie-Division*.[15] The battlegroup made up of elements of *11. Luftwaffen-Felddivision* was led by Major von Saldern, the commander of *II. Bataillon, Luftwaffen-Jäger-Regiment 22*. The battalion was charged with taking the eastern region of the island of Leros. The battalion would then seize the heights overlooking Alinda Bay and Leros City itself.[16] One source says that two battalions instead of one were employed from *Luftwaffen-Jäger-Regiment 22* in the taking of Leros.[17] If true, the second *Jäger* battalion may have arrived as part of a reinforcement.

The invasion began on 12 November 1943. The first group of *Luftwaffe* troops had departed from the port at Rafti at 0800 hours on 3 November using nine J-Boats from the *Kriegsmarine 6. Landungsflotille* (6th Landing Flotilla). The principal units of this initial assault force included *6. Kompanie* and *7. Kompanie* of *II. Jäger-Bataillon, Luftwaffen-Jäger-Regiment 22*. The second group departed from Lawrion at the same time. It also included the headquarters of *II. Jäger-Bataillon*, as well as *8. Kompanie*, a communications platoon (*nachrichten zug*) and a *panzerjäger zug* (an anti-tank platoon).[18]

In both instances, British planes strafed the *Luftwaffe* infantrymen while on their way to Leros. The third group, which consisted of seventy-six men and vehicles belonging to *II. Jäger-Bataillon* departed from Lawrion on 13 November in a large transport vessel. They, too, were strafed before they arrived at Calino on 18 November 1943. The battle for Leros lasted four days and cost the British around 1,000 casualties, while the Germans lost 400 men. The German garrison left on Leros held out until the end of the war, but proved as useful to the German war effort as the isolated pockets of German forces trapped in numerous French ports between 1944 and 1945 – in other words, not useful at all.

The other thing of importance that occurred in November was the absorption of *11. Luftwaffen-Felddivision* into the German Army. At this time the division could count on about 10,000 men in its ranks.[19] The division was renamed

Felddivision 11 (L) and began to reorganize. *Luftwaffe Flak-Bataillon 11* was completely withdrawn from the division and returned to *Luftwaffe* service. It was eventually redesignated *I. Flak-Bataillon* of *Flak-Regiment 28 (motorisiert)*.[20] While this was a heavy loss, it was by no means the only one that the division suffered: it also lost 700 officers and men who volunteered for the paratroopers, and therefore were also withdrawn from the division. The *Luftwaffe* took another 400 men, ostensibly because they had specialized training, which the Air Force said was vital. To replace these major losses, *Felddivision 11 (L)* received 1,250 older-age recruits who were of limited service because of former injuries or existing medical conditions.[21] The major changes that now occurred included the expansion of the *Radfahr Kompanie*, which had been acting as the divisional reconnaissance unit, into a battalion-sized formation. The anti-tank battalion was also changed, as was *III. Artillerie-Bataillon* of *Artillerie-Regiment 11 (L)*. The *Nachrichten Kompanie* was also expanded to battalion size. In addition, a *Feldersatz Bataillon 11 (L)* was raised to supply replacements for the division. The various medical and field hospital units were all grouped together into a medical battalion. All of this took time to implement, but by 24 April 1944 the changes were complete and the divisional organization was as follows:

Artillerie-Regiment 11 (L)
   III. Artillerie-Abteilung
      7. *Artillerie-Batterie* (4 × Yugoslav 105mm howitzers)
      8. *Artillerie-Batterie* (4 × Yugoslav 105mm howitzers)
      9. *Artillerie-Batterie* (4 × Russian 152mm howitzers)
Fusilier-Bataillon 11 (L)
   1. *Fusilier-Kompanie*
   2. *Fusilier-Kompanie*
   3. *Fusilier-Kompanie*
   4. *Fusilier-Kompanie (schwer)*
Panzerjäger-Abteilung 11 (L)
   1. *Panzerjäger-Kompanie* (12 × 75mm PAK-40 L-48 anti-tank guns)
   Sturmgeschütz-Batterie 11 (10 × STUG-IV assault guns with 75mm L-48 guns)
Feldersatz-Bataillon 11 (L)
   1. *Feldersatz-Kompanie*
   2. *Feldersatz-Kompanie*
Sanitäts-Abteilung 11 (L)
   1. *Feldlazarret-Kompanie (motorisiert)*
   2. *Feldlazarret-Kompanie (motorisiert)*
   Feldlazarret-Versorgungs-Kompanie
Nachrichten-Abteilung 11 (L)
   1. *Telefon-Kompanie*
   2. *Radio-Kompanie*
   3. *Signal-Kompanie*

On 16 January 1944 the division sent two battalions to the city of Kymi in the region of Euboea. On 12 February *Jäger-Regiment 21 (L)* sent a reinforced company to the island of Skyros, just off the coast of Kymi. Between March and August the division took part in numerous anti-partisan operations extending as far as Tripolis on the Peloponnese peninsula and Larissa on the mainland.[22] In these operations the men of *Felddivision 11 (L)* were combined with other German Army formations. The division also took part in *Unternehmen Wildente* (Operation Wild Duck) on 19 March in the northern part of Euboea and the region of Gythio. Next followed *Unternehmen Krebs* (Operation Cancer) on 29 March 1944, in the region north of Megara, and *Unternehmen Geyer* on 26 April.

On 18 May part of *Felddivision 11 (L)* was also used to launch a drive against guerrillas north of Megara and northwest of Athens. In this last operation *117. Jäger-Division* also took part. The next major operation in which the division saw action was *Unternehmen Kondor* (Operation Condor). This drive was launched in an area north of Tripolis, on the highway between Arta and Agrinion. On 11 August a unit of the division was combined with one rifle battalion and two artillery batteries of *SS und Polizei-Gebirgsjäger-Regiment 18*.[23] and together, they launched a drive in the region of Amphissa and Karutia on 28 August 1944.

The organization of some units in the division changed once again in the summer of 1944. In the divisional artillery regiment, *I.* and *II. Artillerie-Abteilung* were upgraded when their 75mm guns were exchanged for German 105mm howitzers. *Feldersatz-Bataillon 11 (L)* was also reorganized. By August 1944 the final reorganization had been completed:

Artillerie-Regiment 11 (L)
   I. Artillerie-Abteilung
      1. Artillerie-Batterie (4 × 105mm German howitzers)
      2. Artillerie-Batterie (4 × 105mm German howitzers)
      3. Artillerie-Batterie (4 × 105mm German howitzers)
   II. Artillerie-Abteilung
      4. Artillerie-Batterie (4 × 105mm German howitzers)
      5. Artillerie-Batterie (4 × 105mm German howitzers)
      6. Artillerie-Batterie (4 × 105mm German howitzers)
   III. Artillerie-Abteilung
      7. Artillerie-Batterie (4 × 105mm Yugoslav howitzers)[24]
      8. Artillerie-Batterie (4 × 105mm Yugoslav howitzers)
      9. Artillerie-Batterie (4 × 152mm Russian howitzers)[25]
Feldersatz-Bataillon 11 (L)
   1. Feld-Ersatz-Kompanie
   2. Feld-Ersatz-Kompanie
   3. Feld-Ersatz-Kompanie
   4. Feld-Ersatz-Kompanie
   5. Feld-Ersatz-Kompanie
   Panzerjäger Zug (3 × 75mm PAK-40 anti-tank guns)

11. Luftwaffen-Felddivision 109

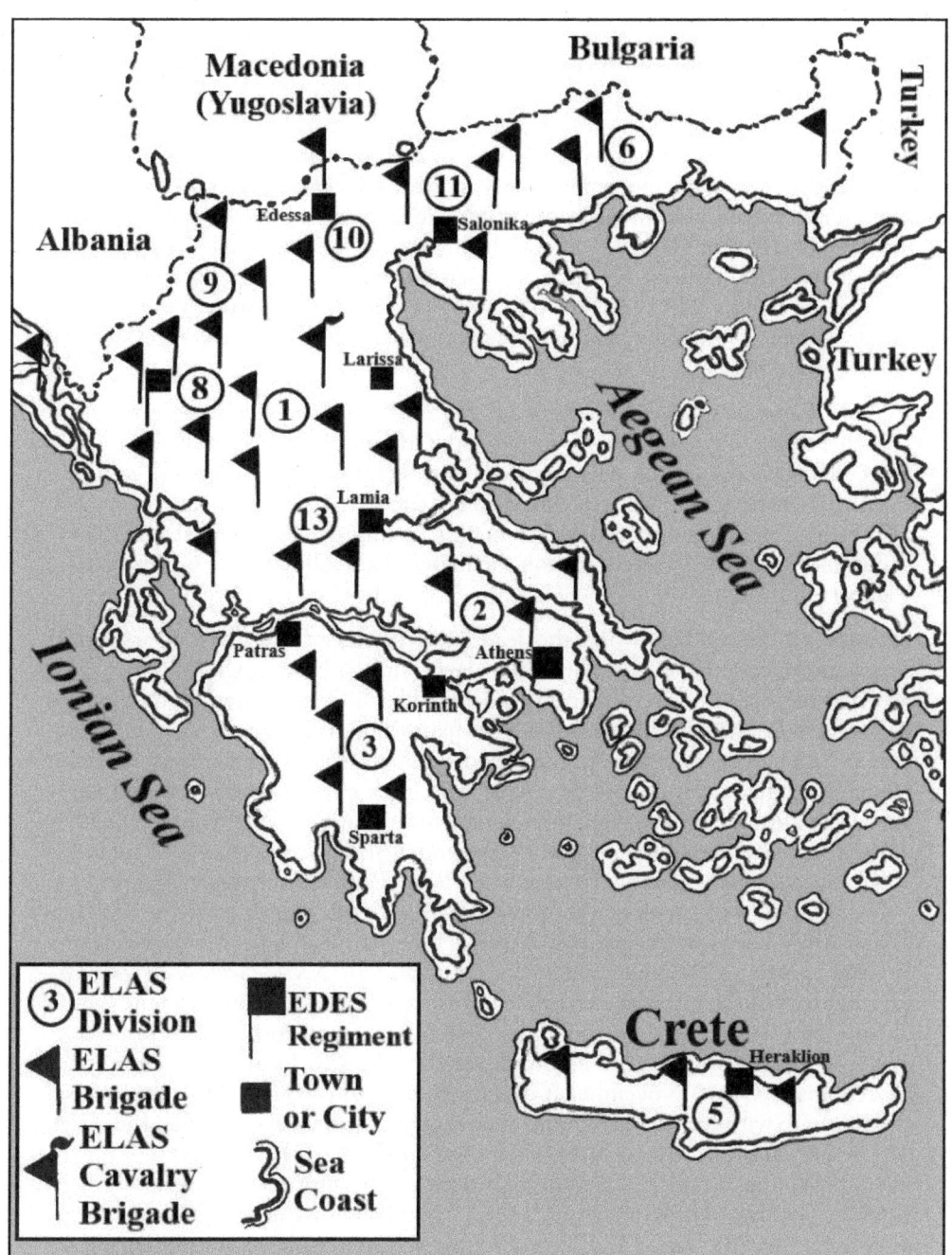

Greek guerrilla units and their location in late 1943. The (communist) ELAS organization had about 20,000 men, while the (monarchist) EDES group contained around 8,000. A third guerrilla movement, named EKKA and republican in nature, existed from 1943 to 1944.

In the first week of September 1944 *Felddivision 11 (L)* began its move northwards, withdrawing from Greece with the rest of the German Army. Part of the unit was shifted by rail to Salonika on 9 September, while another part that was transported by sea had left on 6 September. They landed in Thessalonica, and from there the column headed for Veria to link up with the rest of the withdrawing division. This movement was part of the German general retreat from Greece and would culminate in the complete withdrawal of all German forces from the Balkans by May 1945. It was during this move that an incident occurred that showed the haste with which the German forces were trying to withdraw from Greece and avoid being cut off by the advancing Red Army. It seems that the divisional commander, General Henke, made a deal with the ELAS (communist) guerrillas:

> Major General Gerhard Henke's *11. Luftwaffen-Felddivision* made good its escape through areas heavily infested with Communist guerrillas in a unique manner: it supplied the partisan Reds with certain heavy arms and equipment in exchange for free passage through their territory. The Reds – more interested in equipping themselves for the upcoming [Greek] civil war than in fighting the Wehrmacht – took the material and allowed the Germans to depart unmolested.[26]

Between 10 September, when the leading elements of the division arrived at Skopje in Macedonia, in southern Yugoslavia, and 16 November 1944, the units of *Felddivision 11 (L)* were transported by rail and road under the control of *Wehrmacht-Befehlshaber Mazedonien* (German Military Commander in Macedonia).[27] As described above, one report asserts that *Generalmajor* Gerhard Henke arranged a clandestine deal with the Greek guerrillas which would allow his division unhindered passage in exchange for his unit's heavy weapons.[28] Other units under the command of the *Wehrmacht-Befehlshaber Mazedonien* included *4. SS-Polizei-Panzergrenadier-Division* and *SS und Polizei-Gebirgsjäger-Regiment 18*.

In the middle of October the division clashed with elements of the 1st Bulgarian Army between Vranye and Zletovo. The unit also fought near Kriva and Palanka, north of Skoplje, under the command of *XXII. Gebirgs-Armeekorps*. Another part of the division, probably *Jäger-Regiment 21 (L)*, fought in the region of Stip, by Carevo Selo and the highway between Kumanovo and Buyanovce.[29] At the beginning of November *Felddivision 11 (L)* was located east of Vardar, Macedonia.[30] On 10 November it was in the area of the Kumanovo bridgehead and began to withdraw from Skoplje after holding off several combined Bulgarian and Soviet divisions. By 16 November the rearguard of the division was northwest of Skoplje, while the leading elements of the unit were moving through Kraljevo, southwest of Kragujevac.[31] On 17 November parts of *Felddivision 11 (L)* as well as the *104.* and *117. Jäger-Divisionen* began to be evacuated from the Kraljevo airfield via Ju-52 transport planes towards Cacak.[32] While this was going on, *III. Jäger-Bataillon* of *Jäger-Regiment 21 (L)*, with *Festungs-Infanterie-Bataillon 1001, 1010* and *1012* reached Rogacica. Also arriving with the *Luftwaffe*

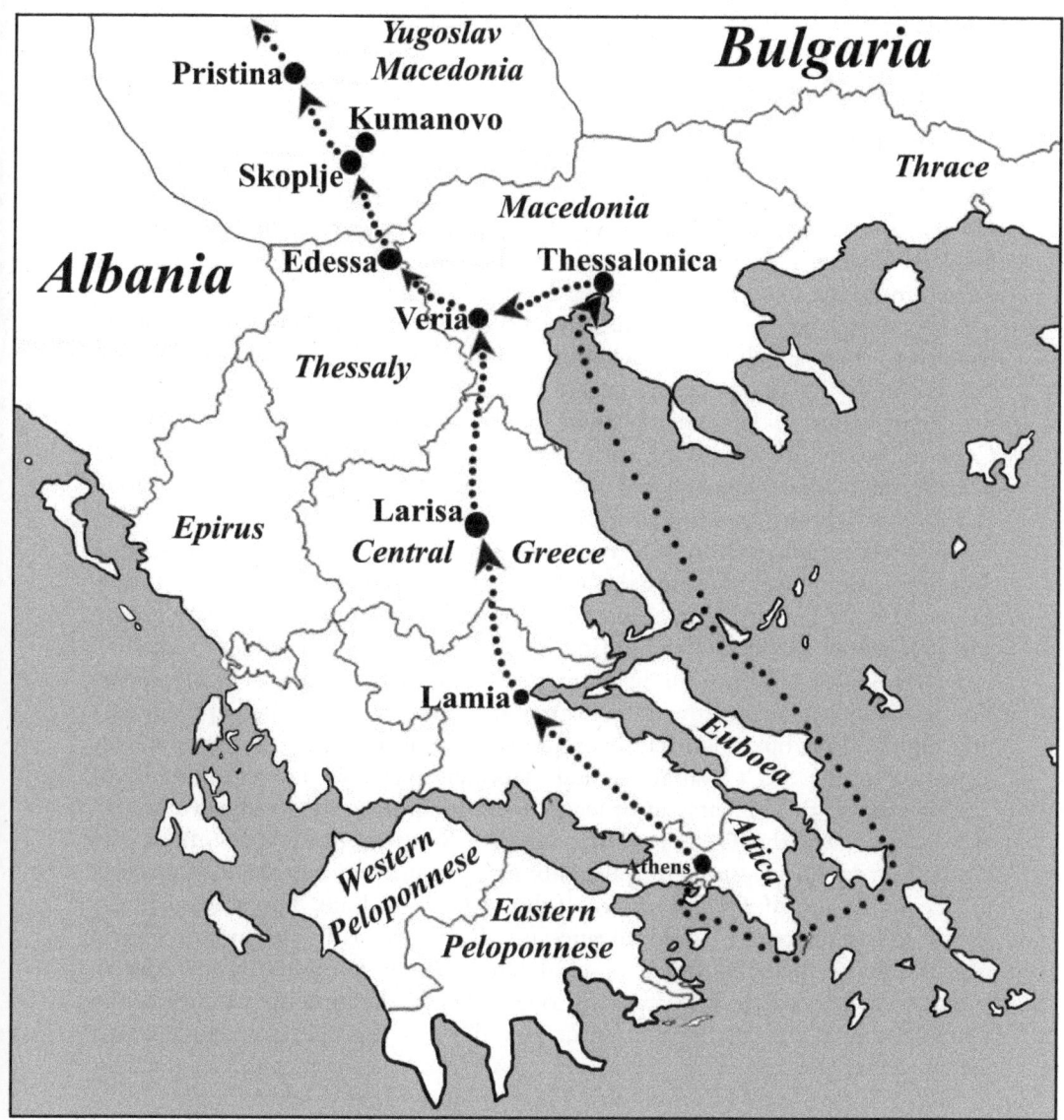

Route of withdrawal for *Felddivision 11 (L)* in the late summer and autumn of 1944.

division was *SS-Feld-Ersatz-Bataillon* 7. The air force troops were assigned security duty in and around Rogacica.[33]

Between 27 November and 7 December 1944 the bulk of *Felddivision 11 (L)* travelled from Zvornik to Janya, east of Tuzla. *Oberst* Alexander Bourquin, the army officer who had led the division in November–December 1943 (after *Generalmajor* Drum left the division), now left the unit and went on to a new assignment: heading the War School in Wiener Neustadt.[34] In his place General Wilhelm Kohler assumed command. Kohler had been promoted on 1 June 1944 to *Generalleutnant*.[35] On 18 December *SS-Freiwilligen-Gebirgs-Infanterie-Regiment 13 Artur Phleps*, from 7. *SS-Freiwilligen-Gebirgs-Division Prince Eugen*, relieved *Jäger-Regiment 21 (L)*, which had been holding positions in and around

Brcko since the end of November.[36] The division found itself attached to *XXXIV. Armeekorps* in late November. Other divisions in this corps included *104. Jäger-Division* and *7. SS-Freiwilligen-Gebirgs-Division Prinz Eugen*.[37] On 23 December 1944 *Felddivision 11 (L)* reached Otok and by 2 January 1945 the unit's defence lines were located southeast of Osijek near the Danube river.[38]

Three days later the division launched a counterattack in a region south of the Save river. This attack was launched in conjunction with *1. Kosaken-Kavallerie-Division* of *XV. Kosaken-Kavalleriekorps*.[39] On 6 January *Jäger-Regiment 22 (L)*, which happened to be available, was moved west to cover the advance of a Cossack cavalry brigade, along with *Kampfgruppe Fischer*. This battlegroup had been formed in late January and early February 1945 by removing *III. Jäger-Bataillon* from both *Jäger-Regiment 21 (L)* and *Jäger-Regiment 22 (L)* and forming a totally new regiment from these two battalions.[40] The new regiment was named *Jäger-Regiment 111 (L)* but was also referred to by its commander's name, *Major Fischer*. On 27 January *XCI. Armeekorps* assumed control of *Kampfgruppe Fischer* and *Felddivision 11 (L)*.[41] The location held by the division in January remained relatively unchanged until the beginning of February, when a large-scale operation was launched against the Tito partisan divisions located in the Papuk mountain region. This operation had been prepared in anticipation of enemy moves against Zagreb, the Croatian capital. German plans to move the bulk of *2. Panzerarmee* to Hungary, in order to assist in an upcoming offensive, would eventually dilute the German forces on the Syrmien front.[42] In effect, the German Army was planning to leave only *117. Jäger-Division* in this region, so as to free up the rest of *2. Panzerarmee*. If this were to be done, Tito's forces in the Papuk mountain region could advance on Zagreb virtually unopposed. It was vital, therefore, that this threat be eliminated, if only temporarily, in order to allow *2. Panzerarmee* to withdraw without adversely affecting the defence of the Croatian capital and the Syrmien front as well.[43] For this operation, codenamed *Unternehmen Werwolf*, *XCI. Armeekorps*, *XXXIV. Armeekorps* and *XV. Kosaken-Kavallerie-Korps* would be employed. The formations that would take part in the offensive included the following:

- *Kampfgruppe Fischer*: *Jäger-Regiment 111 (L)*
- *104. Jäger-Division*
- *SS-Freiwilligen-Gebirgs-Division Prinz Eugen*[44]
- *297. Infanterie-Division*
- *2. Kosaken-Kavallerie-Division*
- Croatian *5. Domobran-Ustashe Division*

The date set for the attack was 15 February 1945.[45] Preparations should have been completed by 6 February, and the initial drives were begun on that day. By 8 February the attack units had taken Podravska Slatina, Grubisno Polje, Pletenica and Velika Bama. Some positions on the Bilo mountain were also seized. It was hoped that the expulsion of Tito's forces from the Papuk hills would delay any enemy advance towards the Croatian capital; it was also thought that several enemy military depots, believed to be in the area, could be captured.

The operation proved partly successful, and some weapons and foodstuffs were seized, although no military depots. By 6 March *Felddivision 11 (L)* had been ordered to cross the Drava river by Valpovo, just west-northwest of Osijek, in small landing boats.[46] At Osijek the division came under attack from the Partisan 51st Vojvodina Assault Division and the Osijeka Brigade of the 12th Partisan Assault Division. Elements of *Felddivision 11 (L)* remained north of the Drava river, with the unit's left wing positioned as far forward as Miholjac. A day later, on 7 March, a Cossack regiment made its appearance on the division's left flank.

The attack on Soviet forces in southern Hungary began on 6 March 1945. Codenamed *Unternehmen Frühlingserwachen* (Operation Spring Awakening), this last German offensive employed *6. Armee*, *6. Panzerarmee* and *2. Panzerarmee*. While this was going on, the Yugoslav forces did their best to try to relieve the pressure on the Soviet armies by launching attacks of their own from Yugoslav territory. The brunt of these attacks was borne by the units of *2. Panzerarmee*, now mostly occupied in assisting the offensive spearheaded by *6. Panzerarmee* and its two *SS* armoured corps. The OKW War Diary recorded the events:

> Army Group South (attack in Hungary): the advance forces that had formed two bridgeheads on the Drava river now had to be withdrawn. A depth of 4 to 6 kilometres had been gained. Since afternoon *104. Jäger-Division* had held a position across the river. The bridges were under enemy fire. Air forces were employed. The 36th Partisan Division was committed against Osijek, and the 11th Luftwaffe Field Division was opposed by the 16th Partisan Division.[47]

On 7 March 1945 there were some significant changes. Despite several Russian and Yugoslav counterattacks launched against *2. Panzerarmee*, *Felddivision 11 (L)* on the Drava river front was able to gain 2km of ground near Valpovo, although the enemy continued to attack the division. Hitler himself had ordered the division to go over to the attack, alongside *2. Kosaken-Kavallerie-Division*, in an order dated 14 March 1945. The purpose of this attack was to throw the enemy off balance and consolidate the Drava river bridgehead: 'The Führer orders the participation of *2. Kosaken-Kavallerie-Division* east of the Drava river bridgehead, in an attack in a northwesterly direction together with parts of *Felddivision 11 (L)*, in order to unite the bridgehead over the Drava river.'[48]

The failed German attack in the direction of Lake Balaton and Budapest in the second week of March signalled yet another withdrawal of German forces. Beginning on 18 March 1945 the units of *2. Panzerarmee* pulled back:

> On the night of 20 March 1945, the artillery and Cossack cavalrymen crossed the Drava river by Valpovo. On the night of 22 March part of *Felddivision 11 (L)* also crossed, in spite of enemy pressure. *Felddivision 11 (L)* marched to its old defensive positions along the Drava, while the

297th Infanterie-Division moved to Koprivnika under *2. Panzerarmee* and *104 Jäger-Division* under *XV. Gebirgs-Armeekorps*.[49]

At the end of March *Felddivision 11 (L)* was still under *XCI. Armeekorps*. The division was shifted from Slivosevei, north of Benicani, towards Karlovac. On 18 March an attack northwest of Valpovo by the division against partisan forces failed to make any progress. By 21 March the withdrawal across the Drava river was under way. At Valpovo on that day *1. Kosaken-Kavallerie-Division*, the artillery battalion of *2. Panzerarmee* and the motor vehicles of *Felddivision 11 (L)* were withdrawn.[50]

On 12 April, when the Tito partisans launched their final offensive, the division was located in and around Nasice. One source, however, states that part of the division was located between Vukovar and Dalj on that date, alongside *41. Festungs-Division*. This is confirmed by another source.[51] On 14 April, after a day of fierce and heavy street fighting, the 51st and 12th Partisan Divisions finally expelled *Jäger-Regiment 21 (L)* from Osijek. On 15 April the Yugoslav partisans on the Syrmien front launched an attack from south and north of Nasice with the aim of trapping the entire division. The Germans, therefore, withdrew westwards, retreating through the towns of Dalij (Donji), Dl. Miholjac, Dyakovo and Podgorica.[52] The fighting in and around Dyakovo proved especially gruesome and tough for the unit, but its front lines held. In the middle of April 1945 the Armed Forces High Command praised *Felddivision 11 (L)* for its defence of Dyakovo, the Command diary recalling: 'After the unit was renamed *Felddivision 11 (L)* we awaited its help with expectations, and from Dyakovo indeed it came.'

A few records indicate that in April the division was attached to *15. Kosaken-Kavallerie-Korps*.[53] This is confirmed in an order of battle for April 1945.[54] However, another source states that *Felddivision 11 (L)* was not transferred over to *XV. Kosaken-Kavallerie-Korps* until May 1945.[55] By 2 May, however, the division had been reduced to a mere battle group under the command of *Generalmajor* Gerhard Henke, the former Head of the German Military Legal Court.[56] The Germans were now evidently so short of leaders that they were reduced to promoting judges to command divisions. The divisional 'Ia' had been changed for a fourth time due to attrition. By May 1945 it was *Major* Bauernstätter, who had formerly been on the staff of *Panzergrenadier-Regiment 10*.[57]

On 21 April the remnants of the division were attached to *22. Infanterie-Division (Luftlande)* as *Kampfgruppe Henke*. From 2 to 7 May these formations made a fighting withdrawal around Pragovac and the Varazdin-Zagreb highway. By 8 May 1945 the remnants of *Felddivision 11 (L)* were at Cilli in Slovenia, and two days later were in the region of St Georgian north of the Austrian city of Klagenfurt. There they surrendered to British forces advancing from the west.

Compared to other *Luftwaffe* field divisions, *11. Luftwaffen-Felddivision/ Felddivision 11 (L)* had a long combat history. It also operated with greater success than about ten *Luftwaffe* field divisions: *2., 3., 4., 5., 6., 7., 8., 9., 10.* and *15.*

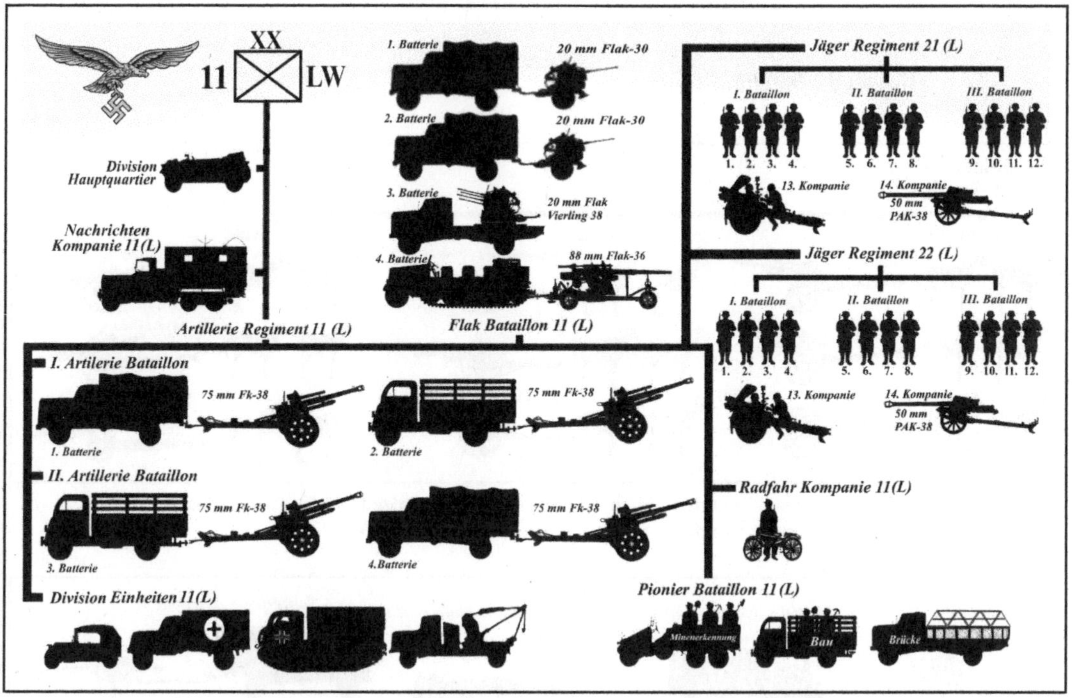

11. Luftwaffe Felddivision, December 1942.

Luftwaffen-Felddivisionen. Of course, we can attribute its success partly due to the fact that the division was fighting Greek and Yugoslav partisans (although in the case of the Yugoslav guerrillas, by 1944 they were fighting like a regular army). In any event, not having to fight on the Russian Front probably helped this air force unit to survive for as long as it did. In spite of this, there is no doubt that the division was one of the better *Luftwaffe* field divisions, since its performance was far superior to many others.

Initially, the anti-tank battalion only contained one anti-tank company. The plan was to add two more anti-tank companies. However, in the end *Panzerjäger-Abteilung 11 (L)* managed to establish only a second company, albeit equipped with ten assault guns.

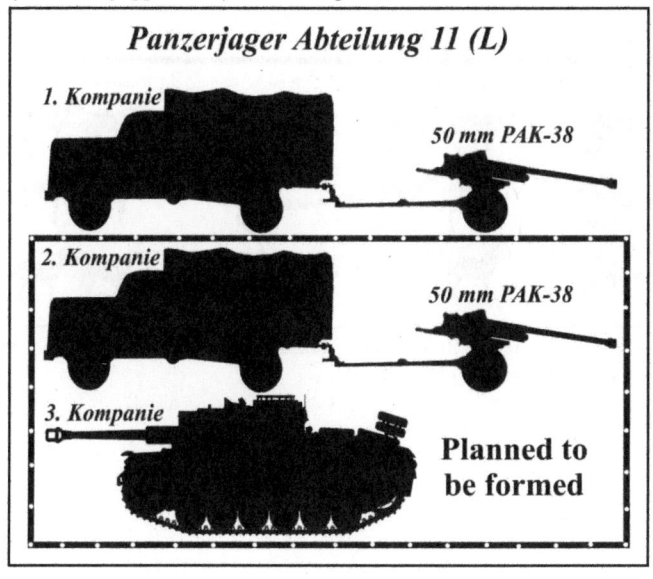

116   Hitler's *Luftwaffe* Infantry

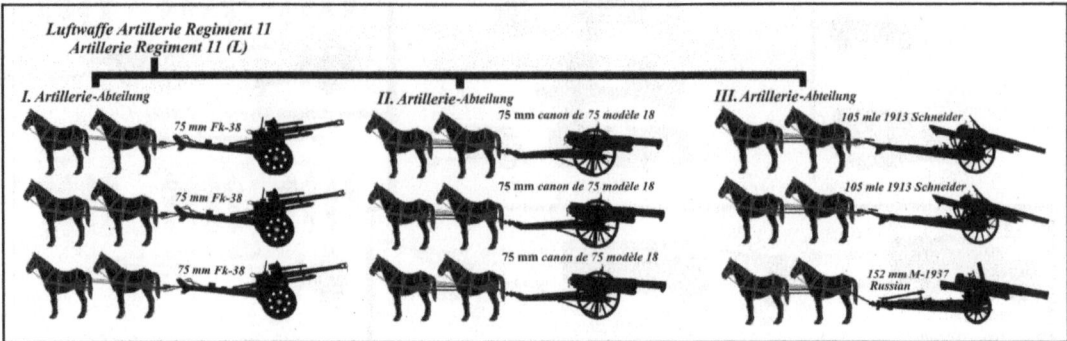

In April 1944 the artillery regiment of the division was reorganized. The anti-tank battalion was expanded and other service battalions were added to the divisional TO&E.

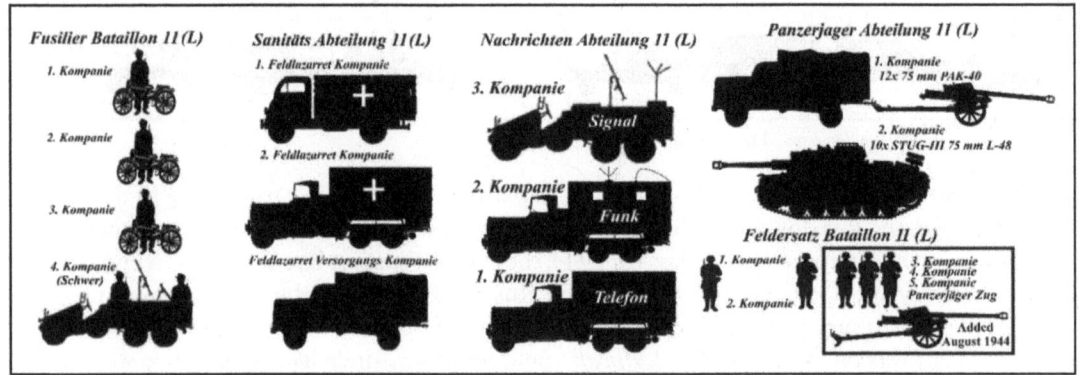

In April 1944 the *Radfahr-Kompanie* was expanded into a *Fusilier-Bataillon*. The anti-tank battalion received enough assault guns to create a second company, and medical and signals battalions were also added. A replacement battalion of two companies was created and in August 1944 it was expanded from two companies to five, plus an anti-tank platoon of 75mm PAK-40 anti-tank guns.

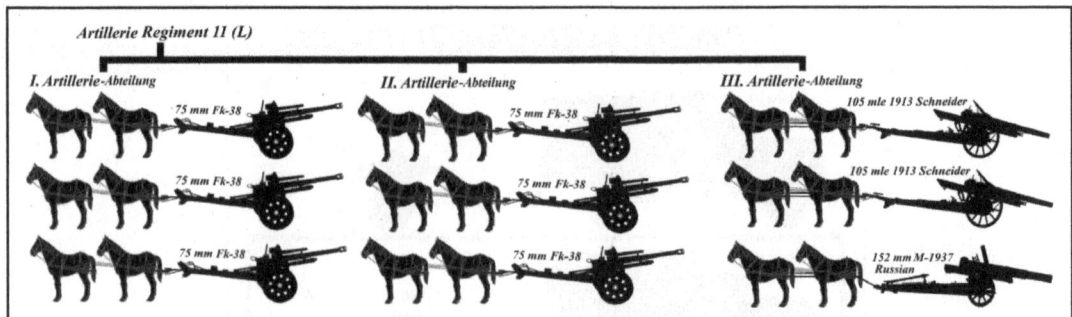

In August 1944 the artillery regiment was reorganized once again. The first and second artillery battalions received German artillery pieces.

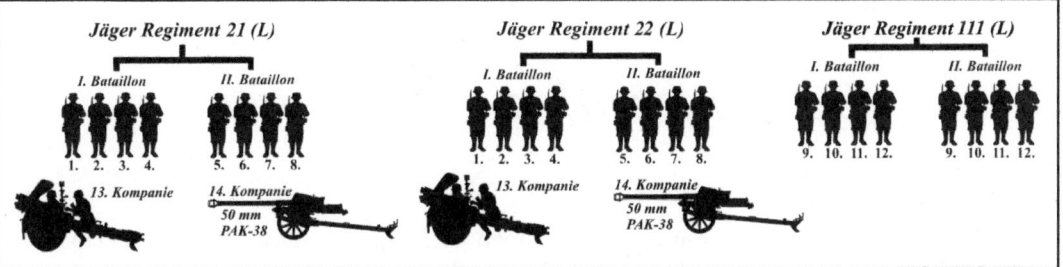

In February 1945 the decision was made to take the 3rd Battalion from each of the two *Jäger* regiments and create a third regiment, designated *Jäger-Regiment 111 (L)*. There was insufficient weaponry for a 13th and 14th Company to be created for this new regiment.

Organization of *11. Luftwaffen-Felddivision*

Commanders:
  Divisional Commander:
    Generalleutnant Karl Drum, 10/42–09/11/43
    Oberst Alexander Bourquin, 10/11/43–01/12/43
    Generalmajor Wilhelm Kohler, 01/44–10/44
    Generalmajor Gerhard Henke, 01/11/44–05/45
  Ia:
    Hauptmann Volrath Gerlach, 12/42–01/43
    Oberstleutnant Heinz Alewyn, 01/43–10/43
    Major i.G. Wolfgang Binder-Krieglstein, 01/12/43–10/44
    Major i.G. Bauernstätter, 01/11/44–05/45
  IIa:
    Hauptmann Roy, 10/12/43–05/45[58]
  CO *Luftwaffen-Artillerie-Regiment 11*:
    Oberstleutnant Herbert Roehler
  CO *Luftwaffen-Jäger-Regiment 21*:
    Oberst Walther Pawelke, 01/01/43–30/09/43
    Oberst Friedrich Edler von Braun, 10/43–01/11/43
  CO *Luftwaffen-Jäger-Regiment 22*:
    Oberst Mueller, 12/42–01/44
  CO *II. Bataillon / Luftwaffen-Jäger-Regiment 22*:
    Major von Saldern

On 10 November 1942 *Hauptmann* Wilhelm Thormeier was transferred to the divisional staff of *11. Luftwaffen-Felddivision*. He served in the division until 9 June 1944, when he was transferred to the *Flak* service of *Luftflotte 3*. *Major* Konrad Stapelfeld, who had also made a career in the *Flak* units, was transferred to *11. Luftwaffen-Felddivision* on 10 May 1943.

12. Luftwaffen-Felddivision

The cadre for this division came from men of *Flieger-Regiment 12*, which had been stationed initially in Handorf in Lower Saxony, but in 1942 was moved to Douai, about 45km south of Lille, near the Belgian-French border.[1] The division was initially formed at Troop Training Ground Bergen by Celle, also in Lower Saxony.[2] Sources state that the unit actually began organizing in December 1942, although elements for the division had begun to be assigned as early as October. One source states that the division was formed in *Wehrkreis XVIII*, the headquarters of which was in Salzburg, Austria.[3] *12. Luftwaffen-Felddivision* was initially formed around two principal infantry regiments: *Luftwaffen-Jäger-Regiment 23* and *Luftwaffen-Jäger-Regiment 24*. These two regiments each contained three *Jäger* battalions, each comprising four companies. While the line companies contained two heavy and thirteen light machine guns each, the *4. Kompanie* (4th Company) in each battalion was intended to be the *schwer* (heavy) company, equipped with six heavy machine guns and three light machine guns, plus four 120mm and six 80mm mortars.[4] The artillery regiment initially contained three artillery battalions. *I.* and *II. Artillerie-Abteilungen* of *Luftwaffen-Artillerie-Regiment 12* each possessed twelve French model 1897 75mm artillery howitzers, split up into three batteries of four guns apiece. *III. Artillerie-Abteilung* of *Luftwaffen-Artillerie-Regiment 12* was the divisional *Flak* battalion. *Flak* guns, no matter their calibre, cannot be used in the indirect fire role that artillery is designed for, therefore it was ludicrous to call the divisional *Flak* battalion the 3rd artillery battalion. It may have worked for administrative purposes, to have the *Flak* battalion attached to the artillery regiment, but in effect the division only had two battalions of actual artillery. The divisional anti-tank battalion contained one company of towed 75mm L-40 Pak anti-tank guns (12 guns), one light *Flak* company (12 × 20mm *Flak* guns) and an assault gun battery of ten *Sturmgeschütz-IV* assault guns carrying the 75mm L-48 anti-tank gun. The engineer battalion contained three companies. Each of these three companies was equipped with two heavy machine guns, nine light machine guns, six flamethrowers, two 80mm *Granatwerfer-34* (mortars) and an engineer column with engineer equipment.[5]

The communications battalion initially contained only one company, but in November 1943 it was expanded to three companies.[6] It was completely motorized and contained a signals supply column, radio company and telephone company. When the division reached the Russian Front in February 1943, it lacked a reconnaissance battalion, having only one *radfahr* (bicycle) company to act as its eyes and ears. The rest of the formation was composed of support and supply troops. Thus, initially, *12. Luftwaffen-Felddivision* looked like this:

Luftwaffen-Jäger-Regiment 23:
  I., II., III. Jäger-Bataillonen
Luftwaffen-Jäger-Regiment 24:
  I., II., III. Jäger-Bataillonen
Luftwaffen-Artillerie-Regiment 12:
  I., II., III. Artillerie-Abteilungen[7]
Luftwaffen-Panzerjäger-Abteilung 12
Luftwaffen-Radfahr-Kompanie der Luftwaffen-Felddivision 12
Luftwaffen-Nachrichten-Kompanie der Luftwaffen-Felddivision 12
Kommandeur von Nachschubtruppen und Versorgungs-Einheiten der
  Luftwaffen-Felddivision 12

After three short months of training, *12. Luftwaffen-Felddivision* was rushed by train to the sector of the Russian Front controlled by Army Group North and assigned to *XXVIII. Armeekorps, 18. Armee*. The division was posted to a defensive sector along the Volkhov Front and first saw action on 4 March 1943, west of the Kirischi bridgehead and south of Lake Ladoga.[8] The division was to remain in this region for the rest of 1943. It was partly responsible for helping to halt Soviet drives in the area of Kirischi in the spring of 1943. By June 1943, *18. Armee* had stabilized its front lines. *Luftwaffen-Felddivision 12* was located between

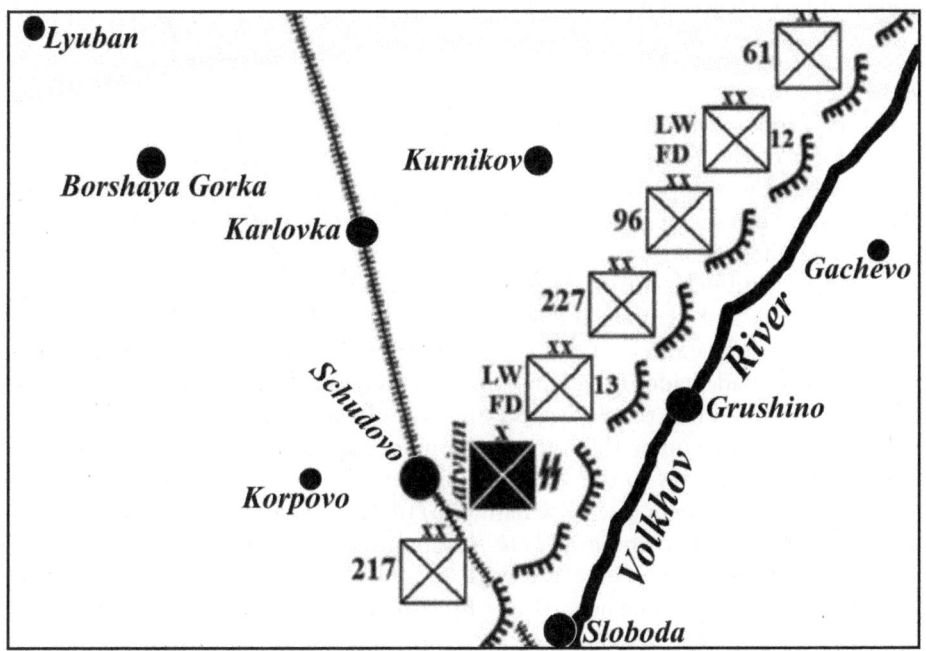

12. Luftwaffen-Felddivision, 4 June 1943.

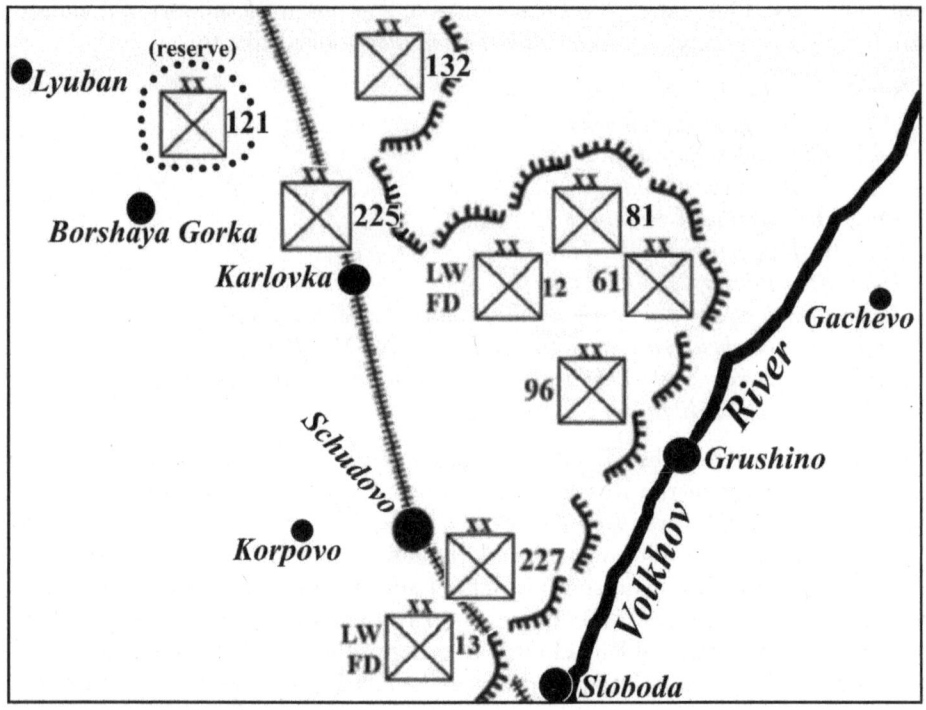

Positions of *12. Luftwaffen-Felddivision*, 1 July 1943.

61. and *96. Infanterie-Divisionen* around the Kirischi bridgehead and Pogoste pocket. The division was in the region of the Pogoste pocket northeast of Ljuban.

The division was engaged in stationary trench warfare around Didvino and Dubovik for most of 1943. In November 1943 two lieutenants of the divisional anti-tank battalion were awarded the German Cross in Gold for actions undertaken in the autumn of that year. These were *Oberleutnant* Günter Ohme, the commander of *4. Kompanie, Luftwaffen-Panzerjäger-Abteilung 12*, and *Oberleutnant* Werner Stuhlick, also of *Luftwaffen-Panzerjäger-Abteilung 12*.[9] Aside from probing attacks and artillery duels, the lines of *12. Luftwaffen-Felddivision* had remained relatively static for most of 1943, although towards the end of the year the Red Army had made inroads northwest of Grushino, by Karlovka, where a bulge was created after the Soviet penetration of the area.

Beginning in November 1943, the division once again underwent some reorganization. Major changes to the divisional artillery regiment included the transfer of *III. Artillerie-Abteilung* (the *Flak* battalion) of *Luftwaffen-Artillerie-Regiment 12* to *Luftwaffe* service, becoming *II. Flak-Abteilung* of *Flak-Regiment 6*. In February 1944 the artillery regiment received a new *III. Artillerie-Abteilung* and *IV. Artillerie-Abteilung*. The new *III. Artillerie-Abteilung* was originally *I. Artillerie-Abteilung* of *Luftwaffen-Artillerie-Regiment 13*. It contained four German 105mm artillery pieces, while *IV. Artillerie-Abteilung* was formed from scratch, using twelve French 155mm howitzers split into three batteries.[10] This reorganization basically expanded the division and gave it additional firepower. By 24 April 1944 *OKH* records showed the unit's Order of Battle as follows:

Jäger-Regiment 23 (L)
   I., II., III. Jäger-Bataillonen
Jäger-Regiment 24 (L)
   I., II., III. Jäger-Bataillonen
Jäger-Regiment 25 (L)[11]
   I., II. Jäger-Bataillonen
Artillerie-Regiment 12 (L)
   I., II., III., IV. Artillerie-Abteilungen
Panzerjäger-Abteilung 12 (L)
Fusilier-Bataillon 12 (L)[12]
   1., 2. Fusilier-Kompanie
   3. Radfahr-Kompanie
   4. Schwer Kompanie
Nachrichten-Abteilung 12 (L)
   Telefon-Kompanie
   Funk-Kompanie
   Signals-Versorgungs-Kompanie

On 3 December 1943 the forwardmost elements of the division were holding the city of Ssalzy. On 11 December *18. Armee* reported Red Army probing attacks against the lines of *Felddivision 12 (L)*, *96.* and *1. Infanterie-Divisionen*, but these were repulsed by the Germans. Thereupon, the Soviets resorted to heavy artillery barrages on the front lines of these divisions.[13] These Red Army probes were almost certainly geared to detect any weak positions along the German defence lines prior to their planned offensive in January 1944. The Luftwaffe division was listed at the end of 1943 as one of the stronger divisions of Army Group North. According to German documents, it was scheduled as a Category III formation – that is, capable of full defence.[14] Certainly it would feature prominently in the defensive battles against the Russian offensive that began on 14 January 1944. At this time the entire northern German army group had almost no reserves, since those few units that they had managed to hoard had been committed to the fighting at the so-called Panther positions.

Only two regiments of *Felddivision 12 (L)* had been withdrawn from the front lines and placed in reserve at the disposal of the army group. These two regiments had been immediately split into two combat groups. One was located in reserve southeast of Irboska, while the other was similarly in reserve southwest of Pskov.[15] As for the remainder of the division, it covered the front-line positions with an estimated nine to thirteen anti-tank guns and seven batteries of artillery of varying calibre and quality.[16] It staged a strong defence from 14 to 19 January, and then made a fighting withdrawal on 20 January 1944 to the Mga-Ssalzy railway line by Lipovik, Lyady and Grustynya. On 24 January *XXVIII. Armeekorps*

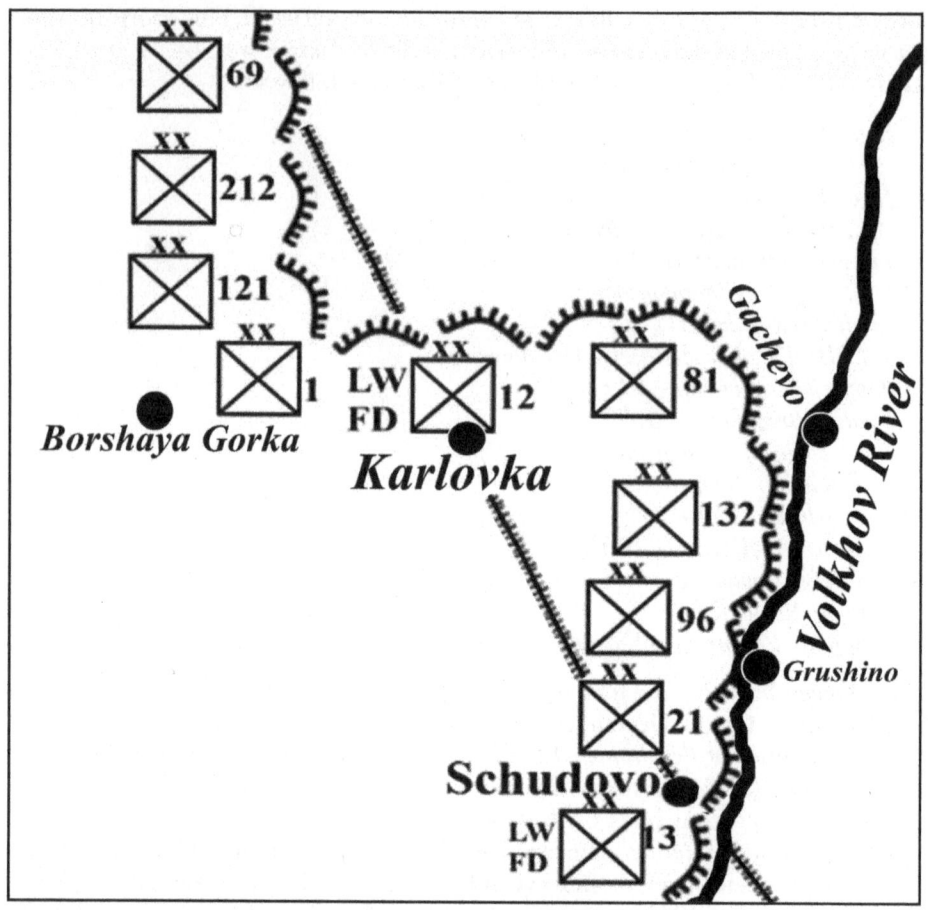

Detail of *12. Luftwaffen-Felddivision* positions in October 1943.

began to experience Soviet infantry attacks of regimental size. On that same day a breakthrough occurred in the defence lines of *Felddivision 12 (L)*. However, a rapid counterattack led personally by the divisional commander with a reserve *Jäger* battalion managed to temporarily stabilize the front lines.[17]

One day later *Felddivision 12 (L)* suffered breakthroughs in the areas by Drosdovo and Dubrovy,[18] and was forced to withdraw on 26 January 1944 to the area of Grushino and Schudovo.[19] On that same day Red Army tank units once again penetrated the division's lines at Tschudski-Bor and Dubrovy, affirming the rightness of the decision by the divisional commander, Gottfried Weber, to order the withdrawal of his division, lest it be surrounded.[20] The Soviet attack had been particularly heavy against the divisions of *XXVIII. Armeekorps*, but losses were even greater in the neighbouring positions of *XXXVIII. Armeekorps*. In fact, by the last week of January the divisions under *XXXVIII. Armeekorps* had been reduced to mere battle groups. These included *Kampfgruppe Schuldt*

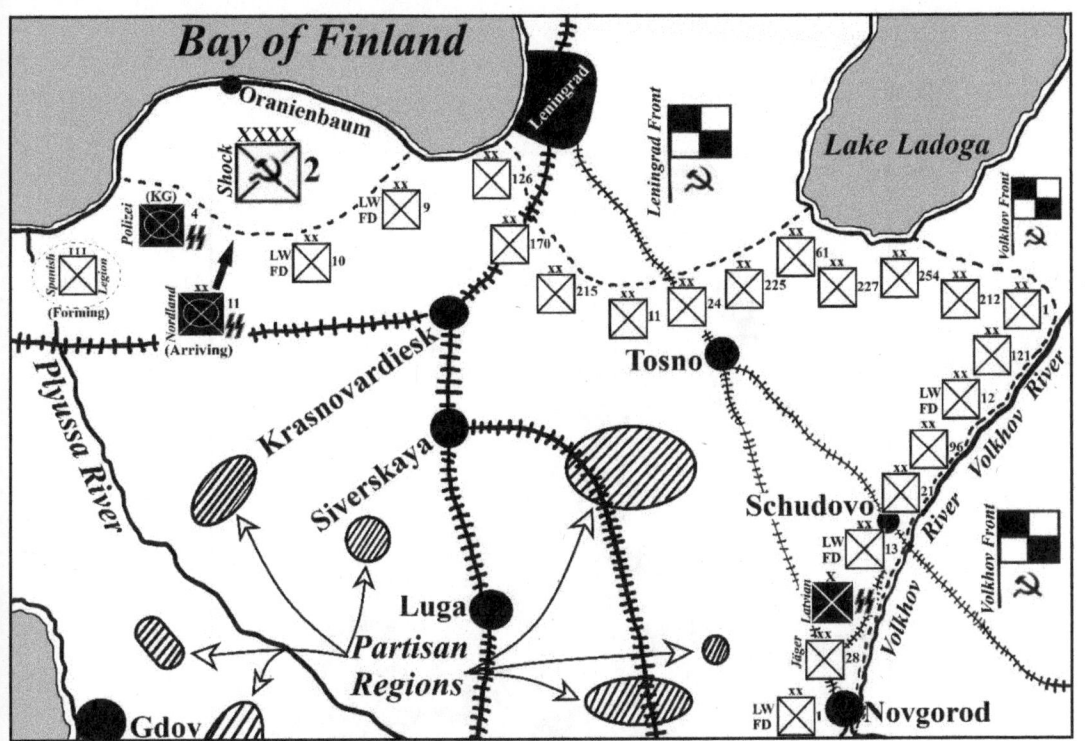

Location of divisions under Army Group North, from the Bay of Finland to Lake Ilmen, 3 December 1943. 12. *Luftwaffen-Felddivision* was located northeast of Schudovo, along the Volkhov river front.

(five battalions from *2. (lettische) SS-Freiwilligen-Brigade*, plus one reserve regiment from *Felddivision 12 (L)*, parts of *Felddivision 13 (L)*, Kampfgruppe *Speth* (the intact *Felddivision 1 (L)*), *28. Jäger-Division*, parts of *Kavallerie-Regiment Nord*, a few Estonian *Schuma* battalions, and *Kampfgruppe Bock* and *Kampfgruppe Pohl*, both of which were at regimental strength. In total, the strengths of these battle groups included 4,500 men for *Kampfgruppe Schuldt*, 2,200 for *Kampfgruppe Speth* and 1,200 each for *Kampfgruppe Bock* and *Kampfgruppe Pohl*. On 30 January half of the 9,100-man strength of *XXXVIII. Armeekorps* was withdrawn when *Kampfgruppe Schuldt* was shifted to *XXVIII. Armeekorps*.[21] On 2 February the division was located by the railway line between Ssalzy and Baleskaya; it then moved to Oredesh on 8 February and was by Luga on 9 February. From 10 to 13 February it defended Luga. The German forces formed a semicircle around that important north Russian city. On 3 February *Felddivision 12 (L)* was detached temporarily from the front lines and was moved to cover the junction between *XXVIII. Armeekorps* and *I. Armeekorps*.[22]

Similarly, the remnants of *Felddivision 13 (L)* were shifted to the same locality, and placed on the western flank in the area between the Luga positions and *58. Infanterie-Division*. A German document dated 7 February 1944 listed the division as having incurred heavy losses during the fighting withdrawal from the Volkhov Front. In almost a month of heavy fighting, the entire division had been reduced to a mere 7,424 men, out of whom only 1,481 men were the actual bayonet strength.[23] It had begun the withdrawal with around 11,000 men; during

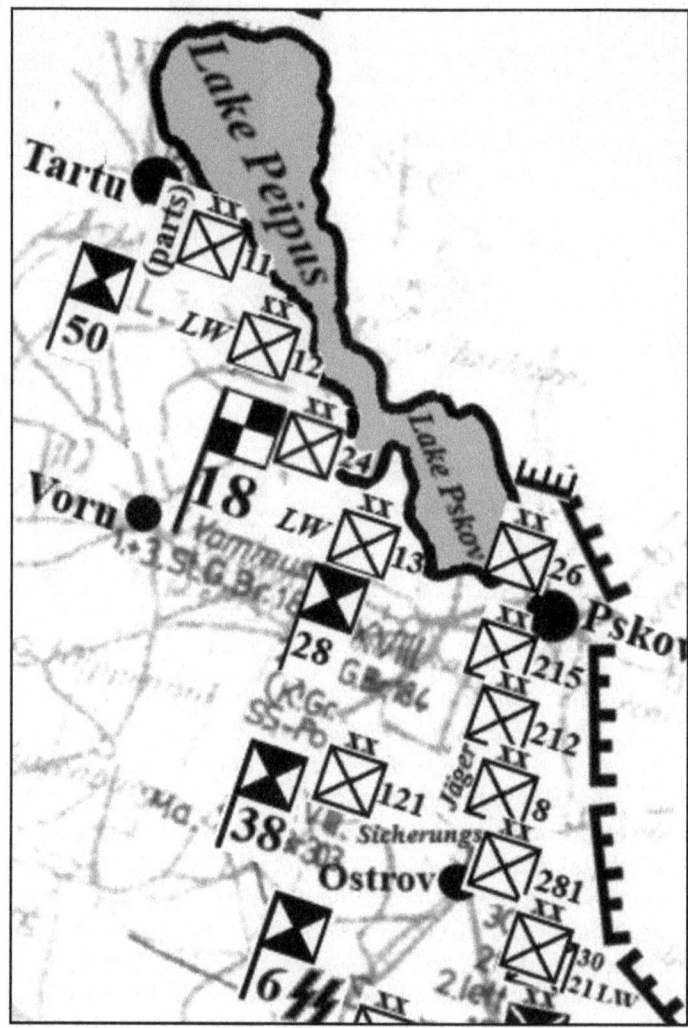

Positions of *18. Armee*, including *Felddivision 12 (L)*, as of 4 March 1944.

the withdrawal it had lost around 3,576 men. On 13 February *Felddivision 12 (L)* lost some ground on its left flank while fighting alongside *21.* and *58. Infanterie-Divisionen*. Red Army attacks against these three German divisions were particularly heavy on this date. In addition, the German units also had to deal with Soviet guerrilla bands that were attacking many German rear area units and positions.[24]

Three days later, on 16 February, it was the turn of the line companies defending the right flank of *Felddivision 12 (L)* to bear the brunt of the enemy attack.[25] One day later the division was reporting heavy enemy tank attacks, with a number of T-34 tanks destroyed by the *Landsers*.[26] The withdrawal of Army Group North continued throughout February. The retreat to the so-called *Bamberg Verteidigungslinie* (Bamberg Defence Line) began on 19 February 1944. During this withdrawal the Red Army placed heavy pressure on the units of *XXVIII. Armeekorps*. Continued heavy pressure on the right flank of *Felddivision 12 (L)* continued throughout that day.[27] As if targeted, *Felddivision 12 (L)* was particularly hardhit.[28] By 23 February the division had withdrawn to Pleskau (Pskov). On 25 February *Felddivision 12 (L)* and other units of *XXVIII. Armeekorps* began to launch local counter-attacks which managed to keep the attacking Red Army units temporarily off balance.[29]

By 27 February the division was located near Plyussa. The positions around Pskov were protected by Lake Peipus immediately to the north. Between 23 February and 14 August 1944 the division successfully defended Pskov. This was quite an achievement, given that the division was actually the strength of a brigade. Initially, *Felddivision 12 (L)* remained split up into two groups, one fighting alongside *8. Jäger-Division* while the other fought alongside parts of *126.* and *212. Infanterie-Divisionen* just south of Pskov. Two days later units of the division were shifted north and placed under *L. Armeekorps*.[30]

The division remained north of Pskov until August 1944. During that time it successfully blocked all Red Army attempts to break through north to Pskov. The second battle for Pskov occurred from 30 March to 17 April 1944. The Red Army initially gained a span of territory in the area of the greatly weakened *212. Infanterie-Division*, whose lines cracked in four different places. The men of one of the *Luftwaffe Jäger* regiments of *Felddivision 12 (L)* were immediately employed in a counterattack and succeeded in reaching the Lobany-Vanukha line, closing the hole in the lines. The other *Luftwaffe Jäger* regiment, stationed further north, was also employed in the counterattack but only managed to gain a few hundred metres of ground.[31]

In March *Felddivision 13 (L)* was finally disbanded and parts of this unit were used to reinforce the weakened *Felddivision 12 (L)*. During March the division was attached to *L. Armeekorps*, while the remnants of *Felddivision 13 (L)* were under *XXVIII. Armeekorps*. On 3 April the Soviets launched a total of four army corps, with a further three corps in reserve, against *215. Infanterie-Division*, *8. Jäger-Division* and *Felddivision 12 (L)*. The Soviet 53rd, 86th and 326th Rifle Divisions, which attacked the defence lines of *215. Infanterie-Division* in the region of Krapivinka and Letovo, were repulsed by the exhausted Swabian line companies from Wurtemberg.[32] *Felddivision 12 (L)* was holding the right flank of *215. Infanterie-Division*. On the right flank of the *Luftwaffe* infantrymen was *8. Jäger-Division*, in the region of Vernavino. There, *8. Jäger-Division* managed to give some ground to the six Red Army rifle divisions of 6th and 119th Rifle Corps. The greatest amount of territory lost occurred in the middle of these three divisions, that is, in the front lines of *Felddivision 12 (L)*. The division, which was holding the region of Podvorove and Sapatkino-Pavlona, was hit by no fewer than six rifle divisions (the 18th, 46th, 56th, 224th, 275th and 311th Rifle Divisions). A small bulge developed in the centre of the line, and for a time it seemed

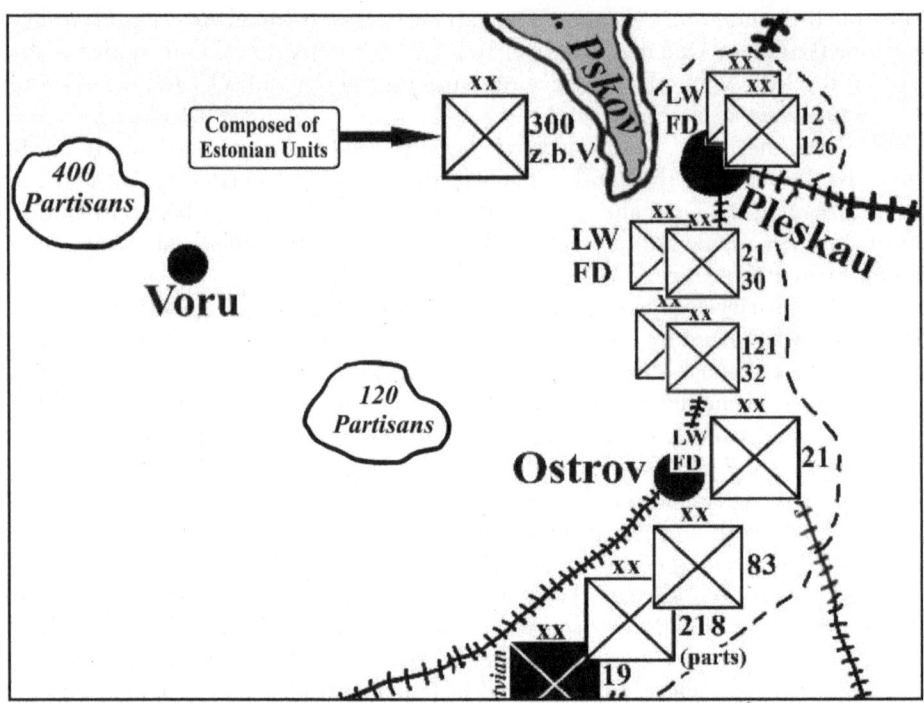

The defence of Pleskau (Pskov) by *Felddivision 12 (L)* and *30. Infanterie-Division* in June 1944.

that *215. Infanterie-Division* and *8. Jäger-Division*'s flanks would be enveloped. The town of Podvorove changed hands several times before the grenadiers of *Felddivision 12 (L)* finally halted the enemy assault.[33]

This victory was not without heavy losses, however. *Felddivision 12 (L)* had been in the hardest-hit positions and needed to be replenished. That fact alone meant that the German Army High Command considered this former *Luftwaffe* division to be a reliable unit. Between 4 and 8 April the Pomeranian regiments of *32. Infanterie-Division* took over the front-line positions that had recently been held by *215. Infanterie-Division* and *Felddivision 12 (L)*.[34] The division now shifted its location once again, when the East Prussian *21. Infanterie-Division* switched positions with it on 9 April 1944. By 15 April *Felddivision 12 (L)* was back under *XXVIII. Armeekorps*. In mid-April *Felddivision 13 (L)* ceased to exist[35] and *18. Armee* used its remnants to replenish and reinforce *Felddivision 12 (L)*.[36] *Division z.b.V. 300*, which controlled several regiments of Estonian frontier guard units, also received parts of *Felddivision 13 (L)*.[37] The divisional headquarters for *Division z.b.V. 300* was actually formed using the staff from *Felddivision 13 (L)*.[38] The line regiments could no longer sustain three *Jäger* battalions. There simply weren't enough replacements to support a three-battalion regiment. The decision was therefore made to reduce the size of *Jäger-Regiment 23 (L)* and *Jäger-Regiment 24 (L)* to two battalions apiece. In order to make up for the loss of the third battalion in each of the two regiments, the *1. Bataillon* of *Jäger-Regiment 25 (L)* and *Jäger-Regiment 26 (L)*, from the now-defunct *Felddivision 13 (L)*, were merged to become *I. Jäger-Bataillon* and *II. Jäger-Bataillon* of *Jäger-Regiment 25 (L)*. In addition, *I. Bataillon* of *Grenadier-Regiment 374* was now redesignated *Fusilier-Bataillon 12 (L)* of *Felddivision 12 (L)*.[39] The divisional artillery regiment, *Artillerie-Regiment 12 (L)*, was also reinforced by the addition of a fourth artillery battalion. All these efforts made it possible for *Felddivision 12 (L)* to continue as one of the most effective formations of *18. Armee*. It is certain that had it not been effective, Army Group North would have disbanded it.

On 2 May 1944 *Felddivision 12 (L)*, alongside *126.* and *215. Infanterie-Divisionen*, was still holding Pskov. Estonian frontier guard regiments, under the command of *Division z.b.V. 300*, were now guarding the left flank of the city, behind the west bank of Lake Pskov. *21.* and *30. Infanterie-Divisionen* covered the right flank of Pskov, while *Heeresgruppe Nord* assigned *XXVIII. Armeekorps* two armoured units as reserves: *schwere Panzer-Abteilung 502* and *Sturmgeschütz-Abteilung 184*. On 13 May *Heeresgruppe Nord* records listed that only seven out of its thirty-two divisions, including infantry, armour, security, etc., were at full combat readiness.[40] *Felddivision 12 (L)* was one of those seven divisions.[41] The rest of the divisions of Army Group North were in various stages of effectiveness. This report on the condition of *Felddivision 12 (L)* was confirmed on 18 July when *Heeresgruppe Nord* stated in their daily War Diary that *Felddivision 12 (L)* was considered one of the best of the seven divisions in the entire army group.[42] There is no clear explanation for this, given that most of the *Luftwaffe* field divisions performed so miserably. Was it because the division had a higher calibre of officers and NCOs? Was it weaponry? We will never really know. On 24 July 1944 *Heeresgruppe Nord* listed their divisions according to combat worthiness, as shown in Table 2.[43]

The spring and summer battles proved the worth and value of the men and officers of *Felddivision 12 (L)*. Those who were rewarded with acknowledgement included the following officers:[44] *Oberleutnant* Edwin Herian of *4. Kompanie/ Jäger-Regiment 24 (L)* and *Hauptmann* Hermann Gerken, CO of *1. Kompanie/*

Table 2. Combat readiness of divisions under Army Group North.

Combat effectiveness	Divisions under Army Group North
Fully combat effective	*11., 21., 30., 58., 61., 227. Infanterie-Divisionen* and *Felddivision 12 (L)*
Partially combat effective	*126., 225., 263., 389. Infanterie-Divisionen, 20. (estnische) Waffen-Grenadier-Division der SS, Felddivision 21 (L)*
Exhausted, only partially effective	*24., 32., 81., 83., 87., 93., 121., 132., 205., 215., 218., 290., 329. Infanterie-Divisionen* and *281. Sicherungs-Division*
Completely combat ineffective	*23. Infanterie-Division, 15.* and *19. (lettische) Waffen-Grenadier-Division der SS*

Jäger-Regiment 25 (L). After months of fighting, Army Group North also rewarded the divisional commander of *Felddivision 12 (L)*, *Generalmajor* Gottfried Weber, by bestowing on him the Oakleaves to his Knight's Cross. This award was presented to him on 9 June 1944. It was given to him for his excellent employment of the division during the difficult fighting withdrawal.[45] Weber was by now so well thought of that when Army Group North launched an attack to try to re-establish a land-link with German forces in East Prussia, after the army group had been cut off, he was given command of the armoured spearhead after the initial commander was severely injured in an auto accident, just before the counterattack was to start. Weber took command of the preparation and organization for the counteroffensive, but refused to lead the attack units because he claimed not to know the formation.[46]

By the beginning of September, the German divisions of Army Group North had been pushed back to Courland in Latvia, but they still held the Latvian capital, Riga. A bulge in the German divisions of *XXVIII., X., L.* and *I. Armeekorps* protected the Latvian capital in a semi-circle from northeast to southwest. *Felddivision 12 (L)* was still part of *XXVIII. Armeekorps*, which also included *21., 30.* and *61. Infanterie-Divisionen* and *31. Volksgrenadier-Division*. On 14 September 1944 the Red Army launched an offensive to retake the Latvian capital. While one Soviet army attacked the divisions of *16. Armee*, with the intention of tying them down, no fewer than eleven Soviet armies threw themselves against the German divisions in the Riga bridgehead across the Duna river. *Felddivision 12 (L)* repulsed a total of thirteen major Red Army assaults in as many days, but by 10 October losses had been so great that it was forced to withdraw from the front lines, along with *30., 122., 126., 215.* and *225. Infanterie-Divisionen*, which had been similarly mangled.[47]

The Soviets, for their part, had suffered grievous losses. Taking Riga had cost the Red Army about 72,000 casualties (killed, wounded or missing). It was a terrible butcher's bill, but one that the Russian Army could afford. The threat of being caught in a large pocket worried *Heeresgruppe Nord*. Chief of the Army General Staff Kurt Zeitzler and *Generalfeldmarschall* Walter Model were eventually able to convince the *Führer* to withdraw Army Group North west of Riga in order to avoid encirclement.[48] Nevertheless, *Heeresgruppe Nord* only got as far as Courland, as the Red Army was able to cut off its retreat to East Prussia and Poland.

During the battle for Riga the Germans had also taken heavy losses – losses that, unlike the Red Army, the *Heer* could not replace. *Felddivision 12 (L)* had been almost bled white. The unit needed to be replenished and given time to refresh, so the decision was made to place it on coastal defence duty in Courland. The division was transferred to the Vidale area (the northern part of Domesnäs) opposite the Sworbe peninsula separating the island of Saaremaa from the northern tip of Courland. Although this sounded like an easy duty, in reality the Red Army had been attempting to outflank the German defences by landing forces on the islands of Hiumaa and Saaremaa. On 13 October *Felddivision 12 (L)*

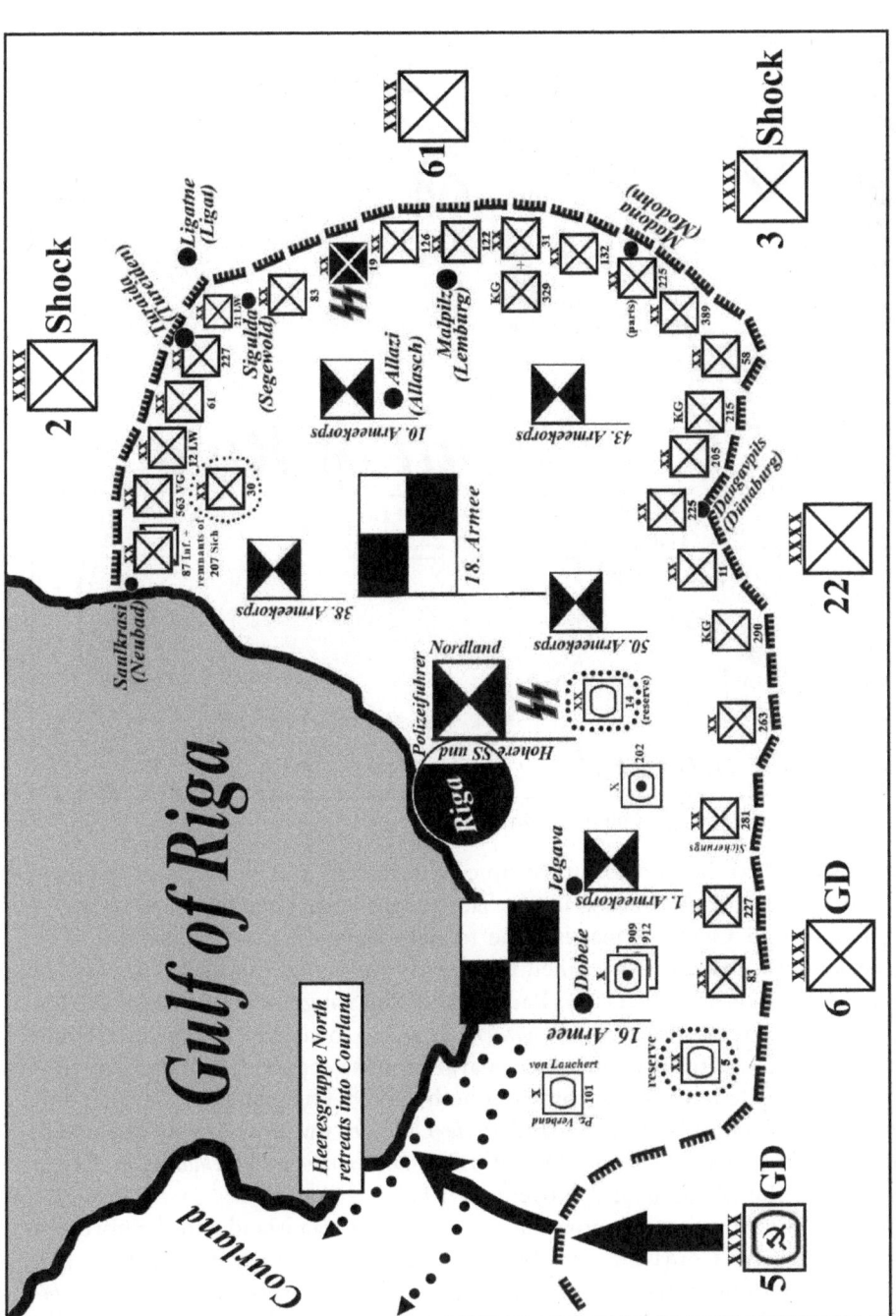

Location of XXVIII. *Armee* and XXVI. *Armee* divisions in and around the Latvian capital Riga, 4 October 1944. At this time, *Felddivision 12 (L)* was located between Saulkrasi (Neubad) and Turaida (Tureiden).

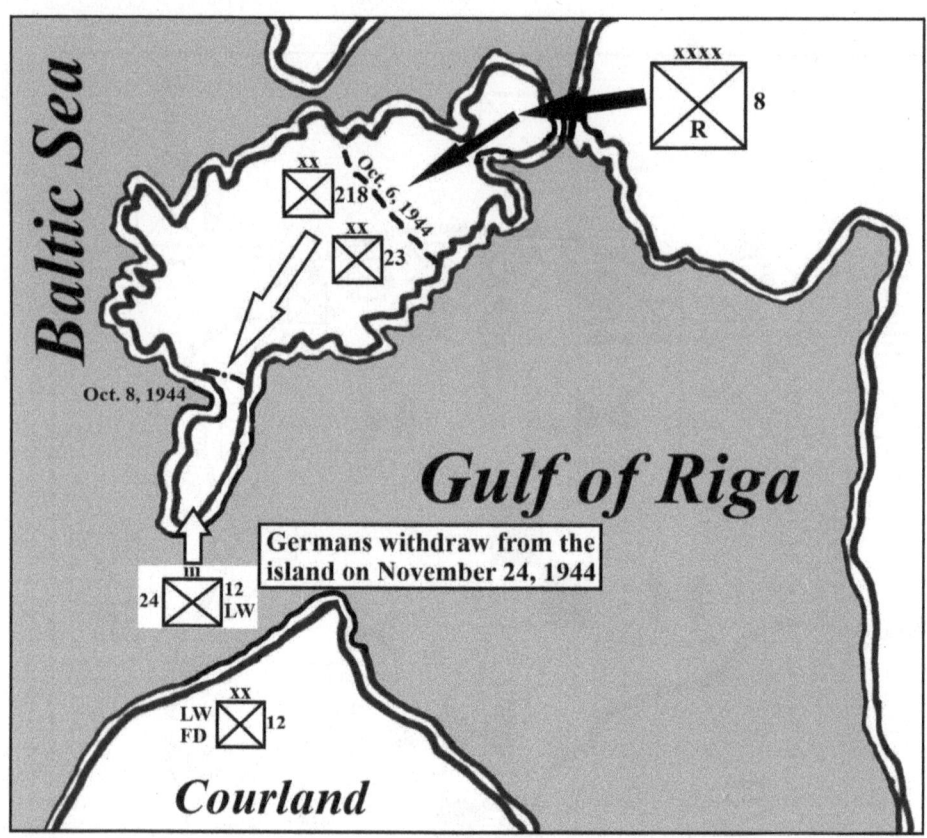

Employment of *Jägerregiment 23* on Saaremaa island.

was transferred to the northernmost tip of Courland[49] and elements of the division now began the task of crossing to Saaremaa island. They began to arrive on the island on 23 October, just in time to help stave off another disaster. The Soviets had just about overwhelmed the greatly weakened German defenders of *23.* and *218. Infanterie-Divisionen*. Bad weather and rough seas prevented the use of large ferries to transport *Jäger-Regiment 23 (L)* to the island and the men could only be sent across from Courland in naval mine-sweepers. The regiment thus arrived in a trickle but was welcomed nonetheless.[50] The principal German unit garrisoning Saaremaa island, *218. Infanterie-Division*, was now mostly evacuated, although elements of *23.* and *218. Infanterie-Divisionen* and *Felddivision 12 (L)* were still on the island as of 2 November 1944.

The *Luftwaffe* division was now stationed on Saaremaa island and the northern Latvian coast of Courland. It evacuated the island three weeks later, on 23 November 1944. Nine days earlier, on 14 November, those elements of *Felddivision 12 (L)* that had not been transported to the island were once again moved to the front lines in order to relieve the battle-weary Bavarian regiments of

*132. Infanterie-Division.*⁵¹ *Felddivision 12 (L)* was not strong enough to cover the front lines of *132. Infanterie-Division* alone, so *96. Infanterie-Division* assumed part of the front line. The division took part in fighting around Dzukste, Lestene and Frauenburg on both sides of Avotini. It launched attacks and performed defensive duties in the region of Pienava and Rozukalni east of Frauenburg and in the Vartaja positions in the area of Preekuln.⁵² *Oberleutnant* Heinz Hartogh, serving in the staff company of *Jäger-Regiment 25 (L)*, was acknowledged in writing for his bravery in action during the battles in November. He received this commendation on 7 December 1944.

On 1 December 1944 *Luftwaffe* forces in Courland stood as follows: under *16. Armee* there were a total of 7,680 personnel, while *18. Armee* had 25,039 men. Altogether, there were 32,719 *Luftwaffe* personnel in Courland. This figure included not only the members of *Felddivision 12 (L)* and *Felddivision 21 (L)*, but also *Luftwaffe* personnel from fighter, reconnaissance and bomber squadrons, ground crews, airfield defence, as well as units of anti-aircraft artillery, observation, command and control staffs, and communications units.⁵³ Some of these excess *Luftwaffe* personnel would end up helping to replenish not only the *Luftwaffe* divisions trapped there but other *Heer* divisions as well. The Third Battle of Courland began in earnest on 21 December at 7.20am. The initial attack was aimed at the German divisions of *I.* and *XXXVIII. Armeekorps*, but four days later, on Christmas Eve, the German divisions holding the town and surrounding region of Tuckum, among which was *Felddivision 12 (L)*, were the subject of heavy Soviet infantry and tank attacks. The Soviets launched two entire tank corps against the defence lines of *19. Waffen-Grenadier-Division der SS (lettische Nr. 2)*. This Latvian SS division had recently shown great combat spirit, but its men were overwhelmed by the sheer numbers of Russian tanks. Only through a swift counterattack, involving *Infanterie-Regiment 272* and *Infanterie-Regiment 366*, as well as *Jäger-Regiment 24 (L)*, was the front line stabilized and the situation saved. One report described the actions of the *Luftwaffe* soldiers: 'The 24. Luftwaffe Light Infantry Regiment under its excellent commander, Kretzschmar, stood like a rock in the surf. The Luftwaffe soldiers gave no ground without exacting a price. Kretzschmar died a soldier's death with his weapon in his hand.'⁵⁴ For his courageous leadership of *Jäger-Regiment 24 (L)* and his bravery in combat, *Oberst* Kretzschmar was posthumously awarded the Oakleaves and Crossed Swords to the Knight's Cross on 12 January 1945.⁵⁵

Unfortunately for the division, these successes did not come without heavy losses. During the month of December the divisional commander had to disband the following units:⁵⁶ *I. Bataillon/Jäger-Regiment 23 (L)*, *II. Bataillon/Jäger-Regiment 24 (L)* and *II. Bataillon/Jäger-Regiment 25 (L)*. In order to keep the division at a fairly normal level of effectiveness, a Latvian security battalion was absorbed into *Jäger-Regiment 24 (L)*, becoming *II. Bataillon* in the regiment. In addition, *Feldersatz-Bataillon 12 (L)* was reorganized into a combat school for possible employment. In all, *Felddivision 12 (L)* could now only count on six combat battalions.

January 1945 brought the launching of yet another Soviet offensive against the trapped German divisions in Courland. This, the Fourth Battle of Courland, eventually bogged down in snow and the first mud of spring. Between 1 January and 3 February 1945 the Soviets lost 40,000 men, 541 tanks and 178 planes – during a period when no major Red Army attacks were being conducted. When the Red Army launched what would be called the Fifth Battle of Courland, the brunt of this major assault fell on both sides of the Latvian city of Preekuln (Priekule). This region was held by *121., 126., 263.* and *290. Infanterie-Divisionen*, as well as *Felddivision 12 (L)*. A total of 21 Soviet rifle divisions and 7 tank brigades now threw themselves against the lines of five tired and weakened German divisions. *121. Infanterie-Division*, which was holding Priekule itself, was particularly hard-hit. Slowly the German lines were pushed back. Only through the arrival and employment of the Saxon *14. Panzer-Division* and the Prussian *11. Infanterie-Division*, as well as *Sturmgeschütz-Brigade 912* – the entire armoured and infantry reserve of Army Group Courland – was this fifth major Russian assault halted. Although heavily engaged, Army Group Courland had been used by Adolf Hitler as a ready source of reinforcements for the crumbling front in Prussia and Poland.

The Soviets had launched their invasion of Prussia and Poland on 12 January 1945. This offensive soon placed Red Army units on the eastern border of the *Reich*. The Germans were desperate to defend the *Heimat* (homeland) but lacked the troops to do so properly. Those who remained in the crumbling *Reich* were training and replacement units, men on convalescent leave, and *Volkssturm* and *Hitler Jugend* units made up of the very old and the very young. Hitler, running short on reinforcements, once again called on the beleaguered Courland Army Group to supply further divisions for the main front. It wasn't long before *Felddivision 12 (L)*, as weakened as it now was, was recalled home in order to take part in the final agonizing defence of the *Reich*.[57] The division received its marching orders on 4 March 1945, and withdrew through the port of Libau (Liepaja) on the western Latvian coast.[58] Having involved himself increasingly in the minutest details of just about every military operation, Hitler personally ordered where exactly *Felddivision 12 (L)* was to be placed after its arrival in Danzig: 'The Führer has ordered that the 12. Air Force Field Division, after arriving, is to be sent from Gotenhafen harbour directly to the area south of Preussich-Stargard.'[59]

On 8 March 1945 two freighters were en route to the port city of Danzig with the initial batch of soldiers from *215. Infanterie-Division* and *Felddivision 12 (L)*. This preliminary group of *Luftwaffe* troops consisted of the following men and equipment:[60] 519 men, 56 motor vehicles, 142 horses, 80 wagons and 14 guns of various calibres. The bulk of the division (what was left of it) began arriving in Danzig harbour two days later, beginning on 10 March 1945. It was on this date that *4. SS-Panzergrenadier-Division 'Polizei', 215. Infanterie-Division* and *Felddivision 12 (L)* were officially transferred from Army Group Courland to Army Group Vistula.[61] The Germans pressed into action the initial group from *215. Infanterie-*

Division and *Felddivision 12 (L)* as soon as the men stepped off the boats. *Felddivision 12 (L)* was placed between *252. Infanterie-Division* and *542. Volksgrenadier-Division* on 13 March, when the advance guard of *Felddivision 12 (L)* reached the front lines.[62] By then, however, the Red Army had captured most of Eastern Pomerania, thus effectively cutting off the retreat of German forces in West Prussia. Inside Danzig were 1.5 million terrified German civilians, about 100,000 wounded soldiers and the remnants of the German *2. Armee*.[63] The units in this pocket extended in a semi-circle from just northwest of Gotenhafen to southeast of Neustadt and east of Schönwalde. The lines then ran south to an area east of Karthaus and through the front-line towns of Rheinfeld and Löblau.

On the eastern half of the pocket, the lines extended from Löblau to Dirschau, then northeast to Neuteich, Tiegenhof and finally Stutthof on the Bay of Danzig by the Frisches Haff. Between 10 and 17 March 1945 further troops and equipment reached Danzig: 1,075 men, 127 motor vehicles, 651 horses and 271 wagons.[64] A *Funk-Fernschreiben* (radio-telex) dated 17 March 1945 ordered that those elements of *215.* and *389. Infanterie-Divisionen*, alongside *Felddivision 12 (L)*, that had not yet arrived at Danzig but were no longer a part of Army Group Courland – that is, those troops en route to Danzig but still at sea, were to be diverted to Swinemünde and other ports west of the Oder river.[65] This order does not seem to have been followed immediately, however, since the Luftwaffe division arrived and was deployed under *2. Armee* as stated. Eventually the whole division would arrive in Danzig. The entire divisional strength of *Felddivision 12 (L)* was about average for a German unit at this late stage in the war, especially one which had been so heavily engaged (see Table 3).[66]

The telex order was eventually acted upon on 19 March, and the remnants of *Felddivision 12 (L)* were finally withdrawn from the Danzig pocket on 31 March through the port of Gotenhafen.[67] The decision to move had been reached for a simple reason: the Russians were already on the Oder river, threatening the German capital. Allowing those arriving German divisions to remain in the Danzig pocket would be militarily useless. The initial location of the division's defence line was in the region of Löblau-Prangenau but was later switched to the area in and around Klein Saldau. On 15 March the division was holding positions 12–14km southwest of Danzig.[68] Between 15 and 19 March remnants of the Bavarian *4. Panzer-Division* began to be inserted between the defensive positions of the Silesian *252. Infanterie-Division*, fighting around Zuckau, and *Felddivision*

Table 3. Strength of *Felddivision 12 (L)*, March 1945.

	Strength	% of full strength
Manpower	4,571	88%
Motor vehicles	443	78%
Horses	1,203	58%
Wagons	483	40%

134 Hitler's *Luftwaffe* Infantry

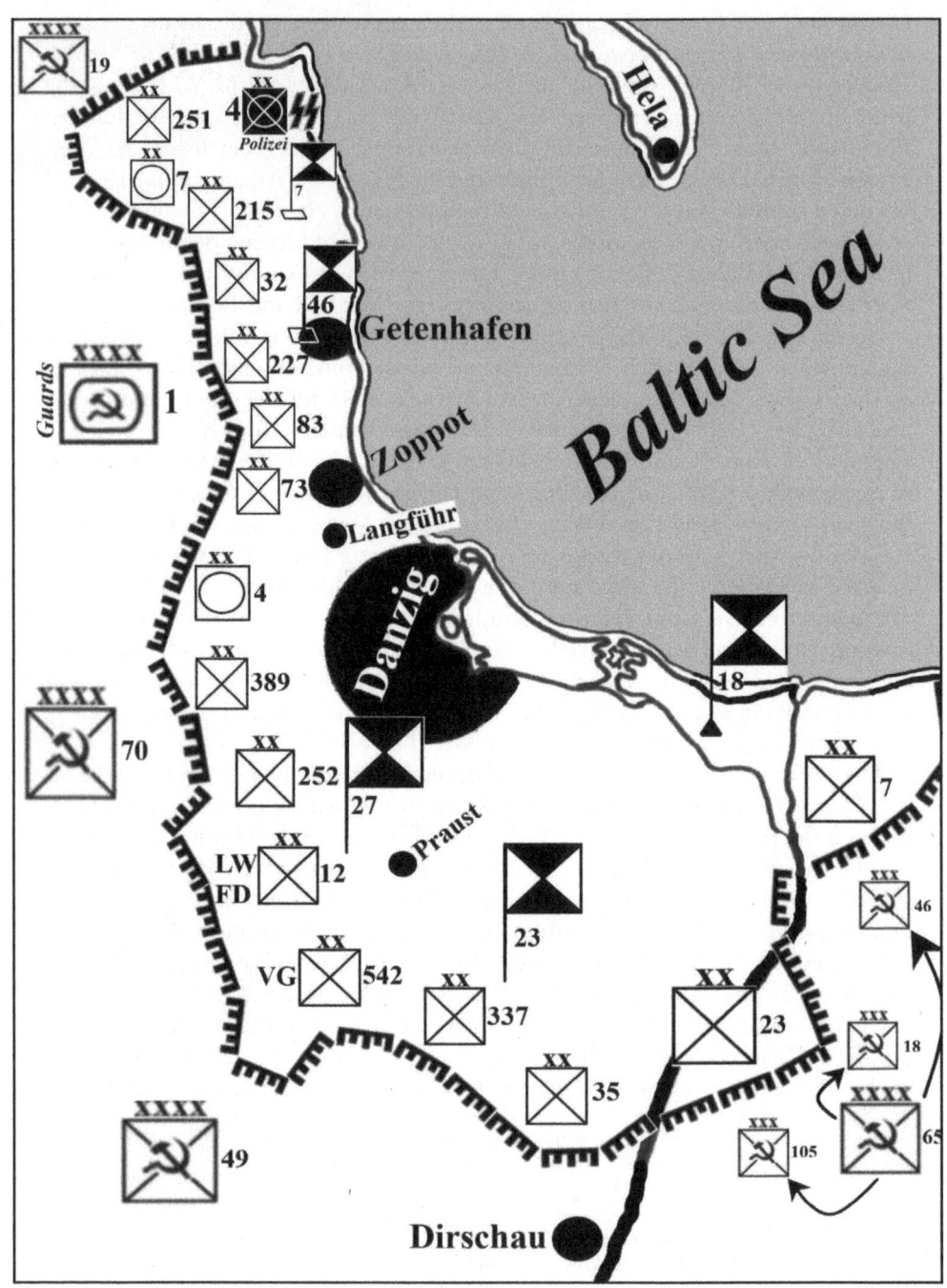

Felddivision 12 (L) and the defence of Danzig, March 1945.

12 (L). In this way, the *Luftwaffe* field division was shifted down to a defence line which stood about 9–10km southwest of Praust.[69] The division was still part of *XXIII. Armeekorps / 2. Armee* on 23 March. This corps not only included *Felddivision 12 (L)* but also contained *4. Panzer-Division*, and *23., 35.* and *252. Infanterie-Divisionen*.[70] However, by 25 March communications between the corps and army headquarters had been completely disrupted. On their own initiative, the surviving battlegroups of *252.* and *389. Infanterie-Divisionen*, as well as *Felddivision 12 (L)*, immediately subordinated themselves to the headquarters of *4. Panzer-Division*. These units had been fighting around Danzig.[71]

On 25 March the main line of resistance for the division was around the town of Praust, just south of Danzig. *Felddivision 12 (L)* was finally destroyed between 23 and 30 March 1945. A small group of men from the division did manage to make a fighting withdrawal through Löblau-Prangenau, then via Klein Saldau, Müggenhal, Danzig-Langführ and Zoppot to Gotenhafen (Gdingen), where they managed to board an evacuation ship on 31 March and reached the German province of Schleswig-Holstein in April 1945.[72]

Thus, the end finally came for this German *Luftwaffe* field division. It had existed from December 1942 until the end of March 1945, a span of 28 months. It fought in some of the fiercest battles of the Eastern Front and acquitted itself well. Its officer corps was deemed excellent and the division was considered by both Army Group North and Army Group Courland as one of the best divisions they had. It received army commanders from November 1943, plus army and air force reinforcements and replacements in 1944, but its performance before then was equally good. Its combat history can be considered unusual since it performed less like a typical mediocre *Luftwaffe* field division, and more like a

12. Luftwaffe Felddivision in December 1942.

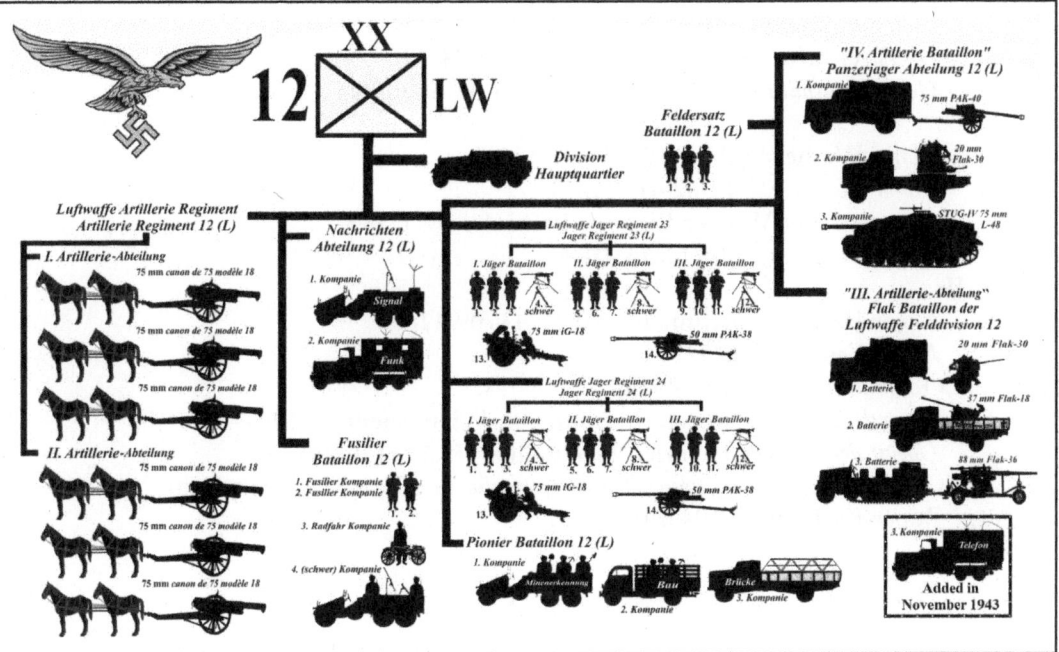

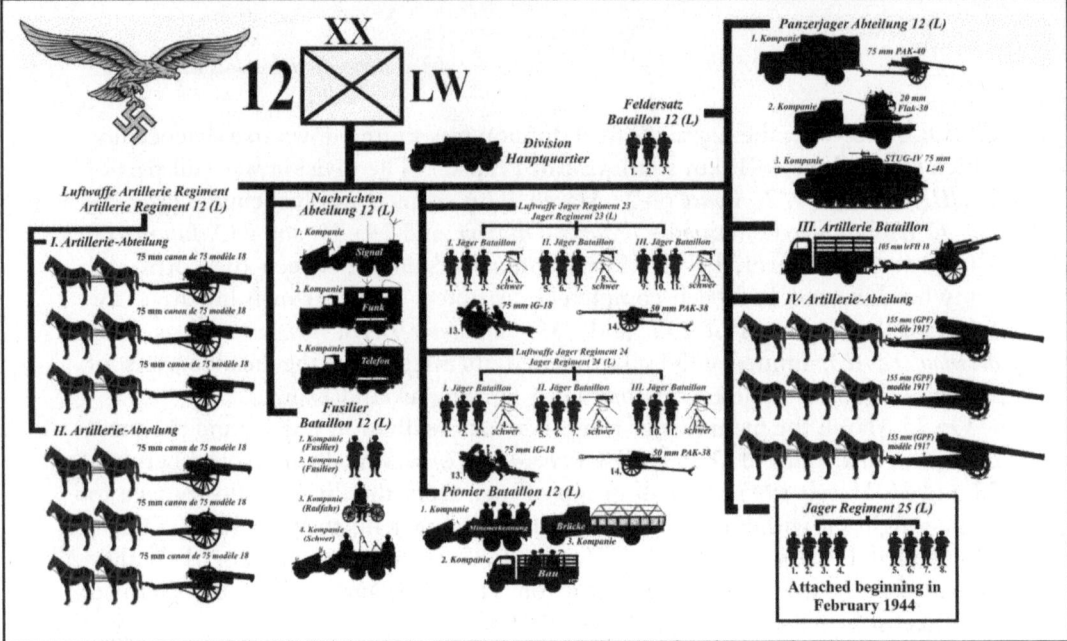

Felddivision 12 (L) in January 1944.

regular *Heer* infantry division. We can therefore consider *12. Luftwaffen-Felddivision*/*Field Division 12 (L)* as either the best or second-best division out of the twenty-two *Luftwaffe* field divisions raised by the *Luftwaffe*. The only other *Luftwaffe* field division that performed as well as *12. Luftwaffen-Felddivision* was *Luftwaffen-Felddivision 'Meindl'/21. Luftwaffen-Felddivision*.

Organization of *12. Luftwaffen-Felddivision*

Commanders:
  Divisional Commanders:
    Generalleutnant Herbert Kettner, 14/12/42–15/11/43
    Oberst Gottfried Weber,[73] 15/11/43–10/04/45
    Generalleutnant Franz Schlieper, 10/04/45–08/05/45
  Ia:
    Major Werner Stubbe, 10/42– 01/12/42
    Major Steuer, 02/12/42–09/12/43
    Oberstleutnant Werner Richter, 10/12/43–09/12/44
    Major i.G. Fox,[74] 10/12/44–04/45
  IIa:
    Major Herbert Furchtmann, 10/12/43–09/12/44
    Major Fasel, 10/12/44–04/45
  CO *Artillerie-Regiment 12 (L)*:
    Oberstleutnant der Reserve Joachim von Wietersheim, 3/1943–05/1944[75]
    Oberst der Reserve Heinrich Fronmüller, 05/1944–05/45
  CO *III. Artillerie-Abteilung/Artillerie-Regiment 12 (L)* [*Flak* battalion]:
    Major Karl Feiler, 1944/45

CO *Jäger-Regiment 23 (L)*:
   Oberst Günther Jordan
CO *II. Bataillon / Luftwaffen-Jäger-Regiment 23*:
   Major Georg Schreiber, 20/01/42–12/44
CO *Jäger-Regiment 24 (L)*:
   Oberstleutnant Wolfgang Kretschmar, 03/43–27/12/44[76]
   Oberstleutnant Eduard Kreuzer, 28/12/44–22/02/45[77]
CO *I. Jäger-Bataillon / Jager Regiment 24 (L)*:
   Major der Reserve Hermann Warnecke,[78] 17/06/43–?
CO *Jäger-Regiment 25 (L)*:
   Major Kilian Otto Weimar, 1943–1944
CO *1. Jäger-Bataillon / Jäger-Regiment 25 (L)*:
   Hauptmann Franz Piehler, 1943–1944

One source listed the commanders of *Luftwaffen-Jäger-Regiment 24* as the following:[79]

CO *Luftwaffen-Jäger-Regiment 24*:
   Oberst Anton Longin, 04/43–09/43
   Oberstleutnant Hans-Günther von Obernitz, 11/09/43–12/43

Major Josef Steffen (b. 17 December 1908) was an officer in the division. He was promoted to *Major* on 1 April 1942 and on 19 June 1943 was transferred to *12. Luftwaffen-Felddivision*. *Major* Richard Witt was transferred to the general staff of *16. Luftwaffen-Felddivision* on 12 June 1943. *Major* Hugo Wiebe was transferred to *12. Luftwaffen-Felddivision* on 2 April 1943.

13. Luftwaffen-Felddivision

13. Luftwaffen-Felddivision was raised on 15 November 1942, using *Flieger-regiment 13*, at Troop Training Ground Fallingbostel, near Neubiburg. The core of this division was formed around six *Jäger* battalions split into two regimental headquarters. To support the two infantry regiments, the division was given a four-battalion artillery regiment and an anti-tank battalion, plus engineer, bicycle and signals companies.[1] The division also received a company of *Sturmgeschütz III* (assault guns), which became part of the divisional anti-tank battalion.[2] Actual training was later shifted to Troop Training Ground Gross-Born in Pomerania, where the two *Jäger* regiments of the division were formed. These two regiments were deemed ready in January 1943.[3] The division began moving to the Eastern Front, in the area of Army Group North, as early as January 1943. This was a concerted move by the Germans to reinforce the entire Eastern Front in the midst of the Soviet winter offensive which began on 19 November 1942 and had encircled *6. Armee* in the south, but had also caused lots of trouble for the Germans all across the front lines. The southern German army group had drawn no fewer than four *Luftwaffe* field divisions: the *5.*, *7.*, *8.* and *15. Luftwaffen-Felddivisionen*.

The Red Army applied pressure to other parts of the Eastern Front in an attempt to draw as many German reinforcements as possible away from the southern regions of the front. This included launching offensive operations in the regions of *Heeresgruppe Nord* and *Heeresgruppe Mitte*. Because of this, both army groups had to be reinforced. *Heeresgruppe Nord* received the *1.*, *9.*, *10.*, *12.*, *13.* and *21. Luftwaffen-Felddivisionen*. Another air force field division, *22. Luftwaffen-Felddivision*, was scheduled to be assigned to *Heeresgruppe Nord*, but it was disbanded before it could be fully established. *Heeresgruppe Mitte* eventually received *2.*, *3.*, *4.* and *6. Luftwaffen-Felddivisionen*. Clearly, the majority of these new air force infantry formations were directed to *Heeresgruppe Nord*, where they were needed the most, for several reasons. First, it was believed that because the front lines in the north were more or less fixed, these new and largely untrained *Luftwaffe* units would have a better chance to gain combat experience, with a minimal risk to the German lines breaking. Initially, this proved to be the case, although the Red Army soon began to launch probing attacks against these divisions, testing their combat abilities. The Soviets rapidly learned their weaknesses, and from then on coordinated their offensives with the intention of driving the main brunt of their assaults against these weak air force field divisions. The intent was obvious: overwhelm these weak *Luftwaffe* divisions and guarantee a breakthrough.

Secondly, the German Army High Command did not have much confidence in the fighting value of these new air force infantry divisions, so they sent the vast majority of them north, in order to divert more experienced combat divisions to Army Group South, which was in desperate need of veteran formations. As it turned out, the shortage of German divisions was so great that eventually four of these untried air force units were sent to *Heeresgruppe Süd* (Army Group South) anyway. Thirdly, the Germans diverted regular German divisions from Army Group North to Army Group South because better quality units were needed in the south, and this contributed to the demand to replace those divisions in the north. The *Luftwaffe* field divisions seemed a likely choice, given the few options available to the German Army in the winter of 1942/43. Fourthly, the terrain in which Army Group North operated was mainly composed of rivers, lakes, swamps and forest regions, with some hills interspersed throughout. This afforded weaker formations natural defences to augment their defensive value. Since the *Luftwaffe* units were considered inexperienced and weak, OKH hoped that they would stand a better chance of surviving Eastern Front in the northern region of the Soviet Union. It was hoped that *13. Luftwaffen-Felddivision* would fare better in the region of Army Group North on account of the region's numerous rivers, forests, swamps, and even some hills. Topography that would benefit a unit on the defense. In addition, The front lines of the army group had been and up until 1943, relatively static[4]

The bulk of the division arrived in February 1943, although advance elements had reached Schudovo on the Volkhov river front in late January. The division was placed under the control of *I. Armeekorps/18. Armee* from February to September 1943. In July its neighbouring German divisions included the *(lettische) Waffen-Grenadier-Brigade der SS* of *XXXVIII. Armeekorps* and *227. Infanterie-Division* of *I. Armeekorps*.[5] Beginning in October, the division was transferred to *XXXVIII. Armeekorps/18. Armee*.[6]

In the course of 1943, the division took part in several key battles. The most notable, which occurred in July, was the Third Battle of Lake Ladoga. The division was located south of the Kirichi bridgehead and Pogoste pocket, on the Volkhov river.[7] It was not at the centre of the fighting, most of which took place between Mga and Schlüsselburg, but defended the eastern approaches to the city of Schudovo (aka Chudovo).[8] The division held its river line positions throughout 1943, but was never used in any major attack, given that its strength never exceeded that of a large brigade. The German command was also probably afraid that the unit might break apart, as reports were coming in from all of the army groups of the collapse of many of these *Luftwaffe* field divisions in combat.

In November 1943 the division was absorbed into the *Heer*, alongside the other existing *Luftwaffe* field divisions. Reorganization started, and the transfer of some German Army officers and NCOs began in order to increase the combat effectiveness of the division. The divisional *Flak* battalion, which had acted as the

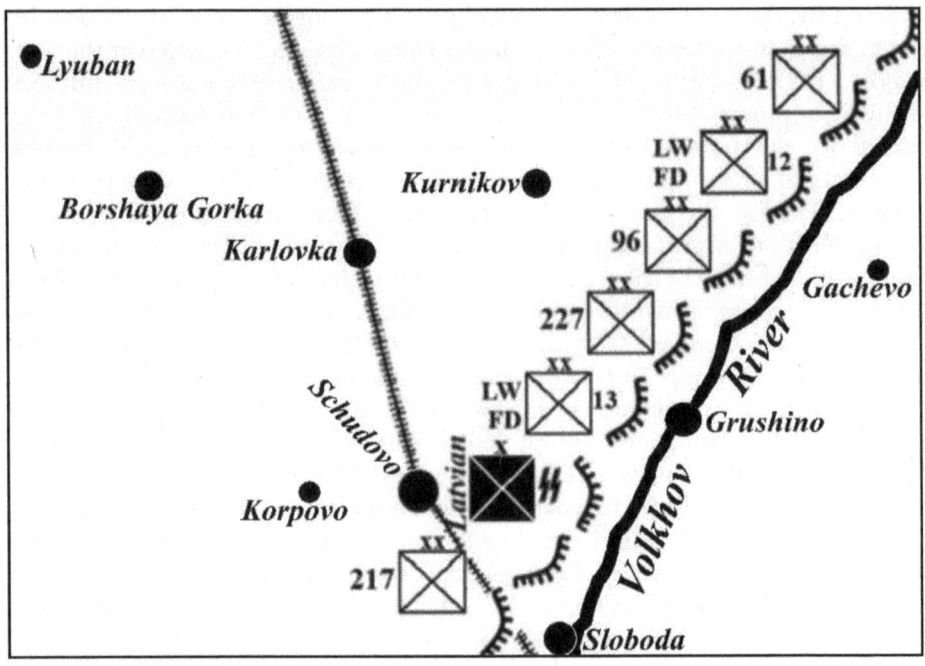

Location of *13. Luftwaffen-Felddivision*, June 1943.

IV. Artillerie-Abteilung in the artillery regiment, was detached and returned to *Luftwaffe* service. It eventually became *I. Flak-Abteilung* of *Flak-Regiment 54 (motorisiert)*.[9] The real change occurred within the *Jäger* regiments, as the third battalions of both regiments were disbanded. Now each regiment contained two battalions apiece.[10] In addition, *Luftwaffen-Jäger-Regiment 26* was renamed *Jäger-Regiment 24 (L)* and assigned to *Felddivision 12 (L)* because of heavy losses suffered by *Luftwaffen-Jäger-Regiment 24*. It seems that the divisional bicycle company, *Radfahr-Kompanie der Luftwaffen-Felddivision 13*, remained active even after the *Heer* assumed control.[11] Aside from these changes, the table of organization for the division remained the same. In effect, its power had not really been increased. In fact, its anti-tank strength as of January 1944 stood at only twelve anti-tank guns – totally inadequate for defensive operations, let alone offensive moves.[12] This figure would later rise to sixteen anti-tank guns shortly before the start of the Red Army offensive in January 1944.[13] However, the addition of four extra anti-tank guns would not substantially increase the division's defensive capacity. From the start of its operational history, the command staff of Army Group North never considered *Felddivision 13 (L)* as an offensive formation. But the almost continuous crisis in their sector of the Russian Front prevented their making any real effort to reinforce this former *Luftwaffe* unit with anything more than a transfusion of some *Heer* officers and NCOs. In fact, the withdrawal of the *Flak* battalion weakened the division further. In some cases, the

Army was able to reinforce the air force divisions, but in many cases these changes were only window dressing. This was the case with *Felddivision 13 (L)*.

This inability to properly reinforce the division would lead directly to its destruction when it was faced with a determined and prolonged Red Army attack. As stated earlier, the disasters in the southern regions of the Russian Front had necessitated the transfer of German forces from Army Group North to the south at the end of 1942. This thinning of German units from the northern part of the Eastern Front continued through 1943. For example, in the second half of 1943 no fewer than thirteen divisions were withdrawn from *Heeresgruppe Nord*, with two additional divisions leaving in December 1943 and January 1944.[14] The Red Army was not blind to these transfers, and adjusted their offensives accordingly. When the Germans reinforced one sector of the Eastern Front with forces removed from another part of the front, the Soviets would launch an offensive in the region of the front lines that had just been weakened. Thus, the stage was set for yet another disaster, this one in the north. The constant shifting of the few available forces from one critical point to another typified the German reaction to Soviet offensive operations from mid-1943 onwards. The German decision to transfer what few available divisions they had from one region of the Eastern Front to another was borne out of necessity. However, it was a recipe for more German military reversals. Given the lack of proper German reinforcements for the Russian front, there was little that *OKH* could do. German reinforcements to the Eastern Front continued to be a mere trickle until the spring of 1945, when *6. Panzerarmee* was shifted from the Western to the Eastern Front. However, by then the war in the East was lost. *Generalleutnant* Hellmuth Reymann, a *Heer* officer, was assigned as the new divisional commander, while *Major* Koch became the operations officer.[15] Reymann would go on to be the last commander of the Berlin Defence Area, which in April 1945 Hitler decreed was a *festung* (fortress).[16]

When the Soviet offensive began in January 1944 in the region of Army Group North, *Felddivision 13 (L)* was still located behind the Volkhov river by Chudovo. The Red Army had waited until the Volkhov river became frozen before launching their attack, thus negating this natural defensive barrier. *Felddivision 13 (L)* had to cover a front line about 25km long. This meant that the *Luftwaffe* men had only one anti-tank gun for almost 2km of frontage. Given this and other discrepancies that greatly weakened the division, coupled with the fact that the Red Army attacked with overwhelming numbers of men and tanks, the outcome of the battle along the Volkhov river was decided even before combat began. For the Red Army, the attack against *Felddivision 13 (L)* was part of the greater plan to oust the Germans from the Leningrad region and free the city for ever from the threat of attack. But the region held by *Felddivision 13 (L)* had great significance since it was at Chudovo three years earlier, in August 1941, that the Germans had initially cut the Leningrad–Moscow railway line, setting the stage for the siege of Leningrad. The German command was well aware of the deficiencies in the front lines. In fact, in the area of Army Group North a total of 46,500 people (of whom

24,000 were civilians) were working on the so-called Panther positions, a fortified area behind the front lines that the Germans could withdraw to.

In January 1944, however, these defensive works were not yet completed. The initial attack along the Volkhov river front did not fall against *Felddivision 13 (L)* at Chudovo, but rather struck *Felddivision 1 (L)* further south at Novgorod. The assault also involved Red Army attacks against the neighbouring *28. Jäger-Division*, which the Red Army soon defeated, although it took grievous losses in the process. The biggest losses came when the division's artillerymen concentrated their fire on the frozen Volkhov river, breaking the ice into smithereens and drowning untold numbers of Soviet soldiers. This costly victory against *Felddivision 1 (L)* and *28. Jäger-Division* made attacks against the right flank of *2. (lettische) Freiwilligen Brigade der SS* further north a lot easier. The Latvian SS battalions were pushed back under intense artillery and tank fire. As the Latvian SS brigade was overwhelmed, it began a hasty withdrawal, which in turn signalled the defeat of *XXXVIII. Armeekorps* along the Volkhov River.

The entire right flank of the Volkhov Front was now shattered. In order to tie down and encircle *XXVIII. Armeekorps*, stationed north of *XXXVIII. Armeekorps*, the Red Army launched a frontal assault aimed at *Felddivision 13 (L)*, alongside *21.* and *96. Infanterie-Divisionen*. Meanwhile, the 2nd Shock Army had broken out of the Oranienbaum pocket and linked up with other Red Army units that were attacking from the city of Leningrad. The first ten days of the Soviet offensive completely decimated *XXXVIII. Armeekorps* and parts of *I. Armeekorps*. In fact, *XXXVIII. Armeekorps* was reduced to the strength of four regimental-sized battlegroups – i.e., equivalent to a reinforced infantry division. As the war dragged on, more and more German divisions were operating with an average strength somewhere between a regiment and a brigade. The first of these battlegroups, *Kampfgruppe Schuldt*, contained 4,500 men from what remained of the Latvian SS

Route of withdrawal of *Felddivision 13 (L)* from the Volkhov river front, January–February 1944.

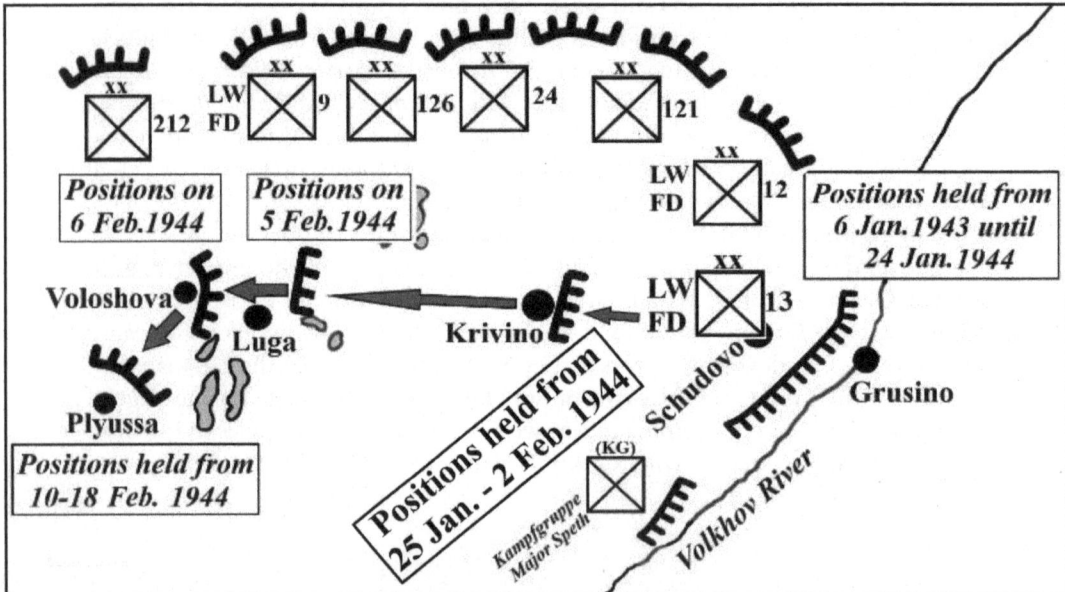

brigade, plus elements of *Felddivision 12 (L)* and *Felddivision 13 (L)*. The Soviet offensive in January 1944 caused *Felddivision 13 (L)* to crack and break. *Jäger-Regiment 25 (L)* made a fighting withdrawal, under heavy pressure, fighting its way through Krivino, Tessovo, Sapolje-Uschnitza and Orodezh-Beloye to the Luga region. From here it moved across the Plyussa to the Pskov area. After a temporary deployment on the southern edge of Lake Pskov, the regiment moved to the area south of Ostrov. At the end of March 1944 the remnants of the regiment fought along the Opochka–Pskov railway line. In April what was left of the regiment was absorbed into *Jäger-Regiment 24 (L)* of *Felddivision 12 (L)*.

Kampfgruppe Speth comprised the surviving infantry from *Felddivision 1 (L)*, *28. Jäger-Division*, parts of *Kavallerie-Regiment Nord* and a few Estonian *Schuma* battalions – around 2,200 men in total. The third and fourth battlegroups, named Bock and Pohl respectively, could count on about 1,200 men each. Thus, ten days after the Soviet offensive began on 2 February 1944, *XXXVIII. Armeekorps* had been reduced to a fighting strength of about 9,500 men, or a small division.[17] The divisions of *XXVI. Armeekorps* that were located further north by the Kirichi bridgehead and Pogoste pocket had to withdraw quickly lest they be cut off by the quick and violent Soviet offensive. In this way *Felddivision 12 (L)* found itself defending Chudovo, alongside *Felddivision 13 (L)*, in late January 1944. The whole northern army group position was coming unhinged. By mid-January 1944 the entire army group was in retreat. This caused heavy casualties but General Reymann was able to make a fairly orderly withdrawal with *Felddivision 13 (L)*, beginning on 29 January 1944.

This withdrawal nevertheless cost the formation dearly, and by the time the unit had left Chudovo, it was a mere battle group in strength. On 3 February an attempt by the Red Army to cut off *XXVIII. Armeekorps* near Oredesh proved unsuccessful, but Army Group North was forced further back. At this time the remnants of *Felddivision 13 (L)* were freed up and placed around Luga for the defence of that city.[18] The division's defence of Luga, a city partly surrounded by lakes and swampy marshes, was not completely successful.

The leading regiment of the division was forced back by a Red Army attack launched through the heavy marshes that the Germans believed were impassable.[19] By 5 February the remains of *Felddivision 13 (L)* were stationed in Luga. The rest of the divisions of Army Group North had also withdrawn. By 4 March 1944 *Felddivision 13 (L)* was located west of Pskov (Pleskau), along the south-western tip of Lake Pskov. The survivors continued to serve as a combat group through February and March 1944. The division was effectively destroyed between Chudovo and Luga. The division was finally disbanded in early April and the surviving units were assigned to other divisions. On 1 April the divisional staff was used to create the staff for *Division z.b.V. 300* (Division for Special Employment No. 300). This formation would control the *(estnisches) Grenzschutz-Regimenter 1, 4* and *6* (1st, 4th and 6th Estonian Frontier Guard Regiments), which had been quickly assembled and grouped into a division-sized unit.[20]

IM NAMEN DES FÜHRERS
VERLEIHE ICH
DEM

Unteroffizier

Karl Adolf Zimmerschied

4./A.R.13 (L)

DAS
EISERNE KREUZ
2. KLASSE

Div.Gef.Std. , 31. 1. 19 44

Generalleutnant u. Div. Kdr.
(DIENSTGRAD UND DIENSTSTELLUNG)

Award certificate for the Iron Cross, Second Class given to Sergeant Karl Adolf Zimmerschied, of *4. Kompanie, Artillerie-Regiment 13 (L)*, dated 31 January 1944.

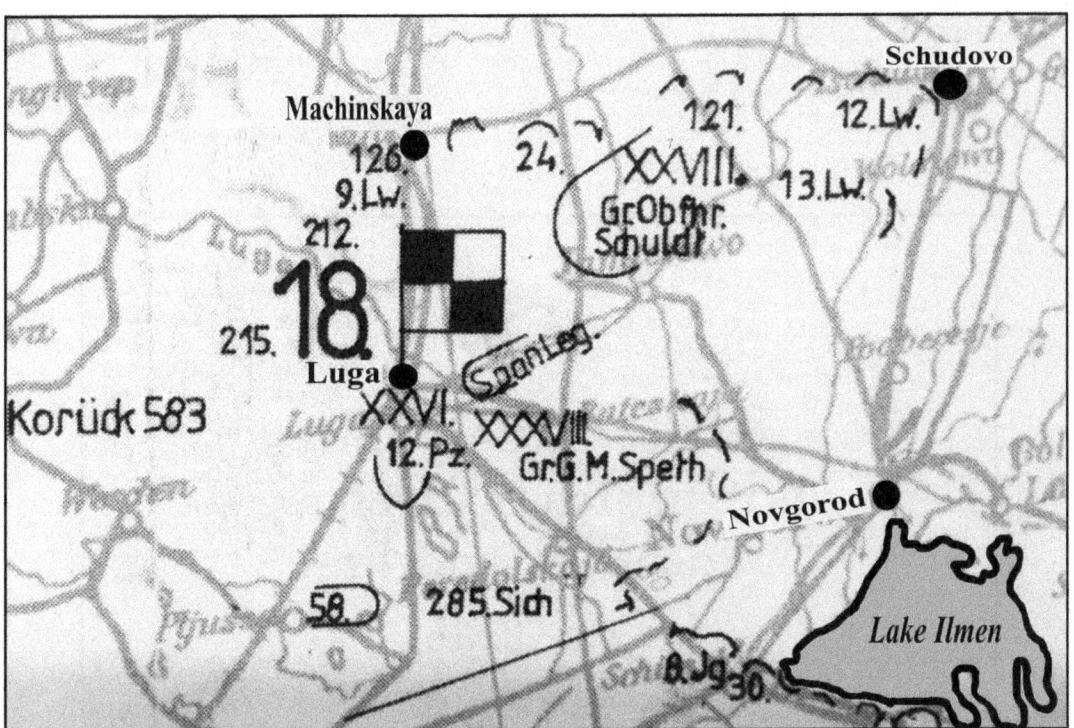

A German *kriegsgliederung karte* listing the positions of *18. Armee* in and around the city of Luga on 31 January 1944. The locations of various German divisions, including *Felddivision 9 (L)*, *12 (L)* and *13 (L)* are clearly listed.

II. *Artillerie-Abteilung* of *Artillerie-Regiment 13 (L)* was now redesignated I. *Artillerie-Abteilung* of '*unabhängines*' [independent] *Artillerie-Regiment 1016* of *18. Armee*.[21] This unit would eventually provide artillery support in the Courland pocket. Later on, this same battalion would once again be redesignated, this time as I. *Artillerie-Abteilung, Artillerie-Regiment 281* of *281. Sicherungs-Division*.[22] This division eventually fought under *3. Panzerarmee* along the Oder river and took part in the battle for Berlin.[23] The staff and I. *Bataillon, Jäger-Regiment 25 (L)* and *Jäger-Regiment 26 (L)* were merged to form a new I. *Bataillon* and II. *Bataillon* of a newly reformed unit: *Jäger-Regiment 25 (L)*, which was now attached to *Felddivision 12 (L)*.[24] *Jäger-Regiment 25 (L)* went on to serve in *Felddivision 12 (L)* well into 1945. As the sample documents show, the surviving men of *Felddivision 13 (L)* went on to serve in various other *Luftwaffe* field divisions, including *Felddivision 19 (L)* and *Felddivision 12 (L)*, as well as non-*Luftwaffe* units such as *Division z.b.V. Nr. 300* and *281. Sicherungs-Division*. *13. Luftwaffen-Felddivision* served fairly well in the defensive role and behind natural defensive barriers like the Volkhov river, but it was undergoing Army reorganization when it was heavily attacked in January 1944. The fact that the Army did not have sufficient forces to augment the division's strength meant that the unit could only count on a small transfusion of *Heer* officers and NCOs, who, although experienced, could not possibly make up for the loss of units like the divisional *Flak* battalion. It thus suffered the fate of most *Luftwaffe* field divisions: it was soon destroyed and eventually disbanded.

Im Namen des Führers und Obersten Befehlshabers der Wehrmacht

verleihe ich

dem

Unteroffizier

Karl-Adolf Zimmerschied

4./A.R.13(L)

das

Eiserne Kreuz 1. Klasse

.....Div.Gef.Std....., den .....1. 3.........1944

In Vertretung des Div.Kdr.

Generalmajor
(Dienstgrad und Dienststellung)

This award was given to Sergeant Zimmerschied after *Felddivision 13 (L)* had been disbanded. The date of the award is 1 May 1944.

Organization of *13. Luftwaffen-Felddivision*

Commanders:
Divisional CO:
  Generalleutnant Herbert Olbrich, 11/42–25/01/43
  Generalmajor Hans Korte, 26/01/43–01/10/43
  Generalleutnant Hellmuth Reymann,[25] 01/10/43–01/04/44[26]
Ia:
  Major Heinz Koch, 10/12/43–04/44
Ib:
  Oberstleutnant Erich Barkowski, 04/43–01/11/43
IIa:
  Hauptmann Fritz Mahler, 11/42–01/11/43
  Hauptmann Freiherr von Puttkamer, 10/12/43–04/44
CO *Luftwaffen-Artillerie-Regiment 13*:
  Oberst Hans Frielinghaus, 02/43–24/09/43
  Oberstleutnant Dr Walter Weiss, 01/08/43–01/11/43
CO *IV. Abteilung/Luftwaffen-Artillerie-Regiment 13*:
  Oberstleutnant Fritz Strube,[27] 04/06/43–01/11/43
CO *Luftwaffen-Jäger-Regiment 25*:
  Oberst Willi Westphal, 12/42–28/03/43
  Major Werner Fabig, 29/03/43–28/07/43
  Oberst Willi Westphal, 29/03/43–?
CO *Luftwaffen-Jäger-Regiment 26*:
  Oberst Theodor Greve, 01/04/43–12/43

Oberstleutnant Friedrich Wolf served in the division from the autumn of 1942. On 12 April 1943 he was ordered to *battalionsführerschule* in France. On 1 June 1943 he returned to *13. Luftwaffen-Felddivision* and was given command of a *Jäger* battalion.

14. Luftwaffen-Felddivision

The 14th Air Force Field Division was raised using *Flieger-Regiment 61*, which had been stationed in Oschatz in northern Saxony. The men were gathered together in *Luftgau III* (Berlin-Brandenburg region). This *Luftwaffe* division was destined to become one of a select few units to garrison Norway. As a result, it would never see combat and would survive the war completely intact. There was another unique factor, too: it would be fully armed and manned and would even have a large number of men and weapons above and beyond its authorized table of organization strength. This would be accomplished by a full use of captured foreign weapons from French, Yugoslavian, Dutch and Norwegian Army stocks.[1] The creation of *14. Luftwaffen-Felddivision* initially followed the same table of organization formula that had been created for all the *Luftwaffe* field divisions. Initially, the division was formed around two *Jäger* regiments – *Luftwaffen-Jäger-Regiment 27* and *Luftwaffen-Jäger-Regiment 28* – of three battalions apiece. The division also had an artillery regiment, *Luftwaffen-Artillerie-Regiment 14*, which contained three artillery battalions. The division also had an anti-tank battalion with three companies. There was also an engineer battalion with three companies, and a *Luftnachrichten-Kompanie* (air communications company), plus divisional support essentials including a *radfahr* (bicycle) company acting as the reconnaissance element, a veterinary company, a bakery company and a butchery company.[2] *14. Luftwaffen-Felddivision* began to depart from Germany in December 1942. It began to arrive in Norway in January 1943, and assembled near Oslo in February.[3]

Even though the division had arrived as a reinforcement of the army of occupation in Norway, it still continued to be equipped and trained there.[4] When it initially arrived, some of its units had taken part in border guard duty between Norway and Sweden. It began to move north in mid-March, in order to take over responsibility for the coastal defences that were currently held by *196. Infanterie-Division* in the Namsos-Bodö region. This was to allow *196. Infanterie-Division* to move deeper inland to become a ready reserve.[5] Another reason for the transfer was a plan that called for the possible occupation of Sweden.[6]

This plan required that the few mobile and infantry forces available in Norway would be freed from coastal and guard duties in order to be employable for this possible invasion of Sweden. With this in mind, *14. Luftwaffen-Felddivision* was soon moved north to Trondheim. Strangely, *Grenadier-Regiment 340* of *196. Infanterie-Division* remained south of Narvik and was still located there in July 1943. Part of *196. Infanterie-Division* would eventually leave Norway in July 1944 when it was transferred to Army Group Centre. The rest of the division

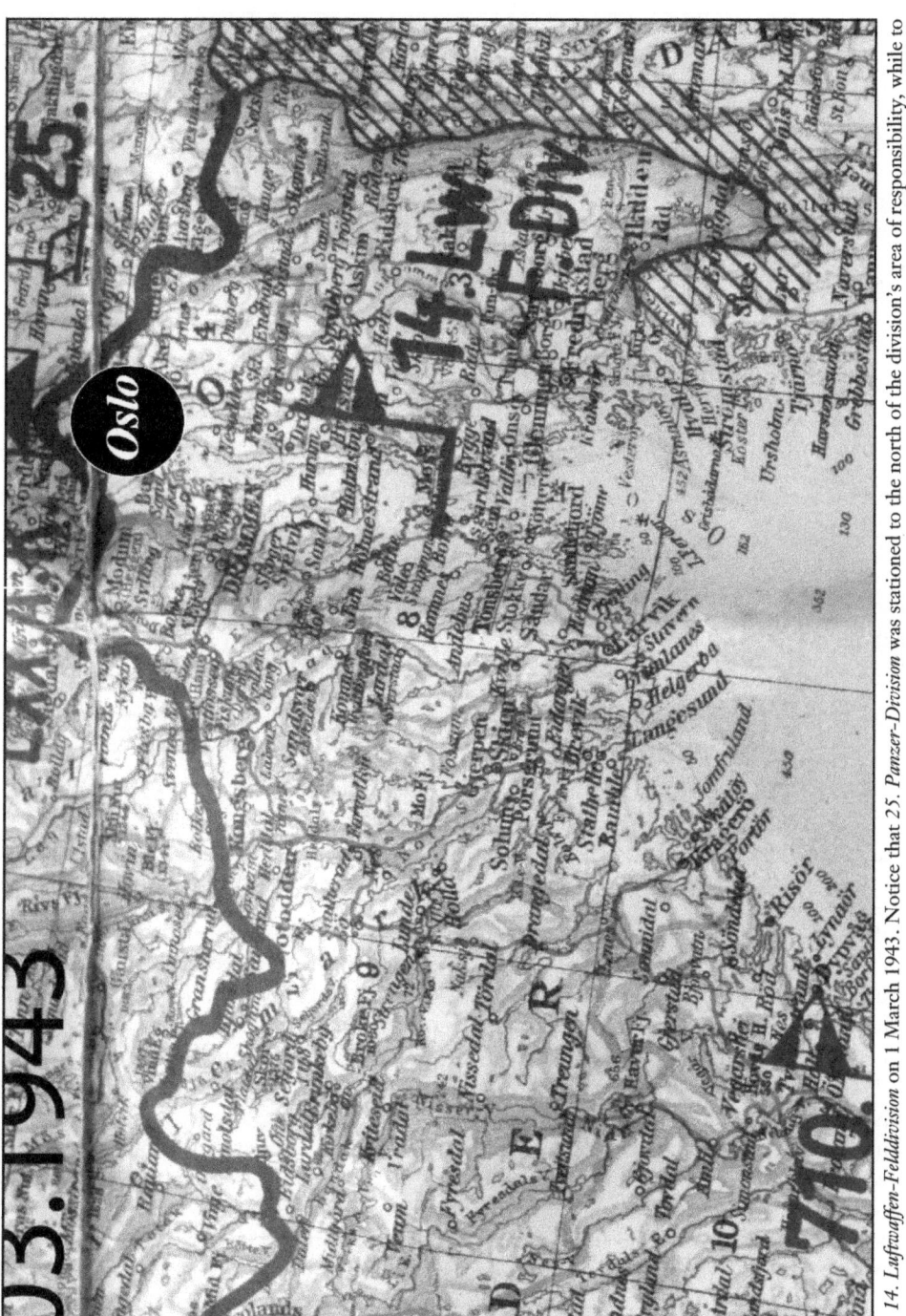

14. *Luftwaffen-Felddivision* on 1 March 1943. Notice that 25. *Panzer-Division* was stationed to the north of the division's area of responsibility, while to the southwest was 710. *Infanterie-Division*.

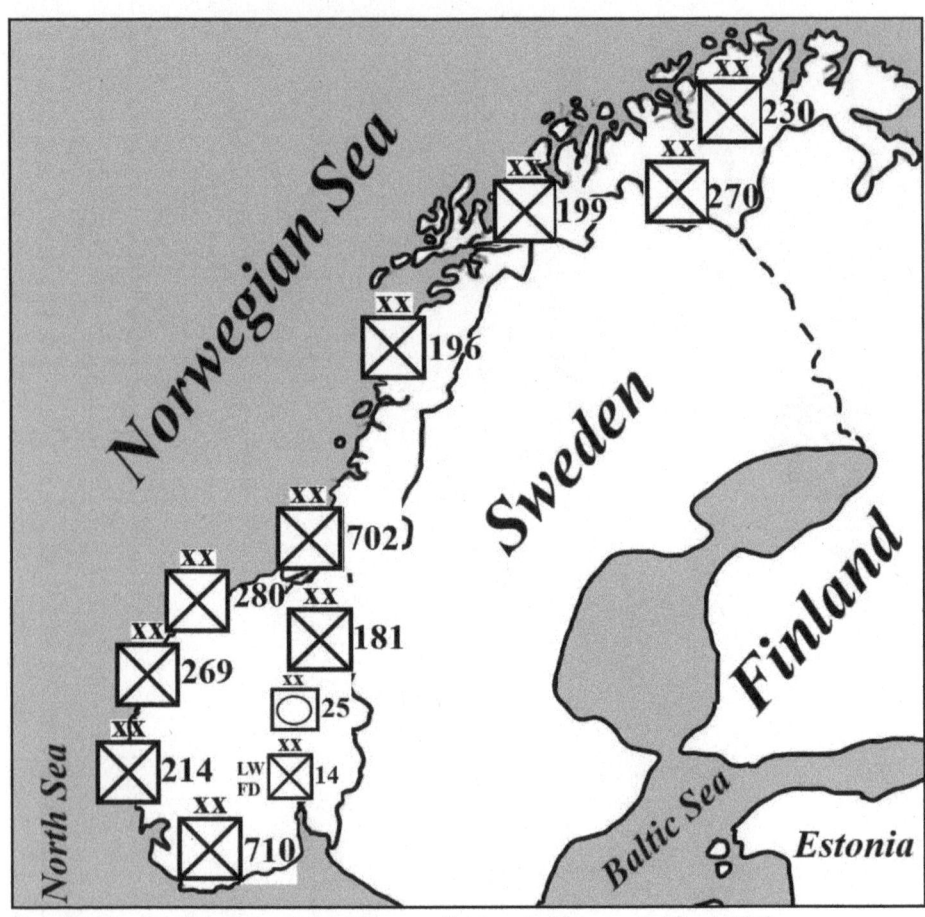

Map showing the general location of German divisions in Norway, in March 1943.

followed in August.[7] Its initial engagement on the Russian Front was just east of the Polish town of Wiżajny. The division withdrew in August and ended up operating in the region of Vilnius, Lithuania. Meanwhile, *14. Luftwaffen-Felddivision* did not complete the transfer north until April 1943.[8] A month later, in May, the Army of Norway reached its peak strength of fifteen divisions.[9]

According to German records, *14. Luftwaffen-Felddivision* was placed at the disposal of the German Army commander in Norway from January to June 1943, but in reality it was under the control of *XXXIII. Armeekorps* from the moment its first units began arriving in the Namsos-Bodö region of Norway, south of Narvik. It remained under the control of this corps throughout 1943 and 1944.[10] In the winter of 1942/1943 the German *Luftwaffe* command in Norway organized three regiments of air force men to act as infantry. One of these regiments was already operating in the region where the men of *14. Luftwaffen-Felddivision* were posted. This was *Luftwaffen-Feld-Regiment 501*, which was stationed in the major

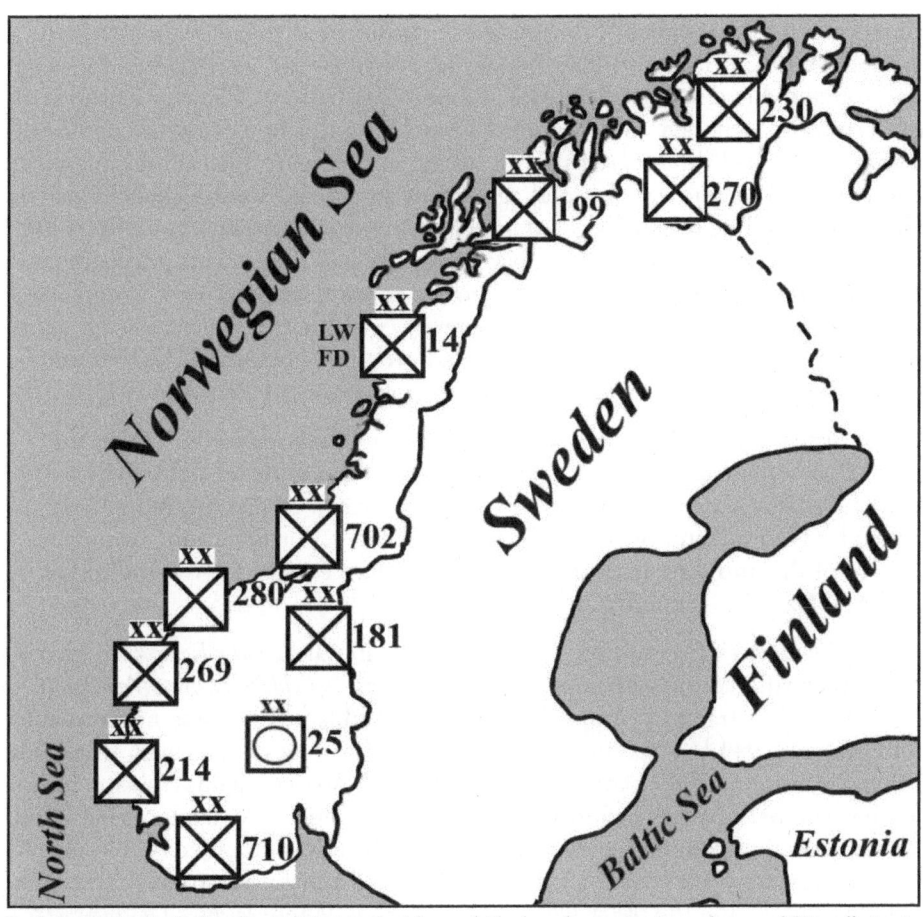

By July 1943, *14. Luftwaffen-Felddivision* had been shifted to the region in and around Trondheim in northern Norway.

islands just west of Narvik. The commander of this regiment from 5 December 1942 until 26 June 1943 was *Oberst* Maximilian Müller. This independently raised regiment contained three *Jäger* battalions. *I.* and *III. Jäger-Bataillone* were located on the islands, but *II. Jäger-Bataillon* was stationed on the mainland, just south of Narvik. In November 1943, *14. Luftwaffen-Felddivision* was absorbed into the *Heer* and was renamed *Felddivision 14 (L)*. It was also reorganized. The division still contained two *Jäger* regiments of three battalions apiece, renamed as *Jäger-Regiment 27 (L)* and *Jäger-Regiment 28 (L)*.

Additionally, each *Jäger* battalion was outfitted with captured French 25mm and 37mm anti-tank guns, and Norwegian-manufactured M-27 model 1911 75mm mountain howitzers. It is interesting to note that the Norwegians only manufactured twenty-four of these mountain howitzers.[11] The *Jäger* regiments were also issued with French heavy machine guns,[12] flame-throwers and even some French fortress guns.[13] The artillery regiment, *Artillerie-Regiment 14 (L)*, was reduced from three artillery battalions down to two. *I. Artillerie-Abteilung* now contained two artillery batteries and one *Flak* battery. The two batteries of artillery were equipped with captured French 155mm howitzers. *II. Artillerie-Abteilung* now had three *Flak* batteries of 88mm *Flak* guns instead of howitzers. These heavy *Flak* guns were useful against air attack and were especially deadly when employed against tanks, but they were virtually useless as indirect fire weapons. The divisional anti-tank battalion now had one assault gun company of four armoured vehicles and two towed motorized anti-tank companies. *III. Artillerie-Abteilung* of the artillery regiment, which was composed of light and medium *Flak* guns, was now withdrawn and eventually became *I. Flak-Abteilung* of *Flak-Regiment 15 (motorisiert)*.[14] This was ordered on 1 October 1943:

> The Armed Forces Supreme Commander Norway reports to the Führer that from 20 September 1943 for the conversion of the air force field divisions, the measures planned are to take place. The Armed Forces Supreme Commander Norway approves the suggestion of the 5. Air Fleet, on the movement of the anti-aircraft battalion of 14. Air Force Field Division, into the area of Varnika–Bardufoss on 3 October 1943.[15]

Fusilier Bataillon 14 (L) was now created from the initial *Radfahr Kompanie*. It contained four rifle companies, mounted on bicycles.[16] *Feldersatz-Bataillon 14 (L)*, made up of five training companies, was also established but was not available until March 1944.[17] A communications battalion was also formed from the original communications company. It contained two companies plus a headquarters company, which included a signals supply column. An engineer battalion was also raised; it had three companies, one of which was mounted on bicycles.[18] The division now also had two heavy motorized mortar companies, one with 120mm mortars and the other with several German 90mm *leichter Ladungswerfer* mortars. The divisional support units included a veterinary company, a butcher company and a bakery company.[19] By the time the war was over, *Felddivision 14 (L)* would be outfitted with not only German equipment but 'an assortment of French 50mm mortars, French heavy machine guns, and Yugoslav 75mm artillery pieces, beyond its authorized equipment'.[20]

In 1942 *Luftwaffen-Feld-Bataillon 'Finnland'* was established using Finnish volunteers and a German *Luftwaffe* cadre staff in the city of Oulu, in northwestern Finland. This infantry battalion contained four rifle companies and operated in northern Finland and Norway. In October 1943 it was renamed *Landesschützen-Bataillon der Luftwaffe 1* (Regional Defence Battalion of the Air Force No. 1). In the winter of 1942/43 three *Luftwaffe* field regiments – *Luftwaffen-Feld-Regimenter 501, 502* and *503* – were created in Norway.[21] They were established from excess personnel such as ground crews and staff who no longer supported German squadrons. Each of these regiments contained three *Jäger* battalions of infantry. In the case of *Feld-Regiment 502*, one of its three battalions (*III. Jäger-*

Bataillon) was composed of Finnish airmen. On 1 November 1943 *Luftwaffen-Feld-Regiment 501* was renamed *Jäger-Regiment 501 (L)*. It was posted to the Lofoten archipelago, in northern Norway.

Luftwaffen-Feld-Regiment 503 was eventually posted further north, along the Norwegian Arctic coast. In June 1944 *Luftwaffen-Feld-Regiment 503* was renamed *Grenadier-Brigade 503*, although its strength did not change. It was assigned to *20. Gebirgsarmee*.[22] This brigade of former airmen took part in the heavy defensive battles in and around Petsamo and Kirkenes from 7 to 29 October 1944.

The Red Army had launched an offensive there on 7 October, which eventually pushed the Germans back into Norwegian territory. The ultimate success of this operation enabled the Soviets to capture Petsamo, with its important nickel mines. The three Air Force field regiments now faced changes: *Luftwaffen-Feld-Regiment 501* became *III. Jäger-Bataillon / Jäger-Regiment 501 (L)*. *I.* and *II. Jäger-Bataillone* of the regiment were disbanded and their personnel distributed to the surviving *III. Jäger-Bataillon* and parts of *Felddivision 14 (L)*. *Luftwaffen-Feld-Regiment 502* was disbanded. Its *I. Jäger-Bataillon* became *Landesschützen-Bataillon der Luftwaffe 2*, while its *II. Jäger-Bataillon* became *Landesschützen-Bataillon der Luftwaffen-Feld-Regiment 503* was renamed *Jäger-Regiment 503 (L)*. These two *Landesschützen* (regional defence) battalions continued to serve in Norway under *269. Infanterie-Division* until August 1944, when they were dissolved. Noted historian Georg Tessin states that *III. Jäger-Bataillon* of *Feld-Regiment der Luftwaffe 502* was disbanded, but *OKW* situation maps from the period contradict this. The map shows the unit as employed under *702. Infanterie-Division*, and still named *III. Jäger-Bataillon / Jäger-Regiment 502 (L)*.

Jäger-Regiment 503 (L) was shifted to Finland in late 1943 and served there under *20. Gebirgsarmee* throughout all of 1944. In August *III. Jäger-Bataillon* of *Jäger-Regiment 501 (L)* was redesignated *Brigade-Lofoten* under *Festungs-Kommandant Tromsö* (*270. Infanterie-Division*). Together with *Festungs-Bataillone 646, 650* and *662, Brigade-Lofoten* became part of *210. Infanterie-Division* when they merged with *Festung-Infanterie-Regiment 859* in January 1945.[23]

As for *Grenadier-Brigade 503* (previously *Feld-Regiment 503 (L)*), it withdrew into northern Norway when *20. Gebirgsarmee* ordered a general retreat, and left Finland in the autumn of 1944. At the beginning of 1945 this brigade was located southwest of Narvik. As for *Felddivision 14 (L)*, its duty remained that of garrisoning its designated area throughout 1944 and into 1945. The units of the division remained up to full strength until the end of the war, thanks in part to the induction of *Jäger-Regiment 501 (L)*. Although it operated mostly in Norway, it was put on coastal defence duties on the Danish coast in June 1944 when part of the division was shifted to Jutland in Denmark. This small and temporary transfer of units to Jutland caused a lot of confusion for post-war historians, who believed that the whole of *Felddivision 14 (L)* had been shifted to Denmark for a time. Finally, the division came under the command of *20. Gebirgsarmee* when it began to cover the rear-guard of that army as it withdrew into Norway in late 1944.

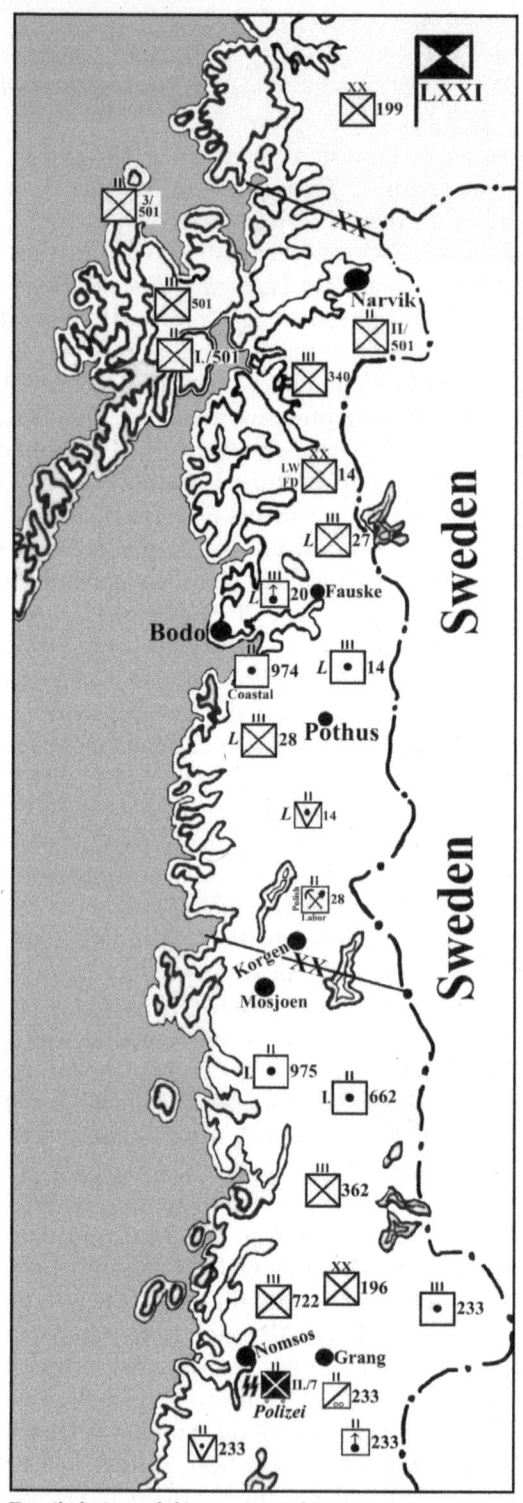

Detailed view of the position of *Felddivision 14 (L)* and neighbouring German forces in July 1943.

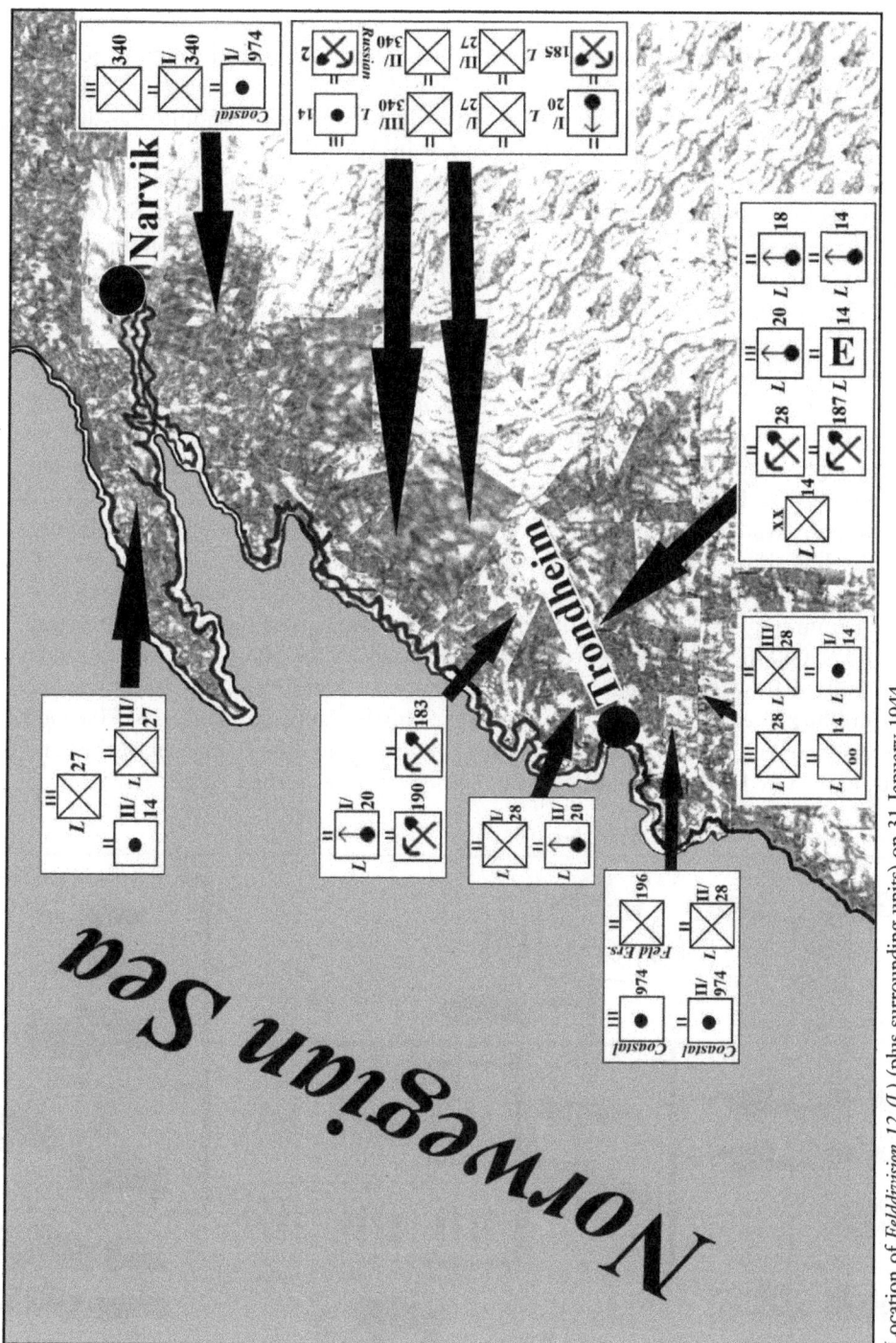

Location of *Felddivision 12 (L)* (plus surrounding units) on 31 January 1944.

156 Hitler's *Luftwaffe* Infantry

In February 1945 a new divisional commander was appointed. *Generalleutnant* Wilhelm Richter, a veteran of the First World War, had been the commander of *Artillerie-Regiment 30* when the Second World War began, serving in that role from 1 April 1938 to 1 October 1941. In early 1943 he was appointed as deputy commander of a *Luftwaffe* field division, but in April that year he was appointed commander of *716. Infanterie-Division*. After his division was decimated in the fighting in southern France in 1944, he was relieved of his command in September and was unemployed until November, when he became the deputy commander of an army division. This was a demotion for him and he was so upset about this that he resigned his post on 25 December 1944. He once again remained unemployed until his posting as commander of *Felddivision 14 (L)* on 1 February 1945.[24] The OKW approved this posting since *Felddivision 14 (L)* was in a relatively quiet sector (Norway). It also allowed Richter's pride some room to restore itself by the fact that he was now once again in command of a division.

In April 1945 the division decided to create a third field regiment. This was accomplished by disbanding *III. Jäger-Bataillon* from both *Jäger-Regiment 27 (L)* and *Jäger-Regiment 28 (L)*. These regiments now contained two *Jäger* battalions each. The third regiment thus formed was *Jäger-Regiment 55 (L)*. This reorganization did not change the overall strength of the division, which remained at an astounding 13,000+ men. In mid-1944 the strength of the Army of Norway was 372,000 men.[25] This figure was reduced towards the end of 1944 when about 80,000 men were transferred from Norway in order to help reinforce the crumbling Western and Eastern Fronts.[26] This left approximately 292,000 men in Norway, with *Felddivision 14 (L)* contributing about 4.5–5 per cent of the total strength. On 18 December 1944, *20. Gebirgsarmee* absorbed *Armee Norwegen*.[27]

14. Luftwaffen-Felddivision in December 1942.

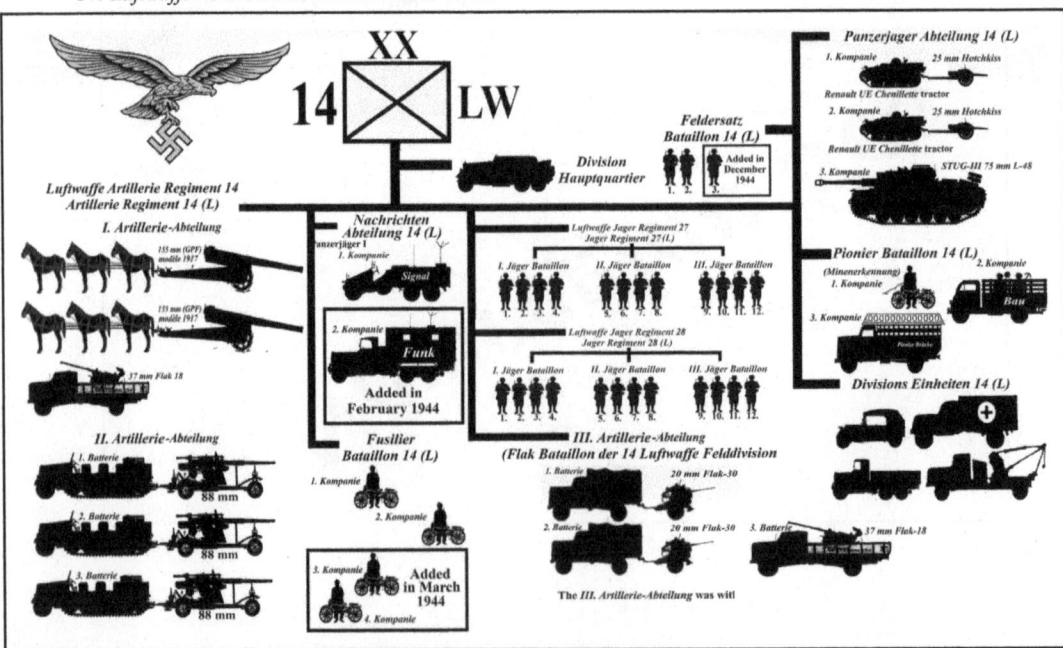

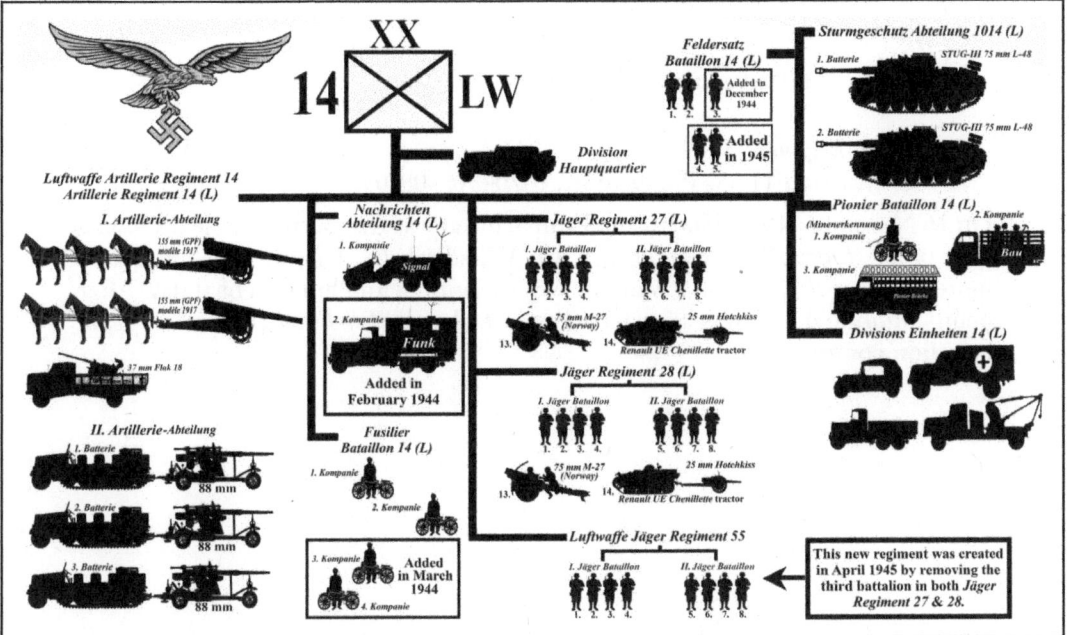

Felddivision 14 (L) in January 1944.

There was no need for two army commands in Norway, and a single command could better organize a defence against the threat of a Soviet invasion of northern Norway.

There is no question that if you were a German airman inducted into *14. Luftwaffen-Felddivision*, you would have considered yourself lucky indeed. The same can be said of all the German units in Norway. The division was never tested in battle, so we will never know whether it would have been one of those exceptional *Luftwaffe* divisions that performed above army expectations.

Organization of *14. Luftwaffen-Felddivision*

Commanders:
  Divisional CO:
    Generalleutnant Günther Lohmann,[28] 28/11/42[29]–31/01/45
    Generalleutnant Wilhelm Richter, 01/02/45–08/05/45
  Ia:
    Oberstleutnant Hugo Poggendorf, 10/12/44–14/02/45
    Major Rudolf Siefart,[30] 15/02/45–08/05/45
  IIa:
    Major der Reserve Brandes,[31] 10/12/43–08/05/45
  CO *IV. Abteilung (Flak)/Artillerie-Regiment 14 (L)*:
    Hauptmann der Reserve Bernhard Schulte-Mattler,[32] 28/07/43–24/08/43
  CO *Jäger-Regiment 28 (L)*:
    Oberst Konstantine von Braun, 11/42–07/09/43
  CO *Luftwaffen-Artillerie-Regiment 14*:
    Oberst Herbert Müller, 11/42–01/11/43

CO *Jäger-Regiment 55 (L)*:
Oberstleutnant Hugo Poggendorf, 01/04/45–08/05/45

On 16 November 1942 *Hauptmann* Emil Schekat was transferred to the divisional staff of *14. Luftwaffen-Felddivision*. Otto Wündisch (b. 1 April 1896) was promoted to *Oberstleutnant* on 9 March 1943, a month before his 47th birthday. After being promoted, he was transferred to *14. Luftwaffen-Felddivision* as a *Jäger* battalion commander.

15. Luftwaffen-Felddivision

This *Luftwaffe* field division is unique in that it began to be formed completely from excess *Luftwaffe* personnel from *Luftflotte 4* and *VIII. Fliegerkorps* in southern Russia. Initially at least, it was titled *Luftwaffen-Division 'Südost'*. The first commander appointed to create and lead this new division was *General der Flieger* a.D. Alfred Mahncke, who at that time was commander of *Luftgaustab z.b.V. XXI* (Air Force Administrative Command Staff for Special Employment No. 21). The commander of *Luftflotte 4*, *Generaloberst* Wolfram von Richthofen, directed *General der Flieger* Kurt Pflugbeil to order Mahncke's command to be disbanded and to start forming what would become *15. Luftwaffen-Felddivision* from its personnel.

Mahncke's career up until then had been long and varied:

1908: Officer Candidate with Railway Regiment No. 1 in Berlin.
1909: Commissioned a second lieutenant (pre-dated to 1907).
1911: Flight training at *Fliegerkommando Doberitz* near Berlin, then test pilot and instructor at the same school.
1913: Adjutant in *Flieger Bataillon 2*, Posen (Poznan).
1914: Flight Staff Officer with *VIII. Armeekorps* in East Prussia.
1915: Promoted to first lieutenant.
1916: Flight Staff Officer with *II. Armeekorps* in Russia. Transferred to Western Front and assigned as a staff officer with *Feldflug France, Kogenluft*.
1917: Promoted to captain and transferred from the *Fliegertruppe* (Air Wing) into the army. Assigned as staff officer with *11. Reserve Division* on the Western Front. Commanded an infantry company at Vimy Ridge.
1918: Transferred as a staff officer to *LVII. Generalkommando z.b.V.* on the Eastern Front. Promoted to a staff officer position within the headquarters of *XXVI. Reservekorps* on the Western Front. Promoted to command *Flieger-Abteilung A-231* on the Western Front. Reassigned as a staff officer at *Feldflug France, Kogenluft*.
1919: Retired from the *Fliegertruppe*.
1920: Was given a commission as a captain in the Security Police in East Prussia. Assignment as a training and instruction officer throughout East Prussia.
1925: Promoted to Major of the Police. Became a senior staff officer and instructor within the East Prussian Police.

1933: Promoted to Lieutenant-Colonel of the Police.
1935: Commissioned in the *Luftwaffe* and promoted to *Reichluftsportführer* (National Sport Flying Leader). In addition, Mahncke also held the post of President of the German Civilian Flying Club (*Luftsportsverband*). His position in the German Air Force was Air Force Reserve Inspector (*Inspekteur der Luftwaffen-Reserve*).
1937: Given the title of commodore and assigned as the commander of *Kampfgeschwader 152 Hindenburg*. This bomber force initially used (Dornier) *Do. 11*, *Do. 17* and *Do. 23* bombers but later switched to *Heinkel 111*, *Junkers Ju-52* and *Junkers Ju-86* planes.[1]
1939: Promoted to *Generalmajor der Luftwaffe* and assigned as commanding officer of *Luftgaustab z.b.V. I*. Took part in the Polish campaign. The unit was equipped with *AR-96* and *Fiesler Storch 156* scout planes.[2]
1940: Appointed commander of *Luftgaustab z.b.V. XII*. Took part in the French campaign.
1941: Appointed as head of *Höhere-Fliegerausbildungs-Kommandeur X* (10th Flight Training Command).
1942: Appointed as *Inspekteur der Flugzeugführer Ausbildung in der Reichsluftfahrtministerium* (Inspector of Pilot Training for the National Air Ministry). Later he went on to command *Luftgaustab z.b.V. XXI* in southern Russia. In November 1942 assigned as commander of *15. Luftwaffen-Felddivision*.
1943: Commander of *Flieger Division Donetz* in southern Russia. Promoted to *General der Flieger* and reassigned as commanding general of *Luftgau-Kommando Süd* in Italy. Later commanded *Luftgaukommando 28*, also in Italy.
1945: Commander of *Luftwaffeauffangstab Nord* in Hamburg. Went into Allied captivity.
1947: Released from POW captivity.

Although Mahncke's military career was impressive with regard to his staff duties, his only infantry experience was his brief stint as a staff officer in *23. Reserve-Division* in 1917 and his short tour of duty that same year as a company commander in the same division. His only other potentially experience in terms of commanding an infantry formation was his tour of duty in the East Prussian Police between 1920 and 1935. Aside from this, the general had spent the bulk of his career in the air wing as an administrator. He was, as his résumé shows, a very talented and highly experienced *Luftwaffe* staff officer. It was therefore quite unfair for him to be given the task of organizing and leading an infantry division – a formation that he admitted openly he was quite unqualified to command. It was, in my estimation, a sheer waste of talented manpower to assign this gifted *Luftwaffe* staff officer to such a mission. But such mismanagement of *Luftwaffe* personnel would be repeated hundreds of thousands of times as a result of *Reichsmarschall* Hermann Göring's desire to create infantry formations from airmen.

The effort to raise infantry units from inadequately trained and equipped *Luftwaffe* personnel proved to be unsound, half-baked, mostly disorganized and militarily criminal. This type of slapdash method crept into use not only in the *Reich*, where the majority of these new divisions were being organized, but at the front as well, where the normal chaos of combat was magnified by the intensity of the fighting, especially during the Soviet winter offensive in and around Stalingrad:

> The Germans cobbled together a line along the Chir using *15. Luftwaffen-Felddivision* (*Generalleutnant* Alfred Mahncke) and the ad-hoc battle groups including one of Luftwaffe ground personnel under Oberst Rainer Stahel, while *Flak* guns from Luftgau 25 (Rostov) added strength as *Flak-Regiment 99* (*Oberst* Eduard Obergethmann) shielded Fiebig's remaining airfields. Behind this line the Luftwaffe regrouped at Morozovskaya, Tatsinskaya and nearby Oblivskaya, where the stocks assembled through Richthofen's foresight enabled the Axis air forces to fly 150 sorties a day on 22 November 1942.[3]

It seems most likely that Mahncke was picked to help create this division not for his skills as an infantry commander but for his command staff and organizational skills. The division he was tasked with organizing had little time for training. It was being formed in southern Russia in the midst of the Soviet winter offensive. As a result, the division was initially employed piecemeal and at the front on an emergency basis. Hundreds of German airmen were armed with infantry weapons, split into companies and battalions by low-ranking Luftwaffe officers with no experience of army organization, and then sent to the front to fight a powerful enemy. The reality for *15. Luftwaffen-Felddivision* was that it was deployed before it was properly established, tasked with covering a portion of the Manych river as far south as Salsk and around Proletarskaya. The personal war diary of General Mahncke describes how he came to command the division during those frantic months in southern Russia, during the winter of 1942/1943:

> Early in November 1942 another change in my career seemed imminent. On orders of the *Flottenchef, Generaloberst* Wolfram von Richthofen, I was told that my *Luftgaustab z.b.V. 21* was to be disbanded, and that I had to expect a new post within *Luftflotte 4*. In my opinion this meant that operations across the Caucasus in a southerly direction would be abandoned. Three days later I was in Ossentuki at Luftflotte H.Q. and had been made *Kommandeur der Luftflottentruppen*, a post which was entirely new. I had to establish a base, find suitable staff officers, and make plans on how to develop it. I was in charge of all units belonging to *Luftflotte 4*, except those already under direct command of army corps or divisions. Evidently there were many small and larger groups from aircraft and signal units operating somewhere in southern Russia between the Caucasus – Don river – Stalingrad, enjoying a fairly unsupervised existence. On the morning of 3 November 1942, I reported to the *Flottenchef*. As was von Richthofen's characteristic,

he spoke animatedly about my new activity and what he wanted me to achieve. At the end he indicated that even this assignment was only temporary and that I could expect to be sent to the front in the very near future. This was in absolute accord with my wishes. Before I began work, I took a few days off to relax and enjoy the blessings of a warm room with central heating, a proper bed with white linen and a clean WC, things I had not seen in the past six months when I had slept in my sleeping bag and performed my ablutions in the open. My room even had a balcony from which I enjoyed a breathtaking view of the snow-covered mountains. This was the southernmost point I had reached in Russia. Four thousand kilometres separated me from home, as the crow flies. I was closer to India's borders than to Germany's. Beyond the mountains there was the colourful orient: Iran, Mesopotamia and Turkey. This was a crazy region. In December the sun rose at four in the morning, and at half past two in the afternoon stars shone brightly in the sky. The reason was simple: in all German-occupied countries, from the Volga to the Atlantic coast, we used the same time. One day after reporting to Richthofen, I received additional orders. I had to form the Luftwaffe Felddivision Südost from surplus soldiers from aircraft units, Flak, signals, staff and others.[4] After four weeks of intensive training, they would be attached to 1. Panzerarmee under Generaloberst von Kleist and used as infantry in a quiet front line. This gave me two hats to wear: (1) Establish and direct the staff of *Kommandeur der Luftflottentruppen*, and (2) form and train the *Luftwaffen-Felddivision 'Südost'*.[5]

It appears, then, that Mahncke assumed the responsibility of creating *Luftwaffen-Division Südost* as well as leading it in early November 1942. General Mahncke's comments on the reasons why these *Luftwaffe* divisions were created are worth mentioning:

It was only after the war that I learned why parts of the *Luftwaffe* were destined to fight side by side with army soldiers. In 1942 the OKW demanded that the *Luftwaffe* transfer excess personnel to those infantry divisions on the Eastern Front that had been bled white. It was no secret that for years Göring's *Luftwaffe* had soaked up soldiers, ostensibly to be used in giant future operations, although there were neither sufficient aircraft available nor pilots to fly them. It was a concession to Göring's vanity as he considered the *Luftwaffe* his private allodium. Rather typically, he refused to hand over any of his soldiers and asked Hitler to consent. Even the *Generalstabschef*, *Generaloberst* Jeschonneck, had his doubts at deploying *Luftwaffe* units with army soldiers but finally agreed, hoping that thereby he would not lose total control in case he required them later on. This was how the *Luftwaffen-Felddivisionen* were born, a botched concept from the start. The aim was to form twenty-two divisions with 170,000 men. Fortunately, it did not come to this. I soon came to realize that *Luftflotte 4* could perhaps raise two *Jäger* regiments (Nr. 29 and Nr. 30) of two battalions each, but only with the greatest difficulty, simply because there were no suitable soldiers available. As far as the many support units were concerned which a division required, these would have to be sent from Germany. A certain measure of clarity was given by an *Aufstellungsbefehl* arriving on 20.11.42 from the *Oberbefehlshaber der Luftwaffe* renaming my division *15. Luftwaffen-Felddivision*. Dreamed up at a comfortable desk in a warm office, the order's outlines were easy to understand. But the writer ignored that we were 4,000km away from Berlin, in the Caucasus steppe, at the onset of winter, expecting to be called to the front at any time. It took me a while to assemble my staff, qualified people were hard to find at this stage of the war, and after I had briefed them in detail, visited units under my command to get first-hand information.[6]

In the midst of this chaos, a relief attempt was being planned in order to free the trapped *6. Armee* at Stalingrad. For that purpose, new headquarters commands had been established and units earmarked for them. On 27 November 1942 *Heeresgruppe Don* (Army Group Don) was activated. Although trapped in the Stalingrad pocket and thus unable to assist, *6. Armee* was made a part of the army group.[7] The now-redesignated *15. Luftwaffen-Felddivision* was earmarked for *LVII. Panzerkorps*. Several *Flak* Regiments were also assigned. Other units slated for this corps included twenty-three tanks that were originally set aside for *13. Panzer-Division* but were now diverted, plus the assault guns of *Sturmgeschütz-Abteilung 203*. These were all earmarked for the relief attempt, but the strength of *LVII. Panzerkorps* proved to be insufficient for various reasons. For one thing, some of the forces allocated to it were not even ready. This was the case with *15. Luftwaffen-Felddivision*:

> The strength of the relief groups proved more unsatisfactory still. *15. Luftwaffe Felddivision*, which was due to join 57 Panzer Corps, had not even been established yet – a process which took several weeks to complete. When finally ready, the division had to be committed to battle at the height of an emergency (at a time, incidentally, when the relief problem had long been decided in the negative sense) and disintegrated during its first few days in action.[8]

General Mahncke described in some detail just how problematic it was to try to establish *15. Luftwaffen-Felddivision* at the front and under such difficult conditions:

> As I expected, the assembly of the *15. Luftwaffen-Felddivision* in the region of Essentuki-Kislovodsk was a slow process due to long distances and poor connections. Training suffered from a lack of combat-experienced instructors, and soldiers arrived piecemeal and without arms. Faced by these drawbacks it was obvious that the division would not be ready soon. As long as I was in Essentuki I attached myself to the immediate staff of Richthofen. The members were the Generalstabschef, Oberst Herhuth von Rhoden, the

Flottenintendant and Flottenarzt, the Chefrichter, the Höhere Nachrichtenführer, Flotteningenieur and the Oberquartiermeister, plus staff officers. Here we were trying to put the *15. Luftwaffen-Felddivision* together; despite my urgings for speed things moved slowly. Here was an opportunity for us to do well, an operation I liked, but everything crawled at a snail's pace. Suddenly, on 22 November an order burst in, highlighting the deteriorating situation on our southern front and upsetting my carefully laid plans. My division (what a euphemistic name) had to relocate to Salsk, 400km to the north, to work with *4. Panzerarmee* (*Generaloberst* Hoth). What had happened? Two days ago, the Russians had begun to attack the German-Romanian front northwest and north of Stalingrad. Cracks in our lines quickly led to breakthroughs, allowing the enemy to push in with tanks and cavalry, gaining ground fast. Whereas German units steadied themselves, the 4. Romanian Army was in total disarray after their senior commander had been killed. Their survivors fled along the railway line Stalingrad–Kotelnikovo–Salsk towards the Manych river sector. German soldiers, supply units, army escorts, police and others used the rampant confusion to clear off, on foot, hitching, or on trucks and trains. My orders read: 'Close the Manych [river] crossings, stop and collect the runaways and integrate them into defensive positions to be erected by the division at Manych; defend the important railway station at Salsk and the equally important airfield.'[9]

The original plan to relieve Stalingrad involved an attack from two directions: *LVII. Panzerkorps* (*4. Panzerarmee*) would attack from the Kotelnikovo area east of the Don bend, while *XLVIII. Panzerkorps* (*Armee-Abteilung Hollidt*) advanced from the middle Chir river towards Kalach. Unfortunately for the Germans, part of the forces assigned to this counterattack had to be diverted. For example, *62. and 294. Infanterie-Divisionen*, which *Armee-Abteilung Hollidt* had been promised, had to be sent to the 3rd Romanian Army in order to stabilize that part of the Axis front lines.[10] In the end, Soviet moves along the Don bend forced *XLVIII. Panzerkorps* onto the defensive and obliged *LVII. Panzerkorps* to withdraw one of its panzer divisions, *6. Panzer-Division*, which had been held in reserve for the expected breakthrough to Stalingrad, and send it to help relieve the pressure along the Don river bend.[11] *Armee-Abteilung Hollidt* had been created on 23 November 1942 using the headquarters of *XVII. Armeekorps*. As of 22 December 1942 it contained the following forces:

XVII. Armeekorps
   62. Infanterie-Division
   294. Infanterie-Division
I Romanian Corps
   7th Romanian Infantry Division
   9th Romanian Infantry Division (only a battlegroup)

11th Romanian Infantry Division
II Romanian Corps
1st Romanian Tank Division
14th Romanian Infantry Division (only a battlegroup)
22. Panzer-Division
Armee-Abteilung Hollidt Reserve: 306. Infanterie-Division

The main striking force of *XLVIII. Panzerkorps*, *11. Panzer-Division*, was still on its way to the front. Similarly, the air force field divisions earmarked for the relief effort were only now arriving in the Kotelnikovski (Kotelnikovo) area, where they were to assemble. Red Army attacks in the region of *Armee-Abteilung Hollidt*, however, forced those German forces to go over to the defense. In the end, only *LVII. Panzerkorps*, comprising *17.* and *23. Panzer-Divisionen*, managed to launch the Stalingrad relief effort. From the start, this small force met stiff Soviet tank and infantry opposition. The peak of success for the operation was reached on 17 December, when *23. Panzer-Division* succeeded in capturing two bridge crossings over the Aksay river, some 70km from the southwest corner of the Stalingrad pocket.[12] That was as far as the relief effort got.

Meanwhile, on 10 December, *17. Panzer-Division* was moved between the Sal and Don rivers in order to counter a thrust by the Soviet 2nd Guards Army. Specifically, the division fought in and around Potemkinskaya, while *11. Panzer-Division* was sent further north, by Nizhna Chirskaya, in an attempt to hold the bridgehead across the Don river. Four days later Red Army attacks along the Chir river forced this bridgehead to be lost. *7. Luftwaffen-Felddivision* and *Luftwaffen-Gruppe Stahel* were brought up to help cover the left flank of *11. Panzer-Division*. Eventually, *11. Panzer-Division*, together with the arriving *336. Infanterie-Division*, resolved the crisis on the Chir by launching a counterattack in the region of Surovkino, supported by elements of *Luftwaffen-Gruppe Stahel* (still being referred to on this date as part of *15. Luftwaffen-Felddivision*).[13] The attack was so successful that the Red Army failed to follow up with more assaults in this region until 22 December 1942. But what was General Mahncke doing during these critical weeks in November and early December to get *15. Luftwaffen-Felddivision* ready to face the Soviets? We return to his recollections:

> About noon on 23.11.42 I flew with my two most senior staff officers and a small sub-staff into an uncertain, even ominous future. I welcomed the prospect of meeting with the enemy, but to attempt this with a deficient unit under difficult circumstances worried me. The last entry in my diary from that time confirmed this: 'I do not know where my fate will lead me. I think of my beloved wife who has been my faithful companion for twenty years, and of my son. They both have made my life worth living and for this I thank them.' When I landed at Salsk I found only a short-range reconnaissance group which flew for 4. Panzerarmee and now fell under my command. An improvised bomber group promised by the Luftflotte never arrived. Want-

ing to have a closer look at the country, I flew to the front on the next day and over the combat zone as well as the rear of 4. Panzerarmee. I needed to study the terrain where my division might have to fight and also look at the worsening chaos on the roads along which the Romanians were fleeing. The ground was flat and featureless, the Manych river had widely overflowed its banks, turned marshy and was frozen in places. Clusters of Romanian soldiers marched to the rear, driving beef cattle, probably hoping to march straight home. However, they did not get that far. They were stopped, reorganized and, after a few days of complete rest, incorporated in the defence of the Manych [river] crossings. Next, I reported to Generaloberst Hoth at his command post in Kotelnikovo. I stood in front of the small, alert and dynamic man; his hair turned white and his face was worry-lined. His composed and assured way of talking showed self-control. We had not seen each other for quite a while; in the meantime, he had become one of the most respected senior panzer leaders. He greeted me in his typical friendly manner but was extremely serious. The outcome of our discussion was the following: although his army's position was secure at the moment despite its problems, surprises and unforeseen crises could suddenly happen. Therefore, any increase in troop strength was more than welcome and a timely gift. What I was compelled to report on the readiness of my division forced him to lower his expectations considerably. Twenty-fifth November was the day that my first Flak batteries were expected to arrive at Salsk, and already calls for help came in from the AOK demanding that we dispatch single batteries to Kotelnikovo for action. I refused point blank because this would only send my Flak to the slaughter. In a number of priority telephone calls with *Luftflotte 4*, the dilemma was discussed and my standpoint basically accepted, but the circumstances had become so desperate that even single guns had to be thrown in. Eventually the guns moved forward one by one, and what I had feared and tried to prevent happened: they went into action in the forward infantry lines and were wasted. Two days later, on 27 November 1942, two full and one-half battalions from my Jäger-Regiment arrived by train in Salsk at last; the rest was on its way. Accommodating them in the few widely scattered villages around Salsk posed a bit of a problem. The battalions were not ready for action. We lacked heavy infantry weapons and ammunition, there was no communication equipment, no transport vehicles, no heavy guns, no sapper battalion and lots more. The division was not motorized and so we were expected to collect materiel required from Heer and Luftwaffe depots hundreds of kilometres away somewhere. We were asked to use horses, of which there were none, and with only a handful of heavy trucks available we certainly faced a desperate dilemma. At the beginning of November frost had been the master, then the weather changed, storms began to blow and we were swamped with rain. Then abruptly it turned to frost for a few hours and the roads became impassable for days. We did not dare send off a truck as we could not be certain when we would see it again, if at all. Of course, this affected ration delivery and the supply of heating fuel, candles and carbide. The latter deficiency was especially annoying because living in the dark depressed the men, when 2pm in the winter the stars were up in the sky. We first had to collect horses from depots and veterinary hospitals in villages not shown on any of our maps, and for this we had to find soldiers who could handle them. When we were ready to send them off, it was discovered that there were no halters and we had to give them pieces of rope. A few days later the party returned, driving herds of horses, many undernourished and suffering from mange. The pride of the regiment, though, was two camels led by locals. They performed very well in the course of their duties. Finding harnesses for the horses was another problem, as was the collection of panje carts to be used as ammunition and supply wagons. Finally, the carts arrived on trucks, dismantled. These were really primitive conditions, and it had to happen to the *Luftwaffe*, of all units. How often did we wish in our anger to have those responsible for hatching *Luftwaffen-Felddivisionen* with us to show them how widely fantasy and reality differed. On the day when parts of my Jäger-Regiment arrived in Salsk, events changed with frightening speed and the situation became critical. Kotelnikovo, Hoth's HQ and the most important supply railway station of 4. Panzerarmee, was threatened by enemy cavalry and tanks, and small groups had already launched attacks. As I expected, calls for help arrived from AOK as they had no reserves left, but I could only reply that I was unable to assist as my division was not yet ready. Fortunately, the place was successfully defended without us, but the situation remained very worrying because the front of 4. Panzerarmee could break at any time with unforeseeable consequences. This was one of the reasons why Richthofen suddenly called for me. Early on 1 December 1942 I flew in a Storch to Kamensk and his mobile command post, 200km north of Rostov on the Donetz river. It was a railway train, consisting of a number of carriages as workrooms, a dining car, a couple of sleepers and a locomotive ready to move off at a moment's notice. The weather was abominable, it rained, low clouds raced across the sky, the temperature was below zero, the ideal weather to ice up any plane. Flying close to the ground and navigating with the aid of telegraph poles, I luckily reached the Don valley and one of the two Rostov airfields occupied by a Romanian squadron. After landing I found to my amazement that lumps of ice had formed along the wing edges and they had to be knocked off with hammers. I actually should have crashed long ago, but all I had felt was the steering become heavy and that the plane lost power and manoeuvrability. This persuaded me not to risk an emergency landing; instead, I tried to struggle through to Rostov. After the ice had been removed, I carried on. Richthofen and I had a long discussion during which he described the military situation in great detail, and although he was not at all a pessimist, he saw things in a very serious light. He said there were no army reserves at our front and therefore every additional battalion and company which could be thrown into battle counted. This was the reason why *4. Panzerarmee* and *Heeresgruppe von Manstein* had made their demands to me. His remarks gave me the welcome opportunity to reveal clearly and in no uncertain terms what unbridgeable complications we faced and what little we had been able to do so far. Richthofen was shocked. He immediately placed a call to Generaloberst Jeschonneck at Hitler's HQ in Rastenburg, informed him about my report and asked him to speed up transport of troops and equipment from Germany, especially the artillery and sapper regiments. Jeschonneck promised support, and although I usually never based my hopes on such noncommittal, vague promises, I assumed that in this case we might see results. I knew Jeschonneck and Richthofen were friends and he had been lucky with his requests a few times in the past. A return trip was out of the question, the weather was still poor. I had dinner with Richthofen in the warm dining car, emptied a bottle of good French wine and, after listening to a discourse on physics and higher mathematics between Richthofen and one of his senior officers which went far above my head, sank exhausted into my bed. By 10 December 1942 officers and soldiers from *Luftflotte 4* had assembled. The reason for the delay was that many soldiers had been rejected as physically unfit and replaced with others. But we secured experienced officers and NCOs from the Panzerarmee, even heavy infantry weapons, and at last began proper battle training. Gradually more soldiers arrived from depots, but they were burdened by too much winter clothing and equipment, more than one man could hope to carry, as the depots wanted to do us a favour. Soldiers en route from the station to their distant barracks often collapsed under the load. Since it was impossible to haul all surpluses with us on our few available carts, we erected a depot in Salsk which required security personnel, cutting into our already insufficient manpower. From the beginning I was almost constantly with my soldiers, looking after them, helping where I could. It was most satisfying to see how they faced and overcame unfamiliar, primitive living conditions, and how team spirit improved. Depending on the weather, training carried on, although the country was absolutely flat without shrubs or trees – not very varied, and plenty of live ammunition was expended. Targets we had none, wood was extremely scarce, but the men managed somehow. Our thoughts still revolved around Stalingrad and the dangers faced by *6. Armee*. The fortified city was at that time oval shaped and measured 40km from east to west and 20km from north to south. Its only useable airfield was in Pitomnik. Our senior command now decided to relieve the encircled garrison, and Hoth's Armeegruppe, reinforced by a Romanian army, was to make the crucial drive. Hoth was ordered to attack east of the Don river and on both sides of the railway line Salsk–Stalingrad and advance along the shortest route to restore the link to *6. Armee*. At the same time *6. Armee* was expected to break out of its southern front line as soon as Hoth's Armeegruppe had reached a point 30km away, and continue its attack in his direction.[14]

15. Luftwaffen-Felddivision 169

It is clear from General Alfred Mahncke's recollections that *15. Luftwaffen-Felddivision* was not committed to battle up until this time. His description of events between 12 and 20 December 1942 also shows that his division was not committed to the relief attempt, but was kept behind at Salsk, continuing to train and organize. As previously stated, Soviet counter moves on the Don and Chir rivers forced the Germans to commit most of the forces earmarked for the Stalingrad relief effort to the defence in those areas. On paper, the forces allocated for the Stalingrad relief attempt looked impressive, but in reality, aside from the weakened *XLVII.* and *LVII. Panzerkorps*, the other units proved too weak or not yet deployed, or were totally insufficient and not capable of offensive operations:

> The *Luftwaffe* divisions which were beginning to appear in the field for the first time had only recently been formed. Von Manstein's force, in spite of its grandiloquent designation, was not an army group since its only offensive element was the under-strength *LVII.* and *XLVIII. Panzerkorps*. It could not in fact be compared with a 1941 German army. Except for *6. Panzer-Division*, its German formations were very much understrength and contained inexperienced Luftwaffe ground staff, headquarters and supply troops fighting as infantry. The Romanian troops were disorganized, and they and the newly formed Luftwaffe field divisions had no offensive capability. In all it was a makeshift, hastily scraped together force inadequate for its task and in the first week of December, until the arrival of the panzer formations, it was hardly in a position to withstand the Soviet probes across the Chir and Aksai [rivers].[15]

Table 4 shows the German order of battle for Heeresgruppe Don, with its subsequent sub-corps and divisional units, in the first week of December 1942.[16]

General Mahncke would not have been able to raise the artillery regiment for his division during this chaotic and difficult time in southern Russia. In fact, his regiments would have to make do with some *Flak* guns for support. It had been a sheer miracle that the *Jäger* regiments had begun organizing at all. But excess *Luftwaffe* personnel had eventually arrived: from *Luftflotte 4* for *Luftwaffen-Jäger-Regiment 29* and from *VIII. Fliegerkorps* for *Luftwaffen-Jäger-Regiment 30*. Mahncke's description of the Stalingrad relief effort is worth noting here, since he mentions not only the actions of the divisions under Hoth's command, but also the air supply effort, as well as the smaller, battalion-sized units employed in the relief, like the new *schwere Panzer-Abteilung 503*, which was equipped with the brand-new Tiger tank. This heavy tank battalion had arrived on the front lines on 1 January 1943 but would be transferred to Kharkov on 11 February 1943:

> Operation Wintergewitter began on 12 December. Although enemy resistance was weak at first, the weather had changed again, making it extremely hard for our panzers to advance. A group of the new Tiger panzers, arrived in Russia for the first time, from which Hitler expected great things, disappointed. Although this panzer was better protected against heavy weapons

Table 4. Axis Order of Battle, Army Group Don, December 1942.

Army Group	Army or Army Abt.	Corps	Division
Don	Hollidt (Created from the HQ of XVII. Armeekorps)	XVII. Armeekorps[17]	Two regiments of 62. Infanterie-Division
		I Romanian Army Corps	294. Infanterie-Division
			7th Romanian Infantry Division
			9th Romanian Infantry Division
			11th Romanian Infantry Division
	320. Infanterie-Division: currently available for special employment. This division was under the direct command of Army Group Don in January 1943. However, by February 1943 it had been assigned to Army Detachment Lanz, which was under Army Group B and was stationed around Izium.	II Romanian Army Corps	1 regiment of 62. Infanterie-Division
			22. Panzer-Division[18]
			1st Romanian Panzer-Division
			7th Romanian Cavalry Division[19]
			14th Romanian Infantry Division
		XLVIII. Panzerkorps	336. Infanterie-Division[20]
			11. Panzer-Division (30 tanks)[21]
			7. Luftwaffen-Felddivision (arriving)
			24. Panzer-Division[22]
		LVII. Panzerkorps[23]	6. Panzer-Division[24]
			15. Luftwaffen-Felddivision[25]
			17. Panzer-Division (30 serviceable tanks)
			23. Panzer-Division[26] (39 serviceable tanks)
		Gruppe Spang supply units protected by security troops	Sicherungs-Regiment 619[27]
			Sicherungs-Regiment 354[28]
	3rd Romanian Army	VI Romanian Army Corps	1st Romanian Infantry Division
			2nd Romanian Infantry Division
			18th Romanian Infantry Division
		VII Romanian Army Corps	4th Romanian Infantry Division
			8th Romanian Cavalry Division (parts)
		Gruppe Stumpfeld[29]	1 regiment of 336. Infanterie-Division
			213. Sicherungs-Division
			403. Sicherungs-Division

For Special Employment under Army Group Don headquarters

Arriving Reinforcements:

To 8th Italian Army
Date	Unit
16 Dec.	27. Panzer-Division (50 tanks)
16 Dec.	385. Infanterie-Division[33]
20 Dec.	387. Infanterie-Division
27 Dec.	19. Panzer-Division (28 tanks)

To LVII. Panzerkorps
Date	Unit
31 Dec.	15. Luftwaffen-Felddivision
9 Dec.	17. Panzer-Division
7 Dec.	23. Panzer-Division
1 Jan.	SS Infanterie-Division Wiking (motorisiert)
1 Jan.	16. Infanterie-Division (motorisiert)
21 Dec.	schwere Panzer-Abteilung 503. Began arriving piecemeal 21–24 Dec.

IV and V Romanian Army Corps (remnants)
Kampfgruppe Stabel[30]
Kampfgruppe Heilman[31]

HQ units and ancillary army corps forces

Unit	Date
VIII. Fliegerkorps	
384. Infanterie-Division	
Heeresabteilung Hollidt (17. Armeekorps HQ)	25 Nov.
8. Luftwaffen-Felddivision[32]	2 Dec.
7. Luftwaffen-Felddivision	21 Dec.
306. Infanterie-Division	22 Dec.
11. Panzer-Division	
6. Panzer-Division	25 Dec.
Heeresgruppe Fretter-Pico (XXX. Armeekorps HQ)	
304. Infanterie-Division	30 Dec.
3rd Italian Infantry Division Ravenna	1 Jan.
Brigade Nere 23 Marzo	1 Jan.
Brigade Dörfler-Schuldt[34]	1 Jan.
Kampfgruppe Nagel	? Jan.
Kampfgruppe Kreising[35] (Represented half of 3. Gebirgs Division)[36]	1 Jan.

than the Russian T-34 and its gun was also of a heavier calibre, its excessive weight made it less manoeuvrable under local conditions: ice and snow, no firm roads, no bridges which could carry its weight. However, the attack gained ground steadily in the face of increasing resistance. By 20 December 1942 Hoth's advance troops had reached the Aksay and Myschkova regions and were only 55km away from the city. At night they could see the flares across the flat featureless Steppe. It raised our hopes for the survival chances of our encircled comrades. Supplying 6. *Armee* was only possible by air. Our airfield at Salsk was one of the few which were suitable. Without pause, our Ju-52 transport planes carried food, ammunition and medical equipment in all kinds of weather – storm, rain, frost, fog and sleet, landed at one of the few crude air strips in the Kessel and returned immediately.[37] On their return flights they carried a bloody load of seriously wounded, each night about 300, who were sent straight on to field hospitals. Not all our aircraft returned. Some were shot down by Russian anti-aircraft, others crashed by icing up or were wrecked landing on the narrow air strips. Here was abundant proof of the silent heroism shown by our aircraft crews. On 23 December Richthofen asked me again to Novocherkassk. He told me about the situation in the area of Heeresgruppe von Manstein. It was bad everywhere, especially south of the Don river, where our Chir front line, maintained with great effort, had collapsed. Our troops retreated to the west, fighting delaying actions. If attacks should threaten us on this sector south of the Don, everybody and everything would have to be thrown into battle, including my division, even if it was not ready. I could not really comment, but described the still unsatisfactory preparedness of my division, and Richthofen granted me an extension of two weeks, provided the situation did not worsen. On Christmas Day I returned to Salsk. I could not use a plane on account of the weather, and the trip by jeep, 500km both ways, took me 15 hours driving time. More bad news was waiting for me. Since early morning Russian tanks occupied our airfield at Tatsinskaya which had been used for supply flights to Stalingrad. This was a heavy blow. But even worse was the report that Operation Wintergewitter had failed shortly before reaching its target due to extremely powerful enemy resistance, impassable roads and our supply deficiencies. Christmas evening was spent under increasing tension and our thoughts on Stalingrad never left us. On 26 December, I flew to Hoth, who was still in Kotelnikovo. It was bitter gallows humour when we wished each other Merry Christmas, with the sound of gunfire nearby. Hoth, the non-smoker, offered me a posh cigar box and said: 'So, mein lieber Mahncke, this is the only and last present I can give you.' We talked about the dangers facing us. The Russians had apparently withdrawn strong tank-supported forces from their Stalingrad front and thrown them against Hoth. At Novoskaisky they had broken through the Romanian front, and on our east flank strong tank units were assembling at Sadovize–Maly Drbaty. In the Elista steppe, parts of Russian divisions waited to attack.[38] They had been shipped across the Caspian Sea to Machatschkala. If our position so far had been serious, it now grew critical. Armeegruppe Hoth had to be taken back to be able to defend itself effectively. The advance command post of 4. Fliegerkorps was situated on the other side of Kotelnikovo: a small wooden hut next to the airfield. As I landed in my Storch, reports arrived that many Russian armoured cars had been bombed and driven off by Stuka dive-bombers at a spot only 5km away, and that nearby at Verchne Yablotschny a group of 20 to 30 tanks massed to attack the airfield. Because our fighters, Stuka and reconnaissance planes were almost defenceless against tanks on the ground, the situation was most unpleasant and the planes took off from the airfield as fast as they could. From remarks made by Hoth and Pflugbeil, I gathered that the hour for my division had come.[39]

Mahncke knew that his division was still nowhere near being fully combat ready or fully organized for combat. In fact, the artillery regiment of the division would not be organized until the early spring of 1943 in Celle, France, and even then it would not arrive until May 1943. Its three battalions were poorly equipped: the Germans had to resort to requisitioning nineteenth-century French 155mm field guns from a local museum.[40] These guns were so old that their barrels were made of bronze instead of steel! Needless to say, the value of the artillery regiment was very low, given these substandard weapons. But deficiencies were apparent not only in the heavy weapons category, but in simple infantry arms as well. In fact, these shortages were encountered throughout the division with regard to all types of equipment. When General Mahncke moved his division forward, he had to disarm one of his line regiments in order to fully equip the other *Jäger* regiment:

> I had just returned to my command post, when the AOK sent orders that all available units from my Jäger regiments, even individual companies, had to move to the front at once. This was alarming, but I could do nothing at the moment as both regiments were not fully equipped. All equipment, as it had arrived, had been divided equally between the regiments to give both a chance to train effectively. Refusing to have my units broken up to be sent into action piecemeal, I ordered that *Jäger-Regiment 29* had to hand over all horses, transport vehicles, arms and equipment to *Jäger-Regiment 30*, to bring it up to full combat strength. My decision was facilitated by the fact that this regiment was commanded by a very active officer with front-line experience in Russia and was better prepared. The restructuring would take a few days, though. When I telephoned Richthofen late on 28 December 1942, I gained the impression that the situation south of the Don had neither improved nor worsened. On 31 December I wrote in my diary: 'The situation at *4. Panzerarmee* has intensified and worsened. Strong Russian tank units have again attacked our unprotected eastern flank and forced the army to withdraw rapidly. The high command is already on this side of the

Manych [river]. Tomorrow morning, *Jäger-Regiment 30* will be employed to protect the important and directly threatened railway and road bridges at Proletarskaya. I will follow with my combat staff one day later.' During the morning of 2 January 1943, I called on the regiment in its position at Proletarskaya. I found a few Tiger panzers which had been placed under its command.[41] The regiment's commander reported his defensive plans, which I approved. In the afternoon, just as I wanted to leave, a priority call came in. Richthofen was on the line. Judging by his manner of speech, I knew immediately that something had happened. Very briefly he told me that I was to take over a Fliegerdivision between the Don and Donetz, and at once. I was flabbergasted. I had weathered all sorts of surprises in the last six months, but this topped everything. I thought of my *15. Luftwaffen-Felddivision* which was at last taking shape and going into battle to prove itself. I felt almost like a deserter if I left them at this point and conveyed my strong feelings to Richthofen. His curt reply was: 'This is all well and good, but I need you here now and as soon as possible. When can you be here?' I replied: 'By tomorrow noon.' Fate had interfered once again. Ten hours after this call, on 3 January 1943, at 2:00 o'clock in the morning I left Salsk in an all-terrain, six-wheeled truck. A sudden thaw had made all roads impassable, but to arrive on time at Luftflotte headquarters in Novocherkassk I had selected this vehicle although it was a petrol guzzler. After a few hours we stopped with a broken axle.[42]

General Mahncke eventually made it to Richthofen's headquarters at Novocherkassk, just outside Rostov, when a German ambulance came by and gave him a lift. His description of the truck suggests it was a *Raupenschlepper Ost*, commonly referred to as an RSO truck. These vehicles were fully tracked and therefore fared much better in snow and mud than regular trucks. Mahncke now assumed command of the new *Fliegerdivision Don*, which had been organized from the close support groups of *VIII. Fliegerkorps*, including *Messerschmitt Bf 109* fighters, tank-destroyer *Stukas* and scout planes. Mahncke was now charged with reorganizing these squadrons and supporting *Armee-Abteilung Hollidt* and the newly raised *Armee-Abteilung Fretter-Pico*.[43] In addition, he was also tasked with finding any surviving elements of a *Flak* division whose batteries had been distributed to forces under *Armee-Abteilung Hollidt* and were badly mauled during the fighting from November 1942 to January 1943.[44] His command of *15. Luftwaffen-Felddivision* had ended just as the unit was about to be committed, leading to speculation that higher German command headquarters had never actually intended him to lead a ground division, merely to help organize it.

This cannot be proven one way or another as all parties involved have long since passed away, but his organizational expertise and staff knowledge were doubtless widely respected. Equally, it could also have been a coincidence, or a matter of necessity, and he was appointed to the role because he was the most qualified. In either case, he served *15. Luftwaffen-Felddivision* well as its commander.

Whoever was to take over from him would have a rough time of it, given the unit's low combat readiness. One source names *Oberst* Rainer Stahel as the new commander of the division, but probably this was because his *Luftwaffe* battlegroup had been earmarked for the division before being absorbed into *8. Luftwaffen-Felddivision*. To add to the confusion, *7.* and *8. Luftwaffen-Felddivisionen* were also absorbed by *15. Luftwaffen-Felddivision* in March and April 1943, so technically at least *Kampfgruppe Stahel* did eventually join 15th Air Force Field Division:

> The *17. Panzer-Division* could finally move out from 10 December into the area northeast of Potemkinskaya on the Don river, while the *11. Panzer-Division* was sent to the Don bend by Nizhna Chirskaya, whose German garrison had been cut off. Here only weak alarm formations and foremost units were trying to secure the area. These were composed of the *8.* and *15. Luftwaffen Felddivisionen*. Russian mechanized units were threatening to advance on Rostov along the Chir river. *LVII. Panzerkorps* (*Generalleutnant* Kirchner) was deadlocked in the area northeast of Kotelnikovo, while *XLVIII. Panzerkorps* (*General der Panzertruppe* Otto von Knobelsdorff, a veteran of the fighting in Demyansk) was on the defensive southeast of Morosovskaya (Morosovsk) fighting under Gruppe Hollidt and 3rd Romanian Army. The *11. Panzer-Division* (*General der Panzertruppe* Hermann Balck) and the arriving *336. Infanterie-Division* (*Generalmajor* Walther Lucht) resolved the crisis in the area of Surovkino/Chir, supported by parts of the *15. Luftwaffen-Felddivision* (Stahel). Here the enemy did not move again until 22 December.[45]

On 15 January 1943 the Red Army's 3rd Mechanized Corps (2nd Guards Army) broke through the German defences at Spornyy, on the upper Manych river, about 40km from where the Manych merges into the Don.[46] At the same time, 37km northwest of Spornyy, the 1st Guard Rifle Corps, supported by tanks from 3rd Guards Tank Corps, broke through the *Flak* and infantry screen at Samodurovka, on the Manych river, about 5km from Manychskaya and the Don river.[47] The city of Rostov and the escape route for *Heeresgruppe A*, which was in the Caucasus, were now directly threatened with falling into Red Army hands. The result of this would be to bag the entire army group: something that would have certainly shortened the war.

Elements of *16. Infanterie-Division (motorisiert)*, which had been withdrawn from Spornyy, now veered northwest and headed towards Samodurovka to try to retake the crossing. Matters became critical when leading elements of 3rd Guards Tank Corps reached the town of Lenin, on the southeastern outskirts of Rostov, on 20 January. The *11. Panzer-Division* had to be recalled from *Armee-Abteilung Hollidt* and sent south to try to prevent the fall of Rostov. Meanwhile, the advance elements of *1. Panzerarmee* were racing north, *XL. Panzerkorps* leading the way. *15. Luftwaffen-Felddivision* had already begun its move north as soon as it was learned that the Soviet Army had broken through the upper Manych river defences. Their withdrawal took from 5 to 13 February 1943. For better

176   Hitler's *Luftwaffe* Infantry

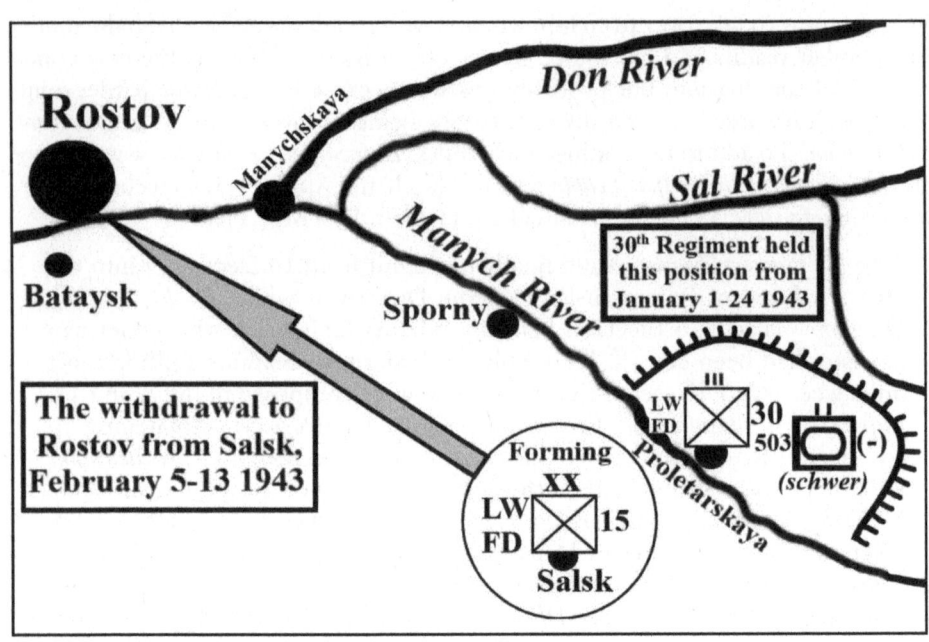

Location of *15. Luftwaffen-Felddivision* from 1 January to 13 February 1943.

The military situation in early February 1943: the race to Rostov-on-Don.

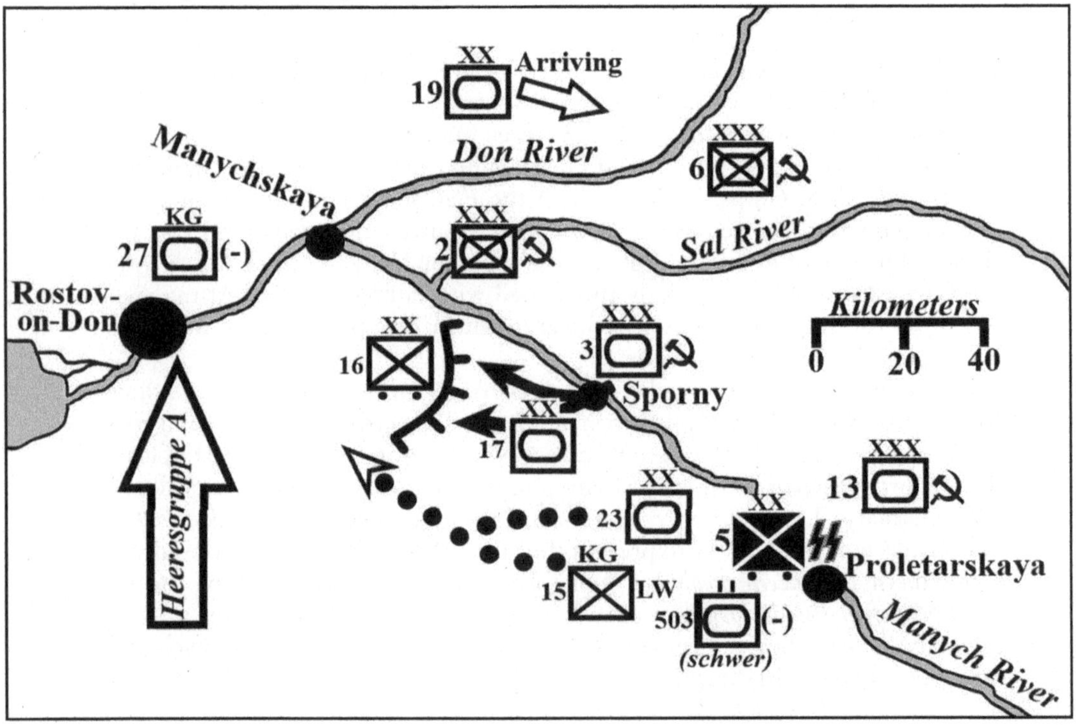

protection, the division attached itself to *111. Infanterie-Division*, which was also retreating northwards.

With the help of *11. Panzer-Division* and *16. Infanterie-Division (motorisiert)*, the Germans were able to retake the Manychskaya–Samodurovka crossing points on 24 January and thus temporarily halted the Red Army advance. This gave parts of *Heeresgruppe A* time to withdraw from the Caucasus, although a large portion of the army group (basically, *17. Armee*) remained trapped in the Kuban region until it could cross the Kerch Strait and into the Crimean Peninsula in early spring. By 13 February 1943 the division had crossed the Don river by Rostov and moved west to the area of Taganrog. *15. Luftwaffen-Felddivision* reached its new defensive positions north of Taganrog much worn out. It was now under the control of *V. Armeekorps*, whose other divisions on 3 February included *444. Sicherungs-Division* and *111. Infanterie-Division*, plus a Cossack unit, *Kosaken-Kavallerie-Regiment von Jungschultz*.[48] On paper, *V. Armeekorps* looked like a full-strength infantry corps. However, these divisions were but mere shadows of themselves. Their combined 'bayonet' strength stood at fewer than 11,000 riflemen.[49] *LVII. Panzerkorps* crossed the front lines of *V. Armeekorps* on the evening of 13 February 1943, together with elements of *23. Panzer-Division* and *16. Infanterie-Division (motorisiert)*.

111. Infanterie-Division and *15. Luftwaffen-Felddivision* covered the withdrawal of *LVII. Panzerkorps*. *23. Panzer-Division* was placed in reserve about 20km north of Taganrog.[50] In March *7.* and *8. Luftwaffen-Felddivisionen* were disbanded and the remnant parts absorbed into *15. Luftwaffen-Felddivision*. This small transfusion aided in keeping the division alive past the spring of 1943. One source

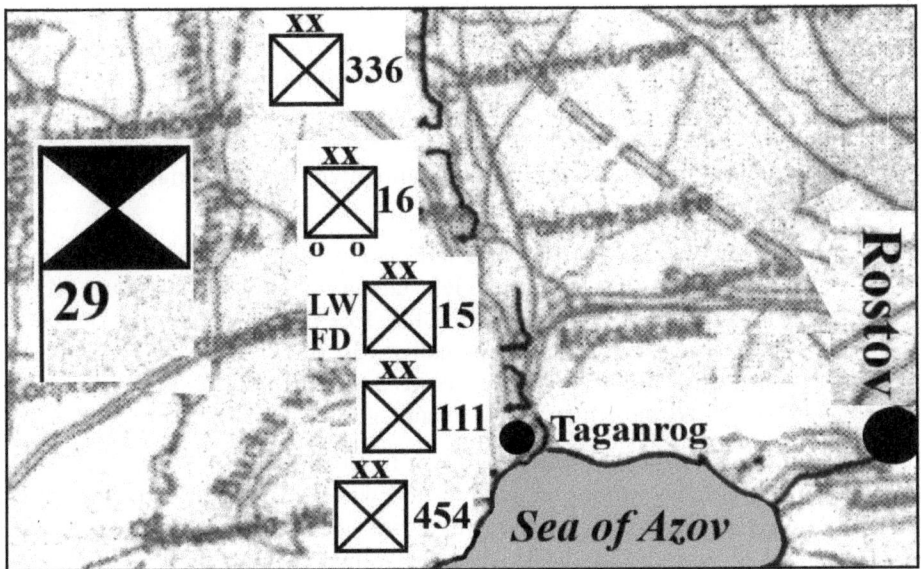

Positions of *15. Luftwaffen-Felddivision* on 27 February 1943.

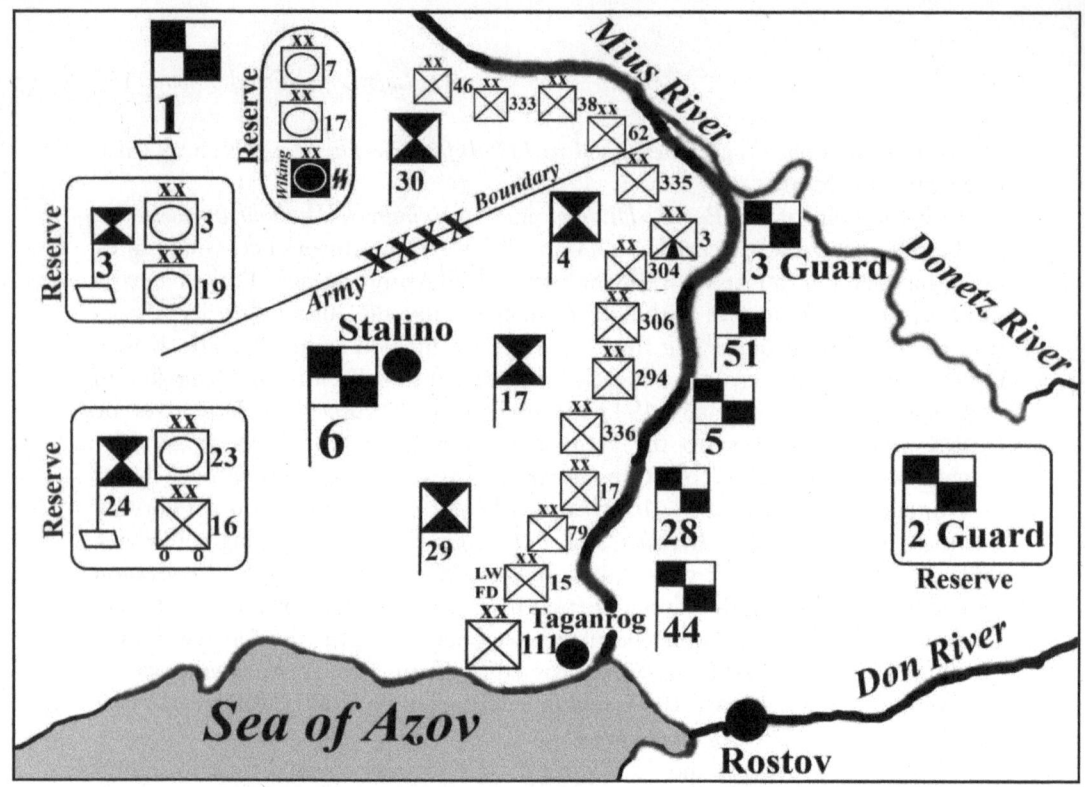

Positions of *15. Luftwaffen-Felddivision*, *6. Armee* and part of *1. Panzerarmee* in April 1943.

states that the remnants of *7. Luftwaffen-Felddivision* were not actually absorbed by the division until May.[51] Whichever is the case, it is clear that the remaining elements of both *7.* and *8. Luftwaffen-Felddivisionen* ended up serving as replacements for *15. Luftwaffen-Felddivision*. On 24 February 1943, *15. Luftwaffen-Felddivision* came under the control of *XXIX. Armeekorps*.[52] Army Detachment Hollidt was renamed the new *6. Armee* at the beginning of April 1943.[53] The so-called divisions of *XXIX. Armeekorps* were divisions in name only. Their weakened condition was typical of units throughout the newly organized *6. Armee*. Its commanding officer, General Hollidt, commented on the strengths of each of his corps and the task they faced:

> My 29. Armeekorps has 8,706 men left. Facing it are 69,000 Russians. My XVII. Armeekorps has 9,284 men left; facing it are 49,500 Russians. My IV. Armeekorps is relatively best off: it has 13,143 men, faced by 18,000 Russians. Altogether 31,133 Germans against 136,500 Russians. The relative strength in tanks is similar: Tolbukhin yesterday had 165 tanks in operation; we have seven tanks and thirty-eight assault guns.[54]

In May 1943 the divisional artillery regiment finally arrived from France but, as stated earlier, its three battalions were armed with old French artillery pieces from the nineteenth century and were therefore of very limited value.

The months of June and July 1943 were relatively quiet ones for *15. Luftwaffen-Felddivision*, especially in July when Soviet interests were concentrated in the

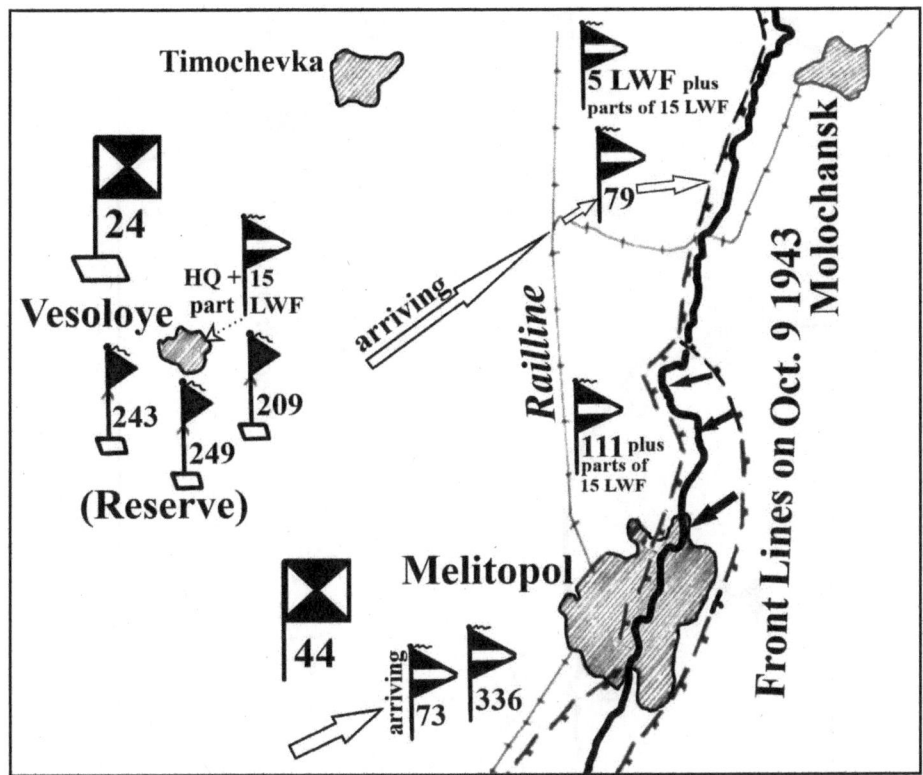

The Soviet attack on Melitopol, October 1943.

region of Kursk, where the Germans had launched their last major offensive of any significance in the East.[55] But in late July the entire southern wing of the Red Army went over to the attack, heralding a terrible period for the *Ostheer* and the German war effort in general. The Germans lost the battle of Kursk, and took heavy losses. The Russians lost even more, however they could replace their losses, while the Germans could not.

In August the Russians in the south also broke through the weak lines of *6. Armee*, near Kyubyshev, and cut off *XXIX. Armeekorps*, effectively defeating this weakened German corps. Once again, *15. Luftwaffen-Felddivision* had to make a hard fighting withdrawal, this time in the direction of Mariupol, which it reached by 10 September 1943. The trapped unit had to attempt to break out of the pocket *XXIX. Armeekorps* now found itself in. *15. Luftwaffen-Felddivision* was surrounded at the mouth of the Mius river, near Taganrog, on 29 August.[56] On the night of 31 August the division, under the personal leadership of *Generalleutnant* Willibald Spange, made its breakout from the *XXIX. Armeekorps* pocket and headed west. The war diary of *6. Armee* noted the extraordinary feats of *Hauptmann* Emil Eitel, the commanding officer of *III. Bataillon/Luftwaffen-Jäger-Regiment 30*, praising his bravery in action. He was killed in action, leading

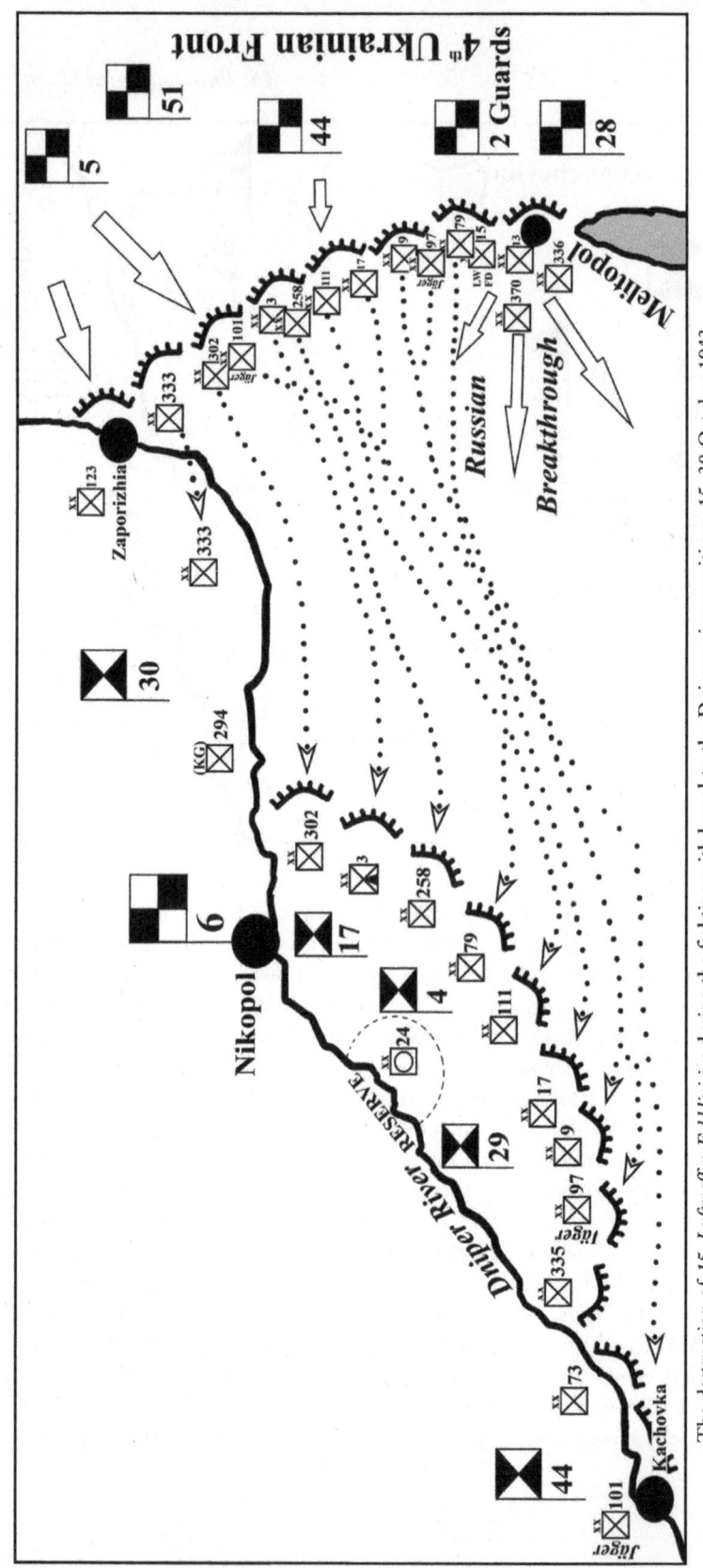

The destruction of 15. *Luftwaffen-Felddivision* during the fighting withdrawal to the Dnieper river positions, 15–30 October 1943.

his men out of the pocket. For his accomplishment, he was posthumously awarded Germany's highest decoration, the much-coveted Knight's Cross:

> 29. Armeekorps, along the Sea of Azov, was surrounded. Desperately the Lower Saxon 111. and the Franconian 17. Infantry Divisions, together with the Central German 13. Panzer-Division, tried to stave off annihilation. Remnants of the 15. Luftwaffen-Felddivision and the Bielefeld 336. Infantry Division, both of which had been smashed, fought their way through to the bulk of the forces in the pocket.[57]

Between 10 September and 15 October 1943 the front lines of *6. Armee* and *1. Panzerarmee* moved westward an average of 40km until they reached the area of Melitopol and Zaporizhzhia. It was in the region between these two Ukrainian cities that the final chapter of the history of *15. Luftwaffen-Felddivision* was written. The artillery regiment, which had not been of much use to the division in the first place, had to leave their ancient artillery pieces during the breakout from the *XXIX. Armeekorps* pocket. The strength of the line regiments had been drained away. For example, *Luftwaffen-Jäger-Regiment 30* had been recently replenished with replacements from 7. and 8. *Luftwaffen-Felddivisionen*, and had begun August with about 2,600 men. By the beginning of September, after the breakout, the regiment was down to only 400 men.[58] The remnants of the division, positioned just north of Melitopol, were ordered to merge with 5. *Luftwaffen-Felddivision*, which now made its appearance in the area after being shifted from the Crimea, where it had been reforming. Another Soviet offensive beginning on 15 October 1943 effectively broke through the German defence lines once again; this time the division was in such a poor condition that it was effectively smashed.[59] What remained was absorbed into 5. *Luftwaffen-Felddivision*, which itself barely managed to escape destruction.

15. Luftwaffen-Felddivision in August 1943.

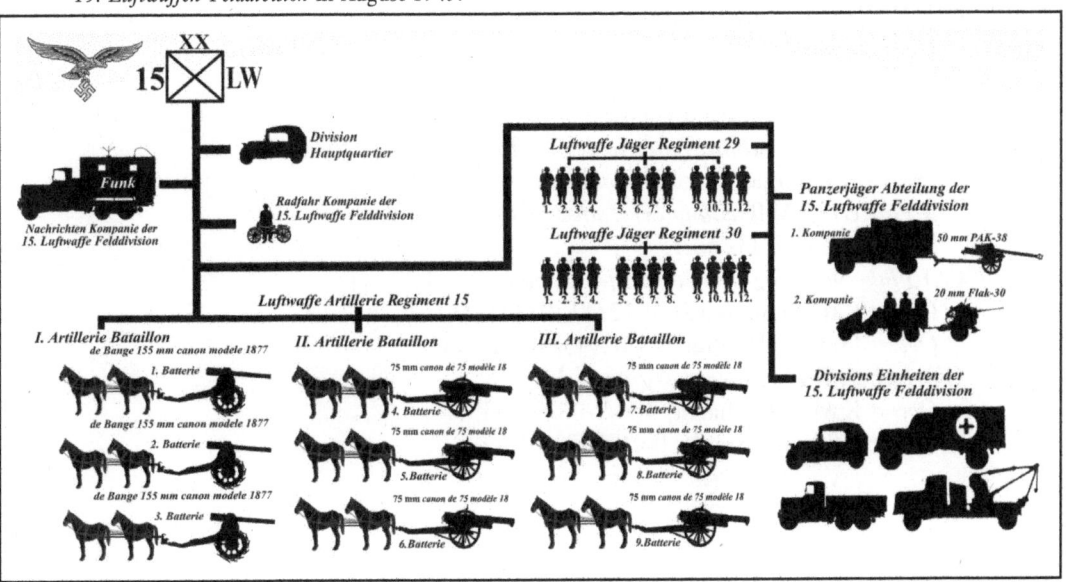

Organization of 15. Luftwaffen-Felddivision
Commanders:
  Divisional Commander:
    Generalleutnant Alfred Mahncke, 01/12/42–02/01/43
    Oberst Heinrich Conrady,[60] 02/01/43–24/01/43
    Oberst Eberhard Dewald,[61] 25/01/43–01/02/43
    Generalleutnant Willibald Spang,[62] 15/01/43–07/11/43[63]
    Oberst Hans-Bruno Schulz-Heyn, 11/12/43–30/12/43
    Generalmajor Eduard Muhr,[64] 01/01/44–07/44
Ia:
    Hauptmann i.G. Dr Hans (Heinrich) Wolf,[65] 10/42–12/42
    Major August Fischer-See,[66] 01/01/43–28/02/43
    Major i.G. Dr Hans (Heinrich) Wolf, 01/03/43–22/03/43
Ib:
    Hauptmann Tuch, 11/42–12/42
    Hauptmann Richter, 01/43–10/43
    Signals Führer:
    Hauptmann Rinow, 11/42–10/43
IIa:
    Hauptmann von Müller, 12/42–10/12/43
CO *Luftwaffen-Jäger-Regiment 29*:
    Oberst Konstantin von Braun, 10/42–12/42
    Oberst Heinrich Conrady, 12/42–10/43
    Oberst Freiherr von Bieberstein, 11/43–03/44
CO *Luftwaffen-Jäger-Regiment 30*:
    Oberst Eberhard Dewald, 12/42–09/07/43
    Oberst Anton Schub, 01/08/43–09/43
    Oberst Kalberlah, 09/43–12/43
CO *III Bataillon / Jäger-Regiment 30 (L)*:
    Hauptmann Emil Eitel, 03/02/43–14/11/43, 20/01/44–14/09/44 (KIA)
CO *Sturmgeschütz-Batterie der Luftwaffen-Felddivision 15*:
    Oberleutnant Friedrich Beutter
Adjutant *Sturmgeschütz Batterie der Luftwaffen-Felddivision 15*:
    Leutnant Andreas von Rackowitsch
CO *Panzerjäger-Abteilung der Luftwaffen-Felddivision 15*:
    Major Dietrich Gerlach
CO *Flak-Abteilung der Luftwaffen-Felddivision 15*:[67]
    Oberst Karl Schuchardt,[68] 12/42–07/02/43
    Oberst Herbert Müller, 08/02/43–05/03/43
CO *Luftwaffen-Artillerie-Regiment 15*:
    Oberst Karl Schuchardt, 1942–08/02/43
    Oberst Wilhelm Mann, 06/03/43–10/43

Somewhere in *Luftwaffen-Artillerie-Regiment 15*:
  Hauptmann Rudolf Freiherr von Schmidtseck, 01/12/42–08/02/43
Somewhere in *IV. Artillerie-Abteilung, Artillerie-Regiment 15 (L)*:
  Oberleutnant Hans-Reinhardt Kukuk
Other officers in the division:
  Leutnant Alfred Schröppel, in *11 Kompanie / Luftwaffen-Jäger-Regiment 30*

The following officers were transferred to *15. Luftwaffen-Felddivision* on the date listed:
  Leutnant Heinz Raddatz, 07/05/43
  Hauptmann Willi Vater, 07/05/43
  Hauptmann der Reserve Ludwig Thome, 08/06/43
  Major Bernhard Warnecke, 08/06/43 (promoted to *Oberstleutnant*, 01/08/43)

16. Luftwaffen-Felddivision

16. Luftwaffen-Felddivision was the first *Luftwaffe* formation earmarked for employment in France and the Low Countries. Up until then, all the air force field divisions had been sent to, or established on, the Eastern Front except for the 11th (sent to Greece) and the 14th (Norway). This division was ordered to be formed shortly after the fall of Stalingrad, when Hitler was attempting to replace the sixteen divisions lost during the battle for that Russian city. On 4 February 1943 Hitler issued a new plan for rebuilding the *Heer*. This called for twenty-six divisions to be refitted, and five new ones to be created in the West. Of these thirty-one planned divisions, those lost at Stalingrad were to be re-established using rear area elements from each formation. The cadre for each of these units was the elements from each division that had not been destroyed when Stalingrad fell. There are always rear area units that are part of a division but are not necessarily with the division itself. Examples include training and replacement formations, repair and maintenance units, men on leave or convalescing, etc. In addition, the German Army in France would provide the necessary recruits to fill out the ranks of these cadre units. The programme also resulted in the creation of eight new occupation divisions that would be handed over to *Oberbefehlshaber West* (Supreme Commander West) in order to make up for the loss of manpower drained by the replenishment of the Stalingrad divisions with soldiers from France.

The new occupation divisions included not only *343., 344., 346., 347.* and *348. Infanterie-Divisionen (bodenständige)* but also *16., 17., 18.* and *19. Luftwaffen-Felddivisionen*.[1] Later, another seven static divisions were delivered to the West in June, July and September 1943: *242., 243., 244., 245., 264., 265.* and *266. Infanterie-Divisionen (bodenständige)*.[2] The static divisions were created using men from the older age group. The four *Luftwaffe* field divisions were different from the other occupation divisions, in that the men tended to be younger and physically fitter, because they had been drawn from excess personnel not needed by the *Luftwaffe*. On average, the age and physical condition of these men was good to excellent. Even before the war began, Hermann Göring's ego had propelled him to make grandiose plans to increase the size of the *Luftwaffe*. He therefore ordered the German recruitment system to draft more personnel than were actually needed for the available aircraft and ground installations. In other words, there were too many ground crews, as well as men from observation, communications, supply and *Flak* units, and even excess air crews. The airmen were there for those squadrons and air wings that had not yet been created, but the *Luftwaffe* simply did not have enough planes to employ them. Again, we see

German troops inspect a French 155mm *modèle* 1917 heavy artillery piece. The *Luftwaffe* field divisions made extensive use of captured foreign artillery pieces. (*Bundesarchiv*)

A father and son duo. These two men were allowed to serve in the same air force field unit. (*Author's collection*)

Marching to the front, 1944. (*Author's collection*)

German Luftwaffe infantry interrogating a suspected partisan, Central Russia, 1942. (*Bundesarchiv*)

A bunker on the Leningrad front, winter of 1942/1943. (*Author's collection*)

Training in the field, 1943. (*Author's collection*)

The commander of
15. Luftwaffen Felddivision,
General Alfred Mahncke.
(*Author's collection*)

Marching to the front, 1943.
(*Author's collection*)

Pre-patrol jitters. The men of a Luftwaffe infantry squad before a patrol, some time in 1943. (*Author's collection*)

(**Opposite, above left**) NCO and later Second Lieutenant Friedrich Sass was a typical German *landser* from the Second World War. Married with three children, Sass was originally a member of the signal corps in the *Luftwaffe*. He fought on the Russian Front before being sent to officer training in France. In the spring of 1944 he visited his wife and children for the last time. As he left for France again, he was teary-eyed because he knew he was probably never coming back. Caught up in the summer 1944 campaign, *Leutnant* Sass and his unit marched from southern France in August–September. On 12 October 1944 Sass was killed in a firefight near the French town of Remiremont, in the Vosges Mountains. (*Author's collection*)

(**Opposite, above right**) *Generalmajor* Eugen Meindl, the commander of *Luftwaffe Felddivision Meindl / 21. Luftwaffe Felddivision*. Meindl was later given command of *I. Luftwaffen-Feldkorps* and in 1943 became commander of *II. Fallschirmjäger-Korps*. (*Bundesarchiv*)

(**Opposite, below**) *Luftwaffe* infantry in the autumn of 1942, during the battle for Stalingrad. (*Bundesarchiv*)

(**Left**) A typical *Luftwaffe* trooper on the Eastern Front, c.1943. (*Bundesarchiv*)

(**Below**) Men from a *Luftwaffe* field division move forward during the 1944 summer battles in France. (*Bundesarchiv*)

Company muster in southern France, spring 1944. (*Author's collection*)

Zwei kameraden. Two comrades from *Flieger-Regiment 13,* summer 1942. (*Author's collection*)

the waste of manpower in the Nazi system, in this case all for the vanity and ego of one man.

Initially, the division was assigned two *Jäger* regiments, *Luftwaffen-Jäger-Regiment 31* and *Luftwaffen-Jäger-Regiment 32*, each of which had three *Jäger* battalions of four companies each. In addition, a three-battalion artillery regiment, *Luftwaffen-Artillerie-Regiment 16*, was also organized. *I. Artillerie-Abteilung* comprised three batteries, each with four heavy 105mm *Flak* guns. *1.* and *2. Artillerie-Batterie* of *II. Artillerie-Abteilung* had four French-made 155mm artillery pieces each, while *III. Artillerie-Abteilung* was fully tracked, with four 105mm artillery guns mounted on outdated French Hotchkiss tank chassis. In the German naming and numbering system, these vehicles were designated as *Hotchkiss 105mm le-FH 18 (Sf.) auf Geschutzwagen 39H(f)*). These oddly shaped mobile artillery guns were slow and clumsy, but slightly better than towed artillery. The division also had a *Flak* battalion, with four batteries. *1.* and *2. Flak-Batterie* each had four 88mm *Flak-18* anti-aircraft guns, while *3.* and *4. Flak-Batterie* had a complement of twelve 20mm *Flak-38* guns apiece. The divisional anti-tank battalion was made up of three companies of towed 75mm PAK-40 and 50mm PAK-38 guns. The entire battalion had 16 50mm and 18 75mm anti-tank guns (12 PAK-40 and 6 PAK-38 guns). The division also contained several company-sized support units, such as signals, bakery, butcher, truck repair, administration, supply, etc. At this time it lacked a reconnaissance battalion, but had a reconnaissance platoon mounted on bicycles. The engineer battalion was fully motorized and had three engineer companies. Table 5 gives a brief list of authorized and available weapons in the division as of 12 February 1943.

The division began organizing at Troop Training Ground Gross-Born using a forming staff from *Fliegerkorps XIII*.[3] It shifted by rail to the area of Ljmuiden,

Table 5. Available weaponry, 12 February 1943.

Weapon	Authorized	On hand
Light MG	446	486[4]
Heavy MG-42	166	125
80mm mortar	60	60
Rifle Grenade Launcher	189	243
88mm *Flak*	8	8
20mm *Flak* 60	24	34
20mm *Flak* 38	30	30
50mm PAK guns	16	15
75mm PAK 38 guns	–	6
75mm PAK 40 guns	16	12
76.2mm Russian guns	–	4
105mm *Flak*	12	12
Bazookas (*Panzerbusche*)	3	0
Hotchkiss 75mm (mech.)	6	4
French 155mm (towed)	8	7

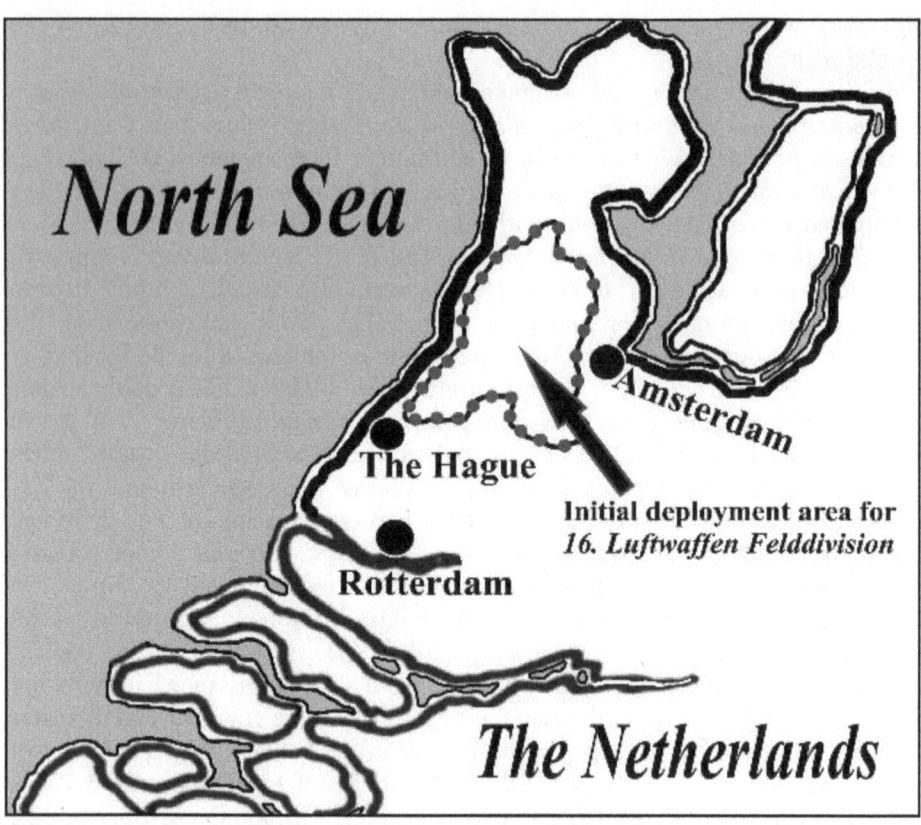

The region bordering Ljmuiden, Haarlem, Leiden and Scheveningen, where *16. Luftwaffen-Felddivision* would train and perform coastal guard duty in 1943. *(Author)*

Haarlem, Leiden and Scheveningen in Holland in early February 1943 to perform coastal security duty while continuing to undergo training.[5] Its personnel were accommodated in the villages, towns and cities in the aforementioned localities. A *Truppendienstliche Befehlsgliederung* (Military Command Structure) document, dated 1 February 1943, listed four divisions under the control of the commander of *LXXXVIII. Armeekorps*. These divisions were described as forming units.[6] They included *16. Luftwaffen-Felddivision*, along with *167., 347.* and *719. Infanterie-Divisionen*. In early March 1943 the division completed its transfer to Holland.[7] Although the division was considered as still forming, *16. Luftwaffen-Felddivision* was charged with coastal guard duty from the start of its tour. In April it was still under *LXXXVIII. Armeekorps* and listed as an occupation division.[8] Another document, dated 1 June 1943, listed the location of most of *16. Luftwaffen-Felddivision* in Holland[9] (see Table 6).

The second half of 1943 was spent undergoing infantry training, with some specialized manoeuvres directly geared for defence against invasion by sea and against air landings. On 1 November 1943, in accordance with the general order

16. Luftwaffen-Felddivision 187

Table 6. Location of *16. Luftwaffen-Felddivision* units on 1 June 1943.

Formation	Location
16. Luftwaffen-Felddivision Headquarters	Amstelveen
Luftwaffen-Jäger-Regiment 31	
Regimental Headquarters	Wassenaar
I. Jäger-Bataillon Headquarters	Wassenaar
1. Kompanie / I. Jäger-Bataillon	Oud Wassenaar
2. Kompanie / I. Jäger-Bataillon	Meijen Del
3. Kompanie / I. Jäger-Bataillon	Wassenaar
4. Kompanie / I. Jäger-Bataillon	Wassenaar
II. Jäger-Bataillon Headquarters	Noordwijk
5. Kompanie / II. Jäger-Bataillon	Noordwijk
6. Kompanie / II. Jäger-Bataillon	Noordwijk
7. Kompanie / II. Jäger-Bataillon	Katwijk
8. Kompanie / II. Jäger-Bataillon	Noordwijk
III. Jäger-Bataillon Headquarters	Scheveningen
9. Kompanie / III. Jäger-Bataillon	Scheveningen
10. Kompanie / III. Jäger-Bataillon	Scheveningen
11. Kompanie / III. Jäger-Bataillon	Scheveningen
12. Kompanie / III. Jäger-Bataillon	Scheveningen
Luftwaffen-Jäger-Regiment 32	
Regimental Headquarters	Bloemendaal
I. Jäger-Bataillon Headquarters	Ijmuiden
1. Kompanie / I. Jäger-Bataillon	Ijmuiden
2. Kompanie / I. Jäger-Bataillon	Wijk
3. Kompanie / I. Jäger-Bataillon	Ijmuiden
4. Kompanie / I. Jäger-Bataillon	Ijmuiden
II. Jäger-Bataillon Headquarters	Overveen
5. Kompanie / II. Jäger-Bataillon	Driehuis
6. Kompanie / II. Jäger-Bataillon	Santpoort
7. Kompanie / II. Jäger-Bataillon	Bloemendaal
8. Kompanie / II. Jäger-Bataillon	Overveen
III. Jäger-Bataillon Headquarters	Hillegom
9. Kompanie / III. Jäger-Bataillon	Hillegom
10. Kompanie / III. Jäger-Bataillon	Lisse
11. Kompanie / III. Jäger-Bataillon	Langeveld
12. Kompanie / III. Jäger-Bataillon	Hillegom
Luftwaffen-Artillerie-Regiment 16	
Regimental Headquarters	Amstelveen
I. Artillerie-Abteilung Headquarters	Wassenaar
1. Batterie / I. Artillerie-Abteilung	Ruigenhoek
2. Batterie / I. Artillerie-Abteilung	Kotwijk
3. Batterie / I. Artillerie-Abteilung	Wassenaar
II. Artillerie-Abteilung Headquarters	Bloemendaal
4. Batterie / II. Artillerie-Abteilung	Bloemendaal
5. Batterie / II. Artillerie-Abteilung	Zandvoort
6. Batterie (Hotchkiss) *le-FH 18 (Sf.) / II. Artillerie-Abteilung*	Removed from the division in June 1943

III. Artillerie-Abteilung Headquarters (*Flak-Bataillon Hauptquartier*)	Sassenheim
7. *Flak Batterie / III. Artillerie-Abteilung*	Oosterdvinen
8. *Flak Batterie / III. Artillerie-Abteilung*	Katwijk
9. *Flak Batterie / III. Artillerie-Abteilung*	Aardenhout
10. *Flak Batterie / III. Artillerie-Abteilung*	Voorschoten
Luftwaffen-Panzerjäger-Abteilung 16	
Panzerjäger-Abteilung 16 Headquarters	Haarlem
1. *Kompanie / Panzerjäger-Abteilung 16*	Haarlem
2. *Kompanie / Panzerjäger-Abteilung 16*	Haarlem
3. *Kompanie / Panzerjäger-Abteilung 16*	Haarlem
4. *Kompanie / Panzerjäger-Abteilung 16*	Haarlem
Pionier-Bataillon 16	
Pionier-Bataillon Headquarters	A'dam
1. *Kompanie / Pionier-Bataillon 16*	A'dam
2. *Kompanie / Pionier-Bataillon 16*	Velsen
3. *Kompanie / Pionier-Bataillon 16*	Noordwijk
Panzerjäger-Abteilung 16	
Panzerjäger-Abteilung Headquarters	A'dam
1. *Kompanie / Panzerjäger-Abteilung 16*	A'dam
2. *Kompanie / Panzerjäger-Abteilung 16*	A'dam
3. *Kompanie / Panzerjäger-Abteilung 16*	A'dam
Versorgungs-Einheiten der Luftwaffen-Felddivision 16	A'dam
Nachrichten-Kompanie der Luftwaffen-Felddivision 16[10]	A'dam
Radfahr-Aufklärungs-Schwadron der Luftwaffen-Felddivision 16[11]	Lisse
Bekerei-Kompanie der Luftwaffen-Felddivision 16	A'dam
Sclachterie-Kompanie der Luftwaffen-Felddivision 16	A'dam
Verwaltungs-Kompanie der Luftwaffen-Felddivision 16	A'dam
Hauptverbandplatz der Luftwaffen-Felddivision 16[12]	Leiden
Krankenkraftwagen-Zug der Luftwaffen-Felddivision 16[13]	Leiden
Versorgungs-Kompanie der Luftwaffen-Felddivision 16[14]	A'dam
Veterinars-Kompanie der Luftwaffen-Felddivision 16[15]	A'dam

from the *OKW*, the division was absorbed into the *Heer*. At the beginning of January 1944 *Felddivision 16 (L)*, as it was now called, was still under the command of *LXXXVIII. Armeekorps*. Allied estimates of the corps listed it as consisting of three weak divisions, one of which, of course, was *Felddivision 16 (L)*. Clearly the division was not rated very highly.[16]

The division was reorganized as soon as it was absorbed into the army. The 105mm *Flak* guns of *I. Artillerie-Abteilung* were detached from the division and returned to the *Luftwaffe*. In their place *I. Artillerie-Abteilung* received Russian-made 76mm field guns. The divisional *Flak* battalion, which was acting as *III. Artillerie-Abteilung* of the artillery regiment, was also detached from the division and transferred back to *Luftwaffe* service, becoming *I. Flak-Abteilung* of *Flak-Regiment 53*.[17] In February 1944 the division began organizing a third line regiment. This was created by detaching the *III. Jäger-Bataillon* from both

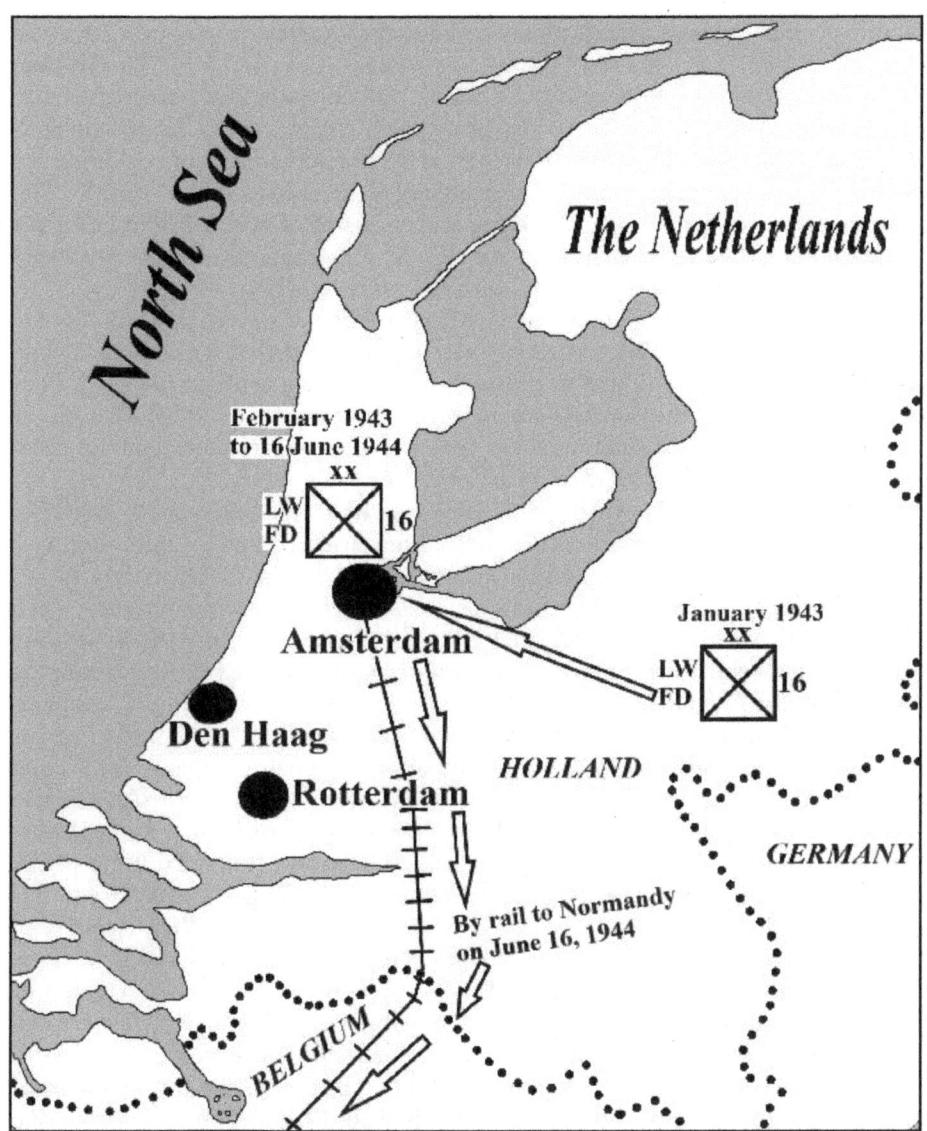

Location of *Felddivision 16 (L)* in Holland, 1943–1944. (*Author*)

Jäger-Regiment 31 (L) and *Jäger-Regiment 32 (L)*, and redesignating them *I.* and *II. Jäger-Bataillonen* of *Jäger-Regiment 46 (L)*.[18]

In addition, while the original two *Jäger* regiments each had a *13. (Infanterie Geschütz)* and *14. (Panzerjäger) Kompanie, Jäger-Regiment 46 (L)* only had a *14. (Panzerjäger) Kompanie*. The divisional anti-tank battalion continued unchanged. It had an assault gun company of ten *Sturmgeschütz III K-40 (L-48 PAK)* anti-tank guns mounted on Panzer-III tank chassis. The battalion was divided into three batteries of three vehicles apiece. The tenth vehicle was reserved for the battalion commander, and also served as a mobile command post. By the time the division arrived in Normandy, the assault gun company had been reduced to two vehicles. What happened to the other eight *Sturmgeschütz III* assault guns is open to conjecture. They may have been given to another division, or destroyed by Allied strafing. The other two companies in the battalion varied. The *2. Panzerjäger-Kompanie* was fully tracked and consisted of twelve 20mm *Flak* guns mounted on armoured half-tracks. Finally, *3. Panzerjäger-Kompanie* possessed twelve 75mm towed anti-tank guns, with *Opel Blitz* trucks to tow them.

On 15 April 1944 the divisional artillery regiment was composed of only two battalions: *I. Artillerie-Abteilung* was equipped with 76mm guns, while *II. Artillerie-Abteilung* still had the French-made 155mm artillery pieces. A divisional fusilier battalion, *Fusilier-Bataillon 16 (L)*, was also established. One of its four companies was mounted on bicycles; this was the original *Radfahr-Aufklärungs-Schwadron der Felddivision 16 (L)*.

One report, dated 24 April 1944, listed *I. Artillerie-Abteilung* of *Artillerie-Regiment 16 (L)* as containing Russian 76.2mm artillery guns.[19] Although one source states that the division left for Normandy on 16 June 1944 with only two artillery battalions, it is possible that a new *I. Artillerie-Abteilung* could have been established between 15 and 24 April 1944 using these captured Russian artillery guns. Another report states that this exchange of guns occurred shortly before the division left for France, which contradicts some previous documents. The signals (communications) company was expanded to a small, two-company signals battalion, *Signals-Bataillon 16 (L)*. Like the original signals company, the second radio company was also fully motorized. A *Feldersatz-Bataillon 16 (L)* was also established to supply replacements for the division. According to a *Kriegsgliederung Karte* dated 15 April 1944, this replacement battalion contained five replacement companies, although again, another source lists only two companies in this reserve battalion on 24 April 1944.[20] On 10 May 1944, LXXXIV. *Armeekorps* established a new coastal defence area that was to be assigned to the control of the *Befehlshäber der Waffen-SS Niederlande*, who at this time was *SS-Obergruppenführer und General der Waffen SS* Karl Demelhuber.[21] This new order created and detailed the reorganization of the Dutch coastal defences in the region of *719. Infanterie-Division* and *Felddivision 16 (L)*.[22] Basically, the Supreme Commander of the *Waffen SS* in the Netherlands would be accountable for coastal defences from the zone defended by *Felddivision 16 (L)*, whose area of responsibility now ran from Noordwijk/Katwijk to Oude Rijn, then Hoogmade, to the area covered by *719. Infanterie-Division* and its coastal defence positions. The first page of this four-page document stated that the following units were to be located in the region of Scheveningen: *Jäger-Regiment 31 (L)*, *4. Kompanie / Festungs-Stamm-Trupp LXXXVIII*,[23] *I. Artillerie-Abteilung / Artillerie-Regiment 16 (L)* and *Polizei-Batterie Scheveningen*.[24]

The second page of the document named *SS-Oberführer der Reserve* Erwin Tzschoppe as responsible for the area of Scheveningen and all German forces there, which now included *II. Jäger-Bataillon* of *Jäger-Regiment 31 (L)*, plus the regimental staff. Thus, for tactical reasons these units were under the command of *SS-Oberführer* Tzschoppe. In support of *Felddivision 16 (L)*, *SS-Obergruppenführer und General de Waffen-SS* Karl Maria Demelhuber brought up two formations: *Ersatz-und-Ausbildungs-Regiment Hermann Göring* and *SS-Ersatz und Ausbildungs-Bataillon 4*.[25] Page three of the document is interesting since it mentions that part of *Felddivision 16 (L)* would help replenish the *Ersatz-und-Ausbildungs-Regiment Hermann Göring*. The commander of LXXXVIII. *Armeekorps* and the divisional commanders at this time were as follows:

Armed Forces Commander Netherlands:
   General der Flieger Friedrich Christiansen
LXXXVIII. Armeekorps:
   General der Infanterie Hans Reinhard
Felddivision 16 (L):
   Generalmajor Karl Sievers
347. Infanterie-Division (bodenständig):
   Generalleutnant Wolf Trierenberg
719. Infanterie-Division:
   Generalmajor Carl Wahle[26]

Felddivision 16 (L) may well have contributed some replacement personnel for the reserve and training unit for the elite *Hermann Göring* formation, for a strength report dated 15 May 1944 listed *Felddivision 16 (L)* as having a total of 9,354 men. This number is significantly smaller than the strength report of 9,873 men for January 1944. It is possible that these 500 or so men left the division individually and for various reasons, but it is also equally possible that several groups of the most physically fit personnel could have been transferred to the *Hermann Göring* reserve and training regiment in early May 1944. In any event, *Felddivision 16 (L)*

Travel route of the division to the Normandy front. (*Author*)

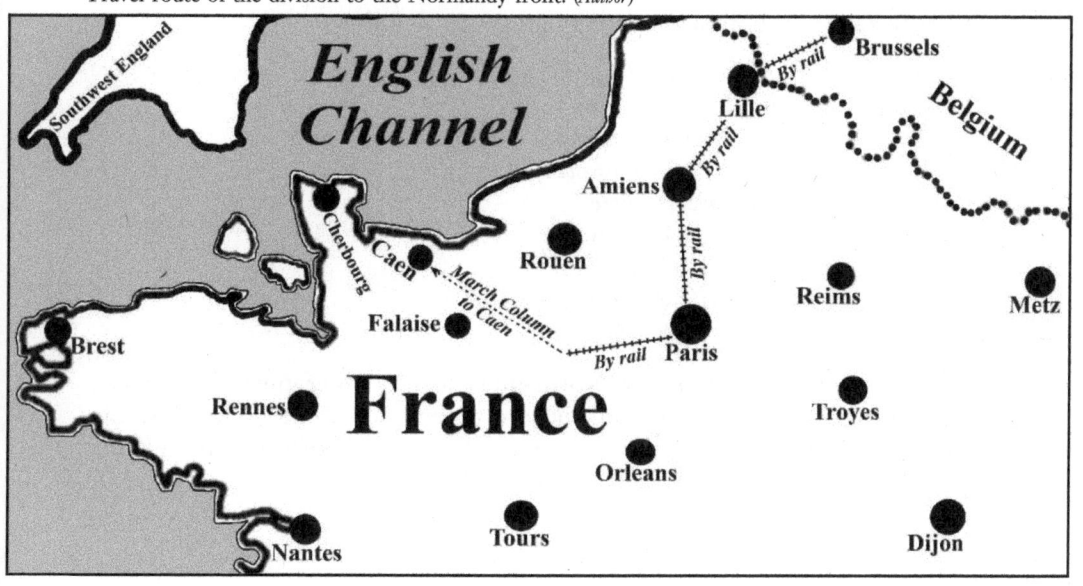

received more men before its move to Normandy in mid-June, since a subsequent strength return listed it as having reached a level of around 9,800 men. The strength report for May 1944 did not change significantly in June.

On 6 June 1944 the Allies landed in Normandy. The Allied deception plan, titled 'Fortitude', kept the bulk of German divisions looking at the *Pas de Calais* region for more than a week, believing that the Normandy landings were a feint and that the real invasion would come further north.[27] This meant the invading troops encountered fewer German divisions, which it was hoped would guarantee their success. Eventually the Allied deception faded under the reality of Allied advances in Normandy, and Hitler finally ordered more German forces to move to the new battle front there. One of the divisions ordered to Normandy was *Felddivision 16 (L)*, which began to move south on 16 June. Movement to Normandy proved extremely difficult. Allied air bombardment had largely destroyed or damaged major railways, bridges and communications centres, thus impeding the arrival of German reinforcements. *Felddivision 16 (L)* had left Holland with slightly fewer men than its official strength, as some remained to operate the guns on the Dutch coast. Having crossed the Seine river and detrained somewhere west of the French capital, the various elements then moved westwards on foot. Thus, the division reached Normandy with 9,816 men, 28 artillery pieces and about 32 anti-tank guns of various calibres. The artillery regiment had been dramatically altered before the division left for Normandy. The large 105mm *Flak* guns of I. *Artillerie-Abteilung* were traded in for captured Russian 76.2mm artillery pieces. Similarly, the French 155mm pieces of II. *Artillerie-Abteilung* were left on coastal guard duty in Holland and the battalion was re-equipped with Russian guns:

6. *Batterie/II. Artillerie-Abteilung* – four 76.2mm guns
7. *Batterie/II. Artillerie-Abteilung* – four 122mm guns
8. *Batterie/II. Artillerie-Abteilung* – four 122mm guns
9. *Batterie/II. Artillerie-Abteilung* – four 122mm guns

The organization of both artillery battalions was as follows:

1. *Batterie* – kein artilleriegeschütze (no artillery pieces)
2. *Batterie* – 76.2mm M1933 (*russische*)
3. *Batterie* – 76.2mm M1933 (*russische*)
4. *Batterie* – 76.2mm M1933 (*russische*)
5. *Batterie* – kein artilleriegeschütze
6. *Batterie* – 76.2mm M1933 (*russische*)
7. *Batterie* – 122mm M1938 (*russische*)
8. *Batterie* – 122mm M1938 (*russische*)
9. *Batterie* – 122mm M1938 (*russische*)

The German military situation in Normandy was becoming graver by the day. The Allies were pouring more and more divisions into Normandy while the Germans were struggling to move their reinforcements forward through the heavy Allied fighter and bomber screen that dominated the skies. It was extremely slow going trying to advance along roads littered with destroyed or damaged tanks and other vehicles, or via damaged rail lines, or across destroyed bridges. The need for troops was so great that a planned German attack east of the Orne river was contingent upon the prompt arrival of *Felddivision 16 (L)* and the withdrawal of Allied naval forces, which had allowed the Allies to use hundreds of naval guns in support of the landings.[28] As the Allied forces advanced deeper into French territory, the naval guns became less of a problem for the Germans. Leading elements of *Felddivision 16 (L)* arrived in the Caen sector as early as 25 June, although the bulk of the division did not arrive until early July. One report states that the division relieved *21. Panzer-Division*, taking over its defence sector.

This allowed the badly mauled *21. Panzer-Division* the opportunity to refit, and it became an operational reserve immediately behind the Caen front lines.[29] In addition, *276. Infanterie-Division* was to link up with *Felddivision 16 (L)* to the west in order to relieve the bulk of *12. SS-Panzer-Division 'Hitler Jugend'*.[30] While *Felddivision 16 (L)* comprised just under 10,000 men, a roster for *276. Infanterie-Division* states that on 4 June 1944 its strength was 11,658 men, plus 1,704 *Hiwis* (*Hilfswilliger*: volunteers, mostly from the USSR). On 1 July, 7,416 men of *Felddivision 16 (L)* arrived in the area of Caen. The remainder of the formation, a smaller group of 2,400 men, would arrive two weeks later on 14 July.[31] By 2 July both *II. Jäger-Bataillon* of *Jäger-Regiment 46 (L)* and *I. Jäger-Bataillon* of *Jäger-Regiment 32 (L)* were fully committed. Meanwhile, *I. Jäger-Bataillon* of *Jäger-Regiment 46 (L)* and *II. Jäger-Bataillon* of *Jäger-Regiment 32 (L)* were preparing for action.[32] In its first engagement against British forces *Felddivision 16 (L)* was bloodied. It had committed two small battalions west of the Orne river. This totalled about 500–600 infantrymen, since it involved only two battalions, each of four companies, with each company having an average strength of just 70–80 men. It was widely reported that these two battalions suffered about 75 per cent casualties during this initial battle, with some 375–380 men killed, wounded or captured. It seems Field Marshal Erwin Rommel had called in the two battalions of *Felddivision 16 (L)* to relieve the equally battered *Panzer-Lehr-Division* in this sector, but the British 3rd Armoured Division attacked the positions of the *Panzer-Lehr-Division* just as the Luftwaffe men came forward:

> On 2 July Rommel (in hopes of forming some kind of mobile reserve) had taken the battered Panzer Lehr Division out of the line and replaced it with the newly arrived *Felddivision 16 (L)*, which had just come down from the Netherlands. The next day Montgomery struck with his veteran British 3. Division at the exact point Panzer Lehr had vacated. Despite the support of the *12. SS-Panzer-Division 'Hitler Jugend'* – itself a mere skeleton – the green air force unit broke and ran. It was a complete rout. The Luftwaffe unit lost 75 per cent of its men (most captured) and almost all of its artillery. The remainder of the unit was so demoralized that Rommel attached it to

21. *Panzer-Division*, probably in the hope that the latter could restore some fighting spirit to the survivors.[33]

The transfer of at least some of the battalions of *Felddivision 16 (L)* to *21. Panzer-Division* is confirmed by its divisional commander, *Oberst* Hans von Luck, who states that early in July he allocated a battalion of *Luftwaffe* troops from *Felddivision 16 (L)* to his armoured combat group. In addition, other *Luftwaffe* battalions were under his divisional control. These were used as blocking forces for *I.* and *II. Bataillonen* of *Panzergrenadier-Regiment 125*.[34] In fact, *General der Panzertruppen* Heinrich von Eberbach, the commander of *Panzergruppe West*, went on to suggest on 23 July 1944 that *Felddivision 16 (L)* should be used to rebuild *21. Panzer-Division*.[35] His proposal was later partly taken up. The attack against the German defenders at Caen continued on the evening of 7 July, when 467 British Lancaster and Short Stirling bombers pummelled the German defence lines. Although greatly weakened, *12. SS-Panzer-Division 'Hitler Jugend'* made the British 59th Infantry Division pay dearly for every village. The British 3rd Armoured Division fared much better, against what British Intelligence was referring to as a low-grade *Luftwaffe* division that had already been severely shaken.[36] Of course, it was never a fair fight to match the stunned *Felddivision 16 (L)* against a full-strength British armoured division.

It was hardly surprising that the unit was 'severely shaken'. During its actions at Caen, *Felddivision 16 (L)* had been attached to *LXXXVIII. Armeekorps*, which was holding the easternmost tip of the German defence lines at Normandy. To the division's right were the remnants of *346. Infanterie-Division (bodenständige)*, while on its left flank was *12. SS-Panzer-Division 'Hitler Jugend'*. Author and former panzer commander Hubert Mayer described the events of 8 July:

> The Hitler Jugend Division was not informed of these considerations. It prepared for the defence of Caen in its sector. Its border on the right, also the right border of I. SS-Panzerkorps, was the railway line Caen–Luc sur Mer. Its neighbour on the right was 16. Luftwaffen-Felddivision, part of LXXXVI. Armeekorps. The border to the south ran along the western edge of Caen and then along the Orne river. It was reasonable to allocate the city of Caen to 16. Luftwaffen-Felddivision since a panzer division is less efficient than an infantry division during fighting inside a town. On the other hand, it was clear that the combat-inexperienced Luftwaffe field division, inadequately equipped with anti-tank weapons, would have great difficulties withstanding an enemy attack supported by tanks. For this reason, one panzer abteilung of 21. Panzer-Division was attached to the division.[37]

The British 3rd Armoured Division was making steady progress against *Felddivision 16 (L)*. In the early morning hours of 7 July it had launched an attack to clear out several companies of *Felddivision 16 (L)* from the wooded region east of the village of Lebisey. The attack began at 6:30am and within two hours the mission was successful.[38] The attack continued on 8 July, when the Canadian 3rd Infantry Division joined in the attack on Caen:

> At 4:20 hours on 8 July, the major attack on Caen started with a surprise fire attack by all the artillery of the 59th Division, the 3rd Canadian Division, the 105th Field Regiment, parts of 4th AGRA, 3rd AGRA and the 107th Heavy Anti-Aircraft Regiment on the la Bijude and Galmanche sectors, and, simultaneously, by the artillery of the 3rd British Division on the adjoining sector to the east. The fire on the sector of 16. Luftwaffen-Felddivision at la Bijude also took in the positions of I./25. The positions of II./25. near Galmanche were the target of the fire there. At the same time, the 6th North Staffords and the 2/6th South Staffords, together with supporting tanks and heavy weapons, crossed the start line for the attacks on la Bijude and Galmanche respectively. The capture of la Bijude was reported at 07:30 hours. At 09:30 hours the last nest of resistance there had been wiped out.[39]

Felddivision 16 (L) began to withdraw on 8 July 1944 as the British 1st Corps began to close in on the town of Caen from the north and northeast. On 9 July it received some much-needed reinforcements when eight *Sturmgeschütz III* assault guns were brought up for the division's anti-tank battalion.[40] On that same day the division took up new makeshift defensive positions behind the Orne and Odon rivers. One *panzergrenadier* regiment from *21. Panzer-Division* was already committed to bolstering the defences of the *Luftwaffe* division, while the bulk of *21. Panzer-Division* was trying to regroup and refresh immediately behind the front lines.[41] Meanwhile, *272. Infanterie-Division*, which arrived at the front on 11 July, had assumed responsibility for the defence of the southern half of the city of Caen behind the Orne river. The remnants of *1. SS-Panzer-Division 'Leibstandarte Adolf Hitler'* were placed right behind *272. Infanterie-Division* as a ready reserve. This all occurred between 13 and 17 July.

On 10 July *Felddivision 16 (L)* took stock of its condition and its situation. All through higher German headquarters it was expected that the main brunt of the next Allied attack in the Caen sector would fall on the division's grenadiers. The unit had already suffered heavy losses since its arrival at the front, especially during Operation Charnwood (the Anglo-Canadian offensive that took place from 7 to 9 July 1944 and was geared to capture Caen), and in the process the British had acquired a very low opinion of its capabilities, making it an obvious target.[42] *Generalmajor* Karl Sievers, the divisional commander, also believing that his formation would be the main target of Allied aggression when the next phase of the Caen battle began, attempted to prepare the division's front lines for a defence in depth. Based on past experience, the forward elements of *Felddivision 16 (L)* were reduced to a small infantry screen in order to avoid losses during the expected heavy bombardment of the front lines by Allied preparatory fire. In addition, the reconnaissance battalion and armoured engineer battalion of *21. Panzer-Division* were positioned immediately to the rear of the remnants of

Artillerie-Regiment 16 (L), which could count on some 88mm *Flak* guns but few artillery pieces. The Flak guns were apparently acquired in Normandy.

Thus, Rommel tried to saturate the rear of *272. Infanterie-Division* and *Felddivision 16 (L)* with sufficient *Flak* and armour to counter the inevitable British attack. On 15 July, three days before the beginning of Operation Goodwood (the final breakout attempt in the region of Caen), the last elements of *Felddivision 16 (L)* arrived at the front. These 2,400 men were well received by the division and its much-depleted line regiments. By mid-July the entire *LXXXVI. Armeekorps*, which on paper contained four divisions – *21. Panzer-Division, Felddivision 16 (L), 346.* and *711. Infanterie-Divisionen (bodenständige)* – was actually no larger than a reinforced division, as each of its divisions had been reduced to a battlegroup. The only unit still more or less intact was *schwere SS-Panzer-Abteilung 103 (503)*, which was in corps reserve.[43] Rommel had established five lines of *Flak*, infantry and tank defences east of the Orne river. He had already decided that the infantry companies of *272. Infanterie-Division* and *Felddivision 16 (L)* would be the first line, referring to them coldly as expendable; it seems he was willing to sacrifice them in order to slow the Allied advance.[44] The forwardmost defence lines had a small screen of infantry with the main line of resistance about 200 metres behind the front lines. Here Rommel had instructed the infantry forces to dig in, especially near deep hedgerows that would cover their trenches from observation or air attack.[45] *Felddivision 16 (L)* was to cover the line from the edge of Vaucelles to Toufreville, where the trench lines of *346. Infanterie-Division* began. Behind the 'cannon fodder' infantry lay the divisional anti-tank and reserve units, and behind them were the artillery positions. Immediately behind the artillery units was the *Flak* screen, while the panzers of *1. SS-Panzer-Division* and *21. Panzer-Division* were to be the final and fifth line of defence. Allied carpet bombing of the area began on 17 July 1944 at exactly 5:00 am. For two days the Germans sat back and took a pounding that included over 60,000 shells expended in the region of *LXXXVI. Armeekorps*, equating to 1,250 shells per hour, or 20 shells a minute. Another 40,000 shells landed on the adjacent *I. SS-Panzerkorps*. More than 2,200 bombers dropped an estimated 7,800 tons of munitions over the projected breakout region. Under this terrific hammering, *Felddivision 16 (L)*, already greatly weakened, folded like so much cardboard.[46] All its battalion and regimental commanders were either killed or wounded. The fifty remaining tanks of *21. Panzer-Division* were buried where they stood. After this savage assault, not a single tank appeared intact to oppose the Allied drive:

> These air attacks, the heaviest flown in support of ground troops until that time, completely smashed the forward lines of *Felddivision 16 (L)* and also hit the panzer assembly area. Many of the panzers were put out of action by hits, others were rendered useless for an extended period of time because of sand in their engine compartments and optical mechanisms. At 07:45, after the medium bombers had turned away, the tanks of the 11th Armoured Division started their attack behind a moving wall of fire from approximately

700 Allied guns. In addition, 48 heavy anti-aircraft guns and 21 battleship guns fired on various targets. The tanks overran the positions of *Felddivision 16 (L)* and the strong points close behind.[47]

Felddivision 16 (L) was effectively and finally destroyed during the eight days between 18 and 25 July. The *OKW* listed the division as having been lost from 23 to 25 July 1944.[48] The division was officially dissolved on 3 August 1944,[49] although one source states that this happened a day later, on 4 August.[50] Both sources, however, agree that the remnants of *Felddivision 16 (L)* were taken into the ranks of the much-reduced *21. Panzer-Division* and the newly established *16. Infanterie-Division*, which began organizing on 4 August 1944.[51] This new division was established from *158. Reserve-Division*, plus some elements from the

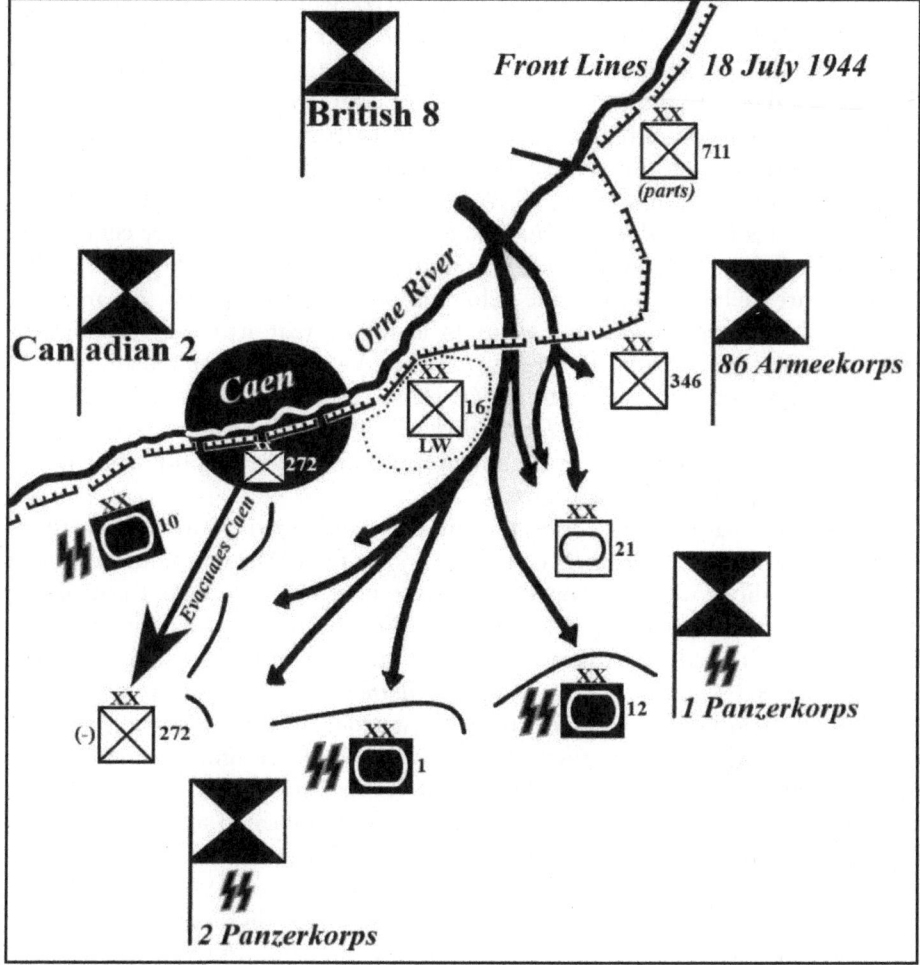

Operation Goodwood, 18–22 July 1944. *(Author)*

Table 7. Ground and air losses, 6 June–29 September 1944.

	Killed	Wounded	Missing[52]	Total
Luftwaffe	2,600	4,400	22,500	29,500
Osttruppen	160	340	7,900	8,400
Heer	26,000	78,000	259,000	363,000[53]
Kriegsmarine	?	?	?	60,000
Total	28,760	82,740	289,400	460,900

now-defunct *Felddivision 16 (L)*. It was part of the thirtieth wave of German divisions.[54] *16. Infanterie-Division* was redesignated *16. Volksgrenadier-Division* in October 1944. This *16. Infanterie-Division* should not be confused with the Prussian-raised *16. Infanterie-Division (motorisiert)*, which was upgraded in 1944 to become *116. Panzer-Division*. *Felddivision 16 (L)* had lost around 2,500 men killed, wounded or captured between 1 July and 3 August 1944, or an average of 78 men per day – roughly the strength of the average line company when the division was first committed. It is interesting to compare the *Luftwaffe* losses (including ground and air losses) with the figures for other services on the Western Front between 6 June and 29 September 1944[55] (see Table 7).

The fatalities incurred by *Felddivision 16 (L)* amounted to 8.5 per cent of the total *Luftwaffe* losses for the period. This is quite a large percentage given that the 29,500 figure includes not only the field divisions in the West (*16., 17.* and *18.*), but also all the support, *Flak* and air units, as well as rear area and headquarters personnel. The total *Luftwaffe* strength in the West had amounted to 340,000 men, of whom 100,000 served in the *Flak* forces, 30,000 in the parachute troops and another 28,000 or so in the *Luftwaffe* field divisions[56] *Felddivision 16 (L)* was always a third-rate formation, even though it contained a large proportion of the healthier recruits of the 30 age-group.[57]

There were many reasons why the division performed poorly, not least of which was the fact that during its combat history it faced Allied armoured units of the highest calibre while equipped with substandard or insufficient armament, especially anti-tank guns and heavy artillery. For example, it was armed almost completely with Russian artillery pieces. The strength of the division fluctuated and was reduced several times, as when *Felddivision 16 (L)* was taken over by the *Heer* on 1 November 1943. At that time it lost around 2,000 men who remained with the *Luftwaffe* and were transferred to other air force units. Some of these men were also transferred to the *Fallschirmjäger* or *Flak* forces.[58] It didn't help, either, that close to 500 men from the division were allocated to the reserve and training regiment of the *Panzergrenadier-Division 'Hermann Göring'* in May 1944, about a month before it was sent into battle.

The constant fluctuation of personnel in and out of the division did nothing for unit cohesion. Additionally, the German High Command, in trying to maintain the division's strength, had sent replacements who turned out to be *Volksdeutsche* (ethnic Germans) from various parts of Europe. These were drafted men, whose motivation and loyalty – and therefore their fighting value – were always mediocre and questionable.[59] They were forced to bond quickly with their German cousins, although some *Volksdeutsche* personnel surrendered as soon as they got the chance. In many cases there was also a language barrier, because many of the newer ethnic German recruits spoke very little German. In the process, officers lost experienced NCOs whom they had trusted to carry out their orders and relied on to react correctly in any given situation. NCOs lost trained men only to receive new recruits whom they did not know at all. In addition, the Air Force field divisions earmarked for operations in France and Italy (that is, *Felddivisionen 16 (L), 17 (L), 18 (L), 19 (L)* and *20 (L)*) were basically foot formations that were dependent primarily on horses to move their men and equipment. Very few of their respective divisional units were ever motorized. This made them greatly inferior to the fully motorized, fully equipped Allied divisions.

In retrospect, it was no surprise that *Felddivision 16 (L)* was destroyed after being committed to battle for just over a month. The unit was inferior in all respects to any Allied division it ever faced. Add to this the fact that it experienced some of the worst fighting and the heaviest bombardments from Allied bomber fleets, followed by hours of intensive artillery barrages and massed tank and mechanized assaults, and we come to the conclusion that the obliteration of the unit was inevitable. In fact, it is a wonder that, given its crippling deficiencies and formidable adversaries, the division fought for as long as it did. We can attribute this to the fact that almost from the beginning Rommel and all the other commanding officers ordered local army units to mix with the *Luftwaffe* men. This gave the division a chance to survive, at least for a while, despite the fact that the unit was virtually tied down in heavy fighting from the very day that it was committed. Stories about the deficiencies and weaknesses of these *Luftwaffe* field divisions had travelled from the Eastern Front to France, so those in command knew what they were getting. The *16. Luftwaffen-Felddivision/Felddivision 16 (L)* also suffered from all the deficiencies that the other *Luftwaffe* field divisions

16. Luftwaffen-Felddivision in August 1943.

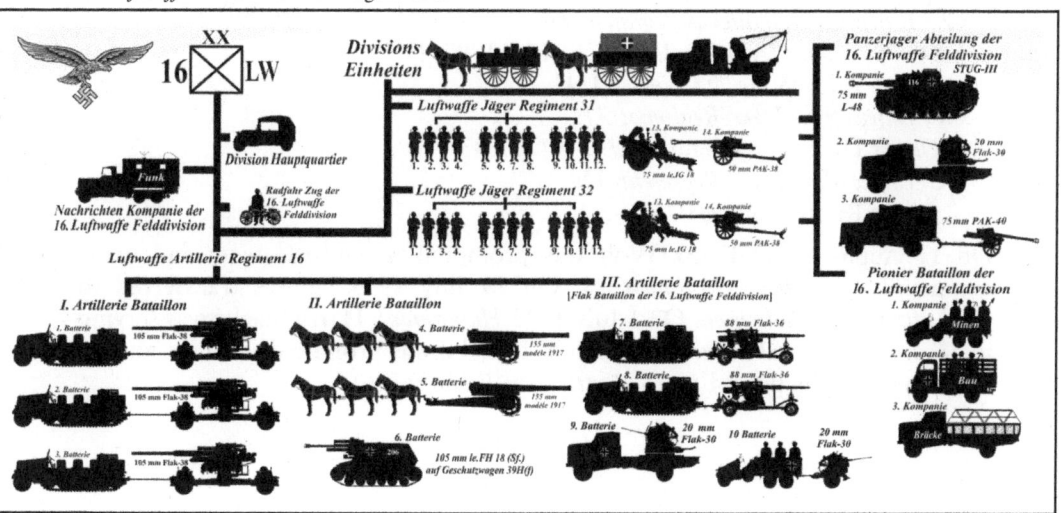

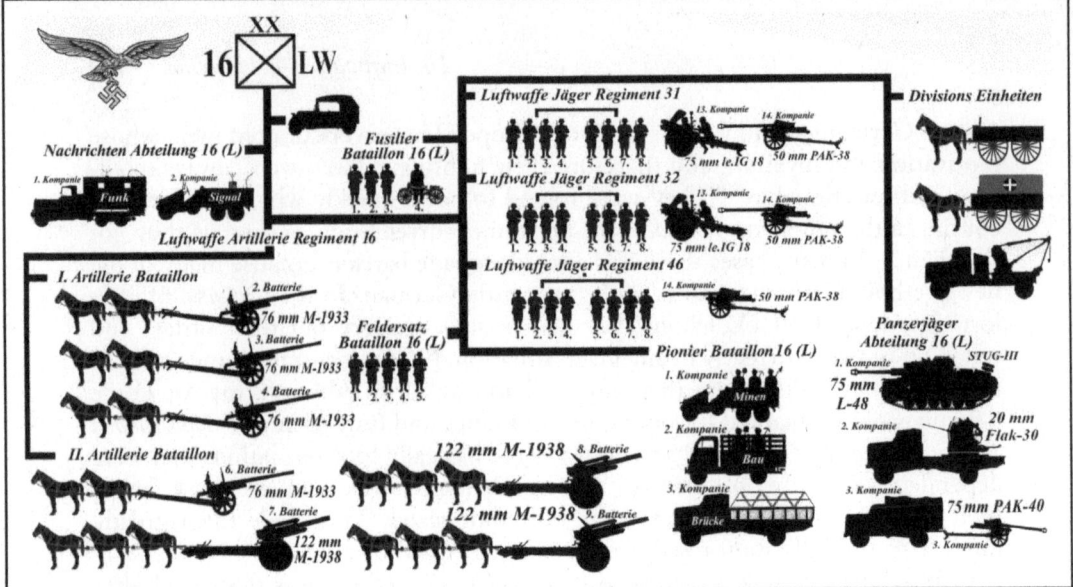

Felddivision 16 (L) in June 1944.

experienced, with the added disadvantages of serving in France against a vastly superior enemy with unlimited supplies in men and materiel, and complete command of the air. Given all of these drawbacks, and the division's limited combat value, a survival rate of a little over a month is not surprising.

Organization of *16. Luftwaffen-Felddivision*

Commanders:
  Divisional Commander:
    Oberst Otto von Lachemair, 12/42–21/08/43
    Generalmajor Karl Sievers,[60] 22/08/43[61]–25/07/44[62]
  Ia:
    Hauptmann Otto Wilhelm,[63] 12/42–09/12/43[64]
    Oberstleutnant Hans Biekel, 10/12/43–?
  IIa:
    Oberstleutnant Theiß, 10/12/43–?
  CO *Luftwaffen-Artillerie-Regiment 16*:
    Oberstleutnant Walther Palitzsch, 12/42–07/43[65]
    Oberst Kurt Wille,[66] 07/43–11/43
  CO *Luftwaffen-Jäger-Regiment 31*:
    Oberst Dr Edgar Johann, 12/42–01/11/43
  CO *Luftwaffen-Jäger-Regiment 32*:
    Oberst Rudolf Junge, 07/43–?

On 12 August 1942 Franz Wolf was promoted to *Oberstleutnant* and made commander of *Flieger-Regiment 23*. On 29 July 1943 he was transferred to *16. Luftwaffen-Felddivision*. On 1 July 1943 *Hauptmann* Harry Staake was serving in *16. Luftwaffen-Felddivision*. On 8 July 1943 he was promoted to *Major* and on the same day was posted to *18. Luftwaffen-Felddivision*.

17. Luftwaffen-Felddivision

This division was formed at the end of 1942 from men in *Luftwaffe* units originally located in *Luftgau VII* (Munich). It seems some or all parts of the division were initially trained and/or organized in Pomerania.[1] From the very beginning, the division was earmarked as one of eight brand-new occupation divisions that were to be assigned to the German Army to serve as static divisions in France and the Low Countries.[2] In addition, it was also designated as a *bodenständige* (static) formation. In practical terms, this meant the division would require minimal motor transport, given that its missions were occupation duty and manning the Atlantic Wall defences. The further significance of the term 'static division' was that it would include a larger percentage of older age reservists. The logic was that less physically fit men would serve better if they did not have to force march or be used in attacks, which requires more stamina, strength and agility. They would be better off sitting in a bunker, manning a machine gun. Although *17. Luftwaffen-Felddivision* was categorized as a static unit, it was in slightly better condition than most army static divisions, given that its personnel came from the *Luftwaffe*, where the average age (about 30) and physical condition of the men was far younger and stronger than the type of men (aged 38–40) the *Wehrmacht* was typically drafting into service by 1943.

17. Luftwaffen-Felddivision was allocated two *Jäger* line regiments, *Luftwaffen-Jäger-Regiment 33* and *Luftwaffen-Jäger-Regiment 34*, of three battalions each. This was the standard *Luftwaffe* field division organization, although it changed when the army assumed control of these air force units. An artillery regiment, *Luftwaffen-Artillerie-Regiment 17*, was also established. It had three artillery battalions. As was standard practice, *III. Artillerie-Abteilung* of the artillery regiment was the divisional *Flak* battalion. The artillery regiment was said to have been organized in Arys, East Prussia.[3] The rest of the division consisted of an engineer battalion and an anti-tank battalion, plus smaller units including a communications (signal) company and a reconnaissance company. Support units included an administrative company, a butcher company, etc. The small size of the division's communications unit and its reconnaissance company was sufficient for the purpose of static defence, but would have been totally inadequate if the division were to be employed as a regular infantry formation. However, this organization was standard practice among the Air Force field divisions.

On 28 December 1942, *7. Armee* in France assigned the divisional headquarters staff of *17. Luftwaffen-Felddivision* to the town of Coetquidan, in Brittany. The train carrying the leading elements of *17. Luftwaffen-Felddivision* reached the area of *7. Armee* on 2 January 1943.[4] The next day four large trains brought additional forces, and on 4 January seven more trains arrived from the *Reich* carrying men and equipment for the forming division. Eight more trains reached Brittany on 5 January, and twelve more a day later. By 7 January 1943 the transfer of *17. Luftwaffen-Felddivision* to Brittany was completed.[5] It had taken just thirty-two transport trains to bring the *Luftwaffe's* 17th Division to Brittany in less than a week. By comparison, the transfer of *320. Infanterie-Division* had required no fewer than fifty-eight trains.[6] These numbers indicate that the *Luftwaffe* division was significantly smaller (in terms of men and equipment) than *320. Infanterie-Division*, which was a regular infantry formation in the *Heer*. The simple assumption that can be drawn is that *17. Luftwaffen-Felddivision* was about half the size of a regular German infantry division. Thus, although labelled a division, it was probably little more than a brigade. This conclusion is reinforced by the unit's organization, which was far smaller in scale than any army TO&E for that period. In addition, strength returns for the *Luftwaffe* field divisions, with few exceptions, never exceeded more than 8,000–9,000 men at any one time.

17. Luftwaffen-Felddivision came initially under the direct control of *7. Armee* headquarters in January 1943 but towards the end of the month it was reassigned to *XXV. Armeekorps*. An order dated 7 February 1943, however, allotted the unit to *15. Armee*, requesting that preparations be made to move the unit to the area

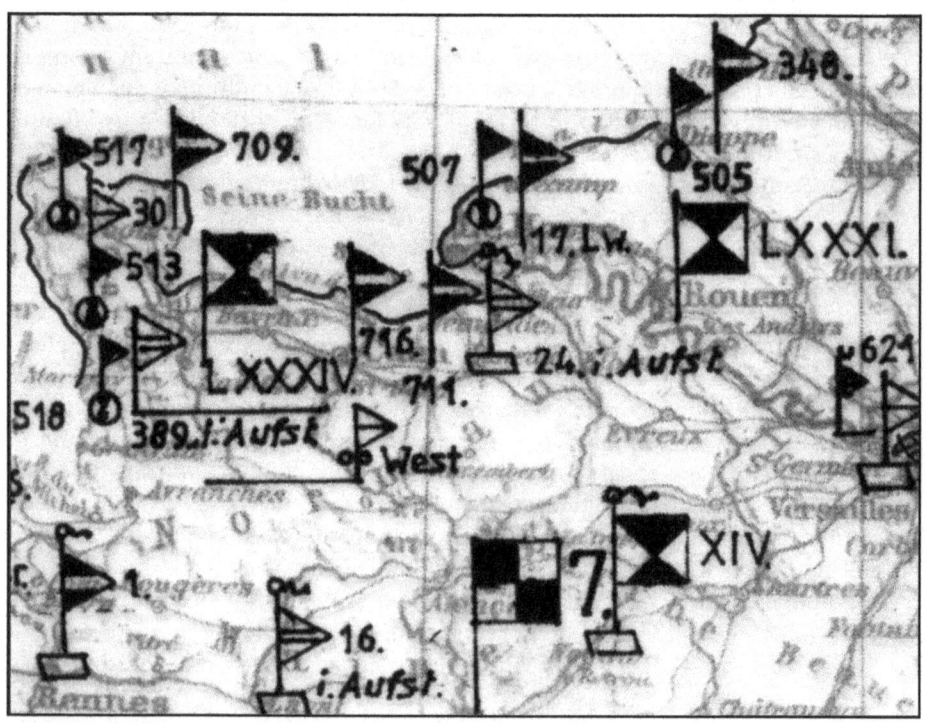

A German *Kriegsgliederung Karte* showing the location of *17. Luftwaffen-Felddivision* and surrounding units on 7 April 1943.

between Dieppe and Le Havre,[7] where it was to take up coastal guard duty.[8] On 8 February, *17. Luftwaffen-Felddivision* noted that an initial batch of four platoons had begun the move. That same day, the commander of the division reported that one recruit had been killed and four others wounded during a training exercise. On 9 February a work detail of four platoons was detached and assigned to *332. Infanterie-Division*.

Between March and October 1943, *17. Luftwaffen-Felddivision* was located just east of Le Havre, near the mouth of the River Seine.[9] On 10 February the division began to move towards the region of *15. Armee*, and its new assignment near Le Havre. It was also on this date that the division was officially transferred over to *15. Armee*. On 12 February the first units began to arrive on the coast. A day later, another twenty platoons left for Le Havre. The primary mission of the unit was now coastal watch duty, but the towns of Le Havre and Dieppe were not to come under the command of the unit:

> In terms of permanent fortifications, the Germans continued to concentrate a substantial portion of their heavy construction work near the major ports, and Hitler went so far as to declare eleven of them as 'fortresses' *(festungen)* on January 19, 1944. The areas singled out were Ijmuiden and the Hook of Holland in the Netherlands; Dunkirk, Boulogne, and Le Havre in the *15. Armee* sector along the Channel; Cherbourg, St. Malo, Brest, Lorient, and St. Nazaire in the *7. Armee* zone; and the Gironde river estuary that led to Bordeaux in the *1. Armee* area. *Wehrmacht* staff officers added three more fortresses – the Channel Islands and the coastal harbours of Calais and La Pallice-La Rochelle – during February and March.[10]

In fact, the towns and cities that were declared fortresses had their own guard troops. Of course, the idea of making these coastal towns fortresses was nonsensical, and the argument that such a move deprived the Allies of port space did not justify the loss of personnel ordered to defend them, notably the *Festungs-Stamm-Truppen* (Fortress Cadre Troops) (see Table 8).

The combat readiness of *17. Luftwaffen-Felddivision* was very poor, basically because it had very few officers and NCOs with combat experience, or any training skills in order to properly instruct the recruits in the line companies. In order to alleviate this situation, and help speed up the preparedness of the division, *65. Infanterie-Division*, which had already provided similar help for

Table 8. Declared fortresses by the German High Command.

Town/City	Troops	Town/City	Troops
Cherbourg	1,355	Brest	2,001[11]
Dinard	900	St Nazaire	761[12]
Lorient	953	St Michel	109
Plouhinec	172	Vannes	305
Ause de Pouldu	395	Guerrance	501

44. Infanterie-Division Hoch und Deutschmeister, was ordered on 19 February 1943 to provide training for the *Luftwaffe* soldiers:

> On February 19, the Sixty-fifth was ordered to provide training personnel for the Seventeenth Luftwaffe Field Division. In exchange for privates and junior officers, the Sixty-fifth was to send an infantry battalion commander, an artillery battalion commander, a machine gun company commander, five infantry platoon leaders, and fourteen squad leaders, about 10 per cent of its leadership.[13]

The division now spent a lot of time preparing for an Allied invasion, laying down tens of thousands of anti-tank and beach obstacles, while simultaneously undergoing training. During the summer of 1943 it settled down to a routine of garrison and coastal guard duty, sprinkled with training exercises whenever possible, in order to try to bring the unit up to speed. Building up Hitler's Atlantic Wall was also a job that every German division in the West needed to perform. By 1943 Hitler's *Festung Europa* (Fortress Europe) was no longer a propaganda myth, but a reality. The term *Festung Europa* referred to a series of fortifications and obstacles of all kinds that the Nazis either built or embedded into the French and Dutch coast lines and beaches. Some of these obstacles were simple, but ingeniously effective and deadly. Many were also armed with hidden mines that would explode on contact. By 1943 a total of 1,992,895 mines had been laid in the West. By 30 May 1944 that number had increased to 6,508,330. In addition, strong concrete fortifications were built along the coast. In May 1942 about 110,000 cubic metres of concrete had been poured in helping to turn what Field Marshal von Rundstedt initially called (in 1941) the 'Atlantic Wall myth' into a series of static concrete fortifications for troops and artillery pieces. In April 1943 a whopping 780,000 cubic metres of concrete was poured.[14] Thus, the average monthly concrete output for the wall in 1943 was some seven times greater than the average output in 1942.

Even though the *Organization Todt* was in overall control of building the major concrete structures for Hitler's Atlantic Wall defences, the German divisions themselves were responsible for laying out a lot of the minor and medium strength barricades, tank obstacles, barbed wire fences, mine fields, etc. For example, *17. Luftwaffen-Felddivision* and its neighbour, *346. Infanterie-Division*, together installed a total of 200,000 camouflaged anti-glider landing stakes, complete with concertina wire. The *Luftwaffe* men also built numerous bunkers and pillboxes for heavy weapons and machine guns.[15] They performed relatively well in outfitting their part of the Atlantic Wall with deadly obstacles and defences, so much so that when the time came to design a divisional emblem, the divisional command chose an image of an anti-invasion obstacle superimposed on a divisional shield. In April 1943, *17. Luftwaffen-Felddivision* had plenty of backup divisions to support its defence of Le Havre. However, many of these units were in France temporarily refreshing and would eventually be sent back to

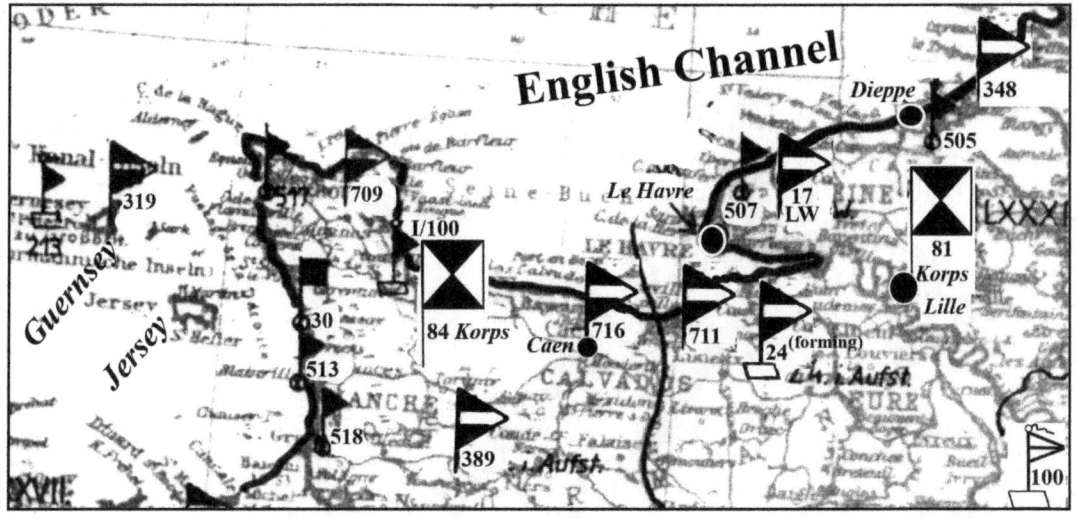

A German *Kriegsgliederung Karte* showing the location of *17. Luftwaffen-Felddivision* in June 1943.

fight in Russia. Three months later, on 1 July 1943, the number of German forces in the area around Le Havre had been reduced.

On 1 November 1943 the army assumed control of the surviving *Luftwaffe* field divisions and *17. Luftwaffen-Felddivision* was now redesignated *Felddivision 17 (L)*.[16] Immediately, many changes were instituted in the division. A third regiment was planned that would be raised by taking a *Jäger-Bataillon* from each regiment. Now *Jäger-Regiment 33 (L)* and *Jäger-Regiment 34 (L)* were to have two *Jäger* battalions instead of three. A divisional fusilier battalion was also formed, with four rifle companies. The divisional *Flak* battalion was withdrawn and eventually became *I. Flak-Abteilung* of *Flak-Regiment 20*.[17] Although two sources state that the divisional anti-tank battalion in 1944 was composed of three companies, one German *Kriegsgliederung Karte* for November 1943 listed only two: the first was the 75mm towed anti-tank company, and the second was a small assault gun battery of four *Sturmgeschütz III* assault guns armed with the L48 75mm anti-tank gun. Each of the two artillery battalions contained twelve barrels. One source says that *II. Artillerie-Abteilung*, which was originally armed with Czech-made 155mm artillery pieces, replaced those guns with older model 150mm guns.[18] The French-made 105mm guns of *I. Artillerie-Abteilung* were said to have remained in the regiment.

On 15 February 1944 *Jäger-Regiment 47 (L)* was finally organized and activated.[19] Strangely, the German command ended up using the *I. Bataillon* from both *Jäger-Regiment 33 (L)* and *Jäger-Regiment 34 (L)*. Normally the third battalion in each of the two *Jäger* regiments would be used to create the third regiment, but this was not the case here. In April a battalion made up of men from the Caucasus region, originally designated as *Nordkaukasische-Infanterie-Bataillon 835*, arrived in the area of *Felddivision 17 (L)*, and was integrated into the division as *III. Jäger-Bataillon* of *Jäger-Regiment 34 (L)*.[20] When the division was transferred to the front lines, this battalion of volunteers from the Soviet Union would be left behind. One report states that the North Caucasian battalion was eventually converted into a construction unit and may have helped

Fighting along the Seine river, 13–19 August 1944. (*Author*)

supply recruits for the *Kaukasicher Waffen-Verbände der SS* in late 1944.[21] Apparently, another foreign battalion, which was under the command of a German officer, *Hauptmann* Keilig, was also attached to the division's artillery regiment during this time.[22]

By May 1944 the division had been able to establish an anti-invasion defensive position that stretched 4–5km in length along the coast line. The divisional headquarters was now located in Auberville la Renault, about 14km northwest of Belbec. On 1 June 1944 the strength of *Felddivision 17 (L)* was exactly 9,543 officers, NCOs and enlisted men. Since November 1943 the division had received a greater influx of army officers and NCOs, which it was hoped would help raise the level of preparedness of the division. One of these officers was *Oberstleutnant* Elmar Warning, now the divisional Ia (operations officer). Warning had served with *Feldmarschall* Erwin Rommel in North Africa, and the story goes that Rommel had relieved Warning of his duties on the staff of the Afrika Korps in November 1942 for questioning his decisions.[23] Now, however, Rommel visited Warning and his new command on 16 July 1944. He would soon commit *Felddivision 17 (L)* to the heavy fighting in Normandy, and wanted to gauge its abilities. He was not impressed, but his forces in Normandy were losing an average of 2,500–3,000 men per day killed, wounded, missing or captured. Since the D-Day landings, total losses had been 97,000 men, with 225 tanks destroyed. Up until 17 July, only 10,000 men and 17 tanks had arrived as replacements.

On 23 July 1944 *Felddivision 17 (L)* assumed command of the city of Le Havre, although this was only temporary, since the division would leave for the invasion front in the first week of August, a development prompted by the break-out of the Allied armies from Normandy. Indeed, it was a drastic decision since the division, as a static formation, lacked proper motor vehicles and had less horse-drawn transport than usual.[24] As a result, the division didn't reach the front lines until 19 August 1944. Before the division left Le Havre the Czech-manufactured 150mm artillery pieces of *II. Artillerie-Abteilung* were replaced with antiquated First World War guns of 150mm calibre. Upon its arrival in Normandy, *Felddivision 17 (L)*, still under *LXXXI. Armeekorps*, was sent to the front lines and assumed responsibility for the defence of the corps' left flank on 20 August.[25]

When the *Luftwaffe* men left Le Havre on 13 August, *226. Infanterie-Division* was made responsible for the defensive positions in and around the town.[26] This division would lose a part of its complement when the 7th Canadian Brigade surrounded and then captured Calais in early September 1944. What was left of the division eventually withdrew to Dunkirk, where it remained (trapped) for the rest of the war.

One day later, on 21 August 1944, Allied divisions broke through the defence lines of *344. Infanterie-Division* and *Felddivision 17 (L)*.[27] By 23 August *Felddivision 17 (L)* had been so shaken that part of the unit was operating separately, while the bulk of the division had withdrawn and taken up defensive positions behind the River Seine, near Elbeuf. On 25 August *Felddivision 18 (L)* received some very badly needed reinforcements when the elements of *Felddivision 17 (L)* that had been left behind in Le Havre finally began to arrive at the front. They were

The military situation on 23 August 1944. (*Author*)

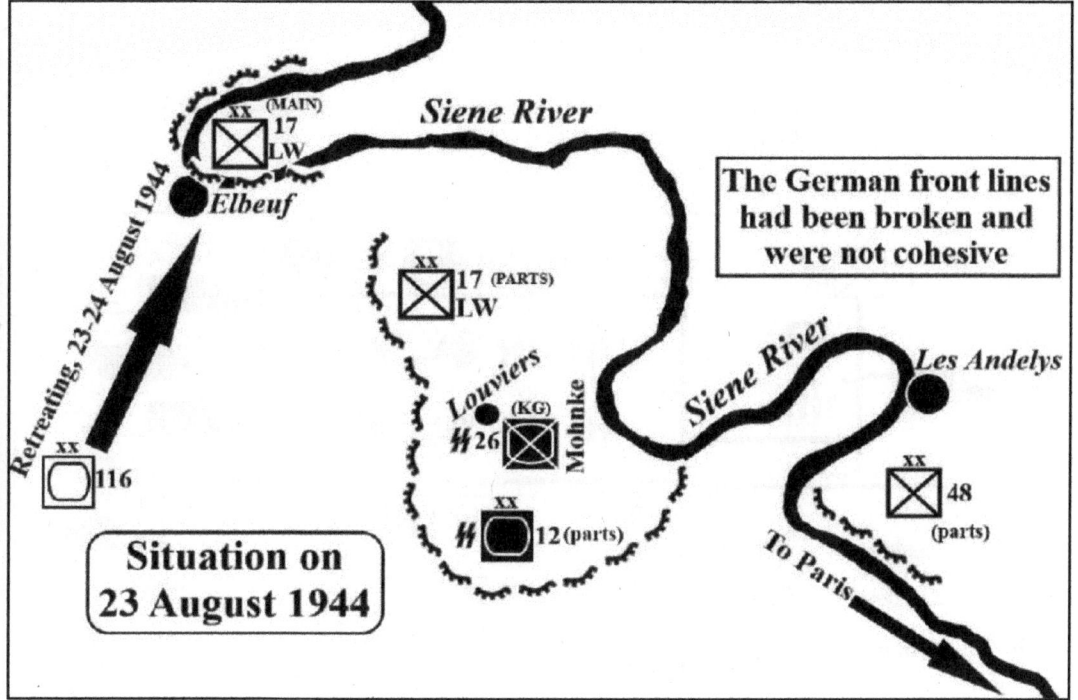

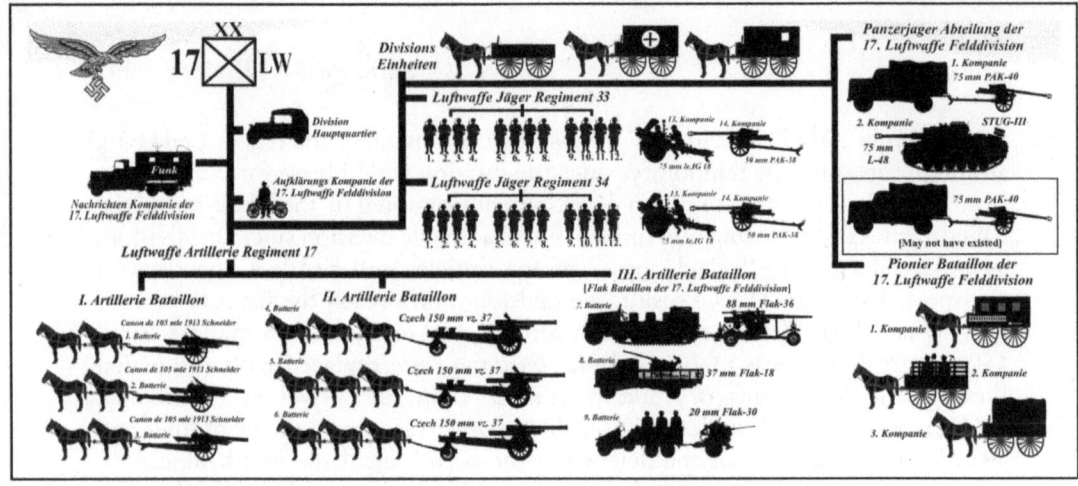

17. Luftwaffen-Felddivision in August 1943.

quickly picked up by *Felddivision 18 (L)*, which was now attached to *I. SS-Panzerkorps* and had recently taken part in a counterattack when *Fusilier-Bataillon 18 (L)* had fought American forces to a standstill northeast of Mantes. By the end of August the division had been so badly mauled that the decision was made to disband it,[28] the official order following on 22 September 1944. The remains of the unit were transferred to *167. Volksgrenadier-Division*, which was in the process of being reformed.[29]

Organization of 17. *Luftwaffen-Felddivision*

Commanders:

Divisional Commander:
- *Oberst* Hans Korte,[30] 12/42–25/01/43
- *Generalleutnant* Herbert Olbrich, 25/01/43–29/06/43[31]
- *Oberst* Erich Baeßler,[32] 30/06/43–04/11/43
- *Oberst* Hans Kurt Höcker,[33] 05/11/43–28/09/44[34]

Ia:
- *Major* Gundolf *Freiherr* Schenk zu Schweinzberg, 12/02/43–31/10/43
- *Major* Elmar Warning,[35] 10/12/43–08/44

Organization of *Felddivision 17 (L)* in March 1944.

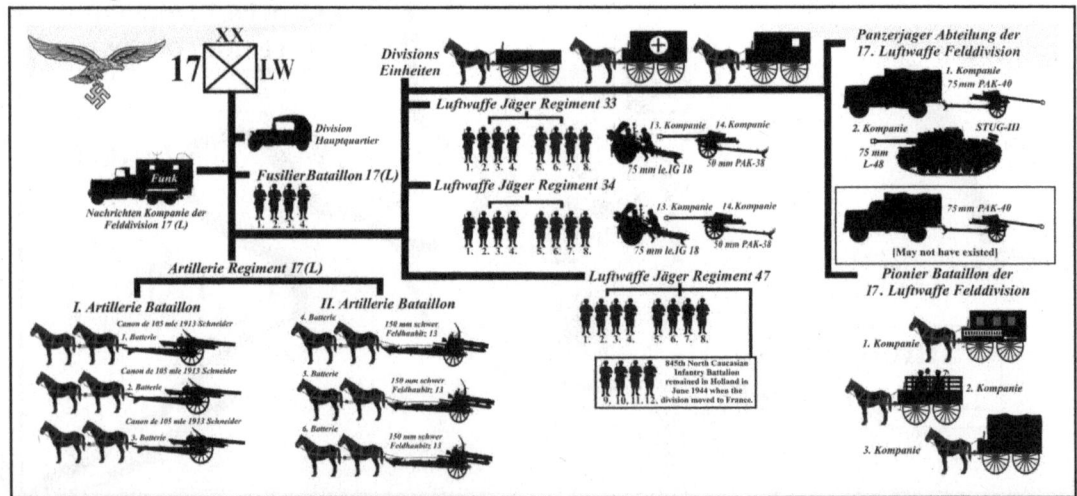

IIa:
  Major Breuninger, 10/12/43–?
IVb:
  Oberstabarzt Dr Hans Weichert,[36] 17/08/43–07/02/44
O3:
  Leutnant Paul Keller, 10/43–?
CO *Luftwaffen-Jäger-Regiment 33*:
  Oberst Dipl. Ing. Dr Robert Fuchs,[37] 28/12/42–05/43
  Oberst Oskar Pinagel, 05/43–19/07/43
  Oberst Fritz Müller,[38] 19/07/43–01/11/43
  Oberst Maximilian Köppel, 01/11/43–?
CO *Luftwaffen-Jäger-Regiment 34*:
  Oberst Hans Belau, 03/43–01/04/43
  Oberstleutnant Kurt Hübel, 13/05/43–12/43
CO *Luftwaffen-Artillerie-Regiment 17*:
  Oberstleutnant Herbert Keilhold, 03/43–01/11/43
Luftnachrichten-Kompanie der Felddivision 17 (L):
  Hauptmann Walter Tarnowski,[39] 14/05/43–09/44
Division surgeon:
  Oberstabsarzt Dr Johan Scherak

18. Luftwaffen-Felddivision

18. Luftwaffen-Felddivision was formed with the help of *Flieger-Regiment 52* in Soissons, France. This training unit, led by *Oberst* Günther Hartung,[1] helped to supply personnel for *Luftwaffen-Jäger-Regiment 35* and *Luftwaffen-Jäger-Regiment 36*. As was standard practice, each of the regiments comprised three *Jäger* battalions. The division also had an artillery regiment, *Luftwaffen-Artillerie-Regiment 18*, composed of two artillery battalions. *I. Artillerie-Abteilung* had three batteries of four 76.2mm Russian artillery guns (twelve barrels), while *II. Artillerie-Abteilung* had three batteries of four French-made 155mm artillery guns (twelve barrels).[2] The division also possessed an anti-tank battalion, *Luftwaffen-Panzerjäger-Abteilung 18*, with two towed 75mm anti-tank companies of six guns each, and four *Sturmgeschütz III* assault guns (*Sturmgeschütz-Batterie 1018*).[3] The anti-tank battalion was considered as *III. Artillerie-Abteilung* within the division, while the divisional *Flak* battalion, *Luftwaffen-Flak-Bataillon 18*, was considered *IV. Artillerie-Abteilung* in the artillery regiment. Nevertheless, the only two artillery battalions capable of indirect fire were *I.* and *II. Artillerie-Abteilungen*. Initially, the division only had one company of signal troops and one company of engineers. It also had a *radfahr* (bicycle) company, which acted as the reconnaissance unit. The divisional support elements were also company sized.

The division was sent to France at the beginning of January 1943 and was initially placed at the disposal of *1. Armee*.[4] The unit was part of a series of static formations earmarked for garrison and coastal guard duty. As a result, just like *17. Luftwaffen-Felddivision*, *18. Luftwaffen-Felddivision* had limited mobility as it was felt that the unit's mission negated the need for motorized transport. In fact, the division also lacked proper horse-drrawn transport. In February and March 1943, *18. Luftwaffen-Felddivision* was placed under the command of *LXXVI. Armeekorps*, *1. Armee*, and situated in the Rochefort area. One month later it was shifted to the coastal area of Dunkirk and attached to *LXXXII. Armeekorps*, *15. Armee*.[5] It was now responsible for Dunkirk itself and the surrounding region.[6] The divisional area of defence was soon expanded, so that by April the division was also guarding a slice of the French coast extending from Dunkirk to Calais.[7] On 1 November 1943 the German Army assumed control of the existing *Luftwaffe* field divisions, and the unit's name became *Felddivision 18 (L)*. There were some changes in the divisional organization, too. The *Flak* battalion was detached and returned to Luftwaffe service, where it became *II. Flak-Abteilung* of *Flak-Regiment 52*.[8] The engineer company was expanded into a battalion with three companies, and the signals company was also expanded. However, the new *Nachrichten-Abteilung 18 (L)* only possessed two communications companies.

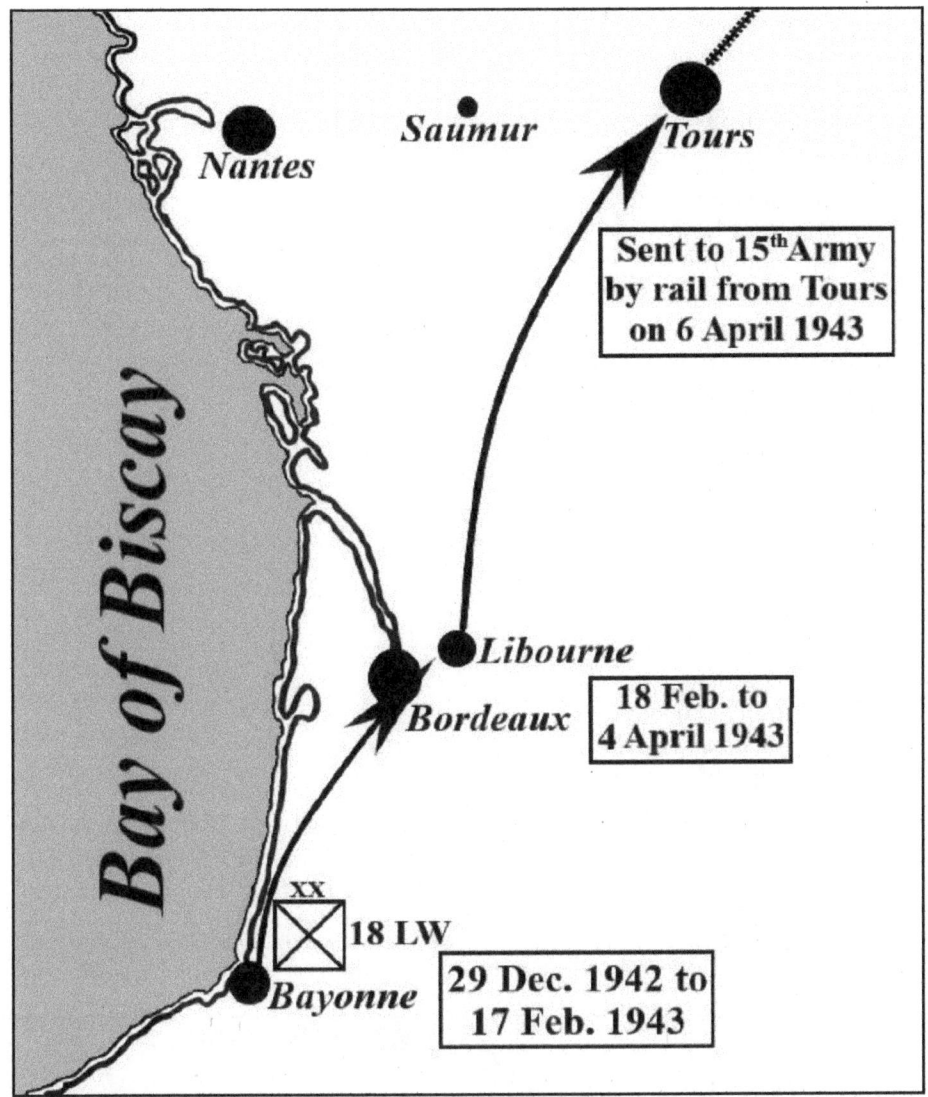

Transfer of the cadre units of *Luftwaffen-Felddivision 18* to the region of Rochefort, then Dunkirk-Calais, in 1943. *(Author)*

In addition, the division's two regiments were to lose their third *Jäger* battalion so that a third *Jäger-Regiment* could be established. This occurred on 12 February 1944, when *III. Jäger-Bataillon* of *Jäger-Regiment 35 (L)* became *I. Jäger-Bataillon* of *Jäger-Regiment 48 (L)*. Similarly, *III. Jäger-Bataillon* of *Jäger-Regiment 36 (L)* became *II. Jäger-Bataillon* of *Jäger-Regiment 48 (L)*. The bicycle company was expanded into a three-company *Fusilier* battalion. Plans were in the works to add a third artillery battalion to the divisional artillery regiment, but this does not seem to have occurred until the division was close to being disbanded,[9] with *III. Artillerie-Abteilung* probably becoming operational in late July or early August 1944.

By April 1944 the division's TO&E was as follows:

Jäger-Regiment 35 (L)
  2 *Jäger* battalions
Jäger-Regiment 36 (L)
  2 *Jäger* battalions
Jäger-Regiment 48 (L)
  2 *Jäger* battalions
Artillerie-Regiment 18 (L)
  2 artillery battalions
Fusilier-Bataillon 18 (L)
  1 bicycle and 2 'foot' companies
Panzerjäger-Abteilung 18 (L)
  1 assault gun company
  2 towed anti-tank companies
Pionier-Bataillon 18 (L)
  3 engineer companies
Signals-Bataillon 18 (L)
  1 Radio company
  1 Telephone company
Versorgungs-Verwaltungs-Einheiten 18 (L)
  Various support companies

Field Marshal Erwin Rommel constantly toured the Atlantic Wall defences and the units defending it. Between 17 and 19 April 1944 he visited *348., 344., 47., 49.* and *712. Infanterie-Divisionen*, plus *Felddivision 18 (L)*.[10] His assessment of

A German *Kriegsgliederung Karte* showing the position of *18. Luftwaffen-Felddivision* in and around Dunkirk, April 1943. The divisions shown with an 'f' in parentheses were being replenished and reformed.

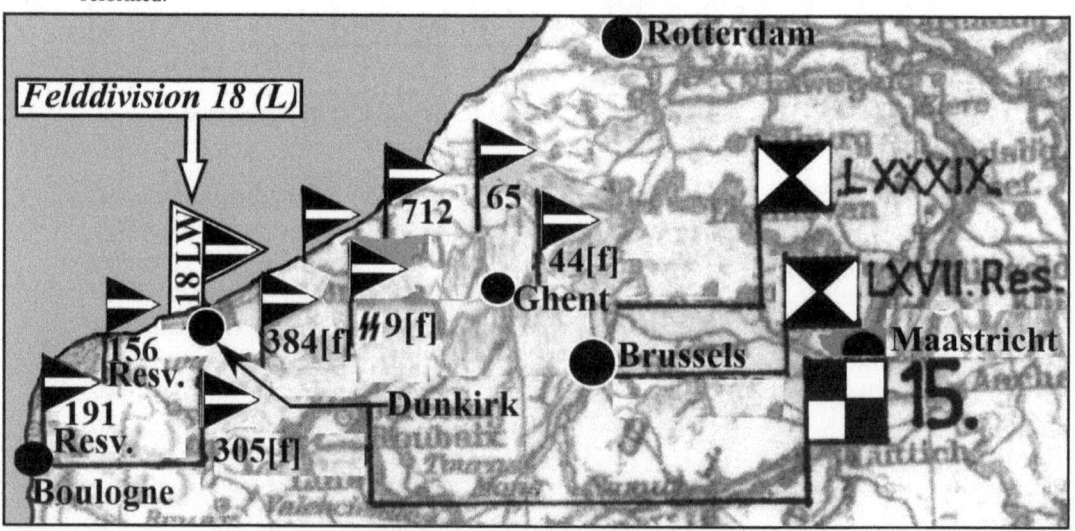

the *Luftwaffe* division was not encouraging. During the tour he found that it had only 9,000 poorly trained men, with few NCOs and not enough young officers. Von Treskow, the divisional commander, told Rommel that his unit would never become a fighting formation until more young officers and NCOs were supplied. It's not known whether Rommel was able to meet von Treskow's request before the division was committed that summer, but an attempt was made to try to improve the division's arms, especially in anti-tank weapons:

> On 27 May 1944 orders were sent out for the divisional anti-tank artillery equipment to be replaced. The panzerjäger battalion's (motorized) companies were changed from six 75mm PAK 40 and six 75mm PAK 97/38 guns to twelve 75mm PAK 40 guns. The grenadier regiment's anti-tank companies were reequipped from three 50mm PAK 38 to three 75mm PAK 40, three 75mm PAK 97/38, and thirty-six 88mm Panzerschreck.[11]

How far these plans were implemented, however, is not known although it appears that the division's artillery regiment had its artillery pieces replaced with better equipment in June. The beneficiary was *I. Artillerie-Abteilung*, which traded in its Russian guns for German field pieces. The division remained in the Dunkirk-Calais region throughout the months of June and July 1944. On 1 June 1944 the divisional strength had reached 9,400 men. This would be its peak strength. It was finally ordered committed to action on 14 August, when the leading elements of the division began moving towards Paris, which was now in danger of falling to the advancing US and Free French forces. Parts of the division reached Mantes-la-Jolie on the Seine river on 19 August 1944.

On 23 August the division came under the operational control of *I. SS-Panzerkorps, 5. Panzerarmee*.[12] These two higher-level formations sounded powerful, but in reality they were mere shadows of themselves after suffering greatly in the Normandy fighting and the failed counterattack at Mortain in July and August. The Mortain offensive quickly turned into the Falais pocket, the final burial ground of German armoured forces in France in 1944.[13]

Felddivision 18 (L) had moved from the coast at Dunkirk into the region of Mantes-la-Jolie basically on foot, although some horse-drawn transport was available, especially for the artillery batteries. The division had first moved towards Amiens, but was soon redirected to the Mantes region. It took the division about eight days to complete the move, but by 23 August the bulk of *Felddivision 18 (L)*, as well as part of *49. Infanterie-Division* and the headquarters staff of *116. Panzer-Division*, were located just north of Mantes-la-Jolie.[14] While the division moved southwards along the west bank of the Seine river, it encountered no opposition from Allied units but soon after its arrival in the city of Mantes, American forces crossed the river, threatening once again to cut off German forces south of the Seine. The division was ordered to launch a counterattack to throw the US forces back across the river, just southeast of Mantes.

The division committed only one of its *Jäger* regiments, *Jäger-Regiment 48 (L)*, plus *Fusilier-Bataillon 18 (L)*, which was used as the main striking force in this counterattack. This small force, however, could not throw American forces back across the Seine. They did, however, manage to halt the US advance momentarily.[15] Continued US strikes, geared to break through the *Luftwaffe* defence, eventually drew the rest of the division into battle during the next few days. This eventually cost the division heavy casualties. Orders were eventually received to withdraw. In order to disengage from the enemy, *Jäger-Regiment 36 (L)* was ordered to launch an attack, supported by a few tanks, on the morning of 27 August 1944. The plan was to convince the Americans that the division was still on the offensive and had no plans to withdraw. The assault met with initial success, but the attacking battalions eventually lost 50 per cent of their original strength. Meanwhile, *Felddivision 18 (L)* began to pull back towards Rouen, but the unit was unable to completely withdraw as an organized division. The divisional commander, *Generalleutnant* von Tresckow, decided to split the division into two combat groups. An additional regimental-sized unit composed of men from the destroyed *Felddivision 17 (L)*, now attached to *Felddivision 18 (L)*, also came under Tresckow's command. Tresckow's two combat groups were formed from *Jäger-Regiment 35 (L)* and *Jäger-Regiment 48 (L)* and were named after their regimental commanders: *Kampfgruppe Schmidt* of *Jäger-Regiment 35 (L)* and *Kampfgruppe Mangold* of *Jäger-Regiment 48 (L)*. The battle group from *Felddivision 17 (L)* was named *Kampfgruppe Koppel* and had been created around

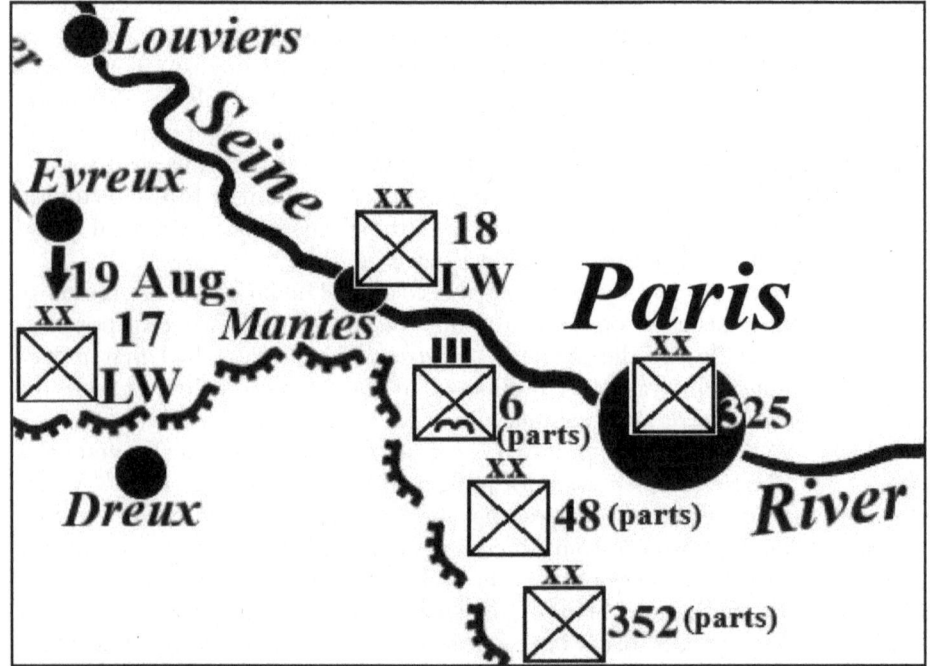

The leading elements of *Felddivision 18 (L)* began arriving at Mantes-la-Jolie around 19 August 1944. *(Author)*

Jäger-Regiment 33 (L). Remnants of *Jäger-Regiment 36 (L)*, plus the artillery batteries, were divided among these three *kampfgruppen*.[16]

The regimental battle groups began to withdraw towards Beauvais, and all went well until an American armoured division caught up with *Kampfgruppe Mangold* on 20 August. It was carnage. The supply wagons and horse-drawn artillery were either squashed or blown apart. Horses lay dead or dying, whining from shrapnel wounds, while the *Landsers* who weren't immediately killed or blown apart were desperately trying to outrun the enemy armour. The expression on most of these *Luftwaffe* men was that of panic. Dead men and horses lay everywhere, strung along the road. The artillery pieces, still hitched to the horse carriages, lay where their teams of horses had fallen. What the armoured division failed to destroy was strafed and eliminated by American *Jabos* (fighter-bombers).

On 1 September 1944 the remnants of the division was on the Franco-Belgian border near the Somme Canal at Ham, in the region of St Quentin. The following day, after a day of reorganizing, the division moved again, this time in the direction of Cambrai. It was there, along the Amiens–Cambrai–Mons road, that the final chapter of *Felddivision 18 (L)*'s brief history began. The leading elements of 3rd US Armored Division, in cooperation with other American and British forces, were able to encircle a large batch of German troops between Cambrai and Mons. Inside the pocket, extending from Mons to the forest of Compiégne, were 25,000 men of *47., 49., 331.* and *353. Infanterie-Divisionen*, as well as what remained of *Felddivision 18 (L)*. Most of the men from these divisions eventually went into captivity, with another 11,000 additional German troops being captured by Allied forces a day later, between the cities of Namur and Mézières.[17] *Generalmajor* von Tresckow did not want to surrender and decided to break out from the Mons pocket with those men of his division who felt the same. Once again he split the survivors into two groups. He himself led one of the groups, comprising about 300 men. With his group further divided into assault platoons of forty men each, they began their breakout attempt on the evening of 3 September.[18] Von Tresckow instructed them to try to make their way northeast towards Mons:

> Von Tresckow's small band of soldiers faced other problems. They suffered from lack of food and water, and had to ford many rivers and streams in Belgium, including the Sambre and Maas rivers, where enemy soldiers were on the lookout for escaping German troops. The band managed to cross the Maas in a small boat (which sank after the last members reached the eastern bank five kilometres south of Dinant). This was accomplished within yards of enemy patrols during a stormy night. The following day, 8 September, Belgian troops surrounded the woods where the Germans were resting and opened fire. Von Tresckow received wounds in both legs from a hand grenade and another soldier was also injured. The group immediately scattered, re-assembled a few kilometres away, and continued the march. By the morning of 15 September, a handful of bedraggled survivors entered the

Malmedy-Eupen region of Belgium and were greeted by German-speaking natives.[19]

Belgian troops made one more attempt to capture von Tresckow's group on 16 September but were fought off, fundamentally because the Belgians were not supported by armour. In fact, when the Americans reached Mons, their lines of supply were stretched to breaking point. Fetching their gas, food and ammunition meant travelling over 725km to the closest usable deep-water port. The British forces further north were a little better off since they only had to drive 400km from Bayeux for their petrol and provisions.[20] The Allied advance had by now almost run out of steam due to a lack of supplies.

On 16 September the *OKW* officially dissolved *Felddivision 18 (L)*, considering it to have been completely destroyed between Mantes and Mons. Von Tresckow and his few hundred survivors of the division finally reached the safety of the German front lines near Hallschlag on the night of 18 September 1944. Their trek had lasted seventeen days and had covered some 260km. Tresckow's exploits won him the Knight's Cross and he was appointed commander of a corps in the autumn of 1944. The remnants of the division were assigned to *18. Volksgrenadier-*

The Mons pocket, 1–4 September 1944. (*Author*)

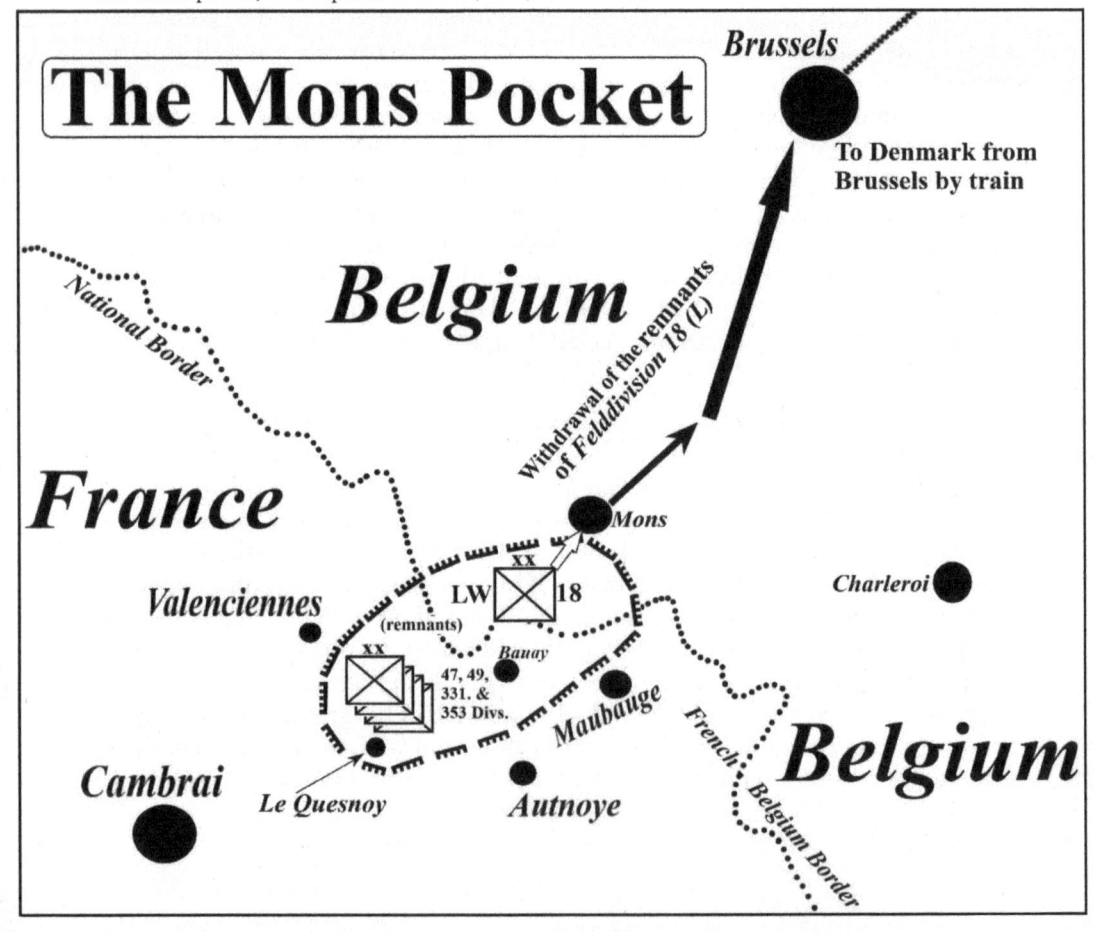

Division and transferred to Denmark at the beginning of October, where the unit was being organized.[21]

The division had performed during its lifespan like a third-rate static infantry outfit – exactly how it had been raised, organized and trained. It was impossible for it to have performed in any other manner. Had it been used to counter an Allied invasion along the coast, it is likely that its performance would have been better – that is, it would have caused more casualties among the enemy and lasted as an intact formation for a bit longer – but this is just mere speculation. The fact remains that once it was committed to battle in mid-August it only took three to four weeks for the division to be completely wiped out. Thus, we can consider *18. Luftwaffen-Felddivision / Felddivision 18 (L)* as one of the poorest units formed by the *Luftwaffe*. Even the German Army was unable to improve the division's combat effectiveness.

Location of the three air force field divisions as they were stationed in the West on 6 June 1944. (*Author*)

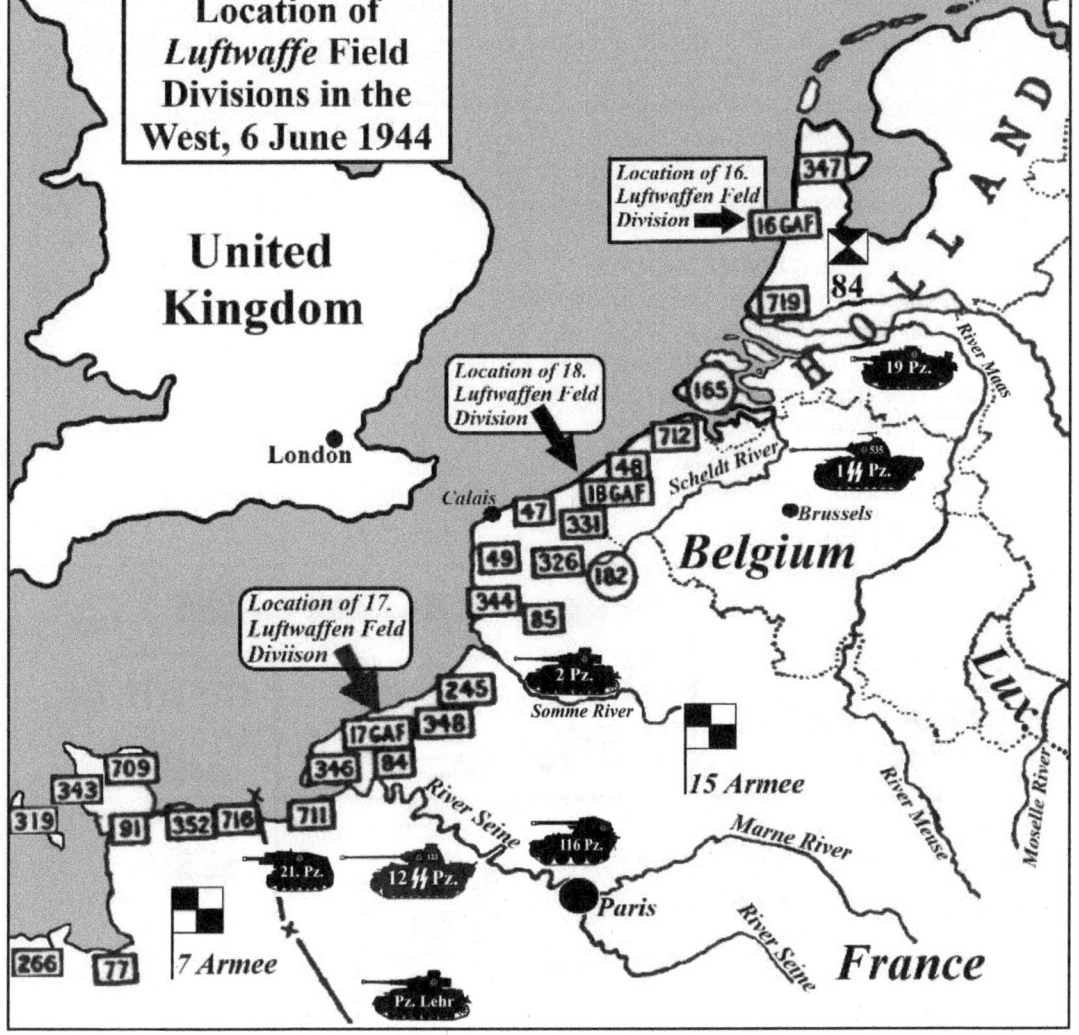

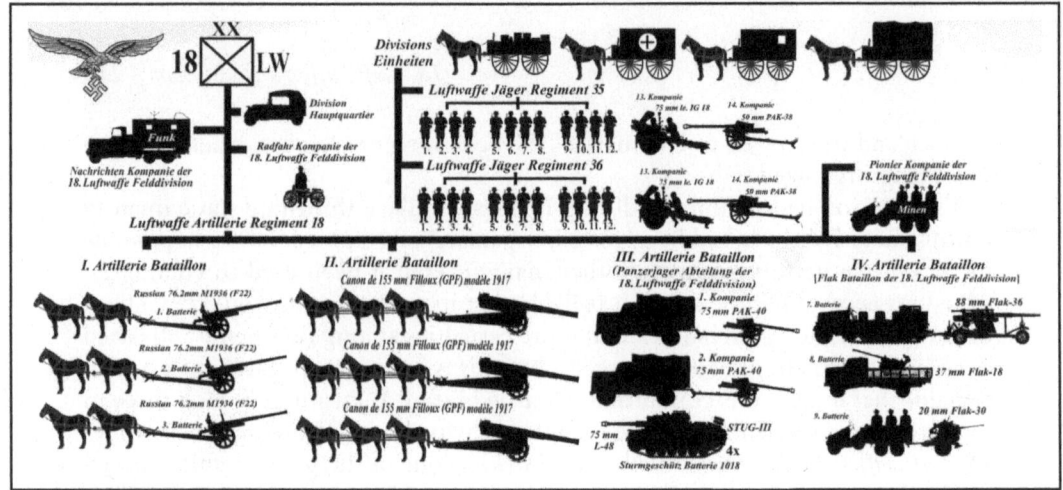

18. Luftwaffen-Felddivision in April 1943.

Organization of *18. Luftwaffen-Felddivision*

Commanders:
  Divisional Commander:
    Oberst Ferdinand Wilhelm Freiherr von Stein-Libenstein zu Barchfeld,[22] 12/42–05/04/43
    Generalmajor Dr Wolfgang Erdmann (*Luftwaffe*),[23] 20/04/43–29/08/43
    Generalmajor Fritz Reinshagen (*Luftwaffe*),[24] 29/08/43–27/10/43
    Generalleutnant Wilhelm Rupprecht (*Heer*),[25] 28/10/43–01/02/44
    Generalleutnant Joachim von Treskow (*Luftwaffe*),[26] 02/02/44–09/44
  Ia:
    Major Steuer, 09/12/42–01/43
    Hauptmann Volrath Gerlach,[27] 01/43–22/02/43
    Oberstleutnant Alexander Olbrichs, 23/02/43–24/05/43
    Oberstleutnant Gerhard Hildebrant, 25/05/43–14/12/43
    Major (later *Oberst*) Albert Hobusch,[28] 15/12/43–?
    Major Windt, 12/43–1944
  Divisional Supply Officer:
    Oberstleutnant Wolfgang Rogalla von Bieberstein,[29] 10/08/43–01/11/43

Felddivision 18 (L) in February 1944.

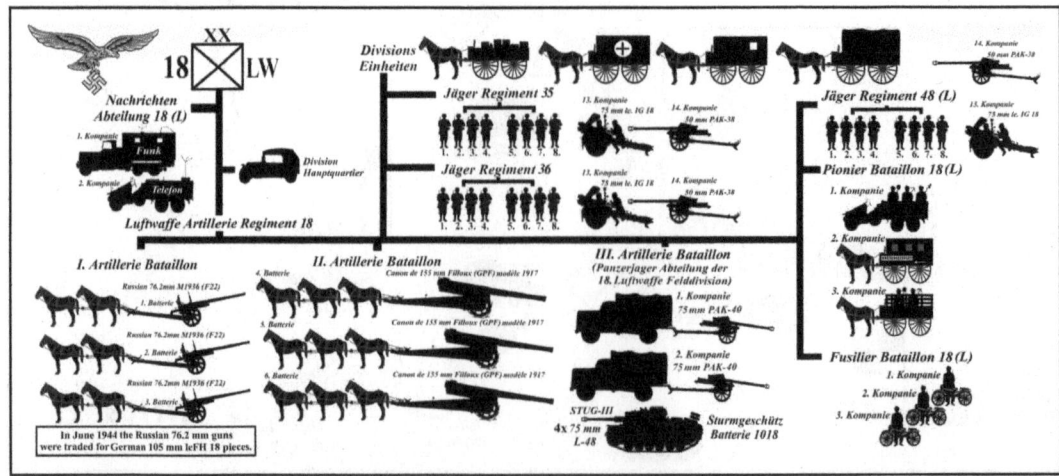

IIa:
Major Freiherr von Aschauer, 10/12/43
CO *III. Artillerie-Abteilung/Artillerie-Regiment 18 (L)*:
Major Godde, ?-09/44
CO *Luftwaffen-Jäger-Regiment 35*:
Oberst Karl Drewes, 12/42-31/10/43
Oberst Schmidt, 11/43-09/44
CO *Luftwaffen-Jäger-Regiment 36*:
Generalmajor Fritz Reinshagen,[30] 04/43-25/08/43
Oberstleutnant Walter Lehnert, 13/09/43-11/43
CO *III. Bataillon/Jäger-Regiment 36 (L)*:
Major Harry Staake, 05/08/43-11/43
CO *Jäger-Regiment 48 (L)*:
Oberstleutnant Mangold, 02/44-09/44
CO *Panzerjäger-Abteilung 18 (L)*:
Hauptmann Ernst Speiser, 22/07/43-12/43
CO *Flak-Kompanie/Panzerjäger-Abteilung 18 (L)*:
Hauptmann Hans-Werner Staunau, 01/06/42-10/01/43
Major Josepf Stift served as a *Flak* commander. He was transferred on 1 December 1942 to *18. Luftwaffen-Felddivision* and served with the division until early May 1943.

19. Luftwaffen-Sturm-Division

Originally titled *19. Luftwaffen-Felddivision*, this was the first of the so-called 'third wave' field divisions of the *Luftwaffe*. Although its cadre units were actually available in January and February 1943, it only began forming in earnest in March 1943 at Troop Training Ground Bergen by Celle, France.[1] Part of the division was created using a cadre from *Luftwaffen-Infanterie-Regiment Moskau*, which had been in existence (as a single battalion) since the winter of 1941/1942. Beginning in March 1942, it contained two battalions and was led by *Luftwaffe Oberst* Karl-Eduard Wilke. It undertook partisan operations in the Roslavl-Bryansk area, as well as in the region of Kletnya and Rzhev. It existed until December 1942.[2] After its withdrawal from the Eastern Front, the remnants were sent to France. In addition to this unit, recruits and officers came from *XIII. Fliegerkorps*. As with the other field divisions, two *Jäger* regiments were created: *Luftwaffen-Jäger-Regiment 37* and *Luftwaffen-Jäger-Regiment 38*. As was standard, each regiment comprised three *Jäger* battalions. *Luftwaffen-Artillerie-Regiment 19* was also formed with four battalions, with *IV. Artillerie-Abteilung* being the divisional *Flak* battalion.

There was also an anti-tank battalion (*Luftwaffen-Panzerjäger-Abteilung 19*), a signals company (*Signals-Kompanie der 19 Luftwaffen-Felddivision*) and a bicycle company that was later expanded to a battalion (*Luftwaffen-Radfahr-Bataillon 19*), plus corresponding supply and support companies, all of which used the ancillary number 19. *1. Kompanie* of *Panzerjäger-Abteilung 19 (L)* was outfitted with the *Marder III* tank-destroyer armoured vehicle. There were various versions of this tank destroyer, armed with either the ex-Soviet 76.2mm F-22 Model 1936 anti-tank gun or the German 75mm PAK L-40 gun. The type employed by the division was the *Sd. Kfz. 138 Ausf. M* version, which carried the German 75mm PAK L-40 anti-tank gun. These small but rugged vehicles were built on the tank chassis of the Czech 38(t) tank, combined with an open superstructure. When supplied to the division, these vehicles had been freshly painted in ordnance tan, but later they would be painted in a camouflage scheme. The anti-tank battalion's *2. Panzerjäger Kompanie* was equipped with *Sturmgeschütz III* assault guns, while *3. Panzerjäger Kompanie* had 37mm and 20mm *Flak* guns.

Interestingly, before *19. Luftwaffen-Felddivision* began to form, some of the men earmarked for the unit were used to help reform the so-called 'Stalingrad' divisions: that is, those formations that had been lost at Stalingrad in February 1943 and whose reactivation had been personally ordered by Hitler. *24. Panzer-Division*, for example, was to be reformed from some survivors of the old division, together with men from the division's rear area training and support units that

19. Luftwaffen-Sturm-Division 221

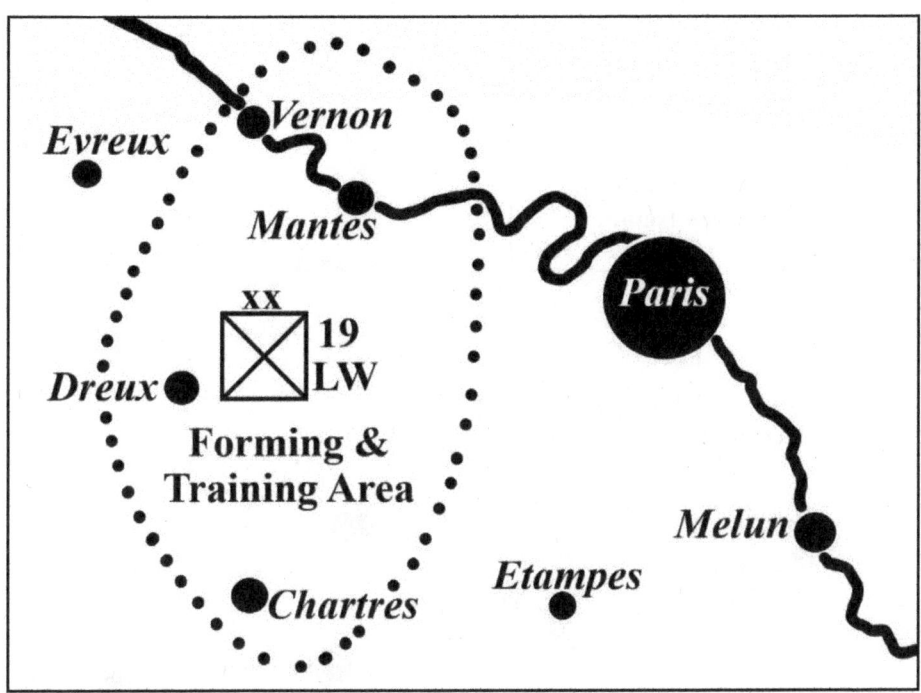

Forming and training area for *19. Luftwaffen-Sturm-Division*, west of Paris. The division began arriving in the area between Chartres and Vernon in the middle of April 1943. *(Author)*

had escaped destruction. In addition, other army units were to contribute men and materiel. *19. Luftwaffen-Felddivision*, although not yet ordered to be raised, was one of those units called on to provide personnel for this reconstructed armoured division and it actually made substantial contributions of men and weapons.[3] On 24 February 1943, for example, *OKW* records state that two artillery batteries earmarked for *Luftwaffen-Artillerie-Regiment 19* were instead diverted to *24. Panzer-Division*.[4] On the following day an additional two artillery batteries were transferred to *44. Reichsgrenadier-Division 'Hoch und Deutschmeister'*, another of the 'Stalingrad' divisions being reformed in France. On 26 February 473 *Luftwaffe* recruits from the 15th and 19th *Luftwaffe* divisions were handed over to *24. Panzer-Division*.[5] The next day, an additional 458 men from these *Luftwaffe* units were transferred to *24. Panzer-Division*.[6] An even greater sacrifice of men was made by the nascent *19. Luftwaffen-Felddivision* on 28 February when 1,109 men were handed over to the line companies of *44. Reichsgrenadier-Division 'Hoch und Deutschmeister'*.[7]

In accordance with the necessary training and organizational requirements, *19. Luftwaffen-Felddivision* was transferred in April 1943 to France, the whole division moving in just two days. On 16 April twenty-six trains brought the bulk of the division to the region of Paris and on the next day the transfer of the division was completed. The divisional units were billeted between Chartres and

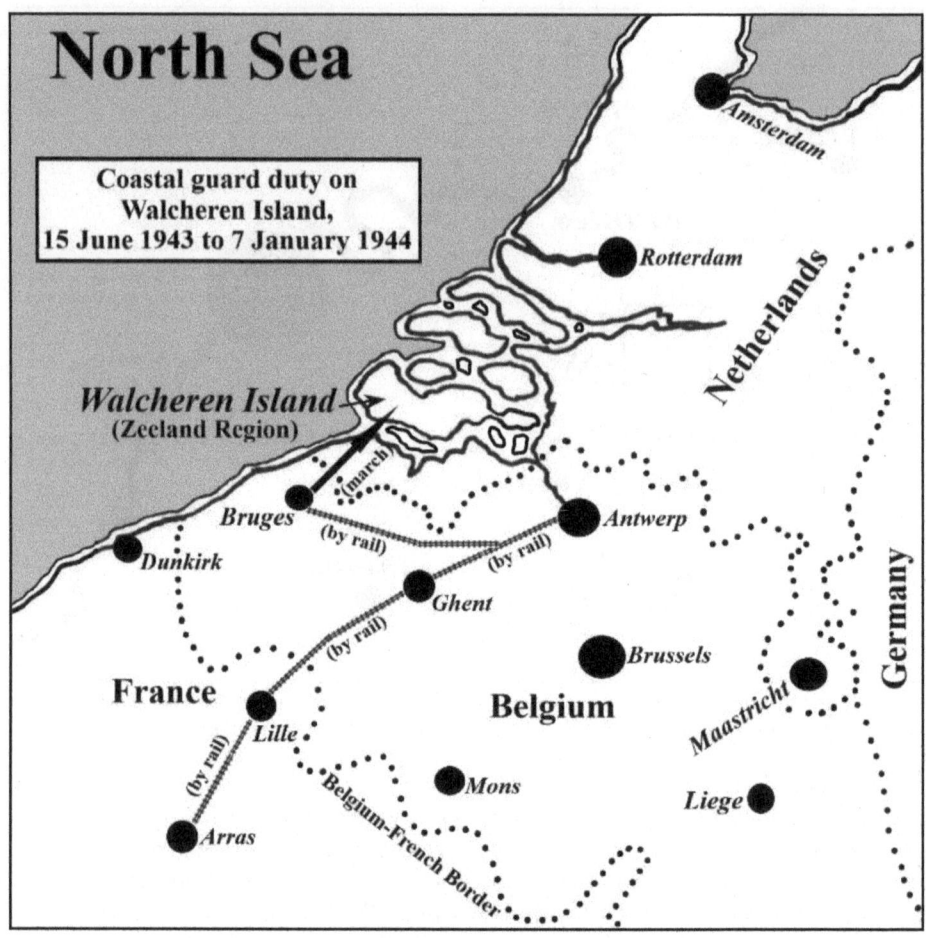

Movements and assigned areas of *19. Luftwaffen-Felddivision*, June 1943–January 1944. (*Author*)

Vernon for further training and there followed several months of intense training, which included live fire exercises. Most of the divisional units were created during these months. After their training was completed, the division was transferred to *15. Armee* in the Netherlands in June.

On 6 June 1943, in preparation for its transfer to active service in Italy, *65. Infanterie-Division* began getting rid of any personnel within the unit who were deemed unfit for combat. As a result, 450 men from this army division were transferred to *19. Luftwaffen-Felddivision*, while another 932 men ended up in static, fortress units.[8] The order for *19. Luftwaffen-Felddivision* to take over the coastal defence positions of *65. Infanterie-Division* arrived on 8 June 1943, although the division did not arrive there until 15 June.[9] On that day five trains carrying the initial batch of men arrived in the coastal region of South Beveland in Holland.[10] On 17 June another eleven trains arrived.[11] On 19 June the bulk of

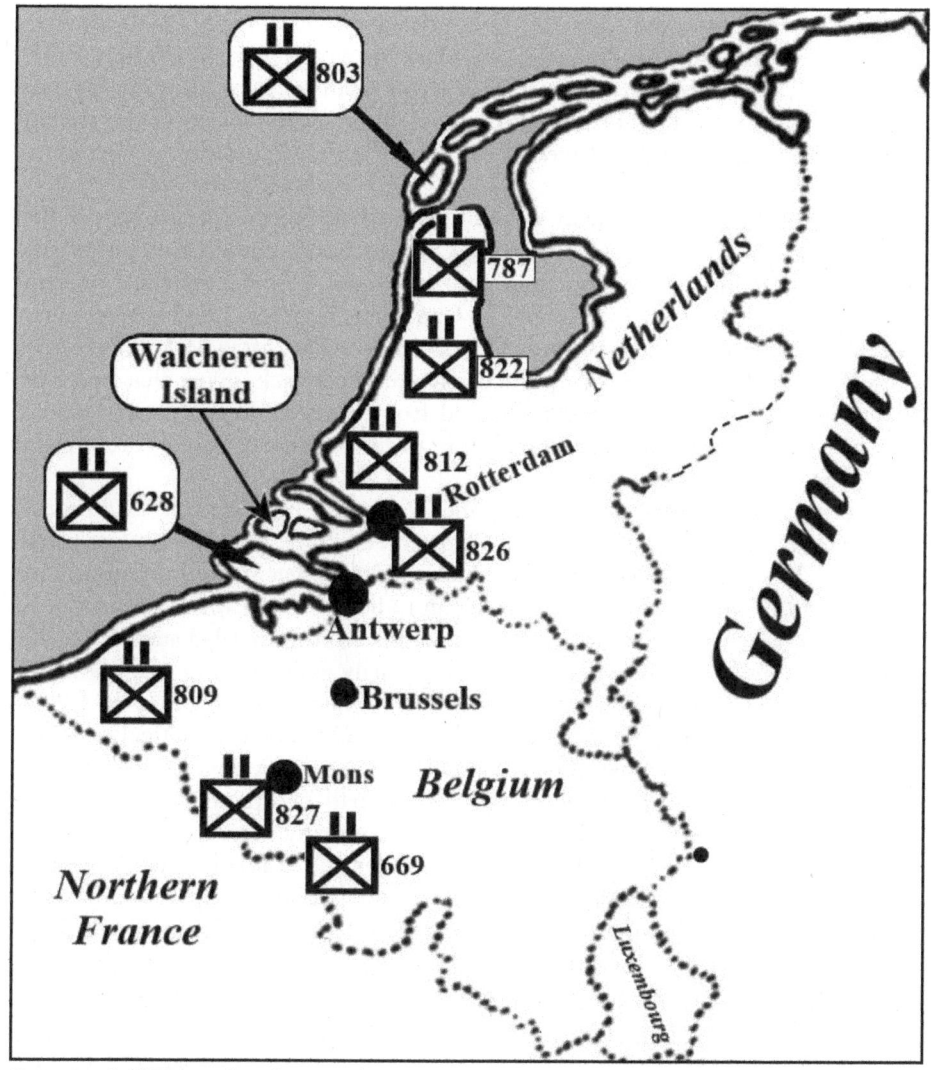

German-raised Eastern battalions in the Low Countries, November 1943. (*Author*)

the division reached Holland in another twenty-six trains. The last elements of the division reached Holland on 18 June, when the final nineteen trains arrived. Eventually, part of the division would also be posted to Walcheren Island[12] and it was there that members of *19. Luftwaffen-Division* encountered Eastern troops. These were volunteers recruited from the numerous peoples that made up the Soviet Union. This region of Holland saw the arrival of several Eastern battalions raised by the Germans. Some of these Eastern troops would rebel against the Germans in 1945, but between 1943 and 1944 the Eastern battalions sent to the West were merged into existing German infantry divisions. For example,

Ost-Bataillon 628 became part of *Grenadier-Regiment 745 (712. Infanterie-Division)*. The divisional headquarters was placed at Middleberg on 20 June 1943. Although *65. Infanterie-Division* was now freed from garrison duty, it did not immediately move to Italy, but instead remained for several weeks in the area of St Omer as a reserve for *15. Armee*. It was finally ordered to move to Ferrara in Italy on 15 July 1943.

In late 1944 the Canadian Army was ordered to dislodge the Germans from the island of Walcheren since German artillery on the island could easily target any Allied ships moving nearby, on their way in or out of the important port of Antwerp. The island was captured by the Canadians between 1 and 8 November 1944. Defending the island was *70. Infanterie-Division (bodenständige)*. This region of the Netherlands would prove particularly hard to attack, given that much of the terrain was, in essence, land reclaimed from the sea. The Germans would eventually flood many parts of the region in order to prevent Allied forces from advancing.

A German *Kriegsgliederung* for 1 June 1943 did not list *19. Luftwaffen-Felddivision* in the West but three weeks later, on 21 June, the division was listed under *LXXXIX. Armeekorps*, categorized as a *bodenständige* (static) division. The war diary of *LXXXIX. Armeekorps* now began to list *19. Luftwaffen-Felddivision* as part of its organic complement. A diary report for 24 August 1943 stated that the division's *3. Pionier Kompanie* had been temporarily assigned to a neighbouring division: '24.8.43 – tactical record. *3. Kompanie, Pionier-Bataillon 19 (L)* on 1.9. to be moved to Ostend to reinforce the *171. Reserve-Division* as a tactical reserve.' This small note proves that the divisional engineer unit for *19. Luftwaffen-Felddivision* had already been raised, not as a small company, as with earlier *Luftwaffe* divisions, but as a full strength three-company battalion.

On 1 November 1943 the division came under the control of the *Heer* and changes in the organization of the unit were ordered. The principal modification was the reduction of the line regiments from three *Jäger* battalions to two *Jäger* battalions. *III. Jäger-Bataillon* in each of the two *Jäger* regiments were detached and redesignated as *I.* and *II. Jäger-Bataillone* of a new regiment, *Jäger-Regiment*

347. (bodenst.) 16. Lw. F.D. (bodenst) 719. (bodenst.)	LXXXVIII.	W.B. Niederlande 376. (i. Aufst.)
19. Lw. F.D. (bodenst.) 712. (bodenst.) 771. Res	LXXXIX.	
18. Lw. F.D. (bodenst.) 156. Res	LXXXII.	15.

Part of a German *Kriegsgliederung* table of units for 21 June 1943. It shows *19. Luftwaffen-Felddivision* under the command of *LXXXIX. Armeekorps*. Notice also that at this time *16. Luftwaffen-Felddivision* was under *LXXXVIII. Armeekorps*, while *18. Luftwaffen-Felddivision* was under *LXXXII. Armeekorps*.

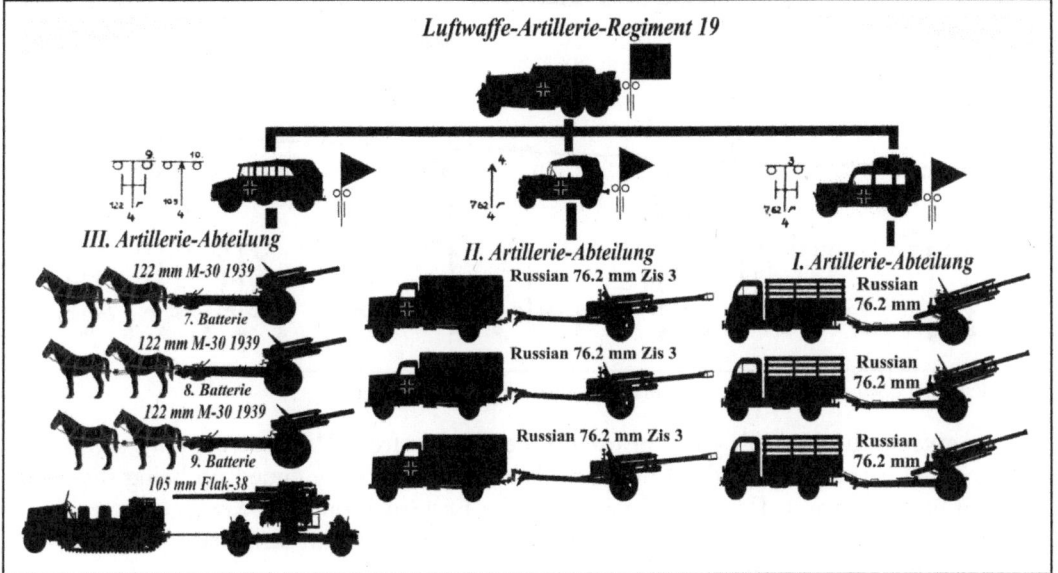

The initial artillery component of *19. Luftwaffen-Felddivision.*

45 (L). A *Kriegsgliederung* for January 1944 showed that the *Radfahr-Kompanie der 19. Luftwaffen-Felddivision*, which had been acting as the divisional reconnaissance unit, had been expanded to four companies: one remained mounted on bicycles, one was the heavy machine-gun company, and the other two were regular infantry companies. Although listed as a static division, it appears that *I.* and *II. Artillerie-Abteilungen* in the artillery regiment were not horse-drawn but motorized. These two artillery battalions were equipped with Russian 76.2mm field guns. *III. Artillerie-Abteilung* initially had *Flak* guns.

IV. Artillerie-Abteilung, considered the divisional *Flak* battalion, was now removed and returned to the *Luftwaffe*, and became *I. Flak-Bataillon* of *Flak-Regiment 35*. Evidently *II. Artillerie-Abteilung* was a separate *Flak* battalion and not the divisional *Flak* unit. However, another *Kriegsgliederung*, this one dated 1 April 1944, clearly shows that the guns of *II. Artillerie-Abteilung* were Russian-made M1942 (Zis 3) 76.2mm artillery pieces. In addition, *I. Artillerie-Abteilung* was equipped with Russian 76.2mm M1902 light field guns, while *III. Artillerie-Abteilung* also had three artillery batteries using 122mm M1939 (M30) Russian howitzers. A tenth artillery battery, attached to *III. Artillerie-Abteilung*, contained four *Armata Wz. 29* 105mm artillery guns of Polish origin. Altogether, the division's artillery regiment could count on twelve 76.2mm Russian M1942 (Zis 3) howitzers, twelve 76.2mm M1902 guns, twelve 122mm M1939 (M 30) Russian howitzers and four 105mm Polish *Armata Wz. 29* howitzers.

The division formed a reserve (*Feldersatz*) battalion of five companies. This unit would provide replacements for the formation. One source states that the division signals company was expanded to a battalion of three companies, but in January 1944 the table of organization listed only two communications companies.[13] The divisional support units were also expanded slightly. Unfortunately for the division, January 1944 was also the month when an order came through that forced the *326.*, *346.* and *348. Infanterie-Division*, as well as *Felddivision 19 (L)*,

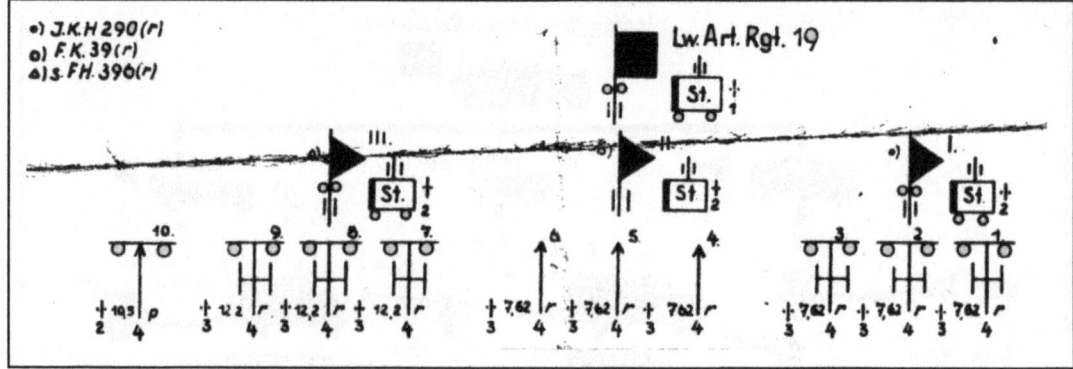

Part of a document detailing the initial divisional artillery component.

to give up their assault guns for use on the Russian front.[14] These weapons were initially earmarked for the Romanian Army but eventually ended up being distributed to various German divisions on the Eastern Front.[15] A *Kriegsgliederung* dated 1 April 1944 showed that the 19th Division's anti-tank battalion was missing its assault guns.

Also in January 1944 the division, although still under *LXXXIX. Armeekorps*, was shifted from the Walcheren-Beveland area of Holland to Belgium, where it was stationed between Ghent and Brugge.[16] A month later it remained in Belgium, but had moved to Thielt.[17] Its roster of weapons on 1 April 1944 is shown in Table 9.

It is puzzling that *Sturmgeschütz-Abteilung 1019* was said to have been a component of the division from April to September 1944 as part of the anti-tank battalion, despite the division having been ordered to give up its assault guns in January. It was said to have been outfitted with one battery of assault guns that came from *Sturmgeschütz-Abteilung 1016*.[18] An assault gun battery usually had six armoured fighting vehicles, divided into three platoons of two vehicles each.

On 15 May 1944 *Felddivision 19 (L)* was listed as a reserve unit of *15. Armee*.[19] Another source contradicts this, claiming that the division was listed directly as an Army Group B reserve.[20] On 1 June 1944 the division was renamed: it was

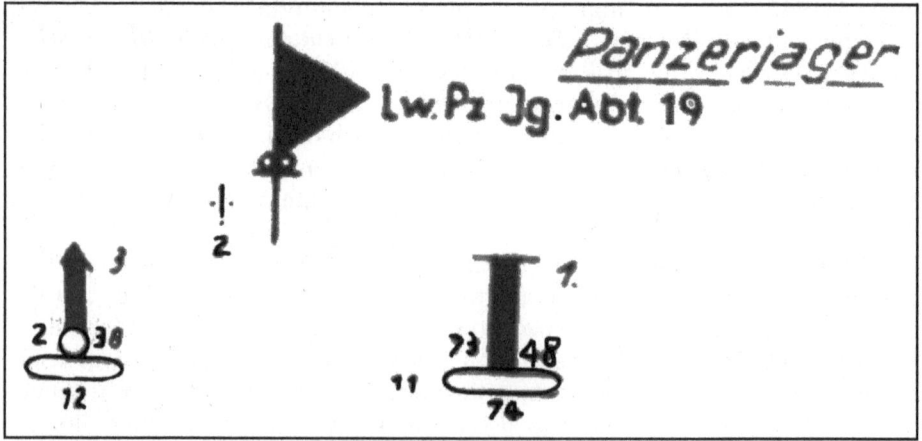

Luftwaffen-Panzerjäger-Abteilung 19 (L).

Table 9. Weapons in *Felddivision 19 (L)*, 1 April 1944.

Divisional Arms	Quantity	Divisional Arms	Quantity
Infantry Weapons		Artillery Pieces	
Light Machine Guns	554	7.62mm JKH 290 (Russian)	12
Heavy Machine Guns	102	7.62mm FK 39 (Russian)	12
Mortars, type 34	79	105mm K29 (Polish)	4
Flame-throwers	18	122mm sFH 396 (Russian)	12
Heavy Infantry Weapons		*Sturmgeschütz III* (7.5cm KwK 40)	6
20mm *Flak* Guns	24		
50mm anti-tank Guns	15		
75mm PAK-40 anti-tank Guns	9		
75mm PAK-97/38 anti-tank Guns	9		
75 PAK-40 (Sf)	14		

now to be referred to as *19. Luftwaffen-Sturm-Division*.[21] This title change would seem to indicate that the formation was now an elite unit, but its organization, structure and weaponry do not seem to have been upgraded or improved at all. Nor was there any increase in the division's manpower strength, which on 1 June totalled of around 9,400 men.[22] Was there a plan to upgrade the unit and make it an elite division? Perhaps the title 'assault division' was merely symbolic, or was it a deliberate deception, intended to mislead Allied intelligence as to the strength and condition of the division? The title of the division was changed three times. In March 1943 it was *19. Luftwaffen-Felddivision*. In November 1943 it became *Felddivision 19. (L)*, and on 1 June 1944 it was renamed *19. Luftwaffen-Sturm-Division*.

This last possible explanation for the change in the division's title may have been the correct one, for on 3 June 1944 the formation was ordered to move to Italy.[23] The Allies had long since broken the German cipher system and knew that the division was being moved there. In fact, by 5 June, just two days after *Generalmajor* Bäßler had received his marching orders, British intelligence was already well aware that *Felddivision 19 (L)/19. Luftwaffen-Sturm-Division* was being brought up by rail for coastal defence duty south of Leghorn (Livorno).[24] In fact, Allied intelligence had reports that a total of five divisions were arriving in Italy from other theatres. Two were coming from the West (*19. und 20. Luftwaffen-Sturm-Divisionen*), one from the Balkans (*42. Jäger-Division*), one from central Europe (*16. SS-Panzergrenadier-Division 'Reichsführer SS'*) and one from Ukraine (*34. Infanterie-Division*).[25] Thus the Allies knew almost immediately the exact German order of battle. Obviously, breaking the German cipher code aided the Allied war effort tremendously. This achievement, early in the war, can be considered a key element in Germany's defeat.

Before the division left for Italy, its *III. Artillerie-Abteilung* of the divisional artillery regiment was detached to become an independent army artillery battalion. It was redesignated *Heers-Artillerie-Abteilung 1154*, which later became *IV. Artillerie-Abteilung* of the artillery regiment in *157. Gebirgs-Division*.[26]

One report stated that when *19. Luftwaffen-Sturm-Division* arrived in Italy, it was initially placed under the control of *LXXV. Armeekorps* of *Armeeabteilung von Zangen*;[27] the latter was a formation raised using the staff of *LXXXVII. Armeekorps* to control Italian and German rear area and coastal security units in the Ligurian region of northern Italy. However, another source states that on 17 June 1944 the forces under *LXXV. Armeekorps* included only *42. Jäger-Division* and *135. Festungs-Brigade 'Doehla'* (CO: *Oberst* Almers), which contained five fortress battalions (*Festungs-Bataillone 902, 905, 906, 907* and *908*).

To add to the confusion, a *Kriegsgliederung* dated 15 June 1944, two days earlier, placed *19. Luftwaffen-Sturm-Division* alongside *Festungsbrigade Döhla* and *42. Jäger-Division*, all under *LXXV. Armeekorps*.[28] The corps was still listed under *Armeeabteilung von Zangen*.[29] General Zenger und Etterlein, the commander of *XIV. Panzerkorps* in Italy, states that he assumed control of both the 19th and 20th *Luftwaffe* Divisions in June 1944.[30] This is confirmed by US Army reports that show its army units encountering and fighting elements of *19. Luftwaffen-Sturm-Division* near the town of Grosseto. This is confirmed by one German author, who also mentions Grosseto as the initial combat of *19. Luftwaffen-Sturm-Division* in Italy.[31] Another US Army account perhaps explains the confusion over exactly which German army corps controlled the division in June. It seems that Zenger's *XIV. Panzerkorps* was in the process of being shifted from *10. Armee* to *14. Armee*. In the interim period before the arrival of the panzer corps to the area of *14. Armee*, *LXXV. Armeekorps* had been shifted south with *19. Luftwaffen-Sturm-Division* as a stop-gap measure until the corps, and its accompanying tank and mechanized divisions, could be deployed:

> The regrouping had begun on the twelfth with the transfer of Senger's XIV Panzer Corps headquarters from the Tenth to the Fourteenth Army sector, where the panzer corps took command of the 19. and 20. Luftwaffe Field Divisions on the coastal flank, pending the arrival of its former divisions – the 26. Panzer and the 29. and 90. Panzer Grenadier Divisions from the Tenth Army zone.[32]

Both the *19.* and *20. Luftwaffen-Sturm-Divisionen* had been sent to Italy after the Allies had captured Rome and were threatening to break through the numerically inferior German units in central Italy. *20. Luftwaffen-Sturm-Division* had preceded *19. Luftwaffen-Sturm-Division*, arriving a month earlier, in May. *Generalfeldmarschall* Albert Kesselring, who was in overall command of German forces in Italy, initially used the latter division for rear area security. In early June it was in the Italian region of Liguria, under *LXXV. Armeekorps*. As stated earlier, it was employed for coastal defence in the Grosseto area. However, the worsening German military situation required that the division be sent to support *XIV. Panzerkorps*. At that time, the Germans had established and were counting on the so-called Frieda Line, employing both *19. Luftwaffen-Sturm-Division* and its sister unit, *20. Luftwaffen-Sturm-Division*, on the right flank of *14. Armee*, near

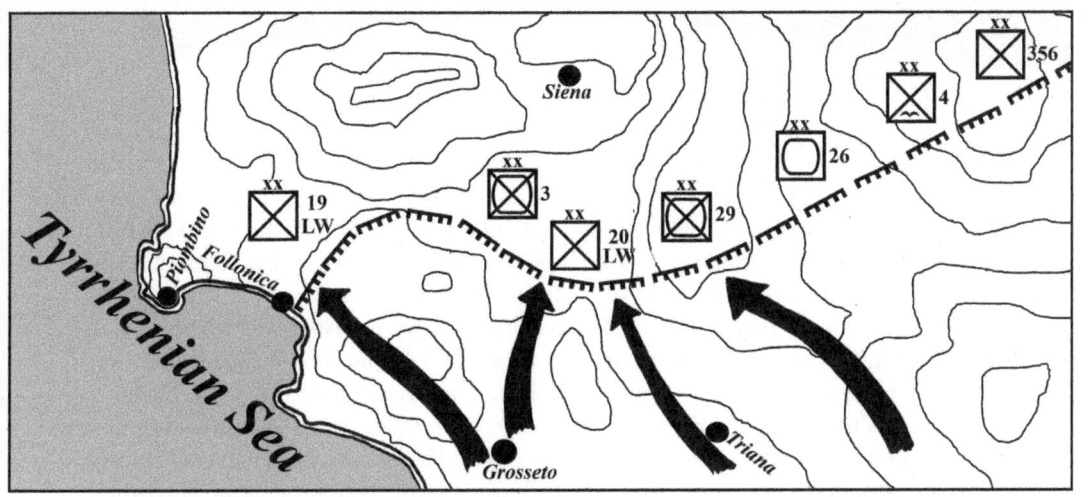

Location of *19. Luftwaffen-Sturm-Division* in the Frieda Line positions near Piombino, Italy, in mid-June 1944.

Piombino.[33] Although Kesselring hoped that these divisions of *Luftwaffe* men would be able to hold off the Allied advance for some time, General Frido von Senger und Etterlein, who had fought in southern Russia and was aware of the performance of these air force field divisions, was not of the same opinion:

> Since there was yet no corps HQ staff in the zone that I had taken over, the divisions had been subordinate to a so-called corps command, which was nothing more than a divisional command entrusted with controlling the operations of the other associated divisions, and therefore lacked the requisite facilities for communications. Two of these divisions were so-called *Luftwaffen* field divisions, which had been constituted from redundant air force personnel and had retained this appellation although they had been incorporated into the army. Lacking fighting experience, they were not battle-worthy. One of them, the *19. Luftwaffen-Sturm-Division*, was disbanded during the fighting withdrawal. The other, whose officers consisted mainly of former cavalry officers, did better but it too was later disbanded.[34]

The US Army's 36th (Texas) Infantry Division initially fought *19. Luftwaffen-Sturm-Division* from mid-June and into July:

> As *14. Armee* on the right flank of *Heeresgruppe C* fell back toward the Cecina river and lateral Route 68, Kesselring prepared to occupy this terrain in strength by assigning to the *XIV. Panzerkorps* the newly arrived *16. SS-Panzergrenadier-Division 'Reichsführer SS'* and the *19. Luftwaffen-Sturm-Division*, the latter replacing the *20. Luftwaffen-Sturm-Division*, which then moved to Tenth Army. Kesselring also relieved the *162. (turkestanisch) Infanterie-Division*, which had been in action on the coastal flank almost continuously since 8 June, with the veteran *26. Panzer-Division*, thus returning the panzer division to Senger's *XIV. Panzerkorps*.[35]

Fierce rearguard battles were fought by *19. Luftwaffen-Sturm-Division*, particularly in the region of Castagneto and Monteverdi.[36] American forces launched an attack on 21 June, deploying the Texas 36th Infantry Division around Highway No. 1, which ran parallel to the Ligurian Sea on Italy's west coast. Their advance was briefly held up by the Frieda Line, but by nightfall on 24 June two of the 36th's regiments had crossed the Ombrone river by Grosseto and advanced as far as Montepescali, an important road junction on the road to Piombino.[37] On 25 June 1944 the Texas 36th Infantry Division was withdrawn in anticipation of its employment in the invasion of southern France, and was replaced by the 34th US Infantry Division. Two days later the 34th Division launched its first attack in the area held by *19. Luftwaffen-Sturm-Division*. On that very same day the Americans pushed the *Luftwaffe* men back to within 25km of their intermediate objective: Route 68. The Cecina river now came into their sights, and *19. Luftwaffen-Sturm-Division* had to abandon Piombino in order to avoid being cut off.[38]

Behind the Cecina river, by the town of the same name, *19. Luftwaffen-Sturm-Division* attempted to make a new defence line. The Americans were aware that although the little Cecina river represented only a minor military obstacle, it could become a formidable defence if the Germans were allowed time to occupy the range of low hills just behind the river. It was for this reason that 34th Infantry Division's attack was continued in cooperation with the 1st US Armored Division on its right flank. By now elements of *26. Panzer-Division* had begun to arrive, but these meagre forces were still insufficient to significantly hold up the US advance. On the coastal flank *19. Luftwaffen-Sturm-Division* prepared to meet the continued American drive:

> The terrain over which these several routes led favored the defence. Ridge lines on the flanks of the main routes of approach rose to peaks of over 1,500 feet on the left and over 2,000 feet on the right, offering the Germans vantage points from which they might rake the advancing columns with flanking fire. Seven miles north of Cecina and lateral Route 68 the reinforced 19. Luftwaffen Division prepared to make a stand just north of a lateral road which connected the coastal highway with Route 206, the westernmost of the 34. Division's two main routes of approach.[39]

On the front lines of *19. Luftwaffen-Sturm-Division*, units of *65. Infanterie-Division* were beginning to arrive, but when the US attack began on 3 July, they were still not yet in a position to help in the defence:

> Deployed on the high ground opposite 4th [US] Corps' front two enemy divisions of varying quality awaited the attack. On the Fourteenth Army's right flank, General von Senger's *XIV. Panzerkorps* was controlling *19. Luftwaffen-Sturm-Division* and *26. Panzer-Division*, both of which had given such a good account of themselves in the defence of the Cecina sector, but in so doing had suffered considerable losses. To the left and holding a comparatively narrow front was *20. Luftwaffen-Sturm-Division*.[40]

The American attack was so swift and so violent that *19. Luftwaffen-Sturm-Division* was almost immediately forced to withdraw into the coastal town of Rosignano-Solvay. Fighting for the town raged from the evening of 3 July until 10 July as the *Luftwaffe* troops desperately tried to hold on to the town and positions leading to Route 206 further inland. They launched several fierce and desperate counterattacks that held off the Americans for over a week.[41]

On 10 July 1944, however, *19. Luftwaffen-Sturm-Division* was finally outflanked when the US 135th Infantry Regiment broke through its left flank just outside the town of Rosignano-Solvay and the air force men were forced to withdraw northwards. With its right flank broken, the rest of *XIV. Panzerkorps*, which now included *19.* and *20. Luftwaffen-Sturm-Divisionen, 26. Panzer-Division* and *3. Panzergrenadier-Division*, was also forced to withdraw. *19. Luftwaffen-Sturm-Division* headed towards the coastal city of Leghorn (Livorno), with the 135th and 133rd US Infantry Regiments of 34th Infantry Division following close behind.

19. Luftwaffen-Sturm-Division, which had apparently given a good account of itself in the battles for Cecina, was to all intents and purposes smashed after the battle for Rosignano-Solvay.[42] Indeed, the right flank of *14. Armee* had been so battered that no serious attempt was made to hold the important port city of Leghorn (Livorno). The Germans found time to try to destroy the port facilities but could do no more. The *19. Luftwaffen-Sturm-Division* withdrew north, laying down scattered minefields, and booby-traps behind them in order to try to slow down the US advance,[43] and by the evening of 19 July the German main line of resistance was just north of Livorno, where the Germans were able to temporarily stabilize the front with the arrival of *65. Infanterie-Division, 90. Panzergrenadier-Division* and *16. SS-Panzergrenadier-Division 'Reichsführer SS'*. The decision to disband *19. Luftwaffen-Sturm-Division* was made by *OKW* in the second half of July.

Parts of *19. Luftwaffen-Sturm-Division* were now ordered to Denmark, to be used as the basis for a new division, *19. Volksgrenadier-Division*, being formed there.[44] They arrived in Denmark on 3 August and were immediately incorporated into the new division.[45] They included the remains of the *Jäger* regiments, minus *Fusilier-Bataillon 19 (L)*, as well as *II. Artillerie-Abteilung* of *Artillerie-Regiment 19 (L)*, which was absorbed into *Artillerie-Regiment 719* of *19. Volksgrenadier-Division*.[46] In addition, some elements of the division were handed over to *20. Luftwaffen-Sturm-Division*.[47] These included *I. Artillerie-Abteilung* and *Fusilier-Bataillon 19 (L)*, which was now redesignated *Fusilier-Bataillon 20 (L)*. The official date of disbandment appears to have been 15 August 1944,[48] exactly a week after the new *19. Volksgrenadier-Division*[49] was ordered to be formed (8 August 1944) in Denmark.[50]

Thus ended the brief history of *19. Luftwaffen-Sturm-Division*. Initially formed as a static infantry formation in March 1943, it had been armed with various German as well as captured Russian and Polish artillery pieces. It underwent

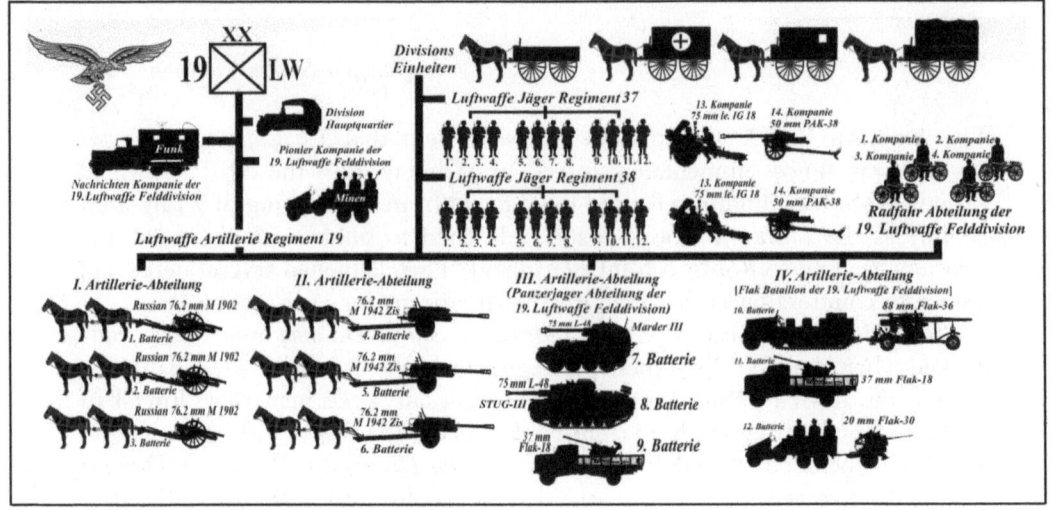

19. Luftwaffen-Felddivision in August 1943.

several reorganizations throughout its seventeen-month existence, but in the end it proved to be wholly inadequate as a regular combat infantry division, disintegrating less than two months after being committed to battle. That it gave a fairly good account of itself, especially in the latter half of June at Cecina and the early part of July at Rosignano-Solvay, can most likely be attributed to the addition of German Army NCOs and junior officers after the unit was officially absorbed into the German Army on 1 November 1943. Given enough good equipment and properly trained officers, these excess *Luftwaffe* personnel certainly had the potential to make good the horrendous losses suffered by the German Army on the Eastern Front from the summer of 1941 to the spring of 1942, but the warnings of the German Army High Command about the *Luftwaffe* field divisions had come true. As with so many other *Luftwaffe* field divisions, the 19th Division's history is one of waste – of both men and equipment – that occurred simply because of one power-hungry and vain man, at a time when the *Wehrmacht* (and Germany as a whole) could ill afford to lose more than 200,000 fit, strong, young men.

Felddivision 19 (L) in April 1944.

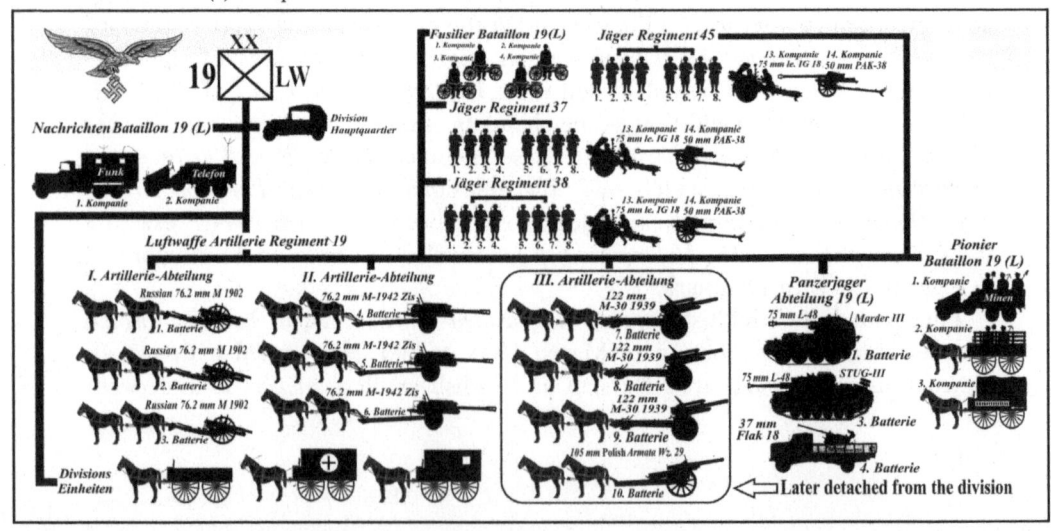

Organization of *19. Luftwaffen-Sturm-Division*
Commanders:
Divisional Commander:
  Generalmajor Gerhard Bassenge,[51] 01/12/42–01/02/43
  Generalmajor der Flakartillerie Hermann Plocher (b. 5 January 1901),[52] 02/02/43–17/08/43
  Generalmajor Hermann Muggenthaler (b. 12 February 1888), 17/08/43–12/10/44
  Generalmajor Erich Bäßler (b. 5 August 1890),[53] 12/10/43–15/07/44[54]
  Oberst Albert Henze (b. 7 August 1894),[55] 06/44–08/44
Personal Adjutant:
  Oberleutnant Siebert, 06/43–08/44
Ia:
  Hauptmann Gerhard Hildebrand,[56] 25/05/43–10/07/44
O1:
  Oberleutnant Küllmer, 07/43–07/44
Ib:
  Oberstleutnant Richard Seifert, 03/03/43–07/44
O2:
  Oberleutnant Franke, 07/43–07/44
O3:
  Oberleutnant Brücker, 07/43–07/44
IIa:
  Major Humer, 06/43–11/43
  Hauptmann Junghans, 10/12/43–07/44
IIb:
  Major Rattey, 07/43–07/44
Ic:
  Major Roland von Örtzen, 06/43–09/07/43
  Hauptmann Fischer, 10/07/43–07/44
IVa:
  Oberstabsintendant Vogel, 07/43–07/44
IVb:
  Oberstarzt Dr Eduard König, 01/03/43–17/08/43
  Oberstarzt Dr Gustav Papcke, 17/08/43–12/43
IVc *Stabsveterinär*:
  Dr Friesen, 07/43–08/44
Kdt. Div. St. Qu.:
  Oberleutnant Würke, 07/43–08/44
Divisional Supply Officer [*Divisions-Nachschubtruppen 19 (L)*]:
  Oberstleutnant Theodor Hirschling, 06/43–07/44
Company Chief, Medical Company [*Sanitäts-Kompanie 19 (L)*]:
  Stabsarzt Dr Jäntsch, 07/43–07/44

Surgeon [*Chirurg*]:
  Stabsarzt Dr Dieter, 07/43–07/44
Internist:
  Oberarzt Dr Berg, 07/43–07/44
  Oberarzt Dr Eckert, 07/43–07/44
Artillery Regiment Officers:
  CO *Luftwaffen-Artillerie-Regiment 19/Artillerie-Regiment 19 (L)*:
    Oberstleutnant Hans Winter, 06/03/43–07/43
    Oberstleutnant Ferdinand-Ernst Nord, 07/43–07/44
  CO *I. Artillerie-Abteilung*:
    Major Hermann Kunz-Krause, 06/43–07/44
  CO *II. Artillerie-Abteilung*:
    Major Lambert Kreuter, 06/43–07/44
  CO *III. Artillerie-Abteilung*:
    ?
  CO *IV. Artillerie-Abteilung*:
    Major Mätze, 06/43–07/44
  CO *Panzerjäger-Abteilung 19*:
    1.–3. Kompanie
    ?
    Sturmgeschütz-Batterie der Sturmgeschütz-Abteilung 1016
    ?
  CO *Pionier-Bataillon 19 (L)*:
    Major Heinrich Schmid, 22/12/42–24/01/44
  CO *1. Kompanie/Pionier-Bataillon 19 (L)*:
    Leutnant Maiwald
  CO *2. Kompanie/Pionier-Bataillon 19 (L)*:
    Leutnant Bauer
  CO *3. Kompanie/Pionier-Bataillon 19 (L)*:
    Leutnant Sander
  CO *Nachrichten-Kompanie der 19. Luftwaffen-Sturm-Division*:
    Oberleutnant Bennecke, 06/43–07/44
  CO *Luftwaffen-Jäger-Regiment 37/Jäger-Regiment 37 (L)*:
    Oberst Wilhelm Dannenberg, 03/43–07/44
  CO *I. Jäger-Bataillon/Luftwaffen-Jäger-Regiment 37*:
    Major Kleye, 03/43–07/44
  CO *II. Jäger-Bataillon/Luftwaffen-Jäger-Regiment 37*:
    Oberstleutnant Müller, 03/43–02/44
  CO *III. Jäger-Bataillon/Luftwaffen-Jäger-Regiment 3 became III. Jäger-Bataillon/Luftwaffen-Jäger-Regiment 37*:[57]
    Hauptmann Horst Wolff, 18/05/43–19/09/43
    Major Roland von Örtzen, 20/09/43–07/44

20. Luftwaffen-Sturm-Division

The order to raise this division was given on 8 March 1943 and it was initially formed at *Truppenübungsplatz Munsterlager* using Cadre Staff No. 2 from *XIII. Fliegerkorps*.[1] The majority of the men who would make up the initial core of the division came from *Flieger-Ausbildungs-Regiment 13* (Air Training Regiment 13). For command-and-control purposes, this regiment was attached to *Luftflotte 3*. The various training regiments for the *Luftwaffe* were organized as follows:

Luftflotte 1:
  Flieger-Ausbildungs-Regimente 10, 11, 21, 31, 41, 51, 61, 71
Luftflotte 2:
  Flieger-Ausbildungs-Regimente 12, 32, 42, 52, 62, 72, 82
Luftflotte 3:
  Flieger-Ausbildungs-Regimente 13, 23, 33, 43, 53, 63
Luftflotte 4:
  Flieger-Ausbildungs-Regimente 14, 24

In July 1943 *Flieger-Ausbildungs-Regiment 13* was completely absorbed into the newly forming division. Between the autumn of 1942 and 3 August 1943 this training regiment was led by *Generalmajor* Josef Pultar,[2] who was officially relieved of his command on 3 August. The officer initially placed in charge of the forming division was *Oberst* Hermann Aue, who held command for the entire month of March 1943. Thereafter he was assigned as commander of *Luftwaffen-Jäger-Regiment 39*. Command of the division would be given to no fewer than eleven more officers, ranging in rank from colonel to general. Before its absorption into *20. Luftwaffen-Felddivision, Flieger-Ausbildungs-Regiment 13* had been sent (as a whole unit) to the central sector of the Russian Front in November 1942. The men who made up the regiment were mostly air force ground crew, with some air crews from bombers and a few pilots thrown in as platoon commanders. During the winter of 1942/1943 the regiment had been committed to front-line fighting. As was standard, the new *Luftwaffe* division was to contain two *Jäger* regiments, *Luftwaffen-Jäger-Regiment 39* and *Luftwaffen-Jäger-Regiment 40*, with three battalions apiece. For artillery support, a three-battalion regiment, *Luftwaffen-Artillerie-Regiment 20*, was created. Later a fourth artillery battalion was added, but in reality this was the divisional anti-aircraft battalion: *Luftwaffen-Flak-Abteilung 20*.

III. Artillerie-Abteilung only had a single artillery battery, instead of the usual three or four. This unit wasn't even a regular artillery battery but was in fact a

120mm mortar company. When no further companies could be obtained for the battalion, it was redesignated *Luftwaffen-Granatwerfer-Kompanie der Luftwaffen-Felddivision 20*.[3] The division was also provided with an anti-tank battalion, *Panzerjäger-Abteilung 20 (L)*, of three companies. *1. Kompanie* and *2. Kompanie* were equipped with anti-tank guns, while *3. Kompanie* had *Flak* (anti-aircraft) guns. The anti-tank guns included a mixture of 50mm PAK-38 and 75mm PAK-97/38 guns. The *Flak* guns, in certain instances, could serve in the anti-tank role, provided that their calibre round was sufficient to penetrate armour. The division also contained a bicycle company, *Luftwaffen-Radfahr-Kompanie der Luftwaffen-Felddivision 20*, acting as the division's reconnaissance unit, and a communication company, *Luftwaffen-Signals-Kompanie der Luftwaffen-Felddivision 20*. Rounding out the rest of the divisional elements were *Luftwaffen-Sanitätskompanie der Luftwaffen-Felddivision 20* and *Luftwaffen-Versorgungskompanie der Luftwaffen-Felddivision 20*. Normally, German divisions would have a reconnaissance battalion as well as a *signals* (communications) battalion, but in the *Luftwaffe* divisions this was not always the case. In fact, quite often it was difficult even to establish an entire anti-tank battalion. The German Air Force was not able to supply sufficient support formations to equip each division with full-strength battalions, so they were significantly smaller than regular infantry divisions. This is one reason why the *Luftwaffe* divisions (for the most part) performed so poorly.

After a three-month period of organizing and training in Fallingbostel, a military camp in the Lüneberg Heath area of Germany, the division was sent to Denmark. It arrived in July 1943 and continued training while also performing garrison duty. Using rear-area, convalescent, forming and training units to garrison occupied lands had become part of the *modus operandi* of the German Army. When the division was sent to Denmark, the only other large German formation in that country was *416. Infanterie-Division*.

As previously stated, the various air force field divisions were transferred to the *Heer* on 1 November 1943. By then it was perfectly clear to the German Armed Forces High Command how utterly substandard these air force infantry divisions were in combat. The failure of Göring's airmen to perform well in the ground fighting role – something they had not trained to do, and had been given only a few months to master – was a serious humiliation for the *Reichsmarschall*. Hermann Göring had lost face. As a result, he also lost interest in his infantry divisions. In fact, when the order came for their transfer to the *Heer*, he didn't make much of a fuss. Instead, he concentrated on making sure that his *fallschirmjäger* (paratrooper) units, as well as *Fallschirm-Panzer-Regiment 'Hermann Göring'*, were well armed and supplied with the best men and equipment. In particular, he took a special interest in the tank regiment that bore his name. This regiment had been established in southern France in February 1943, and as the war progressed it would be expanded to a division. Göring pushed for, and received, approval for a second mechanized formation, *Fallschirm-Panzergrenadier-Division 2 'Hermann Göring'*, which was established in September 1944. One month later, in October,

20. Luftwaffen-Felddivision in Denmark, 30 November 1943.

both of 'his' divisions were merged into a new corps-sized formation, *Fallschirm-Panzerkorps 'Hermann Göring'*.

The German Army wasted no time in trying to salvage what it could from the mess created by Göring's ill-advised *Luftwaffe* infantry. The *Reichsmarschall*'s insistence, in the spring of 1942, that the *Heer* would not get 'his' airmen eventually led to the loss of a valuable source of recruits that, at the time, were desperately needed by the *Ostheer*.[4] On a 'quiet' day on the Russian Front, Hitler was losing around 5,000 men killed, wounded, captured or missing. Göring's refusal to give up around 200,000 airmen to the army was, in practical terms, an unforgivable act of military malpractice. The German Army ordered that more men and equipment be provided for these former *Luftwaffe* divisions. They were also to receive additional training. All of this was supposed to improve the quality of these former *Luftwaffe* divisions. In point of fact, many good quality officers and NCOs were retained by the *Luftwaffe* High Command and transferred to other air force units, such as the *Fallschirmjäger* branch. The additional recruits now added to these divisions were also, for the most part, of poor quality. Some good quality officers and NCOs were transferred into the air force field divisions, but never in sufficient numbers to make an appreciable difference. These *Heer*

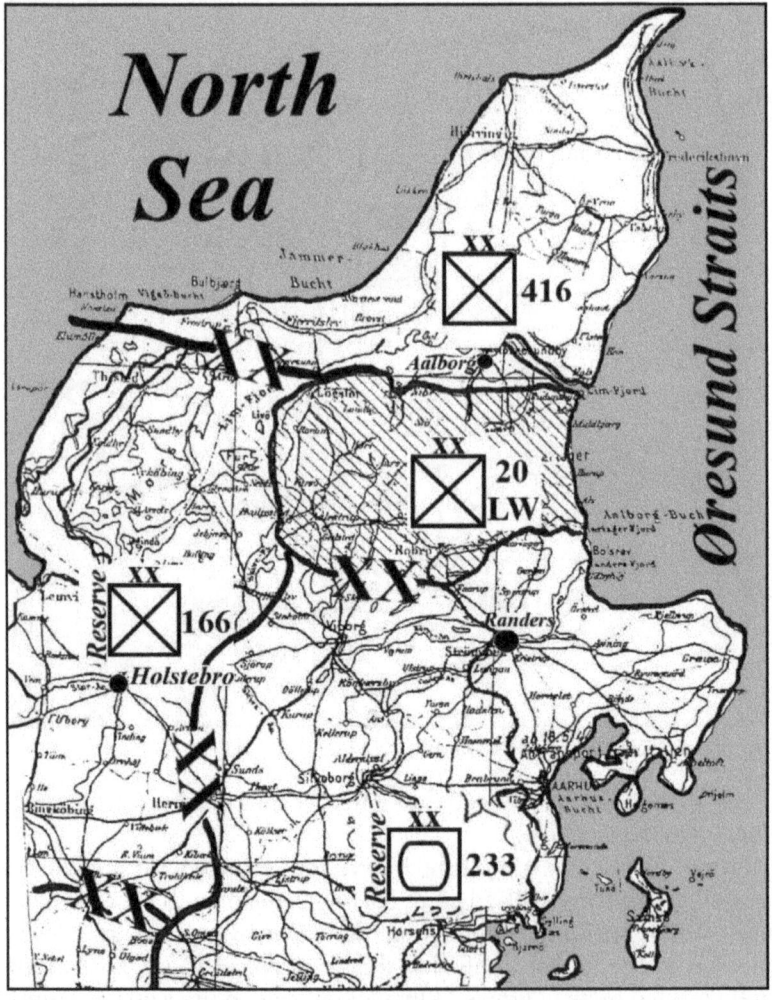

The shaded region is the area of Jutland where *20. Luftwaffen-Sturm-Division* was on garrison duty. The division remained in Denmark until May 1944, when it was transferred to Italy.

transfers came mostly from the cavalry/bicycle branches of the German Army and in most cases the units that these men came from were glad to be rid of them, for one reason or another.

In spite of the Army High Command's insistence that all air force field divisions be disbanded and their personnel used to flesh out the army's battered and skeletal divisions, Hitler forbade it. One can only assume that in the *Wolfsschanze* (Wolf's Lair) in Rastenburg, East Prussia, or perhaps in Hitler's Berlin bunker, these extra divisional battle flags pinned to a war map must have looked very impressive. But Hitler's delusion went even further. He insisted on keeping divisions that were mere skeletal battlegroups on the active divisional rolls. With regard to *Felddivision 19 (L) and Felddivision 20 (L)*, he decreed that instead of keeping the new title for both, they were to be referred to as *19. and 20. Luftwaffen-Sturm-Divisionen* (19th and 20th Air Force Assault Divisions). This title change occurred on 1 June 1944. Again, on paper, having two assault divisions looked great, even though in reality these two units were, in essence, static formations. They had fewer horses than were normally allotted to a 1944 German infantry division, and about 70 per cent of the division still depended on either horse transport or marching on foot, so even the nomenclature of the division, *Radfahr* (bicycle), was incorrect. At one point, Hitler even wanted to fully motorize *20. Luftwaffen-Sturm-Division* by assigning it a full complement of motor vehicles, like a motorized division. However, due to a shortage of trucks and other vehicles, this proved impossible, in spite of the *Führer's* insistence. In lieu of trucks, Hitler pushed to supply *20. Luftwaffen-Sturm-Division* with bicycles. This wish could be realized, and soon the division was fully equipped. However, only six out of the ten infantry companies were outfitted with bicycles. The infantry contingent in the division was reduced to four battalions, divided equally between two *Jäger* regiments. Even though not every infantryman in the division had a bicycle, the infantry regiments were now redesignated as *Jäger-Regiment 39 (L)* and *Jäger-Regiment 40 (L)*.[5]

Thus, even though Hitler insisted on calling the formation an assault division, the strength of the unit as far as combat was concerned was only four infantry battalions instead of the usual six or nine. Both regiments contained one anti-tank company and one machine-gun company. These companies were equipped with some vehicles that could tow or carry the heavy equipment.

The division was now considered bicycle-mobile, even though many of its component parts were not equipped with either bicycles or motor vehicles. Horses were still a necessity within the division. On 17 November 1943 the division was retitled *Felddivision 20 (L)*. The final designation of the division was *20. Luftwaffen-Sturm-Division*. This occurred in February 1944. In the meantime, the division suffered another blow to its combat capability when *IV. Artillerie-Abteilung* of its artillery regiment (i.e. the *Flak* battalion) was withdrawn from the division and returned to *Luftwaffe* service, where it was redesignated *I. Flak-Abteilung* of *Flak-Regiment 48*. In order to make up for this loss, an army artillery battalion that had been stationed in Denmark, *schwere Artillerie-Abteilung 995*, was added to the division's artillery regiment on 11 December 1943, becoming its *III. Artillerie-Abteilung*. This battalion did not have to depend completely on horses to pull its artillery pieces, as it was partially motorized.

On 23 May 1944 the 6th US Corps broke out of the Anzio beachhead and advanced on Cisterna, where it joined up with the 11th US Corps, which had begun to advance from Terracina on 25 May. On that same day German military trains began moving *20. Luftwaffen-Sturm-Division (Radfahr)* from northern Jutland in Denmark to Italy, and in Britain MI6 had learned of the division's movement through an intercepted German military message sent through their cypher machine.[6] The British had broken the German cypher code in 1941 and were able to intercept military messages. The British referred to this Intelligence unit as 'Ultra'[7] and it was one of the most closely guarded secrets of the war, because the Allies always knew ahead of time what the German military commanders were planning. It was a key factor that shortened the war by years and played a part in winning the war for the Allies.[8] Further decrypted messages sent between 31 May and 5 June showed that *20. Luftwaffen-Sturm-Division* was being sent to the area between Civitaveccia and Ortebello, along the coastline of the Tyrrhenian Sea.[9] On 1 June 1944 the division was located between Terracina and San Olivia.[10] Terracina is southeast of the Anzio bridgehead, about 65km away, while San Olivia is located approximately 40km northeast of the Anzio bridgehead. The division then moved to Orvieto as a reserve unit alongside *26. Panzer-Division, 162. (turkistanische) Infanterie-Division* and *356. Infanterie-Division*.[11] The division did not remain in reserve long. It was sent to aid the beleaguered German *14. Armee*.[12] By 6 June *Jäger-Regiment 39 (L)* was operating just south of Civitaveccia, while *Jäger-Regiment 40 (L)* was located near Bracciano.[13] Two days later the division reported suffering heavy losses. Beginning on 8 June 1944, the division began a fighting withdrawal. One source described the fighting from the American side:

> As night fell, and against little opposition, the 133rd Infantry came within 5 miles of Tarquinia. But the next morning, 8 June, in hilly country just south of Tarquinia, the regiments encountered the first elements of *20. Luftwaffen-Sturm-Division*; a unit that Kesselring had sent south from Orvieto to reinforce *14. Armee*. The enemy infantrymen had established themselves on the sides of a ravine overlooking the highway. Backed by mortars and artillery, they held until shortly before dark, when the Americans, using newly issued 57mm anti-tank guns as direct fire weapons, blasted the positions. Instead of sending the 133rd Infantry into Tarquinia that night, Ryder relieved it with an attached unit, Rudolf W. Broedlow's 361st Regimental Combat Team, the first contingent of the 91st Infantry Division to arrive in Italy.[14]

20. Luftwaffen-Stürm-Division made a fighting withdrawal through Caprani, Vetralla, Tuscany, Manziana and Tarquinia, by Lake Bolsano, just west of Siena, which was reached on 12 June 1944. On that date the German command underwent a regrouping with the transfer of *XIV. Panzerkorps* from *10. Armee* to the extreme right-hand sector of *14. Armee* (by the coast). *XIV. Panzerkorps* assumed control of both *19. Luftwaffen-Sturm-Division* and *20. Luftwaffen-Stürm-Division*, pending the arrival of three further divisions: *26. Panzer-Division, 29. Panzergrenadier-Division* and *90. Panzergrenadier-Division*. By the third week of June, *20. Luftwaffen-Sturm-Division* was operating under *I. Fallschirmjäger-Korps*, fighting southwest of Siena. The division had suffered especially heavy losses during the battle for Grosseto, which began on 14 June. It continued to suffer losses in men and equipment during the battle for Paganico (19–21 June). As the US 4th Corps was making its way up Route No. 68, General Alphonse Juin's French Expeditionary Force (comprising around 112,000 men) was located on the right flank of the American 5th Army.[15] Using Route No. 2, the French were attacking in the direction of Siena. The main formations during this drive included the 3rd Algerian Infantry Division on the left flank and the 2nd Moroccan Infantry Division on the right. This French drive against Siena began towards the end of June:

> Starting to attack on 21 June, the French soon found themselves bogged down opposite the German left wing of *14. Armee*, one of the most heavily defended sectors of the German front. There General Schlemm's *I. Fallschirmjäger-Korps* had deployed from east to west *356. Grenadier-Division, 4. Fallschirmjäger-Division*, a regiment of *26. Panzer-Division*, elements of *20. Luftwaffen-Sturm-Division*, and a regiment of *29. Panzergrenadier-Division*. For the next five days, from 22 through the 26 June, this strong enemy force held the French to a 2-mile advance. Not until 26 June, after the neighbouring [US] 1. Armored Division had outflanked the enemy positions, did the Germans begin to withdraw and the French to make appreciable progress.[16]

On 3 July 1944 Algerian troops captured the town of Siena. *Jäger-Regiment 40* was said to have been attached to *90. Panzergrenadier-Division* during the battle for Volterra, just west of Siena. In the last week of June *20. Luftwaffen-Sturm-Division* was ordered to be relieved, pending the arrival of additional German forces in the operational area of *XIV. Panzerkorps*. These reinforcements included *16. SS-Panzergrenadier-Division 'Reichsführer SS', 162. (turkistanische) Infanterie-Division* and *90. Panzergrenadier-Division*. The military situation was so dire, however, that *20. Luftwaffen-Sturm-Division* had to remain on the front line until 30 June 1944. On that date the division was attached to *3. Panzergrenadier-Division*. What remained of the unit now began fighting under *Kampfgruppe Crisolli*, named after its commander. In July this battlegroup received some much-needed replacements when elements of the newly disbanded *19. Luftwaffen-Sturm-Division* were absorbed into *20. Luftwaffen-Sturm-Division*, which helped to increase the latter's strength. These elements included:

Fusilier-Bataillon 19 (L)
Feldersatz-Bataillon 19 (L)

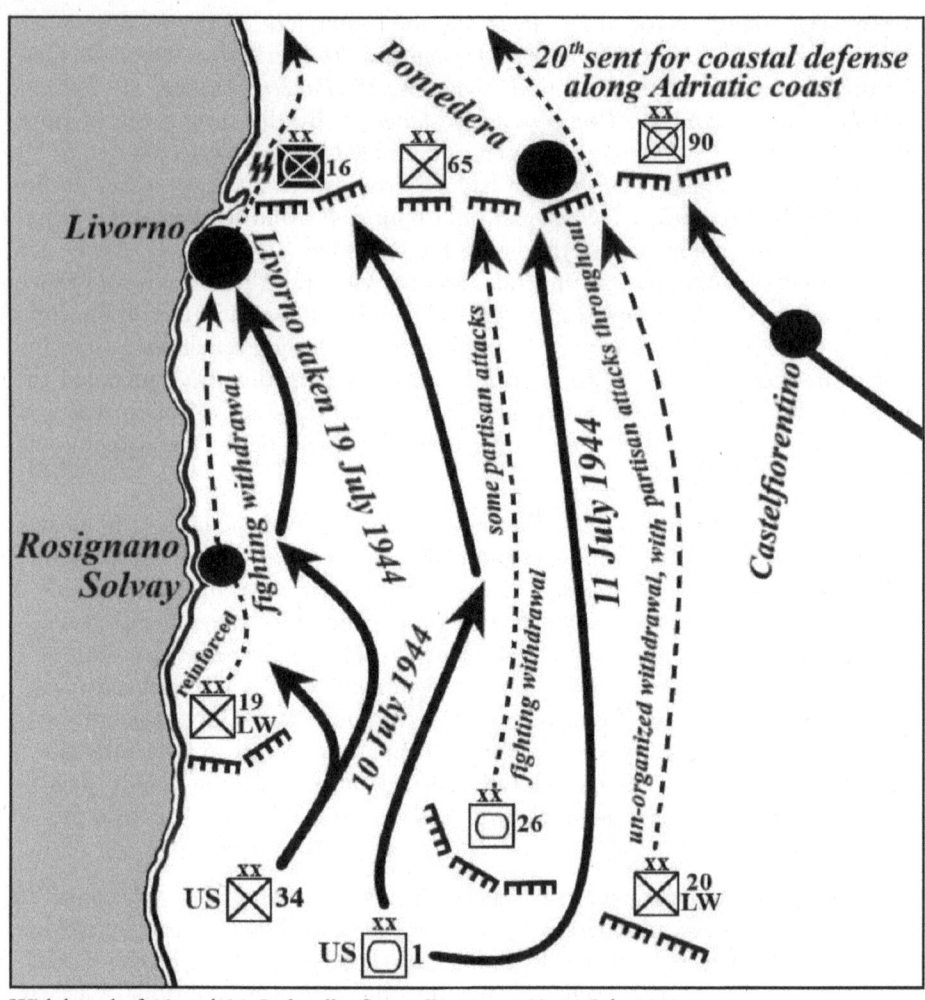

Withdrawal of *19.* and *20. Luftwaffen-Sturm-Divisionen*, 10–19 July 1944.

Panzerjäger-Abteilung 19 (L)
Pionier-Bataillon 19 (L)
I. Artillerie-Abteilung/Artillerie-Regiment 19 (L)
Versorgungseinheiten 19 (L)

Of course, these units were renamed, so that, for example, *I. Artillerie-Abteilung/ Artillerie-Regiment 19 (L)* became *I. Artillerie-Abteilung/Artillerie-Regiment 20 (L)*.[17] In July *Jäger-Regiment 39 (L)* was fighting on the front lines near Lucca, but the bulk of *20. Luftwaffen-Sturm-Division* was stationed between Viareggio and La Spezia.[18] It had been sent there to perform coastal guard duty, while at the same time reforming and regrouping. A third mission was soon added, when *Jäger-Regiment 40 (L)* was assigned to fight the pro-Allied Italian

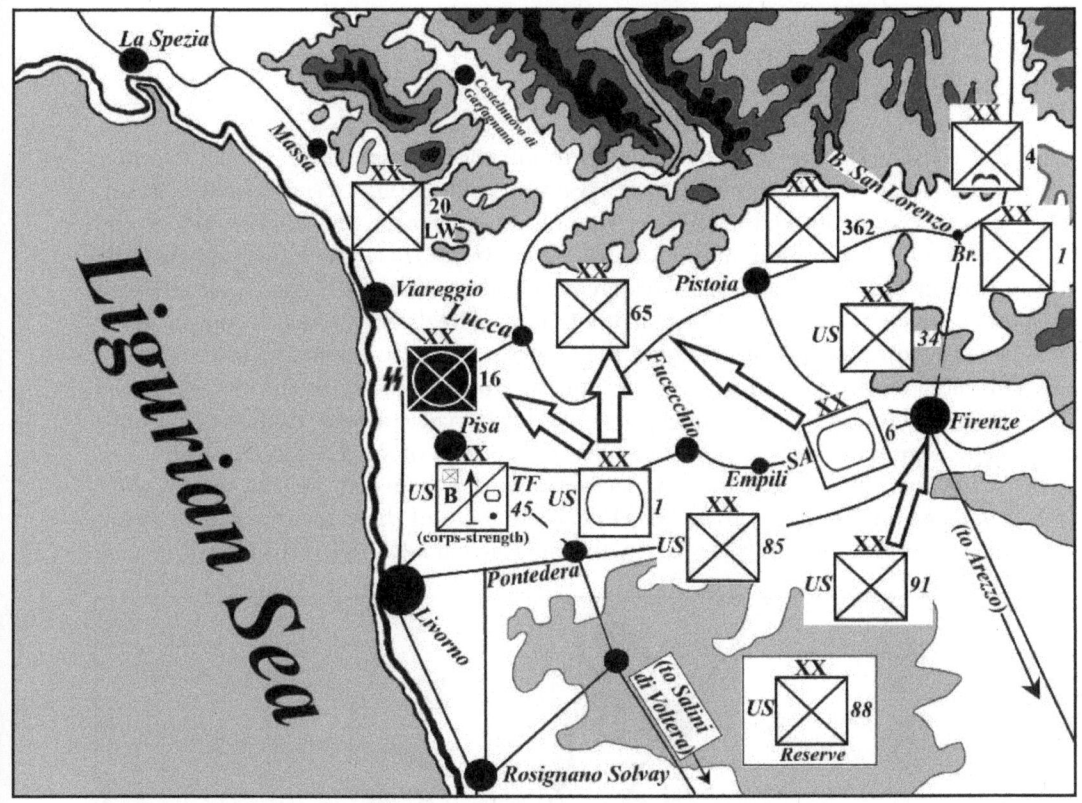

The military situation on 25 August 1944. The map shows elevation levels. The highest peaks north of the town of Pistoia are the Corno alle Scale (6,381ft above sea level) and the Alpe Tre Potenze.

partisans operating north of the town of Lucca.[19] This guerrilla activity often extended to the German front lines:

> Driving the Germans from the mountain, the battalion continued toward Monte Battaglia, a mile and a half to the northeast. Passing the night short of the objective, the men on the next day, 27 July, encountered a group of partisans who claimed to be already in possession of Monte Battaglia. Guided by the partisans along a mule trail, the battalion saw no evidence of the enemy other than sporadic artillery fire. Reaching Battaglia's crest in midafternoon, Williamson established his command post on the reverse slope. Because he was well in front of the rest of the division, he posted only one company on the summit, and deployed the rest to cover a long and tenuous line of communication to the regimental command post. While a few partisans remained with the Americans, the others vanished into the mountains, presumably to harass the enemy.[20]

During September 1944, *20. Luftwaffen-Sturm-Division* continued to perform security duty between Viareggio and La Spezia. In addition, it was charged with expanding its anti-partisan operations above the Gothic Line positions. On 12 September 1944 the divisional commander, *Generalmajor* Wilhelm Crisolli, was assassinated by an Italian partisan dressed in civilian attire, a disguise which had enabled him to get close enough to kill the German commander.[21] Immediately after Crisolli was killed, his operations officer (Ia), *Oberst* Kaspar Völcker, assumed command of the division. In mid-September the division was moved and placed under the command of *LXXVI. Panzerkorps* (*10. Armee*) along the Adriatic coast, in the Rimini and San Arcangelo area and south of Cesena. There it faced off against elements of the British 8th Army.[22] The division was not committed as a whole unit, for obvious reasons: the German High Command feared that if the division was employed as a whole unit, it would collapse under the weight of enemy attack and the German line would be pierced. Instead, both the division's *Jäger* regiments were employed under the control of *26. Panzer-Division*.

The rest of the divisional units were divided between *29. Panzergrenadier-Division* and *90. Panzergrenadier-Division*. In spite of these measures, units from the division took heavy losses in the area around Rimini, especially the area

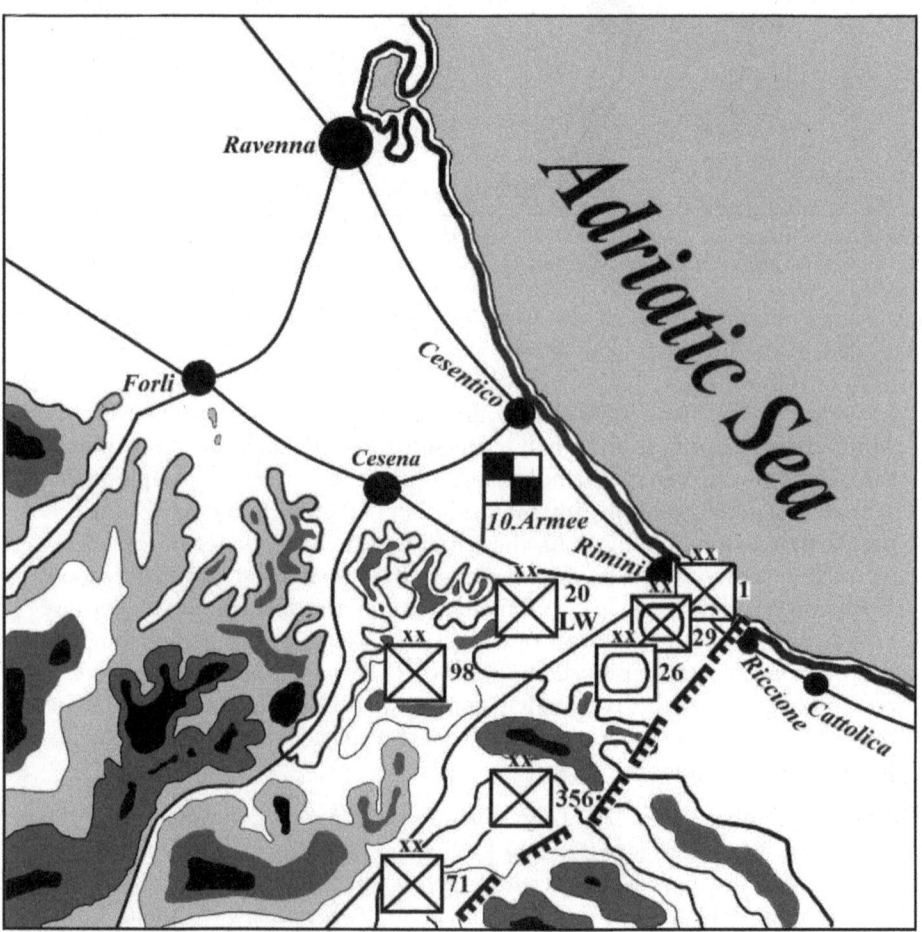

10. Armee positions, mid-September to November 1944.

surrounding San Marino. On 5 October 1944 what remained of *20. Luftwaffen-Sturm-Division* withdrew to Cesena, following a general retreat of *10. Armee*. In the autumn of 1944 the division took part in difficult defensive battles in the region between Faenza and Via Emilia, just southeast of Bologna. The German commanders, aware of the military situation, understood that the division could not take much further punishment. Disbandment seemed likely. The first indication of this was Field Marshal Albert Kesselring's decision to employ the air force field division in guarding the Italian coast line and fighting the partisans. Only when the military situation became critical did he authorize its employment on the front lines. Splitting up the component parts of the division in September 1944 was the second indication. In October the 20mm *Flak* guns were taken from each of the two *Jäger* regiments and given to *148. Infanterie-Division*.[23] This was another sign that the unit was headed for dissolution.

One month later, on 28 November 1944, the axe fell and OKW made the unit's disbandment official, although the order to do so was not signed until 8 December 1944.[24] The remaining divisional elements were absorbed into various *Heer* formations in late November, primarily *155. Feldausbildungs-Division*,[25] although the two *Jäger* regiments, *Jäger-Regiment 39 (L)* and *Jäger-Regiment 40 (L)*, remained attached to *26. Panzer-Division* for a while longer. On 11 February 1945 the *Jäger* regiments were both officially incorporated into *155. Feldausbildungs-Division*, which at that time was forming in northern Italy and on that same day was redesignated as an infantry division. On 1 March 1945 the two former *Jäger* regiments were redesignated as *Feldausbildungs-Grenadier-Regiment 1128* and *1129*. Similarly, the division's field reserve battalion was absorbed into *Feldausbildungs-Grenadier-Regiment 1127*, which was also part of *155. Infanterie-Division*. Specifically, it became *I. Bataillon* in the regiment.[26]

As for the artillery element, *I. Artillerie-Abteilung/Artillerie-Regiment 20 (L)* was also absorbed by *155. Feldausbildungs-Division* and renamed *155. Feldausbildungs-Artillerie-Abteilung*, while the other parts of *Artillerie-Regiment 20 (L)* went to other units. For example, *II. Artillerie-Abteilung/Artillerie-Regiment 20 (L)* became *II. Artillerie-Abteilung/Artillerie-Regiment 661* (of *114. Jäger-Division*), and *III. Artillerie-Abteilung/Artillerie-Regiment 20 (L)* became *III. Artillerie-Abteilung/Artillerie-Regiment 650* (of *710. Infanterie-Division*). Likewise, *IV. Artillerie-Abteilung/Artillerie-Regiment 20 (L)* became *IV. Artillerie-Abteilung/Artillerie-Regiment 661* (of *114. Jäger-Division*). *Fusilier-Bataillon 20 (L)* was renamed *Aufklärungs-Abteilung 1057*, and now became part of *157. Gebirgs-Division*. The headquarters and two remaining anti-tank companies of *Panzerjäger-Abteilung 20 (L)* became *Panzerjäger-Abteilung 1048* of *148. Infanterie-Division*. *Nachrichten-Abteilung 20 (L)* was renamed *Nachrichten-Abteilung 630*, and placed under *155. Feldausbildungs-Division*.[27] Finally, 2. and 3. *Artillerie-Batterie* of *Artillerie-Regiment 20 (L)* were absorbed into *Artillerie-Regiment 142* of *42. Jäger-Division*.

20. Luftwaffen-Sturm-Division had existed from its inception in March 1943 until its disbandment in November 1944. Its military service lasted around twenty months, with the division in combat for the last seven of those months.

Table 10. Corps and Army Posting for *20. Luftwaffen-Sturm-Division*.

Date	Corps	Army or Detachment	Army Group or Higher Command
21/06/43	Befehlshaber der deutschen Truppen in Dänemark		Chef der Ersatzheer
20/11/43	”		”
03/12/43	”		”
26/12/43	”		”
15/05/44	”		”
24/05/44	In transit to Italy		”
15/06/44	XIV. Panzerkorps	14. Armee	Heeresgruppe C
15/07/44	XIV. Panzerkorps	14. Armee	”
15/08/44	LXXV. Armeekorps	14. Armee	”
31/08/44	XIV. Panzerkorps	14. Armee	”
16/09/44	LXXVI. Panzerkorps	10. Armee	”
05/11/44	LXXVI. Panzerkorps	10. Armee	”
26/11/44	LXXVI. Panzerkorps	10. Armee	”

Note also that almost as soon as it was committed, the division began to fragment. Its performance was below average when compared to a regular German infantry division of that period. The *Heer* had made an attempt at strengthening the division when it was being established by an infusion of seasoned army troops. But this proved insufficient, and the unit behaved like most of the air force field divisions: mediocre to poor, in spite of Hitler's elevation of the formation to the status of an 'assault division'.

Organization of *20. Luftwaffen-Sturm-Division*

Commanders:
  Divisional Commander:
    Oberst Hermann Aue, 01/03/43–31/03/43
    Generalmajor Wolfgang Erdmann
    Oberst August Kleßmann, 05/04/43–06/43
    Oberst Hermann Aue, 06/43–07/43
    Generalmajor Robert Fuchs, 08/43–31/10/43
    Oberst Helmuth Wachsen, 01/11/43–24/11/43
    Generalmajor Wilhelm Crisolli, 25/11/43–12/09/44
    Oberst Kaspar Völcker,[28] 12/09/44–11/44
    Generalmajor Erich Fronhöfer, 11/44–01/45
  Ia:
    Major Hans Delinsky, 09/12/42–19/11/43
    Oberst Kaspar Völcker, 20/11/43–12/09/44
    Oberstleutnant Werner Lämpe,[29] 10/12/43–01/06/44
  IIa:
    Hauptmann Maak,[30] 09/12/42–19/11/43

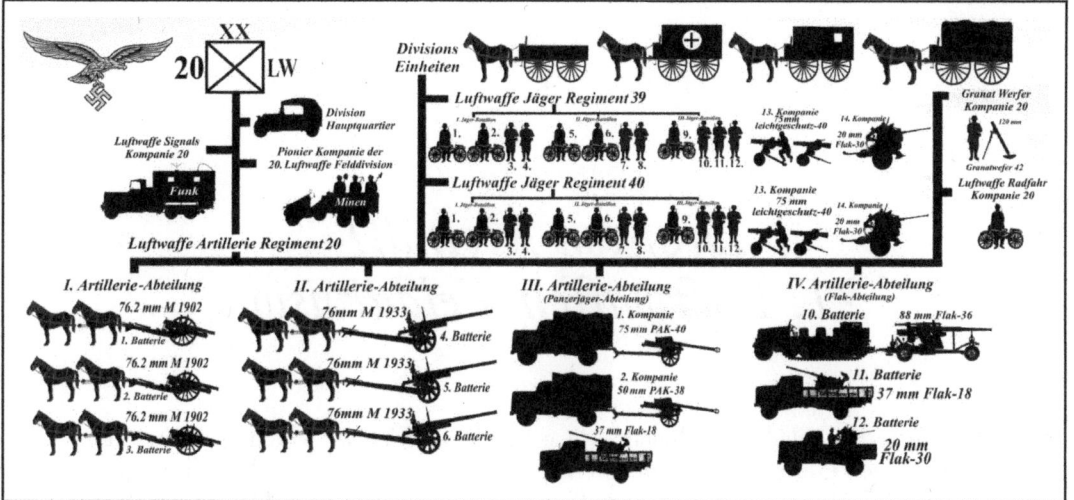

20. Luftwaffen-Felddivision in August 1943.

CO *Luftwaffen-Jäger-Regiment 39*:
Oberst Hermann Aue
CO *Luftwaffen-Jäger-Regiment 40*:
Oberst August Kleßmann
CO *I. Jäger-Bataillon / Jäger-Regiment 40 (L)*:
Oberstleutnant Eugen Triep,[31] 10/06/43–30/06/43
CO *Luftwaffen-Artillerie-Regiment 20*:
Oberst Schaper, 03/43–?
Oberst Kurt Wäntig, ?–01/11/43
Luftwaffen-Panzerjäger-Abteilung 20:[32]
Major Castening
Pioneer-Abteilung 20 (L):[33]
Oberst Anstett
Feldersatz-Abteilung 20 (L):[34]
Oberstleutnant Gillitze

20. Luftwaffen-Sturm-Division in June 1944.

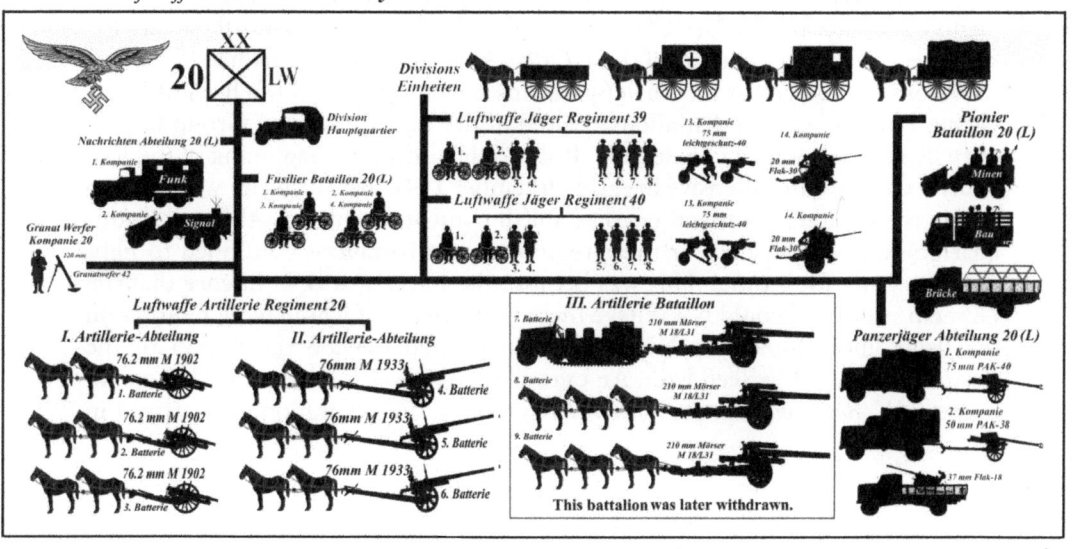

Division Meindl/
21. Luftwaffen-Felddivision

21. Luftwaffen-Felddivision began life as *Division Meindl*, which was the first division-sized German *Luftwaffe* infantry formation to be established. In preparation for the Soviet winter counteroffensive, which began on 5 December 1941, Stalin had brought together eighteen divisions with 1,700 tanks and over 1,500 aircraft, all from Siberia and the Far East. These Siberian divisions were veteran troops who, in the 1930s, had fought border battles with the Empire of Japan. These men had trained in winter warfare and possessed an abundance of cold weather gear, equipment and ski troops, complete with white camouflage to blend in with the snowy countryside. While the transmission fluid and oil of German vehicles froze in weather that averaged –30 degrees Fahrenheit, the Siberian divisions had specialized lubricants that allowed their tanks and vehicles to keep functioning. Unprepared for winter weather, and with long and fragile lines of supply, the German Army reeled back as the fresh Red Army divisions threw themselves in front of Moscow. During these winter months of 1941/1942, the Red Army made advances in most sectors of the Russian Front. Desperate to find additional forces to plug the numerous gaps in its front lines, the *Ostheer* began to scrape together all available rear area forces for combat.

In the case of *Division Meindl* (as it was initially known), the troops were gathered together from various *Luftwaffe* sources. German air force bases and installations were always guarded by companies of air force personnel acting as guards. Now, these men were pressed into several regiments with the addition of excess ground personnel and staff. The earliest creation of such 'emergency' regiments took place in October 1941 in the region of Army Group North, where the rear area commander employed these *Luftwaffe* personnel in individual battalion-sized formations against the Soviet partisans operating behind the lines of Army Group North. Air force battalions created in the region of Army Group Centre were likewise employed individually. It was only during the beginning of the Red Army winter counteroffensive in early December 1941 that the order was given to merge these battalions together to establish combat regiments. Although headquarters were established for these regiments, the battalions continued to fight independently for a time. This was because the fighting was so intense that the German command could not relieve these units, many of whom were fighting on the front lines. Some battalions had been created outside the region of the Eastern Front, and arrived later. An example of this was the battalion that would become *IV. Bataillon* of *Luftwaffen-Feldregiment 4*. This battalion only arrived in

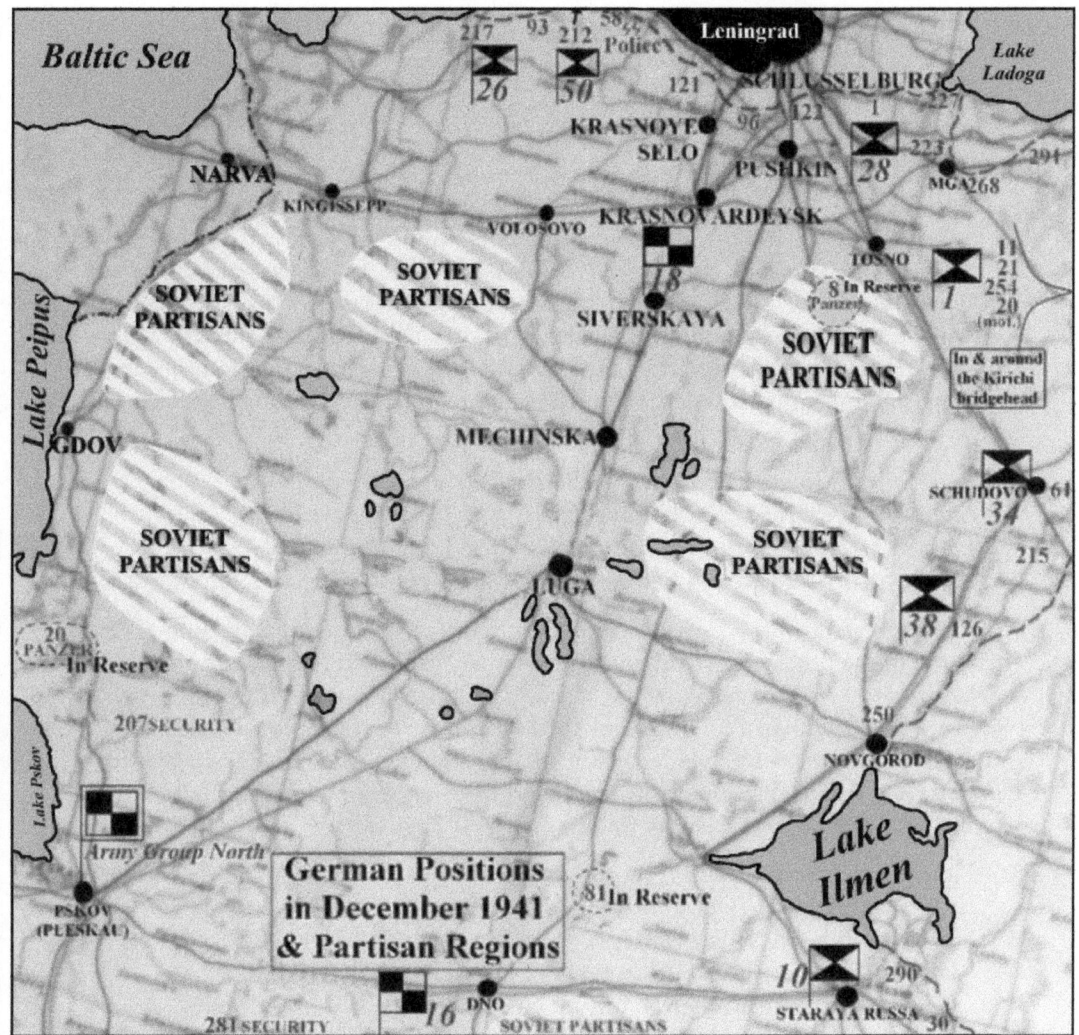

The regions of partisan activity in the area of Army Group North, December 1941.

the region of the Volkov Front (under *18. Armee*) in February 1942. Therefore, although these air force field regiments were created in the months of December 1941 and January 1942, their employment as regimental combat groups would occur much later. The five regiments that were created during this time each had four battalions:

Luftwaffen-Feldregiment 1
  I., II., III., IV. Bataillonen
Luftwaffen-Feldregiment 2
  I., II., III., IV. Bataillonen
Luftwaffen-Feldregiment 3
  I., II., III., IV. Bataillonen
Luftwaffen-Feldregiment 4
  I., II., III., IV. Bataillonen

Luftwaffen-Feldregiment 5
  I., II., III., IV. Bataillonen

Later on, these five air force field regiments would be used as the basis for *Luftwaffen-Felddivision 21* and *Luftwaffen-Felddivision 22*. In the case of *Luftwaffen-Felddivision 22*, the division was not yet completely formed when the decision was made to disband it and send whatever troops it had to flesh out *Luftwaffen-Felddivision 21*. As the structure of the various German air force divisions began to be imposed, the numerical designation of these regiments was altered and in 1942 they were renumbered as follows:

Luftwaffen-Feldregiment 1 became *Luftwaffen-Jäger-Regiment 43*
Luftwaffen-Feldregiment 2 became *Luftwaffen-Jäger-Regiment 42*
Luftwaffen-Feldregiment 3 became *Luftwaffen-Jäger-Regiment 44*
Luftwaffen-Feldregiment 4 became *Luftwaffen-Jäger-Regiment 41*

Luftwaffen-Feldregiment 5 was disbanded in February 1943 and its personnel distributed to the other four regiments. Another air force field regiment, *Luftwaffen-Feldregiment 14*, was created on 6 March 1942 and was sent to operate in the region of the German *16. Armee*. In April 1943 this regiment was also disbanded and its personnel were handed over to the forming *21.* and *22. Luftwaffen-Felddivision*. As for the officers in command of these regiments, their names and service as commanders were as follows:

Luftwaffen-Feldregiment 1
  Oberst Max Voitl (December 1941–March 1942)
  Oberst Wilhelm Völk (March–7 June 1942)
  Oberst Hermann Fricke (8 June 1942–31 May 1943)
  Oberst Max Schirmacher (1 July–1 November 1943)
Luftwaffen-Feldregiment 2
  Oberst Wilhelm Völk (December 1941–February 1942)
  Oberst August Klessmann (February–September 1942)
  Oberst Wilhelm Völk (October 1942–24 March 1943)
  Oberst Wolfgang Neudörfer (25 March–1 November 1943)
IV. Jäger-Bataillon / Luftwaffen-Feldregiment 2
  Hauptmann Heinz *Freiherr von* Wangenheim
Luftwaffen-Feldregiment 3
  Oberst Hermann Aue (December 1941–June 1942)
  Oberstleutnant Graf Kerssenbrock (June 1942–29 March 1943)
  Oberst Fritz Hencke (30 March–April 1942)
  Oberst Hermann Schütze (April–December 1943)
Luftwaffen-Feldregiment 4
  Oberst Friedrich Leesemann (December 1941–October 1942)
  Oberst Ludwig Engel (October–November 1942)
  Oberst Werner Krahl (November 1942–1 November 1943)

Luftwaffen-Feldregiment 5
 Oberstleutnant Fritz Hencke (December 1941–April 1942)
 Oberst Anton Schub (April–July 1942)
 Oberst Hermann Aue (July 1942–February 1943)[1]

The records for the commanders of *Luftwaffen-Feldregiment 14* are incomplete and in some instances we only know the surname of the officers:

Luftwaffen-Feldregiment 14
 Oberst Erich Munske (February–March 1942)
 Oberst Techel (March–April 1942)
 Oberst Otto Jordan (April 1942–April 1943)

As stated earlier, initially these men were committed in battalion-sized units in the region of Army Group North. Most of the battalions were employed under *16. Armee*, but some served under *18. Armee*. As the battalions were merged into regiments, they operated in the following areas:

Luftwaffen-Feldregiment 1
 Attached to *218. Infanterie-Division*, both inside and outside the Cholm pocket. One battalion (the 3rd) was trapped inside the Cholm pocket, while the rest of the regiment operated outside it. This regiment was initially employed in the region of Nagovo, by Staraya Russa from 20 February 1942.

Luftwaffen-Feldregiment 2
 Attached to *5. Jäger-Division* in the region of Staraya Russa and Kalitnika, just south of Lake Ilmen, on the left flank of the Demyansk pocket.

Luftwaffen-Feldregiment 3
 Attached to *12. Infanterie-Division*, inside the Demyansk pocket.

Luftwaffen-Feldregiment 4
 This regiment, minus its *IV. Jäger-Bataillon*, was attached to *18. Panzergrenadier-Division* and located near Staraya Rusa, south of Lake Ilmen. Parts of this division were inside the Demyansk pocket, including part of *Luftwaffen-Feldregiment 4*. *IV. Bataillon / Luftwaffen-Feldregiment 4* was attached to *58. Infanterie-Division* in the region of the Volkhov Front and also inside the Volkhov pocket. The battalion was first employed fighting partisan forces behind the lines of the German *I. Armeekorps* and *XXXVIII. Armeekorps* in February 1942.

Luftwaffen-Feldregiment 5
 This regiment was attached to *290. Infanterie-Division*, which had divisional elements inside and outside the Demyansk pocket. The air force field battalions inside the pocket fought in and around Fedorovka. One source says that two of its battalions were employed at Cholm and two in Demyansk.[2]

Luftwaffen-Feldregiment 14
 This regiment was formed on 6 March 1942 with the help of the staff of *Luftwaffen-Feldregiment 4*. The regiment contained only two battalions in

The Cholm commemorative shield, issued on 1 July 1942.
(*Author's collection*)

October 1942. It is possible that the regiment never had more than two battalions, instead of the normal complement of four.

During the second week of January 1942 the military situation became increasingly precarious for the Germans in the area bordering Army Group Centre and Army Group North, where the Soviet 3. Shock Army of the Kalinin Front managed to break through the lines of *XXXIX. Armeekorps* (renamed *XXXIX. Panzerkorps* in July 1942). Supporting this drive was the 4th Shock Army, on the left flank of the 3rd Shock Army. The 4th Shock Army soon captured Toropets, and with it the huge German food and munitions depots located there.

In the meantime, the 3rd Shock Army barrelled down towards Cholm, which was the most important communications hub in the region. The town of Cholm itself stood on solid ground but it was surrounded mostly by marshes, swamps and forests. In order for the Red Army to continue moving forward, this town had to be taken. The Germans were well aware that the capture of Cholm would greatly facilitate the enemy's advance on Nevel, a town further south in the rear

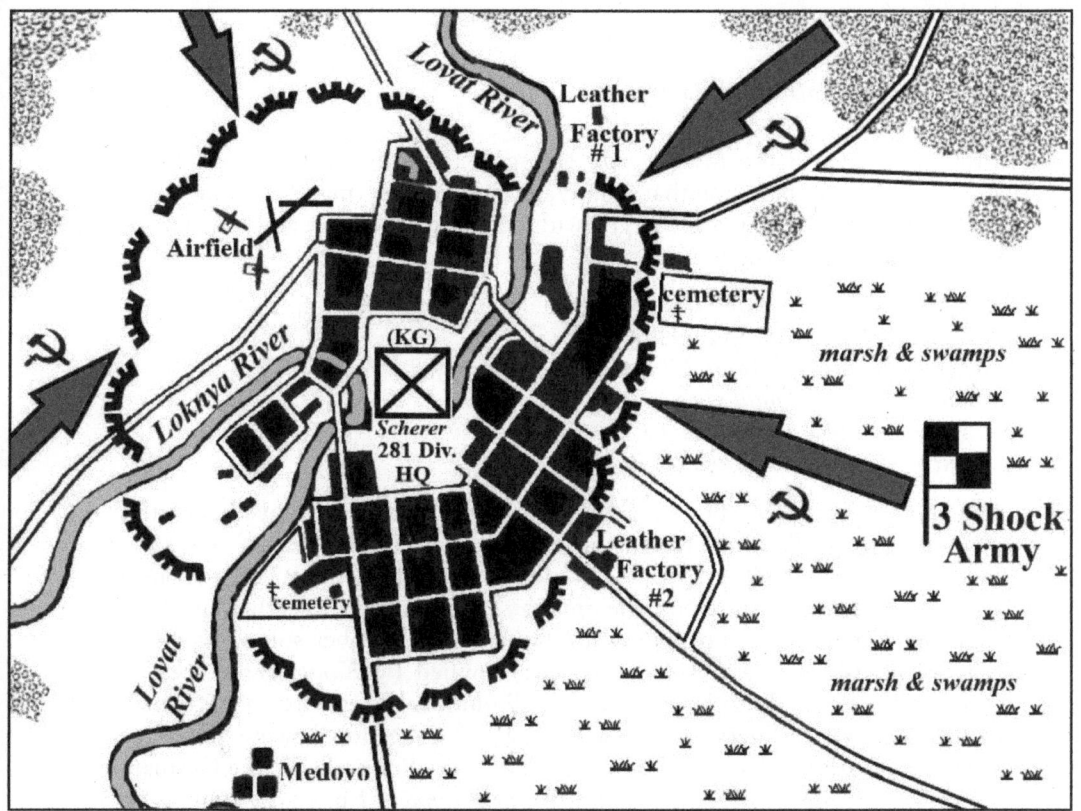

Close-up view of the town of Cholm and the surrounding area on 18 January 1942. At one point in the battle the Red Army captured half the town.

of Army Group Centre. If the Red Army could break through at Nevel, then the entire rear area of Army Group Centre would be in peril. Cholm, therefore, had to be held at all costs. Unfortunately for the Germans, the units available for the defence of the town were limited and comprised a mixed bag of formations. The Soviet winter counteroffensive which had begun on 7 December 1941 had done a great job of shattering many German divisions, and had already forced the German Army High Command to activate non-combat, rear area units for front-line service.

The troops that were presently available to defend Cholm, therefore, were few. The Germans had no illusions about holding a viable front line in this area. They knew the town would soon be surrounded by elements of the 3rd and 4th Shock Armies. They therefore planned accordingly for a siege of the town. The Germans had no idea that this siege would last for 105 days, and those three months saw some of the fiercest fighting on the whole Russian Front. This battle was so important that after it was all over, the OKW issued a special badge eligible to be worn by those soldiers who served during the siege. Given that only around 5,500 men took part in the defence of the town, this commemorative shield would turn out to be the rarest of all the badges and shields established by the *Ostheer* during the Russian campaign. The German forces that took part in the defence of Cholm included a hodge-podge of *Heer*, *Luftwaffe* and *Polizei* units, with some men of the *Kriegsmarine* acting as truck drivers. There was even a Latvian volunteer battalion that fought alongside the German garrison.[3] *Generalmajor* Theodor Scherer was charged with defending the town and the main units under his command included:

Infanterie-Regiment 386 (elements)
Infanterie-Regiment 553 (elements)
Jagdkommando 8 (about 200 men from *Gebirgsjäger-Regiment 8*)[4]
Reserve-Polizei-Bataillon 65
Maschinengewehr-Bataillon 10
(lettische) Schutzmannschaft-Bataillon 16

For the headquarters command to lead them, Scherer employed the staff of *281. Sicherungs-Division*. He had been appointed commander of this security division back in October 1941.[5] The initial strength of the town garrison was around 3,500 men, although by the time the battle was over in early May 1942 the total number of men who fought at Cholm would number some 5,000–5,500. The German defenders at Cholm were supplied by *Kampfgruppe z.b.V. 172* (Junker Ju-52 transport planes), and a small number of reinforcements were sent in the same way. Gliders were later employed.[6] Other forces were added to the defence of the town during the course of the battle. For example, the German Air Force brought in *III. Bataillon / Luftwaffen-Feldregiment 1* in eighty Junkers Ju-52 transport planes (*KG z.b.V. 172*) that landed the men on the airfield just outside the town. This battalion was led by *Luftwaffe Major* Thoms. Another unit that actually fought its way into the town after being surrounded by superior Russian forces was *Maschinengewehr-Bataillon 10*. This machine-gun battalion entered the town as the Russians surrounded the settlement.

On the night of 17/18 January 1942 the 2nd Leningrad Partisan Brigade (800–1,000 men), acting on the orders of the Soviet Chief of Staff of the Northwestern Front, Lieutenant General N.F. Vatutin, surrounded Cholm and cut off access in and out of the town. The plan was to keep the Germans bottled up in the town until the leading elements of the 3rd Shock Army could arrive. However, the Germans were able to beat back the partisan encirclement. It was only on 21 January 1942 that the town was finally surrounded and effectively cut off.

Unfortunately for the German defenders, as the Russians made progress and advanced on the town, the pocket grew smaller and the airfield on the outskirts of the town soon came under heavy artillery fire, prohibiting the landing of further reinforcements by fixed-wing aircraft. The *Luftwaffe* command made the decision to employ large Gotha Go-242 gliders in order to bring in further reinforcements. During the entire siege the *Luftwaffe* would lose twenty-seven Junkers Ju-52 transport planes and fifty-six Gotha Go-242 gliders.[7] According to one source, during the siege of the town two battalions from *280. Infanterie-Division* were brought in by air.[8] This division spent the war garrisoning Norway, but it's possible that some of its elements could have been sent to Russia, given the military emergency faced by the Germans during the winter of 1941/1942.

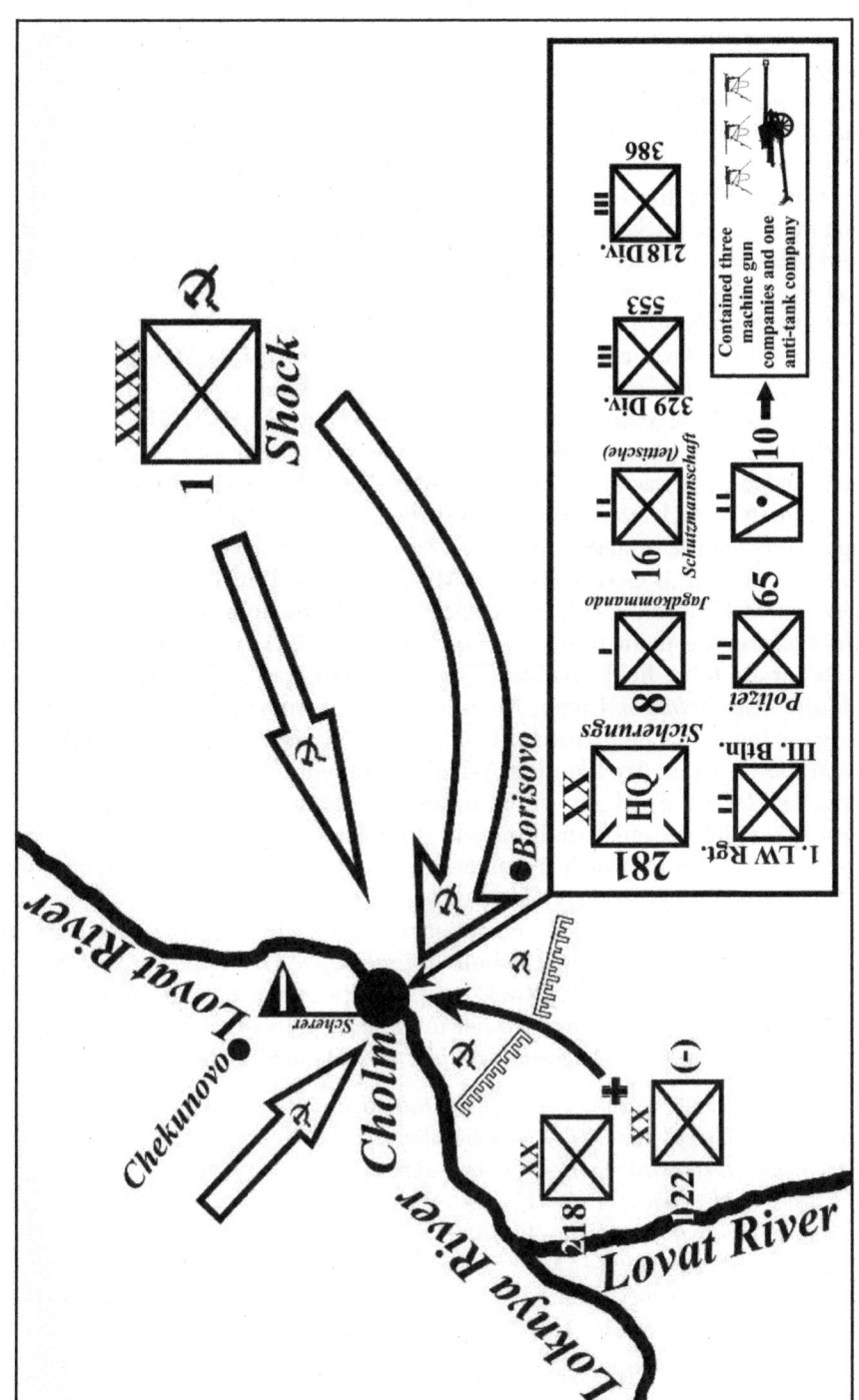

Encirclement of German forces at Cholm, 21 January 1942.

The Germans made several unsuccessful attempts to relieve the beleaguered garrison, but it was not until early May 1942 that the siege was finally broken. German casualties numbered 2,200 killed and 1,500 wounded. When the Germans re-entered the town, only 1,200 of the town's defenders were still fit for duty.[9]

When the battle for Cholm began to develop, there were German forces fighting outside the pocket. As the siege began to strengthen, two *Jäger* battalions of *Luftwaffen-Feldregiment 5* were positioned just northwest of the town, tasked with blocking the Cholm–Staraya Rusa road. Also operating in this region were units of *281. Sicherungs-Division* that had not been surrounded in Cholm. To the southwest of the town, elements of two German divisions, *218. Infanterie-Division* and *122. Infanterie-Division*, were organizing a relief attack. *Oberst* Horst Freiherr von Uckermann, the commander of *Grenadier-Regiment 386 (218. Infanterie-Division)*, led a battlegroup, *Kampfgruppe Uckermann*, which sought to relieve the trapped garrison but was unable to fully break through the Soviet line. However, about 200 men from *Maschinengewehr-Bataillon 10* (10th Machine Gun Battalion) managed to reach the besieged town on 27 January. For his bravery, Uckermann would be promoted to *Generalmajor* in March 1942 and made a divisional commander. On 26 February 1942, as the encirclement of Cholm was about a month old, the decision was made to bring together the various *Luftwaffe* field regiments to create an air force field division. The formation was initially titled *Division Meindl* after *Generalmajor* Eugen Meindl, its first commander, who was tasked with organizing it.[10] The divisional HQ was created using the staff of *Luftlande-Sturm-Regiment 1* (1st Air Landing Assault Regiment).[11]

Three days later the order went out to bring these air force regiments together, but given that the various battalions and regiments were operating in different sectors of Army Group North it was not possible for them to comply immediately. For example, *I. Jäger-Bataillon / Luftwaffen-Feldregiment 4* was serving under *18. Armee* and *III. Jäger-Bataillon / Luftwaffen-Feldregiment 1* was fighting inside the town of Cholm. In addition, the bulk of *Luftwaffen-Feldregiment 2* and *4* were fighting in and around Staraya Rusa, etc. In spite of the fact that the division could not be physically brought together immediately, its organization continued on paper. By 6 March 1942 *Division Meindl* was planned as follows:

Luftwaffen-Feldregiment 1 (I.–IV. Jäger-Bataillonen)
Luftwaffen-Feldregiment 2 (I.–IV. Jäger-Bataillonen)
Luftwaffen-Feldregiment 3 (I.–IV. Jäger-Bataillonen)
Luftwaffen-Feldregiment 4 (I.–IV. Jäger-Bataillonen)
Luftwaffen-Feldregiment 5 (I.–IV. Jäger-Bataillonen)
Luftwaffen-Feldregiment 14 (I.–II. Jäger-Bataillonen)
Luftwaffen-Nachrichten-Abteilung
Schi-Bataillon der Luftflotte 1[12]

In the meantime, on 20 March 1942 the Germans launched a coordinated counterattack aimed at breaking through the Russian lines and opening a land

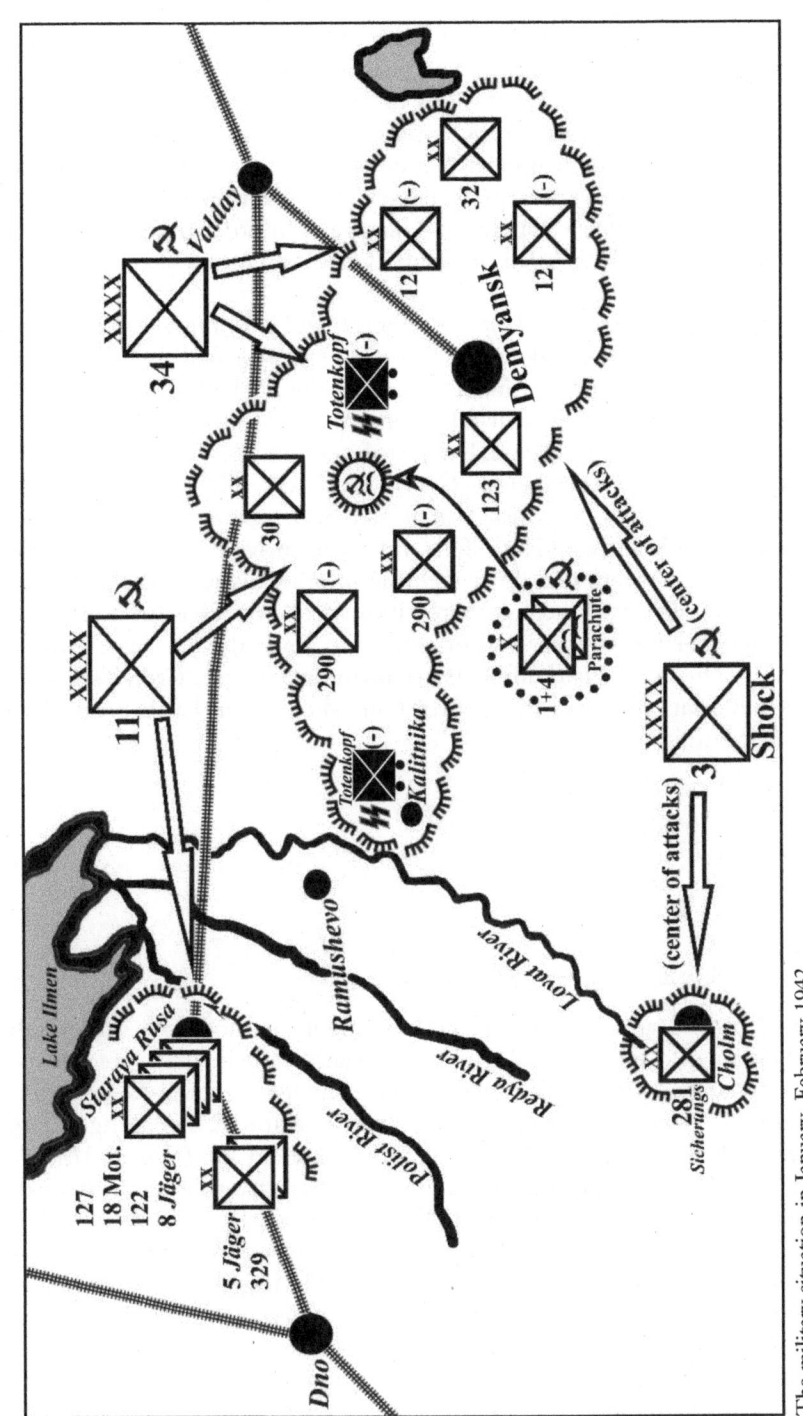

The military situation in January–February 1942.

corridor to another encircled German force in and around Demyansk. The codename for the operation was *Brückenschlag* ('Bridge Build'). The bulk of the attack was to be carried out by four divisions under the command of *Generalleutnant* Walther von Seydlitz (*Korpsgruppe Seydlitz*), while two more divisions under X. *Armeekorps* were to lend support. Simultaneously, the trapped German forces inside the Demyansk pocket were to launch their own breakout attempt to the west, *Unternehmen Fallreep* (Operation Gangway), in order to reach the German divisions moving east. If the plan were successful, both forces would link up in the town of Ramushevo.

SS-Infanterie-Division 'Totenkopf' (motorisiert) and *290. Infanterie-Division* were earmarked to launch the breakout attempt under *Gruppe Eicke*, which was named after the *Totenkopf* divisional commander, Theodor Eicke. *SS-Infanterie-Division 'Totenkopf' (motorisiert)* was not at full strength, and would lose 80 per cent of its personnel during the battle for the Demyansk pocket. *290. Infanterie-Division* was not much better off. Nevertheless, *Gruppe Eicke* was able to break out in early April 1942. Meanwhile, *Division Meindl* had been earmarked to reinforce the attack from outside the cauldron. This, however, proved impossible, as most of the *Jäger* regiments were tied down fighting in other areas. In the end, only two *Luftwaffe Jäger* regiments were gathered into an ad-hoc 'division' to support the advance. Another *kampfgruppe* was organized to cover the left flank of what was being called *Division Meindl* (after its commanding officer, *Generalmajor* Eugen Meindl) as it attacked in the direction of Ramushevo. This battle group included the following units:[13]

Kompanie / Panzer-Regiment 208
II. Bataillon / Luftwaffen-Feldregiment 3
Baubataillon 132
Sturmgeschütz-Batterie 666
Sturmgeschütz-Batterie 659
Zwei Züge der 3. Kompanie / Luftverteidigungs-Bataillon 745
Eine Kompanie des Luftverteidigungs-Bataillon 31

The attack proved successful and a land link, albeit a tenuous one, was established to the beleaguered forces holding the Demyansk salient. This precarious land link was in danger of collapsing at any time. The fear that the Red Army might counterattack and cut off once more the German forces defending Demyansk was ever present. By June 1942 more units earmarked for *Division Meindl* were brought together between the Redya and Lovat rivers, although not all the air force units assigned to the division could be extracted. In effect, for the duration of 1942 *Division Meindl* operated in pieces and not as a whole unit. Throughout 1942 its component parts were either being used in the front lines or behind the lines fighting a growing partisan threat. For example, the bulk of *Oberst* Kerssenbrock's *Luftwaffen-Feldregiment 3* was still attached to and operating under *8. Panzer-Division* east of the Cholm–Staraya Rusa road, in the Masury–Lobvantyknie sector, about 3km to the north of the Cholm–Radelskoye and Lake

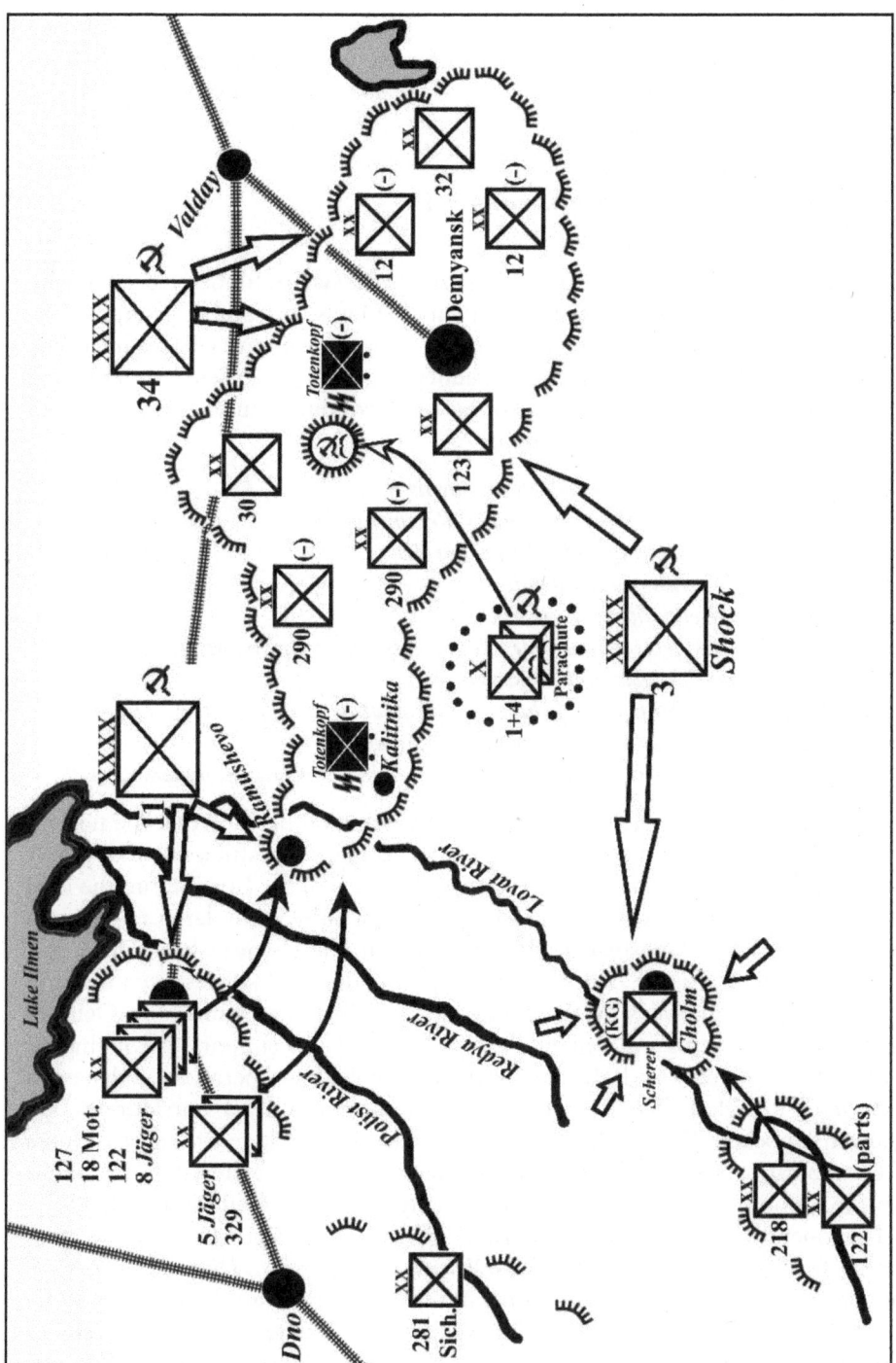

The military situation in mid-March 1942, during *Unternehmen Brückenschlag* (Operation Bridge Blow).

Navolok areas.[14] A security regiment located just south of *Division Meindl* kept a line of communication open with German forces further south, by Cholm. This ad-hoc security regiment was composed of the following units:

Panzerjäger-Abteilung 290
Aufklärungs-Abteilung 290
Ein Bataillon des Luftwaffen-Feldregiment 5
Kradschützen-Bataillon 5[15]

As late as 19 September 1942 parts of *Division Meindl* were still being used behind the front lines, fighting various partisan bands. One such combat group, led by *Oberst* Wagner, was operating in and around several towns and villages including Grichnovo, Ossipovo, Sselo, Borki, Sseredneye, Ignatov, Goruschka, Loknya and Roshnovo. *Oberst* Wagner's combat group was a combination of units from both *8. Panzer-Division* and *Division Meindl*:[16]

Ein Kompanie des Panzergrenadier-Regiments 8
3. und 5. Kompanie des Panzergrenadier-Regiments 28
Ein Kompanie des Luftwaffen-Feldregiment 3
Eine estnische Freiwilligen-Kompanie
Eine usbekische Freiwilligen-Kompanie
Eine gemischte Artillerie-Batterie des Panzer-Artillerie-Regiment 80
Ein leichter Flak-Zug von Flak-Regiment 111
Zwei Infanterie-Geschützzüge, Schützen-Regiment 8, 218. Infanterie-Division
Jagdkommando 207 der 207. Sicherungs-Division
Ein gemischt SD (Sicherheitsdienst) Bataillon des SS-Sonderkommandos

In September 1942 the German Army High Command decided that the neck of the Demyansk cauldron needed to be widened as there was still a risk that Soviet forces could once again cut off the German divisions there. In addition, the land corridor through the town of Ramushevo was not sufficiently large for enough supplies to reach the approximately 90,000 men in the Demyansk cauldron. For this reason, the *Luftwaffe* continued to make hundreds of sorties per month in order to bring in supplies by air. These air force flights terminated in October 1942, given the increasing demands on the *Luftwaffe* to support the Stalingrad battle. On 27 September 1942 the Germans launched an operation, codenamed *Winkelried* ('Angled Reed'), aimed at expanding the land corridor to the Demyansk pocket. The southern neck of the Demyansk bulge would be the area of concentration for this attack. The German command believed that without this expansion of the land corridor, the Demyansk bulge could not be held.[17]

The operation involved four German divisions: *5. Jäger-Division* (recently arrived from France), *126. Infanterie-Division, SS-Infanterie-Division 'Totenkopf'* and *Luftwaffendivision Meindl*. The operation, which lasted until 9 October 1942, proved a success and the corridor was expanded. At the beginning of November 1942 a new commander, *Generalleutnant der Flakartillerie* Job Odebrecht, was

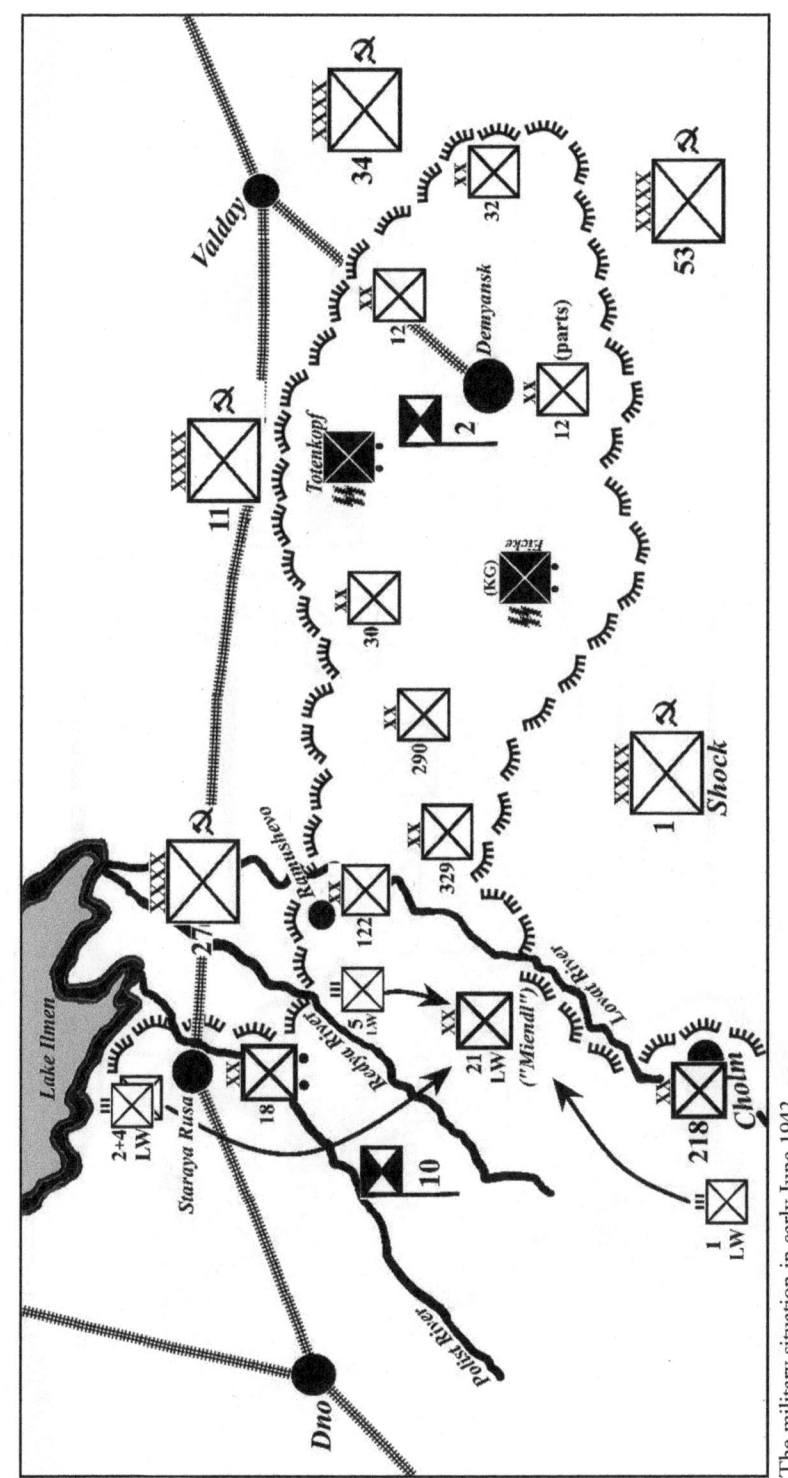

The military situation in early June 1942.

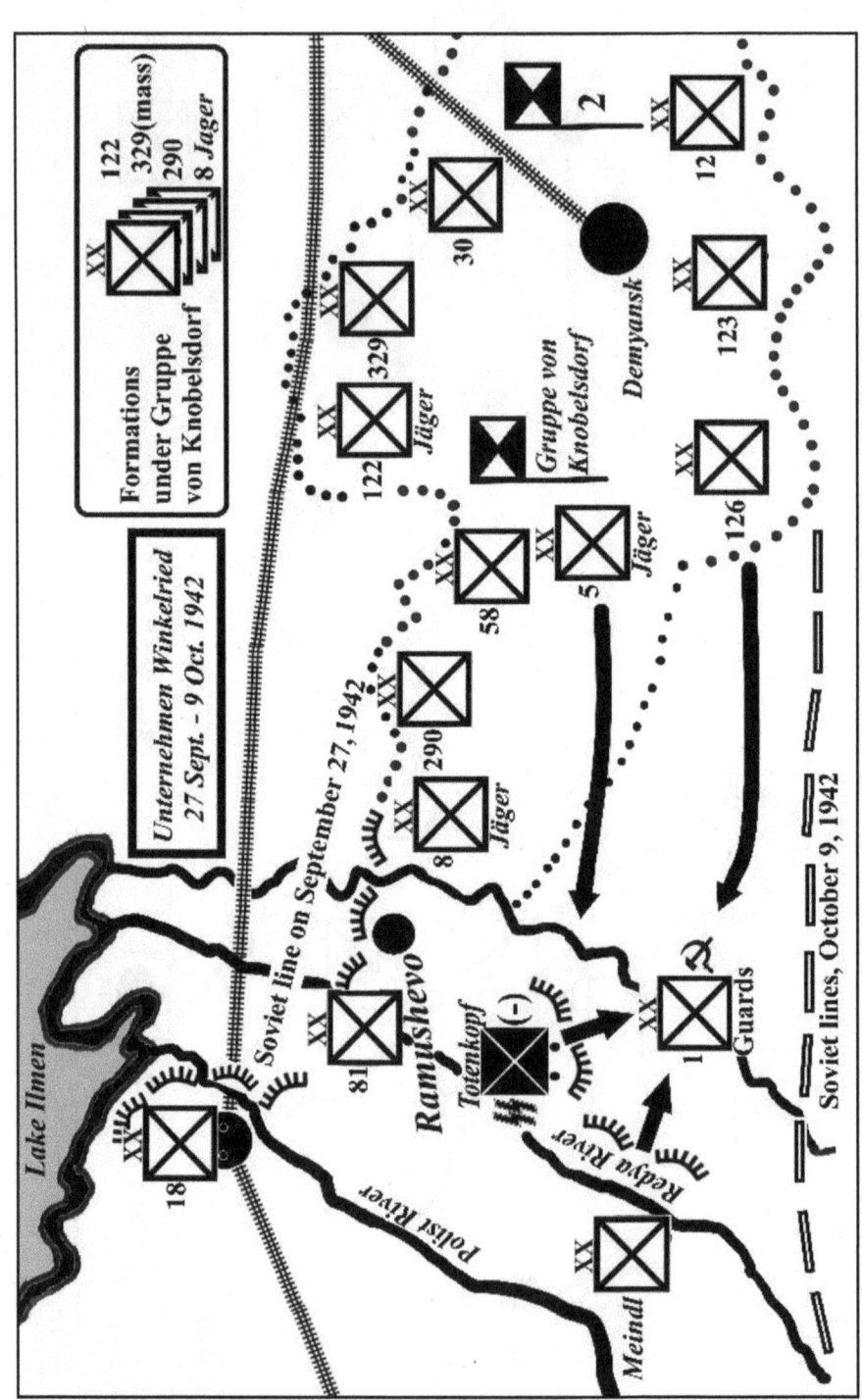

Operation *Winkelried*, 27 September–9 October 1942.

assigned to *Luftwaffendivision Meindl* and in December the division itself was redesignated *21. Luftwaffen-Felddivision*. In addition to changing the name of the division, its various regiments were also renumbered. *Oberst* Neudorffer's regiment was redesignated *Luftwaffen-Jäger-Regiment 42*, while *Feldregiment 3* became *Luftwaffen-Jäger-Regiment 44* and *Feldregiment 4* became *Luftwaffen-Jäger-Regiment 41*. The new organization for *21. Luftwaffen-Felddivision* was as follows:

Luftwaffen-Jäger-Regiment 41 (I.–III. Jäger-Bataillone)
Luftwaffen-Jäger-Regiment 42 (I.–III. Jäger-Bataillone)
Luftwaffen-Jäger-Regiment 43 (I.–III. Jäger-Bataillone)[18]
Luftwaffen-Artillerie-Regiment 21 (I.–IV. Artillerie-Abteilung)
Panzerjäger-Abteilung 21
Luftwaffen-Pionier-Bataillon 21
Luftwaffen-Nachrichten-Abteilung 21
Feldersatz-Bataillon 21
Aufklärungs-Kompanie der 21. Luftwaffen-Felddivision
Versorgungseinheiten der 21. Luftwaffen-Felddivision

In January 1943 *21. Luftwaffen-Felddivision* was located in positions behind the Lovat river, in the region where it had operated in 1942, deployed as follows: *Feldregiment 1* and *3* were located north of Cholm, while *Feldregiment 4* was just south of the town of Minzewa. As such, it was considered a lynchpin unit holding the Demyansk corridor open. In February the decision was made to withdraw from the Demyansk bulge, and between 18 and 26 February the Germans made an orderly retreat from the bulge. This decision had been made for several reasons. First, the danger that the Red Army could once again cut off the salient was growing day by day. Second, withdrawing from the bulge drastically shortened the German front lines and enabled the creation of a large pool of reserve German divisions.

From March 1943 the Red Army began to apply increasing pressure to *21. Luftwaffen-Felddivision*. It began as a series of small probing attacks, but soon increased to battalion and regiment-sized operations. These attacks were meant to test the fighting capacity of the division because by this time the Soviets were aware of the apparent weakness of these new German air force field divisions, and wanted to take advantage of it by launching full-scale operations in the sectors where these divisions were located. This was a sound strategy that was employed by the Soviets countless times throughout the course of the Russian campaign.

The only problem, however, was that in the case of *21. Luftwaffen-Felddivision* the clean and quick breakthrough never occurred. Throughout 1943, the division held its own against probing attacks of increasing size and strength. One academic with whom I had the opportunity to communicate, Professor Michael Stout, whose interest also focused on the history of the German air force field divisions, agreed with me that throughout the war *21. Luftwaffen-Felddivision* performed far better than most of the other air force field divisions.

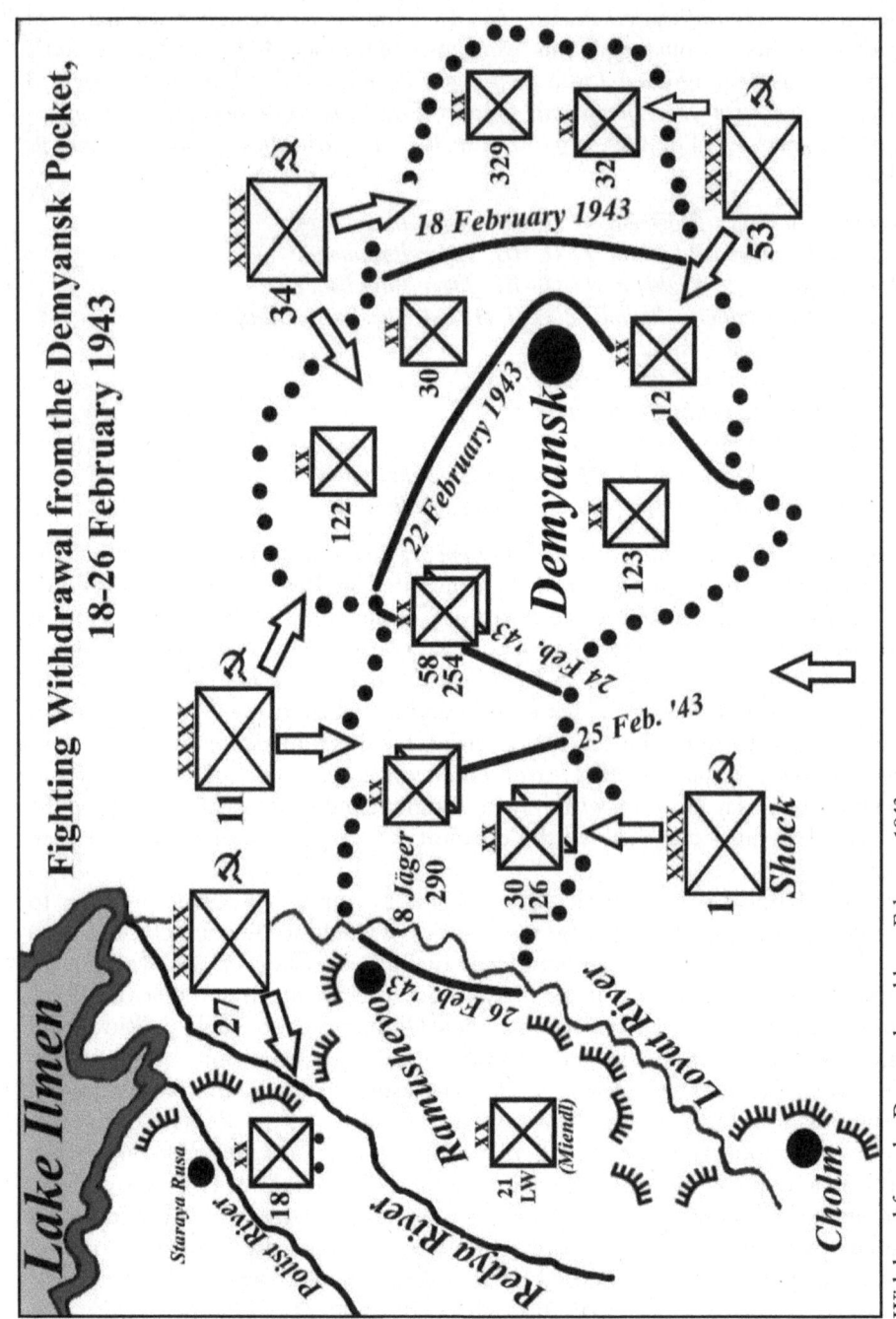

Withdrawal from the Demyansk cauldron, February 1943.

The explanation for this may be derived from *how* the division was employed, which, I believe, inadvertently aided its eventual better-than-expected military record. During its first year of combat as *Division Meindl* (October 1941– December 1942), the various battalions and regiments were never merged together into one cohesive division-sized unit. Instead, they were all employed piecemeal and (most importantly) alongside regular German Army units, which

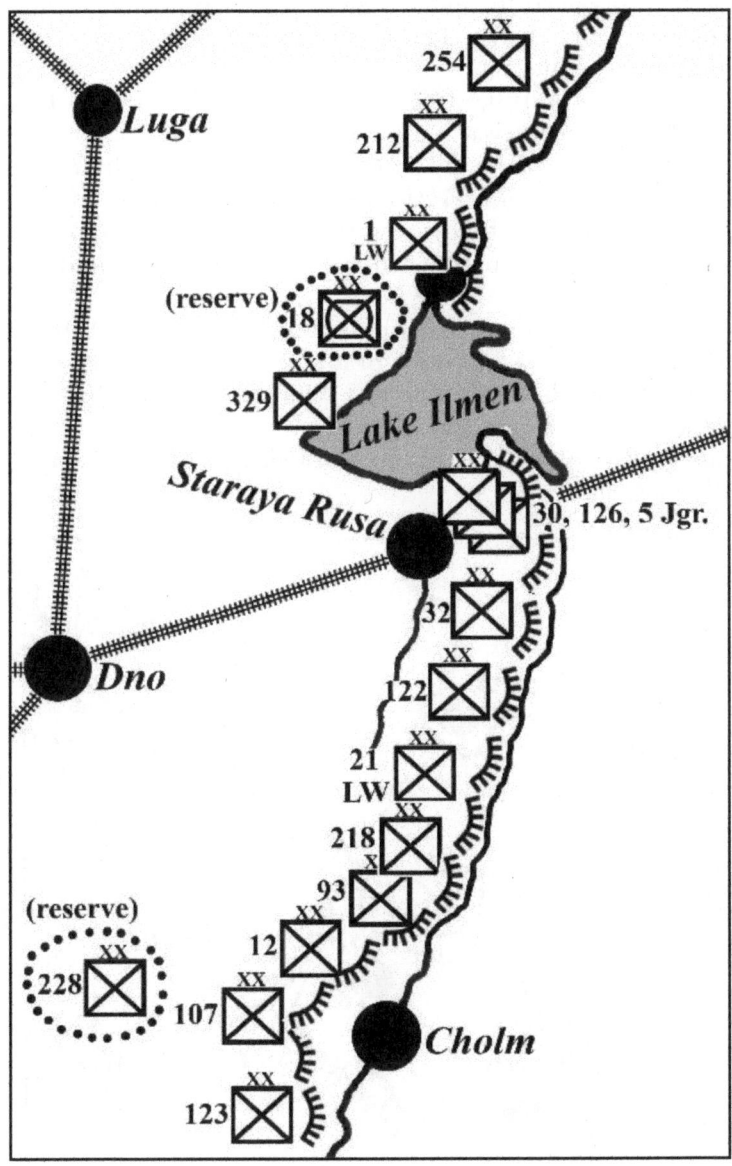

The military situation, 4 June 1943.

acted as stiffening for the *Luftwaffe* units and prevented them from being destroyed, which would have most likely occurred had the division been employed as a whole unit. Deployment alongside *Heer* formations also allowed the men to develop the military skills necessary for a front-line unit to function properly. In other words, they gained much valuable experience during that initial year so that by the time the division finally came together as a complete formation, its men and units had gained the military knowledge and experience necessary to acquit themselves well in battle. This is most likely the reason why this division performed as well as it did.

As far as the division's artillery regiment is concerned, it was not formed until the summer of 1943 and the way it came together was unusual. For example, the *Flak* battalion in most of these divisions was designated *IV. Artillerie-Abteilung*, but in the case of *21. Luftwaffen-Felddivision* the *Flak* component was *II. Artillerie-Abteilung*. This is attested to by a wartime German *Kriegsgliederung* dated 14 October 1943. On that date the artillery regiment was organized as follows:[19]

I. *Artillerie-Abteilung* – three batteries of four truck-towed 105mm guns;
II. *Artillerie-Abteilung* – one battery of four truck-towed 88mm guns, one battery of four halftrack-mounted 20mm guns and one battery of four halftrack-mounted 37mm *Flak* guns;
III. *Artillerie-Abteilung* – three batteries of four truck-towed 75mm French guns; and

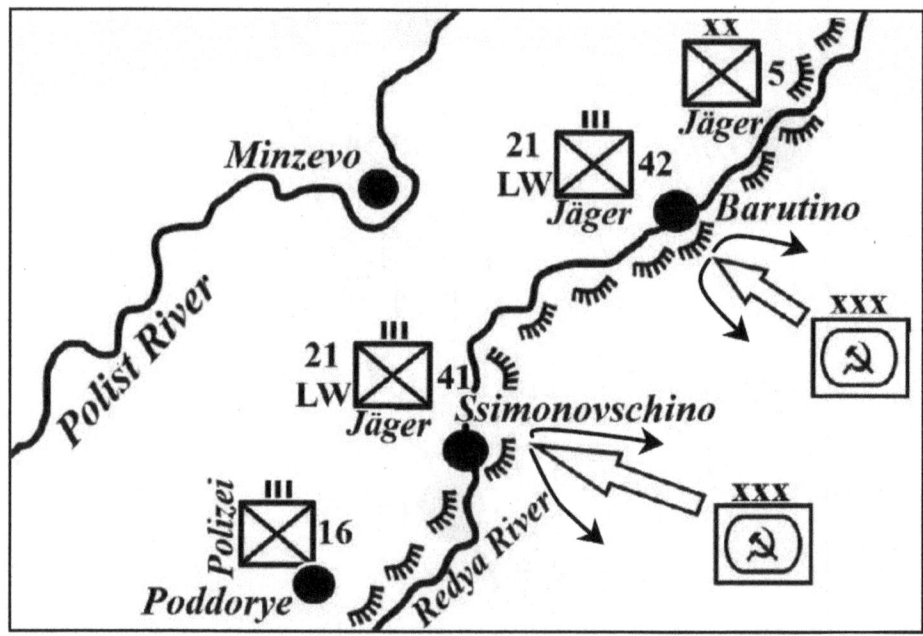

Defence along the Redya river, October 1943.

IV. Artillerie-Abteilung – three batteries of four truck-towed 155mm French guns.

On 1 November 1943, when the *Luftwaffe* field divisions were officially inducted into the German Army, the *Flak* contingent of the artillery regiment (*II. Artillerie-Abteilung*) was withdrawn. *Korporal* Georg Jagolski, who served in *9. Kompanie der Jäger-Regiment 41 (L)* during this time, states that the divisional artillery regiment was composed of German 105mm guns, as well as French-made 105mm and 155mm guns.[20] In October 1943 Jagolski's regiment was located behind the Redya river, in and around the village of Ssimovnovsschino. Earlier in the year, in March, this regiment had borne the brunt of a full-scale Russian assault. Its sister regiment *Jäger-Regiment 42 (L)*, which was located further north along the Redya river by Barutino, also held off a Russian attack in the same month. The Russian attacks in March were led by armoured units but because the division had an ample supply of anti-tank guns in its *panzerjäger* and *Flak* contingents, the regiments were able to hold off the Soviet attacks. Their anti-tank guns had actually come from what remained of the anti-tank battalion of the now-disbanded *15. Luftwaffen-Felddivision*. *Panzerjäger-Abteilung 21* was established in the summer of 1943 using those remnant forces.

The assault gun battery of *15. Luftwaffen-Felddivision* was transferred (intact) to *21. Luftwaffen-Felddivision* to become *Panzerjäger-Abteilung 21 (L)*, which initially contained three companies, until the *Flak* contingent was withdrawn in November 1943. After this, the battalion operated with only two companies.[21] One anti-tank company contained the *sturmgeschütz* (assault guns), while the other was equipped with towed 75mm anti-tank guns. According to one source, in the *sturmgeschütz* company there were ten assault guns, equipped with the 75mm L48 anti-tank gun. The other anti-tank company contained ten (towed) 75mm L40 anti-tank guns. According to the testimony of *Korporal* Georg Jagolski, *21. Luftwaffen-Felddivision*, now redesignated *Felddivision 21 (L)*, could count on fifty anti-tank guns as of October 1943. He also claims that the division possessed four *Sturmgeschütz III* assault guns.

Further, Jagolski stated that the commander of *Panzerjäger-Abteilung 21* (at the time) was *Major* Schmidtseck, while *Oberleutnant* Witte and *Oberleutnant* Hallweg led *1.* and *2. Panzerjäger-Kompanie* respectively.[22] *Major* Schmidtseck would be replaced by *Oberleutnant* Kuhbacher in February 1944.[23] Jagolski also says that the fifty anti-tank guns included not only German-made 75mm guns but also Russian-made 76.2mm guns. Later in the year the division received six additional *Sturmgeschütz III (StuG. III)* assault guns, making a total of ten assault guns in the division. This large number of anti-tank and assault guns made *Felddivision 21 (L)* the most powerful *Luftwaffe* field division in existence. Another reason why *Felddivision 21 (L)* was so powerful, compared to other *Luftwaffe* field divisions, is that it contained three *Jäger* regiments instead of the normal complement of two.

A document stamped 'Secret' and dated '14.12.43' includes a list of transfers of some 3,500 personnel from six of the air force field divisions to the parachute

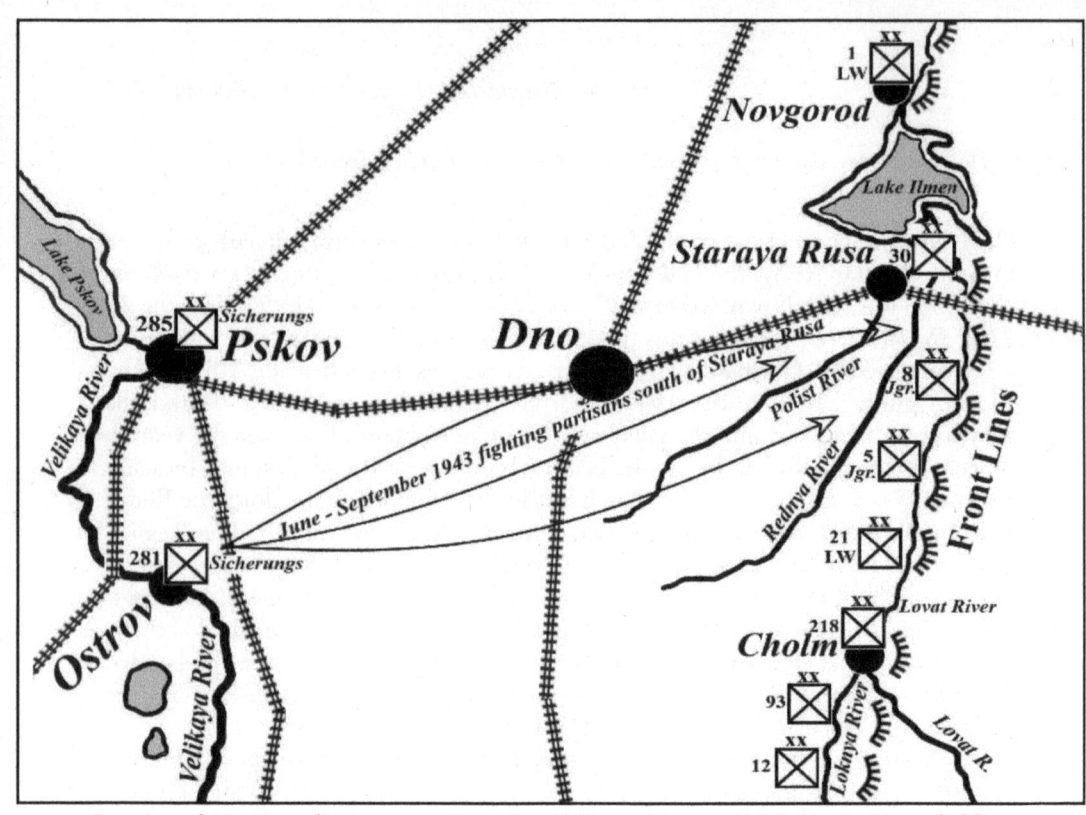

Location of *16. Armee* divisions on 3 December 1943. At this time *Felddivision 1 (L)* was holding defensive positions in and around Novgorod.

troops.[24] *Felddivision 1 (L)* and *Felddivision 21 (L)* both lost over a thousand men, while the other four lost several hundred men apiece. Although hard to read, beside the official numbers per division listed there are handwritten numbers that may perhaps represent the actual number of men withdrawn from each of the divisions.[25] It is possible that the men who were withdrawn from these field divisions were the physically fittest for service, and therefore ideal candidates for the paratroopers. The document also states that these men were replaced in the divisions by new recruits.

The battles fought all along the front lines of the Eastern Front were fierce and bloody. Throughout the year, however, *Felddivision 21 (L)* was able to hold onto

Table 11. *Luftwaffe* field division men transferred into the paratroopers, 14 December 1943.

Field Division	Typed number	Handwritten number
Felddivision 1 (L)	1,397	1,346
Felddivision 9 (L)	323	348
Felddivision 10 (L)	286	266
Felddivision 12 (L)	186	158
Felddivision 13 (L)	305	219
Felddivision 21 (L)	1,203	1,165
Total:	3,700	3,502

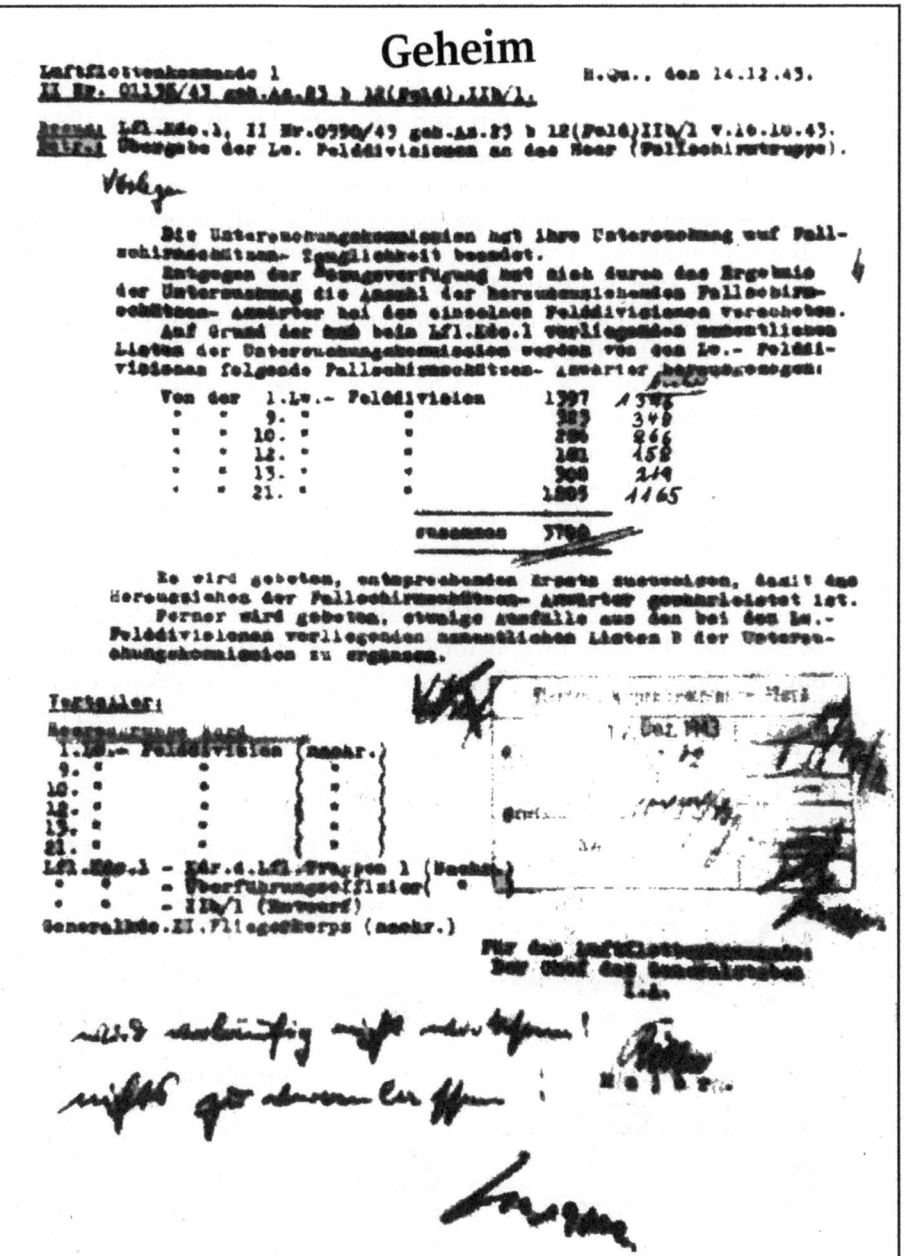

Copy of the document dated 14 December 1943.

its positions along the Redya river between Staraya Rusa and Cholm, although it paid a heavy price for its success. Nowhere was this more visible than in the division's loss of anti-tank guns between November 1943 and January 1944: in November 1943 it had a total of fifty anti-tank guns but by January 1944 this number had been reduced to just eight.[26]

German defensive preparations in the area bordering Army Groups North and South included creating a defensive line that would take advantage of the natural barrier afforded by the Narva river, as well as Lake Peipus and Lake Pskov. This was especially true after the failed Kursk offensive of 4–11 July 1943. An estimated 50,000-man workforce eventually managed to create about 6,000 bunkers (800 of them concrete), 40km of tank traps and trenches, and 200km of barbed wire obstacles. The work was directed by units of the *Reichsarbeitsdienst* (*Reich Labour Service*) and *Organization Todt*, but the bulk of the manual labour was done by tens of thousands of conscripted Russian civilians. In January 1944 *Felddivision 21 (L)* was attached to *X. Armeekorps*. Other divisions in this corps included *8. Jäger-Division* and *30. Infanterie-Division*. As was typical along the entire length of the Eastern Front, *X. Armeekorps* was responsible for holding an incredibly lengthy defence line, which at this point in time was some 110km long. This averaged out to around 55km of front-line positions for each of its three divisions: an impossible task. Luckily for *Felddivision 21 (L)*, when the Red Army winter offensive began in January 1944 the bulk of the Soviet forces were directed around the Oranienbaum pocket, as well as the Chudovo and Novgorod areas, with the intention of breaking the German siege of the city of Leningrad. That same month, as part of the so-called Leningrad-Novgorod Offensive, the Soviets hit the German positions around the Novgorod area in an attempt to pile further pressure on Army Group North. The point of the Russian attack centred on

Location of divisions under 16. Armee, from Lake Ilmen to Cholm and Ostrov, 3 December 1943.

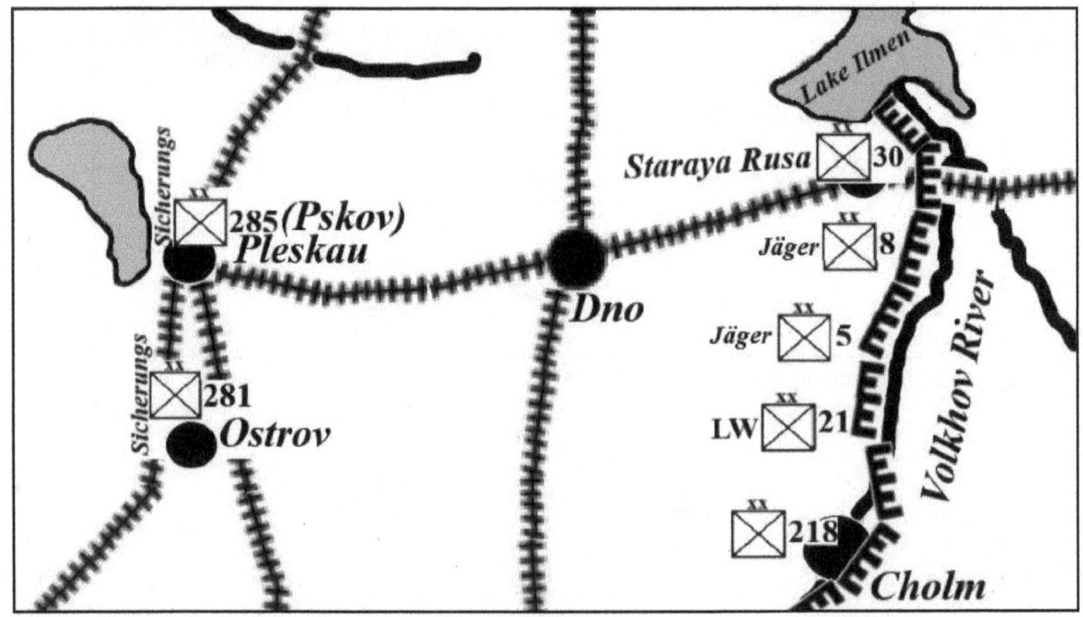

Novgorod in an attempt to break the connection between *16. Armee* and *18. Armee*, which would facilitate breaking the lynchpin connecting Army Group North and Army Group Centre. By the end of January 1944 a rift was beginning to form between the divisions of *16. Armee* and *18. Armee*. On 28 October 1943 the strength of *Felddivision 21 (L)* was only 6,429 men, of whom only 2,779 were combat troops. By December 1943 that number had dropped dramatically to around 4,540 men, of whom 1,378 were combat troops. During the month of January 1944 the division lost another 1,300 men trying to hold its positions in and around Novgorod. Against this small force the Red Army threw the following formations: the 34th, 44th, 58th and 299th Rifle Brigades and the 225th and 337th Rifle Divisions.

To the north of *Felddivision 21 (L)*, *5. Jäger-Division*, brought up from its positions south of Staraya Rusa, was not doing well either. It was under pressure from no fewer than four rifle divisions (the 191st, 239th, 310th and 378th) and a tank brigade (the 29th). Against such overwhelming numbers, *5. Jäger-Division* was forced to withdraw, while *Felddivision 1 (L)* was effectively destroyed in defending Novgorod. The city became the division's graveyard. The only reinforcements that *Felddivision 1 (L)* received were *Grenadier-Regiment 503* (the only corps reserve available) and *II. Artillerie-Abteilung/Artillerie Regiment 290*. Together, this small German force held the city until 19 January 1944, when the order to break out was given. Not all the men in the city managed to escape. It was clear by 15 February 1944 that the German lines had been irrevocably broken and the order was now given by Army Group North to withdraw to the so-called *Panther-Wotan* positions, which the Germans had nicknamed the *Ostwall*.

This defence line included wooden as well as cement bunkers, trenches, wooden roads and prepared artillery positions. However, it was nowhere near completion and lacked the depth to hold back a determined Soviet offensive. In theory, the Panther Line was to be thousands of kilometres long and would run all across the Russian Front, from Narva in the north to the Black Sea in the south. In fact, it was more hope than reality. The German positions around the Panther Line were adjusted between 25 and 27 February 1944 when *Gruppe Herzog*, formerly known as *Gruppe Friessner*, was ordered to withdraw to the so-called *Darmstadt Linie* (Darmstadt Line). General Herzog was the current commander of *XXXVIII. Armeekorps*, to which *Felddivision 21 (L)* was now attached. The front lines of *XXXVIII. Armeekorps* extended to the southeast, where *VI. SS-Freiwilligen-Armeekorps (lettische)* was operating.[27] By 4 April 1944 *Felddivision 12 (L)* and *Felddivision 21 (L)* were still fighting around Pskov (Pleskau, in German).[28]

Felddivision 21 (L) was located south of Ostrov, north of Opochka and west of Novorzhev. To the north of its positions was *Kampfgruppe Schulz*, which contained the remnants of *Felddivision 12 (L)*, *126. Infanterie-Division*, *212. Infanterie-Division* and *8. Jäger-Division*. Further north, by Pskov, was *Gruppe Generalmajor Gothsche*, which contained what remained of *207. Sicherungs-Division*, as well as *estnische Grenzschutz-Regiment 1.* and *estnische Grenzschutz-Regiment 4*. (Estonian

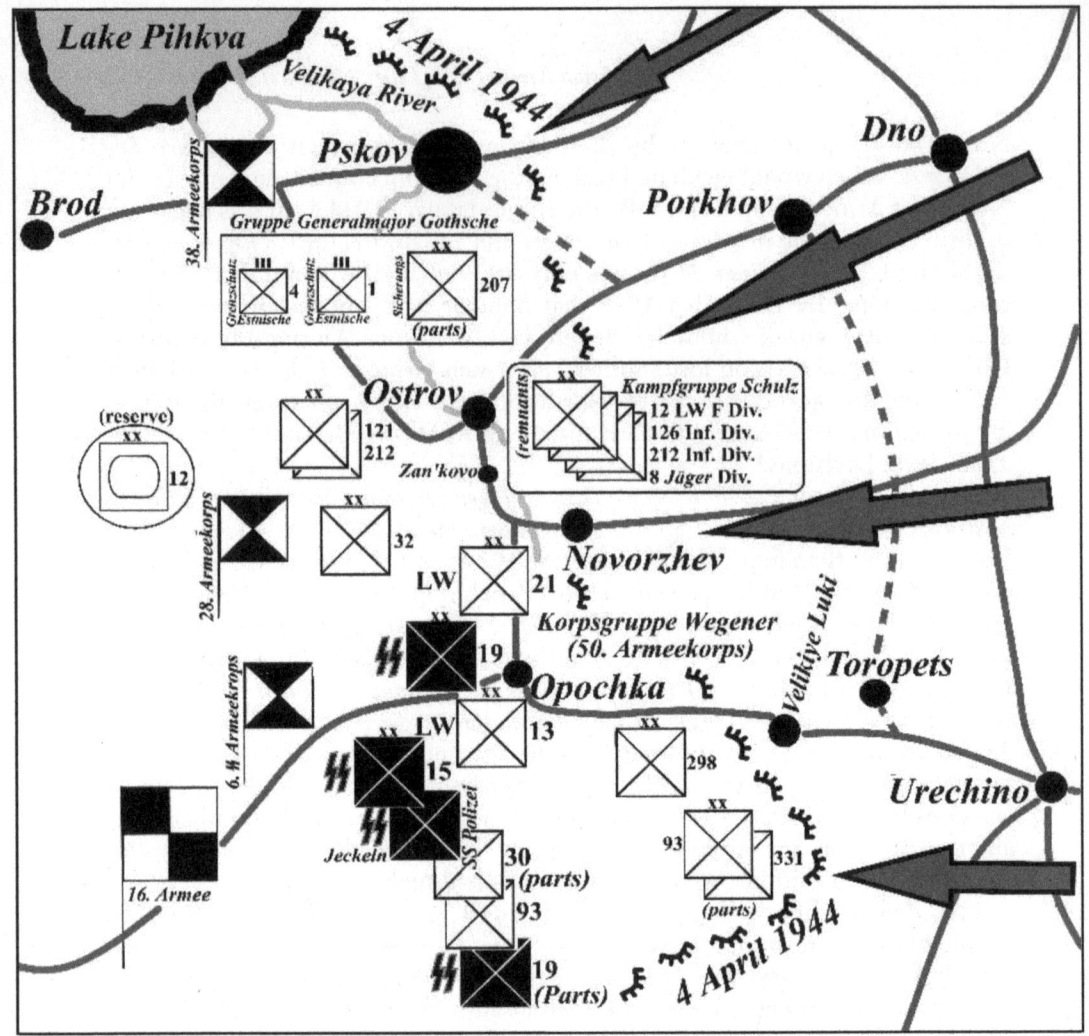

Positions of *16. Armee*, 4 April 1944.

1st and 4th Frontier Guard Regiments). It was clear that by the beginning of April *16. Armee* had taken a heavy beating. Many of its divisions had been reduced to mere battlegroups. In May *Felddivision 21 (L)* continued to serve under *XXXVIII. Armeekorps* and in June the divisional front lines were still located south of Ostrov. The left flank of the division was now manned by men of the Pomeranian *32. Infanterie-Division*, while the right flank was held by the greatly reduced Hanoverian regiments of *83. Infanterie-Division*. By July the front lines of *16. Armee* stretched from Pskov to as far south as Volki. In July 1944 the Red Army once again attempted to outflank the German defences in and around Pskov, the Soviets concentrating their efforts on the front lines of *XXXVIII. Armeekorps*, which they knew had been battered and greatly weakened. In particular, they sent armoured units to try to break through the lines of *Felddivision 21 (L)*. The division had begun to take heavy losses as early as February 1944, as it withdrew from its positions along the Lovat river, between Cholm and Staraya

Rusa. A chronicler writing the combat history of *32. Infanterie-Division* described the situation:

> Actually, the front of 21. Luftwaffen-Felddivision cracked under strong enemy pressure during the evening of 20 July. As the advanced elements of 32. Infanterie-Division arrived in the Utroya sector, early on 21 July, they found it occupied by enemy forces. The crossings were either destroyed or in the hands of the enemy. The regiments crossed the river under difficult conditions, fighting their way through enemy troops and occupying a position between Utroya and Kukhva, in which they continued to fight bitterly with the enemy. 21. Luftwaffen-Felddivision was completely exhausted, and there was also spotty contact with the 121. Infanterie-Division, which was also in heavy combat.[29]

The Soviet offensive gained its intended consequence, which was to force a break in the lines of *XXXVIII. Armeekorps*. Four days after the Red Army launched its attack, the headquarters of Army Group North rated *Felddivision 21 (L)* as only partially combat effective, meaning that the division was only capable of limited defensive action.[30]

By 2 August the division had withdrawn into northeastern Latvia, between Alüksne (Marienberg) by Lake Alüksnes and Ape (Hoopendorf). Their next major movement occurred in early October, when *18. Armee* was ordered to withdraw to the so-called *Segewald Stellungen* (Sigulda Positions).[31] This was a defensive area which resembled a half-circle and began north of the town of Ligat (Ligatne), near the Gulf of Riga, and stretched just north of Segewald (Sigulda). It was *XXXVIII. Armeekorps – 11. Infanterie-Division, 30. Infanterie-Division, 32. Infanterie-Division, 225. Infanterie-Division* and *Felddivision 21 (L)* – that covered the withdrawal to

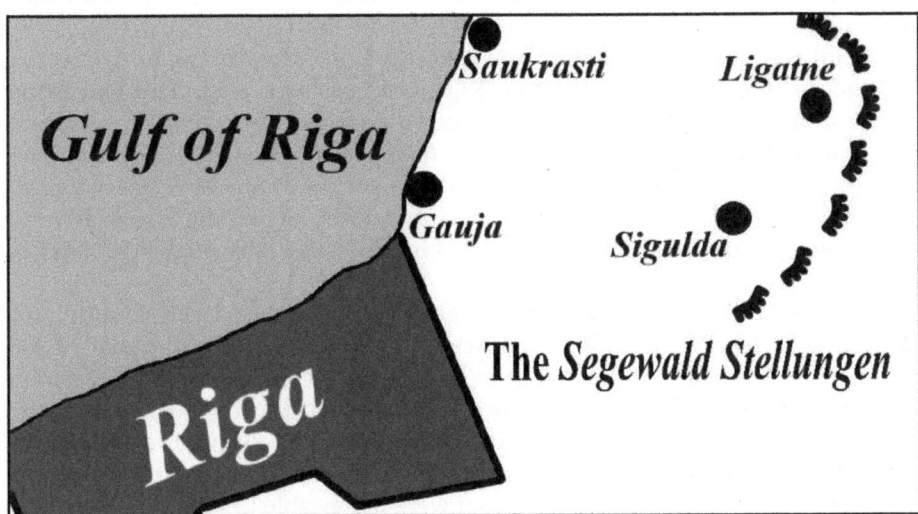

The *Segewald Stellungen* (Sigulda Positions).

these new positions. *Felddivision 21 (L)* played a major role in this and suffered accordingly.

Once the divisions of *18. Armee* were in place, what remained of *Felddivision 21 (L)* withdrew to a predetermined position between Sigulda and Turaida. The division was already not in the best shape, and was now located in a part of the new defensive positions that was vulnerable to attack. The Red Army wished to capture the Zagare (Schagarren) to Pampali (Palperm) road, but *Felddivision 21 (L)* was in their way. In order to better position the unit and prepare it for defence, Army Group North ordered *Felddivision 21 (L)* to shorten its defence lines with its neighbour, *329. Infanterie-Division*.[32] By now it was clear that the divisions of Army Group North would most likely be forced further west. Before the end of the month, its divisions had been forced back to the region of Courland (Kurland), after having been unable to withdraw into East Prussia. From October 1944 until the end of the war on 8 May 1945, Army Group North (redesignated Army Group Courland on 15 January 1945) would repel a total of six major Red Army offensives, geared to destroy the German forces. In mid-October 1944 the division received some badly needed replacements when *Waffen-Grenadier-Regiment der SS (lettische Nr. 7)*, mustering two battalions of Latvian SS infantry, was temporarily attached.[33] There is no mention of this Latvian SS regiment being officially incorporated into the ranks of either *15. Waffen-Grenadier-Division der SS (lettische Nr. 1)*, or *19. Waffen-Grenadier-Division der SS (lettische Nr. 2)*. Most likely, it was disbanded during the autumn of 1944 and its men used as replacements for both Latvian SS divisions. The Latvian volunteers appear to have got along well with the men of *Felddivision 21 (L)*. Between mid-October and the third week of December 1944 the division, as well as the attached Latvian SS regiment, suffered few losses.

The First Battle of Courland began on 9 October 1944 and had two major concentration points of attack: the first was led by 6th Guards Army against the important and vital port of Livau (Liepāja), while the second was a drive by the 2nd and 3rd Baltic Fronts to capture Riga, the Latvian capital. The Red Army entered Riga on 13 October, just days after the start of the offensive. Covering the withdrawal of German forces were *87. Infanterie-Division* and *227. Infanterie-Division* – both of which blew up the bridges over the Daugava river leading to the Latvian capital on the night of 12 October 1944. While the Soviet drive to capture Riga proved successful, the 6th Guards Army was unable to capture Liepāja.

The Second Battle of Courland began on 22 October 1944. During this battle *Felddivision 21 (L)* suffered particularly heavy losses at the hands of the 10th Guards Army. The divisional front lines gave way and a retreat was ordered. The division made a fighting withdrawal to the town of Autz (Auce). During the initial Red Army attack on the division's front lines, and during the subsequent extraction, the divisional elements began to break apart. What reached Auce was a chaotic series of subdivisional units that were barely able to organize a defence. The Soviet 10th Guards Army merely bypassed the town and as a result a portion

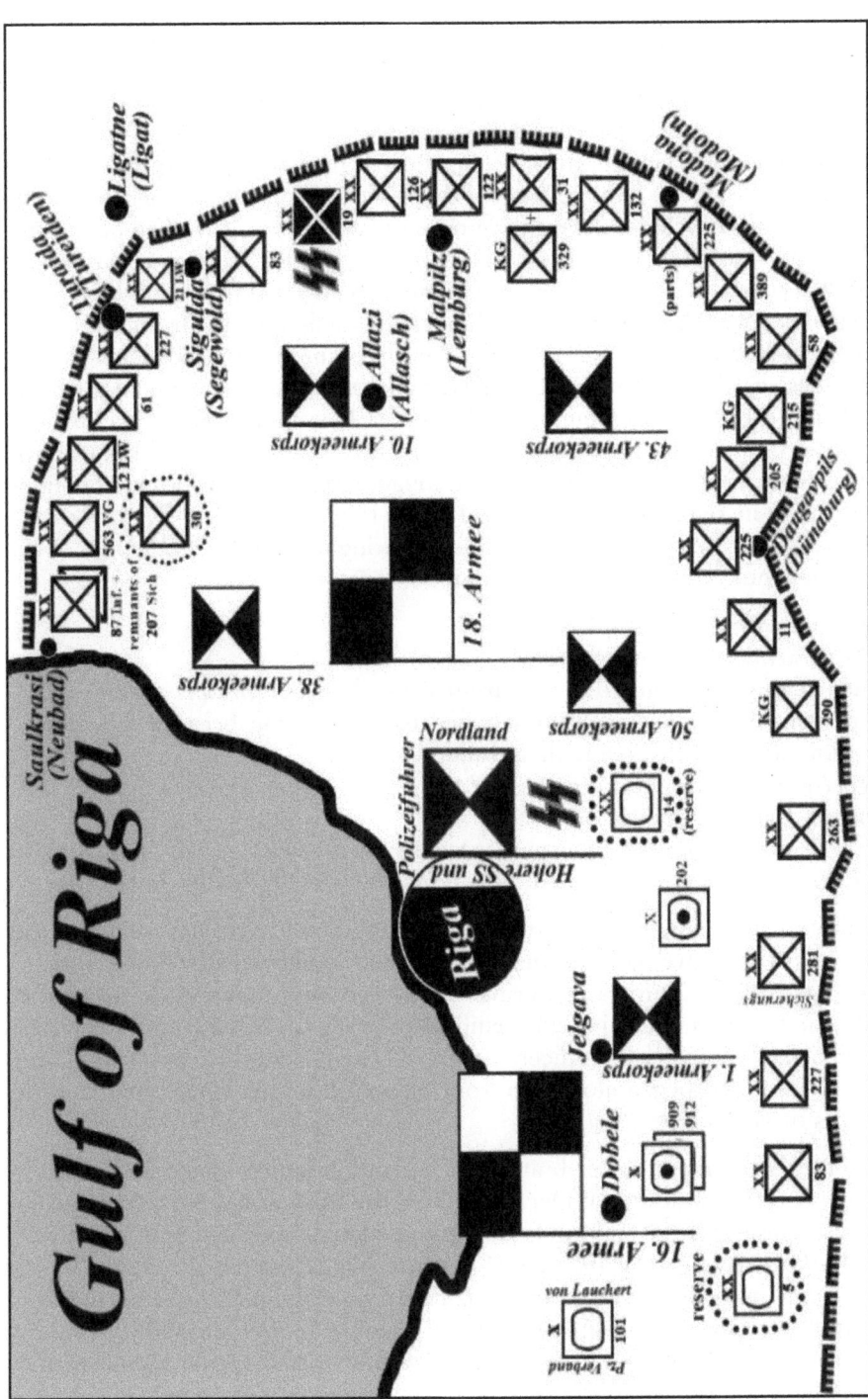

Location of 18. Armee and 16. Armee divisions on 4 October 1944. Felddivision 21 (L) had covered the withdrawal of 18. Armee to the Sigulda Positions.

of *Felddivision 21 (L)* remained trapped there while other units withdrew further north. On 1 November 1944 the division's remnants, alongside *83. Infanterie-Division* and *329. Infanterie-Division*, withdrew to a new defence line, the *Brunhilde Stellungen*, situated between Lake Lielauce and Lake Zebres. With both flanks protected by a large body of water, the beleaguered divisions of *XXXVIII. Armeekorps* were able to halt the Soviet drive. By 25 November the Second Battle of Courland was over. However, the damage to *Felddivision 21 (L)* had been done and by mid-November the division was shattered. The survivors were earmarked for coastal watch duty near the port of Windau (Ventspils) because the German command believed the division was no longer able to fight on the front lines. This plan did not materialize, however, because at this point the Soviets launched their third offensive, which required all available German forces to remain on the front lines. The Third Battle of Courland began on 21 December 1944. This time the main focal point of the Red Army drive was the Latvian town of Frauenburg (Saldus). Since *Felddivision 21 (L)* could no longer function as a cohesive and independent unit, its remnants were assigned to *19. Waffen-Grenadier-Division der SS (lettische Nr. 2)*. By 25 December 1944 the following units from *Felddivision 21 (L)* were under the command of this Latvian SS division:

HQ staff of *Felddivision 21 (L)*
HQ of Artillerie-Regiment 21 (L)
One battalion of around 450 men from a squadron of *Luftwaffe* ground and air personnel who had been assigned to the division because a lack of planes and fuel had made them redundant
Signal-Kompanie der Felddivision 21 (L)
Sanitäts-Kompanie der Felddivision 21 (L)
Two *Jäger* battalions of infantry that had originally belonged to *Felddivision 12 (L)* but had been absorbed into *Felddivision 21 (L)* earlier in the year.

The division, therefore, could barely muster a regiment in strength. During the seven weeks of relative quiet between the end of the Second Battle of Courland and the start of the Third, the Germans had been busy building defensive fortifications, trenches, machine-gun emplacements and barbed wire defences. A high-ranking Latvian SS officer, Arturs Silgailis, described how the Third Battle of Courland began along the front lines of the Latvian SS men and the remnants of *Felddivision 21 (L)*:

The men were about to celebrate their fourth Christmas of the war, when suddenly on the morning of December 23rd the Russian opened a tremendously intense artillery and air force barrage along the entire sector of the *19. Waffen-Grenadier-Division der SS (lettische Nr. 2)* and the *21. Luftwaffen-Felddivision* as well as in the rear areas. There were about 500 aircraft in the air at times. The assault, supported by an armoured corps, smashed into the left wing of the *19. Waffen-Grenadier-Division der SS (lettische Nr. 2)* and with its center into the *21. Luftwaffen-Felddivision*. By noon, the enemy tanks had penetrated well into the German division's positions and its infantry had reached the line of Priezusarse-Rumbinas-Krimunas-Pienava-Irbes. The situation became extremely critical due to lack of reserves.[34]

The *Waffen-Grenadier-Regiment der SS 106 (lettische)*, on the left flank of what remained of *Felddivision 21 (L)*, suffered 60 per cent casualties, but still grimly hung on to their positions, thus preventing the Red Army from outflanking the air force infantrymen. Direct artillery fire by the artillery regiment of *19. Waffen-Grenadier-Division der SS (lettische Nr. 2)*, and what few guns remained of *Feld Artillerie-Regiment 21 (L)*, finally repulsed the Soviet tank and infantry attack by the evening of 25 December 1944. Pockets of surrounded Latvian SS men and *Luftwaffe* soldiers, who had managed to avoid being overrun for three days, were finally relieved by 8pm. Three days later the Red Army launched another attack that was able to break through the lines of *19. Waffen-Grenadier-Division der SS (lettische Nr. 2)*. By then, the Latvians and German *Luftwaffe* troops had managed to destroy eighty-seven Soviet tanks. In January 1945 what was left of *Felddivision 21 (L)* was absorbed into *Division z.b.V. 300*,[35] which was stationed in Tuckums (Tukum).[36] This division was holding the extreme left flank of *16. Armee*, along the coast of the Gulf of Riga. This German divisional headquarters controlled four Estonian volunteer border guard regiments:

(estnische) Grenzschutz-Regiment 2 (Polizei);
(estnische) Grenzschutz-Regiment 4 (Polizei);
(estnische) Grenzschutz-Regiment 5 (Polizei); and
(estnische) Grenzschutz-Regiment 6 (Polizei).

On 16 February 1945 *Generalmajor* Otto Barth, the last commander of the divisional battlegroup from *Felddivision 21 (L)*, assumed command. Other staff officers in the combat group included *Major i.G.* Flor, the operations officer (Ia), *Hauptmann* Gerlicher, *Oberleutnant* Hohn and *Major* Bräunig, who was the 'divisional' adjutant.[37] This battlegroup remained basically independent from late February until the capitulation of German forces in Courland on 8 May 1945.

On 1 March 1945 the battlegroup fought a bitter battle for the defence of the region in and around Dondagen (Dungaga). After that, March and April were relatively quiet until the Red Army launched its Fifth Courland Offensive and then the Sixth (and final) Offensive. This time the Red Army concentrated on the German front lines around the town of Funkenhof (Bunka), from where they hoped to break through and reach Liepaja. The attack began to gain momentum but was eventually stopped in its tracks by the combined effects of the artillery barrels of *Nebelwerfer-Regiment 70*, *Heer-Flak-Abteilung 276*, the few remaining tanks of *14. Panzer-Division* and the *Felddivision 21 (L)* battlegroup infantry, who had been detached from *Division z.b.V. 300* and sent west to help counter the offensive.[38] When the end came on 8 May 1945, the battlegroup was located just west of Tuckum and under the command of *XVI. Armeekorps, 16. Armee*.[39] On that same day the last divisional commander, *Generalmajor* Otto Barth, committed

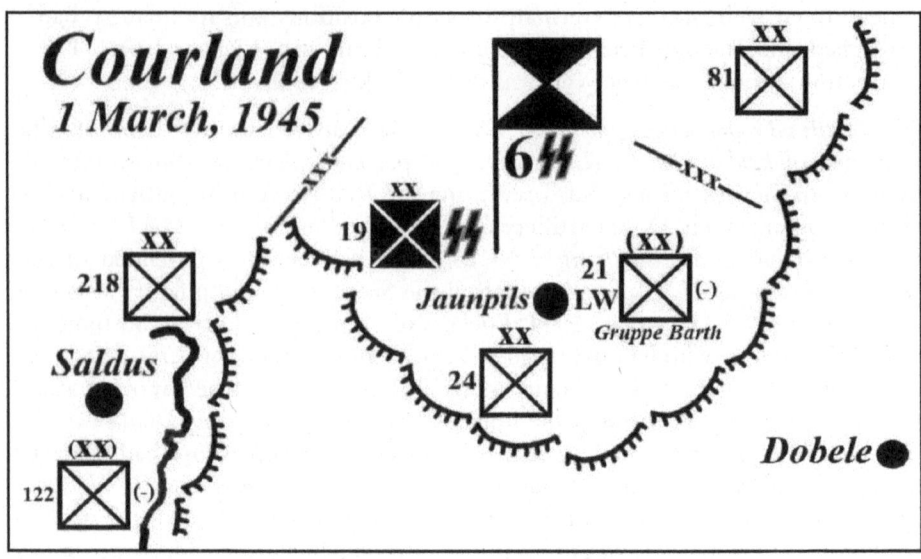

Positions of the *Felddivision 21 (L)* battlegroup on 1 March 1945.

suicide. So ended the history of *Division Meindl/21. Luftwaffen-Felddivision/ Felddivision 21 (L)*. It had actually performed far better than all of the other air force infantry divisions. As stated earlier, the most likely reasons were as follows:

1. For the first year of service, the division did not fight as a whole unit. Instead, its battalions and regiments operated independently of one another, attached to *Heer* formations. The German Army units 'stiffened' the green and inexperienced *Luftwaffe* men, allowing their units to remain intact long enough for the *Luftwaffe* troops to gain much valuable combat experience.
  a. The division was well equipped and had far more heavy weapons, such as anti-tank guns, *Flak* guns and artillery pieces, than were allotted to the other German air force field divisions.

Whatever the reason, it can be said unequivocally that this unit was one of the best, if not *the* best, of the *Luftwaffe* divisions.

Command Structure of *21. Luftwaffen-Felddivision*

Commanders:
  Divisional Commander:
    Generalmajor Eugen Meindl, 02/1942–10/1942
    Generalleutnant Job Odebrecht, 10/1942–10/11/1942
    Generalleutnant Richard Schimpf, 10/11/1942–24/10/1943
    Generalmajor Rudolf-Eduard Licht, 12/10/1943–01/04/1944
    Oberst Rudolf Goltzsch, 01/04/1944–08/04/1944
    Generalleutnant Rudolf-Eduard Licht, 08/04/1944–30/08/1944

Table 12. Employment of *Division Meindl/21. Luftwaffen-Felddivision/Felddivision 21 (L)*.

Date	Corps	Army or Army Detachment	Army Group
22/12/1942	X. Armeekorps	16. Armee	North
01/01/1943	X. Armeekorps	16. Armee	North
09/04/1943	Gruppe Höhne (VIII. Armeekorps)	16. Armee	North
01/06/1943	Gruppe Höhne	16. Armee	North
17/07/1943	Gruppe Höhne	16. Armee	North
25/07/1943	VIII. Armeekorps	16. Armee	North
08/11/1943	VIII. Armeekorps	16. Armee	North
20/11/1943	X. Armeekorps	16. Armee	North
26/12/1943	X. Armeekorps	16. Armee	North
15/04/1944	XXXVIII. Armeekorps	18. Armee	North
15/06/1944	XXXVIII. Armeekorps	18. Armee	North
15/07/1944	XXVIII & XXXVIII. Armeekorps	18. Armee	North
15/08/1944	XXVIII & XXXVIII. Armeekorps	18. Armee	North
31/08/1944	XXXVIII. Armeekorps	18. Armee	North
16/09/1944	XXXVIII. Armeekorps	18. Armee	North
28/09/1944	XXXVIII. Armeekorps	18. Armee	North
13/10/1944	XXXVIII. Armeekorps	Armee-Abteilung Grasser (LIV. Armeekorps)	North
05/11/1944	XXXVIII. Armeekorps	Armee-Abteilung Grasser (LIV. Armeekorps)	North
26/11/1944	VI. SS Armeekorps	16. Armee	North
31/12/1944	XVI. Armeekorps	16. Armee	North
21/01/1945	XLIII. Armeekorps	16. Armee	Courland
26/01/1945	XLIII. Armeekorps	16. Armee	Courland
19/02/1945	XLIII. Armeekorps	16. Armee	Courland
01/03/1945	XVI. Armeekorps	16. Armee	Courland
08/05/1945	XVI. Armeekorps	16. Armee	Courland

Oberst Albert Henze,[40] 30/08/1944–16/02/1945
Generalmajor Otto Barth, 16/02/1945–08/05/1945
Ia:
Oberstleutnant i.G. Heinz-Friedrich Rüden, 12/1942–01/11/1943
Major Otto Heckel, 01/11/1943–03/11/1943
Oberstleutnant Heinz-Friedrich Rüden, 03/11/1943–01/12/1944
Major Hartwig Flor, 01/01/1945–08/05/1945
Ib:
Major Otto Thomas,[41] 06/12/42–30/05/44
IIa:
Major z.V. Clauss, 10/12/1943–10/12/1944
Major Bräunig, 10/12/1944–1945
CO *Luftwaffen-Jäger-Regiment 41*:
Oberst Werner Krahl, 29/03/1943–10/1943
CO *I. Bataillon/Luftwaffen-Jäger-Regiment 41*:
Hauptmann Kunze, 1943–1944

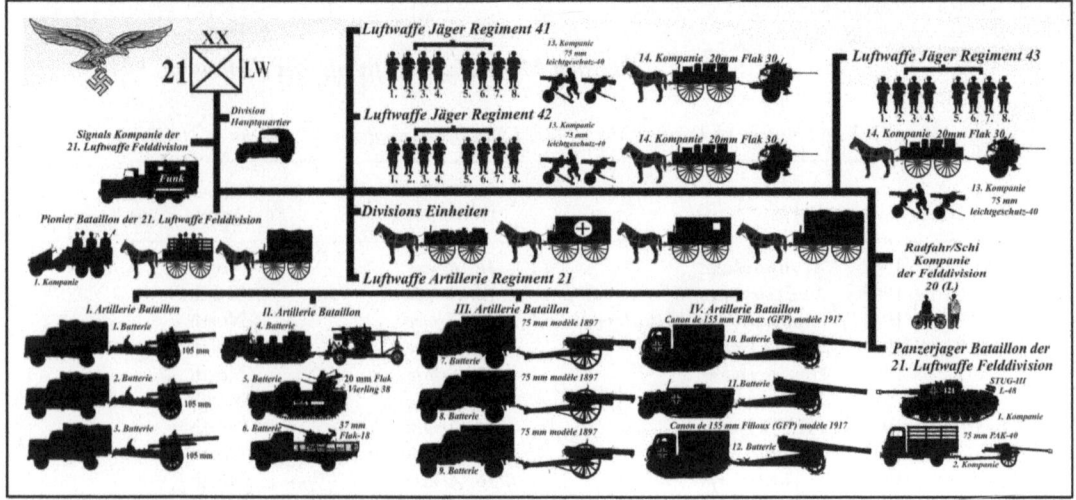

Division Meindl / 21. Luftwaffen-Felddivision in August 1943.

CO *4. Kompanie / I. Bataillon / Luftwaffen-Jäger-Regiment 41*:
  Hauptmann Sodeik, 1943–1944
CO *Luftwaffen-Jäger-Regiment 42*:
  Oberst Neudörfer, 03/1943–01/11/1943
  Oberst Findeisen, 01/11/1943–1944
CO *Luftwaffen-Jäger-Regiment 43*:
  Oberst Max Schirmacher, 03/1943–01/11/1943
CO *III. Jäger-Bataillon, Luftwaffen-Jäger-Regiment 43 (L)* – formerly
    III. Jäger-Bataillon, Luftwaffe Feldregiment 3:
  Hauptmann Karl Utpatel,[42] 29/03/43–13/05/43
  Hauptmann Heinz Freiherr von Wangenheim,[43] 03/07/43–11/43
  Hauptmann Willi Schrader, 11/43–10/44

Felddivision 21 (L) in June 1944.

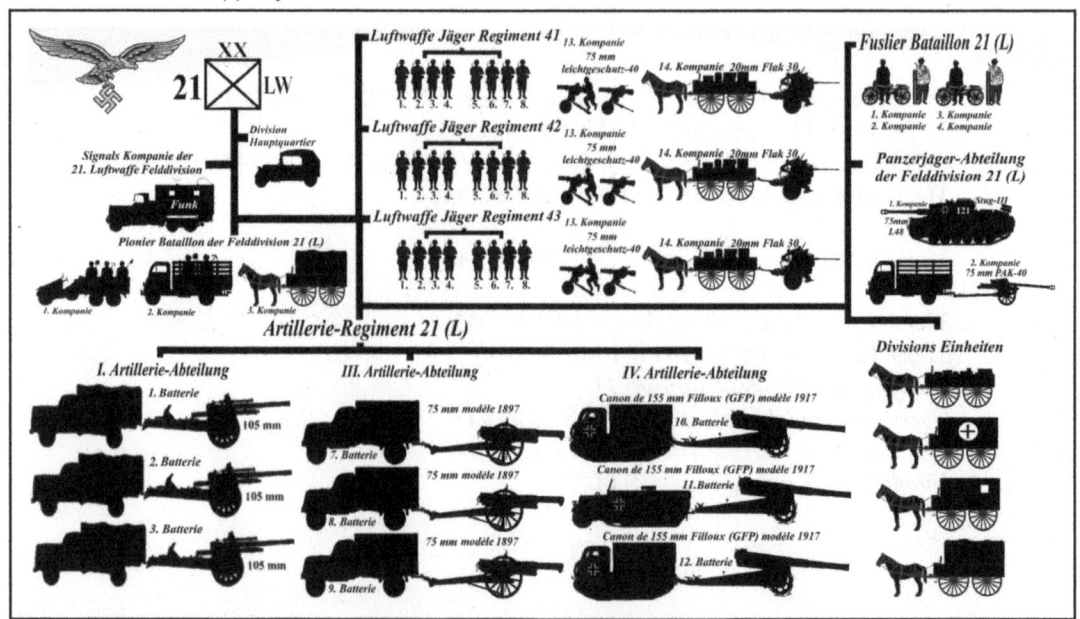

CO *Luftwaffen-Artillerie-Regiment 21*:
 Oberst Karl Schuchardt, 08/02/1943–26/06/1942
 Oberst Sebastian Mahrle, 26/06/1943–01/11/1943
CO *Luftwaffen-Panzerjäger-Abteilung 21*:
 Major Rudolf Freiherr von Schmidtseck,[44] 09/02/43–1944
CO *Feldersatz-Bataillon 21 (L)*:
 Hauptmann Schwöppe, 1944–1945

22. Luftwaffen-Felddivision

22. *Luftwaffen-Felddivision* began forming in the spring of 1943 but shortly before 1 November 1943, the day the *Heer* assumed control of these *Luftwaffe* field divisions, the decision was made to disband the unit. Thus, it never became *Felddivision 22 (L)* but continued to be referred to as *22. Luftwaffen-Felddivision*. Several divisional elements had already been established before the order to disband came through. One such was *Luftwaffen-Pionier-Bataillon 22*, which was sent to Italy to serve as a special unit directly under the control of *14. Armee*. Similarly, *Luftwaffen-Panzerjäger-Abteilung 22* was formed entirely with *Flak* guns. After disbandment, this battalion became *(leicht) Flak-Abteilung 88 (motorisiert)*, or 88th Light AA Battalion (motorized),[1] and was, uniquely, retained by the German Army. (In all other cases, the *Luftwaffe* field divisions' *Flak* battalions were returned to *Luftwaffe* control, in accordance with Hermann Göring's demands.) Perhaps surprisingly, the planned division's support services were also created. They included the following units:

1. *(l.) Transport-Kolonne der Luftwaffen-Felddivision 22*
2. *(l.) Transport-Kolonne der Luftwaffen-Felddivision 22*
3. *(l.) Transport-Kolonne der Luftwaffen-Felddivision 22*

Nachrichten-Kompanie der Luftwaffen-Felddivision 22
Werkstatt-Kompanie der Luftwaffen-Felddivision 22
Versorgungs-Kompanie der Luftwaffen-Felddivision 22
Versorgungs-Kolonne (mot.) der Luftwaffen-Felddivision 22
Bäckerei-Kompanie der Luftwaffen-Felddivision 22
Schlächterei-Kompanie der Luftwaffen-Felddivision 22
Verpflegungsamt der Luftwaffen-Felddivision 22
Sanitäts-Kompanie der Luftwaffen-Felddivision 22
Sanitäts-Zug (mot.) der Luftwaffen-Felddivision 22
Veterinär-Kompanie der Luftwaffen-Felddivision 22

When the division was ordered to disband, all the support units were immediately split, apart from two. *Versorgungs-Kompanie der Luftwaffen-Felddivision 22* was transferred intact to *Felddivision 17 (L)* and redesignated *Versorgungs-Kompanie der Luftwaffen-Felddivision 17*. *Nachrichten-Kompanie der Luftwaffen-Felddivision 22* became *Luftnachrichten Betriebs Kompanie 140*. This communications company was assigned to *20. Flak-Division*, which was in Belgrade, Serbia, in the process of being reconstituted. In November 1943 *Jäger-Regiment 43 (L)* was transferred to *Felddivision 21 (L)*. *Jäger-Regiment 44 (L)*, the other regiment earmarked for *22. Luftwaffen-Felddivision*, was disbanded and its personnel transferred to other active regiments in *21. Luftwaffen-Felddivision*. The divisional headquarters staff was removed in December 1943 and used as the basis for the new headquarters staff of *20. Flak-Division*, which at this time was being reformed in Belgrade, Serbia. The original *20. Flak-Division* had been sent to Tunisia in early 1943, where it surrendered to the Allies with the rest of *5. Panzerarmee*.

Luftwaffen-Artillerie-Regiment 22 comprised four artillery battalions. *I.* and *II. Artillerie-Abteilung* were outfitted with the 75mm FK18 cannon. These two battalions were fully equipped with RSO (*Raupenschlepper-Ost*) light, fully tracked vehicles to tow the guns. As such, they were fully mobile. *III. Artillerie-Abteilung* was armed with the 105mm le-FH 18 artillery piece, while *IV. Artillerie-Abteilung* was equipped with the heavy 155mm French model 1917 GPF artillery gun. The artillery pieces of *III.* and *IV. Artillerie-Abteilung* were horse-drawn.

Although the transfer of personnel from the division began as early as November 1943, units that had been earmarked for it were still being withdrawn through December and into early February 1944.

Command Structure of *22. Luftwaffen-Felddivision*

Commanders:
Divisional Commander:
 Generalmajor Robert Fuchs, 01/07/1943–01/11/1943
 Oberst Fichter, 09/1943–10/1943
Ia:
 Oberleutnant Heinz Heinsius, 04/1943–11/1943
CO *Luftwaffen-Jäger-Regiment 43*:
 Oberst Max Schirmacher, 03/1943–01/11/1943
CO *III. Bataillon/Jäger-Regiment 43 (L)*:
 Hauptmann Willi Schrader, 02/09/43–11/43
CO *Luftwaffen-Jäger-Regiment 44*:
 Oberst Fritz Hencke, 03/1943–04/1943
CO *Luftwaffen-Artillerie-Regiment 22*:
 Oberst Wulff, 02/1943–03/1943
 Oberst Herbert Müller
 Oberstleutnant Heinrich Kiewitt, 04/05/1943–01/11/1944

Appendix I

Active *Luftwaffe* divisions as of 1 November 1943

The air force field divisions that were still active in the combat rolls when the German Army assumed control of the *Luftwaffe* field divisions on 1 November 1943 included the following:

Division	Front or Region	Area	City or Town	Condition
1.	Russian	North	Novgorod	Division
2.	Russian	Centre	Nevel	Battlegroup
3.	Russian	Centre	Gorodok	Brigade
4.	Russian	Centre	Vitebsk	Division
5.	Russian	South	Nogay Steppe	Battlegroup
6.	Russian	Centre	Vitebsk	Division
9.	Russian	North	Korovino to Peterhof	Division
10.	Russian	North	Zasstrove to Korovino	Division
11.	Balkans	Boetia	Athens	Division
12.	Russian	North	Ssazy	Division
13.	Russian	North	North of Schudovo	Division
14.	Norway	North-Central	Trondheim	Division
15.	Russian	South	Melitopol	Battlegroup
16.	Holland	Holland	Amsterdam	Division
17.	France	North Coast	Le Havre	Division
18.	France	North Coast	Dunkirk–Calais	Division
19.	Holland	Zeeland	Walcheren Island	Division
20.	Denmark	Jutland	Aalborg	Division
21.	Russian	North	Between Cholm and Staraya Russa	Division

Source: Mehner, *Die Geheimen Tagesberichte*, vol. 8, p. 109.

Appendix II

Insignia of the Luftwaffe field divisions

(a) (b) (c) (d)

(a) *1. Luftwaffen-Felddivision*: a diving eagle holding a rifle. (b) *2. Luftwaffen-Felddivision*: a number 2 inside a large L (*Luftwaffe*). (c) *3. Luftwaffen-Felddivision*: a trident above a circle with the letter L. (d) *4. Luftwaffen-Felddivision*: the Luftwaffe eagle and the number 4.

(e) (f) (g) (h)

(e) *5. Luftwaffen-Felddivision*: the Roman numeral for 5 with an eagle. (f) *9. Luftwaffen-Felddivision*: a German jackboot with wings. (g) *10. Luftwaffen-Felddivision*: a watchtower. (h) *12. Luftwaffen-Felddivision*: two oak leaves sprouting from an oak.

(i) (j) (k) (l)

(i) *Felddivision 13 (L)*: the talon of a white-tailed eagle (the national bird of Germany). (j) Although not official, this insignia was employed by the communications company of *14. Luftwaffen-Felddivision* when it transferred to Trondheim in the spring of 1943. (k) *15. Luftwaffen-Felddivision*: a white circle cut diagonally by a black line. (l) *16. Luftwaffen-Felddivision*: a soaring *Luftwaffe* eagle holding a rifle above the number 16.

Appendix II: Divisional insignia of the Luftwaffe field divisions 287

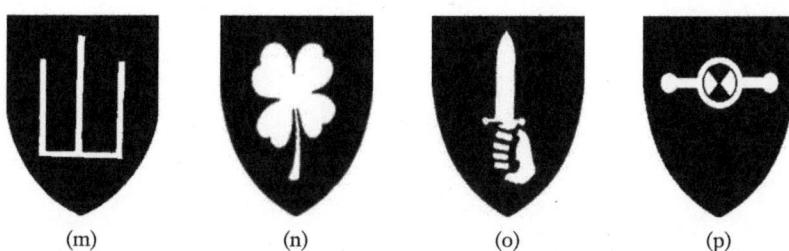

(m)　　　　　(n)　　　　　(o)　　　　　(p)

(m) *17. Felddivision (L)*: the symbol resembles an anti-tank barrier of the type employed by the Germans along the beaches of France and the Low Countries.　(n) *19. Luftwaffen-Sturm-Division (Radfahr)*: a four-leaf clover.　(o) *19. Volksgrenadier Division*: a hand holding a bayonet. (When *19. Luftwaffen-Sturm-Division (Radfahr)* was disbanded in October 1944, its remaining elements were used to form this division.)　(p) *20. Luftwaffen-Sturm-Division*'s shield.

(q)　　　　　(r)

(q) *Luftwaffendivision Meindl*: a letter M (for Meindl).　(r) *21. Luftwaffen-Felddivision / Felddivision 21 (L)*: a diving golden eagle holding a German grenade (nicknamed the 'potato masher') in its talons.

Notes

Introduction

1. The change in strategy was made by Hitler on account of the British air raid on Berlin on the night of 25 August 1940. The British claimed they were targeting arms factories in the city but the *Führer* was incensed. Shortly thereafter, he ordered the *Luftwaffe* to target British cities, like London. This change in the strategy of the campaign saved the RAF, because the English airfields and radar installations were no longer targeted.
2. Milch was demanding that aircraft production be quadrupled virtually overnight – an impossible task.

1. Luftwaffen-Felddivision

1. *Generalleutnant* Robert Pistorius was killed near Vitebsk on 27 June 1944, while leading the *4. Feld Division (L)*.
2. The *Sturmgeschütz III* assault gun was created in 1940 for two main reasons: (1) to give heavy firepower support for the infantry and (2) for anti-tank defence.
3. Wolf Keilig, *Das Deutsche Heer 1939–1945*. 3 vols. Bad Nauheim: Podzun-Verlag, 1960, vol. III, p. 6.
4. The division was completely manned by Spanish volunteers, most of whom were members of the Spanish Fascist 'Falange' Party, whose official title was *'Falange Española de las Juntas de Ofensiva Nacional Sindicalista'*.
5. Kevin C. Ruffner, *Luftwaffe Field Divisions 1941–45*. Oxford: Osprey Publishing, 1998, p. 11.
6. The Red Army drive also included the Gostilzi region of the Oranienbaum Pocket.
7. Ruffner, *Luftwaffe Field Divisions*, p. 37.
8. The *Grenadier-Regiment 503* and *II. Bataillon/Artillerie-Regiment 290* belonged to the *290. Infanterie-Division*.
9. *Kampfgruppe Furguth* was what remained of *Grenadier-Regiment 503*.
10. Kurt Mehner, *Die Geheimen Tagesberichte der Deutschen Wehrrnachtführung Im Zweiten Weltkrieg, 1939–1945*. 12 vols. Osnabrück: Biblio Verlag, 1988, vol. 8, p. 267.

2. Luftwaffen-Felddivision

1. Calvin University, German Propaganda Archive, 'Hermann Göring on National Socialism.'
2. Franz Kurowski, *The Brandenburgers Global Mission*. Winnipeg: J.J. Fedorowicz Publishing, 1997, p. 195.
3. Albert Seaton, *The Russo-German War 1941–45*. New York: Praeger Publishers, 1970, p. 389.
4. Werner Haupt, *Army Group Center*. Atglen: Schiffer Publishing Ltd., 1997, p. 176.
5. Seaton, *The Russo-German War*, p. 389.
6. OKH: [German] Army High Command.
7. Otto Heidkämper, *Vitebsk. The Fight and Destruction of the Third Panzer Army*. Havertown: Casemate Publishers, 2017, p. 8.
8. Werner Haupt, *Army Group North*. Atglen: Schiffer Publishing Ltd., 1997, p. 187.
9. Heidkämper, *Vitebsk*, p. 13.
10. Ibid., p. 14.
11. Seaton, *The Russo-German War*, p. 389.
12. Haupt, *Army Group North*, p. 187.

13. Werner Haupt, *Die Deutschen Luftwaffen-Felddivisionen, 1941–1945*. Friedberg: Podzun Pallas, 1993, p. 40.
14. Burkhart Mueller-Hillebrand, *Das Heer 1933–45*. Frankfurt am Main: E.S. Mittler & Sohn GmbH, 1969, p. 224.
15. By August 1943 this corps was operating under *16. Armee* of Army Group North.
16. The *II. Luftwaffen-Feldkorps* was officially disbanded on 8 November 1943 and its remnant parts withdrawn to the Reich. In January 1944 it was reorganized as the *I. Fallschirmjägerkorps*.
17. Eugon Denzel, *Die Luftwaffen-Felddivisionen, 1942–1945*. Neckargemund: Kurt Vowinckel Verlag, 1976, p. 25.
18. George F. Nafziger, *The German Order of Battle. Waffen-SS and other units in World War II*. Conshohocken: Combined Publishing, 2001, p. 148.
19. Steven H. Sandman et al., *Hitler's Army*. Conshohocken: Combined Publishing, 1996, p. 101.
20. Mueller-Hillebrand, *Das Heer*, p. 306.
21. Haupt, *Die Deutschen Luftwaffen-Felddivisionen*, p. 40.
22. Kurt Mehner and Reinhard Tauber, *Abbreviations of the German military language: from the imperial army to the German armed forces*. Norderstedt: Militär-Verlag Patzwall, 1994, p. 84.
23. *Hauptmann* Schmidt was promoted to *Major* on 1 July 1943 and transferred to the staff of *2. Luftwaffen Feldkorps*.
24. *Oberstarzt* – Colonel of the Medical Service.
25. WuG: *Waffen und Gerät* – the ordnance officer in charge of weapons and equipment.
26. *Oberst* Waldschmidt was initially assigned to *II. Luftwaffen-Feldkorps*, but shortly thereafter became the commander of *III. Jäger-Bataillon / 2. Luftwaffen-Felddivision*. On 15 June 1943 he became the commander of *II. Jäger-Bataillon / 6. Luftwaffen-Felddivision*. On 1 August 1943 he became the commander of an independent battalion serving directly under *II. Luftwaffen-Felddivision*. This unit was referred to as '*Korps Bataillon / II. Luftwaffen-Feldkorps*'.
27. On 25 July 1943 Schmitz was transferred to the staff of the artillery regiment in *13. Luftwaffen-Felddivision*.
28. Sarnitz was transferred to *Flak-Ersatz-Abteilung 99* as of 1 June 1943.
29. On 1 February 1943 *Hauptmann* Scheloske was transferred from *2. Luftwaffen-Felddivision* to *Flak-Ersatz-Abteilung 12*.

3. Luftwaffen-Felddivision

1. BA-RW 48/305, *3. Luftwaffen-Felddivision, Blatt 1–2, 19.09.42*.
2. Ibid., *MsG 175/157. Stand von 1 Nov. 1942*.
3. Haupt, *Die Deutschen Luftwaffen-Felddivisionen*, p. 41.
4. Edgar Howell, *The Soviet Partisan Movement*. Washington DC: Center of Military History, 1956, pp. 117–18.
5. Ruffner, *Luftwaffe Field Divisions*, p. 12.
6. Georg Tessin, *Verbände und Truppen der Deutschen Wehrmacht und Waffen-SS*. 14 vols. Osnabrück: Biblio Verlag, 1973–1980, vol. 2, p. 202.
7. Approximately 30km east of Lake Losvida.
8. Egon Kleine and Volkmar Kühn, *Tiger: Die Geschichte Einer Legendären Waffe, 1942–45*. Stuttgart: Motorbuch Verlag, 1985, p. 140.
9. Haupt, *Army Group Center*, p. 180.
10. *Der Chef des Generalstabes des Heeres. Org. I/4852/43 g. Kdos. v. 21.10.43*.
11. Brian L. Davis, *Uniforms and Insignia of the Luftwaffe. Vol. 2: 1940–1945*. London: Arms & Armour Press, 1995, p. 223.
12. Heidkämper, *Vitebsk*, p. 61.
13. Haupt, *Army Group Center*, p. 182.
14. Mueller-Hillebrand, *Das Heer*, p. 224.
15. Heidkämper, *Vitebsk*, p. 89.
16. Nafziger, *The German Order of Battle*, p. 148.
17. Samuel W. Mitcham, *Hitler's Legions*. New York: Dorset Press, 1985, p. 428.

18. Kurt Mehner, *Die Deutsche Wehrmacht 1939–1945*. Norderstedt: Militair Verlag Klaus D. Patzwall, 1993, p. 124.
19. This was not a *Luftwaffe* officer. He was in fact, a *Heer* officer.
20. On 1 December 1942 Schwarz left the division. On 15 January 1943 *Major* Schwarz returned to *3. Luftwaffen-Felddivision*, this time as the divisional supply officer (*Nachschubführer*). On 6 May 1943 he was appointed the 'Ib' in the divisional staff of *4. Luftwaffen-Felddivision*. On 2 September 1943 he became the divisional 'Ib' for *2. Luftwaffen-Felddivision*.

4. Luftwaffen-Felddivision

1. NARA T-78, Roll 398, *Blatt 1-38, OKH Befehl datiert 17 Januar, 1944*.
2. Ruffner, *Luftwaffe Field Divisions*, p. 11.
3. Ibid., p. 9.
4. E.R., *Eagle in Flames. The Fall of the Luftwaffe*. London: Arms & Armour Press, 1997, p. 182.
5. Surash was located northeast of Vitebsk.
6. Dated 12 October 1943.
7. Ruffner, *Luftwaffe Field Divisions*, p. 10.
8. Haupt, *Die Deutschen Luftwaffen-Felddivisionen*, p. 42.
9. Mehner, *Die Geheimen Tagesberichte*, vol. 6, p. 198.
10. Keilig, *Das Deutsche Heer*, pt. 130, p. 7.
11. Tessin, *Verbände und Truppen*, vol. 2, p. 267.
12. Werner Haupt, *Die Schlachten Der Heeresgruppe Mitte*. Friedberg: Podzun Pallas Verlag, 1984, p. 247.
13. Mueller-Hillebrand, *Das Heer*, p. 306.
14. Nafziger, *The German Order of Battle*, p. 149.
15. Gerd Niepold, *Battle For White Russia*. London: Brassey's Defence Publishers, 1987, p. 29.
16. Corps Detachment 'D'. This was basically a grouping of several shattered German divisions, of about regimental strength each, which Hitler refused to disband. Throughout the campaign numerous *Korpsabteilung* were formed.
17. Niepold, *Battle For White Russia*, pp. 40–1.
18. Ibid., p. 80.
19. Haupt, *Die Deutschen Luftwaffen-Felddivisionen*, p. 43.
20. Niepold, *Battle For White Russia*, p. 82.
21. Gollwitzer was captured by the Red Army on 26 June 1944. He remained in Soviet captivity until October 1955, when he was finally released.
22. Paul Adair, *Hitler's Greatest Defeat*. London: Arms & Armour Press, 1994, p. 95.
23. Alex Buchner, *Ostfront 1944*. West Chester: Schiffer Military History, 1991, p. 151.
24. Niepold, *Battle For White Russia*, p. 101.
25. *Generalmajor* Peter von der Groeben. *The Collapse of German Army Group Center*. US Army Historical Division: Europe, 1947. MS# T-31, p. 27.
26. Haupt, *Die Deutschen Luftwaffen-Felddivisionen*, p. 43; Buchner, *Ostfront*, p. 151.
27. Andris J. Kursietis, *The Fallen Generals. The Destruction of the German Officer Corps in World War II and its Aftermath*. Milwaukee: Ark Publications, 1994, p. 38.
28. Adair, *Hitler's Greatest Defeat*, p. 98.
29. Rolf Hinze, *East Front Drama – 1944*. Winnipeg: J.J. Fedorowicz Publishing, 1996, pp. 340, 347.
30. This man was an army officer.
31. Klepp was promoted to *Generalleutnant* (lieutenant general) in 1943 and was posted to command *133. Festungs-Division* (133rd Fortress Division) on the Greek island of Crete.
32. Mehner, *Die Deutsche Wehrmacht*, p. 124.
33. On 28 April 1943 *Hauptmann* Strackerjahn was no longer a member of *4. Luftwaffen-Felddivision*. Instead, he was serving in *Flieger-Ersatz-Bataillon VII*. After leaving *4. Luftwaffen-Felddivision*, he was ordered to take a quartermaster course in France. On 1 June 1943 he was promoted to *Major* and ordered to report to *III. Luftwaffen-Feldkorps* for temporary duty. On 29 June 1943 he was

posted to the division staff of *2. Luftwaffen-Felddivision* as *divisionsquartiermeister* (divisional quartermaster).
34. The headquarters for this regiment was created using the staff company of *Grenadier-Regiment 486 (262. Infanterie-Division)*.
35. Wenzel was commander of *II. Bataillon / Flieger-Regiment 22*. He was promoted to *Oberstleutnant* on 16 December 1942 and immediately transferred to *4. Luftwaffen-Felddivision* to lead *IV. Jäger-Bataillon*.
36. The headquarters for this regiment was created using the staff company of *Grenadier-Regiment 268 (113. Infanterie-Division)*; BA RW 48/316, *Luftwaffen Jäger-Regiment 50-4, 111, 268, 471, 486, 501, 503*, MSG 175/168, BA Freiburg.
37. The headquarters for this regiment was created using the staff of *3. Luftwaffen-Felddivision*.

5. Luftwaffen-Felddivision

1. Keilig, *Das Deutsche Heer*, pt. 7, p. 130.
2. Haupt, *Die Deutschen Luftwaffen-Felddivisionen*, p. 44.
3. Denzel, *Die Luftwaffen-Felddivisionen*, p. 42.
4. Mark Axworthy, *Third Axis Fourth Ally*. London: Arms & Armour Press, 1995, p. 116.
5. Georges Bernage and Francois de Lannoy, *La Luftwaffe / La Waffen SS 1939–1945*. Bayeux: Editions Heimdal, 1998, p. 259.
6. Didier Lodieux, 'Des Sturmgeschütz dans les divisions de campagne de la Luftwaffe', in *39/45 Magazine*, Nr. 148. Bayeux: Editions Heimdal, Septembre à Octobre 1998, p. 5.
7. Bernage and de Lannoy, *La Luftwaffe/La Waffen SS*, p. 259.
8. Lodieux, 'Des Sturmgeschütz dans les divisions', p. 5.
9. Haupt, *Die Deutschen Luftwaffen-Felddivisionen*, p. 44.
10. This battlegroup was led by *Oberstleutnant* Karl Busche, the commander of *Jäger-Regiment 228*. For his actions while leading this *kampfgruppe*, Busche would be awarded the much-coveted Knight's Cross.
11. Wilhelm Tieke, *The Caucasus and the Oil. The German-Soviet War in the Caucasus, 1942–1943*. Winnipeg: J.J. Fedorowicz Publishing, 1995, p. 307.
12. OKW – *Oberkommando der Wehrmacht* (Armed Forces High Command).
13. Paul Carrell, *Scorched Earth: The Russo-German War, 1943–1944*. Boston: Little, Brown & Company, 1970, p. 136.
14. John A. Armstrong, *Soviet Partisans in World War II*. Madison: University of Wisconsin Press, 1964, p. 585.
15. Tieke, *The Caucasus and the Oil*, p. 311.
16. Carrell, *Scorched Earth*, pp. 158, 167.
17. This involved *Panzergrenadier-Regiment 66* of *13. Panzer-Division*, which had been unable to withdraw with *1. Panzerarmee*.
18. Tieke, *The Caucasus and the Oil*, p. 342.
19. Mehner, *Die Geheimen Tagesberichte*, vol. 6, p. 544.
20. Tieke, *The Caucasus and the Oil*, p. 345.
21. *OKW Situation-Landkarte* (Armed Forces High Command Situation Map).
22. Nafziger, *The German Order of Battle*, p. 150.
23. Located in Norway.
24. Mehner, *Die Geheimen Tagesberichte*, vol. 8, p. 109.
25. Ruffner, *Luftwaffe Field Divisions*, p. 16.
26. Rolf Hinze, *Rückzugskämpfe in der Ukraine 1943/44*. Neustadt: Verlag Dr Rolf Hinze, 1991, p. 112.
27. Andreas Hillgruber, *Die Raumung Der Krim 1944*. Berlin: Verlag E.S. Mittler & Sohn GmbH, 1959, pp. 11, 23.
28. Haupt, *Die Deutschen Luftwaffen-Felddivisionen*, p. 45.
29. Two batteries. This unit was to become the 3rd Battalion in the Artillery Regiment.
30. Nafziger, *The German Order of Battle*, p. 150.

31. This *Flak* battalion was to become *IV. Artillerie-Abteilung* in the forming *Artillerie-Regiment 5 (L)*, but was detached from the division in November 1943. The *Flak* battalion became *I. Abteilung* of *Flak-Regiment 17 (mot.)*, which was an independent air force unit.
32. 5th Field Division (L), where the 'L' stood for *Luftwaffe*.
33. Tessin, *Verbände und Truppen*, vol. 3, p. 6.
34. Hinze, *Rückzugskampfe in der Ukraine*, p. 287.
35. Haupt, *Die Deutschen Luftwaffen-Felddivisionen*, p. 45.
36. Mueller-Hillebrand, *Das Heer*, p. 224.
37. In relation to the brief combat histories of other Air Force field divisions.
38. Schaefer was promoted to *Oberstleutnant* on the same day he was transferred (26 January 1943) to *Flak-Ersatz-Abteilung 12*.
39. Lodieux, 'Des Sturmgeschütz dans les divisions', p. 27.

6. Luftwaffen-Felddivision

1. Haupt, *Die Deutschen Luftwaffen-Felddivisionen*, p. 45.
2. Haupt, *Army Group Center*, p. 135.
3. Werner Haupt, *Die Deutschen Infanterie-Divisionen*. 3 vols. Friedberg: Podzun Pallas Verlag, vol. 1, p. 130; Franz Kurowski, *Deadlock Before Moscow. Army Group Center 1942/1943*. West Chester: Schiffer Military History, 1992, pp. 296–7.
4. Peter Schmitz, Klaus-Juergen Thies, Guenter Wegmann and Christian Zweng, *Die Deutschen Divisionen 1939–1945*. 6 vols. Osnabrück: Biblio Verlag, 1994, vol. 2, p. 289.
5. Haupt, *Die Schlachten Der Heeresgruppe Mitte*, p. 267.
6. Ibid.
7. Haupt, *Die Deutschen Luftwaffen-Felddivisionen*, p. 28.
8. Nafziger, *The German Order of Battle*, p. 151.
9. Tessin, *Verbände und Truppen*, vol. 3, p. 37.
10. Schmitz et al., *Die Deutschen Divisionen*, vol. 2, p. 20.
11. Mueller-Hillebrand, *Das Heer*, p. 224.
12. Formerly known as *Luftwaffen-Jäger-Regiment 11*.
13. Formerly known as *Luftwaffen-Jäger-Regiment 12*.
14. Tessin, *Verbände und Truppen*, vol. 13, p. 212.
15. Schmitz et al., *Die Deutschen Divisionen*, vol. 2, p. 21.
16. Nafziger, *The German Order of Battle*, p. 151.
17. Walter Scott Dunn, *Second Front Now 1943*. Tuscaloosa: University of Alabama Press, 1980, p. 260.
18. Schmitz et al., *Die Deutschen Divisionen*, vol. 1, p. 288.
19. Haupt, *Army Group Center*, p. 179.
20. Ibid., p. 183.
21. Schmitz et al., *Die Deutschen Divisionen*, vol. 1, p. 21.
22. At the time, *20. Panzer-Division* was in reserve. When released, it was committed to halting the Soviet attack in the region of *LIII. Armeekorps*.
23. Haupt, *Die Deutschen Luftwaffen-Felddivisionen*, p. 47.
24. Niepold, *Battle For White Russia*, p. 81.
25. Buchner, *Ostfront*, p. 151.
26. Peter von der Groben, *The Collapse of German Army Group Center*. US Army Historical Division: Europe, 1947. MS# T-31, p. 27.
27. Later promoted to *Generalmajor* (Major General).
28. *Generalleutnant* Peschel was killed fighting alongside his division in the encircled city of Vitebsk, on either 27 or 28 June 1944. Peschel was the former commander of *52. Infanterie-Division*. He had led this unit with the rank of *Generalmajor*: Haupt, *Die Deutschen Infanterie-Divisionen*, vol. 2, p. 11.
29. On 1 August 1943 he became the commander of an independent battalion serving directly under *II. Luftwaffen Feldkorps*. This unit was referred to as *Korps Jäger-Bataillon / II. Luftwaffen Feldkorps*.

30. This regimental headquarters was created from the staff company of *Grenadier-Regiment 471* (*251. Infanterie-Division*).
31. This regimental headquarters was created from the staff personnel of *2. Luftwaffen-Felddivision*.
32. This regimental headquarters was created from the staff company of *Grenadier-Regiment 459* (*251. Infanterie-Division*).

7. *Luftwaffen-Felddivision*

1. Mitcham, *Hitler's Legions*, p. 430.
2. For a history of *Division Meindl*, please see the chapter on the history of the *22. Luftwaffen-Felddivision*.
3. Haupt, *Die Deutschen Luftwaffen-Felddivisionen*, p. 48.
4. Nafziger, *The German Order of Battle*, p. 151.
5. Ruffner, *Luftwaffe Field Divisions*, p. 11.
6. Bernage and de Lannoy, *La Luftwaffe/La Waffen SS*, p. 259.
7. Denzel, *Die Luftwaffen-Felddivisionen*, p. 26.
8. Erich von Manstein, *Lost Victories*. Novato: Presidio Press, 1982, pp. 295–6.
9. Earl F. Ziemke and Magna Bauer, *Moscow to Stalingrad: Decision in the East*. Washington, DC: Center for Military History, United States Army, 1987, p. 479.
10. Percy Ernst Schramm, *Kriegstagebuch des Oberkommandos der Wehrmacht 1939–1945*. 8 vols. München: Bernard & Gräfe Verlag, 1982, vol. 4, pp. 1392–3.
11. Bernage and de Lannoy, *La Luftwaffe/La Waffen SS*, p. 259.
12. Tessin, *Verbände und Truppen*, vol. 3, p. 76.
13. Rolf Stoves, *Die 22. Panzer-Division, 25. Panzer-Division, 27. Panzer-Division, und die 233. Reserve-Panzer-Division*. Friedberg: Podzun-Pallas Verlag, 1985, pp. 73–5.
14. Earl F. Ziemke, *Stalingrad to Berlin: The German Defeat in the East*. Washington DC: Center of Military History, 1968, p. 62.
15. Mitcham, *Hitler's Legions*, p. 430.
16. Major General F.W. von Mellenthin, *Panzer Battles. A Study of the Employment of Armor in the Second World War*. Norman: University of Oklahoma Press, 1971, p. 175n.
17. Ibid., p. 325.
18. Ibid., p. 179.
19. Haupt, *Die Deutschen Luftwaffen-Felddivisionen*, p. 48.
20. Ruffner, *Luftwaffe Field Divisions*, p. 12.
21. Carrell, *Scorched Earth*, pp. 181–3. Corps 'Mieth' would later be redesignated as *IV. Armeekorps*.
22. On 20 July 1943 *Korps Mieth* was redesignated as *IV. Armeekorps*.
23. NARA Microfilm T-174, Roll 785, Frames 812–874.
24. BA-MA *OKH Kriegsgliederung, Dislokation Heeresgruppe Süd nach Lage Ost, Stand 2.6.43*.
25. Nafziger, *The German Order of Battle*, p. 152.
26. Denzel, *Die Luftwaffen-Felddivisionen*, p. 26.
27. Axworthy, *Third Axis Fourth Ally*, p. 116.
28. Schmitz et al., *Die Deutschen Divisionen*, vol. 2, p. 68.
29. One report said that General August Klessmann assumed command of the division from 28 November 1942 until 28 February 1943.
30. Bernage and de Lannoy, *La Luftwaffe/La Waffen SS*, p. 259.
31. He was promoted to *Generalleutnant* on 1 January 1942. On 15 February 1943 Spange became the commander of *8. Luftwaffen-Felddivision*. However, the order was rescinded and he was appointed commander of *15. Luftwaffen-Felddivision* on the same day.
32. Kurt Mehner and Reinhard Teuber, *Die Luftwaffe 1939–1945*. Schönau: Klaus D. Patzwall Verlag, 1989, p. 84.
33. In March 1943 *Major* Guido von Suchodol-Maculan was transferred to Slovakia, to serve under *167. Volksgrenadier Division* (then currently forming near Bratislava).

8. Luftwaffen-Felddivision

1. Haupt, *Die Deutschen Luftwaffen-Felddivisionen*, p. 49.
2. Ibid., p. 51.
3. Nafziger, *The German Order of Battle*, p. 152.
4. Denzel, *Die Luftwaffen-Felddivisionen*, p. 27.
5. Tessin, *Verbände und Truppen*, vol. 14, p. 110.
6. David M. Glantz, *From the Don to the Dnieper. Soviet Offensive Operations, Dec. 1942–Aug. 1943*. London: Frank Cass, 1991, p. 380.
7. Ruffner, *Luftwaffe Field Divisions*, p. 12.
8. Haupt, *Die Deutschen Luftwaffen-Felddivisionen*, p. 49.
9. Carrell, *Scorched Earth*, p. 121.
10. Stoves, *Die 22. Panzer-Division*, p. 82.
11. Tessin, *Verbände und Truppen*, vol. 9, p. 84; vol. 4, p. 118; vol. 3, p. 61.
12. Nafziger, *The German Order of Battle*, p. 152.
13. Schmitz et al., *Die Deutschen Divisionen*, vol. 2, p. 116.
14. Stoves, *Die 22. Panzer-Division*, p. 100.
15. Richard C. Lukas, *Forgotten Holocaust. The Poles Under German Occupation 1939–1944*. Lexington: University Press of Kentucky, 1986, pp. 184–5.
16. On 18 June 1943 *Hauptmann* Steuer (b. 14 December 1913) was serving in the *Feldausbildungs-Bataillon* of *2. Luftwaffen-Felddivision*.
17. *Hauptmann* Christian von Steiglitz was wounded on this date.
18. *Major* Kurt Ulmer, who had served in *Luftwaffen-Infanterie-Regiment 'Moskau'*, was posted to the staff of *8. Luftwaffen-Felddivision* on 16 November 1942. He remained with *8. Luftwaffen-Felddivision* until 15 February 1943, when he was transferred to the divisional staff of *19. Luftwaffen-Sturm-Division*. By 1 May 1943 Ulmer was once again in the divisional staff of *8. Luftwaffen-Felddivision*. Towards the end of May 1943 he was posted to the divisional staff of *13. Luftwaffen-Felddivision*. He remained in this division until November 1943.

9. Luftwaffen-Felddivision

1. Bernage and de Lannoy, *La Luftwaffe/La Waffen SS*, p. 259.
2. Haupt, *Die Deutschen Luftwaffen-Felddivisionen*, p. 100.
3. Bernage and de Lannoy, *La Luftwaffe/La Waffen SS*, p. 259.
4. Haupt, *Army Group North*, p. 152.
5. Haupt, *Die Deutschen Luftwaffen-Felddivisionen*, p. 50.
6. Denzel, *Die Luftwaffen-Felddivisionen*, p. 27.
7. Haupt, *Die Deutschen Luftwaffen-Felddivisionen*, p. 50.
8. Ibid.
9. Ibid.
10. Steven H. Newton, *Retreat from Leningrad*. Atglen: Schiffer Publishing, 1995, p. 36.
11. Haupt, *Die Deutschen Luftwaffen-Felddivisionen*, p. 51.
12. Haupt, *Army Group North*, p. 174.
13. Haupt, *Die Deutschen Luftwaffen-Felddivisionen*, p. 52.
14. Jonathan House and David Glantz, *When Titans Clashed. How The Red Army Stopped Hitler*. Lawrence: University Press of Kansas, 1995, p. 192.
15. Patrick McTaggart, 'The Battle of Narva, 1944'. San Luis Obispo: *Command Magazine*, January–February 1992, 14:56.
16. David Glantz, *Soviet Military Deception in the Second World War*. London: Frank Cass, 1989, p. 299.
17. Newton, *Retreat from Leningrad*, p. 60.
18. Richard Landwehr, 'Soldiers of Europe: The III SS-Panzerkorps (part 1)', Glendale: *Siegrunen Magazine*, July 1979, 3(3-15):9.

19. Werner Haupt, *Leningrad. 900 Tage Schlacht 1941–1944*. Friedberg: Podzun Pallas Verlag, n.d., p. 227.
20. Richard Landwehr and Holger Thor Nielsen, *Nordic Warriors. SS Panzer Grenadier-Regiment 24 Danmark, Eastern Front, 1943–45*. Halifax: Shelf Books, 1999, p. 66.
21. Where *Felddivision 1 (L)* was 'coincidentally' stationed.
22. Haupt, *Army Group North*, p. 174.
23. Newton, *Retreat from Leningrad*, p. 59.
24. Ibid., p. 63.
25. Mehner, *Die Geheimen Tagesberichte*, vol. 9, p. 227.
26. Haupt, *Leningrad*, p. 229.
27. Ibid., p. 230.
28. Haupt, *Die Deutschen Luftwaffen-Felddivisionen*, p. 54.
29. NARA Microfilm Roll T-311, Roll 70, Frames 349–350, 'Heeresgruppe Nord, Ia, 159/44, 17 January 1944'.
30. Nafziger, *The German Order of Battle*, p. 152.
31. Haupt, *Die Deutschen Luftwaffen-Felddivisionen*, p. 54.
32. Keilig, *Das Deutsche Heere*, pt. 130, p. 8.
33. NARA Microfilm Roll T-311, Roll 72, Frames 0109–0218, *Heeresgruppe Nord Ia* entries dated 14 March, 5 April, 10 April, 19 April and 21 April.
34. Mueller-Hillebrand, *Das Heer*, p. 224.
35. BA MA, RW 48/309, MSG 175/161 – 9. – 10. *Luftwaffen-Felddivision*.
36. Mehner, *Die Geheimen Tagesberichte*, vol. 7, p. 360.
37. Assumed temporary command of the division from 12–25 August 1943.
38. On 29 March 1943 Emil Stephan was appointed commander of *Luftwaffen-Jäger-Regiment 26*. On 1 October 1943 he was promoted to *Generalmajor*.
39. On 1 November 1942 Stein was promoted to *Oberstleutnant*.

10. Luftwaffen-Felddivision

1. Mehner and Teuber, *Die Luftwaffe*, p. 91.
2. Bernage and de Lannoy, *La Luftwaffe/La Waffen SS*, p. 259.
3. Haupt, *Die Deutschen Luftwaffen-Felddivisionen*, p. 54.
4. Ruffner, *Luftwaffe Field Divisions*, p. 11.
5. Denzel, *Die Luftwaffen-Felddivisionen*, p. 27.
6. Jason von Zerneck, Internet posting dealing with the military career of his grandfather in the *Luftwaffe*. German Armed Forces in WWII on-line forum message board. Posted on 16 November 1999 at 11:49pm.
7. Kursietis, *The Fallen Generals*, p. 50.
8. Wolf Keilig, *Rangliste Des Deutschen Heeres 1944/45*. Bad Nauheim: Hand-Henning Podzun Verlag, 1955, pp. 38, 61.
9. Tessin, *Verbände und Truppen*, vol. 3, p. 184.
10. Haupt, *Army Group North*, p. 152.
11. Ziemke and Bauer, *Moscow to Stalingrad*, pp. 411–12.
12. Ibid.
13. Alan Wykes, *The Siege of Leningrad*. New York: Ballantine Books, 1968, p. 145.
14. Carrell, *Scorched Earth*, p. 239; Wykes, *The Siege of Leningrad*, p. 140.
15. Gerald R. Kleinfeld and Lewis A. Tambs, *Hitler's Spanish Division. The Blue Division in Russia*. Carbondale: Southern Illinois University Press, 1979, pp. 347–441.
16. Up until January 1943 the three companies of *Panzerjäger-Abteilung 563* had been armed with the outdated 37mm anti-tank gun. Each company possessed twelve of these obsolete guns. In January 1943 the battalion was re-equipped with the more effective 75mm L-48 anti-tank gun.
17. Kleine and Kühn, *Tiger*, p. 23.
18. Carlos Caballero Jurado, *La Division Azul*. Madrid: Defensa Editorial, 1999, p. 45.
19. Ibid.

20. Carrell, *Scorched Earth*, p. 246.
21. Jurado, *La Division Azul*, p. 45; Carrell, *Scorched Earth*, p. 246.
22. Haupt, *Die Deutschen Luftwaffen-Felddivisionen*, p. 54.
23. This battalion was formed from the core of *Luftwaffen-Radfahr-Aufklärungs-Kompanie 10*.
24. Newton, *Retreat from Leningrad*, p. 305.
25. Wilhelm Tieke, *Korps Steiner. Nordland-Nederland. Nachträge zu den Truppengeschichten*. Malbeck: Kleinoffsetdruckerei Otto Dittmer, 1987, p. 23.
26. Wilhelm Tieke, *Tragodie um die Treue. Kampf und Untergang des III. (germanische) SS-Panzerkorps*. Osnabrück: Munin Verlag GmbH, 1968, p. 20.
27. Haupt, *Leningrad*, p. 161.
28. Ferdinand Müller, *Vom Kessel von Oranienbaum bis zu den Endkämpfen in Ostpreuben: Meine Ereibnisse als Funker bei der 10. Luftwaffen-Felddivision und der 170. Infanteriedivision*. Bremen: Mix Verlag GmbH, 2013, p. 74.
29. Haupt, *Die Deutschen Luftwaffen-Felddivisionen*, p. 55.
30. Testimony of Herbert Poller, member of *SS Aufklärungs Abteilung 11*, from his unpublished manuscript, 'Die Panzer Aufklärungs Abteilung der Freiwilligen Panzergrenadier Division 11.' Available at: http://www.sno.No/files/documents/118257.pdf.
31. Tieke, *Tragodie um die Treue*, p. 51.
32. Landwehr, 'Soldiers of Europe', pp. 9–10.
33. McTaggart, 'The Battle of Narva, 1944', p. 56.
34. Haupt, *Die Deutschen Luftwaffen-Felddivisionen*, p. 55.
35. Newton, *Retreat from Leningrad*, p. 36.
36. Tieke, *Tragodie um die Treue*, p. 51.
37. Kleine and Kühn, *Tiger*, p. 66.
38. Landwehr, 'Soldiers of Europe', p. 11.
39. Schmitz et al., *Die Deutschen Divisionen*, vol. 2, p. 239.
40. Horst Scheibert, *Die Träger des Deutschen Kreuzes in Gold. Heer-Kriegsmarine-Luftwaffen-Waffen-SS*. Friedberg: Podzun Pallas Verlag, n.d., p. 293.
41. Bernage and de Lannoy, *La Luftwaffe/La Waffen SS*, p. 259.
42. Mitcham, *Hitler's Legions*, p. 431.
43. Landwehr, 'Soldiers of Europe', p. 12.
44. Haupt, *Army Group North*, p. 206.
45. Mueller-Hillebrand, *Das Heer*, p. 224.
46. Mehner, *Die Deutsche Wehrmacht*, p. 124, says that Wedel held this post until 29 January 1944.
47. In February 1943 51-year-old *Major* Waibel (b. 17 January 1891) was transferred to the *OKL Führerreserve*.
48. On 1 December 1942 *Major* Dr Walter Weiss (b. 27 March 1896) was transferred to *10. Luftwaffen-Felddivision*. Previously, he had been the commander of *Reserve-Flak-Abteilung 153*. In February 1943 he was made commander of *II. Jäger-Bataillon/10. Luftwaffen-Felddivision*. On 1 August 1943 he was promoted to *Oberstleutnant* and given command of *Artillerie-Regiment 13 (L)/13. Luftwaffen-Felddivision*.
49. *Oberst* Mehnert was also awarded the German Cross in Gold, but did so after leaving *Felddivision 10 (L)*. He received the award on 1 January 1945 while leading another *Luftwaffen Jäger* regiment.

11. Luftwaffen-Felddivision

1. Haupt, *Die Deutschen Luftwaffen-Felddivisionen*, p. 56.
2. Nafziger, *The German Order of Battle*, p. 155.
3. Ruffner, *Luftwaffe Field Divisions*, p. 33.
4. *Feldpost nummer ab Apr/45 45809 A/B Bataillon stab u. 1. Panzerjäger Kompanie*.
5. J. Lee Ready, *The Forgotten Axis. Germany's Partners and Foreign Volunteers in World War II*. Jefferson: McFarland & Co., 1987, p. 414.
6. Schramm, *Kriegstagebuch des Oberkommandos*, vol. 4, p. 1,206.
7. Tessin, *Verbände und Truppen*, vol. 14, p. 62.

8. Dunn, *Second Front Now*, p. 246.
9. Andre Gerolymatos, *Guerrilla Warfare and Espionage in Greece 1940–1944*. New York: Pella Publishing Co., Inc., 1992, p. 174.
10. Tessin, *Verbände und Truppen*, vol. 14, p. 63.
11. Schmitz et al., *Die Deutschen Divisionen*, vol. 3, p. 258.
12. Gerolymatos, *Guerrilla Warfare*, p. 174.
13. Haupt, *Die Deutschen Luftwaffen-Felddivisionen*, p. 56.
14. Ruffner, *Luftwaffe Field Divisions*, p. 33.
15. Tessin, *Verbände und Truppen*, vol. 4, p. 176.
16. Ruffner, *Luftwaffe Field Divisions*, p. 34.
17. Adam Geibel, 'Taking Leros: The Fight for the Dodecanese Island Fortress'. New York: *Europa Magazine*, 1998, 14:31.
18. Ruffner, *Luftwaffe Field Divisions*, p. 34.
19. Ibid., p. 17.
20. Denzel, *Die Luftwaffen-Felddivisionen*, p. 27.
21. Ruffner, *Luftwaffe Field Divisions*, p. 18.
22. Schmitz et al., *Die Deutschen Divisionen*, vol. 3, p. 259.
23. Hermann Franz, *Gebirgsjäger der Polizei. Polizei Gebirgsjäger-Regiment 18 und Polizei Gebirgs Artillerie-Abteilung 1942 bis 1945*. Bad Nauheim: Verlag Hans Henning Podzun, 1963, p. 152.
24. This was the French-made *Canon de 105mle 1913 Schneider* artillery piece, employed during the First World War.
25. This was the 152mm M1937 (ML-20) Russian artillery piece, produced by the Soviet Union between 1937 and 1947.
26. Samuel W. Mitcham, *Crumbling Empire. The German Defeat in the East, 1944*. Westport: Praeger Publishers, 2001, p. 206.
27. Tessin, *Verbände und Truppen*, vol. 14, p. 158.
28. Mitcham, *Crumbling Empire*, p. 206.
29. Schmitz et al., *Die Deutschen Divisionen*, vol. 1, p. 260.
30. Haupt, *Die Deutschen Luftwaffen-Felddivisionen*, p. 56.
31. Otto Kumm, *Vorwärts Prinz Eugen. Geschichte Der 7. SS Freiwilligen Gebirgs Division 'Prinz Eugen'*. Osnabrück: Munin Verlag GmbH, 1978, p. 314.
32. Ibid., p. 315.
33. Otto Kumm, *Prinz Eugen. The History of the 7. SS Mountain Division 'Prinz Eugen'*. Winnipeg: J.J. Fedorowicz Publishing, 1995, p. 238.
34. Keilig, *Rangliste Des Deutschen Heeres*, p. 40.
35. Mehner, *Die Deutsche Wehrmacht*, p. 124.
36. Kumm, *Prinz Eugen*, p. 239.
37. Tessin, *Verbände und Truppen*, vol. 14, p. 64.
38. Haupt, *Die Deutschen Luftwaffen-Felddivisionen*, p. 56.
39. Schramm, *Kriegstagebuch des Oberkommandos*, vol. 4, p. 993.
40. Ibid., p. 1041.
41. Nafziger, *The German Order of Battle*, p. 156.
42. This would prove to be the last major offensive by the German Army in the Second World War.
43. Kumm, *Prinz Eugen*, p. 256.
44. Schramm, *Kriegstagebuch des Oberkommandos*, vol. 4, p. 1054.
45. Ibid., p. 1079.
46. Hermann Frank, *Geschichte der XXI. Gebirgs Armeekorps*. Heidelberg: Kurt Vowinckel Verlag, 1957, p. 101.
47. Major der Reserve a. D., Dr Ernst Percy Schramm. *The German Wehrmacht in the Last Days of the War (1 January–7 May 1945)*. Europe: Historical Division, Headquarters United States Army, MS# C-020, n.d., p. 515.
48. NARA Microfilm T-78, Roll 645, Frame 000807. *Notiz nach Führervortrag, am 14.3.45*.

49. Ibid.
50. Frank, *Geschichte der XXI. Gebirgs Armeekorps*, p. 103.
51. Schramm, *The German Wehrmacht in the Last Days of the War*, p. 538.
52. Schmitz et al., *Die Deutschen Divisionen*, vol. 1, p. 262.
53. Samuel J. Newland, *Cossacks in the German Army 1941–1945*. London: Frank Cass, 1991, p. 164.
54. Schramm, *Kriegstagebuch des Oberkommandos*, vol. 1, p. 1145.
55. Tessin, *Verbände und Truppen*, vol. 14, p. 64.
56. Keilig, *Rangliste Des Deutschen Heeres*, p. 35.
57. Ibid., p. 175.
58. Haupt, *Die Deutschen Luftwaffen-Felddivisionen*, p. 103. *Hauptmann* Roy was eventually promoted to the rank of *Major* before the end of the war.

12. Luftwaffen-Felddivision

1. Haupt, *Die Deutschen Luftwaffen-Felddivisionen*, p. 57.
2. Tessin, *Verbände und Truppen*, vol. 3, p. 251.
3. Haupt, *Die Deutschen Infanterie-Divisionen*, p. 102.
4. Nafziger, *The German Order of Battle*, p. 157.
5. BA MA, RH 38, blatt 14, *Divisionsstärke: 12. LFD, H. Gr. Nord, Operationsabteilung Nr.314/42, 17.12.42*.
6. Haupt, *Die Deutschen Luftwaffen-Felddivisionen*, p. 57.
7. The 3rd Artillery Battalion was in reality the division's *Flak* battalion.
8. Haupt, *Die Deutschen Luftwaffen-Felddivisionen*, p. 57.
9. Schmitz et al., *Die Deutschen Divisionen*, vol. 3, p. 58.
10. Keilig, *Das Deutsche Heer*, pt. 130, p. 9.
11. *Jäger-Regiment 25 (L)* was created in February 1944 by the absorption of parts of *Felddivision 13 (L)*. Specifically, *II. Bataillon* of *Jäger-Regiment 25* and *I. Bataillon* of *Jäger-Regiment 26* became *I.* and *II. Bataillone* of *Jäger-Regiment 25* in *Felddivision 12 (L)*.
12. The Fusilier Battalion was organized in March 1944 by redesignating the 1st Battalion of Grenadier-Regiment 374 of the 207th Security Division.
13. Mehner, *Die Geheimen Tagesberichte*, vol. 9, p. 59.
14. NARA Microfilm T-311, Roll 70, Frames 00357-8 '*HG Nord, Ia./Abt.III – 19 Dezember 1943*'.
15. Newton, *Retreat from Leningrad*, p. 103.
16. Ibid., pp. 37, 120.
17. Mehner, *Die Geheimen Tagesberichte*, vol. 9, p. 247.
18. Ibid., p. 251.
19. Haupt, *Leningrad*, p. 235.
20. Mehner, *Die Geheimen Tagesberichte*, vol. 9, p. 255.
21. NARA Microfilm T-311, Roll 70, Frames 00567-8, '*Armeeoberkommando 18, Ia, 732/44 5 Februar 1944*'.
22. Newton, *Retreat from Leningrad*, p. 72.
23. Ibid., p. 120.
24. Ibid., p. 76.
25. Mehner, *Die Geheimen Tagesberichte*, vol. 9, p. 372.
26. Ibid., p. 331.
27. Ibid., p. 339.
28. Newton, *Retreat from Leningrad*, p. 343.
29. Ibid., p. 349.
30. Ibid., p. 76.
31. Mehner, *Die Geheimen Tagesberichte*, vol. 9, p. 372.
32. Newton, *Retreat from Leningrad*, p. 95.
33. Ibid., p. 105.
34. Haupt, *Die Deutschen Infanterie-Divisionen*, vol. 2, p. 97.
35. Newton, *Retreat from Leningrad*, p. 108.

36. Mueller-Hillebrand, *Das Heer*, p. 224.
37. Newton, *Retreat from Leningrad*, p. 109.
38. 'Division for Special Employment No. 300'.
39. Landwehr and Nielsen, *Nordic Warriors*, p. 118.
40. Haupt, *Die Deutschen Luftwaffen-Felddivisionen*, p. 58.
41. Mitcham, *Crumbling Empire*, p. 124.
42. The other six divisions that were fully combat ready were the 11th, 21st, 30th, 58th, 61st and 227th Infantry Divisions.
43. Haupt, *Die Deutschen Luftwaffen-Felddivisionen*, p. 58; Haupt, *Army Group North*, p. 240.
44. BA MA RH-41, blatt 13, *Kriegsgliederungen d. LFD 12., H. Gr. Nord, Operationsabteilung Nr. 517/44*, 24.7.44.
45. Mitcham, *Crumbling Empire*, p. 125.
46. Schmitz et al., *Die Deutschen Divisionen*, vol. 2, p. 57.
47. Mitcham, *Crumbling Empire*, p. 142.
48. Haupt, *Army Group North*, p. 277.
49. Seaton, *The Russo-German War*, p. 443.
50. Ibid., p. 297.
51. Ibid., p. 298.
52. Gottlob Herbert Bidermann, *In Deadly Combat. A German Soldier's Memoir of the Eastern Front*. Lawrence: University of Kansas Press, 2000, p. 203.
53. Schmitz et al., *Die Deutschen Divisionen*, vol. 2, p. 207.
54. Haupt, *Army Group North*, p. 340.
55. Ibid., pp. 344–5.
56. Schmitz et al., *Die Deutschen Divisionen*, vol. 2, p. 57.
57. Nafziger, *The German Order of Battle*, p. 158.
58. Schramm, *Kriegstagebuch des Oberkommandos*, vol. 8, pt. II, pp. 1,142–3.
59. Ibid., p. 1,143.
60. NARA Microfilm T-78, Roll 645, Frame 000925. *Fernschreiben – 4 Marz, 1945*.
61. NARA Microfilm T-78, Roll 645, Frame Frame 00990, *Vortragsnotiz 9. Marz 1945*.
62. Ibid., Frame 00793, *Fernschreibenvermittlung, 10 Marz 1945*.
63. Hans Schäufler, *1945 – Panzer an der Weichsel. Soldaten der Letzten Stunde*. Stuttgart: Motorbuch Verlag, 1986, p. 79.
64. Christopher Duffy, *Red Storm on the Reich. The Soviet March on Germany, 1945*. New York: Atheneum, 1991, p. 220.
65. NARA Microfilm T-78, Roll 645, Frame 00990, *Vortragsnotiz 9. Marz 1945*.
66. NARA Microfilm T-78, Roll 645, Frame 00736, *Vortragsnotiz – Abtransport Kurland 10.3.45–17.3.45*.
67. Ibid., Frame 00769, *Funk-Fernschreiben. 17 Marz 1945. General Stab des Heeres/Organisations-Abteilung. Oberst i.G. Bennecke, Abteilungs-Chef*.
68. Schmitz et al., *Die Deutschen Divisionen*, vol. 2, p. 313.
69. Schäufler, *1945 – Panzer an der Weichsel*, p. 81.
70. Horst Grossmann et al., *Der Kampf um Ostpreussen*. München: Gräfe und Unzer Verlag, 1960, p. 163.
71. Werner Haupt, *Als Die Rote Armee Nach Deutschland Kam. Die Kämpfe in Ostpreussen, Schlesien, und Pommern 1944/45*. Friedberg: Podzun-Pallas Verlag, 1970, p. 37.
72. Peter Schmitz and Klaus J. Thies, *Die Truppenkennzeichen der Verbände und Einheiten der Deutschen Wehrmacht und Waffen-SS und Ihre Einzätze Im Zweiten Weltkrieg 1939–1945*. Biblio Verlag: Osnabrück, 1987, p. 207.
73. *Oberst* Weber was promoted to *Generalmajor* on 1 February 1944. Weber eventually reached the rank of *Generalleutnant* by war's end. He was considered a particularly energetic and seasoned divisional commander.
74. Major Fox had served previously in the staff headquarters of *Artillerie-Regiment 56*.

75. In October 1942 *Oberstleutnant der Reserve* Joachim von Wietersheim was transferred to *12. Luftwaffen-Felddivision*. He was transferred to *Luftflottenkommando 3* on 12 January 1943. On 1 March 1943 he became the commander of *Flak-Regiment 79 (motorisiert)* but in that same month he was transferred back to *12. Luftwaffen-Felddivision* and given command of *Artillerie-Regiment 12 (L)*. He led this divisional artillery regiment until November 1943.
76. *Oberstleutnant* Kretschmar was killed on 27 December 1944.
77. *Oberstleutnant* Kreuzer was killed on 22 February 1945.
78. *Major der Reserve* Warnecke had been transferred from *II. Bataillon/Flieger Regiment 52* to *12. Luftwaffen-Felddivision* on 1 April 1943.
79. Mehner and Teuber, *Die Luftwaffe*, p. 87.

13. Luftwaffen-Felddivision

1. Tessin, *Verbände und Truppen*, vol. 3, p. 279.
2. Lodieux, 'Des Sturmgeschütz dans les divisions', p. 27.
3. Tessin, *Verbände und Truppen*, vol. 4, p. 232.
4. Ruffner, *Luftwaffe Field Divisions*, p. 17.
5. Haupt, *Army Group North*, p. 173.
6. Tessin, *Verbände und Truppen*, vol. 3, p. 279.
7. Haupt, *Army Group North*, p. 173.
8. Newton, *Retreat from Leningrad*, p. 54.
9. Haupt, *Die Deutschen Luftwaffen-Felddivisionen*, p. 60.
10. Nafziger, *The German Order of Battle*, p. 158.
11. NARA Microfilm T-78, Roll 646, Frame 000576.
12. Newton, *Retreat from Leningrad*, p. 37.
13. NARA Microfilm T-311, Roll 70, Frame 000593.
14. Haupt, *Army Group North*, p. 185.
15. During the retreat from Leningrad and the Volkhov and Ladoga positions, Reymann would temporarily command the 11th Infantry and 20th SS Divisions.
16. Cornelius Ryan, *The Last Battle*. New York: Simon & Schuster, 1966, pp. 375–6.
17. NARA Microfilm T-311, Roll 70, Frame 000794.
18. Newton, *Retreat from Leningrad*, p. 72.
19. Ibid., p. 73.
20. Antonio Muñoz, *Hitler's Eastern Legions. Vol. I – The Baltic Schutzmannschaft 1941–1945*. New York: Europa Books, 1998, p. 45.
21. Tessin, *Verbände und Truppen*, vol. 13, p. 222.
22. Ibid., vol. 8, p. 30.
23. Ibid., vol. 9, p. 1.
24. Haupt, *Die Deutschen Luftwaffen-Felddivisionen*, p. 60.
25. Reymann was a *Heer* (Army) officer.
26. Keilig, *Das Deutsche Heer*, pt. 130, p. 9.
27. *Oberstleutnant* Fritz Strube was transferred to *12. Luftwaffen-Felddivision* on 15 November 1942. On 4 June 1943 he became the commander of *IV. Bataillon/Artillerie-Regiment 12 (L)*. This was in fact the *Flak* battalion of the division. In November 1943 he and the *Flak* battalion were detached from *12. Luftwaffen-Felddivision*, which had now been redesignated as *Felddivision 12 (L)*. The *Flak* battalion formerly under *12. Luftwaffen-Felddivision* went on to become *II. Bataillon/Flak-Regiment 6*. *Oberstleutnant* Strube continued to lead this unit as its CO.

14. Luftwaffen-Felddivision

1. Nafziger, *The German Order of Battle*, p. 159.
2. Tessin, *Verbände und Truppen*, vol. 13, p. 310.
3. Earl F. Ziemke, *The German Northern Theater of Operations 1940–1945*. Washington DC: Department of the Army, 1959. Department of the Army Document No. 20-271, p. 254.
4. Ibid.

5. Ibid., p. 255.
6. 'Spared: Sweden During the Second World War', in San Luis Obispo: *Command Magazine*, September 1996, 39:37.
7. Tessin, *Verbände und Truppen*, vol. 7, p. 277.
8. Ziemke, *The German Northern Theater of Operations*, p. 262.
9. Riochard S. Fuegner, *Beneath the Tyrant's Yoke: Norwegian Resistance to the German Occupation of Norway 1940–1945*. St Paul: Beaver Pond Press, 2002, p. 137.
10. Ibid.
11. Terry Gander and Peter Chamberlain, *Infantry, Mountain and Airborne Guns*. London: MacDonald Jane's Publishers Ltd, 1975, p. 24.
12. The *Mitrailleuse Automatique Hotchkiss Modèle 1914* heavy machine gun, taken from Norwegian Army stocks.
13. Again, from Norwegian Army stocks.
14. Haupt, *Die Deutschen Luftwaffen-Felddivisionen*, p. 61.
15. Mehner, *Die Geheimen Tagesberichte*, vol. 8, p. 163.
16. Haupt, *Die Deutschen Luftwaffen-Felddivisionen*, p. 61.
17. Tessin, *Verbände und Truppen*, vol. 3, p. 295.
18. Nafziger, *The German Order of Battle*, p. 159.
19. BA MA *OKL, Kriegsgliederungen Luftwaffen-Felddivision 14. 55/51 T-207 – 1943.*
20. Ibid.
21. For more information on the *landesschützen* battalions of the *Luftwaffe*, see the *Bundesarchiv, Koblenz*, file: *RL-43* (available online). A brief listing of the known regional defence battalions of the *Luftwaffe* follows: **Landesschützen-Bataillon der Luftwaffe 2** was formed on 1 November 1943 in Norway. Only the staff for the battalion could be created. The headquarters staff of *I. Jäger-Bataillon* of *Feldregiment der Luftwaffe 502* was used to create this battalion staff. The battalion never achieved active status and was disbanded in the summer of 1944. **Landesschützen-Bataillon der Luftwaffe 3** was formed on 1 November 1943 in Norway. Only the staff for the battalion could be created. The headquarters staff of *II. Jäger-Bataillon* of *Feldregiment der Luftwaffe 502* was used to create this battalion staff. The battalion never achieved active status and was disbanded in the summer of 1944. **Landesschützen-Bataillon der Luftwaffe 4** was created in April 1944 in Holland. It contained five rifle companies. In December 1944 it was renamed *Luftwaffen-Festungs-Bataillon XXI*. **Landesschützen-Bataillon der Luftwaffe 5** was formed in the winter of 1943/1944 in Holland with five companies. It was renamed *Luftwaffen-Festungs-Bataillon XXII* in October 1944. The battalion served in Holland and contained three companies. **Landesschützen-Bataillon der Luftwaffe 6** was established in the winter of 1943/1944 with four rifle companies. It may have been employed in the city of Breslau in 1944–1945.
22. Tessin, *Verbände und Truppen*, vol. 11, p. 10.
23. Ibid., vol. 8, p. 43.
24. Samuel W. Mitcham, *The Desert Fox in Normandy. Rommel's Defense of Fortress Europe*. Westport: Praeger Publishers, 1997, p. 91.
25. Ziemke, *The German Northern Theater of Operations*, p. 310.
26. In December 1944 General Rendulic assumed command of German forces in Norway, and General Falkenhorst returned to Germany. The *20. Gebirgsarmee* now absorbed the Army of Norway. The forces shifted back to Germany included: *XVIII. Gebirgsarmeekorps* (January 1945), *6. SS Gebirgs Division 'Nord'* (November 1944), *2. Gebirgs Division* (January 1945), *163. Infanterie-Division* (January–February 1945), *169. Infanterie-Division* (February–March 1945) and *199. Infanterie-Division* (April 1945).
27. Schramm, *Kriegstagebuch des Oberkommandos*, vol. 7, p. 920.
28. Schmitz et al., *Die Deutschen Divisionen*, vol. 3, p. 121.
29. One source (Mehner and Teuber, *Die Luftwaffe*) states that Lohmann did not assume command of the division until 24 December 1942, or fully one month after Schmitz claims that he took over control.

30. Mehner, *Die Deutsche Wehrmacht*, p. 124.
31. Mehner, *Die Geheimen Tagesberichte*, vol. 12, p. 459.
32. On 25 August 1943 Schulte-Mattler became the commander of *Flak Abteilung 781*.

15. Luftwaffen-Felddivision

1. Barry C. Rosch, *Luftwaffe Codes, Markings and Units 1939–1945*. Atglen: Schiffer Publishing Ltd, 1995, p. 259.
2. Ibid., p. 301.
3. Hooton, *Eagle in Flames*, p. 182.
4. *Luftwaffen-Felddivision 'Südost'* would soon be redesignated *15. Luftwaffen-Felddivision*.
5. Excerpt from the personal war diary of *General der Flieger* Alfred Mahncke.
6. Jochen Mahncke, *For Kaiser and Hitler: From Military Aviator to High Command – The Memoirs of Luftwaffe General Alfred Mahncke 1910–1945*. Sussex: Tattered Flag, 2012.
7. Seaton, *The Russo-German War*, p. 322.
8. Manstein, *Lost Victories*, p. 321.
9. Excerpt from the personal war diary of *General der Flieger* Alfred Mahncke.
10. Mellenthin, *Panzer Battles*, p. 193.
11. Ibid., p. 191
12. Stoves, *Die 22. Panzer-Division*, p. 83.
13. Ibid.
14. Excerpt from the personal war diary of *General der Flieger* Alfred Mahncke; Mahncke, *For Kaiser and Hitler*, pp. 331–3.
15. Seaton, *The Russo-German War*, pp. 323–4.
16. NARA, T-314, Roll 45, Frame 0417, *Anlagen zum KTBB, Blatt 3, Eingegangene Meldungen, 28/12/42, Nr. 29711/7*.
17. These two German divisions had to be diverted to the 3rd Romanian Army before the Stalingrad relief effort was launched.
18. This Panzer-Division, which was thrown in to help the 3rd Romanian Army at the beginning of the Soviet offensive, proved to be a mediocre unit, incapable of full offensive action after the heavy losses it incurred in November 1942.
19. Effectively destroyed in a fighting withdrawal on 19 December 1942.
20. Arriving from Army Group Don reserve. One regiment was used under *Kampfgruppe Stumpfeld*, operating by the 3rd Romanian Army.
21. Moving forward to attack.
22. This division was trapped inside the Stalingrad pocket. It was supposed to launch a breakout attempt from inside the pocket when the relief forces came within 30km of the cauldron.
23. Placed 'for special employment' directly under Army Group Don.
24. *6. Panzer-Division* never took part in the Stalingrad relief effort, having been diverted to the Don bend to counter Soviet tank attacks in that area.
25. Although earmarked for *LVII. Panzerkorps*, the division was not ready by the time the offensive was launched.
26. On 27 November 1942 the tank strength of this division was sixty-seven tanks (all types).
27. Glantz, *From the Don*, p. 380.
28. This regiment was part of *403. Sicherungs-Division*.
29. Composed mainly of German artillerymen.
30. *Oberst* Rainer Stahel, a German *Luftwaffe* officer who organized ground crews, *Flak* and rear area support units. Initially earmarked as part of the forming *15. Luftwaffen-Felddivision*, but later absorbed into *8. Luftwaffen-Felddivision*. Stahel would later take part in the suppression of the Warsaw Uprising in August and September 1944.
31. The unit was used independently under Army Group Don, but was part of *384. Infanterie-Division* (as was *Kampfgruppe Adam*). These two battlegroups were created on 12 December 1942. On 14 December, after a heavy Russian tank assault against the defence lines of the division by 7th Tank Corps, between the Don bridge at Werchne-Tschirskij and the town of Erickij, the

384. Infanterie-Division split into four separate battlegroups: *Kampfgruppe Heilman*, *Kampfgruppe Adam*, *Kampfgruppe Mikosch* and *Kampfgruppe Goebel*.
32. The bulk of the division arrived in the first week of December 1942 and operated basically together with *294. Infanterie-Division*. Elements were still arriving on 22 December 1942.
33. The division included *Panzerjäger-Kompanie 11*.
34. This emergency SS brigade was created in November 1942 using the following units: *VII. SS-Wach-Bataillon der Leibstandarte Adolf Hitler* (Berlin SS Guard Battalion No. 7 'Adolf Hitler'); *I. Bataillon der SS Panzergrenadier-Regiment 3 (SS Das Reich Division)*; *I. Bataillon der SS Panzergrenadier-Regiment 7 (SS Polizei Division)*; *Luftwaffen-Feldbataillon 100 'Hermann Göring'*; *Panzerjäger Kompanie 518* (*Oberleutnant* Wilde). On 1 January 1943 it was attached to *6. Panzer-Division*. The brigade was disbanded on 6 March 1943.
35. For anti-tank support, *Gruppe Kreysing* contained *Panzerjäger-Kompanie 515* and *Panzerjäger-Kompanie 516*.
36. Schramm, *Kriegstagebuch des Oberkommandos*, vol. 5, p. 5.
37. *Kessel* – German word meaning 'cauldron.'
38. This was a region between Stalingrad and the Caucasus, where the Kalmuck people lived. Elista was the capital of the Kalmuck SSR. The Kalmuck people aided the Germans by forming a cavalry formation which served under German control from 1942 to 1945. For a complete history of this and other esoteric formations from the Soviet Union, see Antonio Munoz, *Hitler's Muslim Allies: German Army and Waffen-SS Islamic Volunteers 1941–1945*. Barnsley: Frontline Books, 2025.
39. Excerpt from the personal war diary of *General der Flieger* Alfred Mahncke.
40. Haupt, *Die Deutschen Luftwaffen-Felddivisionen*, p. 62.
41. Ibid.
42. Excerpt from the personal war diary of *General der Flieger* Alfred Mahncke.
43. *Armee-Abteilung Fretter-Pico* had been established on 23 December 1942, by upgrading the existing *XXX. Armeekorps* headquarters. Its mission was to seal the gap between Army Groups 'B' and 'Don' after the Soviet breakthrough near the Don River and the collapse of the Italian 8th Army. As of 1 February 1943, *Armee-Abteilung Fretter-Pico* contained: *3. Gebirgs-Division* (part of *Kampfgruppe Kreysing*), *304. Infanterie-Division* (recently arrived from France), *305. Infanterie-Division*, the Italian Ravenna Infantry Division, *SS-Brigade Schuldt*, *Kampfgruppe Nagel* (various battlegroups), and the Italian Black Shirt (CCNN) 'XXIII Marzo' Legion, which was the size of a brigade.
44. Excerpt from the personal war diary of *General der Flieger* Alfred Mahncke.
45. Stoves, *Die 22. Panzer-Division*, p. 83.
46. This bridge at Sporny was being held by weak elements of *16. Infanterie-Division (motorisiert)*.
47. Ibid.
48. Carrell, *Scorched Earth*, p. 132. *Kosaken-Kavallerie-Regiment von Jungschultz* was led by *Oberstleutnant* Werner Jungschultz von Roebern. This regiment attached itself to *444. Sicherungs-Division* in February 1943. It would end up serving as a cavalry regiment in the German-sponsored *XV. Kosaken-Kavallerie-Korps* (15th Cossack Cavalry Corps) in 1944.
49. The bayonet strength of a formation is the number of men actually fighting on the front lines.
50. Werner Haupt, *Die Schlachten der Heeresgruppe Süd*. Friedberg: Podzun Pallas Verlag, 1987, p. 281.
51. Keilig, *Das Deutsche Heer*, pt. 130, p. 9.
52. Glantz, *From the Don*, p. 388.
53. Tessin, *Verbände und Truppen*, vol. 3, p. 5.
54. Carrell, *Scorched Earth*, page 314.
55. Karl Ullrich, *Wie Ein Fels im Meer. Kriegsgeschichte der 3. SS Panzer-Division 'Totenkopf'*. Osnabrück: Munin Verlag, 1987, vol. 2, pp. 235–6.
56. Ruffner, *Luftwaffe Field Divisions*, p. 16.
57. Haupt, *Die Deutschen Luftwaffen-Felddivisionen*, p. 62; Carrell, *Scorched Earth*, p. 316.
58. Haupt, *Die Deutschen Luftwaffen-Felddivisionen*, p. 62.

59. Mueller-Hillebrand, *Das Heer*, p. 224.
60. When *Luftwaffen-Jäger-Regiment 29* was activated and deemed combat ready, Eberhard Dewald's *Jäger-Regiment 30* was already heavily engaged in Proletarskaya and beginning to withdraw. This left *Oberst* Heinrich Conrady, the commander of *Jäger-Regiment 29*, to assume unofficial and temporary command of *15. Luftwaffen-Felddivision* until General Spang could arrive and assume control.
61. Dewald was not the designated divisional commander at this time (Spange was), but while Spange was only just arriving at the front, it was Dewald who ran the division while Conrady was fighting for his life at Proletarskaya. Operational control first fell on *Oberst* (Colonel) Eberhard Dewald, since he led *Luftwaffen-Jäger-Regiment 30*, the first unit deemed combat ready. This was also confirmed by Jochen Mahncke, the son of *Generalleutnant* Mahncke, who was kind enough to share his father's war diary with me in order to research the history of the *15. Luftwaffen-Felddivision*.
62. Although *Generalleutnant* Willibald Spange had officially assumed command of the division as of 14 January 1943, it took him nearly two weeks to reach his new post. In the interim, Dewald continued to hold command.
63. On 7 November 1943 Spange was placed on the *OKL Führerreserve* list, but he did not leave the division until 12 December 1943.
64. Mehner, *Die Deutsche Wehrmacht*, p. 189.
65. *Hauptmann* Wolf left the division on 22 March 1943 and was reassigned as the commander of *Feldersatz Bataillon / Luftflotte 1*.
66. Parachute commander *Major* August Fischer-See was born on 4 December 1911 in the town of Konjik, in Bosnia-Herzegovina, of an Austrian father and Hungarian mother.
67. Since the artillery regiment was not yet formed at this time, we can readily surmise that this was the divisional *Flak* battalion which was operational in early 1943. In October 1943 it was permanently detached from the division and became *I. Flak-Bataillon, Flak-Regiment 46*; Keilig, *Das Deutsche Heer*, pt. 130, p. 10.
68. Mehner and Teuber, *Die Luftwaffe*, p. 89.

16. Luftwaffen-Felddivision

1. Dunn, *Second Front Now*, p. 239.
2. Tessin, *Verbände und Truppen*, vol. 1, p. 67.
3. Schmitz et al., *Die Deutschen Divisionen*, vol. 3, p. 221.
4. Of this number, 279 were MG-15 and 207 were MG-34 light machine guns.
5. Keilig, *Das Deutsche Heer*, pt. 130, p. 10; Haupt, *Die Deutschen Luftwaffen-Felddivisionen*, p. 63.
6. BA MA, M-34, *Truppendienstliche Befehlsgliederung*, WBN 1.2.1943.
7. Dunn, *Second Front Now*, p. 235.
8. Ibid., p. 244.
9. BA MA, M-34, *Truppendienstliche Befehlsgliederung*, WBN 1.6.1943.
10. This was the communication company.
11. *Radfahraufklärungs-Schwadron* – 'Bicycle Reconnaissance Squadron'.
12. Main dressing station.
13. Ambulance platoon.
14. Supply company.
15. Veterinary company.
16. Mitcham, *The Desert Fox in Normandy*, p. 12.
17. Haupt, *Die Deutschen Luftwaffen-Felddivisionen*, p. 63.
18. Tessin, *Verbände und Truppen*, vol. 5, p. 135.
19. Nafziger, *The German Order of Battle*, p. 161.
20. Ibid.
21. Brün Meyer, *Dienstalterliste der Waffen SS. SS-Obergruppenführer bis SS-Hauptsturmführer. Stand vom 1. Juli 1944*. Osnabrück: Biblio Verlag, 1987, p. 11.
22. BA MA, M-36, *Generalkommando LXXXVIII.A.K. Abt.Ic. Nr.1262/44 gKdos., K.H.Qu., den 10.5.44*.

23. 4th Company of Fortress Cadre Troop, *LXXXVIII. Armeekorps*.
24. Police Artillery Battery 'Scheveningen'.
25. Reserve and Training Regiment 'Hermann Göring' and SS Training and Replacement Battalion 4.
26. Mitcham, *The Desert Fox in Normandy*, p. 39.
27. F.W. Winterbotham, *The Ultra Secret*. New York: Harper & Row Publishers, 1974, p. 127.
28. Gordon A. Harrison, *The United States Army in World War Two. The European Theater of Operations – Cross Channel Attack*. Washington DC: Office of the Chief of Military History, 1951, p. 446.
29. Hubert Meyer, *The History of the 12. SS Panzer-Division Hitler-Jugend*. Winnipeg: J.J. Fedorowicz Publishing Inc., 1994, p. 96.
30. Ibid.
31. NARA Microfilm Series T-311, Roll 28, Frame 7034124. *OB West Ia Nr. 5185/44 g. Kdos, 1.7.44*.
32. Ibid., Frame 7034134. *OB West Ia Nr. 5197/44 g. Kdos, 2.7.44*.
33. Mitcham, *The Desert Fox in Normandy*, p. 160.
34. Hans von Luck, *Panzer Commander. The memoirs of Colonel Hans von Luck*. Westport: Praeger Publishers, 1989, p. 169.
35. NARA Microfilm T-313, Roll 420, Frame 8713976, *Panzer Gruppe West Ia Nr. 522/44 g. Kdos. v. 23.7.44*.
36. Mitcham, *The Desert Fox in Normandy*, p. 351.
37. Meyer, *The History of the 12. SS Panzer-Division*, p. 141.
38. Ibid., p. 144.
39. Ibid., p. 143.
40. BA-MA RH 10/349, *Lieferungen der Pz.Fahrzeuge*.
41. Meyer, *The History of the 12. SS Panzer-Division*, p. 151.
42. Ibid., p. 155.
43. Mitcham, *The Desert Fox in Normandy*, p. 170.
44. Chester Wilmot, *The Struggle for Europe*. New York: Carrol & Graf Publishers, 1954, p. 356.
45. Ibid.
46. Mitcham, *The Desert Fox in Normandy*, p. 173.
47. Meyer, *The History of the 12. SS Panzer-Division*, p. 157.
48. Schramm, *Kriegstagebuch des Oberkommandos*, vol. 7, p. 334.
49. Mueller-Hillebrand, *Das Heer*, p. 307.
50. Mitcham, *The Desert Fox in Normandy*, p. 177.
51. Tessin, *Verbände und Truppen*, vol. 4, p. 32.
52. The missing figures were most likely soldiers who were taken prisoner.
53. Of this number, 198,616 were lost between June and August. The month of September was even more disastrous; total losses for the month of September alone numbered 164,384 men killed, wounded or missing.
54. Haupt, *Die Deutschen Infanterie-Divisionen*, vol. 3, p. 95.
55. Schramm, *Kriegstagebuch des Oberkommandos*, vol. 7, p. 376.
56. Seaton, *The Fall of Fortress Europe*, p. 107.
57. This age was considered good since many static and fortress divisions in France and the Low Countries contained men of an even older age group.
58. Ruffner, *Luftwaffe Field Divisions*, p. 19.
59. Ibid., p. 20.
60. Mehner, *Die Deutsche Wehrmacht*, p. 124.
61. One source proposes that Sievers assumed command of the division on 22 August 1943.
62. Denzel, *Die Luftwaffen-Felddivisionen*, p. 29. One source, Mehner and Teuber, *Die Luftwaffe*, p. 85, says that Sievers held this post until 23 September 1943.
63. BA MA, M-45, *Kriegsgliederung, Luftwaffen-Felddivision 16*, OOB WBN 12.02.43.

64. Otto Wilhelm was promoted to *Hauptmann* on 1 March 1942. In December 1942 he was appointed as 'Ia' of *16. Luftwaffen-Felddivision*. On 15 March 1943 he was temporarily detached from the division so he could attend the *Heereskriegsakademie*. He returned before the end of 1943.
65. Mehner and Teuber, *Die Luftwaffe*, p. 89, says that Palitzsch held this post until November 1943.
66. Ibid., p. 266.

17. Luftwaffen-Felddivision

1. Mitcham, *Hitler's Legions*, p. 434.
2. Dunn, *Second Front Now*, p. 239.
3. Tessin, *Verbände und Truppen*, vol. 4, p. 73.
4. Mehner, *Die Geheimen Tagesberichte*, vol. 6, p. 68.
5. Ibid., p. 77.
6. Ibid.
7. Ibid., p. 139.
8. Haupt, *Die Deutschen Luftwaffen-Felddivisionen*, p. 64.
9. Tessin, *Verbände und Truppen*, vol. 4, p. 73.
10. Ruffner, *Luftwaffe Field Divisions*, p. 19; Alan F. Wilt, *The Atlantic Wall. Hitler's Defenses in the West, 1941–1944*. Ames: Iowa State University Press, 1975, p. 117.
11. The Brest garrison was just over 2,000 men. When Brest became surrounded, the remnants of *2. Fallschirmjäger-Division*, plus the *266.* and *343. Infanterie-Divisions*, withdrew into the port city. The number of men who now defended Brest included 11,444 Army, 11,718 Navy, 4,261 *Luftwaffe* personnel and 1,922 'other' force troops (*Organization Todt, Polizei, SS, Gestapo, NSKK*, etc.). In total the strength of the garrison increased to 29,000+ men.
12. On 21 August 1944 this small garrison force was augmented by troops who became trapped and withdrew to the French coastal port. These included 11,200 men from the *Heer*, 2,000 from the *Luftwaffe* and 8,900 from the *Kriegsmarine*, including naval coastal artillery units. In addition, there were also 2,500 Eastern troops, plus 2,800 'other' service and support troops (*Organization Todt, Polizei, SS, Gestapo, NSKK*, etc.). In total, about 29,900 German troops were surrounded there as of 21 August 1944.
13. Dunn, *Second Front Now*, p. 126.
14. Wilt, *The Atlantic Wall*, p. 98.
15. Ruffner, *Luftwaffe Field Divisions*, p. 20.
16. Denzel, *Die Luftwaffen-Felddivisionen*, p. 29.
17. Haupt, *Die Deutschen Luftwaffen-Felddivisionen*, p. 64.
18. Nafziger, *The German Order of Battle*, p. 163.
19. Tessin, *Verbände und Truppen*, vol. 14, p. 143.
20. Ruffner, *Luftwaffe Field Divisions*, p. 20.
21. Tessin, *Verbände und Truppen*, vol. 13, p. 43; Muñoz et al., *The East Came West*, p. 176.
22. Ruffner, *Luftwaffe Field Divisions*, p. 20.
23. Mitcham, *The Desert Fox in Normandy*, p. 185.
24. Ruffner, *Luftwaffe Field Divisions*, p. 21.
25. Mehner, *Die Geheimen Tagesberichte*, vol. 10, p. 438.
26. Ibid., p. 460.
27. Ibid., p. 463.
28. Haupt, *Die Deutschen Infanterie-Divisionen*, vol. 3, p. 89.
29. Mueller-Hillebrand, *Das Heer*, p. 307.
30. He was later promoted to *Generalmajor*.
31. Mehner, *Die Deutsche Wehrmacht*, p. 189, claims that Olbrich was a *Generalmajor* and that he held the post of divisional commander until 30 October 1943.
32. Schmitz et al., *Die Deutschen Divisionen*, vol. 1, p. 11.
33. Later reached the rank of *Generalleutnant*.
34. Denzel, *Die Luftwaffen-Felddivisionen*, p. 29, claims that Höcker held this post until October 1944.

35. Warning was promoted to *Oberstleutnant* (lieutenant colonel) in the summer of 1944. Mehner, *Die Deutsche Wehrmacht*, p. 124.
36. On 7 February 1944 Dr Hans Weichert was transferred out of *Felddivision 17 (L)* and made divisional doctor for *1. Jagddivision*, a unit of German ME-109 and FW-190 fighter planes.
37. Colonel Fuchs had a doctorate degree in engineering.
38. Mehner and Teuber, *Die Luftwaffe*, p. 88.
39. *Hauptmann* Walter Tarnowski served in this capacity until September 1944, when *Felddivision 17 (L)* was disbanded and the remnants used to help flesh out *167. Volksgrenadier Division*, which was being organized in Slovakia. *Hauptmann* Tarnowski was inducted into the *Heer*, and his signals company now became the basis for the communications company in *167. Volksgrenadier-Division*.

18. Luftwaffen-Felddivision

1. Mehner and Teuber, *Die Luftwaffe*, p. 91.
2. Nafziger, *The German Order of Battle*, p. 164.
3. Keilig, *Das Deutsche Heer*, pt. 130, p. 10.
4. Tessin, *Verbände und Truppen*, vol. 4, p. 105.
5. Schmitz et al., *Die Deutschen Divisionen*, vol. 3, p. 53.
6. Haupt, *Die Deutschen Luftwaffen-Felddivisionen*, p. 81.
7. Denzel, *Die Luftwaffen-Felddivisionen*, p. 30.
8. Mitcham, *The Desert Fox in Normandy*, p. 210.
9. Nafziger, *The German Order of Battle*, p. 165.
10. Mehner, *Die Geheimen Tagesberichte*, vol. 10, p. 469.
11. Matthew Cooper, *The German Army 1933–1945*. Chelsea: Scarborough House, 1978, p. 510.
12. Mehner, *Die Geheimen Tagesberichte*, vol. 10, p. 466.
13. Ruffner, *Luftwaffe Field Divisions*, p. 23.
14. Ibid.
15. Milton Shulman, *Defeat in the West*. New York: E.P. Dutton & Co. Inc., 1948, pp. 174–5.
16. Ruffner, *Luftwaffe Field Divisions*, p. 24.
17. Ibid.
18. Wilmot, *The Struggle for Europe*, p. 471.
19. Mueller-Hillebrand, *Das Heer*, p. 307.
20. Haupt, *Die Deutschen Luftwaffen-Felddivisionen*, p. 81.
21. Ibid.
22. *Oberst* Ferdinand Wilhelm Freiherr von Stein-Libenstein zu Barchfeld. Prior to being the divisional commander of *18. Luftwaffen-Felddivision*, he had been the commander of *Luftwaffen-Infanterie-Regiment 'Moskau'* in 1942. On 5 April 1943 he was reassigned to the *OKL Führerreserve* and left *18. Luftwaffen-Felddivision* on 19 April.
23. Mueller-Hillebrand, *Das Heer*, p. 307.
24. Andries J. Kursietis, *The Wehrmacht at War 1939–1945. The Units and Commanders of the German Ground Forces during World War 2*. Soesterberg: Uitgeverij Aspekt B.V, UK edition, 1999, p. 244. One source, Haupt, *Die Deutschen Luftwaffen-Felddivisionen*, p. 82, says that *Generalmajor* Fritz Reinshagen never assumed command of the 18th *Luftwaffe* Division, although another source, Mitcham, *Hitler's Legions*, p. 435, mentions that he assumed command in 1943.
25. Rupprecht was formerly commandant of Regensburg *(Wehrkreis XIII)* and later directed *327. Infanterie-Division* on the Russian Front in 1942. One source, Haupt, *Die Deutschen Luftwaffen-Felddivisionen*, p. 82, says that *General* Rupprecht (*Heer*) commanded *18. Luftwaffen-Felddivision* from August 1943. Additionally, it also states that *Generalmajor* Fritz Reinshagen never assumed command of the division.
26. Not to be mistaken with Army *Generalmajor* Henning von Treskow, who was involved in the 20 July 1944 bomb plot to kill Hitler and committed suicide the following day.
27. Mehner and Teuber, *Die Luftwaffe*, p. 266.

28. Schmitz et al., *Die Deutschen Divisionen*, vol. 3, p. 54.
29. Mehner and Teuber, *Die Luftwaffe*, p. 85; Haupt, *Die Deutschen Luftwaffen-Felddivisionen*, p. 82; Mitcham, *Hitler's Legions*, p. 435.
30. Apparently, Reinshagen held the post of regimental commander and was appointed to command the entire division in August 1943.

19. Luftwaffen-Sturm-Division

1. Tessin, *Verbände und Truppen*, vol. 4, p. 125.
2. Haupt, *Die Deutschen Luftwaffen-Felddivisionen*, p. 82. NARA T-312, Roll 300, Frames 0070–0071.
3. Dunn, *Second Front Now*, p. 98.
4. Mehner, *Die Geheimen Tagesberichte*, vol. 6, p. 174.
5. Ibid., p. 177.
6. Ibid., p. 179.
7. Ibid., p. 181.
8. Ibid., p. 183.
9. Dunn, *Second Front Now*, pp. 129, 130; Mitcham, *The Desert Fox in Normandy*, p. 12.
10. Mehner, *Die Geheimen Tagesberichte*, vol. 7, p. 19.
11. Ibid., p. 43.
12. Ibid., p. 47.
13. Haupt, *Die Deutschen Luftwaffen-Felddivisionen*, p. 82.
14. Nafziger, *The German Order of Battle*, p. 166.
15. Mitcham, *The Desert Fox in Normandy*, p. 38.
16. Harrison, *Cross Channel Attack*, p. 235.
17. Mitcham, *Hitler's Legions*, p. 436.
18. Denzel, *Die Luftwaffen-Felddivisionen*, p. 30.
19. Mitcham, *The Desert Fox in Normandy*, p. 82.
20. When the German Army absorbed these *Luftwaffe* infantry divisions on 1 November 1943, it ordered the transfer of the assault guns from *16. Luftwaffen-Felddivision* to be incorporated into the forming *19. Felddivision (L)*.
21. Mitcham, *The Desert Fox in Normandy*, p. 39.
22. Haupt, *Die Deutschen Luftwaffen-Felddivisionen*, p. 82.
23. Schramm, *Kriegstagebuch des Oberkommandos*, vol. 7, p. 309; Donald S. Detwiler, ed., with Charles Burdick and Jürgen Rohwer, *World War Two German Military Studies. A Collection of 213 Special Reports on the Second World War Prepared by Former Officers of the Wehrmacht for the United States Army*. 24 vols. Vol. 10: *The OKW War Diary Series, part IV (April–December 1944)*. New York: Garland Publishing, 1979, p. 24.
24. F.H. Hinsley, ed., with E.E. Thomas, C.F.G. Ransom and R.C. Knight, *British Intelligence in the Second World War*. London: Her Majesty's Stationery Office, 1984, vol. 2, pt. I, p. 205.
25. Ralph Bennett, *Ultra and Mediterranean Strategy*. New York: William Morrow & Co., Inc., 1989, pp. 294–6.
26. *157. Gebirgs Division* had been created by simply renaming *157. Reserve Division* on 1 October 1944.
27. Haupt, *Die Deutschen Luftwaffen-Felddivisionen*, p. 83.
28. At this time a third unit under the control of the corps was *16. SS Panzer Grenadier Division Reichsführer SS*.
29. Mehner, *Die Geheimen Tagesberichte*, vol. 10, p. 503.
30. General Frido von Senger und Etterlein, *Neither Fear nor Hope. The Wartime Memoirs of the German Defender of Cassino*. Novato: Presidio Press, 1989, p. 259.
31. Ernest C. Fisher, *Cassino to the Alps. The Mediterranean Theater of Operations. United States Army in World War Two*. Washington DC: Center of Military History, United States Army, 1989, p. 24.
32. Fisher, *Cassino to the Alps*, p. 24.
33. Ruffner, *Luftwaffe Field Divisions*, p. 36.

34. Senger und Etterlein, *Neither Fear nor Hope*, pp. 259–60.
35. Fisher, *Cassino to the Alps*, p. 262.
36. Haupt, *Die Deutschen Luftwaffen-Felddivisionen*, p. 83.
37. Fisher, *Cassino to the Alps*, p. 260.
38. Ruffner, *Luftwaffe Field Divisions*, p. 36.
39. Fisher, *Cassino to the Alps*, p. 273.
40. Ibid., p. 274.
41. Ruffner, *Luftwaffe Field Divisions*, p. 36.
42. Haupt, *Die Deutschen Luftwaffen-Felddivisionen*, p. 83.
43. Ruffner, *Luftwaffe Field Divisions*, p. 36.
44. Schramm, *Kriegstagebuch des Oberkommandos*, vol. 7, p. 583.
45. Mueller-Hillebrand, *Das Heer*, p. 307; Denzel, *Die Luftwaffen-Felddivisionen*, p. 30; Keilig, *Das Deutsche Heer*, pt. 130, p. 11.
46. Tessin, *Verbände und Truppen*, vol. 4, p. 116.
47. Denzel, *Die Luftwaffen-Felddivisionen*, p. 30.
48. Haupt, *Die Deutschen Luftwaffen-Felddivisionen*, p. 83.
49. *Volksgrenadier* – the literal translation is 'People's Grenadier'.
50. Haupt, *Die Deutschen Infanterie-Divisionen*, vol. I, pp. 75–6; Müller-Hillebrand, *Das Heer*, vol. 3, p. 307; Denzel, *Die Luftwaffen-Felddivisionen*, p. 30.
51. Kursietis, *The Wehrmacht at War*, p. 244.
52. Plocher was an *Oberst* (colonel) until 1 March 1943 when he was promoted to general. He was holder of the Knight's Cross, which he had won while holding the post of Chief of Staff of a *Fliegerkorps* on 20 April 1942: Scheibert, *Die Träger des Deutschen Kreuzes in Gold*, p. 333.
53. Erich Bäßler was an army general. He was promoted to the rank of *Generalleutnant* on 1 January 1944.
54. BA MA, M 37, *Personalakte gibt ab 16.09.43. Tätigkeitbericht für den Monat September 1943, Generalkommando LXXXIX A.K. Abt. IIa gibt am 11.9.43: 'GenMaj. Bäßler, Erich, wird ab 16.9.43 zur 19.Lw.Felddiv. zur Einareitung als Führer einer Stellungsdiv. Kommandiert.*
55. Henze was the former commander of *Panzergrenadier-Regiment 63*. He was awarded the Knight's Cross on 15 January 1944. Keilig, *Rangliste Des Deutschen Heeres*, p. 60.
56. Mehner, *Die Deutsche Wehrmacht*, p. 124. Hildebrand was promoted to *Major* on 1 November 1943.
57. In February 1944 a third *Jäger-Regiment* was raised by removing *III. Jäger-Bataillon* in *Jäger-Regiments 37 (L)* and *38 (L)* and renaming them as *I. and II. Jäger-Bataillon / Jäger-Regiment 45 (L)*. Tessin, *Verbände und Truppen*, vol. 15, p. 127.

20. Luftwaffen-Sturm-Division

1. Haupt, *Die Deutschen Luftwaffen-Felddivisionen*, p. 83.
2. Mehner, *Die Deutsche Wehrmacht*, p. 267.
3. Tessin, *Verbände und Truppen*, vol. 15, p. 127.
4. *Ostheer*: the German Army on the Eastern Front.
5. *Radfahr*: bicycle.
6. MI6 – British foreign intelligence.
7. Bennett, *Ultra and Mediterranean Strategy*, p. 296.
8. Hinsley et al., *British Intelligence*, vol. 3, pt 1, p. 204.
9. Ibid.
10. Haupt, *Die Deutschen Luftwaffen-Felddivisionen*, p. 84.
11. Fisher, *Cassino to the Alps*, p. 232.
12. Ibid., p. 233.
13. Schmitz et al., *Die Deutschen Divisionen*, vol. 4, p. 550.
14. Fisher, *Cassino to the Alps*, p. 239.

15. The French expeditionary force was grouped into a corps command. It contained four divisions, of which three were colonial units made up of Moroccans and Algerians led by a core of French officers and NCOs. The corps contained the 1st Free French Division, the 2nd Moroccan Infantry Division, the 3rd Algerian Infantry Division and the 4th Moroccan Infantry Division.
16. Fisher, *Cassino to the Alps*, p. 265.
17. *Fusilier-Bataillon 19 (L)* now became *Fusilier-Bataillon 20 (L)*, while the other component units from *19. Felddivision (L)* were likewise renumbered with the ancillary '20' number.
18. Haupt, *Die Deutschen Luftwaffen-Felddivisionen*, p. 85.
19. Denzel, *Die Luftwaffen-Felddivisionen*, p. 31.
20. Haupt, *Die Deutschen Luftwaffen-Felddivisionen*, p. 85.
21. Denzel, *Die Luftwaffen-Felddivisionen*, p. 31.
22. Fisher, *Cassino to the Alps*, p. 348.
23. Ready, *The Forgotten Axis*, p. 360.
24. Schramm, *Kriegstagebuch des Oberkommandos*, vol. 7, p. 584.
25. Mueller-Hillebrand, *Das Heer*, p. 307.
26. Tessin, *Verbände und Truppen*, vol. 13, p. 338.
27. Ibid.
28. *Oberst* Völcker was the 'Ia' of the division, and assumed command when *Generalmajor* Crisolli was killed. *Oberst* Völcker was captured by the Allies in November 1944.
29. There is an unresolved contradiction as to who was 'Ia' of the division: Völcker or Lämpe.
30. Mehner, *Die Deutsche Wehrmacht*, p. 124.
31. Shortly after taking over command of *I. Jäger-Bataillon*, *Oberstleutnant* Eugen Triep transferred to the divisional staff of *20. Luftwaffen-Sturm-Division*, where he was given the divisional staff position of 'IIa'.
32. The initial supply of 75mm anti-tank guns was a blend of the French 75mm guns mounted on German 75mm gun carriages. In the autumn of 1943 these French guns were withdrawn and replaced with the German 75mm anti-tank gun Pak 40, the abbreviation for *Panzerabwehrkanone 40*.
33. One company was motorized, another was horse-drawn. The engineering equipment employed by this battalion included captured French bridge-building hardware.
34. This replacement battalion had around 1,000 men.

Division Meindl / 21. Luftwaffen-Felddivision

1. *Oberst* Aue went on to command *Jäger-Regiment 39 (L)* of *20. Luftwaffen-Sturm-Division*.
2. Ruffner, *Luftwaffe Field Divisions*, p. 8.
3. Oskars Perro, *Fortress Cholm*. Ontario: Kurland Publishing, 1981, p. 89.
4. This company-strength unit was led by *Hauptmann* Spittäler.
5. Lukas, Richard C. *Forgotten Holocaust. The Poles Under German Occupation 1939–1944*. Lexington: University Press of Kentucky, 1986, p. 75.
6. Georg Schlaug, *Die Deutschen Lastensegler Verbänd 1937–1945*. Stuttgart: Motorbuch Verlag, 1985, p. 70.
7. Ibid., p. 82.
8. Perro, *Fortress Cholm*, p. 76.
9. Ibid., p. 191.
10. Denzel, *Die Luftwaffen-Felddivisionen*, p. 32.
11. Tessin, *Verbände und Truppen*, vol. 2, p. 64.
12. Translation: 'Ski Battalion of Air Fleet 1'.
13. Haupt, *Die Deutschen Luftwaffen-Felddivisionen*, p. 126.
14. Werner Haupt, *Die 8. Panzer-Division im Zweiten Weltkrieg*. Friedberg: Podzun Pallas Verlag, 1987, p. 221.
15. Translation: '5th Motorcycle Battalion.'
16. Haupt, *Die 8. Panzer-Division*, p. 221.
17. Ziemke, *Stalingrad to Berlin*, p. 421.

18. *Luftwaffen-Jäger-Regiment 43* and *Luftwaffen-Jäger-Regiment 44* were originally earmarked for a second air force field division, 22. *Luftwaffen-Felddivision*, which was in the process of being established. However, it ended up being disbanded before it was fully established. It was at this time that one of its assigned regiments, *Luftwaffen-Jäger-Regiment 43*, was assigned to 21. *Luftwaffen-Felddivision*.
19. BA MA, M-68, Blatt 13, *Schematische Kriegsgliederung, Stand: 14.10.1943*, OKH Gen. Stand Heeres Op. Abt. III, Nr. 17934.
20. Lodieux, 'Des Sturmgeschütz dans les divisions', p. 8.
21. Nafziger, *The German Order of Battle*, p. 169.
22. Lodieux, 'Des Sturmgeschütz dans les divisions', p. 10.
23. Tessin, *Verbände und Truppen*, vol. 5, p. 113.
24. BA MA, M52, Luftkommando I – II Nr. 0113K/43 geh. Ab. 23 der 12 (Feld). IIa 1.
25. BA MA, M35, II Nk Meldung, Luftflottenkommando 1, 01195/43 geh. AS g.3 12 (Feld.) IIb/1, H. Qu. 14.12.43.
26. Newton, *Retreat from Leningrad*, p. 37.
27. Haupt, *Leningrad*, p. 261.
28. BA, RL34, *Verbände und Einheiten der Luftwaffen-Infanterie Überlieferungsverweis*: RS 2-1/15: *Tagesmeldungen und Befehle*, Aug. 1944.
29. J. Schröder and Joachim Schultz-Naumann, *Geschichte der Pommeranische 32. Infanterie-Division*. Bad Neuheim: Podzun Pallas Verlag, 1956, p. 229.
30. Haupt, *Army Group North*, p. 240.
31. *Segewald* is the German spelling for the Latvian town of Sigulda, in the Vidzeme region. It lies about 53km northeast of the Latvian capital, Riga.
32. Newton, *Retreat from Leningrad*, p. 284.
33. Ibid.
34. Arturs Silgailis, *Latvian Legion*. San Jose: R. James Bender Publishing, 1986, p. 126.
35. *Division z.b.V. 300 (Division zur Besondere Verwendung 300)* translates to: 'Division for Special Employment 300'.
36. Silgailis, *Latvian Legion*, p. 136.
37. Haupt, *Die Deutschen Luftwaffen-Felddivisionen*, p. 91.
38. Bidermann, *In Deadly Combat*, p. 280.
39. Newton, *Retreat from Leningrad*, p. 294.
40. Henze would be promoted to *Generalmajor* on 9 November 1944.
41. On 6 December 1942 *Major* Otto Thomas was transferred to form part of the divisional staff of *Luftwaffen-Felddivision Meindl* (aka 21. *Luftwaffen-Felddivision*). Upon arrival, he was made the 'Ib' of the division. On 1 June 1944 he was promoted to *Oberstleutnant*.
42. On 20 May 1943 *Hauptmann* Utpatel was transferred to the staff of 16. *Luftwaffen-Felddivision*.
43. On 1 December 1943 *Hauptmann* Wangenheim was posted to the headquarters staff of 21. *Luftwaffen-Felddivision*, now referred to as *Felddivision 21 (L)*.
44. *Hauptmann* Schmidtseck was transferred to *Luftwaffen-Artillerie-Regiment 21* of 21. *Luftwaffen-Felddivision* from 15. *Luftwaffen-Felddivision* on 9 February 1943. On that date he was also promoted to *Major*. He was given command of *Panzerabwehr-Abteilung 21*, which formed part of *Luftwaffen-Artillerie-Regiment 21*.

22. *Luftwaffen-Felddivision*

1. Tessin, *Verbände und Truppen*, vol. 3, p. 187.

Bibliography

Primary Sources

National Archives, College Park, Maryland
NARA Microfilm T-78, Roll 398, *Blatt 1-38, OKH Befehl datiert 17 Januar, 1944.*
NARA Microfilm T-78, Roll 645, Frame 000736. *Vortragsnotiz – Abtransport Kurland 10.3.45–17.3.45.*
NARA Microfilm T-78, Roll 645, Frame 000769. *Funk-Fernschreiben. 17 Marz 1945. General Stab des Heeres/Organisations-Abteilung. Oberst i.G. Bennecke, Abteilungs-Chef.*
NARA Microfilm T-78, Roll 645, Frame 000793. *Fernschreibenvermittlung, 10 Marz 1945.*
NARA Microfilm T-78, Roll 645, Frame 000807. *Notiz nach Führervortrag, am 14.3.45.*
NARA Microfilm T-78, Roll 645, Frame 000925. *Fernschreiben – 4 Marz, 1945.*
NARA Microfilm T-78, Roll 645, Frame 000990. *Vortragsnotiz 9. Marz 1945.*
NARA Microfilm T-78, Roll 645, Frame 000990-1. *Vortragsnotiz 9. Marz 1945.*
NARA Microfilm T-78, Roll 646, Frame 000576.
NARA Microfilm T-311, Roll 28, Frame 7034124. OB West Ia Nr. 5185/44 g. Kdos, 1.7.44.
NARA Microfilm T-311, Roll 28, Frame 7034134. OB West Ia Nr. 5197/44 g. Kdos, 2.7.44.
NARA Microfilm T-311, Roll 70, Frame 000593.
NARA Microfilm T-311, Roll 70, Frame 000792, '*Heeresgruppe Nord, Ia, 159/44, 17 January 1944*'.
NARA Microfilm T-311, Roll 70, Frame 000794.
NARA Microfilm T-311, Roll 70. '*HG Nord, Ia./Abt.III – 19 Dezember 1943*'.
NARA Microfilm T-311, Roll 70. "*Armeeoberkommando 18, Ia, 732/44 5 Februar 1944*'.
NARA Microfilm T-311, Roll 72. Numerous *Heeresgruppe Nord Ia* entries dated 14 March, 5 April, 10 April, 19 April and 21 April.
NARA Microfilm T-313, Roll 420, Frame 8713976. *Panzer Gruppe West Ia Nr. 522/44 g.Kdos. v. 23.7.44.*
NARA Microfilm T-314, Roll 45, Frame 0417. *Anlagen zum KTBB, Blatt 3, Eingegangene Meldungen, 28/12/42, Nr. 29711/7.*
NARA Microfilm T-501, Roll 253, Frame 00078.

Bundesarchiv, Koblenz u. Freiburg
BA MA AOK 4, Ia Kriegstagebuch Nr.13, 16-21 Jun 42, AOK 4 24336/1.
BA MA Operations Abteilung, NO. 5645/42, Heeresgruppe Mitte. 15.07.42.
BA MA OKH Kriegsgliederung, Dislokation Heeregruppe Süd nach Lage Ost, Stand 2.6.43.
BA MA OKL, Kriegsgliederungen Luftwaffen-Felddivision 14. 55/51 T-207-1943.
BA MA Truppendienstliche Befehlsgliederung, WBN 1.6.1943.
BA MA Generalkommando LXXXVIII.A.K. Abt.Ic. Nr.1262/44 gKdos., K.H.Qu., den 10.5.44.
BA MA Personalakte gibt ab 16.09.43. Tätigkeitbericht für den Monat September 1943, Generalkommando LXXXIX A.K. Abt. IIa gibt am 11.9.43: 'GenMaj. Bäßler, Erich, wird ab 16.9.43 zur 19.Lw.Felddiv. zur Einareitung als Führer einer Stellungsdiv. Kommandiert.
BA MA OKL, Kriegsgliederungen Luftwaffen-Felddivision 14. 55/51 T-207-1943.
BA MA, M-34, Truppendienstliche Befehlsgliederung, WBN 1.2.1943.
BA MA, M-34, Truppendienstliche Befehlsgliederung, WBN 1.6.1943.
BA MA, M-36, Generalkommando LXXXVIII.A.K. Abt.Ic. Nr.1262/44 gKdos., K.H.Qu., den 10.5.44.
BA-MA OKH Kriegsgliederung, Dislokation Heeregruppe Süd nach Lage Ost, Stand 2.6.43

BA MA, RL34, *Verbände und Einheiten der Luftwaffen-Infanterie Überlieferungsverweis: RS 2-1/15: Tagesmeldungen und Befehle, Aug. 1944.*
BA MA, RW48/309, MSG 175/161 – 9. – 10. *Luftwaffen-Felddivision.*
BA-MA RH 10/349, *Lieferungen der Pz.Fahrzeuge.*
BA-MA, *Heeresgruppe Mitte, Ia. Nr.14550/43 g. Kdos., 8.XII.43., Anlage zur Kriegstagebuch, Heeresgruppe Mitte, Führungsabteilung, Akte XXIII, Heft 12, 1.X.-31.XII.43. 65002/24. Bundesarchiv, Frieburg. Chef der Sicherungstruppen - Rückwartigen Heeresgebiet 102, Operationsabteilung Nr.272/43, 25.1.43. 23.*
BA-MA (Koblenz). BAK-NS19-11. 470.
BA-MA (Koblenz). *RH 22-229. Berück, Kriegstagebuch 07.04.42.*
BA-MA (Koblenz). *AOK 4, Ia Kriegstagebuch Nr. 13, 16-21 Jun 42, AOK 4 24336/1.*
BA-MA (Koblenz). *Operations Abteilung, NO. 5645/42, Heeresgruppe Mitte. 15.07.42.*

Diaries
Personal war diary of *General der Flieger* Alfred Mahncke.

Secondary Sources
Published Studies
Adair, Paul. *Hitler's Greatest Defeat.* Arms & Armour Press: London, 1994.
Armstrong, John A. *Soviet Partisans in World War II.* University of Wisconsin Press: Madison, 1964.
Axworthy, Mark. *Third Axis Fourth Ally.* Arms & Armour Press: London, 1995.
Bernage, Georges and Francois de Lannoy. *La Luftwaffe/La Waffen-SS 1939–1945.* Editions Heimdal: Bayeux, 1998.
Bidermann, Gottlob Herbert. *In Deadly Combat. A German Soldier's Memoir of the Eastern Front.* University of Kansas Press: Kansas, 2000.
Buchner, Alex. *Ostfront 1944.* Schiffer Military History: West Chester, 1991.
Carrell Paul. *Scorched Earth: The Russo-German War, 1943–1944.* Little, Brown & Company: Boston, 1970.
Cooper, Matthew. *The German Army 1933–1945.* Scarborough House: Chelsea, 1978.
Davis, Brian L. *Uniforms and Insignia of the Luftwaffe, Volume 2: 1940–1945.* Arms & Armour Press: London, 1995.
Denzel, Eugon. *Die Luftwaffe Felddivisionen, 1942–1945.* Kurt Vowinckel Verlag: Neckargemund, 1976.
Duffy, Christopher. *Red Storm on the Reich. The Soviet March on Germany, 1945.* Atheneum: New York, 1991.
Fisher, Ernest C. *Cassino to the Alps. The Mediterranean Theater of Operations. United States Army in World War Two.* Centre of Military History, United States Army: Washington DC, 1989.
Frank, Hermann. *Geschichte der XXI. Gebirgs Armeekorps.* Kurt Vowinckel Verlag: Heidelberg, 1957.
Franz, Hermann. *Gebirgsjäger der Polizei. Polizei Gebirgsjäger-Regiment 18 und Polizei Gebirgs Artillerie-Abteilung 1942 bis 1945.* Verlag Hans Henning Podzun: Bad Nauheim, 1963.
Fuegner, Richard S. *Beneath the Tyrant's Yoke: Norwegian Resistance to the German Occupation of Norway 1940–1945.* St Paul: Beaver Pond Press, 2002.
Gander, Terry and Peter Chamberlain, *Infantry, Mountain and Airborne Guns.* London: MacDonald Jane's Publishers Ltd, 1975.
Geibel, Adam. *Taking Leros: The Fight for the Dodecanese Island Fortress.* Axis Europa Magazine: New York, 1998.
Gerolymatos, Andre. *Guerrilla Warfare and Espionage in Greece 1940–1944.* Pella Publishing Co. Inc.: New York, 1992.
Glantz, David M. From the *Don to the Dnieper. Soviet Offensive Operations, Dec. 1942–Aug. 1943.* Frank Cass: London, 1991.
——. *Soviet Military Deception in the Second World War.* Frank Cass: Totowa, 1989.
Groeben, *Generalmajor* Peter von der. *The Collapse of German Army Group Centre.* US Army Historical Division: Europe, 1947, MS # T-31.

Grossmann, Horst et al. *Der Kampf um Ostpreussen*. Gräfe & Unzer Verlag: München, 1960.
Guillaume, General Augustin. *The German Russian War 1941–1945*. London: HMSO, 1956.
Harrison, Gordon A. *The United States Army in World War Two. The European Theater of Operations – Cross Channel Attack*. Office of the Chief of Military History: Washington DC, 1951.
Haupt, Werner. *Als Die Rote Armee Nach Deutschland Kam. Die Kämpfe in Ostpreussen, Schlesien, und Pommern 1944/45*. Podzun-Pallas Verlag: Friedberg, 1970.
——. *Leningrad die 900-Tage Schlacht 1941–1944*. Podzun Pallas Verlag: Friedberg, 1980.
——. *Die Schlachten Der Heeresgruppe Mitte*. Podzun Pallas Verlag: Friedberg, 1984.
——. *Die 8. Panzer-Division im Zweiten Weltkrieg*. Podzun Pallas Verlag: Friedberg, 1987.
——. *Die Deutschen Luftwaffe Felddivisionen, 1941–1945*. Podzun Pallas: Friedberg, 1993.
——. *Army Group Centre*. Schiffer Publishing Ltd: Atglen, 1997.
——. *Army Group North*. Schiffer Publishing Ltd: Atglen, 1997
——. *Die Deutschen Infanterie-Divisionen*, Podzun Pallas: Friedberg, n.d. 3 vols.
——. *Leningrad. 900 Tage Schlacht 1941–1944*. Podzun Pallas Verlag: Friedberg, n.d.
Hillgruber, Andreas. *Die Raumung Der Krim 1944*. Verlag E.S. Mittler & Sohn GmbH: Berlin, 1959.
Hinsley, F.H., editor, with E.E. Thomas, C.F.G. Ransom and R.C. Knight. *British Intelligence in the Second World War*. HMSO: London, 1984. Numerous volumes.
Hinze, Rolf. *East Front Drama – 1944*. J.J. Fedorowicz Publishing: Winnipeg, 1996.
Hooton, E.R. *Eagle in Flames. The Fall of the Luftwaffe*. Arms & Armour Press: London, 1997.
House, Jonathan and David Glantz. *When Titans Clashed. How The Red Army Stopped Hitler*. University Press of Kansas: Lawrence, 1995.
Howell, Edgar. *The Soviet Partisan Movement*. Centre of Military History: Washington DC, 1956.
Husemann, Friedrich. *Die Guten Glaubens Waren. Geschichte Der 4. SS Polizei Division*. Munin Verlag GmbH: Osnabrueck, 1973. 2 vols.
Jagorski, Georg. *Chronik der 21. Luftwaffen-Felddivision 1942–1945*. Selbstpubliziert: Cuxhaven, 1992.
Jurado, Carlos Caballero. *La Division Azul*. Defensa Editorial: Madrid, 1999.
Keilig, Wolf. *Rangliste Des Deutschen Heeres 1944/45*. Hand-Henning Podzun Verlag: Bad Nauheim, 1955.
——. *Das Deutsche Heer 1939–1945*. Podzun-Verlag: Bad Nauheim, 1960. 3 vols.
Kleine, Egon and Volkmar Kühn. *Tiger: Die Geschichte Einer Legendären Waffe, 1942–45*. Motorbuch Verlag: Stuttgart, 1985.
Kleinfeld, Gerald R. and Lewis A. Tambs. *Hitler's Spanish Division. The Blue Division in Russia*. Southern Illinois University Press: Carbondale, 1979.
Kumm, Otto. *Vorwarts Prinz Eugen. Geschichte Der 7. SS Freiwilligen Gebirgs Division 'Prinz Eugen'*. Munin Verlag GmbH: Osnabrück, 1978.
——. *Prinz Eugen. The History of the 7. SS Mountain Division 'Prinz Eugen'*. J.J. Fedorowicz Publishing: Winnipeg, 1995.
Kurowski, Franz. *Deadlock Before Moscow. Army Group Centre 1942/1943*. Schiffer Military History: West Chester, 1992.
——. *The Brandenburgers Global Mission*. J.J. Fedorowicz Publishing: Winnipeg, 1997.
Kursietis, Andris J. *The Fallen Generals. The Destruction of the German Officer Corps in World War II and its Aftermath*. Ark Publications: Milwaukee, 1994.
——. *The Wehrmacht at War 1939–1945. The Units and Commanders of the German Ground Forces during World War 2*. Uitgeverij Aspekt B.V: Soesterberg (UK edition), 1999.
Landwehr, Richard and Holger Thor Nielsen. *Nordic Warriors. SS Panzer Grenadier-Regiment 24 Danmark, Eastern Front, 1943–45*. Shelf Books: Halifax, 1999.
Leverkühn, Paul. *German Military Intelligence*. Ebenezer Baylis & Sons Ltd: London, 1954.
Luck, Hans von. *Panzer Commander. The memoirs of Colonel Hans von Luck*. Praeger Publishers: Westport, 1989.
Lukas, Richard C. *Forgotten Holocaust. The Poles Under German Occupation 1939–1944*. University Press of Kentucky: Lexington, 1986.

Mahncke, Jochen. *For Kaiser and Hitler: From Military Aviator to High Command – The Memoirs of Luftwaffe General Alfred Mahncke 1910–1945.* Sussex: Tattered Flag, 2012.
Manstein, Erich von. *Lost Victories.* Presidio Press: Novato, 1982.
Mehner, Kurt. *Die Geheimen Tagesberichte der Deutschen Wehrmachtführungs Im Zweiten Weltkrieg, 1939–1945.* Biblio Verlag: Osnabrück, 1988. 12 vols.
——. *Die Deutsche Wehrmacht 1939–1945.* Militair Verlag Klaus D. Patzwall: Norderstedt, 1993.
Mehner, Kurt and Reinhard Teuber. *Die Luftwaffe 1939–1945.* Klaus D. Patzwall Verlag, 1989.
——. *Abbreviations of the German military language: from the imperial army to the German armed forces.* Norderstedt: Militär-Verlag Patzwall, 1994.
Mellenthin, Major General F.W. von. *Panzer Battles. A Study of the Employment of Armor in the Second World War.* University of Oklahoma Press: Norman, 1971.
Meyer, Brün. *Dienstal vvvterliste der Waffen SS. SS Obergruppenführer bis SS Hauptsturmführer. Stand vom 1. Juli 1944.* Biblio Verlag: Osnabrück, 1987.
Meyer, Hubert. *The History of the 12. SS Panzer-Division Hitler Jugend.* J.J. Fedorowicz Publishing Inc.: Winnipeg, 1994.
Mitcham, Dr Samuel W. *Hitler's Legions.* Dorset Press: New York, 1985.
——. *Crumbling Empire. The German Defeat in the East, 1944.* Praeger Publishers: Westport, 2001.
——. *The Desert Fox in Normandy. Rommel's Defense of Fortress Europe.* Cooper Square Press: New York, 2001.
Mueller-Hillebrand, *Das Heer 1933–45.* E.S. Mittler & Sohn GmbH: Frankfurt am Main, 1969.
Müller, Ferdinand. *Vom Kessel von Oranienbaum bis zu den Endkämpfen in Ostpreußen: Meine Ereibnisse als Funker bei der 10. Luftwaffen-Felddivision und der 170. Infanteriedivision* Mix Verlag GmbH: Bremen, 2013.
Muñoz, Antonio. *Hitler's Eastern Legions, Vol. I – The Baltic Schutzmannschaft 1941–1945.* Europa Books: New York, 1998.
—— et al. *The East Came West. Muslim, Hindu and Buddhist Volunteers in the German Armed Forces 1941–1945.* Europa Books: New York, 2001.
Nafziger, George F. *The German Order of Battle. Waffen-SS and other units in World War II.* Combined Publishing: Conshocken, 2001.
Newland, Samuel J. *Cossacks in the German Army 1941–1945.* Frank Cass: London, 1991.
Newton, Steven H. *Retreat from Leningrad.* Schiffer Publishing: Atglen, 1995.
Niepold, Gerd. *Battle For White Russia.* Brassey's Defence Publishers: London, 1987.
Perro, Oskars. *Fortress Cholm.* Kurland Publishing: Ontario, 1981.
Ready, J. Lee. *The Forgotten Axis. Germany's Partners and Foreign Volunteers in World War II.* McFarland & Co.: Jefferson, 1987.
Ruffner, Kevin C. *Luftwaffe Field Divisions 1941–45.* Osprey Publishing: Oxford, 1998.
Ryan, Cornelius. *The Last Battle.* Simon & Schuster: New York, 1966.
Sandman, Steven H. et al. *Hitler's Army.* Combined Publishing: Conshocken, 1996
Schäufler, Hans. *1945 – Panzer an der Weichsel. Soldaten der Letzten Stunde.* Motorbuch Verlag: Stuttgart, 1986.
Scheibert, Horst. *Die Träger des Deutschen Kreuzes in Gold. Heer-Kriegsmarine-Luftwaffen-Waffen-SS.* Podzun Pallas Verlag: Friedberg, n.d.
Schmitz, Peter and Klaus J. Thies. *Die Truppenkennzeichen der Verbände und Einheiten der Deutschen Wehrmacht und Waffen-SS und Ihre Einzätze Im Zweiten Weltkrieg 1939–1945.* Biblio Verlag: Osnabrück, 1987.
Schmitz, Peter, Klaus-Juergen Thies, Guenter Wegmann and Christian Zweng. *Die Deutschen Divisionen 1939–1945.* Biblio Verlag: Osnabrück, 1994.
Schraml, Franz. *Kriegsschauplatz Kroatien: Die deutsch-kroatischen 369., 373., 392. Infanterie-Division (kroatische) – ihre Ausbildungs und Ersatzformationen.* Kurt Vowinckel Verlag: Neckargemünd, 1962.
Schramm, Percy Ernst. *Kriegstagebuch des Oberkommandos der Wehrmacht 1939–1945.* Bernard & Gräfe Verlag: München, 1982. 8 vols.

———. *The German Wehrmacht in the Last Days of the War (1 January–7 May 1945)*. Historical Division, Headquarters United States Army: Europe, MS# C-020, n.d.
Schröder, J and Joachim Schultz-Naumann. *Geschichte der Pommeranische 32. Infanterie-Division*. Podzun Pallas Verlag: Bad Neuheim, 1956.
Seaton, Albert. *The Russo-German War 1941–45*. Praeger Publishers: New York, 1970.
———. *The Fall of Fortress Europa 1943–1945*. Holmes & Meier Publishers Inc.: New York, 1981.
Senger und Etterlein, General Frido von. *Neither Fear nor Hope. The Wartime Memoirs of the German Defender of Cassino*. Presidio Press: Novato, 1989.
Shulman, Milton. *Defeat in the West*. E.P. Dutton & Co. Inc.: New York, 1948.
Silgailis, Arturs. *Latvian Legion*. R. James Bender Publishing: San Jose, 1986.
Steenberg, Sven. *Vlasov*. Alfred A. Knopf: New York, 1970.
Stoves, Rolf. *Die 22. Panzer-Division, 25. Panzer-Division, 27. Panzer-Division, und die 233. Reserve-Panzer-Division*. Podzun-Pallas Verlag: Friedberg, 1985
Tessin, Georg. *Verbände und Truppen der Deutschen Wehrmacht und Waffen-SS*. Biblio Verlag: Osnabrueck, 1973–1980. 14 vols.
Tieke, Wilhelm. *Korps Steiner. Nordland-Nederland. Nachträge zu den Truppengeschichten*. Kleinoffsetdruckerei Otto Dittmer, 1987.
———. *The Caucasus and the Oil. The German-Soviet War in the Caucasus, 1942–1943*. J.J. Fedorowicz Publishing: Winnipeg, 1995.
Ullrich, Karl. *Wie Ein Fels im Meer. Kriegsgeschichte der 3. SS Panzer-Division 'Totemkopf'*. Munin Verlag: Osnabrück, 1987.
Wilmot, Chester. *The Struggle for Europe*. Carrol & Graf Publishers: New York, 1954.
Wilt, Alan F. *The Atlantic Wall. Hitler's Defenses in the West, 1941–1944*. Iowa State University Press: Ames, 1975.
Winterbotham, F.W. *The Ultra Secret*. Harper & Row Publishers: New York, 1974.
Wykes, Alan. *The Siege of Leningrad*. Ballantine Books: New York, 1968.
Ziemke, Earl F. *The German Northern Theater of Operations 1940–1945*. Department of the Army: Washington DC, 1959, document 20-271.
———. *Stalingrad to Berlin: The German Defeat in the East*. Centre of Military History: Washington DC, 1968.
Ziemke, Earl F. and Magna Bauer. *Moscow to Stalingrad: Decision in the East*. Centre for Military History, United States Army: Washington DC, 1987.

Magazine articles
Frankson, Anders. 'SPARED. Sweden During the Second World War', in *Command Magazine*: San Luis Obispo. September 1996, issue 39.
Landwehr, Richard. 'Soldiers of Europe: The III SS-Panzerkorps (part 1)', *Siegrunen Magazine*: Glendale, July 1979, vol. 3, no. 3, no. 15.
Lodieu, Didier. 'Des Sturmgeschütz dans les divisions de campagne de la Luftwaffe', *39/45 Magazine*, Editions Heimdal: Bayeux, September 1998, no. 147.
Lodieu, Didier. 'Des Sturmgeschütz dans les divisions de campagne de la Luftwaffe', *39/45 Magazine*, Editions Heimdal: Bayeux, September–October 1998, no. 148.
McTaggart, Patrick. 'The Battle of Narva, 1944', *Command Magazine*: San Luis Obispo, issue 14, January–February 1992.

Name Index

Alewyn, Heinz, 117
Almers, Kurt, 228
Anstett, *Oberst*, 247
Arnim, Hans-Joachim von, 52
Arns, Wilhelm, 67
Aschauer, *Major* Freiherr von, 219
Aue, Hermann, 235, 246–7, 250–1

Bach, Wolfgang, 54
Baeßler (Bäßler), Erich, 208, 227, 233
Balck, Hermann, 175
Barkowski, Erich, 147
Barth, Otto, 277, 279
Basedow, Hans, 25
Bassenge, Gerhard, 233
Bauer, *Leutnant*, 234
Bauer, Andreas, 33
Bauernstätter, *Major*, 114, 117
Becker, Carl, 25
Belau, Hans, 209
Bennecke, *Oberleutnant*, 234
Berg, *Oberarzt Dr.*, 234
Beutter, Friedrich, 182
Bieberstein, Wolfgang Rogalla Freiherr von, 182, 218
Biedermann, Wolf Freiherr von, 76
Biehler, Ernst-Friedrich, 91
Biekel, Hans, 200
Binder-Krieglstein, Wolfgang, 117
Bluhm, Reinhold, 76
Bodemann, *Leutnant*, 32
Bogert, *Hauptmann*, 26
Borckenhagen, Hans, 53
Bourquin, Alexander, 111, 117
Bräunig, *Major*, 277, 279
Brandes, *Major der Reserve*, 157
Braun, Friedrich Edler von, 117
Braun, Konstantine von, 157, 182
Breuninger, *Major*, 209
Briegel, Johann, 33
Brücker, *Oberleutnant*, 233
Burbach, Karl, 101
Bureck, Paul, 67
Busche, Karl, 292

Castening, *Major*, 247
Christ, Hermann, 54
Clauss, *Major z.V.*, 279
Clodius, Guenther, 101
Conrady, Heinrich, 182, 305
Crisolli, Wilhelm, 241, 243–4, 246, 311
Christiansen, Friedrich, 191

Dannenberg, Wilhelm, 234
Darge, Werner, 40, 53
Deffner, Emil, 40
Dehn-Rotfelser, *Hauptmann der Reserve* von, 91
Delinsky, Hans, 246
Demelhuber, Karl Maria, 190–1
Dewald, Eberhard, 182, 305
Dieketter, Hermann, 33
Dieter, *Stabsarzt Dr.*, 234
Drewes, Karl, 219
Drobeck, Richard, 101
Drum, Karl, 103, 117

Eckert, *Oberarzt Dr.*, 234
Egeler, *Major*, 32, 91
Eicke, Theodor, 258
Eitel, Emil, 76, 179, 182
Emmerich, *Hauptmann*, 66
Engel, Ludwig, 101, 250
Eppendorff, Henning, 101
Erbe, Heinz, 33
Erdmann, Hans, 91
Erdmann, Wolfgang, 218, 246
Etterlein, Frido von Senger und, 229–30

Fabig, Werner, 147
Fasel, *Major*, 136
Fedyuninsky, Ivan Ivanovich, 87
Feiler, Karl, 136
Fichter, *Oberst*, 283
Findeisen, *Oberst*, 280
Fischer, Gottfried, 25
Fischer, Gotthard, 89
Fischer, *Hauptmann*, 233
Fischer, Karl, 67
Fischer, *Major*, 112

Fischer-See, August, 76, 182
Fliesbach, Horst, 26
Flor, Hartwig, 277, 279
Foch, Ferdinand, 3
Fox, *Major i.G.*, 136
Franke, *Oberleutnant*, 233
Fricke, Hermann, 250
Friedrichsen, Ernst, 66
Frielinghaus, Hans, 147
Friesen, *Stabsveterinär Dr.*, 233
Frohn, Heinrich, 54
Fronhöfer, Erich, 246
Fuchs, Robert, 209, 246, 283
Furchtmann, Herbert, 136

Gareis, Wilhelm, 28, 33
Geerkens, Heinrich, 91-2
Gerlach, Dietrich, 182
Gerlach, Volrath, 117, 218
Gerlicher, *Hauptmann*, 277
Gerndt, Joachim, 32
Gillitze, *Oberstleutnant*, 247 Gillitze,
Glaesel (Gläsel), Karl, 32-3
Godde, *Major*, 219
Gollwitzer, Friedrich, 37, 64
Goltzsch, Rudolf, 278
Göring, Hermann Wilhelm, 1, 3-7, 12, 17, 21, 34, 47, 73, 85, 160, 162, 184, 236-7, 282
Govorov, Leonid, 95
Graepel, Walter, 67
Greve, Theodor, 147

Hallweg, *Oberleutnant*, 267
Hartogh, Heinz, 131
Hartung, Günther, 55
Heckel, Otto, 279
Hedenus, Paul, 26
Heidemeyer, Hans, 77
Heidkämper, Otto, 21-2
Heinemann, *Oberleutnant* Dr, 40
Heinsius, Heinz, 283
Helbig, Hermann, 53
Hemmer, Hasso, 26
Hencke, Fritz, 250-1, 283
Henke, Gerhard, 110, 114, 117
Henze, Albert, 233, 279
Herian, Edwin, 127
Heyking, Rüdiger von, 66
Hildebrant, Gerhard, 218, 233
Hindenburg, Paul von, 4
Hirschling, Theodor, 233

Hitler, Adolf, 1, 3-7, 21, 64-5, 81, 132, 169, 184, 192, 203, 237, 239, 246
Hobusch, Albert, 218
Höcker, Hans-Kurt, 91, 208
Hoffmann, Walter, 40
Hohn, *Oberleutnant*, 277
Hollunder, Georg, 40
Holtz, Bruno, 81
Hoth, Hermann, 164, 172
Hübel, Kurt, 209
Hülsen, Botho Graf von, 52
Huhmann, *Hauptmann*, 67
Humer, *Major*, 233

Jäntsch, *Stabsarzt Dr.*, 233
Jagolski, Georg, 267
Jena, Axel Freiherr von, 34
Jeschonneck, Hans, 162
Johann, Edgar, 200
Jordan, Günther, 137
Jordan, Otto, 251
Juin, Alphonse, 241
Junge, Rudolf, 200
Junghans, *Hauptmann*, 233

Kalberlah, *Oberst*, 182
Keilig, *Hauptmann*, 206
Keller, Paul, 209
Kerssenbrock, Graf, 250
Kesselring, Albert, 229, 240, 245
Kettner, Herbert, 136
Keynes, John Maynard, 3
Keilhold, Herbert, 209
Kiewitt, Heinrich, 283
Kirchner, Friedrich, 175
Klepp, Dr Ernst, 40
Kleßmann, August, 246-7, 250
Kleye, *Major*, 234
Kment, Alfred, 40
Knobelsdorff, Otto von, 175
Koch, Heinz, 141, 147
König, Eduard, 233
Köppel, Maximilian, 209
Kohler, Wilhelm, 117
Korovnikov, Ivan- 14
Korte, Hans, 147, 208
Krahl, Werner, 250, 279
Kretschmer, Hermann, 101
Kretzschmar, Wolfgang-Hans, 131, 137
Kreuter, Lambert, 234
Kreuzer, Eduard, 137
Küllmer, *Oberleutnant*, 233

Kuhbacher, *Oberleutnant*, 267
Kukuk, Hans-Reinhardt, 183
Kunz-Krause, Hermann, 234
Kunze, *Hauptmann*, 279

Lachemair, Otto von, 200
Lämpe, Werner, 246
Lampe, Friedrich, 54
Lassmann, *Oberst*, 91
Leesemann, Friedrich, 250
Lehnert, Walter, 219
Licht, Rudolf-Eduard, 278
Lohmann, Günther, 157
Longin, Anton-Carl, 91, 137
Lottens, *Major*, 33
Luck, Hans von, 194

Maak, *Hauptmann*, 246
Maass, Willi, 67
Mätze, *Major*, 234
Mahler, Fritz, 147
Mahncke, Alfred, 159–62, 169, 173, 182, 305
Mahrle, Sebastian, 281
Maiwald, *Leutnant*, 234
Oberstleutnant, 219 Mangold,
Mann, Wilhelm, 54, 182
Manstein, Fritz-Erich von, 70
Massing, Engelbert, 91
Matt, Georg, 101
Matussek, Paul, 98, 101
Mehnert, Karl, 101, 297
Meindl, Eugen, 256, 258, 278
Melitz, Engelbert, 33
Meretskov, Kirill, 95
Meyer, Ludwig, 101
Michael, Ernst, 89, 91
Mieth, Friedrich, 72, 74
Milch, Erhard, 7
Model, Walter, 128
Mueller-Gebuehr, Hans, 76
Mueller (Müller), Herbert, 54, 81
Mueller, *Oberst*, 117
Muggenthaler, Hermann, 233
Muhr, Eduard, 182
Müller, Ferdinand, 97
Müller, Fritz, 209
Müller, *Hauptmann* von, 182
Müller, Herbert, 157, 182, 283
Müller, Maximilian, 151
Müller, *Oberleutnant*, 234
Munske, Erich, 251

Neudörfer, Wolfgang, 250, 280
Nitzschke, Walter, 40
Nord, Ferdinand-Ernst, 234
Nordwig, Dr Carl, 25
Norsen, Alfred, 33
Novak, Hugo, 67

Obergethmann, Eduard, 161
Obernitz, Hans-Günther von, 137
Odebrecht, Job, 260, 278
Olbrich, Herbert, 147, 208
Olbrichs, Alexander, 218
Orthmann, Kurt, 32, 101
Örtzen, Roland von, 233
Ostermeyer, *Hauptmann*, 33
Ostertag, Erich, 92
Ottenberg, Ernst, 76

Palitzsch, Walther, 200
Pätzold, Hellmuth, 17, 25
Papcke, Gustav, 233
Passlick, Paul, 32
Pawelke, Walther, 117
Peschel, Rudolf, 61, 66, 293
Petermann, Alfred, 101
Petrauschke, Rudolf, 10, 14
Pflugbeil, Kurt, 159
Piehler, Franz, 137
Pinagel, Oskar, 209
Pirner, *Hauptmann*, 92
Pistorius, Robert, 10, 32, 38, 40, 289
Plocher, Hermann, 233, 310
Poggendorf, Hugo, 157–8
Pulina, Johannes, 101
Pultar, Josef, 235
Puschner, Karl-Heinz, 53
Puttkamer, (Hasso?) Freiherr von, 147

Rackowitsch, Andreas von, 182
Raddatz, Heinz, 183
Rattey, *Major*, 233
Reichmann, Heinz, 61
Rein, Alfred, 101
Reinhard, Hans, 191
Reinshagen, Fritz, 218–19, 309
Rendulic, Lothar, 302
Reuter, Hans, 81
Reymann, Hellmuth, 141, 147
Richter, *Hauptmann*, 182
Richter, Werner, 136
Richter, Wilhelm, 156–7
Richthofen, Baron Manfred Albrecht von, 1

Richthofen, Wolfram von, 159, 161, 172
Rinow, *Hauptmann*, 182
Roebern, Werner Jungschultz von, 304
Roehler, Herbert, 117
Roesner (Rösner), Erich, 53
Rhoden, Herhuth von, 163
Rommel, Erwin, 193, 206
Rosenthal, Hans-Juergen, 26
Ross, Walter, 67
Rothmayer, Otto, 67
Roy, *Hauptmann*, 117
Rüden, Heinz-Friedrich, 279
Rundstedt, Gerd von, 204
Rupp, Ernst, 45
Rupprecht, Wilhelm, 218, 308
Rütgers, Carl, 92

Saalbach, Rudolf, 98
Saldern, *Major* von, 106, 117
Sander, *Leutnant*, 234
Sarnitz, Alfons, 26
Sartori, Albert, 40
Saß, Eduard von, 55
Sauerbrey, Hans, 40
Schall-Riaucour, Max Graf von, 54
Schaper, *Oberst*, 247
Schawdtke, Hans-Joachim, 33
Schaefer (Schäfer), Tillo, 53
Schekat, Emil, 158
Schenke, *Korvettenkapitän*, 89
Scherak, Johan, 209
Scherer, Theodor, 254
Schimpf, Richard, 278
Schirmacher, Max, 250, 280, 283
Schlieper, Franz, 136
Schmid, Heinrich, 234
Schmidt-Künitz, Walter, 67
Schmidt, *Oberst*, 219
Schmidtseck, Rudolf Freiherr von, 183, 267, 281, 312
Schrader, Willi, 283
Schreiber, Georg, 137
Schröppel, Alfred, 183
Schub, Anton, 182, 251
Schuchardt, Karl, 182
Schulte-Mattler, Bernhard, 157
Schütze, Hermann, 250
Schwarz, Wilhelm, 40
Schwier, Friedrich-Wilhelm, 101
Schwöppe, *Hauptmann*, 281
Scheloske, Bruno, 26
Schiffer, Rudolf, 91

Schlemm, Alfred, 25
Schmidt, Herbert, 25
Schmitz, Carl (Karl), 26
Scholz, Herbert, 25
Schrader, Willi, 280
Schreder, Hans-Georg, 40
Schub, Anton, 53
Schuchardt, Karl, 281
Schuetz, Karl, 40
Schuh, Eduard, 92
Schulz, Alexander, 54
Schulz-Heyn, Hans-Bruno, 52, 182
Schwarz, Wilhelm, 25, 33
Schweinzberg, Gundolf Freiherr Schenk zu, 208
Seibold, Karl, 26
Seydlitz, Walther von, 258
Siebert, *Oberleutnant*, 233
Siefart, Rudolf, 157
Seifert, Richard, 233
Sievers, Karl, 191, 195, 200
Sodeik, *Hauptmann*, 280
Spang, Willibald, 76, 81, 179, 182, 294, 305
Speiser, Ernst, 219
Spiller, Ernst, 101
Staake, Harry, 200, 219
Stahel, Rainer, 40, 74, 78–9, 81, 165, 175, 304
Stapelfeld, Konrad, 117
Staunau, Hans-Werner, 219
Steiglitz, Christian von, 81
Stein, Hans, 81, 92, 296
Stein-Libenstein zu Barchfel, Ferdinand Wilhelm Freiherr von, 218, 308
Stephan, Emil, 92, 296
Steuer, Hans-Helmuth, 81, 136
Stift, Josepf, 219
Stockhaus, Karl-Hermann, 101
Stolle, Otto, 26
Strackerjahn, Hans-Christian, 40
Strube, Fritz, 147, 301–2
Stubbe, Werner, 136
Suchodol-Maculan, Guido von, 76
Suetterlin, Rene, 66

Tarnowski, Walter, 209, 308
Techel, *Oberst*, 251
Tempel, Georg, 40
Theiß, *Oberstleutnant*, 200
Thomas, Otto, 279, 312
Thome, Ludwig, 183
Thoms, *Major*, 254
Thormeier, Wilhelm, 117

Tresckow, Henning von, 214–16, 308
Treskow, Joachim von, 218
Triep, Eugen, 247, 311
Trierenberg, Wolf, 191
Tuch, *Hauptmann*, 182
Tzschoppe, Erwin, 190

Uckermann, Freiherr von, 40
Udet, Ernst, 7
Uckermann, Horst Freiherr von, 256
Ulmer, Adolf, 91
Ulmer, Kurt, 81, 295
Utpatel, Karl, 280

Vater, Willi, 183
Vatutin, Nikolai, 254
Vehlow, Siegfried, 40
Vogel, *Oberstabsintendant*, 233
Völk, Wilhelm, 40, 250
Voitl. Max, 250
Völcker, Kaspar, 244, 246, 311

Wachsen, Helmuth, 246
Wadehn, Walther, 101
Wagner, Ernst, 26
Wagner, *Oberst*, 260
Wahle, Carl, 191
Waibel, Josef, 101
Waldschmidt, Wilhelm, 26, 67
Wahnschaffe, Hans, 40
Wangenheim, Heinz Freiherr von, 280
Wäntig, Kurt, 247
Wangenheim, Heinz Freiherr von, 250
Warnecke, Bernhard, 183
Warnecke, Hermann, 137
Warning, Elmar, 206, 208
Weber, Carl, 101

Weber, Ernst, 66,
Weber, Gottfried, 122, 128, 136, 301
Wedel, Hermann von, 94, 101
Wegener, Wilhelm, 89
Weichert, Hans, 209, 308
Weidling, Helmuth, 21
Weimar, Kilian Otto, 137
Weiss, Walter, 101, 147
Wenzel, Ernst, 40
Westphal, Willi, 147
Wiebe, Hugo, 137
Wietersheim, Joachim von, 136, 301
Wilhelm, Otto, 200
Wilke, Karl-Eduard, 220
Wilke, Gustav, 10
Wille, Kurt, 200
Windt, *Major*, 218
Winkelbauer, Eduard, 81
Winkler, Fritz, 40, 81
Winter, Hans, 234
Winter, Paul, 91
Witt, Richard, 137
Witte, *Oberleutnant*, 267
Wolf, Franz, 199
Wolf, Friedrich, 147
Wolf, Hans (Heinrich), 182
Wolff, Horst, 234, 283
Wündisch, Otto, 158
Würke, *Oberleutnant*, 233

Yeryomenko, Andrey Ivanovich, 21

Zabel, Georg, 66
Zausch, Kurt, 26
Zenker, Fritz, 101
Zerneck, *Obergefreiter* von, 93
Zurmühlen, Walter, 63

Unit Index

Kriegsmarine
6. *Landungsflotille*, 106

W.W.I. German Forces
Fliegerkommando Doberitz, 159
Flieger Bataillon 2, 159
Railway Regiment No. 1, 159
II. *Armeekorps*, 159
XXVI. *Reservekorps*, 159
LVII. *Generalkommando z.b.V.*, 159
11. *Reserve-Division*, 159
23. *Reserve-Division*, 160

Luftwaffe Formations
Luftgau
Luftgaustab z.b.V. I., 160
Luftgau I, 9
Luftgau III, 17, 27, 34, 68, 148
Luftgau IV, 68
Luftgau VII, 201
Luftgau XI, 77
Luftgaustab z.b.V. XII., 160
Luftgaustab z.b.V. XXI, 160–1

Other Luftwaffe Commands
Luftwaffekontrollkomission III, 93
Höhere-Fliegerausbildungs-Kommandeur X, 160
Luftwaffeauffangstab Nord, 160

Luftflotte (Kommando)
Luftflotte 1, 235
Luftflotte 2, 235
Luftflotte 3, 235
Luftflotte 4, 34, 159, 161, 166

Fliegerkorps
IV. *Fliegerkorps*, 173
VIII. *Fliegerkorps*, 169, 174
XIII. *Fliegerkorps*, 34, 185, 220, 235

Fliegerdivision
1. *Jagddivision*, 308
Flieger Division Donetz, 160
Fliegerdivision Don, 174

Jagdgeschwader
Jagdgeschwader 1, 1
6./*Jagdgeschwader 53*, 93
Kampfgeschwader 152 Hindenburg, 160
Kampfgruppe z.b.V. 172, 254

Luftwaffen-Feldkorps
I. *Luftwaffen-Feldkorps*, 72
II. *Luftwaffen-Feldkorps*, 20–2, 25, 28, 57, 59, 290, 294
III. *Luftwaffen-Feldkorps*, 83, 86, 94, 292

Luftwaffen-Felddivision / Felddivision (L)
1. *Luftwaffen-Felddivision / Felddivision 1 (L)*, 9–15, 17, 26, 47, 83, 138, 142–3, 271, 286, 289, 296
2. *Luftwaffen-Felddivision / Felddivision 2 (L)*, 17, 19, 21–3, 25–6, 29–30, 47, 58–9, 114, 138, 286, 289–92, 294–5
3. *Luftwaffen-Felddivision / Felddivision 3 (L)*, 22, 25, 27–33, 37, 41, 47, 58–9, 61, 114, 138, 286, 290–2
4. *Luftwaffen-Felddivision / Felddivision 4 (L)*, 23, 29–30, 34, 40–1, 47, 52, 114, 138, 286, 291–2
5. *Luftwaffen-Felddivision / Felddivision 5 (L)*, 41–3, 45–7, 50, 52, 75, 114, 138, 181, 286, 292–3
6. *Luftwaffen-Felddivision / Felddivision 6 (L)*, 22, 25, 29–30, 32, 37, 41, 47, 55, 57–61, 64–7, 114, 138, 290, 293
7. *Luftwaffen-Felddivision*, 68–9, 72–7, 114, 138, 165, 170–1, 294
8. *Luftwaffen-Felddivision*, 68, 73, 75, 77–9, 81, 114, 138, 171, 175, 177, 181, 294–5, 304
9. *Luftwaffen-Felddivision / Felddivision 9 (L)*, 10, 41, 47, 82–3, 85–6, 88–90, 91, 94, 96–7, 99, 114, 138, 286, 295
10. *Luftwaffen-Felddivision / Felddivision 10 (L)*, 10, 41, 47, 82–3, 85–6, 88, 93–9, 101, 114, 138, 286, 296–97
11. *Luftwaffen-Felddivision / Felddivision 11 (L)*, 47, 102, 103–4, 106–7, 108, 110, 112–14, 117, 297

12. Luftwaffen-Felddivision/Felddivision 12 (L),
    47, 118–22, 124–8, 130–3, 135–8, 140, 143,
    271, 276, 299, 301–2
13. Luftwaffen-Felddivision/Felddivision 13 (L),
    47, 125–6, 138–43, 147, 286, 295, 297, 299,
    301
14. Luftwaffen-Felddivision/Felddivision 14 (L),
    47, 148, 152–3, 156–8, 286, 302
15. Luftwaffen-Felddivision, 47, 72, 74–5, 78–9,
    81, 114, 138, 159–61, 163–5, 170–1, 174–5,
    177–9, 181–3, 267, 286, 294, 303–5, 312
16. Luftwaffen-Felddivision/Felddivision 16 (L),
    47, 137, 184, 186–8, 190–6, 199–200, 286,
    305, 307, 309, 312
17. Luftwaffen-Felddivision/Felddivision 17 (L),
    47, 201–5, 207, 209–10, 214, 282, 307–8
18. Luftwaffen-Felddivision/Felddivision 18 (L)
    47, 200, 207, 210, 212–15, 219, 308
*19. Luftwaffen-Felddivision/19. Luftwaffen-
    Sturm-Division/Felddivision 19 (L)*, 47,
    220–1, 224–5, 227–31, 233–4, 239, 241, 287,
    295, 309
*20. Luftwaffen-Felddivision/20. Luftwaffen-
    Sturm-Division/Felddivision 20 (L)*, 47, 235,
    239–243, 245–6, 310–11
*Luftwaffen Division Meindl/21. Luftwaffen-
    Felddivision/Felddivision 21 (L)* 47, 52, 127,
    131, 136, 138, 248, 256, 258, 260, 263,
    266–7, 270–4, 276–8, 282–3, 287, 294,
    311–12
22. Luftwaffen-Felddivision/Felddivision 22 (L),
    52, 282–3, 312
Luftwaffen-Felddivision 'Südost', 162, 303

Luftwaffe Airborne & Mechanized Units
Fallschirm-Panzerkorps 'Hermann Göring', 237
I. Fallschirmjäger-Korps, 241, 290
2. Fallschirmjäger-Division, 307
4. Fallschirmjäger-Division, 241
8. Fallschirmjäger-Division, 94
Panzergrenadier-Division 'Hermann Göring', 198
*Fallschirm-Panzergrenadier-Division 2 'Hermann
    Göring'*, 236
*Ersatz-und-Ausbildungs-Regiment Hermann
    Göring*, 191
Fallschirm-Panzer-Regiment 'Hermann Göring',
    236
Luftwaffen-Feldbataillon 100 'Hermann Göring',
    304

Luftwaffe Brigades & Regiments
Brigade-Lofoten, 153
Grenadier-Brigade 503, 153

Luftwaffen-Feldregiment 1, 249–51, 263
Luftwaffen-Feldregiment 2, 249–51
Luftwaffen-Feldregiment 3, 249–51, 258, 260,
    263
Luftwaffen-Feldregiment 4, 248–51, 263
Luftwaffen-Feldregiment 5, 250–51, 256, 260
Luftwaffen-Feldregiment 14, 251
Luftwaffen-Infanterie-Regiment Moskau, 220,
    295, 308
Luftlande-Sturm-Regiment 1, 256
Luftwaffen-Feld-Regiment 501, 150, 152–3
Luftwaffen-Feld-Regiment 502, 152–3
Luftwaffen-Feld-Regiment 503, 152–3
Luftwaffen-Jäger-Regiment 9, 47, 51, 53
Luftwaffen-Jäger-Regiment 10, 47, 53
Luftwaffen-Jäger-Regiment 17, 92
Luftwaffen-Jäger-Regiment 19, 93, 95
Luftwaffen-Jäger-Regiment 20, 93, 95
Luftwaffen-Jäger-Regiment 21, 102, 108, 111,
    117
Luftwaffen-Jäger-Regiment 22, 102, 106, 117
Luftwaffen-Jäger-Regiment 23, 118–19, 121
Luftwaffen-Jäger-Regiment 24, 118–19, 121,
    140, 143
Luftwaffen-Jäger-Regiment 25, 121, 143
Luftwaffen-Jäger-Regiment 26, 140, 296
Luftwaffen-Jäger-Regiment 27, 148
Luftwaffen-Jäger-Regiment 28, 148
Luftwaffen-Jäger-Regiment 29, 169, 173, 182,
    305
Luftwaffen-Jäger-Regiment 30, 169, 173–4, 179,
    181–2, 305
Luftwaffen-Jäger-Regiment 31, 185, 187, 199
Luftwaffen-Jäger-Regiment 32, 185, 187, 199
Luftwaffen-Jäger-Regiment 33, 201
Luftwaffen-Jäger-Regiment 34, 201
Luftwaffen-Jäger-Regiment 35, 210, 219
Luftwaffen-Jäger-Regiment 36, 210, 219
Luftwaffen-Jäger-Regiment 37, 220
Luftwaffen-Jäger-Regiment 38, 220
Luftwaffen-Jäger-Regiment 39, 235
Luftwaffen-Jäger-Regiment 40, 235
Luftwaffen-Jäger-Regiment 41, 250, 263, 279
Luftwaffen-Jäger-Regiment 42, 250, 263, 280
Luftwaffen-Jäger-Regiment 43, 250, 263, 280,
    282–3, 312
Luftwaffen-Jäger-Regiment 44, 250, 282–3, 312
Luftwaffen-Jäger-Regiment 49, 40
Luftwaffen-Jäger-Regiment 50, 40
Luftwaffen-Jäger-Regiment 51, 40
Jäger-Regiment 10 (L), 47
Jäger-Regiment 11 (L), 58

Jäger-Regiment 12 (L), 58
Jäger-Regiment 13 (L), 69, 75
Jäger-Regiment 14 (L), 69, 75
Jäger-Regiment 15 (L), 77
Jäger-Regiment 16 (L), 77
Jäger-Regiment 19 (L), 96, 98, 101
Jäger-Regiment 21 (L), 112, 114
Jäger-Regiment 22 (L), 112
Jäger-Regiment 23 (L), 126, 130, 137
Jäger-Regiment 24 (L), 126–7, 131, 137
Jäger-Regiment 25 (L), 127, 131, 137, 145, 299
Jäger-Regiment 26 (L), 127
Jäger-Regiment 27 (L), 151, 156
Jäger-Regiment 28 (L), 151, 156–7
Jäger-Regiment 29 (L), 162
Jäger-Regiment 30 (L), 162
Jäger-Regiment 31 (L), 189–90
Jäger-Regiment 32 (L), 189, 193
Jäger-Regiment 33 (L), 205, 214–15
Jäger-Regiment 34 (L), 205
Jäger-Regiment 35 (L), 211, 214
Jäger-Regiment 36 (L), 211, 214
Jäger-Regiment 37 (L), 310
Jäger-Regiment 38 (L), 310
Jäger-Regiment 39 (L), 239–40, 242, 245, 311
Jäger-Regiment 40 (L), 239–42, 245
Jäger-Regiment 41 (L), 267
Jäger-Regiment 42 (L), 267
Jäger-Regiment 45 (L), 224–5, 310
Jäger-Regiment 46 (L), 189, 193
Jäger-Regiment 48 (L), 211, 213–14, 219
Jäger-Regiment 51 (L), 32, 110
Jäger-Regiment 52 (L), 32, 58, 67
Jäger-Regiment 53 (L), 25, 58, 67
Jäger-Regiment 54 (L), 58, 61, 67
Jäger-Regiment 55 (L), 156, 158
Jäger-Regiment 111 (L), 112
Jäger-Regiment 501 (L), 153
Jäger-Regiment 503 (L), 153
Luftwaffen-Artillerie-Regiment 2, 26, 59
Luftwaffen-Artillerie-Regiment 3, 33, 37
Luftwaffen-Artillerie-Regiment 4, 40
Luftwaffen-Artillerie-Regiment 5, 54
Luftwaffen-Artillerie-Regiment 6, 58–9, 67
Luftwaffen-Artillerie-Regiment 2, 59
Luftwaffen-Artillerie Regiment 3, 28
Luftwaffen-Artillerie-Regiment 11, 102, 117
Luftwaffen-Artillerie-Regiment 12, 118–19, 127
Luftwaffen-Artillerie-Regiment 13, 120
Luftwaffen-Artillerie-Regiment 14, 148, 152, 157
Luftwaffen-Artillerie-Regiment 15, 182–3
Luftwaffen-Artillerie-Regiment 16, 185, 187, 199

Luftwaffen-Artillerie-Regiment 17, 201
Luftwaffen-Artillerie-Regiment 18, 210, 212
Luftwaffen-Artillerie-Regiment 19, 220–1
Luftwaffen-Artillerie-Regiment 20, 235
Luftwaffen-Artillerie-Regiment 21, 263, 281
Luftwaffen-Artillerie-Regiment 22, 283
Artillerie-Regiment 5 (L), 293
Artillerie-Regiment 6 (L), 58
Artillerie-Regiment 9 (L), 91
Artillerie-Regiment 10 (L), 96
Artillerie-Regiment 11 (L), 108
Artillerie-Regiment 12 (L), 136, 301
Artillerie-Regiment 16 (L), 196
Artillerie-Regiment 21 (L), 276–277

Luftwaffe Battalions

Korps Jäger-Bataillon, II. Luftwaffen Feldkorps, 294
Schi-Bataillon der Luftflotte 1, 256
I. Bataillon, Luftwaffen-Feldregiment 1, 249, 256
II. Bataillon, Luftwaffen-Feldregiment 1, 249, 256
III. Bataillon, Luftwaffen-Feldregiment 1, 249, 254, 256, 256
IV. Bataillon, Luftwaffen-Feldregiment 1, 249, 256
I. Bataillon, Luftwaffen-Feldregiment 2, 249, 256
II. Bataillon, Luftwaffen-Feldregiment 2, 249, 256
III. Bataillon, Luftwaffen-Feldregiment 2, 249, 256
IV. Bataillon, Luftwaffen-Feldregiment 2, 249–50, 256
I. Bataillon, Luftwaffen-Feldregiment 3, 249, 256
II. Bataillon, Luftwaffen-Feldregiment 3, 249, 256, 258
III. Bataillon, Luftwaffen-Feldregiment 3, 249, 256, 280
IV. Bataillon, Luftwaffen-Feldregiment 3, 249, 256
I. Bataillon, Luftwaffen-Feldregiment 4, 249, 256
II. Bataillon, Luftwaffen-Feldregiment 4, 249, 256
III. Bataillon, Luftwaffen-Feldregiment 4, 249, 256
IV. Bataillon, Luftwaffen-Feldregiment 4, 248–9, 251, 256
I. Bataillon, Luftwaffen-Feldregiment 5, 250
II. Bataillon, Luftwaffen-Feldregiment 5, 250
III. Bataillon, Luftwaffen-Feldregiment 5, 250
IV. Bataillon, Luftwaffen-Feldregiment 5, 250
I. Jäger-Bataillon, Luftwaffen-Jäger-Regiment 41, 263, 279–80
II. Jäger-Bataillon, Luftwaffen-Jäger-Regiment 41, 263

Unit Index 327

III. Jäger-Bataillon, Luftwaffen-Jäger-
  Regiment 41, 263
I. Jäger-Bataillon, Luftwaffen-Jäger-Regiment 42,
  263
II. Jäger-Bataillon, Luftwaffen-Jäger-Regiment 42,
  263
III. Jäger-Bataillon, Luftwaffen-Jäger-
  Regiment 42, 263
I. Jäger-Bataillon, Luftwaffen-Jäger-Regiment 43,
  263
II. Jäger-Bataillon, Luftwaffen-Jäger-Regiment 43,
  263
III. Jäger-Bataillon, Luftwaffen-Jäger-
  Regiment 43, 263, 280, 283
I. Jäger-Bataillon, Jäger-Regiment 45 (L), 310
II. Jäger-Bataillon, Jäger-Regiment 45 (L), 310
I. Jäger-Bataillon, Luftwaffen-Feldregiment 14,
  256
II. Jäger-Bataillon, Luftwaffen-Feldregiment 14,
  256
I. Jäger-Bataillon, Feld-Regiment der
  Luftwaffe 501, 151
II. Jäger-Bataillon, Feld-Regiment der
  Luftwaffe 501, 151
III. Jäger-Bataillon, Feld-Regiment der
  Luftwaffe 501, 151
I. Jäger-Bataillon, 1. Luftwaffen-Felddivision, 15
II. Jäger-Bataillon, 1. Luftwaffen-Felddivision, 15
I. Jäger-Bataillon, 2. Luftwaffen-Felddivision, 26
II. Jäger-Bataillon, 2. Luftwaffen-Felddivision, 26
III. Jäger-Bataillon, 2. Luftwaffen-Felddivision,
  26, 290
IV. Jäger-Bataillon, 2. Luftwaffen-Felddivision, 26
I. Jäger-Bataillon, 3. Luftwaffen-Felddivision, 33,
  37
II. Jäger-Bataillon, 3. Luftwaffen-Felddivision, 33,
  37
III. Jäger-Bataillon, 3. Luftwaffen-Felddivision, 33
IV. Jäger-Bataillon, 3. Luftwaffen-Felddivision, 33
I. Jäger-Bataillon, 4. Luftwaffen-Felddivision, 40
II. Jäger-Bataillon, 4. Luftwaffen-Felddivision, 40
III. Jäger-Bataillon, 4. Luftwaffen-Felddivision,
  35, 40
IV. Jäger-Bataillon, 4. Luftwaffen-Felddivision, 40
I. Jäger-Bataillon, Luftwaffen-Jäger-Regiment 5,
  32
II. Jäger-Bataillon, Luftwaffen-Jäger-Regiment 5,
  32
I. Jäger-Bataillon, Luftwaffen-Jäger-Regiment 6,
  57, 67
II. Jäger-Bataillon, Luftwaffen-Jäger-Regiment 6,
  57, 67, 290

III. Jäger-Bataillon, Luftwaffen-Jäger-Regiment 6,
  32, 67
IV. Jäger-Bataillon, Luftwaffen-Jäger-Regiment 6,
  32, 67
I. Jäger-Bataillon, Luftwaffen-Jäger-
  Regiment 17 (L), 92
I. Jäger-Bataillon, Luftwaffen-Jäger-
  Regiment 17 (L), 92
IV. Jäger-Bataillon, Luftwaffen-Jäger-
  Regiment 17 (L), 92
I. Jäger-Bataillon, Jäger-Regiment 19 (L), 101
II. Jäger-Bataillon, Jäger-Regiment 19 (L), 101
III. Jäger-Bataillon, Jäger-Regiment 19 (L), 101
I. Jäger-Bataillon, Luftwaffen-Jäger-Regiment 21,
  102, 104
II. Jäger-Bataillon, Luftwaffen-Jäger-Regiment 21,
  102, 104
III. Jäger-Bataillon, Luftwaffen-Jäger-
  Regiment 21, 102, 104, 106, 110, 112
I. Jäger-Bataillon, Luftwaffen-Jäger-Regiment 22,
  102, 112
II. Jäger-Bataillon, Luftwaffen-Jäger-Regiment 22,
  102, 106, 117
III. Jäger-Bataillon, Luftwaffen-Jäger-
  Regiment 22, 102
I. Jäger-Bataillon, Luftwaffen-Jäger-Regiment 23,
  119, 131
II. Jäger-Bataillon, Luftwaffen-Jäger-Regiment 23,
  119, 137
III. Jäger-Bataillon, Luftwaffen-Jäger-
  Regiment 23, 119
I. Jäger-Bataillon, Luftwaffen-Jäger-Regiment 24,
  119, 137
II. Jäger-Bataillon, Luftwaffen-Jäger-Regiment 24,
  119
III. Jäger-Bataillon, Luftwaffen-Jäger-
  Regiment 24, 119
I. Jäger-Bataillon, Jäger-Regiment 25 (L), 127,
  137, 145, 299
II. Jäger-Bataillon, Jäger-Regiment 25 (L), 127,
  131, 145, 299
III. Jäger-Bataillon, Jäger-Regiment 25 (L), 127,
  145
I. Jäger-Bataillon, Jäger-Regiment 26 (L), 299
I. Jäger-Bataillon, Jäger-Regiment 27 (L), 156
II. Jäger-Bataillon, Jäger-Regiment 27 (L), 156
III. Jäger-Bataillon, Jäger-Regiment 27 (L), 156
III. Jäger-Bataillon, Luftwaffen-Jäger-
  Regiment 30, 179
I. Jäger-Bataillon, Luftwaffen-Jäger-Regiment 31,
  187

II. Jäger-Bataillon, Luftwaffen-Jäger-Regiment 31, 187, 191
III. Jäger-Bataillon, Luftwaffen-Jäger-Regiment 31, 187
I. Jäger-Bataillon, Luftwaffen-Jäger-Regiment 32, 187
II. Jäger-Bataillon, Luftwaffen-Jäger-Regiment 32, 187, 193
III. Jäger-Bataillon, Luftwaffen-Jäger-Regiment 32, 187
I. Jäger-Bataillon, Luftwaffen-Jäger-Regiment 34,
II. Jäger-Bataillon, Luftwaffen-Jäger-Regiment 34,
III. Jäger-Bataillon, Luftwaffen-Jäger-Regiment 34, 205
II. Jäger-Bataillon, Jäger-Regiment 48 (L), 211–212
II. Jäger-Bataillon, 7. Luftwaffen-Felddivision, 76
IV. Jäger-Bataillon, 7. Luftwaffen-Felddivision, 68, 76
I. Jäger-Bataillon, 8. Luftwaffen-Felddivision, 81
II. Jäger-Bataillon, 8. Luftwaffen-Felddivision, 81
III. Jäger-Bataillon, 8. Luftwaffen-Felddivision, 81
IV. Jäger-Bataillon, 8. Luftwaffen-Felddivision, 81
III. Jäger-Bataillon, Luftwaffen-Jäger-Regiment 9, 47
I. Jäger-Bataillon, Jäger-Regiment 501 (L), 153
II. Jäger-Bataillon, Jäger-Regiment 501 (L), 153
III. Jäger-Bataillon, Jäger-Regiment 501 (L), 153
III. Jäger-Bataillon, Jäger-Regiment 502 (L), 153
III. Artillerie-Abteilung, Artillerie-Regiment 4 (L), 32, 36
I. Artillerie-Abteilung, Luftwaffen-Artillerie Regiment 3, 28, 32
II. Artillerie-Abteilung, Luftwaffen-Artillerie Regiment 3, 28, 32
III. Artillerie-Abteilung, Luftwaffen-Artillerie Regiment 3, 28
Panzerjäger Abteilung 3, 3. Luftwaffen-Felddivision, 28
Panzerjäger-Abteilung 4 (L), 4. Felddivision (L), 40
Panzerjäger-Abteilung 5 [V. Artillerie-Abteilung], 5. Luftwaffen-Felddivision, 41, 46–7
Panzerjäger-Abteilung 6 (L), 59
Panzerjäger-Abteilung 10 (L), 96
Luftwaffen-Panzerjäger-Abteilung 11, 103, 107
Luftwaffen-Panzerjäger-Abteilung 12, 119–20
Panzerjäger-Abteilung der Luftwaffen-Felddivision 15, 182
Luftwaffen-Panzerjäger-Abteilung 16, 188
Luftwaffen-Panzerjäger-Abteilung 18, 210, 212
Panzerjäger-Abteilung 18 (L), 219

Luftwaffen-Panzerjäger-Abteilung 19, 220
Panzerjäger-Abteilung 19 (L), 220, 242
Luftwaffen-Panzerjäger-Abteilung 20/ Panzerjäger-Abteilung 20 (L), 236, 245
Panzerjäger-Abteilung 21, 263, 267, 281
Panzerjäger-Abteilung 22, 282
I. Bataillon, Luftwaffen-Artillerie-Regiment 2, 59
II. Bataillon, Luftwaffen-Artillerie-Regiment 2, 59
III. Bataillon, Luftwaffen-Artillerie-Regiment 2, 59
I. Artillerie-Abteilung of Luftwaffen-Artillerie-Regiment 3, 59
I. Artillerie-Abteilung of Luftwaffen-Artillerie-Regiment 4, 36
II. Artillerie-Abteilung of Luftwaffen-Artillerie-Regiment 4, 36
III. Artillerie-Abteilung, Luftwaffen-Artillerie 4, 37
III. Artillerie-Abteilung, Luftwaffen-Artillerie-Regiment 5, 46
I. Artillerie-Abteilung, Luftwaffen-Artillerie-Regiment 6 (L), 32, 59, 67
III. Artillerie-Abteilung, Luftwaffen-Artillerie-Regiment 6 (L), 59
Artillerie-Abteilung, 8. Luftwaffen-Felddivision, 81
I. Artillerie Abteilung, 10. Luftwaffen-Felddivision, 93
III. Artillerie-Abteilung, 10. Luftwaffen-Felddivision, 93
I. Artillerie Abteilung, Luftwaffen-Artillerie-Regiment 11, 102–3, 108
II. Artillerie Abteilung, Luftwaffen-Artillerie-Regiment 11, 102–3, 108
III. Artillerie Abteilung, Luftwaffen-Artillerie-Regiment 11, 102–3, 108
III. Artillerie Abteilung, Feld Artillerie-Regiment 11 (L), 107
I. Artillerie Abteilung, Luftwaffen-Artillerie-Regiment 12, 118–19, 121
II. Artillerie Abteilung, Luftwaffen-Artillerie-Regiment 12, 118–119, 121
III. Artillerie Abteilung, Luftwaffen-Artillerie-Regiment 12, 118–119, 121
IV. Artillerie Abteilung, Luftwaffen-Artillerie-Regiment 12, 121
II. Artillerie Abteilung, Artillerie-Regiment 13 (L), 145
I. Artillerie-Abteilung, Luftwaffen-Artillerie-Regiment 14, 152
II. Artillerie-Abteilung, Luftwaffen-Artillerie-Regiment 14, 152

Unit Index

I. Artillerie-Abteilung, Luftwaffen-Artillerie-Regiment 16, 185, 187, 190, 192
II. Artillerie-Abteilung, Luftwaffen-Artillerie-Regiment 16, 185, 187, 190, 192
III. Artillerie-Abteilung, Luftwaffen-Artillerie-Regiment 16, 185, 188
I. Artillerie-Abteilung, Luftwaffen-Artillerie-Regiment 17, 205
II. Artillerie-Abteilung, Luftwaffen-Artillerie-Regiment 17, 205, 207
I. Artillerie-Abteilung, Luftwaffen-Artillerie-Regiment 18, 210, 213
II. Artillerie-Abteilung, Luftwaffen-Artillerie-Regiment 18, 210
I. Artillerie-Abteilung, Luftwaffen-Artillerie-Regiment 19, 225, 231, 242
II. Artillerie-Abteilung, Luftwaffen-Artillerie-Regiment 19, 225
III. Artillerie-Abteilung, Luftwaffen-Artillerie-Regiment 19, 225
I. Artillerie-Abteilung, Artillerie-Regiment 20 (L), 242
II. Artillerie-Abteilung, Artillerie-Regiment 20 (L), 245
III. Artillerie-Abteilung, Luftwaffen-Artillerie-Regiment 20, 235, 245
I. Artillerie-Abteilung, Luftwaffen-Artillerie-Regiment 21, 263
III. Artillerie-Abteilung, Luftwaffen-Artillerie-Regiment 21, 263
IV. Artillerie-Abteilung, Luftwaffen-Artillerie-Regiment 21, 263
I. Artillerie-Abteilung, Luftwaffen-Artillerie-Regiment 22, 283
II. Artillerie-Abteilung, Luftwaffen-Artillerie-Regiment 22, 283
III. Artillerie-Abteilung, Luftwaffen-Artillerie-Regiment 22, 283
IV.. Artillerie-Abteilung, Luftwaffen-Artillerie-Regiment 22, 283
I. Jäger-Bataillon, Jäger-Regiment 10 (L), 47
II. Jäger-Bataillon, Jäger-Regiment 10 (L), 47
III. Jäger-Bataillon-Regiment 30, 75–6, 182
III. Jäger-Bataillon, Jäger-Regiment 35 (L), 211–12
III. Jäger-Bataillon, Jäger-Regiment 36 (L), 211–12, 219
III. Jäger-Bataillon, Jäger-Regiment 37 (L), 224
III. Jäger-Bataillon, Jäger-Regiment 38 (L), 224
II. Jäger-Bataillon, Jäger-Regiment 46 (L), 193
I. Jäger-Bataillon, Jäger-Regiment 49 (L), 37
II. Jäger-Bataillon, Jäger-Regiment 49 (L), 37
III. Jäger-Bataillon, Jäger-Regiment 50 (L), 37
IV. Jäger-Bataillon, Jäger-Regiment 50 (L), 37
I. Jäger-Bataillon, Jäger-Regiment 51 (L), 37
II. Jäger-Bataillon, Jäger-Regiment 51 (L), 37
Fusilier-Battalion 6 (L), 58
Fusilier-Bataillon 10 (L), 96
Fusilier-Bataillon 11 (L), 107
Fusilier-Bataillon 12 (L), 121, 127
Fusilier Bataillon 14 (L), 152
Fusilier-Bataillon 16 (L), 190
Fusilier-Bataillon 18 (L), 212–13
Fusilier-Bataillon 19 (L), 231, 241, 311
Fusilier-Bataillon 20 (L), 231, 245, 311
Luftwaffen-Radfahr-Bataillon 19, 220
Sturmgeschütz-Abteilung 6 (L), 59
Sturmgeschütz-Abteilung 1016, 226
Sturmgeschütz-Abteilung 1019, 226
Feldersatz-Bataillon 6 (L), 59
Feldersatz-Bataillon 11 (L), 107–8
Feldersatz-Bataillon 14 (L), 152
Feldersatz-Bataillon 16 (L), 190
Feldersatz-Bataillon 19 (L), 241
Feldersatz-Bataillon 21, 263, 281
Luftwaffen-Feld-Bataillon 'Finnland', 152
Landesschützen-Bataillon der Luftwaffe 1, 152
Landesschützen-Bataillon der Luftwaffe 2, 153, 302
Landesschützen-Bataillon der Luftwaffe 3, 153, 302
Landesschützen-Bataillon der Luftwaffe 4, 302
Landesschützen-Bataillon der Luftwaffe 5, 302
Landesschützen-Bataillon der Luftwaffe 6, 302
Nachrichten Abteilung 6 (L), 59
Nachrichten- Abteilung 12 (L), 121
Nachrichten-Abteilung 16 (L), 190
Nachrichten-Abteilung 18 (L), 210
Nachrichten-Abteilung 20 (L), 245
Luftwaffen-Nachrichten-Abteilung, 256
Luftwaffen-Nachrichten-Abteilung 21, 263
Pionier-Bataillon 6 (L), 59, 62
Luftwaffe Pionier Bataillon 11, 102
Pionier-Bataillon 16, 188
Pionier-Bataillon 18 (L), 212
Pionier-Bataillon 19 (L), 224, 242
Luftwaffen-Pionier-Bataillon 21, 263
Luftwaffen-Pionier-Bataillon 22, 282

Luftwaffe Flak Units

2. Flak-Division, 99
20. Flak-Division, 282–3
Flak-Regiment 79 (mot.), 301
Flak-Regiment 99, 161
Flak-Regiment 111, 260

330   Hitler's *Luftwaffe* Infantry

Luftverteidigungs-Bataillon 31, 258
Flak-Ersatz-Abteilung 12, 290, 293
(leicht) Flak-Abteilung 88, 282
I. Flak-Abteilung, Flak-Regiment 2 (mot.), 86
II. Flak-Abteilung of Flak-Regiment 6 (mot.), 120, 302
II. Flak Abteilung, Flak-Regiment 8 (mot.), 36
I. Flak-Abteilung, Flak-Regiment 15 (mot.),152
I. Abteilung of Flak-Regiment 17 (mot.), 293
I. Flak-Abteilung of Flak-Regiment 20 (mot.), 205
I. Flak-Bataillon, Flak-Regiment 28 (mot.), 107
I. Abteilung, Flak-Regiment 34 (mot.), 58
II. Flak-Abteilung, Flak-Regiment 32 (mot.), 96
I. Bataillon, Flak-Regiment 40 (mot.), 9
I. Flak-Abteilung, Flak-Regiment 43 (mot.), 32
I. Flak-Bataillon, Flak-Regiment 46 (mot.), 305
I. Flak-Abteilung, Flak-Regiment 48 (mot.), 239
I. Bataillon, Flak-Regiment 50 (mot.), 24–5
II. Flak-Abteilung, Flak-Regiment 52 (mot.), 210
I. Flak-Abteilung, Flak-Regiment 54 (mot.), 140
Flak-Bataillon 3, 3. Luftwaffen Felddivision, 28
IV. (Flak) Artillerie-Abteilung, Luftwaffen-Artillerie-Regiment 3, 32
IV. (Flak) Artillerie-Abteilung, Luftwaffen-Artillerie-Regiment 3, 32
IV. (Flak) Artillerie-Abteilung, Luftwaffen-Artillerie-Regiment 4, 36
IV. (Flak) Artillerie-Abteilung, Luftwaffen-Artillerie-Regiment 5 (L), 46–7, 293
IV. (Flak) Artillerie-Abteilung, Luftwaffen-Artillerie-Regiment 6, 25, 58
Flak-Abteilung, 8. Luftwaffen-Felddivision, 81
IV. Artillerie-Abteilung, 10. Luftwaffen-Felddivision, 93
Luftwaffen-Flak-Bataillon 11, 102, 107
III. Artillerie-Abteilung, Artillerie-Regiment 12 (L), 136
IV. Artillerie-Abteilung, Artillerie-Regiment 12 (L), 301
IV. Abteilung (Flak)/Artillerie-Regiment 14 (L), 157
Flak-Abteilung der Luftwaffen-Felddivision 15, 182
IV. Bataillon /Artillerie-Regiment 15 (L), 183
III. Artillerie-Abteilung, Luftwaffen-Artillerie-Regiment 17, 201
III. Artillerie-Abteilung, Luftwaffen-Artillerie-Regiment 18, 210, 219
Luftwaffen-Flak-Bataillon 18, 210
II. Artillerie-Abteilung, Luftwaffen-Artillerie-Regiment 19, 231
III. Artillerie-Abteilung, Luftwaffen-Artillerie-Regiment 19, 227
IV. Artillerie-Abteilung, Luftwaffen-Artillerie-Regiment 19, 220, 225
Luftwaffen-Flak-Abteilung 20, 235
II. [Flak] Artillerie-Abteilung, Luftwaffen-Artillerie-Regiment 21, 263, 267

Reserve & Field Training Units

Flieger-Ersatz-Bataillon VII, 291
Flieger-Ausbildungs-Regiment 10, 9
Flieger-Regiment 12, 118
Flieger-Regiment 13, 138
Flieger-Ausbildungs-Regiment 10, 235
Flieger-Ausbildungs-Regiment 11, 235
Flieger-Ausbildungs-Regiment 12, 235
Flieger-Ausbildungs-Regiment 13, 235
Flieger-Ersatz-Abteilung 14 (1939), 34
Flieger-Ersatz-Regiment 14 (1942), 34
Flieger-Ausbildungs-Regiment 21, 55, 235
Flieger-Regiment 23, 199
Flieger-Ausbildungs-Regiment 24, 235
Flieger-Ausbildungs-Regiment 31, 102, 235
Flieger-Ausbildungs-Regiment 32
Flieger-Ausbildungs-Regiment 33, 235
Flieger-Ausbildungs-Regiment 41, 235
Flieger-Ersatz-Abteilung 42 (1939), 77
Flieger-Regiment 42 (1941), 77
Flieger-Ausbildungs-Regiment 43, 235
Flieger-Ausbildungs-Regiment 51, 235
Flieger-Regiment 52, 210
Flieger-Ausbildungs-Regiment 53, 235
Flieger-Ausbildungs-Regiment 61, 148, 235
Flieger-Regiment 62, 82
Flieger-Ausbildungs-Regiment 63, 235
Flieger-Ausbildungs-Regiment 71, 235
Fliegerregiment 72, 93
Fliegerregiment 82, 14

Troop Training Centers

Heerestruppenübungsplatz Gross-Born, 9, 17, 34, 55, 68, 138, 185
Truppenübungsplatz Bergen, 220
Truppenübungsplatz Mlawa (Mielau), 41, 77, 82
Truppenübungsplatz Munsterlager, 235
Truppenübungsplatz Obrdruf, 9

German Army Formations
Rear Area Commands

Wehrkreis XVIII, 118
BefehlshaberWest-Taurien, 49
Wehrmacht-Befehlshaber Mazedonien, 110

Unit Index

Army Groups/*Heeresgruppen*

Army Group North/*Heeresgruppe Nord*, 10, 21–2, 60, 82, 89, 94–5, 119, 127–8, 135, 138–41, 143, 270, 273–4
Army Group Courland, 132–3, 135, 248, 251–2
Army Group Centre/*Heeresgruppe Mitte*, 21–2, 25, 27, 29, 63, 79, 138–9, 148, 252–3
Army Group South/*Heeresgruppe Süd*, 60, 70, 78, 95, 139
Army Group Don/*Heeresgruppe von Manstein/Heeresgruppe Don*, 70–2, 77, 79, 163, 168–70, 172, 303–4
Army Group Hoth/*Heeresgruppe Hoth*, 77
Army Group A/*Heeresgruppe A*, 175, 177
Army Group B/*Heeresgruppe B*, 170
Army Group C/*Heeresgruppe C*, 229, 246
Heeresgruppe Fretter-Pico, 171
Panzergruppe West, 194

Armies/*Armeen*

1. *Panzerarmee*, 43, 81, 175, 292
2. *Panzerarmee*, 112–14
3. *Panzerarmee*, 21, 25, 28, 30, 32, 59–61, 64–5
4. *Panzerarmee*, 70, 77, 164, 166–8, 173
5. *Panzerarmee*, 213
6. *Panzerarmee*, 113, 141
1. *Armee*, 203, 210
2. *Armee*, 133
6. *Armee*, 47, 49–50, 70, 72, 77–8, 95, 113, 138, 163, 168, 172, 178–9, 181
7. *Armee*, 201
8. *Armee*, 51
9. *Armee*, 17, 25, 27
10. *Armee*, 229, 244–6
11. *Armee*, 71, 82, 95
12. *Armee*, 104
14. *Armee*, 228–9, 231, 240–1, 246, 282
15. *Armee*, 203, 210, 224, 226
16. *Armee*, 10, 128, 271–2, 277
17. *Armee*, 42–3, 45, 177
18. *Armee*, 10, 83, 87–88, 94, 119, 121, 126–7, 131, 139, 249, 251, 256, 271, 274
20. *Gebirgsarmee*, 153, 156, 302
Armee Norwegen, 156

Army Detachments/*Armee-Abteilungen*

Armee-Abteilung Fretter-Pico, 174
Armee-Abteilung Hoth, 71
Armee-Abteilung Hollidt, 72–3, 77, 164–5, 171, 174–5, 178
Armee-Abteilung Lanz, 170

Armee-Abteilung von Zangen, 228

Corps Detachments/*Korpsabteilungen*

Korpsabteilung D, 37
Korpsabteilung H, 39

Corps/*Korps*

I. *Armeekorps*, 123, 128, 131, 138, 142, 251
III. *Panzerkorps*, 81
Korps Mieth (IV. Armeekorps), 72, 74
V. *Armeekorps*, 42, 45, 177
VI. *Armeekorps*, 17, 25, 27, 37, 64
VIII. *Armeekorps*, 279
IX. *Armeekorps*, 22, 30, 61
X. *Armeekorps*, 10, 128, 258, 270, 279
XIV. *Panzerkorps*, 228–31, 240–1, 246
XV. *Gebirgs Armeekorps*, 114
XVI. *Armeekorps*, 277, 279
XVII. *Armeekorps*, 77, 81, 164, 170–1, 178
XVIII. *Gebirgs-Armeekorps*, 303
XXII. *Gebirgs-Armeekorps*, 110
XXV. *Armeekorps*, 202
XXVI. *Armeekorps*, 83, 95, 143
XXVIII. *Armeekorps*, 15, 119, 121–3, 125–8, 142–3, 251, 279
XXIX. *Armeekorps*, 51, 74, 178–9, 181
XXX. *Armeekorps*, 17, 171
XXXIII. *Armeekorps*, 148, 150
XXXIV. *Armeekorps*, 15
XLIV. *Armeekorps*, 42–3
XXXVIII. *Armeekorps*, 9–11, 83, 122–3, 131, 139, 142, 271–3, 276, 279
XXXIX. *Armeekorps*, 252
XLIII. *Armeekorps*, 279
XLVII. *Panzerkorps*, 169
XLVIII. *Panzerkorps*, 169
XLIX. *Gebirgs Armeekorps*, 43
XL. *Panzerkorps*, 175
XLI. *Panzerkorps*, 25, 27
XLIII. *Armeekorps*, 21, 25
XLVIII. *Panzerkorps*, 72–4, 164–5, 170, 175
L. *Armeekorps*, 83, 89, 94, 125, 128
Korpsgruppe Seydlitz (LI. Armeekorps), 258
LII. *Armeekorps*, 42
LIII. *Armeekorps*, 25, 37–9, 61–2, 64–5, 293
LIV. *Armeekorps*, 95
LVII. *Panzerkorps*, 71–2, 163–5, 169–70, 175, 177, 303
LIX. *Armeekorps*, 35
LXXII. *Armeekorps*, 49
LXXV. *Armeekorps*, 228, 246
LXXVI. *Armeekorps*, 210, 244, 246
LXXXI. *Armeekorps*, 207

LXXXII. Armeekorps, 210
LXXXIV. Armeekorps, 190
LXXXVI. Armeekorps, 196
LXXXVII. Armeekorps, 228
LXXXVIII. Armeekorps, 186, 188, 190–1, 194, 306
LXXXIX. Armeekorps, 224, 226, 310
XCI. Armeekorps, 112, 114
Gruppe Spang, 170
Gruppe Stumpfeld, 170

Divisions

Infanterie-Division 'Groß Deutschland' (mot.), 19
Panzer-Lehr-Division, 193
1. Infanterie-Division, 121
2. Gebirgs Division, 303
3. Gebirgs-Division, 79, 171
3. Panzer-Division, 45
3. Panzergrenadier-Division, 231, 241
4. Panzer-Division, 133, 135
5. Jäger-Division, 251, 260, 271
6. Panzer-Division, 71–2, 164, 169–71, 303–4
7. Panzer-Division, 78
8. Jäger-Division, 125–6, 270–1
8 Panzer-Division, 57, 258, 260
9. Infanterie-Division, 46
11. Infanterie-Division, 132, 273, 300–1
11. Panzer-Division, 71–3, 127, 165, 170–1, 175, 177
12. Infanterie-Division, 251
13. Panzer-Division, 45, 181, 292
14. Infanterie-Division (mot.), 30, 61
14. Panzer-Division, 132, 277
16. Infanterie-Division (mot.), 71, 171, 175, 177, 198
16. Infanterie-Division, 198
17. Infanterie-Division, 181
17. Panzer-Division, 50, 72, 165, 170, 175
18. Panzergrenadier-Division, 251
18. Volksgrenadier-Division, 217
19. Volksgrenadier-Division, 231
19. Panzer-Division, 19, 79, 171
20. Infanterie-Division (mot.), 36
20. Panzer-Division, 19, 22, 61, 293
21. Infanterie-Division, 15, 124, 126–8, 142, 300
21. Panzer-Division, 193–7
22. Infanterie-Division (Luftlande), 106
22. Panzer-Division, 71–2, 74, 165
23. Panzer-Division, 127, 165, 170–1, 177
23. Infanterie-Division, 71–2, 130, 135
24. Infanterie-Division, 96, 127
24. Panzer-Division, 170, 220–1
26. Panzer-Division, 228–30, 241, 244–5

27. Panzer-Division, 171
28. Jäger-Division, 11–12, 15, 82, 123, 142–3
29. Panzergrenadier-Division, 228, 241, 244
30. Infanterie-Division, 127–8, 270, 273, 300
31. Volksgrenadier-Division, 128
32. Infanterie-Division, 56, 94, 126–7, 272–3
34. Infanterie-Division, 227
35. Infanterie-Division, 135
41. Festungs-Division, 114
42. Jäger-Division, 228, 245
44. Infanterie-Division 'Hoch und Deutschmeister', 203, 221
47. Infanterie-Division (bodenstandig), 212
49. Infanterie-Division (bodenstandig), 212–13
50. Infanterie-Division, 45, 82
58. Infanterie-Division, 9, 123–4, 127, 251, 300
61. Infanterie-Division, 90, 119, 127–8, 300
62. Infanterie-Division, 164, 170
65. Infanterie-Division, 222, 224, 230–1
69. Infanterie-Division, 10, 83
70. Infanterie-Division (bodenständige), 224
72. Infanterie-Division, 82
76. Infanterie-Division, 51
79. Infanterie-Division, 50
81. Infanterie-Division, 127
83. Infanterie-Division, 21–2, 55, 272, 276
87. Infanterie-Division, 22, 57, 61, 127
90. Panzergrenadier-Division, 228, 231, 241, 244
93. Infanterie-Division, 127
95. Infanterie-Division, 65
96. Infanterie-Division, 15, 120–1, 131, 142
97. Jäger-Division, 42, 45
101. Jäger-Division, 42–3, 45
104. Jäger-Division, 112–14
111. Infanterie-Division, 45, 177, 181
113. Infanterie-Division, 292
114. Jäger-Division, 245
116. Panzer-Division, 198, 213
117. Jäger-Division, 108, 110
121. Infanterie-Division, 127, 132, 273
122. Infanterie-Division, 128, 256
125. Infanterie-Division, 42
126. Infanterie-Division, 89–90, 125, 127–8, 132, 260, 271
129. Infanterie-Division, 22, 30, 32, 61
132. Infanterie-Division, 82, 127, 131
133. Festungs-Division, 291
148. Infanterie-Division, 245
155. Feldausbildungs-Division, 245
155. Infanterie-Division, 245
156. Infanterie-Division, 19
157. Reserve Division, 309

157. Gebirgs-Division, 227, 245, 309
158. Reserve-Division, 197
162. (turkistanische) Infanterie-Division, 229, 240–1
163. Infanterie-Division, 303
167. Infanterie-Division, 186
167. Volksgrenadier-Division, 208, 308
169. Infanterie-Division, 303
170. Infanterie-Division, 99
196. Infanterie-Division, 148
197. Infanterie-Division, 22, 37, 64–5
198. Infanterie-Division, 42
199. Infanterie-Division, 303
201. Sicherungs-Division, 65
205. Infanterie-Division, 21, 127
206. Infanterie-Division, 37, 64–5
207. Sicherungs-Division, 260, 271, 299
207. Sicherungs-Division, 96
210. Infanterie-Division, 153
212. Infanterie-Division, 96, 125, 271
213. Sicherungs-Division, 170
215. Infanterie-Division, 89, 125–8, 132–3
217. Infanterie-Division, 11
218. Infanterie-Division, 127, 130, 251, 256, 260
225. Infanterie-Division, 90, 127–8, 273
226. Infanterie-Division, 207
227. Infanterie-Division, 90, 127, 139, 300
242. Infanterie-Division (bodenständige), 184
243. Infanterie-Division (bodenständige), 184
244. Infanterie-Division (bodenständige), 184
245. Infanterie-Division (bodenständige), 184
246. Infanterie-Division, 17–19, 37–8, 64–5
250. Infanterie-Division (spanische) 'Blau', 10, 83, 95–6
251. Infanterie-Division, 294
252. Infanterie-Division, 22, 133, 135
263. Infanterie-Division, 21, 30, 127, 132
264. Infanterie-Division (bodenständige), 184
265. Infanterie-Division (bodenständige), 184
266. Infanterie-Division (bodenständige), 184, 307
269. Infanterie-Division, 153
270. Infanterie-Division, 153
272. Infanterie-Division, 195–6
276. Infanterie-Division, 193, 196
280. Infanterie-Division, 254
281. Sicherungs-Division, 145, 254, 256
290. Infanterie-Division, 127, 132, 251, 258
294. Infanterie-Division, 77, 164, 170, 304
297. Infanterie-Division, 112, 114
Division z.b.V. 300, 126–7, 143, 145, 277
304. Infanterie-Division, 50–1, 79, 171
306. Infanterie-Division, 165, 171

320. Infanterie-Division, 51, 170, 202
326. Infanterie-Division, 225
327. Infanterie-Division, 308
328. Infanterie-Division, 55
329. Infanterie-Division, 55, 127, 274, 276
330. Infanterie-Division, 55
331. Infanterie-Division, 55
332. Infanterie-Division, 203
335. Infanterie-Division, 51
336. Infanterie-Division, 71–4, 165, 170, 175, 181
343. Infanterie-Division (bodenständige), 184, 307
344. Infanterie-Division (bodenständige), 184, 207, 212
346. Infanterie-Division (bodenständige), 184, 194, 196, 204, 225
347. Infanterie-Division (bodenständige), 184, 186, 191
348. Infanterie-Division (bodenständige), 184, 212, 225
356. Infanterie-Division, 240–1
370. Infanterie-Division, 45, 50
384. Infanterie-Division, 72, 74, 304
385. Infanterie-Division, 171
387. Infanterie-Division, 171
389. Infanterie-Division, 127, 133, 135
403. Sicherungs-Division, 170, 304
416. Infanterie-Division, 236
444. Sicherungs-Division, 177, 304
542. Volksgrenadier-Division, 133
702. Infanterie-Division, 153
710. Infanterie-Division, 245
711. Infanterie-Division (bodenständige), 196
712. Infanterie-Division, 212, 224
716. Infanterie-Division, 156
719. Infanterie-Division, 186, 190–1

Brigades & Regiments

135. Festungs-Brigade 'Doehla', 228
Brigade Dörfler-Schuldt, 171
Sturmgeschütz-Brigade 249, 46
Sturmgeschütz-Brigade 912, 132
3. Kavallerie-Brigade, 25
Kavallerie-Regiment Nord, 15, 123, 143
Festung-Infanterie-Regiment 859, 152
Jäger-Regiment 49, 11
Jäger-Regiment 83, 11
Gebirgsjäger-Regiment 8, 254
Artillerie-Regiment 28, 12
Artillerie-Regiment 142, 245
Artillerie-Regiment 719, 231
Nebelwerfer-Regiment 70, 277
Panzer-Artillerie-Regiment 80, 260

Panzer-Regiment 208, 258
Panzergrenadier-Regiment 8, 57, 260
Panzergrenadier-Regiment 10, 114
Panzergrenadier-Regiment 28, 57, 260
Panzergrenadier-Regiment 63, 310
Panzergrenadier-Regiment 66, 292
Panzergrenadier-Regiment 125, 194
II. Bataillon, Infanterie Regiment 16, 106
II. Bataillon, Infanterie Regiment 65, 106
Feldausbildungs-Grenadier-Regiment 1127, 245
Feldausbildungs-Grenadier-Regiment 1128, 245
Feldausbildungs-Grenadier-Regiment 1129, 245
Jäger-Regiment 228, 292
Infanterie-Regiment 272, 131
Infanterie-Regiment 366, 131
Infanterie-Regiment 386, 254
Infanterie-Regiment 553, 254
Grenadier-Regiment 4, 94
Grenadier-Regiment 90, 36
Grenadier-Regiment 268, 292
Grenadier-Regiment 286, 37
Grenadier-Regiment 340, 148
Grenadier-Regiment 374, 96, 299
Grenadier-Regiment 386, 256
Grenadier-Regiment 424, 89
Grenadier-Regiment 459, 294
Grenadier-Regiment 486, 37
Grenadier-Regiment 471, 294
Grenadier-Regiment 503, 14, 271, 289
Grenadier-Regiment 547, 22
Grenadier-Regiment 745, 224
Sicherungs-Regiment 619, 170
Sicherungs-Regiment 354, 170

Battalions

Jagdkommando 207, 260
I. Bataillon, Panzergrenadier-Regiment 125, 194
II. Bataillon, Panzergrenadier-Regiment 125, 194
I. Bataillon, Grenadier-Regiment 374, 127
II. Bataillon, Grenadier-Regiment 547, 22
III. Bataillon, Grenadier-Regiment 547, 22
I. Bataillon, 3. Regiment Brandenburg, 17
Panzer-Pionier-Bataillon 59, 57
Panzerjäger-Abteilung 519, 61
Panzerjäger-Abteilung 563, 95, 297
Panzerjäger-Abteilung 1048, 245
Panzerjäger-Abteilung 290, 260
Aufklärungs-Abteilung 1057, 245
Aufklärungs-Abteilung 290, 260
Kradschütz-Bataillon 5, 260
II. Abteilung, Artillerie-Regiment 290, 14, 271, 289

III. Artillerie-Abteilung, Artillerie-Regiment 650, 245
II. Artillerie-Abteilung, Artillerie-Regiment 661, 245
IV. Artillerie-Abteilung, Artillerie-Regiment 661, 245
schwere Artillerie-Abteilung 995, 239
155. Feldausbildungs-Artillerie-Abteilung, 245
Heeres-Artillerie-Abteilung 1154, 227
Heeres-Küsten-Artillerie-Abteilung 708, 85
Marine-Artillerie-Abteilung 530, 89
Flak-Ersatz-Abteilung 99, 290
Reserve-Flak-Abteilung 153, 297
Heer-Flak-Abteilung 276, 277
schwere-Panzer-Abteilung 502, 95, 127
schwere Panzer-Abteilung 503, 169, 171, 196
schwere Panzer-Abteilung 103, 196
Sturmgeschütz-Abteilung 184, 127
Sturmgeschütz-Abteilung 203, 163
Sturmgeschütz-Batterie 659, 258
Sturmgeschütz-Batterie 666, 258
646. Festungs-Infanterie-Bataillon, 153
650. Festungs-Infanterie-Bataillon, 153
662. Festungs-Infanterie-Bataillon, 153
Festungs-Bataillon 902, 228
Festungs-Bataillon 905, 228
Festungs-Bataillon 906, 228
Festungs-Bataillon 907, 228
Festungs-Bataillon 908, 228
Festungs-Infanterie-Bataillon 1001, 110
Festungs-Infanterie-Bataillon 1010, 110
Festungs-Infanterie-Bataillon 1012, 110
Maschinengewehr-Bataillon 10, 254, 256
Nachrichten-Abteilung 630, 245
Baubataillon 132, 258

Eastern Volunteer Formations

XV. Kosaken-Kavalleriekorps, 112, 114, 304
1. Kosaken-Kavallerie-Division, 114
2. Kosaken-Kavallerie-Division, 112–13
Kosaken-Kavallerie-Regiment von Jungschultz, 177, 304
(estnische) Grenzschutz-Regiment 1, 143, 271–2
Estnische-Grenzschutz-Regiment 2, 277
(estnische) Grenzschutz-Regiment 4, 143, 271–2, 277
(estnische) Grenzschutz-Regiment 5, 277
(estnische) Grenzschutz-Regiment 6, 143, 277
(lettische) Schutzmannschaft-Bataillon 16, 254
Ost-Bataillon Hensen, 57
Ost-Bataillon 628, 224
Ost-Bataillon 661, 85
Ost-Bataillon 665, 85

Kosaken-Infanterie-Bataillon *623*, 57
Kosaken-Infanterie-Bataillon *625*, 57
Kosaken-Infanterie-Bataillon *631*, 57
Nordkaukasiche-Infanterie-Bataillon *835*, 205

Kampfgruppen

Kampfgruppe Abel, 57
Kampfgruppe Adam, 72, 304
Kampfgruppe Bock, 123
Kampfgruppe Burgstaller, 74
Kampfgruppe Busche, 43, 292
Kampfgruppe Crisolli, 241
Kampfgruppe Fischer, 112
Kampfgruppe Friessner, 271
Kampfgruppe Furguth, 14–15, 289
Kampfgruppe Goebel, 304
Kampfgruppe Gothsche, 271
Kampfgruppe Heilmann, 72, 304
Kampfgruppe Helling, 99
Kampfgruppe Henke, 114
Kampfgruppe Herzog, 271
Kampfgruppe Hollidt, 77
Kampfgruppe Kohl, 43
Kampfgruppe Kreising, 171
Kampfgruppe Mangold, 214
Kampfgruppe Mikosch, 304
Kampfgruppe Nagel, 171
Kampfgruppe Neise, 57
Kampfgruppe Pohl, 123
Kampfgruppe von Renteln, 57
Kampfgruppe Schafer, 17
Kampfgruppe Schuldt, 122, 142
Kampfgruppe Schulz, 271
Kampfgruppe Speth, 15, 123, 143
Kampfgruppe Stahel, 74, 78–9, 165, 175
Kampfgruppe Stumpfeld, 303
Kampfgruppe Uckermann, 256
Jagdkommando *8*, 254

Waffen-SS Formations

SS Troop Training Ground Beneschau, 96
I. SS-Panzerkorps, 196, 213
III. (germanische) SS-Panzerkorps, 83, 86–7, 89–90, 96–7, 99
VI. SS-Freiwilligen-Armeekorps (lettische), 271, 279
1. SS-Panzer-Division 'Leibstandarte Adolf Hitler', 195
SS 'Das Reich' Division, 304
SS-Infanterie-Division 'Totenkopf' (motorisiert), 258, 260
4. SS-Polizei-Panzergrenadier-Division, 110

SS Infanterie-Division Wiking (motorisiert) / 5. SS-Panzer-Grenadier-Division 'Wiking', 45, 171
6. SS Gebirgs Division 'Nord', 303
SS Kavallerie-Division 'Florian Geyer', 19, 22
7. SS-Freiwilligen-Gebirgs-Division Prince Eugen, 111–12
11. SS-Panzergrenadier Division Nordland, 83, 86, 90, 99
12. SS-Panzer-Division 'Hitler Jugend', 193–4
15. Waffen-Grenadier-Division der SS (lettische Nr. 1), 127, 274
16. SS-Panzergrenadier-Division 'Reichsführer-SS', 227, 229, 231, 241, 309
19. Waffen-Grenadier-Division der SS (lettische Nr. 2), 127, 131, 274, 276–7
20. Waffen-Grenadier-Division der SS (estnische Nr. 1), 90, 301
(lettische) SS-Freiwilligen-Brigade, 11, 139
2. (lettische) SS-Freiwilligen-Brigade, 123, 142
Waffen-Grenadier-Regiment der SS (lettische Nr. 7), 274
Waffen-Grenadier-Regiment der SS *106* (lettische), 277
SS-Panzergrenadier-Brigade 'Nederland', 83, 86, 90
Kaukasicher-Waffen-Verbände der SS, 206
SS-Regiment Norge, 96
SS-Regiment Danmark, 96
SS Pionier-Bataillon *11*, 86, 88, 96–8
I. Bataillon, SS Panzergrenadier-Regiment *7*, 304
I. Bataillon of SS-Panzergrenadier-Regiment *23* Norge, 98–9
SS-Artillerie-Regiment *11*, 98
SS-Pionier-Bataillon *1*, 99
I. Bataillon, SS-Panzergrenadier-Regiment *48* 'General Seyffardt', 99
SS und Polizei-Gebirgsjäger-Regiment *18*, 110
VII. SS-Wach-Bataillon der Leibstandarte 'Adolf Hitler', 304
I. Bataillon, SS Panzergrenadier-Regiment *3*, 304
SS-Feld-Ersatz-Bataillon *7*, 111
SS-Ersatz-und-Ausbildungs-Bataillon *4*, 191
SS-Freiwilligen-Gebirgs-Infanterie-Regiment *13* Artur Phleps, 111
SD-Bataillon, SS-Sonderkommando, 260

Police Units

Reserve-Polizei-Bataillon *65*, 254

Axis Allied Units

8th Italian Army, 171
11th Italian Army, 105

3rd Italian Infantry Division Ravenna, 171
Brigade Nere '23 Marzo', 171
3rd Romanian Army, 70, 72, 164, 170, 175, 303
4th Romanian Army, 70, 164
1st Romanian Army Corps, 164, 170
2nd Romanian Army Corps, 165, 170
3rd Romanian Army Corps, 51, 72, 75, 77–8
4th Romanian Army Corps, 51, 72, 77–8, 171
5th Romanian Army Corps, 171
6th Romanian Army Corps, 71–2, 170
7th Romanian Army Corps, 71–2, 170
Romanian Cavalry Corps, 42–3
5th Romanian Cavalry Division, 72
7th Romanian Cavalry Division, 79
8th Romanian Cavalry Division, 72, 170
1st Romanian Armoured Division, 71–2, 165, 170
1st Romanian Infantry Division, 71, 170
2nd Romanian Infantry Division, 71, 170
4th Romanian Infantry Division, 170
7th Romanian Infantry Division, 164, 170
9th Romanian Infantry Division, 164, 170
11th Romanian Infantry Division, 165, 170
14th Romanian Infantry Division, 165, 170
15th Romanian Infantry Division, 51
18th Romanian Infantry Division, 71, 170
19th Romanian Infantry Division, 45–6
24th Romanian Infantry Division, 50
7th Romanian Cavalry Division, 170
8th Romanian Cavalry Division, 71, 170
9th Romanian Cavalry Division, 42
3rd Romanian Cavalry Regiment 'Rosiori', 42
1st Slovak Division, 50
Croatian 5. Domobran-Ustashe Division, 112

Red Army Formations

2nd Baltic Front, 274
3rd Baltic Front, 274
1st Guards Army, 79
2nd Guards Army, 165
2nd Shock Army, 85–6, 142
3rd Shock Army, 252–4
4th Shock Army, 252–3
2nd Striking Army, 95
4th Shock Army, 32, 62
5th Striking Army, 79
6th Guards Army, 274
8th Army, 95
10th Guards Army, 274
11th Guards Army, 32
33rd Army, 62
39th Army, 37

42nd Army, 95
43rd Army, 37, 88
54th Army, 95
55th Army, 95
56th Army, 43
67th Army, 95
1st Guard Rifle Corps, 175
3rd Guard Tank Corps
6th Rifle Corps, 125
119th Rifle Corps, 125
122nd Army Corps, 88
5th Tank Corps, 30, 32, 61
24th Tank Corps, 79
25th Tank Corps, 79
152nd Tank Division, 88, 97
11th Rifle Division, 88, 97
18th Rifle Division, 125
43rd Rifle Division, 88, 96–7
45th Rifle Division, 96
46th Rifle Division, 125
48th Rifle Division, 97
53rd, Rifle Division, 125
56th Rifle Division, 125
63rd Rifle Division, 96
72nd Rifle Division, 96
86th Rifle Division, 125
90th Rifle Division, 97
98th Rifle Division, 97
131st Rifle Division, 88, 97
168th Rifle Division, 88
191st Rifle Division, 271
196th Rifle Division, 88
224th Rifle Division, 125
225th Rifle Division, 14, 271
275th Rifle Division, 125
239th Rifle Division, 271
310th Rifle Division, 271
326th Rifle Division, 125
337th Rifle Division, 271
372nd Rifle Division, 14
378th Rifle Division, 271
34th Rifle Brigade, 14, 271
44th Rifle Brigade, 14, 271
299th Rifle Regiment, 14, 271
311th Rifle Division, 125
708th Rifle Division, 55
47th Mechanized Rifle Brigade, 55
56th Engineer Brigade, 55
85th Corps Artillery Regiment, 56
793rd Divisional Artillery Regiment, 56
923rd Divisional Artillery Regiment, 56
50th Coastal Brigade, 88

29th Tank Brigade, 271
78th Tank Brigade, 56
– 263rd Tank Battalion, 56
– 264th Tank Battalion, 56
77th BM-13 Katyusha Brigade, 56

Soviet Partisan Units
Alexiev Partisan Brigade, 57
2nd Leningrad Partisan Brigade, 254

Yugoslav Partisan Units
12th Partisan Assault Division, 113–14
16th Partisan Division, 113
36th Partisan Division, 113
51st Vojvodina Assault Division, 113–14
Osijeka Partisan Brigade, 113

Western Allied Units
American 5th Army, 241
American 4th Army Corps, 230, 241
American 6th Army Corps, 240
American 11th Army Corps, 240
American 1st Armored Division, 230
American 34th Infantry Division, 230–1
American 36th ('Texas') Infantry Division, 229–30
American 91st Infantry Division, 240
American 133rd Infantry Regiment, 231, 240
American 135th Infantry Regiment, 231
American 361st Regimental Combat Team, 240
British 8th Army, 244
British 1st Corps, 195
British 3rd Infantry Division, 195
British 3rd Armoured Division, 194
British 11th Armoured Division, 196
British 59th Infantry Division, 194–5
Canadian 3rd Infantry Division, 195
Canadian 7th Brigade, 207
3rd Algerian Infantry Division, 311
2nd Moroccan Infantry Division, 311
4th Moroccan Infantry Division, 311

Operational Codewords
Unternehmen Bettelstab, 94
Unternehmen Brückenschlag, 258
Unternehmen Fallreep, 258
Unternehmen Frühlingserwachen, 113
Unternehmen Geyer, 108
Operation Goodwood, 196
Unternehmen Kondor, 108
Unternehmen Krebs, 108
Unternehmen Moorbrand, 94
Unternehmen Nordlicht, 94
Unternehmen Schlingpflanze, 94
Unternehmen Werwolf, 112
Unternehmen Winkelried, 260
Unternehmen Wintergewitter, 70, 72, 169